ACTIVE DEFENSE

Princeton Studies in International History and Politics

G. John Ikenberry, Marc Trachtenberg, William C. Wohlforth, and Keren Yarhi-Milo, Series Editors

Strategic Instincts: The Adaptive Advantages of Cognitive Biases in International Politics, Dominic D. P. Johnson

Divided Armies: Inequality and Battlefield Performance in Modern War, Jason Lyall

Active Defense: China's Military Strategy since 1949, M. Taylor Fravel

After Victory: Institutions, Strategic Restraint, and the Rebuilding of Order after Major Wars, New Edition, G. John Ikenberry

Cult of the Irrelevant: The Waning Influence of Social Science on National Security, Michael C. Desch

Secret Wars: Covert Conflict in International Politics, Austin Carson

Who Fights for Reputation: The Psychology of Leaders in International Conflict, Keren Yarhi-Milo

Aftershocks: Great Powers and Domestic Reforms in the Twentieth Century, Seva Gunitsky

Why Wilson Matters: The Origin of American Liberal Internationalism and Its Crisis Today, Tony Smith

Powerplay: The Origins of the American Alliance System in Asia, Victor D. Cha

Economic Interdependence and War, Dale C. Copeland

Knowing the Adversary: Leaders, Intelligence, and Assessment of Intentions in International Relations, Keren Yarhi-Milo

Nuclear Strategy in the Modern Era: Regional Powers and International Conflict, Vipin Narang

The Cold War and After: History, Theory, and the Logic of International Politics, Marc Trachtenberg

Liberal Leviathan: The Origins, Crisis, and Transformation of the American World Order, G. John Ikenberry

Worse Than a Monolith: Alliance Politics and Problems of Coercive Diplomacy in Asia, Thomas J. Christensen

Politics and Strategy: Partisan Ambition and American Statecraft, Peter Trubowitz

The Clash of Ideas in World Politics: Transnational Networks, States, and Regime Change, 1510–2010, John M. Owen IV

Active Defense

China's Military Strategy since 1949

M. Taylor Fravel

PRINCETON UNIVERSITY PRESS

PRINCETON AND OXFORD

Published by Princeton University Press
41 William Street, Princeton, New Jersey 08540
6 Oxford Street, Woodstock, Oxfordshire OX20 1TR

press.princeton.edu

Library of Congress Control Number: 2018958697
First paperback printing, 2020
Paperback ISBN 9780691210339
Cloth ISBN 9780691152134

British Library Cataloging-in-Publication Data is available

Editorial: Eric Crahan, Bridget Flannery-McCoy, Alena Chekanov, and Pamela Weidman
Production Editorial: Mark Bellis
Cover Design: Karl Spurzem
Cover Credit: Chinese troops preparing for a military parade at the Zhurihe Training Base in North China's Inner Mongolia Autonomous Region, July 30, 2017. Image courtesy of Zha Chunming/Xinhua/Alamy
Production: Erin Suydam
Publicity: Tayler Lord and Caroline Priday

This book has been composed in Adobe Text Pro and Gotham

Printed in the United States of America

For my parents

CONTENTS

List of Illustrations   ix

Acknowledgments   xi

Abbreviations   xv

Introduction   1

1 Explaining Major Change in Military Strategy   9

2 The CCP's Military Strategies before 1949   39

3 The 1956 Strategy: "Defending the Motherland"   72

4 The 1964 Strategy: "Luring the Enemy in Deep"   107

5 The 1980 Strategy: "Active Defense"   139

6 The 1993 Strategy: "Local Wars under High-Technology Conditions"   182

7 China's Military Strategies since 1993: "Informatization"   217

8 China's Nuclear Strategy since 1964   236

Conclusion   270

Notes   279

Bibliography   339

Index   363

ILLUSTRATIONS

Figure

1.1. Conduct of warfare and party unity in strategic change   25

Maps

I.1. The People's Republic of China   xvi

2.1. CCP base areas and the Long March, 1934–1936   44

2.2. Decisive battles of the Chinese Civil War, 1948–1949   57

3.1. The northeastern strategic direction in the 1956 strategy   85

4.1. Mao Zedong's view of possible invasion routes (June 1964)   124

5.1. The northern strategic direction in the 1980 strategy   159

Tables

1.1. China's military strategic guidelines since 1949   34

3.1. Proposed force deployment by type and region in 1952
(percent of total)   83

ACKNOWLEDGMENTS

When I started my graduate studies, I wanted to write a dissertation on China's military strategy. In the end, however, I turned my attention to cooperation and conflict in China's many territorial disputes with its neighbors. Nevertheless, I'm glad that I put it off. In the past decade, more sources on Chinese military affairs have become available than ever before. These sources make possible studying how the People's Republic of China has approached the formulation of military strategy over the past seventy years, from 1949 to today.

MIT's Department of Political Science and especially the Security Studies Program have provided the ideal intellectual home for researching and writing this book. Since joining the department as a very junior scholar in 2004, Barry Posen and Richard Samuels have provided a unique and magical combination of mentorship and friendship. They have helped me grow not just as a scholar but also as a person. Steven Van Evera without fail has asked the most salient questions, pushing me and many others to pursue scholarship that matters. Owen Cote always finds time to answer all of my basic inquiries about how military hardware and technology does (or does not) actually work. When Vipin Narang and I met at Stanford twenty years ago, I could not have imagined that we would later become colleagues in the same field, much less the same department. He has become my comrade in arms in this business.

Several graduate students at MIT have helped me research various portions of this book. I thank Fiona Cunningham, Kacie Miura, Miranda Priebe, Joshua Shifrinson, Joseph Torigian, and Ketian Zhang for expert research assistance. I would also like to thank two other individuals who have helped me with research on this project, Jonathan Ray and especially Trevor Cook.

Many colleagues generously read the entire manuscript and provided many helpful comments, suggestions, clarifications, and corrections. I am indebted to Fiona Cunningham, David Edelstein, Joseph Fewsmith, Li Chen, Vipin Narang, Barry Posen, Richard Samuels, and Joseph Torigian, along with the anonymous reviewers. More colleagues read portions of the manuscript, and I thank them as well: David Bachman, Dennis Blasko, Jasen Castillo, Jonathan Caverley, David Finkelstein, George Gavrilis, Eugene Gholz, Stacie Goddard,

Avery Goldstein, Eric Heginbotham, Michael Horowitz, Andrew Kennedy, Kevin Narizny, Robert Ross, Randall Schweller, and Caitlin Talmadge.

Special thanks to Steve Goldstein. As a critic, he read several chapters at critical junctures. Each one benefited from his editorial eye. As a colleague, he has helped me better understand the study of Chinese politics and how it has evolved. As a mentor, he has always asked questions that elicited the most helpful guidance and advice. And as a friend, I have always looked forward to our lunches, where we not only talk shop but also discuss the latest gizmos and spy novels.

Participants at forums where I presented drafts of this book also helped to strengthen the final product. These include workshops or seminars at George Washington University, Georgetown University, Harvard University, North-western University, Princeton University, Ohio State University, Tufts University, Tulane University, Stanford University, the University of Chicago, and the University of Washington. I am especially grateful to the participants at the Lone Star Forum, where several chapters of this book were critiqued.

Several foundations provided generous financial support, which allowed me to take time off from teaching to focus on research and writing and to travel to China. I thank the United States Institute of Peace and the Smith Richardson Foundation, whose support helped to launch this project when I was a junior scholar. I thank the Carnegie Corporation, whose support enabled me to finish writing the book. I am also grateful to the Fairbank Center for Chinese Studies at Harvard University for hosting me as a visiting scholar.

This book would not have been possible without the help of a few more people. Since coming to MIT, Lynne Levine's assistance has been indispensable, including in all phases of this project. Philip Schwartzberg of Meridian Mapping created the maps that illustrate the nature of the strategic challenges China faced. At Princeton University Press, I thank Eric Crahan for his continuous support and encouragement (along with ample patience) while I completed the manuscript. I would also like to thank Emily Shelton for outstanding copyediting and Mark Bellis and the rest of the production team for shepherding this project to completion. My thanks to the editors of *International Security* for allowing me to use material from previously published work.

Finally, I would like to thank my family. My wife, Anna, continues to provide more love and support than I can ever hope to repay. She remains my rock and my true north. This book, and so much else, would not have been possible without her. Our daughter, Lana, was born shortly after I started this project. She brings us immense joy and makes us smile every day. We love you to the moon and back. I am blessed to share my life with them. Behan, my sister, and her intrepid family aboard *SV Totem* are a constant reminder of pursuing what matters most. My parents, Maris and Judy Fravel, have supported my interest in international conflict ever since I badgered them into subscribing to the Time-Life series on World War II as a young boy. Later, their courage to move me and my sister to Taiwan when I was sixteen years old opened our eyes to a much wider world from which neither of us has looked back. In so many ways, this book has its origins in that life experience, which they created for us. I dedicate this book to them.

ABBREVIATIONS

AMS Academy of Military Science

CCP Chinese Communist Party

CMC Central Military Commission

COSTIND Commission for Science, Technology, and Industry for National Defense

CSC Central Special Commission

GAD General Armaments Department

GLD General Logistics Department

GPD General Political Department

GSD General Staff Department

ICBM Intercontinental ballistic missile

MIRV Multiple independently targetable reentry vehicle

MR Military Region

NDIC National Defense Industry Commission

NDIO National Defense Industry Office

NDSTC National Defense Science and Technology Commission

NDU National Defense University

PAP People's Armed Police

PLA People's Liberation Army

PLAAF People's Liberation Army Air Force

PLAN People's Liberation Army Navy

PLARF People's Liberation Army Rocket Force

SSF Strategic Support Force

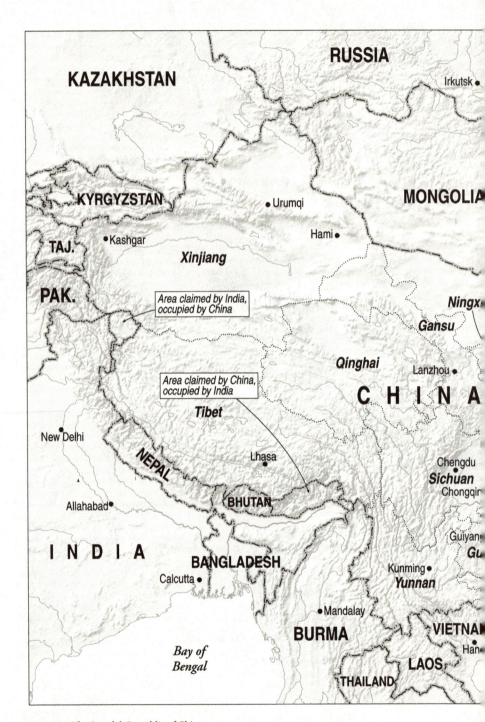

MAP 1.1. The People's Republic of China

Introduction

In September 1980, China's senior military officers convened a month-long meeting to discuss China's strategy for defeating a potential Soviet invasion. At the time, the Soviet Union had almost fifty divisions deployed along China's northern border. On the meeting's last day, Deng Xiaoping spoke. In his straightforward style, he said, "In our future war against aggression, exactly what guideline should we adopt? I approve these four characters—'active defense.'" With those brief remarks, Deng not only endorsed changing the military strategy used by the People's Liberation Army (PLA) since the mid-1960s, which had been based on fighting a protracted war deep inside Chinese territory. He also approved a new strategy to counter a Soviet invasion, which the PLA high command had formulated at the meeting and which sparked an effort to modernize China's armed forces.

Since 1949, China has adopted nine national military strategies, also known as the "strategic guidelines" (*zhanlue fangzhen*). These guidelines provide authoritative guidance from the Central Military Commission (CMC) of the Chinese Communist Party (CCP) for the operational doctrine, force structure, and training of the PLA. The guidelines adopted in 1956, 1980, and 1993 marked efforts to transform the PLA in order to wage war in a new kind of way. When and how has China pursued major change in its military strategy? Why has China pursued major change in its military strategy at these three moments and not at other times?

The answers to these questions are important for several reasons. First, theoretically, the variation in China's approach to military strategy offers a rich set of cases with which to deepen understanding of the sources of change in military organizations. Generally speaking, existing scholarship has examined a relatively small number of cases, limited largely to the advanced militaries in democratic societies and especially the United States and the United Kingdom.[1] In addition, most studies investigate two moments in time: the interwar period between the first and second world wars and the period since the end of the Cold War.[2] Apart from Japan in the interwar period, non-Western states such as China have received less scholarly attention.[3] Similarly, apart from the Soviet Union, military change in socialist states with party-armies remains understudied.[4] Moreover, with the exception of the United States and the Soviet Union, scholars have produced few studies of change over time in the military strategies of individual countries, despite the benefits that this research design offers for explaining strategic change by holding background factors like culture and geography constant.

Examining change in China's military strategy since 1949 represents an opportunity to enrich the existing literature on military doctrine and innovation in several ways. First, it permits the assessment of existing theories in a new and important case—contemporary China. Second, it allows scholars to probe the effects of a broad range of potential variables. Consider many of the attributes of China since 1949: a non-Western state with a distinct and rich cultural heritage, a socialist state with a party-army and not a national one, a revolutionary state with a violent birth, and a late modernizer of its armed forces relative to the other great powers. If theories derived from Western cases can explain military change in China, then they will have passed a series of important and difficult tests. However, if existing theories fail to account for strategic change in China, then scholars should reconsider the scope of their applicability.

Second, empirically, there is no comprehensive and systematic study of change in China's military strategy since 1949. Within the study of contemporary China, a small but vibrant group of scholars across several generations has examined the evolution of the PLA as an organization, its role in society and politics, and in China's defense-related policies.[5] Although existing studies have contributed greatly to understanding China's approach to defense policy, they are limited in three ways.

To start, the empirical scope or the temporal domain of existing studies of China's military strategy is restricted. Typically, China's military strategy has been examined from two perspectives. The first approach is in surveys of the PLA's organizational development that examine strategy alongside other topics such as training, force structure, organization, political work, and civil-military relations.[6] The second, and more common, approach is through book chapters or journal articles that document contemporaneous changes. Since the mid-1970s, Paul Godwin has written more than any other scholar on the subject, along with Li Nan and David Finkelstein, among others.[7] Although these works represent the state of the art at the time of publication, the literature lacks a comprehensive study of China's approach to military strategy, despite its role in guiding most other aspects of force development and modernization.[8]

In addition, most of the existing scholarship on Chinese strategy written before the 2000s relied on a limited number of translated Chinese language sources. In the past decade, however, materials from China on both current and past strategies have become available.[9] The limited availability of Chinese sources in earlier periods matters for two reasons. First, many studies of China's military strategy do not explain the phenomenon in the terms that the PLA itself uses. The importance of the concept of the strategic guideline, which reflects the essence of China's strategy in different periods, has only recently attracted the attention of Western scholars.[10] Despite its importance within the PLA, most previous scholarship has not examined the adoption and content of these strategic guidelines systematically.[11] Second, some of China's past military strategies have inadvertently been mischaracterized. For example, many scholars (this author included) have described the PLA's strategy in the early 1980s as embracing "people's war under modern conditions" because several noteworthy generals used the phrase in the context of a desire to modernize the PLA.[12] The CMC itself, however, never used this label when describing China's military strategy. Moreover, senior Chinese generals first used the phrase in the late 1950s and it remained in use well into the 1990s—both periods when China pursued different military strategies.[13] Similarly, China's military strategy before the 1980s is often characterized as "people's war."[14] During this period, however, the PLA adopted four different strategic guidelines and only two of them could be characterized as approximating what Mao Zedong had described as people's war.

Lastly, existing scholarship on the PLA lacks sufficient integration with the literature on military doctrine and innovation from political science. This lack of integration likely reflects insufficient access to primary sources. Whatever the reason, the lack of integration is costly: it hinders findings from the "China case" from engaging arguments in the broader theoretical literature, inhibits comparisons across cases involving one of the world's great powers, and prevents new frameworks from being applied to the study of Chinese politics.

The third and final reason is that understanding China's military strategy has never been more important than it is today. With four decades of rapid economic growth, China is now the world's second largest economy. Apart from the United States, China now spends more on defense than any other country. With two million soldiers in uniform, the PLA is one of the largest armed forces in the world. Yet some of the most important questions about China, including how it will use its growing military capabilities and for what ends, cannot be answered by simple metrics such as GDP or defense spending. A key part of the answer lies with military strategy. Understanding China's past and present approaches to strategy provides a crucial baseline for assessing future changes. It also carries important implications for the net assessment of

Chinese military power, the role of coercion in Chinese statecraft, the intensity of security competition in East Asia, and the potential for high levels of escalation should conflict erupt between China and the United States.

Overview of the Argument

To explain when, why, and how China has pursued major change in its military strategy, I offer a two-step argument in this book: China has pursued major changes in military strategy in response to shifts in the conduct of warfare—but only when the CCP is united and stable.

The first part of my argument focuses on the motivations for pursuing a change in strategy. In extending arguments that highlight the role of external sources of military change, such as immediate threats, I argue that one reason to pursue strategic change has been overlooked: a significant shift in the conduct of warfare in the international system, as revealed in the last war involving a great power or its clients. Such a shift should create a powerful incentive for a state to adopt a new military strategy if a gap exists between the state's current capabilities and the expected requirements of future wars. The effect of these changes should be particularly salient for developing countries or late military modernizers such as China that are trying to enhance their capabilities. These states are already at a comparative disadvantage and need to monitor closely their capabilities relative to stronger states.

The second part of my argument turns to the mechanism by which a change in strategy occurs, which is shaped by the structure of civil-military relations. In socialist states with party-armies, the party can grant substantial autonomy for the management of military affairs to senior officers, who will adjust military strategy in response to changes in their state's security environment. Because these officers are also party members, the party can delegate responsibility for military affairs without the fear of a coup or concerns that the military will pursue a strategy inconsistent with the party's political objectives. Such delegation, however, is possible only when the party's political leadership is united around the structure of authority and basic policies.

Taken together, a major change in China's military strategy will occur in response to a significant shift in the conduct of warfare that arises when the party is united. If the party is united but no significant shift in the conduct of warfare occurs, then senior military officers are more likely to pursue only minor changes in military strategy. When the party is divided, however, strategic change is unlikely to occur. Even when, externally, there is a significant shift in the conduct of warfare that provides a motive for strategic change, the military may become involved in intraparty politics or top party leaders may disagree about policy, be unwilling to delegate responsibility for military affairs to the armed forces, or seek to intervene in military affairs—all at the expense of the formulation of military strategy and management of military affairs more broadly.

Overview of the Book

Chapter 1 has three objectives. The first is to describe what is being explained: major changes in a state's military strategy. The second goal is to consider the competing motivations and mechanisms that can explain when and why states pursue major changes in military strategy. The chapter emphasizes two variables that are central to understanding changes in China's military strategy. The first is shifts in the conduct of warfare in the international system, which create strong motivations for adopting a new military strategy. The second is the unity of the ruling communist party, which empowers senior military officers to formulate and adopt new strategies without civilian intervention. The final goal of the chapter is to discuss the study's research design, including methods of inference, the measurement of variables, and data sources.

Before turning to the major changes in China's military strategy since 1949, chapter 2 reviews the military strategies adopted by the CCP during the civil war from 1927 to 1949. Some of these strategies were defensive, others were offensive. Most of the strategies emphasized regular units engaging in mobile warfare, while others gave greater prominence to the use of irregular units engaging in guerrilla warfare. This chapter reviews these strategies, along with the key terms that form China's strategic lexicon, such as "active defense" and "people's war," and the challenges the PLA faced when the PRC was established.

Chapter 3 examines the adoption of China's first national military strategy after the establishment of the People's Republic in 1949. The timing of the 1956 strategic guideline is puzzling for two reasons. First, when the strategy was adopted, China did not face immediate or pressing threats to its security and instead focused its resources on economic development through social-ist modernization. Second, although China was allied with the Soviet Union, which made available thousands of military advisors and experts along with enough equipment to arm more than sixty infantry divisions, China did not emulate the Soviet strategy. Instead, China rejected the basic elements of the Soviet model, including the emphasis on first strikes and preemption.

Changes in the conduct of warfare and party unity best explain when and why China adopted its first military strategy in 1956. The principal motivation for the new strategy was an assessment of a shift in the type of war that the PLA would be required to fight. During the early 1950s, China not only sought to absorb the lessons from World War II and the Korean War, but also consid-ered the implications of nuclear weapons for conventional operations. Senior military officers, especially Peng Dehuai, initiated vital military reforms and the formulation of the 1956 strategic guideline. Such military-led change was possible because of the unprecedented unity within the CCP, which created no incentives for the PLA to become involved in party politics and gave the PLA substantial autonomy for the management of military affairs, including military strategy. The chapter concludes by examining alternative explanations for the adoption of the 1956 strategic guideline, especially arguments about emulation.

Chapter 4 examines an anomalous but fascinating change in China's military strategy in 1964. It was an instance of reverting to a previous strategy—in this case, the idea of "luring the enemy in deep" from the Chinese civil war. It was also the only change in strategy initiated by the top party leader and not by senior military officers. Its adoption illustrates how leadership splits that create party disunity can distort strategic decision-making. In May 1964, as Mao became increasingly concerned about revisionism within the CCP, he overturned economic policies focused on agriculture to push for the industrialization of China's hinterland or the "third line." Mao's justification for this reversal was the need to create rear areas in case of a major war. Calling for the development of the third line enabled Mao to take control of economic policy for the first time since the Great Leap Forward and thus attack party leaders and the party's centralized bureaucracy, whom he viewed as revisionist. Yet Mao's justification for the third line—the need to prepare for a large-scale war—required a military strategy consistent with the threat he invoked. The third line as economic policy and luring the enemy in deep as military strategy were complementary efforts to weaken the bureaucracy of the party-state, foreshadowing Mao's frontal assault on the party leadership in 1966.

Chapter 5 examines the second major change in China's national military strategy in October 1980. Representing a stark departure from the strategy of luring the enemy in deep, the 1980 strategic guideline envisioned defeating a Soviet invasion through a forward defensive posture and the development of a mechanized force that could conduct combined arms operations. The timing of this change in strategy, however, presents a puzzle. China had identified the Soviet Union as a potential military adversary in the late 1960s and, after the 1969 clash with Soviet forces over Zhenbao (Damansky) Island, a Soviet invasion from the north was the main national security threat that China faced. Nevertheless, for more than a decade, the PLA did not adjust its strategy to address this threat, even as the Soviet Union deployed more than fifty divisions along China's northern frontier by the late 1970s.

Changes in the conduct of warfare and party unity help explain when and why China changed its military strategy in 1980. Although the Soviet threat was an important factor, a key impetus for adopting a new strategy was China's assessment of the kinds of operations that the Soviets would conduct, which were associated with shifts in the conduct of warfare as revealed in the 1973 Arab-Israeli War. The PLA's veteran generals began pushing for a new strategy as early as 1974 in response to these changes. Disunity in the party, however, delayed a change in strategy. Senior party members were engulfed in the factional conflicts of the Cultural Revolution, as reflected in Deng Xiaoping's short-lived rehabilitation in 1975. In addition, because the PLA had been used to restore order during the Cultural Revolution, it had focused on internal governance at the expense of combat readiness. Moreover, it had become bloated through an expansion of the officer corps in noncombat administrative and political roles. In the late 1970s, unity in the party was gradually restored, first through the arrest of the Gang of Four in October 1976 and followed by Deng's consolidation of power at the historic Third Plenum in December 1978. When PLA officers again pushed for a change in strategy in 1979, they were successful.

The third major change in China's military strategy, the adoption of the 1993 strategic guideline, is examined in chapter 6. This strategy required the PLA to be able to fight and win a local war on its periphery that would be characterized by "high technology." The adoption of this strategy is also puzzling from the standpoint of existing theory. In the early 1990s, China's senior party and military leaders maintained that China's regional security environment was the "best ever" since 1949, owing largely to the dissipation of the Soviet threat. Yet, despite the absence of a clear and present danger to the nation's security, China adopted its most ambitious military strategy to date by seeking to develop the capability to conduct joint operations in a wide range of contingencies on its periphery.

The conduct of warfare and party unity can best explain when and why China changed its military strategy. The principal motivation was an assessment of profound shifts in the conduct of warfare as revealed by the 1990–91 Gulf War. For Chinese strategists, modern warfare was now seen as being characterized by the use of high technology, including precision-guided munitions as well as advanced surveillance and reconnaissance with space-based platforms. China did not change its strategy until 1993, however, because of the conflict within the party and the army after Tiananmen. By late 1992, unity in the party had been restored through Deng's efforts to rebuild consensus around his reform policies. Immediately after the Fourteenth Party Congress, which reflected the restoration of unity in the party, the PLA began to draft the new strategic guideline that was subsequently adopted in early 1993.

Chapter 7 examines recent developments in China's military strategy in two adjustments to the 1993 strategic guideline. In 2004, the strategic guideline was altered to focus on "winning local wars under informatized conditions." In 2014, the strategic guideline was adjusted again to further emphasize informatization in "winning informatized local wars." Limits on the availability of source materials prevent a detailed analysis of the decision-making behind these two changes. Nevertheless, they should be viewed as minor, not major changes in military strategy, as each adjustment further highlighted the role of informatization as the core of high technology in warfare and the need to be able to conduct joint operations. Examination of the 2004 strategy suggests that the PLA was altering its assessments of trends in the conduct of warfare based on the 1999 Kosovo War and the 2003 Iraq War. The 2014 guideline was adopted to provide top-level guidance for the single largest organizational reform of the PLA since the mid-1950s. A primary driver for these reforms is to improve the PLA's ability to conduct joint operations, which had been identified as the future of warfare in the 1993 strategy. Even though the 2014 guideline did not envision waging war in a new way, the reforms it justified are poised to have a significant effect on the PLA's military effectiveness if implemented successfully.

Chapter 8 examines the evolution of China's nuclear strategy. China's nuclear strategy is puzzling for two reasons. One reason is that, based on achieving deterrence through assured retaliation, it has not changed substantially since China exploded its first nuclear device in October 1964. Moreover, China did not seek to change its strategy to overcome its vulnerability to a first strike by the United States or the Soviet Union. This contrasts with the dynamic nature of military strategy for conventional operations in the strategic guidelines. Another reason is the lack of integration between China's nuclear strategy and the many conventional strategies described in this book, even after the adoption of the 1993 strategic guideline.

This chapter suggests that nuclear strategy is the exception that proves the rule. Unlike conventional military operations, top party leaders never delegated authority over nuclear strategy to the PLA. Nuclear strategy was deemed a matter of national policy to be determined by the party leadership, in consultation with senior military officers as well as civilian scientific experts. Although senior military officers, especially in the 1950s, advocated for the development of a large nuclear program, these proposals were consistently rejected. Because nuclear strategy was never delegated to the PLA, the views about nuclear weapons held by China's top party leaders, especially Mao Zedong and Deng Xiaoping, have had an especially powerful effect, even today. Because these leaders viewed the utility of nuclear weapons as limited to deterring nuclear coercion or attacks, nuclear strategy was not integrated with conventional military strategy and has remained focused on achieving assured retaliation.

The conclusion reviews the main findings of the book, the implications of these findings for international relations theory, and the prospects for future changes in China's military strategy.

1

Explaining Major Change
in Military Strategy

Any explanation of why a state pursues a major change in its military strategy must address two questions. First, what factors prompt, spark, or trigger a state to change its strategy? Second, by what mechanism is the new strategy adopted? This chapter seeks to provide answers to these questions and then discuss how they will be used to examine changes in China's military strategy since 1949.

In extending existing arguments that highlight the role of external sources of military change, one likely motivation for why states pursue a change in their military strategy has been overlooked. This motivation is a significant shift in the conduct of warfare in the international system, as revealed in the most recent war involving a great power or its clients. A shift in the conduct of warfare should create a powerful incentive for a state to adopt a new military strategy if it highlights a gap between the state's current capabilities and the expected requirements of future wars it may have to fight.

The mechanism by which a new strategy is adopted depends on the structure of civil-military relations within the state. The structure of civil-military relations shapes whether civilian or military elites are more likely to be empowered to initiate a change in strategy. In socialist states with party-armies and not national ones, the party can grant substantial autonomy for the management of military affairs to senior military officers, who should be more likely to initiate a change in strategy than civilian party leaders. Such delegation, however, only occurs when the party's political leadership is united around the structure of authority and basic policies.

This chapter unfolds as follows. The first section describes what is being explained (military strategy) and the type of change being explored (major change in military strategy). The second section considers competing motivations that can explain when and why states pursue major changes in military strategy, focusing on significant shifts in the conduct of warfare. The third section examines the mechanisms by which military change can occur, emphasizing the structure of civil-military relations and how party unity in socialist states empowers senior military officers to initiate a change in strategy. The fourth and final section discusses the study's research design, including methods of inference and measurement of these variables, and how these will be applied in the study of China's military strategy since 1949.

Major Change in Military Strategy

National military strategy is the set of ideas that a military organization holds for fighting future wars. Military strategy is part of but distinct from a state's grand strategy.[1] Sometimes described as high-level military doctrine, a state's military strategy explains or outlines how its armed forces will be employed to achieve military objectives that advance the state's political goals. Strategy is what connects means with ends by describing which forces are necessary and the way in which they will be used. Strategy then shapes all aspects of force development, including operational doctrine, force structure, and training.[2]

National military strategy refers to the strategy for the use of a state's military as a whole. Locating the level of analysis at the national level is important for several reasons. First, it facilitates comparisons with the process of strategic change in other armed forces by specifying the type of change being examined. Second, it identifies the relevant explanations and arguments from the literature on military doctrine and innovation. A healthy portion of this literature, for example, examines changes within military organizations, especially combat arms and the development of weapons systems. Explanations of these changes often invoke competition within or among the service branches, which might be less salient when examining change in a state's national military strategy.[3]

National military strategy can be analyzed across various dimensions. These include the offensive or defensive content of the strategy or the integration of the strategy with a state's broader grand strategy, among others.[4] This study, however, seeks to explain why and when states decide to adopt a new military strategy that requires substantial organizational change. Although the offensive or defensive content of a strategy can impact stability in the international system, it does not necessarily capture much of what occurs in military organizations, such as changes in concepts of operations, operational doctrine, force structure, and training. In addition, especially after the nuclear revolution and the decline in wars of conquest, many national military strategies combine offensive and defensive operations in the pursuit of limited aims.

Characterizing these strategies as either offensive or defensive is problematic. Similarly, states may have multiple military objectives, some of which require defensive capabilities and others offensive ones. A state may also believe it needs to develop some offensive capabilities for defensive goals. How to categorize a state that plans to use force differently in diverse contingencies presents a challenge for scholars.

Military strategy is associated more broadly with the idea of doctrine. This book, however, is not framed around the concept of doctrine for several reasons. To start, scholars have offered a variety of definitions, which implies a range of different concepts and dependent variables.[5] In addition, a gap exists between how scholars tend to use the term and how military professionals and practitioners conceive of doctrine. Although scholars often use doctrine to refer to the principles of strategic-level activities by a military or a state, many modern militaries use doctrine to refer to the principles or rules that govern any type of activity, at any level, that a military organization conducts, especially operational and tactical activities.[6] Finally, the meaning of the word itself varies from military to military, which can complicate comparative studies. Although widely used within the US military at the tactical level, it was a grand strategic concept for the Soviet Union and is not used at all by the Chinese military.[7]

Major change occurs when the adoption of a new military strategy drives a military organization to alter how it prepares to conduct operations and wage war. Major change requires that a military develop capabilities that it does not already possess to perform activities that it cannot currently undertake. This distinguishes major change from a minor change or an incremental adaptation in strategy, whereby an existing strategy is tweaked or refined but does not require substantial organizational change.

My definition of major change draws on the concept of military reform. According to Suzanne Nielsen, in a military context "reform is an improvement in or the creation of a significant new program or policy that is intended to correct an identified deficiency."[8] Reform does not necessarily require that an organization successfully change how it performs all its core tasks. Nevertheless, if the reforms are successful and deficiencies are addressed, they can substantially improve organizational performance. Nielsen notes that major peacetime components of military reform include not just doctrinal change, but also changes to training practices, personnel policies, organization, and equipment.[9] The concept of reform captures a great deal of what military organizations do, especially in peacetime.

Major change in military strategy contains two components linked with military reforms and can be regarded as high-level military reform. The first is that the strategy articulates a new vision of warfare and a call for change in how a military prepares to fight in the future. The second is that the new strategy must require some degree of organizational change from past practices, including operational doctrine, force structure, and training. Major change highlights the desire to pursue significant organizational reforms over their successful institutionalization. The reasons why a state might decide to adopt a new military strategy are likely to differ from those that explain successful reform within a military organization. Nevertheless, by identifying attempts at organizational reform, major change is much more than just the articulation of an abstract vision of future wars.

Major change is closely associated with the concept of innovation. However, they are different in one important respect. Although many scholars use innovation as another word for change, others define innovation in military organizations as a change that is unprecedented or revolutionary, a significant departure from past practice, and a change that has been successfully institutionalized or implemented within a military organization, usually to improve its effectiveness.[10] In other words, innovation is institutionalized change. Nevertheless, the concept of innovation as institutionalized change may be less helpful for understanding national military strategy because successful institutionalization is likely to be a matter of degree and a continuous process.[11] In addition, as noted, the factors that prompt or trigger a desire to change strategy may not be the same as those that explain its successful institutionalization within a particular organization.

Two final clarifications are necessary before proceeding. One clarification is that major change in military strategy must be distinguished from two other outcomes. The first is no change in military strategy. The second is a minor change in military strategy, defined as adjusting or refining an existing strategy. Here, although a state adopts a new national military strategy, the purpose of the change is to better accomplish the vision contained in the existing strategy.

Another clarification is that I focus on peacetime change in military strategy. This serves to distinguish it from wartime change.[12] It is important to note, however, that the concept of peacetime includes wide variation in the international threat environment. It only excludes military strategies that are devised in wartime for a particular conflict.

Motivations for Major Change in Military Strategy

Within the literature on military doctrine and innovation, a rough consensus exists around the primacy of external motivations for great powers to pursue change in military strategy. As these states develop armed forces to defend against external threats or project power over others, a focus on external factors is unsurprising. These existing external incentives for change should be viewed as forming a general model of external sources of military change. The caveat, however, is that scope conditions, some of which are more restrictive than others, can limit the effect of these incentives in particular cases, and not all of them may apply to China's past strategies.

The first motivation is an immediate or pressing external security threat. If a state's current military strategy is ill suited to meet the threat that it faces, then it will seek to change its strategy. One source of immediate threats can arise through a change in a state's security environment, such as an increase in the capabilities of an opponent or the appearance of a new adversary with a different set of capabilities. Another source can be created by the failure of a state's military to perform as expected during its most recent conflict, especially if it was defeated on the battlefield or failed to achieve its military objectives. Defeat or failure suggests a vulnerability or weakness to be rectified through the adoption of a new military strategy, though defeat could also lead a state to enhance the implementation of its current strategy.[13] The effects of immediate and pressing threats apply to all states and are not limited by many scope conditions—only a gap between the existing strategy and the new threat.

A second motivation for change in strategy, closely related to immediate threats, is assessments of an opponent's military strategy. A military may adopt a new strategy in response to a change in the war plans of its adversary. In a study of Soviet military doctrine, Kimberly Marten Zisk describes this as a "reactive innovation," even in the absence of an immediate threat.[14] The possibility of a reactive innovation is limited to states already in a strategic or an enduring rivalry that would face a greater threat if an adversary changes its strategy.[15] Rivals must closely monitor the war plans and capabilities of their opponents and change their own strategy as circumstances require. Zisk, for example, argues that Soviet doctrine changed in response to changes in American grand strategy and military doctrine. Following the US adoption of "Flexible Response" that increased the role of conventional forces in the defense of Western Europe, for example, Soviet doctrine shifted to emphasizing limited war and the "conventional option."[16]

A third motivation for major change is the creation of new missions and objectives for the military by the state. This source of change can be described as environmental because it occurs independently of any military strategy.[17] New missions can arise for a variety of reasons, such as the acquisition of new interests abroad to be defended, changes in the security needs of an ally, or shifts in a state's political goals for the use of force that require new capabilities (such as a desire to reclaim lost territory or establish buffer zones). In the early twentieth century, for example, the acquisition of the Philippines after the Spanish-American War created new overseas interests for the United States that in turn altered its military strategy. By acquiring a colony in the Pacific, the United States needed to prepare to fight naval battles far from home, which highlighted the importance of amphibious warfare to seize naval bases to support operations in the region.[18] Likewise, Adolf Hitler's broad ambitions required a force capable of mobile offensive operations.[19] New missions can require a military to perform new types of operations, which in turn can require a new military strategy. The impetus for change, however, lies in a state's broader international political environment.[20] New missions as a source of change may be especially relevant to rising powers, which acquire new interests to be defended as their capabilities expand.

The long-term implications for warfare of basic technological change provide a fourth external motivation for change in military strategy. The advent of new technologies may lead states to consider their implications for warfare and to adjust their military strategies accordingly. Here, a state does not face an immediate or pressing threat. Instead, it considers how today's technological advances will impact tomorrow's war. Stephen Rosen, for example, suggests that the invention of the airplane led to the development of aircraft carriers, which ultimately replaced battleships as the main platform of naval firepower.[21] This motivation for change, however, applies primarily to the most advanced states in the system that enjoy a relative abundance of resources for developing military power along with mature industrial and technological capabilities that can develop or apply these technologies to warfare.[22]

These motivations can account for strategic change under different circumstances, but they remain incomplete. Specifically, they cannot account for why a state might change its military strategy when these motivations are absent, such as when the state is not facing an immediate and pressing threat. Another possible motivation for a change in strategy is a shift in the conduct of warfare in the international system, as revealed in the last war that involved one or more great powers or their clients (equipped with their patron's weaponry).[23] Such wars are similar to what Michael Horowitz describes as a "demonstration point" in the context of discrete military innovations.[24] This motivation should be especially powerful if a gap is believed to exist between how a state's military plans to wage war and the requirements of future warfare. Since 1945, for example, the 1973 Arab-Israeli War has attracted a great deal of attention from military professionals because of its implications for armored warfare and the importance of the operational level of war.[25] Likewise, the 1990–91 Gulf War demonstrated the potential of precision-guided munitions when paired with advanced command, control, surveillance, and reconnaissance systems.[26] Of course, not all states will draw the same lessons from the same conflict, as demonstration effects will be filtered by a state's security environment, military capabilities, and resources.[27] Nevertheless, other people's wars may demonstrate the importance or utility of existing practices as well as what some scholars call military revolutions or military innovations.

How does this argument differ from emulation? In *Theory of International Politics*, Kenneth Waltz argues that because international politics is "a competitive realm," states will copy and emulate the most successful military practices in the system. In particular, Waltz suggests, "contending states imitate the military innovations contrived by the country of the greatest capability and ingenuity," including its weapons and strategies. Waltz's argument includes both a potential motivation for change (competition) as well as a mechanism by which such change occurs (emulation, discussed in the next section). As a possible motivation for when and why states pursue change in military strategy, however, Waltz's argument is underspecified. Although Waltz highlights competition as a reason for change in strategy, the specific motivation for change at any one time is unclear. As discussed above, much of the existing literature seeks to identify different motives that the competitive pressures of the international system create for changing strategy. Although competition under anarchy causes states to change their military strategies, the more interesting questions are when and why such change occurs, which can be answered only by looking beyond the general argument that Waltz offers.

Shifts in the conduct of warfare are one such incentive for a major change in military strategy. When a war occurs in the international system, states are likely to assess its key features and implications for their own security. Depending on their strategic circumstances, states may seek to emulate or to develop other responses, such as countermeasures. The 1999 Kosovo War was revealing not just because it highlighted advances in stealth and precision-strike capabilities, but also because it suggested that simple tactics and procedures such as camouflage could blunt the potentially devastating effects of precision-guided munitions.[28] States vulnerable to airstrikes might have focused on the latter and not the former. Waltz also suggests that emulation will most likely occur among peer competitors or "contending states." Yet the lessons from contemporary conflicts should be especially relevant for developing countries or late military modernizers, such as China, that may not yet be peer competitors but that seek to strengthen their armed forces and must allocate their scarce resources for defense with care.

External motivations for change have received the most attention in the scholarly literature because the basic mission for most armed forces of great powers or aspiring great powers is to defend the state against external threats. Nevertheless, internal motivations are also possible triggers for a change in strategy. But the arguments about organizational biases and military culture reviewed briefly below are usually presented to explain stasis or the lack of change in a military organization. For this reason, they are not especially well suited to answering the question posed by this book about when and why China changes its military strategy.

The first internal motive for change is a military's organizational bias or preference for offensive operations that increase its autonomy, prestige, or resources. The logic of this motive draws heavily on organization theory. Such biases can only have an effect on strategy, however, when civilian control is weak or when a benign external environment limits civilian monitoring and allows organizational biases to influence strategy.[29]

The second internal motive is a military's organizational culture apart from an offensive bias. A military's organizational culture can shape its preferences, including for the kinds of strategies it would prefer to adopt. In her examination of the role of organizational culture in the British and French militaries in the interwar period, Elizabeth Kier suggests that when the civilian government in France limited conscription to one year, the military adopted a defensive doctrine because it believed that such recruits would be unable to perform offensive operations required for a more robust defense.[30] More recently, in a detailed study of counterinsurgency operations, Austin Long demonstrates how the deep-rooted cultures of the US Army, US Marines, and British Army shaped how they conducted such operations, regardless of the formal or operational doctrine they adopted. The effect of organizational culture should be especially salient in operational environments where information is ambiguous.[31]

Mechanisms of Major Change in Military Strategy

The second component of any explanation of strategic change is the mechanism by which change occurs, which shapes how a new military strategy is formulated and adopted. In the literature on military doctrine and innovation, much of the debate about how change occurs in military organizations revolves around whether civilian intervention is required or whether change can be led by military officers and occur autonomously. The answer depends on the structure of civil-military relations and whether or not it empowers military leaders. In socialist states like China, with party-armies and not national ones, the structure of civil-military relations empowers senior military officers to initiate changes in strategy under certain conditions—when the party is united and delegates responsibility for military affairs to the armed forces.

CIVILIAN INTERVENTION VERSUS MILITARY-LED CHANGE

Two of the most commonly discussed mechanisms of change in military organizations examine the relative roles of civilian and military elites. Some scholars suggest that major change requires civilian intervention, while others contend that senior military officers can lead such change autonomously and independently.

Civilian intervention as a mechanism for major change in military strategy is most commonly associated with either high threat environments or states with revisionist goals. Both conditions place a premium on the integration of a state's grand strategy with its military strategy to ensure the security of the state or the achievement of its ambitious political objectives.[32] Yet, deductively, no reason exists why other motivations for a change in strategy might not also occur through civilian intervention, except perhaps regarding the long-term military implications of basic technological change. Even here, though, efforts to develop new weapons systems would require funding controlled by civilians.

Civilian intervention for military change can be direct or indirect. In its direct manifestation, a civilian political leader pushes the military to change, such as Hitler's intervention in the Wehrmacht before World War II.[33] In its indirect form, the structure and strength of civilian control mechanisms can create strong incentives for military officers to pursue the change that civilians desire. In a study of counterinsurgency doctrine, Deborah Avant demonstrates that the British military adapted to the counterinsurgency campaigns political leaders wanted to wage because civilian oversight and monitoring was centralized in the cabinet, which controlled military promotions. The US military was less able to adapt to such campaigns because the executive and legislative branches of government shared control of the armed forces, which allowed military elites to resist some civilian oversight.[34]

Military-led change without civilian intervention is another possible mechanism of strategic change. This mechanism stresses military autonomy, positing that change can occur from within, led by senior military officers without a push from civilians.[35] In principle, senior officers could advocate for a change in strategy in response to any of the external motivations identified above. As some scholars have noted, military officers are perhaps more sensitive to changes in the conduct of warfare than civilians because officers must plan to confront these changes on the battlefield.

These two mechanisms—civilian intervention and military autonomy—are usually cast as opposing arguments. Most studies of military innovation begin by contrasting these approaches.[36] Nevertheless, these two mechanisms are probably much more complementary than commonly believed, depending on two scope conditions. The first is the urgency and intensity of external threats that a state faces. The more immediate and greater the threat, the more likely civilian leaders will monitor their military's strategy and intervene if it is ill-equipped to meet the threat.[37] Conversely, the less immediate or intense the threat, the greater the likelihood that a change in strategy will come from within a military organization as it considers the requirements of its future security environment.

The second scope condition concerns the level of organizational change that one seeks to explain. Civilian intervention should be more likely to occur as one moves from the level of tactics and operations to the level of strategy, as information asymmetries decrease, and as formal channels of civilian influence over the armed forces grow. By contrast, military-led change should be more likely to occur as one moves within a military organization from the level of strategy to the level of operations and tactics because of the importance of specialized technical knowledge that most civilians will lack.

National military strategy is perhaps the level of military affairs where civilian and military elites are equally positioned to shape the process of strategic change. Civilians must rely on the professional and technical expertise of the military to devise and implement a strategy, while the military depends on civilians for the necessary resources to implement a new strategy. If this is the case, then the structure of civil-military relations and the degree of delegation to the armed forces should play an important role in creating relatively greater opportunities for either civilians or senior military leaders to initiate a major change in military strategy.

Although the structure of civil-military relations can determine whether civilian or military elites are more likely to push for change in military strategy, scholarship on military innovation and civil-military relations is only loosely integrated. On the one hand, studies of civil-military relations rarely treat the subject as an independent variable that can explain military outcomes of interest, such as operational doctrine, effectiveness, or innovation.[38] Instead, most studies seek to explain the dynamics of civil-military relations and the potential for military intervention in the civilian sphere, such as coups, military influence in politics short of coups, civil-military conflict, military compliance with civilian demands, and the dynamics of civilian delegation.[39] Scholars have only just started to explore civil-military relations as a variable that can explain military as well as political outcomes, and it requires greater attention as both an intervening and independent variable in military affairs.[40]

On the other hand, few studies of military innovation draw explicit links with civil-military relations. To be sure, civilian intervention is discussed, but usually not in the context of theoretical approaches to civil-military relations. For instance, many studies of World War I identify weak civilian control as a key source of the offensive biases displayed by militaries in the run-up to the conflict.[41] Similarly, although Avant casts her argument in terms of institutional theory, its logic is based on the incentives for military change created by different mechanisms of civilian control in democratic systems and how these mechanisms shape the responsiveness of the military to the preferences of civilians.[42] Likewise, in Kier's study of French and British military doctrine in the interwar period, a key variable is the degree of consensus among civilian elites about the role of the armed forces in society. When consensus was absent, political elites sought to intervene more in military affairs.[43] Finally, the struggle for autonomy features prominently in Zisk's study of Soviet military doctrine, but is never discussed in terms of research on Soviet civil-military relations or theories of civil-military relations more generally.[44] These examples are far from exhaustive. Instead, they illustrate how the structure of civil-military relations in a given society creates opportunities for either civilian or military elites to intiate and lead the process of strategic change.

PARTY UNITY AND MILITARY CHANGE IN SOCIALIST STATES

In socialist states such as China, a distinct kind of civil-military relations suggests that senior military officers can be empowered to initiate change in military strategy without civilian intervention. Any discussion of civil-military relations almost always begins with Samuel Huntington's arguments in *The Soldier and the State*.[45] Nevertheless, his framework fits somewhat uncomfortably with socialist states characterized by professional armies that are nevertheless subject to a series of intense political controls and routinely involved in activities beyond the military sphere, and which occasionally participate in internal party conflicts. Put simply, in terms of their relations with the civilian sphere, party-armies differ fundamentally from national armies. In socialist states, the more appropriate subject of study is not civil-military relations, but "party-military" relations.[46] Huntington starts with the premise that an inherent conflict exists between the state and its armed forces, where the greatest danger is military intervention into politics, especially coups. With party-armies in most socialist states, however, this problem does not exist: there have been few if any military-led coups in communist countries, especially those founded through violent revolution.[47] When the military does intervene in politics, it seeks to maintain the hegemony of the ruling communist party, not seize power for itself.

The effect of civil-military relations on the timing and process of strategic change in socialist states such as China reflects the structure of political authority in these societies. Building on various conceptualizations of civil-military relations in the Soviet Union, Amos Perlmutter and William Leogrande sought to develop a unified theory of civil-military relations in socialist states.[48] They explain that socialist states are characterized by the political hegemony of a "vanguard" party. This hegemony requires the subordination of all nonparty institutions, including the military, to the party and not to the state (which the party controls). Subordination of nonparty actors is achieved and sustained through a number of different mechanisms, including the creation of dual elites known as an "interlocking directorate" who hold top positions in the party and the military as well as the construction of a party structure of political commissars and party committees within the armed forces. Subordination of the military to the party, however, does not mean that the military lacks autonomy, especially in the realm of military affairs. The party must grant enough freedom to the military for it to perform the tasks that the party requires. As the technological complexity of war progresses, for example, militaries in socialist states are likely to enjoy greater autonomy in military affairs in order to perform the tasks that are required.[49]

From their analysis, Perlmutter and Leogrande draw several conclusions about civil-military relations in socialist states. First, conflicts over national policy are resolved within the party, not between the party and other institutions such as the state or military. Second, due to this institutional arrangement, the military's participation in politics is the norm and not the exception as in noncommunist states. A party-army can be drawn into politics because a military officer with party membership, as William Odom writes, is an "agent of the party." Third, when the military intervenes decisively in the political sphere, it does so to uphold and maintain the party and its hegemony over the state rather than to seize power. This applies even when the military intervenes to support one faction within the party over another. What prompts intervention is not the military's desire for power, but disunity in the party that threatens its hegemonic position. A final implication that Perlmutter and Leogrande do not discuss is that the military may be required to defend the party not just against external threats to the state but also against internal threats to its continued hegemony. Thus, one should expect the military in socialist states to perform those tasks that the party deems necessary to its continued survival, including the suppression of dissent and opposition movements.

Perlmutter and Leogrande do not consider how party-military relations might influence military or strategic outcomes. Nevertheless, the structure of party-military relations should influence whether and when either party or military elites will push for change in military strategy in socialist states. Because the military in socialist states can enjoy substantial autonomy, it is positioned to initiate the process of strategic change. Yet because the military leaders are also party members, they will formulate new strategies consistent with the party's broader political goals and priorities. As Odom notes, the military in socialist states is an "administrative arm" of the party, as are other state institutions, and "not something separate from and competing with it."[50]

If this view of party-military relations is accurate, the timing and process of strategic change in socialist states will depend on the unity of the party—the condition that enables substantial delegation of military affairs to senior military officers. Party unity refers to the agreement among the top party leaders on basic policy questions (i.e., the proverbial "party line" or general guideline) and the structure of power within the party. When the party is united, it will delegate responsibility for military affairs to the armed forces, with only minimal oversight. As a result, senior officers are likely to play a decisive role in initiating and formulating major changes in military strategy, if required by the state's external security environment. When the party is united, the armed forces remain beholden to only one actor, the party, which sustains its autonomy in the military sphere to pursue strategic change. The party's various control mechanisms ensure that the military will adopt policies consistent with the party's broader political objectives. Debate over military policy and strategy can occur, of course, but does so within the party. In this way, party unity creates an environment similar to Huntington's ideal of objective civilian control, which fosters professionalism, even though a party-army is a politicized armed force. To borrow from Huntington, this might be described as "subjective objective control."[51]

The reasons why party unity enables strategic change in socialist states can be illustrated through Risa Brooks's argument about strategic assessment. Brooks suggests that states are most likely to produce the "best" assessments when the preference divergence between civilian and military elites over questions of strategic assessment is low and when political dominance of the armed forces is high.[52] Party-military relations in many ways reflect such a relationship. As members of the same hegemonic socialist party, preference divergence between the top party leadership and senior military officers should be low. At the same time, a party-army is by definition under the political dominance of the communist party.[53]

By contrast, disunity at the highest levels of the party will likely prevent major strategic change from occurring, even if the state faces strong external incentives for change. Disunity can paralyze strategic decision-making in a party-army for several reasons: first, the military may be required to perform nonmilitary tasks relating to governance or maintaining law and order.[54] If political disunity produces domestic instability (or vice versa), then the military may be given a new primary mission of restoring or maintaining law and order. Second, the military may become the object or focus of political contestation at the highest levels of the party. Because the military is the ultimate guarantor of the party's hegemonic rule, contending groups or factions may seek to increase their influence over the military to prevail in the intraparty struggle. Factional struggle within the party may also spread to the armed forces, hampering their ability to focus on military affairs. Third, as a party-army, the military must also carry out the policies of the party, especially ideological ones such as mass campaigns. Such campaigns would likely interfere with military training and politicize larger policy decisions such as a change in strategy. Fourth, even if the military remained united and depoliticized during periods of disunity, the party may be unwilling to consider proposals for strategic change or, as with any major policy decision, a divided party might be unable to come to any agreement on military change. Fifth, top military leaders may also become involved in intraparty politics—again, at the expense of military affairs such as strategy.

Deductively, periods of party disunity could present the military with an opportunity to back one party faction or group in exchange for support from that faction for its own interests once unity is restored. For example, the military might demand a higher budget or approval of a new military strategy in exchange for their support in order to end the period of disunity. Nevertheless, party-armies should be less able or less willing to engage in these kinds of bargains. Their intervention may not restore unity, and in fact could be a source of greater intraparty tension, further harming the military and the party. The military would be seen as an overt political actor and an independent source of power that could increase disunity and instability in the long term. Moreover, if disunity has created factionalism within the military, then it may be unable to act in a unitary fashion in the intraparty competition. Instead, the military, or a faction in the military, would most likely intervene not to advance its parochial organizational interests, but only to restore unity in the party.

A final question to consider is whether party unity is independent of the external motivations for change. For example, the onset of an immediate or pressing external threat could enhance party unity and thus party unity would be a function of the external environment. External threats are likely to enhance elite cohesion in democracies, as leaders are ultimately accountable to their publics and more likely to set aside partisan differences during periods of duress. Nevertheless, external threats may be less likely to unify a fractured Leninist party in a socialist state, where the party leadership is not accountable to the public and the issues that create disunity involve either the distribution of power within the party or questions relating to the party's basic or fundamental policies. External threats are unlikely to compel leaders to resolve these differences. In the case of China, for example, growing tensions with the Soviet Union after 1969 did little to unify the party leadership that had been divided during the Cultural Revolution.

EMULATION OR DIFFUSION?

The main alternative set of mechanisms to the debate over civilian intervention are the processes of emulation and diffusion. When applied to a change in military strategy, arguments about emulation or diffusion both expect that it occurs because one state seeks to copy or imitate the strategy of another. The relative roles of civilian and military leaders are largely irrelevant, as emulation and diffusion assume elite consensus about the preferred course of action.

Emulation offers one mechanism through which a change in strategy might occur. This draws on the work of Kenneth Waltz, who argues that competition "in the arts and the instruments of force . . . produces a tendency toward the sameness of the competitors." Waltz further claims that states should adopt the practices of the militarily most powerful states: "The weapons of the major contenders, and even their strategies, [will] begin to look much the same all over the world."[55] Competition leads to copying and convergence.[56] Emulation is an especially important potential mechanism for developing countries or late military modernizers such as China. These states not only have the desire to increase their military capabilities, but will also likely search for templates or models to import in order to jump-start their modernization drive.[57]

Although the competitive pressures of the international system no doubt may lead states to adopt new military strategies, emulation as a mechanism for major change in strategy has several limitations (with the caveat that Waltz only devoted two paragraphs to the subject).[58] One limitation is that its logic implies that because states will imitate leading practices, they must face the same set of strategic circumstances and intend to fight the same type of war (most likely industrialized wars of conquest among peer or near-peer great power competitors). Of course, states face a variety of strategic circumstances, and security maximization might be best achieved through countermeasures or counterinnovations, or simply a different strategy, not necessarily by imitating and copying others.[59]

A second limitation is that even if some institutional or organizational similarity among militaries occurs, this may be less helpful in illuminating the choices that states make about their military strategies. Since 1918, most states have moved to adopt elements of what Stephen Biddle calls the "modern system," defined as a set of methods for conducting military operations "in the face of radical firepower."[60] Earlier, as a precursor to the modern system, many states instituted the mass army.[61] In this sense, imitation might explain the choices that states make at the highest level of institutional design and that may be especially relevant during the formation of the modern state and the industrialization of warfare. At the same time, it cannot explain, for example, how a state intends to implement the modern system on the battlefield.[62] Waltz expects military strategies to converge, but this might be precisely where they should diverge because of the different goals, circumstances, and capabilities of states. Perhaps for this reason, Joao Resende-Santos explicitly excludes military strategy in a lengthy study of emulation.[63]

Finally, at the most general level of institutional and organizational forms, what states seem to do is selectively adopt military practices (or innovations) developed by other states. This, in fact, would not be emulation if such selective adoption occurred because of a state's particular threat environment, its resource endowments and capacity to mobilize resources, the level of its own military modernization, or its level of industrialization. States will not engage in wholesale emulation if it breaks the bank. Moreover, it may just not always be practical, given the long lead times for importing innovations from elsewhere. Instead, states will look for the most efficient solution to their security problem. Even if the style of warfare is similar to the modern system, national strategy will still determine how it is employed and for what ends.

The closely related literature on the diffusion of military innovations seeks to understand in more detail when and how the processes of emulation and imitation occur. Although similar, this work differs from Waltz's argument about emulation in several ways. First, it examines the variation in the adoption of military innovations, especially technological innovations such as the development of new weapons systems, as part of a broader effort to understand how the spread of military technology may influence the distribution of power in the system. Second, it typically examines discrete innovations, such as aircraft carriers or nuclear weapons. Third, it moves beyond structural factors to examine variables that might shape the choices of individual states, including those factors that push states to adopt foreign practices as well as those factors, especially cultural ones, that inhibit adoption. The range of potential factors includes geography, financial resources, access to military hardware necessary for the adoption of new operational doctrines or software, the social environment, national culture, organizational capital, organizational culture, and bureaucratic politics.[64]

Like emulation, arguments about diffusion have a teleological quality, a sense that the adoption of military innovations, especially technical ones, is inevitable and will occur when constraints are few and when resources are abundant. The baseline expectation is that states will copy innovations if they have the means and ability to do so. Adoption does not occur when barriers to importation are present, such as culture, the lack of resources, or domestic politics. In one recent study of diffusion, for example, Michael Horowtiz argues that states are much more likely to adopt "major military innovations" when they possess the financial resources to fund development of these technologies and the organizational capital to develop them indigenously. What is missing from many accounts of diffusion, however, is a consideration of a state's assessment of its security environment and its strategic goals, which in turn identify the capabilities required to defend the state and preferences for the adoption of military innovations. States facing different adversaries and pursuing different goals will likely make different choices about how to structure their armed forces and which foreign practices and innovations to adopt.

SUMMARY OF THE ARGUMENT

To sum up, whether China pursues a major change in military strategy depends on whether it encounters a strong external incentive for change and whether politics within the party enables senior military officers to respond to these changes by formulating a new military strategy if necessary. The external stimulus—the shift in the conduct of warfare—is a necessary condition for major change to occur. Party unity is a sufficient condition that allows the military to respond to the external stimulus.

As shown in figure 1.1, four outcomes are possible. If China faces a shift in the conduct of warfare and the party is united, senior military officers will push for a major change in military strategy. If China faces a significant shift

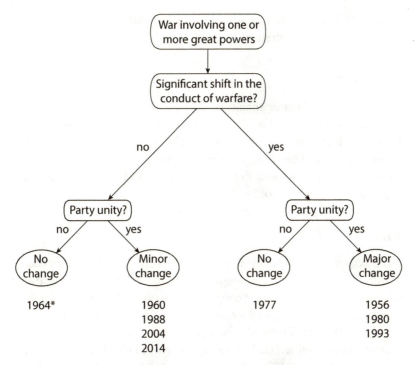

FIGURE 1.1. Conduct of warfare and party unity in strategic change

Note: The years below each node refer to my argument's prediction for each of China's strategic guidelines. The asterisk (*) denotes the adoption of a guideline not predicted by my argument.

in the conduct of warfare, but the party lacks unity, then no change in strategy will occur (major or minor), as disunity prevents the military from responding to the external stimulus. By contrast, if China does not face a significant shift in the conduct of warfare but the party is united, then senior military officers will pursue minor change in their country's military strategy, if external circumstances require it. If China does not face a significant shift in the conduct of warfare and the party lacks unity, then party disunity will prevent the military from undertaking even minor changes in strategy.

This framework can accommodate all external motivations that could prompt a change in military strategy. This book argues that past changes in China's strategy have occurred in response to assessments of a shift in the conduct of warfare. Looking forward, however, China may pursue a major change in its strategy in response to other external factors, such as new missions for its armed forces created by the expansion of its interests overseas. Depending on the intensity of these interests, this process could result in a major change in China's military strategy, so long as the party remains united. Nevertheless, since 1949, a significant shift in the conduct of warfare best explains the reasons why China's senior military officers have pursued major changes in their country's military strategy.

Research Design

Any explanation of major change in military strategy must complete two empirical tasks. The first is to identify those changes in military strategy that can be considered "major" and represent a clear departure from past strategy. The second task is to demonstrate why key decisions were taken at particular points in time and not others. Below I discuss how I will complete these tasks in the remainder of the book.

METHOD

This book uses two methods of inference. First, each of the three major changes in China's military strategy is compared with the minor changes in strategy and periods of no change in strategy to determine which motivations and mechanisms best account for the major changes. Such comparisons are a variant of the method of "structured, focused comparisons."[65] By examining both major changes as well as minor ones and periods of continuity, I explore the full range of variation in China's military strategy, not just the instances of major change (which could bias the findings).

Second, the process by which change occurred is examined to determine which mechanism best accounts for change in military strategy. Examination of primary and secondary sources on military affairs, including official documents and leadership speeches, can help to determine if the decision to adopt a new strategy is consistent with the motivations for adopting a new strategy and if the change was initiated by senior military officers. Such process tracing permits an assessment of the mechanisms by which a change in strategy occurs.[66]

The longitudinal study of change in one country's military strategy over seven decades has several advantages. It controls for many potentially confounding factors, such as regime type, culture, and geography, while also allowing for wide variation in a state's security challenges, threat environment, and wealth. It also permits a complete examination of the process of strategic change by focusing on just one country in detail, and allows scholars to examine periods when change was not pursued and when it might have been expected to occur over a seventy-year period.

This approach improves upon existing longitudinal studies of strategy in two ways. First, it restricts the analysis to the same type of change—the adoption of a new military strategy. This ensures unit homogeneity by holding constant the type of change being examined and the level within a military organization where change should occur. Zisk's study of Soviet doctrinal change, for example, compared both changes in grand strategy (the response to Flexible Response) and changes in operational doctrine (the response to AirLand Battle).[67] Second, by distinguishing among major, minor, and no changes in strategy, it allows for comparisons that reduce selection bias created by examining only instances of major change. This approach can isolate those factors linked with major change in strategy and not minor adaptations.

China presents a rich empirical environment for the study of change in military strategy. Many of the different potential motivations are present. To start, the intensity of threats that China faced since 1949 has varied widely. On one level, there have been several periods when China feared imminent attack, including the spring of 1962, when Taiwan mobilized forces; in 1969 after the clash with the Soviets over Zhenbao Island; and in the 1970s when the Soviets deployed hundreds of thousands of troops on its northern border. There have also been periods of sustained threats to Chinese security, such as during the Cold War, when China squared off against both superpowers, who changed their own military strategies in ways that might have prompted a reactive innovation. Likewise, China's security environment has changed substantially over the past seventy years. Although homeland security and the defense of territorial claims have been the main missions assigned by the CCP to the PLA, these missions have begun to expand in the past two decades as China's economy has grown. Regarding basic technology that might influence the conduct of warfare, China's first military modernization began in the shadow of the revolution in firepower displayed during World War II and the birth of the nuclear revolution. The growing importance of information technology, and the "revolution in military affairs" it purportedly fosters, overlap with the last thirty years of the PLA's modernization. Finally, a significant number of major wars with demonstration effects about the conduct of warfare have occurred over this period, from World War II to the 2003 Iraq War.

MILITARY STRATEGY IN CHINA

In China, the strategic guideline serves as the basis for China's national military strategy. As the Chinese leader Deng Xiaoping stated in 1977, "without a clear strategic guideline, many matters cannot be handled well."[68] After 1988, the "strategic guideline" (*zhanlue fangzhen*) has been described as the "military strategic guideline" (*junshi zhanlue fangzhen*).[69] For the sake of consistency, I will simply use the term "strategic guideline" throughout.

The strategic guidelines are closely linked with the concept of strategy more generally. Within China's approach to military science, the definition of military strategy remains influenced by Mao's own writings. The 2011 edition of the PLA's glossary of military terms defines strategy as "the principles and plans for preparing for and guiding the overall situation of war," including both offensive and defensive strategies.[70] Although the language is different, the essence is the same as the US military's emphasis in its definition of strategy on the "how" of warfare.[71]

The PLA's definition of military strategy, however, remains abstract. Strategy can only be implemented when a series of principles for force planning, training, and operations are articulated and disseminated. China's strategic guidelines contain these principles. As defined by the PLA, a strategic guideline is the "core and collected embodiment of military strategy."[72] Similarly, Chinese military scholars describe the strategic guidelines as the "principal part and heart of strategy."[73] Formally, the guidelines are defined as containing "the program and principles for planning and guiding the overall situation of war in a given period." The guidelines cover both general principles about the whole process of military operations and concrete or specific principles for certain types of operations.[74] In short, the strategic guidelines outline how China plans to wage its next war.

Authoritative Chinese sources indicate that the guidelines have several components. One is the identification of the "strategic opponent" and "operational target," based on a strategic assessment of China's security environment and the perceived threats to China's national interests.[75] Another is the "primary strategic direction," which refers to the geographic center of gravity that will decisively shape the overall conflict as well as military deployments and war preparations. Perhaps the core component is the "basis of preparations for military struggle," which describes the "form" or "pattern" of wars and operations that outline how war will be waged. The final component of a strategic guideline is the "basic guiding thought" for the overall use of military force and for the general operational principles to be applied in a conflict.

The strategic guidelines focus on conventional military operations. Available sources indicate that none of the nine strategic guidelines since 1949 provide explicit guidance for the use of nuclear weapons, though China's nuclear strategy has been formulated to be consistent with the strategic guidelines in a general sense. The guidelines also do not provide guidance for noncombat operations, such as disaster relief or humanitarian operations. At times, such noncombat missions have been assigned to the PLA and were formalized under the rubric of the PLA's New Historic Mission in 2004.

The formulation and implementation of the strategic guidelines should be viewed through the lens of how the CCP makes policy, not Western military planning. With one exception, China's strategic guidelines have been drafted and adopted by the CMC. The CMC is not part of the PLA. Instead, it is a party committee under the Central Committee of the CCP that is responsible for guiding all aspects of military affairs. As a party committee, although the party's top leader has always served as the chairman of this body, most other members (and usually all of them) represent the leadership of the PLA who manage military affairs on behalf of the party. New guidelines are drafted by either the CMC's general office or the leadership of the general staff department, which is often described as the CMC's staff office or "*canmou*." Unlike the drafting of the *National Defense Strategy* in the United States, direct civilian (or party) input is minimal. Party leaders usually approve only the general parameters for new strategic guidelines, usually in response to a suggestion by senior officers to change military strategy.

Once drafted, a new strategic guideline is adopted at an enlarged meeting of the CMC. These enlarged meetings gather together not just members of the CMC but also the leadership of the general departments, services, branches, military regions, and other top-level units in the PLA directly under the CMC. Typically, a new strategic guideline is introduced in a speech or report to the participants at the enlarged meeting. This speech has the same status as a work report to a CCP national party congress and its contents will be viewed as authoritative. Of the nine strategies identified for this book, however, the complete text of speeches introducing new guidelines is only publicly available for those adopted in 1977 and 1993. The 1956 strategic guideline, for example, was contained in a report delivered by Peng Dehuai when he was vice-chairman of the CMC and defense minister, but it has not been published openly.

The PLA, however, has no tradition of published doctrine where any officer (or soldier) can read a strategic-level document. Thus, the content of the speech introducing the new strategic guideline—and thus the new strategy—is transmitted within the PLA through a process of "*chuanda wenjian*" in which excerpts, key quotes, or a condensed version of the speech are distributed to lower-ranking units, usually in meetings convened by the leadership of these units. In 1980, for example, Song Shilun, the president of the Academy of Military Science (AMS), complained that "there are basically no complete written instructions of Comrade Mao Zedong on questions of the strategic guidelines. Instead, they have been mentioned only in parts of speeches from meetings and in conversations with party and military leaders."[76]

The strategic guidelines are just that—guidelines. Like high-level CCP policymaking, the adoption of a new strategic guideline represents only the beginning of a new strategy. They contain the major goals to be achieved and the principles that should guide the achievement of these goals. A new guideline usually does not outline in detail how the new strategy should be implemented or contain a definitive and complete list of the tasks needed to be carried out to accomplish what PLA sources describe as "national defense and army building." The expectation is that the details will be fleshed out afterward in a way consistent with the objectives and principles in the guidelines. In many instances, the programmatic details are often determined when developing the next five-year plan for the armed forces.

To complicate the analysis of strategic decision-making, very little information about the guidelines is made publicly available outside of the PLA.

In general, enlarged meetings of the CMC are not reported in the military or party newspapers, which means that the content of these meetings is also not reported. Thus, a new strategic guideline is not announced outside of the PLA at the time when it is adopted. The 1956 guideline developed by Peng Dehuai, for example, was never announced in either the *Liberation Army Daily* (*jiefangjun bao*), the PLA's main newspaper, or the *People's Daily* (*renmin ribao*), the mouthpiece of the Central Committee of the CCP. Likewise, the first reference to the 2004 revision of the 1993 strategic guideline occurred afterwards, in a footnote in the last entry in Jiang Zemin's *Selected Works* and only indirectly in the 2004 white paper on national defense.[77]

Despite these challenges, several aspects of the process by which new strategic guidelines are formulated and disseminated make them well suited to explaining changes in China's military strategy. First, because the guidelines are issued internally and not announced publicly, analysts can be confident that they are not being adopted as part of an effort to send signals to either foreign adversaries or domestic audiences. Second, unlike in some other militaries, new Chinese strategies are not adopted according to a timetable. The *Quadrennial Defense Review* in the United States and the *National Defense Program Outline* in Japan, for example, are issued according to a semipermanent schedule, every four and ten years, respectively. Instead, China's strategic guidelines are formulated when the PLA's leadership (with the consent of the top party leader) concludes that a change in strategy is necessary. For this reason, it should be easier to isolate those factors that prompt the adoption of a new guideline. Finally, the speed with which a new strategy can be adopted also facilitates identifying those factors that prompt the formulation of a new guideline, as they should be closely correlated in time.

IDENTIFYING MAJOR CHANGES IN CHINA'S MILITARY STRATEGY

Three indicators can be used to determine whether a change in a state's national military strategy can be considered to be major or not. The essence of a major change in strategy is that it requires a military to change how it prepares to fight future wars. Specifically, it requires change in a military's operational doctrine, force structure, and training.

Operational Doctrine. Operational doctrine refers to the principles and concepts that describe how a military plans to conduct operations. Operational doctrine is usually codified in field manuals or regulations and then distributed throughout the organization. A change in operational doctrine is considered a major change, based on two different criteria. The first is the content of the new doctrine and whether it represents a departure from existing doctrine. In 1982, for example, the US Army issued a new edition of FM 100–5, which contained its basic operational doctrine. This edition reflected a dramatic departure from how the United States prepared to defend Western Europe through the adoption of a more offensive- and maneuver-oriented approach when compared with the 1976 edition of that same document.[78] The second is whether the new doctrine is disseminated to all the relevant units. If new doctrine is written, but not disseminated, then it is unlikely to influence how units train or how forces are equipped. In the early 1990s, for example, the British Army drafted a new doctrine for counterinsurgency operations. Only two hundred copies of the document were produced, however, and the British Army failed to adopt the doctrine until the wars in Iraq and Afghanistan.[79] In China, operational doctrine is contained in operations regulations (*zuozhan tiaoling*), which include combat regulations (*zhandou tiaoling*) and campaign outlines (*zhanyi gangyao*).

Force Structure. Force structure refers to the composition of an armed force in terms of both the relative roles of different services (such as the army and the navy) and within a given service, its branches or combat arms (such as infantry and armor). Changes in inter- and intraservice force structure are an important indicator of strategic change because they involve the allocation of scarce resources within an organization and the relative capacity of different services to conduct specified operations. They may also reflect an underlying change in command structure.

A major change in military strategy can be reflected in force structure in different ways. First, strategic change could shift the allocation of resources and the relative importance of the different service branches. One example would be the strengthening of the navy at the expense of the army by reducing the army's budget and shifting resources to the navy. Second, a new strategy could require the creation of new combat arms or other units in order to complete new tasks. Third, a new strategy could alter how units are equipped and armed. An infantry division, for instance, could be light, motorized, or mechanized depending on whether the unit is designed to be carried by vehicles into battle or walk to the fight on foot. Similarly, a navy could be equipped only with submarines, only with surface combatants, or some combination of both. Fourth, strategic change could alter how a particular service is organized. An army, for example, might use a division as the basic unit of organization or it might use smaller brigades. Finally, the types of weapons and equipment that a military provides its troops and whether it invests in the research and development for these weapons or purchases them abroad are also important indicators of organizational change.

Training. Within any military organization, training is a costly and complex activity. How a military trains its troops, and how often, offers another window into major change in military strategy. One component of training is the curriculum of the professional military education system and whether the system provides soldiers and officers with the skills that they need to implement the new strategy. If the curriculum is inconsistent with the content of the strategy, this suggests that the organization has not attempted to pursue major change. A second component of training is the frequency, scope, and content of military exercises and whether they are consistent with what is taught in the classroom and required by the strategy.

In China, the PLA has held fourteen army-wide conferences on military education since 1949. Many of these conferences were held in the 1950s, when China was establishing its professional military education system. These conferences aimed to provide guidance for China's professional military education. As a result, they offer one potential source of data for measuring major military change.[80] Regarding training, the PLA has issued eight training programs (*dagang*) that provide guidance for the entire force in terms of the goals of military training and, in particular, how military exercises should be conducted annually. The issuance of these training programs, as well as the content of exercises held to implement them, can be used to determine whether a change in military strategy is a major one or not.

Table 1.1 provides a list of China's nine strategic guidelines based on these criteria. As the table shows, the PLA has pursued major change in its military strategy in 1956, 1980, and 1993.

SHIFTS IN THE CONDUCT OF WARFARE

One external motivation for a major change in military strategy is a significant shift in the operational conduct of warfare. Assessments of such shifts are most likely to arise when a war occurs in the system that involves at least one of the great powers or a client of a great power who uses its patron's weaponry and equipment. Key elements of change include the way in which military operations are conducted, such as how new equipment is used, how existing equipment is employed in new ways, and, more generally, how operations are executed and force is employed. Through an examination of the secondary literature on warfare after 1945, the key features of these past conflicts that might create a motivation for a state to alter or change its military strategy can be identified and summarized.

These key features, however, are distinct from the lessons that individual states might draw from these conflicts. In other words, even if scholars can agree on the main features of a conflict, states are likely to draw different lessons based on their own strategic circumstances and capabilities. The lessons that China might draw from particular conflicts are not necessarily the same ones that other states will identify. One should probably expect a great deal of variety in the lessons that states draw. A study of reactions to the Gulf War, for example, demonstrates the wide variation in lessons that states inferred shortly after that war.[81]

As this study examines the period after 1949, the context for all the potential shifts in the operational conduct of warfare that might shape military strategy starts with the experience of World War II. Although the key features of this conflict cannot be summarized in a paragraph, several should be noted.[82] The first is the continued mechanization of warfare based on weapons first developed and deployed in World War I, especially tanks and airplanes, in addition to advances in artillery, all of which increased lethality and destructiveness. The second is the vast amounts of ammunition and supplies that were consumed because of the mechanization of warfare and the ability of states with industrialized economies to produce such large amounts of weapons and equipment. The third is the development of combined arms operations in which different types of units such as infantry and artillery were combined to achieve even greater lethality on the battlefield. The fourth is the attention drawn to the operational level of war, especially by the performance of the German Army in the opening years of the conflict.

Since 1949, there have been ten interstate wars involving a great power or its client using the great power's equipment and doctrine. These wars are the 1950–53 Korean War, the 1967 Arab-Israeli War, the 1971 Indo-Pakistani War, the 1973 Arab-Israeli War, the 1980–88 Iran-Iraq War, the 1982 Lebanon War, the 1982 Falklands War, the 1990–91 Gulf War, the 1999 Kosovo War, and the 2003 Iraq War. Counterinsurgency wars, such as those involving the United States in Vietnam or the Soviet Union in Afghanistan, are excluded because these are unlikely to reveal major lessons for conventional wars, which are the focus of great power military strategy.[83] Among scholars of military history and operations, the 1973 Arab-Israeli War and 1990–91 Gulf War are viewed as having the greatest impact on how states viewed the conduct of warfare.[84] China should be most likely to change its military strategy in response to these conflicts.

PARTY UNITY

Unity and stability within a communist party refers to acceptance and support of the party's policies by its leaders as well as consensus among the top leaders about the distribution of power within the party. Of course, party unity is hard to observe, especially in Leninist political parties that abhor public displays of discord or disunity. Moreover, party unity should ideally be measured independent of observable instances of leadership conflict, such as the purge of top leaders, but such measures may not be possible. Nevertheless, the degree of unity can be measured in several different ways.

TABLE 1.1. China's Military Strategic Guidelines since 1949

Year	Name	Guideline Components				Indicators of Major Change		
		Operational Target	Primary Direction	Basis of Preparations for Military Struggle	Main Form of Operations	Operational Doctrine	Force Structure	Training
1956	"Defending the motherland"	United States	northeast	US amphibious assault	positional defense and mobile offense	drafting of operations regulations begins (1958)	creation of new branches and combat arms; reduction of 3.5M troops; formation of general staff system; creation of military regions	draft training program issued (1957)
1960	"Resist in the north, open in the south"	United States	northeast	US amphibious assault	positional defense and mobile offense (north of Xiangshan Bay)	operations regulations issued (1961)	-	-
1964	"Luring the enemy in deep"	United States	-	US amphibious assault	mobile and guerilla warfare	drafting of operations regulations begins (1970)	creation of Second Artillery; expansion to 6.3M troops	-
1977	"Active defense, luring the enemy in deep"	Soviet Union	north-central	Soviet armored and airborne assault	mobile and guerilla warfare	operations regulations issued (1979)	-	training program issued (1978)

1980	"Active defense"	Soviet Union	north-central	Soviet armored and airborne assault	positional warfare of fixed defense	operations regulations drafted and issued (1982–87)	transition from army corps to combined arms group armies; 3M troop reductions (1980, 1982, 1985)	training program issued (1980)
1988	"Dealing with local wars and military conflicts"	-	-	-	-	-	-	training program issued (1989)
1993	"Winning local wars under high-technology conditions"	Taiwan	southeast	warfare under high technology conditions	joint operations	operations regulations and campaign outlines drafted and issued (1995–99)	shift to brigades; creation of GAD; 700,000 troop reductions (1997 and 2003)	training programs issued (1995 and 2001)
2004	"Winning local wars under informatized conditions"	Taiwan (United States)	southeast	warfare under informatized conditions	integrated joint operations	drafting of operations regulations begins (2004)	further shift to brigades	training program issued (2008)
2014	"Winning informatized local wars"	Taiwan (United States)	southeast and maritime	informatized warfare	integrated joint operations	?	reorganization of command and management structures (2016); creation of SSF; 300K troop reduction (2017)	training program issued (2018–19)

One measure of disunity would be change in the appointed successor to lead the party. Such change could be the product of factional politics within the party that are harder to observe.[85] Such change was more common in the Mao era and for most of the Deng era than under Jiang Zemin, Hu Jintao, or Xi Jinping. Liu Shaoqi was Mao's chosen successor until 1966. Then, Lin Biao was anointed as the successor until his mysterious death in a plane crash in 1971. Hua Guofeng became Mao's chosen successor just months before Mao's death in 1976, which sparked a power struggle with Deng Xiaoping. Even the 1980s remained volatile, as two individuals served as general secretary of the CCP, Hu Yaobang (1980–1987) and Zhao Ziyang (1987–1989), but their removals were supported by the top party leadership. Under Jiang Zemin (1989–2002), greater stability emerged, as Hu Jintao, whom Deng chose to succeed Jiang, became general secretary in 2002. The anointed successor to Hu, Xi Jinping, was placed on the Politburo Standing Committee at the Seventeenth Party Congress in 2007.[86] Xi, however, has not yet named a successor.

Another measure of unity in the party is the continuity of membership in the leading bodies of the party. The top governing body is the Central Committee of the CCP, whose members are elected at party congresses. The real power, however, is held by smaller bodies, the Politburo and especially the Politburo Standing Committee. The Politburo is typically composed of top leaders from the most important bureaucracies and provinces. The Politburo Standing Committee is composed of a small group of leaders who assume direct responsibility for different aspects of party and state affairs.[87] Changes in the composition of these bodies offer one indicator of disunity and instability in the party, especially if existing members who meet the criteria for membership are not reelected, if new members are suddenly added, or if large numbers of current members are removed. Likewise, continuity in the membership of these bodies is perhaps an important indicator of unity. A related indicator might be the creation of new leadership bodies outside the existing structure of the party. In the early years of the Cultural Revolution, for example, the Cultural Revolution Group assumed some of the powers of the Central Committee and the Politburo.

A final measure of unity concerns agreement over the party's core policies and guidelines. The greater the debate over policy, the greater the potential disunity. Perhaps the paradigmatic case is Deng's efforts to maintain support for his broad reform agenda after the 1989 massacre in and around Tiananmen Square. Until his "southern tour" in mid-1992, consensus over whether to continue with reform and opening, and at what pace, divided the leadership. Nevertheless, by the Fourteenth Party Congress in October 1992, Deng had managed to rebuild consensus for his policies in the Central Committee and other leading bodies.[88]

SOURCES

This book exploits the increasing availability of Chinese language materials about the PLA. Many of these materials have only been published in the past decade or were published earlier but have only recently become more accessible to scholars outside of China. Perhaps one of the most important sets of Chinese language materials is party history sources published by military and party presses. Several different types are now available, compiled by teams of party historians. The first are official chronologies (*nianpu*), which record the daily activities of top military and party leaders and can contain excerpts of key speeches and reports not always found in other sources in addition to descriptions of important meetings and events. The second party history source is collections of selected documents (*wenxuan*), selected works (*xuanbian*), manuscripts (*wengao*), and expositions (*lunshu*), which include speeches, reports, and other documents, many of which are being published for the first time.

Another, more general type of Chinese language materials used for this study is the biographies and memoirs of military leaders. Most biographies (*zhuan*) are official publications, usually compiled under the direction of either the General Staff Department or the General Political Department and published by the PLA's Liberation Army Press. These biographies are written by compilation teams composed of party and military historians, as well as members of the leader's personal staff. Although biographies are usually published only after a leader has died, many key military leaders since 1949 have published their memoirs (*huiyilu*). Personal recollections also appear in other sources, including oral histories, collections of reminiscences about a particular leader, and historical collections.

Official histories of military affairs are a third type of source tapped for this study. These histories are written by historians affiliated with the party or the PLA. A wide range of subjects is covered, including comprehensive histories of the PLA, during the revolutionary period and after 1949; histories of specific wars and conflicts, such as the Korean War; and histories of particular institutions or particular areas of work within the PLA.

Professional military publications are perhaps one of the newest and fastest growing sources now available regarding Chinese military strategy. Although the PLA started publishing professional military writings in the early 1980s, the volume of material produced increased dramatically from the mid-1990s. The range of topics include strategy (*zhanlue*), campaigns (*zhanyi*), operations (*zuozhan*), tactics (*zhanshu*), political work (*zhengzhi gongzuo*), organization (*zuzhi bianzhi*), army building (*jundui jianshe*), and foreign military history, among others.

These sources provide a rich body of documents and data with which to examine the sources of change in China's military strategy. At the same time, they are not without limitations. The archives of the PLA (and the CCP) remain closed to foreign scholars. Although documents, speeches, and transcripts are available in a variety of sources, they have nevertheless been selected for publication. The motives for including some documents and excluding others are not always clear, which requires that scholars not only treat each published document with some degree of caution, but also remember that they are only seeing a glimpse of the full range of documents. The same general problem applies to other official sources, including biographies and official chronologies. Memoirs, of course, are also colored by the recollection and agenda of the author. Thus, the limited availability of primary sources may bias some of my conclusions because of how these sources were selected. Nevertheless, with the volume of material that is now available, especially from the Mao and Deng periods, the potential for a systematic bias on many issues is reduced because different organizations release materials using different criteria. Scholars can triangulate the information contained in any one document with other sources. The absence of documents or information on particular issues can also be revealing.

Conclusion

The remainder of the book applies the argument developed in this chapter. Each of the nine strategic guidelines or national military strategies that China has adopted since 1949 is examined. One chapter is devoted to each of the three major changes in 1956, 1980, and 1993, and the minor adjustments in strategy that are associated with these major changes. In addition, the book examines the one instance in which the top party leader, Mao Zedong, intervened to change China's military strategy, as a split began to emerge within the party's leadership. Finally, the book examines the continuity in China's nuclear strategy, the one area of China's defense policy that the party leadership never delegated to senior military officers.

2

The CCP's Military Strategies before 1949

Before the founding of the People's Republic in 1949, the leadership of the Chinese Communist Party (CCP) and the party's top military commanders had accumulated more than twenty years of experience on the battlefield. The armed forces under the party's control grew from just a few thousand in 1927 to more than five million at the conclusion of the civil war on the mainland. This battlefield experience would influence how the People's Liberation Army (PLA) approached the development and formulation of military strategy after 1949. During this period, the CCP adopted a variety of military strategies. Some were defensive, others offensive. Most emphasized employing regular units to engage in conventional operations, especially mobile warfare, while other strategies gave greater prominence to the use of irregular forces engaging in guerrilla warfare.

This chapter reviews these strategies, along with the key terms that form China's strategic lexicon. After 1949, these battlefield experiences defined the boundaries for strategic thinking and influenced how senior military officers conceptualized and discussed strategic issues when formulating new military strategies for the PRC. The legacy was also a complex one, involving many different strategies that were contested during the civil war and over which contention would emerge again after 1949 in debates over strategy, in both the mid-1960s and late 1970s. The chapter concludes by outlining the challenges the PLA faced when the PRC was established and senior military officers began to discuss what national military strategy the new country should adopt.

Communist Military Strategies during the Civil War

The CCP's approach to military strategy before 1949 is best understood by an examination of the different phases of the Chinese civil war. In the first phase, during the late 1920s, the CCP attempted to execute urban uprisings and insurrections to seize local power centers in several provinces, starting with the Nanchang Uprising in August 1927. The second followed the failure of these insurrections when the CCP shifted to establishing base areas in the countryside to serve as sanctuaries for developing armed forces known as the Red Army. The third began after the CCP again sought to seize cities in the summer of 1930. In response, the Nationalists launched a series of offensives against these base areas, called "encirclement and suppression" campaigns, to destroy the Red Army. This resulted in the first large-scale conventional engagements of the civil war. Lasting until 1934, this phase ended with the Red Army's defeat in the fifth encirclement campaign and the start of the Long March, when the CCP engaged in a circuitous exodus from Jiangxi province and other base areas that ended in Shaanxi province a year later. The fourth phase covers the period of the Sino-Japanese war. With the exception of the "battle of one hundred regiments" in 1940, the CCP generally avoided direct conventional engagements with Japanese forces so as to conserve its own strength and to establish and expand base areas from which it would seek to gain control over the country following Japan's defeat. The resumption of the contest to control China after Japan's surrender in 1945 marked the fifth and final phase of the civil war, which erupted when the Nationalists launched a general offensive against the CCP in June 1946.

BACKGROUND AND OVERVIEW

Until Japan's surrender in 1945, the CCP's armed forces were composed primarily of light infantry units. These units were armed with rifles, grenades, and some light machine guns, but possessed few heavy weapons such as heavy machine guns, mortars, or field artillery. Typically, the CCP organized its armed forces into three types. The first was conventional or regular forces, which were structured much like many other armies and emphasized the conventional military training of the period. The CCP's conventional forces were first called the Red Army and then changed their name in 1946 to the People's Liberation Army. They are also referred to as main force units (*zhuli budui*) or, in certain configurations, field armies (*yezhan jun*). When the CCP planned to conduct a major military operation against the Nationalists (whose military was called the National Revolutionary Army), it would employ its conventional forces. The second type was local forces (*difang budui*), which were also organized like conventional units, but less well armed and less well trained, focusing only on the conventional defense of a specific area. The third type included militia (*minbing*) and self-defense corps (*ziwei dui*). These were composed of citizen soldiers and would be organized both in areas under CCP control and in areas under Nationalist or Japanese control. They would engage in guerrilla operations and in support activities, especially intelligence, logistics, and supply.

With only light infantry, three forms of warfare (*zhanzheng xingshi*), or ways of fighting, were most prominent before 1949. Mobile warfare (*yundong zhan*) was the use of conventional units to fight on fluid fronts, maneuvering and then attacking enemy units when a local superiority of forces or tactical surprise could be achieved. This was the main form of warfare used by the CCP's armed forces from the early 1930s until the end of the civil war, in both offensive and defensive operations and at the tactical and campaign levels. Positional warfare (*zhendi zhan*) referred to the use of conventional units to defend or attack fixed positions with fighting on a fixed front and not a fluid one. Positional warfare was perhaps the least common form of combat during the civil war, but became somewhat more common after the resumption of hostilities between the Nationalists and Communists in 1946. Guerrilla warfare (*youji zhan*) refers to small-scale harassment and sabotage operations behind enemy lines.[1] To slightly confuse the analysis during this period, the CCP would use both main force units and militia or self-defense corps units to conduct guerrilla operations, depending on the circumstances. The CCP's military strategies adopted before 1949 combined these three forms of warfare, but the most common form was mobile warfare.

During most of the period before 1949, the CCP's armed forces were numerically weaker and technologically inferior to their Nationalist or Japanese opponents. Until the late 1940s, the CCP thus confronted a similar strategic problem: how to defend itself against a superior force to ensure its survival and ultimately to reverse the balance of forces and be able to defeat the Nationalists. Such conditions dictated an emphasis on strategic defense. Only in late 1948 did the CCP for the first time enjoy numerical superiority over the Nationalists. Even then, however, they still lacked superiority in equipment, especially artillery, armor, air power, and transportation. Nevertheless, within this broad orientation of strategic defense, the CCP adopted different strategies to conserve its forces and gradually expand the territory, people, and resources under its control. These approaches are described in the following sections.

The Red Army's inferiority, and the imperative of survival, had several important implications for how it fought during this period. First, CCP forces would sometimes seek to avoid engagements altogether, retreating to remote areas and biding their time to build up their forces. Second, when employing its regular units, the CCP would seek engagements or battles of "quick decision" (*suzhan sujue*). Troops would maneuver to gain local superiority, attack, and then withdraw. The purpose was to destroy or "annihilate" (*jianmie*) enemy units, thus slowly changing the balance of forces while acquiring weaponry, supplies, and soldiers from the destroyed unit. Third, reducing an enemy's effective strength through annihilation operations was often more important than seizing and holding territory. The Red Army would retreat from territory it had conquered if it concluded that it could not defend the area or as part of a ruse to defeat Nationalist units. Finally, the disparity in forces indicated that any conflict would be protracted in nature, as it would take a long time for parity to be reached that would allow the CCP to transition from the strategic defensive to the strategic offensive.

In sum, these varied types of military operations suggest it would be a mistake to view this period simply as dominated by guerrilla warfare, as the concept of "people's war" suggests. Main force units from the Red Army or the PLA would carry out major military engagements. Militia and self-defense forces provided support. Popular support and mass mobilization were essential, producing not only manpower for the Red Army but also supplies, logistics, and intelligence. Areas where the CCP had gained control or influence were often harder for the Nationalists to take back. As the weaker combatant, the support of the people was critical. Nevertheless, the decisive military operations, backed by this popular support, were carried out by conventional units of the Red Army.

URBAN UPRISINGS AND RURAL BASE AREAS

The armed conflict between the Nationalists and Communists began with the Nanchang Uprising on August 1, 1927. Involving many individuals who would rise to prominence at the highest levels of the PLA after 1949, the uprising represented the CCP's first effort to use armed force to achieve its political objectives.[2] The CCP was founded in 1921, and in 1924 it established a united front with the Nationalists with the ambition of unifying China by defeating the warlords who then controlled different parts of the country. In April 1927, however, Chiang Kai-shek turned on the Communists, killing or imprisoning thousands of CCP members in Shanghai. In response, the CCP decided to take up arms and its first military action occurred with its bid to seize Nanchang, a city in Jiangxi province.[3]

The Nanchang Uprising only lasted a few days. Nevertheless, the CCP attempted more armed uprisings in different parts of southeastern China. In September 1927, for example, Mao Zedong led a series of insurrections in Hunan and Jiangxi known as the Autumn Harvest Uprisings. Uprisings occurred in other parts of China, including the city of Guangzhou. All told, official histories indicate that more than one hundred uprisings occurred from July 1927 until the end of 1929.[4] The implied strategy was that the CCP needed to seize control of areas, usually urban ones, from which it would be able to spread its revolution among the working class and peasants, then gradually expand its power throughout the country.

All these early attempts to seize power failed. Some members of the party remained committed to taking control of urban areas deemed most appropriate for a communist revolution based on mobilizing the working class. Others, including Mao Zedong, decided to create bases in rural areas and "encircle the cities from the countryside," while at the same time realizing the more immediate and practical necessity of avoiding major conflicts in order to increase the size and strength of the CCP's armed forces. Although the CCP's ideas about mobilizing the peasantry to support the revolution were not yet fully developed during this period, rural base areas provided a degree of sanctuary for the party, enabling it to develop and organize its armed forces and gradually expand the territory and population under its control.

Between 1927 and 1930, the CCP established more than ten base areas. They were located in the remote border areas of provinces in south-central China, such as Jiangxi, Fujian, Hunan, Henan, Hubei, Anhui, and Sichuan.[5] The base area in the Jinggang Mountains in Jiangxi province, established by Mao Zedong in late 1927, is perhaps the most well known of those created during this period. However, as shown in map 2.1, Mao along with Zhu De would later move south to establish another base area on the Jiangxi-Fujian border.[6] Other significant bases were established along the Hunan-Hubei border and the Hubei-Henan-Anhui border. Official histories attribute the establishment and expansion of these rural base areas to the use of guerrilla warfare, which was well suited to the weaknesses of the Red Army while contributing to its goal of eliminating local power holders in these areas.[7] Still, guerrilla warfare was only a temporary expedient until the party gained sufficient manpower, weapons, and supplies to develop and train regular forces to conduct conventional operations. Because many of the commanders at the time, such as Zhu De, had received modern military training through service in warlord armies, they sought to build similar conventional forces to defeat the Nationalists.[8] Moreover, the majority of the Red Army's leadership subscribed to a conventional military ethic that emphasized regular forces. This was shaped by exposure to either Russian or warlord armies. By contrast, only a minority of the leadership, including Mao Zedong, embraced a guerrilla ethic.[9]

THE ENCIRCLEMENT CAMPAIGNS, 1930-1934

By the summer of 1930, the strategy of establishing rural base areas and avoiding engagements with Nationalist units had appeared to pay off. The CCP forces numbered around one hundred thousand soldiers, with seventy thousand in the Red Army and thirty thousand local forces.[10] The largest base area was located in Jiangxi along the border with Fujian, also known as the

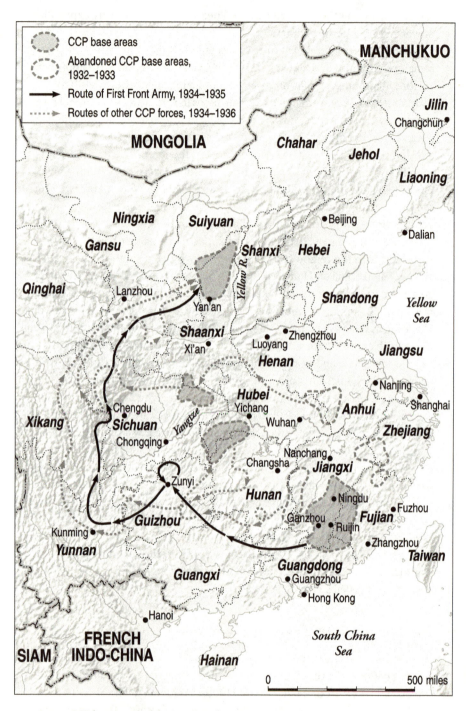

"Central Soviet," with a strength of about forty thousand soldiers. Based on this strength, the CCP leadership decided again to attempt to seize several cities in Jiangxi and Hunan provinces, including Nanchang and Changsha, in the summer of 1930. Like the 1927 uprisings, however, these attempts also failed. Yet they revealed the growing strength of the Communist forces, which represented a renewed challenge to the Nationalists even after Chiang had nominally unified China during the Northern Expedition. In November 1930, Chiang decided to go on the offensive and attack CCP forces in the base areas with "encirclement and suppression" (*weijiao*) or pacification campaigns.

Between October 1930 and October 1934, the Nationalists would launch five offensives against the CCP. The most well-known of those targeted the Central Soviet, which was the Communists' largest base area. The Nationalists also attacked other base areas, including those on the Hunan-Hubei border and the Hubei-Henan-Anhui border.* These campaigns, which the CCP calls counter–encirclement campaigns, offer important examples of the CCP's evolving military strategy. In each campaign, the Red Army was vastly outnumbered, on the defensive, and seeking to ensure its survival. Nevertheless, different strategies were used to defend against the Nationalists' attacks, including a mix of defensive and offensive operations. Mao Zedong, then head of the government in the Central Soviet, was closely involved in the development of the Red Army's military strategy in the first three encirclement campaigns, which would later contribute to the development of Mao's "military thought" (*junshi sixiang*).

Official histories describe Red Army operations during these campaigns as emphasizing mobile warfare. The campaigns involved the Red Army's main force units, drawing directly or indirectly on the populations in base areas for support, supplies, and intelligence.[11] While waiting for the opportune moment to attack and destroy select Nationalist units, Red Army units would maneuver to create ambushes or wear down Nationalist forces who were operating in unfamiliar terrain. When surprise or a local superiority of forces could be achieved, the Red Army would attack.

The first encirclement campaign, from December 1930 to January 1931, highlighted the use of "luring the enemy in deep" (*youdi shenru*). The Nationalists dispatched one hundred thousand soldiers to attack the Red Army's forces, which numbered roughly forty thousand. Under Mao's direction, the basic concept of operations was to draw the Nationalists into the mountains of the base area

---

* The Hunan-Hubei base under He Long was known as the "Xiang-E-Xi Soviet." He Long commanded the Second Front Army in this area. The Hubei-Henan-Anhui base under Zhang Guotao was known as the "E-Yu-Wan Soviet." Zhang commanded the Fourth Front Army. The Red Army forces in the Central Soviet were known as the First Front Army. These were the three main communist forces during the early 1930s.

and then ambush them. The Red Army achieved tactical surprise, destroying one Nationalist division and inflicting significant losses on another, which then withdrew, ending the campaign.[12]

The CCP's strategy in the second encirclement campaign, from April to May 1931, was similar to the first but without the active deception of luring Nationalist forces into the base area. This time, the Nationalists deployed two hundred thousand troops against roughly thirty thousand in the Red Army.[13] CCP forces targeted one of the weaker Nationalist units, the Fifth Division, and laid an ambush as it entered the base area. CCP forces then chased retreating Nationalist units, tripling the area under their control.[14] Poor coordination among the four columns of Nationalist troops contributed to the Red Army's success.[15]

The third encirclement campaign lasted from July to September 1931. Official histories claim that the Nationalists mobilized 300,000 soldiers, but the actual number may have been closer to 130,000, as many Nationalist units were understrength. The CCP fielded between 30,000 and 55,000 soldiers.[16] The CCP strategy was to maneuver within the base area for a month without engaging the Nationalists, thereby wearing down units that were operating in unfamiliar territory that had been deliberately evacuated to deny them supplies. The Red Army avoided the strongest Nationalist armies, attacking and destroying several weaker divisions in the second week of August. Emboldened, the Red Army then attacked one of the strongest Nationalist armies that it had previously sought to avoid, the Nineteenth Route Army. However, CCP forces were defeated and lost about 20 percent of their manpower.

Following the third campaign, the Nationalists paused their attacks against the Central Soviet. Chiang had to divert troops first to deal with the establishment of a rival Nationalist government in Guangzhou allied with several warlords in the summer of 1931, followed by Japan's invasion of Manchuria after the Mukden Incident in September 1931.[17] Given that the Red Army had not destroyed two powerful Nationalist armies involved in the third campaign, this diversion of Nationalist forces likely saved the CCP from even further losses.[18] Nevertheless, with the attention of the Nationalists focused elsewhere, the Central Soviet was able to expand, growing to 50,000 square kilometers with a population of 2.5 million.[19]

After the third encirclement campaign, the CCP's top leadership reconsidered its military strategy. Although militarily successful, the operations in the first three campaigns had been controversial. Some objected that the base areas in which the CCP was trying to mobilize the masses and build a new state around socialist policies such as land reform were ravaged by the fighting. Mao's strategy of luring the enemy in deep was viewed as weakening the image and status of the party in the minds of the people whose support it was trying to mobilize. Following Japan's invasion of Manchuria, along with the apparent success in the third encirclement campaign, the CCP decided to go on the offensive. In January 1932, the party leadership in Shanghai issued instructions "to seize one or two important key cities so as to win an initial victory of the revolution in one or more provinces."[20] The goal was to enlarge the territory under CCP control and integrate isolated base areas, focusing on the provinces of Hunan, Hubei, and Jiangxi. The initial action under this new policy, the siege of the city of Ganzhou in Jiangxi, lasted from late February to late March 1932. Although the attack failed, the party continued with this new approach. By the summer of 1932, party documents described the new strategy as "active offense" (*jiji jingong*).[21]

Mao Zedong opposed these changes to the party's military strategy. Following the instruction to seize one or two key cities in January 1932, he took sick leave. After the failed siege of Ganzhou, he was called back to work. Over Mao's objections, the party leaders in the Central Soviet decided to attack Nationalist areas in northern Jiangxi. In open defiance, Mao led the forces under his command in this two-pronged attack to western Fujian instead. Although Mao's raid of the city of Zhangzhou succeeded, the leadership of the Central Soviet, which now included national party leaders from Shanghai such as Zhou Enlai, decided at the Ningdu Conference in October 1932 to strip him of responsibility for military affairs.[22] Mao was charged with disobeying the party's instructions, advocating a "pure defensive line" (*danchun fangyu luxian*) based on avoiding engagements with the Nationalists outside the Central Soviet, and committing the "rightist risk" of waiting for the enemy to attack (a direct critique of luring the enemy in deep).[23] Thus, the party leadership rejected Mao's strategies used in the first three encirclement campaigns.

The fourth encirclement campaign lasted from January to April 1933. Consistent with the principle of "active offense," the Ningdu Conference also determined that the Red Army would launch preemptive strikes against Nationalist forces that were preparing for another assault on the Central Soviet, targeting Nationalist weak points along the perimeter but not luring them into the base area. Mao later described this approach as "resisting the enemy beyond the gates" (*yudi yu guomen zhiwai*).[24] The campaign also featured what was becoming a familiar CCP tactic of targeting reinforcements dispatched to relieve a besieged unit. When the campaign started, the Nationalists had assembled 154,000 soldiers, with another 240,000 occupying blocking positions around the base area, against 65,000 Red Army troops.[25] In the first phase, Red Army units attacked along the northern and western edge of the base area, driving away Nationalist forces. In the second phase, they besieged the Nationalists at Nanfeng and then attacked two divisions dispatched as reinforcements, destroying one and weakening the other. The campaign ended indecisively, as the bulk of Nationalist forces remained intact.[26]

The fifth and decisive encirclement campaign occurred from October 1933 to October 1934. This time, the Nationalists changed their strategy. Before, their units would seek to drive deep into the Central Soviet. Now, they decided to create a ring of interconnected blockhouses and then gradually tighten a net around the base area to trap and destroy the Red Army inside.[27] The approach was "strategically offensive but tactically defensive."[28] By gradually reducing the territory under CCP control, the Nationalists intended to limit the Red Army's resources and, even more important, its ability to maneuver, which had played a key role in defeating previous Nationalist encirclement campaigns, to gain advantage. Reflecting the importance that Chiang Kai-shek attached to this campaign, the Nationalists deployed about one million soldiers, including 500,000 to invade the base area, against 120,000 Communist forces, creating the largest disparity in forces and thus the harshest conditions to date for the Red Army.[29]

The results of Chiang's new strategy were devastating. Red Army attacks could not break through an east-west line that the Nationalists had created in the northern part of the Central Soviet, which had forced it into a passive position. What became known as "short, swift thrusts" against these fixed positions failed to create any breakthroughs and resulted only in costly engagements. An effort to build "red" blockhouses failed to halt the Nationalist advance in the face of its superior firepower. As Edward Dryer concludes, "It is difficult to imagine any communist strategy that would have prevailed against this combination of factors."[30] The campaign had demonstrated that the Red Army could not wage positional defensive warfare from a position of significant inferiority.[31]

As the net was closing in the summer of 1934, the CCP leadership began to discuss leaving the base area, a move that they called a "strategic transfer" (*zhanlue zhuanyi*). In October 1934, after several months of planning, they embarked on what would later become known as the Long March (as shown in map 2.1). In March 1935, Zhang Guotao's forces, now in Sichuan, began to march to the west, followed by He Long's forces, now in Hunan. Some Red Army units remained behind in Jiangxi to screen the retreating columns and conduct guerrilla operations against the Nationalists.[32]

The strategic goal of the march was to establish a new base area in which the CCP forces could regroup and rebuild. Strategy in the march itself, along with the final destination, changed frequently. The results of the march, however, were devastating. Of the roughly one hundred thousand soldiers that departed from the Central Soviet in October 1934, only ten thousand arrived in northern Shaanxi in October 1935 after traveling more than three thousand miles. The remnants of Zhang Guotao and He Long's forces that began their own long marches from other base areas would only arrive in Shaanxi about a year later.

MAO'S ASSESSMENT OF THE ENCIRCLEMENT CAMPAIGNS

In late 1934 and early 1935, the CCP leadership held a series of meetings during the Long March to discuss strategy and to examine the reasons for the Red Army's defeat in the fifth encirclement campaign. The most well-known meeting was held in the city of Zunyi in Guizhou province. These meetings provided a fortuitous political opening for Mao. Since he had been completely removed from responsibility for military affairs in October 1932, he could not be blamed for the Red Army's defeat in the fifth encirclement campaign. Moreover, he could use the party's defeat to blame others for pursuing a flawed strategy and thereby to elevate his position within the party. Over time, the critique of the military strategy that Mao advocated at Zunyi would eventually form part of the orthodoxy of Mao's military thought.

In his speech and the final Politburo resolution, Mao challenged the view that the Red Army's failure could be attributed to "objective" factors, such as the enemy's overwhelming strength and the CCP's weakness. In a clear jab at those who had critiqued his military strategy at the Ningdu Conference in October 1932, Mao charged that the party had adopted a "pure defensive line" or "purely protective defense" (*zhuanshou fangyu*) of positional warfare and blockhouse warfare. The party should have pursued a "decisive defense" (*juezhan fangyu*), which Mao also termed an "offensive defense" (*gongshi fangyu*), in which superior forces were concentrated to attack an enemy's weak points through mobile operations.[33] In other words, the party should have adopted Mao's strategies from the first three encirclement campaigns.

In December 1936, Mao elaborated on these ideas when he delivered a lecture that would form one of his most influential essays on military affairs. Entitled "Problems of Strategy in China's Revolutionary War," it examined the reasons for the successes and failures during the five encirclement campaigns for the purpose of identifying the "correct" military strategy for the CCP in its revolution.[34] The essay expanded on many of his earlier arguments, but also served the political objective of consolidating Mao's authority on military affairs as part of his struggle for leadership of the party. Eventually, this lecture would become canonized as part of Mao's military thought, endorsed in the 1945 resolution on party history, and would serve as an important point of reference for the formulation of military strategy after 1949.

Mao's starting point was a discussion of the balance of forces. The Nationalists, he argued, were "a big and powerful enemy," while the Red Army was "small and weak."[35] How to prevail under these conditions of extreme inferiority posed the central strategic challenge. Mao identified the "primary problem" while on the strategic defensive as "how to conserve our strength and await an opportunity to defeat the enemy."[36] In the most general terms, Mao advocated for a protracted war at the strategic level and campaigns of "quick decision" at the operational level. Mobile warfare should be the main form of warfare, or "'fight when you can win, leave when you cannot fight and win.'"[37] Operations should combine offense and defense in a flexible way consistent with mobile warfare, which he summarized as follows: "To defend in order to attack, to retreat in order to advance, to move against the flanks in order to move against the front, and to take a circuitous route in order to go the direct route."[38]

Mao highlighted the role of what he termed strategic retreat (*zhanlue tuique*), though it was described in tactical or operational-level terms. The main purpose of strategic retreat was to avoid engagements in which large forces could be defeated. Retreats could create favorable conditions by identifying weak enemy units, creating a local superiority of forces, or inducing an overstretched enemy to make a mistake. Mao then critiqued the strategy adopted by the party in 1932, such as "resisting the enemy beyond the gates" and not luring the enemy in deep; "attacking along the entire front" (*quanxian chuji*) and not focusing one's effort in a particular direction; "seizing key cities" and not enlarging rural base areas; "striking first" (*xianfa zhiren*) and not striking second; and, finally, "setting up defenses everywhere" (*chuchu shefang*) and not maneuvering.[39] Although Mao was quick to blame the failure in the fifth counter–encirclement campaign on others, his own ideas in this essay, such as luring the Nationalists deep into the Central Soviet or using mobile warfare to penetrate the enemy's rear, would also have failed catastrophically. Nevertheless, Mao's assessment of the failure of the fifth encirclement campaign would become part of the party's orthodoxy on military affairs and would be used after 1949 as a rhetorical tool to critique different military strategies.

CCP STRATEGY DURING THE ANTI-JAPANESE WAR (1937-1945)

In late 1935, Red Army units under Mao's leadership reached Shaanxi and gained a relative degree of sanctuary. At the same time, the Japanese threat to China, especially in northern China, had become more acute. In December 1935, the Politburo met in the town of Wayaobu and developed a new military strategy for the coming period that was endorsed by the Central Committee and fore-shadowed the approach that the CCP would take over the coming years.[40]

The first and most important element of the strategy was to use the slogan of national resistance against Japan to strengthen the CCP's position in the civil war with the Nationalists. The resolution passed at the meeting described this as "combining the civil war with the national war."[41] The idea was to portray all CCP actions as part of resisting Japan, with slogans such as "the Red Army is the vanguard of the Chinese people in resisting Japan," while also seeking to recruit sympathetic units from the Nationalists and warlord forces.[42] The immediate goal of this strategy was to attack Chinese forces aligned with Japan while preparing to attack Japanese forces directly. A second goal was to greatly expand the size of the Red Army.[43] The third goal was to create a land bridge with the Soviet Union so that the CCP could receive supplies and support directly from Moscow, while a fourth goal was to use guerrilla warfare to expand areas under CCP control in the main provinces of China.

The next occasion for the CCP to consider its military strategy followed Japan's effort to conquer all of China after the Marco Polo Bridge incident in July 1937. By this point, other Red Army forces under Zhang Guotao and He Long had arrived in Shaanxi and the CCP moved its headquarters to the city of Yan'an, where it would remain until after Japan's surrender in 1945. At this time, the CCP was negotiating a second united front with the Nationalists to cooperate against the Japanese.

In August 1937, the Politburo convened an enlarged meeting at Luochuan in Shaanxi to address the changed situation. The first issue decided was the organization and strategy of the CCP's armed forces during this new phase. As part of the projected united front with the Nationalists, the Red Army's main force units were reorganized into two armies that would nominally be part of the Nationalist-led National Revolutionary Army. The Eighth Route Army would be composed of the units that fled the Central Soviet and other base areas and would operate in northern China, behind Japanese lines or in areas beyond Japan's control. The New Fourth Army would be composed of CCP guerrilla units that had remained in the south after the Long March and was expected to operate in southern China.

A second issue was the CCP's overall military strategy and the military strategy for the Eighth Route Army operating in north China. At the meeting, Mao took up these issues in a report on military affairs, which the Politburo approved. The Red Army would engage in a strategic transformation (*zhanlue zhuanbian*) to a protracted conflict with Japan. The concern was that Chiang would use the opportunity of Japan's invasion to eliminate the CCP, which, along with Japan's invasion, required such a transformation. Regular armies (*zhenggui jun*) engaged in mobile warfare would become guerrilla armies (*youji jun*) engaging in guerrilla warfare, which meant that they would operate in a dispersed fashion, not that they would be composed of irregular forces.[44] The Red Army's goals were to establish base areas in northern China, tie down and destroy Japanese forces, coordinate with "friendly" warlord forces in the area, conserve and enlarge the Red Army's effective strength, and strive for leadership in the resistance against Japan.[45] The slogan for the new military strategy was "independent and self-reliant guerrilla warfare in the mountains."[46] The Red Army units in the north were expected to take the initiative and create base areas in mountainous regions where they could most easily find sanctuary, dispersing their forces to mobilize the population in these areas and only concentrating to attack the Japanese when opportunities arose. This strategy reflected the spirit of Mao's experience building the Jinggangshan base area in the late 1920s, a template he believed was suitable for the current situation.

By December 1937, however, the Politburo had modified the CCP's military strategy. Many of the Red Army's military commanders, such as Zhu De and Peng Dehuai, wanted not only to build new base areas but also to engage in mobile warfare and attack the Japanese.[47] Otherwise, they believed the prestige of the CCP would suffer. Thus, they called for changing the strategy to "mobile guerrilla warfare" (*jundong youji zhan*) or "guerrilla mobile warfare" (*youji yundong zhan*): rhetorical efforts to legitimate such operations within the existing strategy. After the Luochuan meeting, Mao had sent multiple telegrams in September to explain the new strategy to Peng Dehuai (the political commissar of the Eighth Route Army), which was likely a response to Peng's dissatisfaction with the new strategy and emphasis on guerrilla warfare.[48] In December 1937, the Politburo adjusted the military strategy to permit mobile warfare "under favorable conditions."[49] By May 1938, Mao described the CCP's military strategy as "basically . . . guerrilla warfare but not giving up opportunities to conduct mobile warfare under favorable conditions."[50]

In 1938, Mao delivered a series of lectures on strategy in China's war with Japan that again echoed many themes from his assessment of the encirclement campaigns. Mao underscored that, due to the disparity of forces, the war with Japan would be a protracted one that would move through three stages: strategic defense when Japan was on the attack, strategic stalemate when Japan sought to consolidate its gains, and counterattacks that would lead to a strategic offensive to defeat the Japanese. Mao viewed conventional operations, and especially mobile warfare, as the key to ultimately defeating Japan. At the same time, during the period of strategic stalemate, after the enemy had expanded and was seeking to consolidate its gains, guerrilla warfare would take priority. The shift to mobile warfare would only occur after the enemy was weakened by guerrilla operations and the size of Red Army forces had increased to the point that they were able to engage in conventional operations against Japan.[51]

For the next few years, the Red Army focused largely on expanding areas under its control, mostly in northern China. This occurred in areas under Japanese control, as well as those beyond it, in provinces like Shanxi and Shaanxi. The CCP increased the size of its regular and militia forces while avoiding large-scale engagements with Japanese forces that might place those forces at risk. As a de facto or default strategy, this was fairly successful, as the Nationalists were preoccupied defending major cities such as Nanjing and Wuhan. By the end of 1938, the Eighth Route Army in the north had grown to approximately 156,000, while the New Fourth Army in the south numbered more than 25,000.[52] These main force units were augmented by as many as 500,000 local self-defense troops and 160,000 guerrillas.[53] By 1940, the population within the CCP's base areas had grown to 44 million.[54] The Eighth Route Army grew to 400,000 soldiers and the New Fourth Army to 100,000.[55] These forces established and expanded base areas, using primarily mobile and not guerrilla warfare.[56]

The only deviation in the Red Army's approach occurred with the "battle of one hundred regiments" in August 1940. Drawing on these new capabilities, as well as a desire to burnish the CCP's anti-Japanese credentials and weaken Japanese pacification efforts in north China, Peng Dehuai ordered the Eighth Route Army in July 1940 to launch an offensive against the Japanese in parts of Hebei and Shanxi, focusing on the ZhengTai railway from Shijiazhuang to Taiyuan.[57] The goal was to cut the line and disrupt Japanese communications in the area. The offensive was launched on August 20, 1940, and the Red Army scored some impressive victories into early September.[58] Nevertheless, as Japanese reinforcements arrived, the effort fizzled by early October. Official Chinese histories report that the Eighth Route Army suffered 17,000 casualties while destroying 474 kilometers of rail lines and 1,500 kilometers of roads.[59] These same sources indicate that Japan suffered 20,645 casualties, but Japanese sources indicate the number was much lower, with around 4,000 killed in action and an unknown number of wounded and missing.[60] Although the party leadership, including Mao, had approved of the offensive, it did not signal a change in strategy as much as opportunism.

The offensive, however, produced a dramatic change in Japanese strategy. General Yasuji Okamura, the Japanese commander in north China, unleashed the punishing "three alls" campaign (kill all, burn all, loot all) to crush the CCP. The base areas established over the past few years contracted and the population under CCP control fell by almost half, to 25 million.[61] The CCP's main force units were dispersed and focused on small-scale guerrilla operations and generally avoided any engagements with Japanese forces. The size of the Eighth Route Army fell by twenty-five percent, to around 300,000.[62]

Until Japan's surrender in 1945, the Red Army remained focused on rebuilding base areas and carrying out limited guerrilla operations. Aiding them in these efforts was the diversion of Japanese forces for the Ichigo offensive, which sought to create a corridor under Japanese control that would connect Korea with Indochina, and then for operations in other parts of the Pacific Theater. As a result, Japan left a largely garrison force in north China to protect existing Japanese positions, allowing the CCP and the Red Army to rebuild and grow. By April 1945, the CCP's Eighth Route Army in north China had grown to more than 600,000 soldiers and the New Fourth Army to 296,000, although some of this increase occurred as local units were redesignated as main force units.[63]

THE CIVIL WAR (1945-1949)

When Japan surrendered in August 1945, the balance of forces between Nationalists and Communists had changed dramatically. Although the Nationalists had several million soldiers, the Red Army had grown from the remnants of the Long March to approximately 910,000 soldiers, along with two million militia.[64] The party controlled nineteen base areas with a population of 125 million people, or roughly twenty percent of the country's population.[65] Nevertheless, despite the impressive growth of the CCP and the Red Army, it remained in an inferior and tenuous position. The military strategies chosen during this period reflect similar concerns about survival to those that had marked strategic decision-making in earlier periods of the civil war. In the end, the CCP's military victory in the civil war occurred much faster than even the party's leadership had anticipated.

Although hostilities between the Nationalists and Communists did not begin immediately following Japan's surrender, both sides jostled early on for advantage on the ground. The CCP's first strategy for this phase of the civil war was formulated in September 1945, while Mao Zedong and Zhou Enlai were conducting peace talks with the Nationalists in Chongqing. The Central Committee under the leadership of Liu Shaoqi formulated a strategy of "development of the north, defense of the south" (*xiangbei fazhan, xiangnan fangyu*).[66] The goal was to seize control of the northeast or Manchuria. Described by Steven Levine as the "anvil of victory," China's northeast was the most industrialized part of the country and one that had witnessed the least destruction during the period of Japanese occupation.[67] Whoever controlled Manchuria would not only be able to acquire these resources, but would also be well positioned to threaten all of northern China, including Beijing.

Liu's strategy envisioned developing a large base area in the northeast similar to those from the late 1920s and early 1930s. Communist forces would be deployed elsewhere in the north to defend the main approaches to the northeast. By contrast, in the south, Communist forces were instructed to contract their positions to defend against anticipated Nationalist attacks, with some units ordered to shift north and others moved into Shandong to defend access to the north.[68] Some clashes and battles occurred as the Nationalists and Communists raced to control Manchuria in the fall of 1945, but on the whole both sides continued to jockey for position in the peace talks and avoided major military engagements. Although the Communists arrived first in Manchuria, the Nationalists followed in even greater numbers. In late 1945 and into 1946, the Red Army would abandon most of the cities that it had seized a few months earlier and retreated north across the Sungari river into rural areas of Manchuria.

The situation changed when the Nationalists launched a nationwide offensive against the CCP in June 1946. The Nationalist forces were 4.3 million strong against 1.2 million CCP forces, who held approximately 25 percent of the country.[69] At around this time, the Red Army was renamed as the People's Liberation Army (PLA). The offensive marked Chiang Kai-shek's bid to seize control of the country and defeat the Communists once and for all. Perhaps somewhat ironically, Chiang's strategy mirrored Japan's own effort to conquer China by seizing the major cities and communications links between them north of the Yangtze river. This would enable the Nationalists to create strongpoints and transportation corridors from which to launch and sustain attacks against CCP-held areas.

In response, the CCP countered with a strategy of mobile warfare, but on a much larger scale than in the encirclement campaigns of the early 1930s. If expedient, the CCP abandoned cities and other territories it held, which Mao described in July 1946 as "not only unavoidable but also necessary."[70] In this way, CCP strategy reflected a return to both the period of the base areas and the anti-Japanese war in which it avoided large-scale, decisive engagements and withdrew its forces to fight on interior lines. The strategy was later described as "destroying the effective strength of the Nationalists, not holding [baoshou] territory."[71] When engagements occurred, the idea was to concentrate superior forces to achieve tactical victories and gradually reduce the effective strength of the Nationalists.[72] At the strategic and operational level, the PLA returned to modes of warfare that would have been quite familiar to commanders from the late 1920s and early 1930s, focusing on the defense of interior lines.

In the offensive, the Nationalists gained much of the territory they sought. Symbolically, they even captured the CCP capital of Yan'an in March 1947 (after the CCP decided to withdraw and mount only a token defense). Nevertheless, the Nationalists were unable to destroy any large CCP units or to pacify and control any region completely. Nationalist offensives in Shandong and Shaanxi in the first half of 1947, in particular, had failed to destroy any large contingents of CCP forces.[73] The campaign also drew Nationalist forces away from Manchuria, allowing that base area to further develop. By July 1947, the size of the Nationalist forces had shrunk to 3.7 million, while the PLA grew to 1.95 million.[74] Moreover, although the Nationalist forces had gained ground, it became overextended. The need to defend the cities and the communications links between them placed many forces on garrison duty, leaving fewer field forces available for launching attacks against CCP-held areas.[75]

In the summer of 1947, the CCP decided to change its military strategy. In early July, Mao concluded that the Nationalist offensive had been stopped everywhere except in Shandong and the CCP could now counterattack and transition to the offensive. Mao assessed that the Nationalists were losing the support of a war-weary public and becoming increasingly isolated. Reflecting excessive optimism about the changing circumstances, he suggested that the PLA could destroy one hundred brigades in the next twelve months.[76] On September 1, 1947, the CCP outlined its military strategy for the upcoming year.[77] The document indicated what Mao had concluded over the summer:

that the CCP would switch to the offensive by using its main force units to fight on exterior lines or attack areas held by the Nationalists. Some forces would still be assigned to defend CCP-held areas, but others would now take the fight to the Nationalists.

The first major offensive action, however, occurred before the new strategy was formally issued. The target was the central plains of China, in particular the Dabie Mountains in the Hunan-Hebei-Anhui border region that had been abandoned in 1946. The goal was to establish a new base area in the central plains, which could threaten the Nationalists in the south and divert forces from Manchuria. Led by Liu Bocheng and Deng Xiaoping, the offensive involved three army corps and an audacious crossing of the Yellow River.[78] Other battles occurred in the north, including the capture in November 1947 of Shijiazhuang in Hebei, a key communications node, and a series of attacks in the northeast against Nationalist forces connecting Liaodong and Shenyang in Manchuria (known as the LiaoShen corridor). Nevertheless, CCP strategy during this period remained somewhat opportunistic and keyed to regaining what had been lost to the Nationalists since 1946, not significantly weakening the Nationalist forces.

In September 1948, CCP leaders met at Xibaipo in Hebei province to consider plans for military operations for the coming year. They expected that the war would last another three years, until 1951, and that the PLA should be expanded to five million and be able to destroy one hundred Nationalist brigades a year.[79] Operations were mapped out only in areas north of the Yangtze river, including north China and Manchuria. The CMC developed a plan to destroy 128 Nationalist brigades and allocated a rough quota to the regions where the PLA was operating. The highest quota was given to the northeast, where forces under Lin Biao were preparing to attack the LiaoShen corridor in Manchuria again. These plans reflected a view that the war would be protracted and, even though the CCP had shifted to the offensive, victory would be achieved not through decisive battles in the short term but by degrading the effective strength of the Nationalists over several years.

Yet the war ended much more quickly than even the CCP leaders had anticipated. As shown in map 2.2, three major field battles in the fall of 1948 each produced unexpected victories, which generated momentum and turned the tide of the war. From September to November, Lin Biao's forces in Manchuria launched the LiaoShen campaign. It started with a focus on seizing Jinzhou, a smaller city, but succeeded in capturing Nationalist-held territory from Changchun to Shenyang and thus taking control of all Manchuria. It was the largest battle to date in the civil war, pitting 550,000 Nationalist troops against 700,000 Communist ones. The majority of Nationalist forces either defected or were captured, thereby shifting the balance of forces significantly.[80]

In November and December 1948, a second major campaign—known as the HuaiHai Campaign—that would accelerate the CCP's victory in the civil war

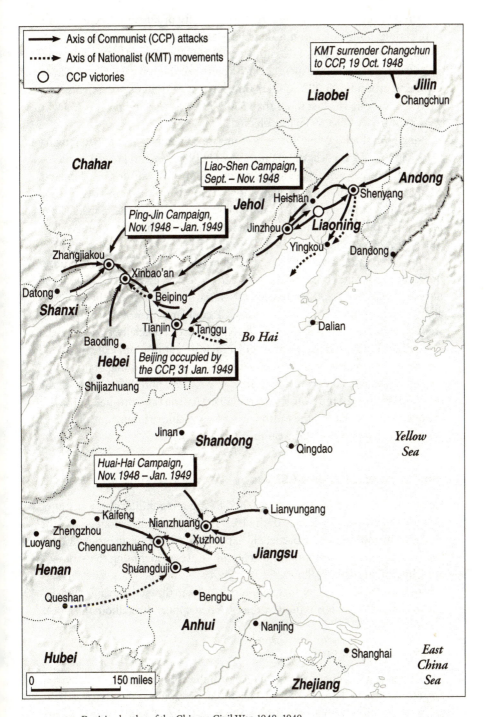

Axis of Communist (CCP) attacks
Axis of Nationalist (KMT) movements
CCP victories

KMT surrender Changchun to CCP, 19 Oct. 1948

Jilin
Changchun

Liaobei

Chahar

Liao-Shen Campaign, Sept. – Nov. 1948

Andong

Jehol   Heishan   Shenyang

Ping-Jin Campaign, Nov. 1948 – Jan. 1949

Jinzhou   Liaoning

Zhangjiakou   Yingkou   Dandong

Xinbao'an

Datong   Beiping   Dalian

Shanxi

Tianjin   Tanggu   Bo Hai

Baoding

Hebei   Beijing occupied by the CCP, 31 Jan. 1949

Shijiazhuang

Jinan   Shandong   Qingdao   Yellow Sea

Huai-Hai Campaign, Nov. 1948 – Jan. 1949

Kaifeng   Nianzhuang   Lianyungang

Zhengzhou   Xuzhou

Luoyang   Chenguanzhuang

Henan   Shuangduji   Jiangsu

Queshan   Bengbu

Anhui   Nanjing

Hubei   Shanghai   East China Sea

0   150 miles

Zhejiang

MAP 2.2. Decisive battles of the Chinese Civil War, 1948–1949

occurred in central China. The target was the city of Xuzhou, a central communications node north of the Yangtze. Although the campaign started with a fairly limited objective of defeating the Nationalist Seventh Army (around 70,000 soldiers), it soon expanded into a battle for the central plains of China, involving around 600,000 soldiers on each side.[81] When the campaign was over, the Nationalists lost more than 550,000 troops, including 320,335 who were captured and 63,593 who defected.[82]

Finally, in the PingJin Campaign from late November 1948 to late January 1949, Lin Biao's forces captured the cities of Beijing and Tianjin. Half a million Nationalist forces were defeated, most of whom were captured or defected. Along with the LiaoShen campaign, the CCP now controlled most of northern China. Thus, at the start of 1949 and in just six months, the Nationalists had lost 1.5 million soldiers and most of their territory north of the Yangtze river. The civil war was effectively over.[83]

The three campaigns were large-scale field battles, larger than any other operations conducted by the PLA to date. They succeeded because of the flexible nature of operations and mobile warfare in all phases of the civil war, along with the popular support that the CCP could mobilize in certain areas, as well as poor command decisions by the Nationalists, especially in the HuaiHai Campaign. What began as a series of large-scale autumn offensives evolved into a series of decisive engagements that marked the beginning of the end of the war. Although major combat operations would last until May 1950, with the seizure of Hainan Island from the Nationalist garrison (and through 1951, with the occupation of Tibet), the Nationalists were unable to mount any meaningful resistance after these three campaigns.

The Chinese Lexicon of Strategy

How senior military officers approached formulating military strategy after 1949 was shaped by the legacy of the PLA's experiences and strategies in the civil war. In addition to the battlefield experience, an important aspect of this legacy was a set of concepts for discussing strategy, including the strategic guideline, active defense, luring the enemy in deep, and people's war. This section reviews these concepts, highlighting their link to the civil war, and then discusses other military terms used by the PLA that appear throughout this book.

STRATEGIC GUIDELINES

After 1949, the PLA has used the concept of the strategic guideline (*zhanlue fangzhen*) to formulate and describe its military strategies. The concept of the strategic guideline, however, has its origins in how the CCP developed military strategies during the civil war. As the civil war progressed through the phases discussed above, the concept of the strategic guideline became synonymous with the CCP's overall military strategy.

The first use of the term "strategic guideline" by the CCP is unknown. Available collections of party documents suggest that it was likely first used in the summer of 1933, before the fifth encirclement campaign, and then more widely during the Long March.[84] In December 1934, for example, the Politburo during the march met at Liping in Guizhou to discuss "the strategic guideline for the Red Army."[85] The main decision taken at the meeting was to abandon previous plans to establish a base area in western Hunan and instead to establish one in the Sichuan-Guizhou border area.[86] In January 1935, the debate at the Zunyi meeting over the party's strategy in the fifth encirclement campaign was framed around the question of whether the party had adopted the correct strategic guideline. The resolution passed at Zunyi concluded that "only with the correct strategic guideline can campaigns be led correctly."[87]

After Zunyi, the CCP's use of the term in the context of strategic decision-making became much more common. In June 1935, after two of the Red Army's main columns on the Long March converged at Lianghekou in Sichuan, the CCP leadership issued a new strategic guideline, to head north and establish a base area in the Sichuan-Gansu-Shaanxi border region. In August 1935, the Politburo revised this guideline to focus on establishing a base area even farther north in the Shaanxi-Gansu border area. In December 1935, after the Red Army forces under Mao had reached Shaanxi, the party leadership issued another strategic guideline, to combine the civil war against the Nationalists with the national war against Japan. In the resolution on military strategy approved by the Politburo at the Wayaobu meeting, the title of the document's first section was the "strategic guideline."[88] Subsequently, all other major decisions on questions of military strategy in the civil war were described as strategic guidelines. These include the strategy formulated at the Luochuan meeting in August 1937 for resisting Japan in north China; Liu Shaoqi's 1945 strategy of "development of the north, defense of the south"; the CCP's response to the Nationalist's nationwide offensive in June 1946; the CCP's decision to go on the offensive in September 1947; and the CCP's strategy for the third year of the war devised in September 1948. Official histories also use the term "strategic guideline" to describe other consequential decisions that were made during the civil war, including the strategies in the encirclement campaigns in the 1930s, the approach for the New Fourth Army's guerrilla operations in south-central China in 1939,[89] and the CCP's overall strategy in the civil war in early 1940.[90]

Thus, when the PRC was established, the concept of the strategic guideline provided the basic framework for how to conceive of military strategy. As Marshal Peng Dehuai stated in 1957, "The strategic guideline affects army building, troop training, and war preparations."[91] As described in the previous chapter, the strategic guideline outlines how China will fight its next war.

After 1949, the components of the strategic guidelines contain most of what Western scholars would describe as high-level military doctrine. Authoritative Chinese sources indicate that the guidelines have four components.[92] The first is the identification of the strategic opponent (*zhanlue duishou*) and the operational target (*zuozhan duixiang*), based on the specific military threat posed by the opponent. The determination of the strategic opponent and operational target would reflect the party's assessment of the country's overall security environment and threats that it faced. Thus, it is the one component of the strategic guidelines that would not be determined primarily by senior military officers. Any "struggle" against the strategic opponent would require mobilizing all elements of national power, not just the military, and would therefore be a party decision. The military would dominate assessments of the specific operational target and development of military plans for countering such an adversary.

The second main component of a strategic guideline is the primary strategic direction (*zhuyao zhanlue fangxiang*). This refers to the geographic focal point for a potential conflict and the center of gravity for the use of force that would decisively shape the overall conflict, including the deployment of military forces and efforts to enhance or maintain operational readiness. In the civil war, the Red Army's weakness often dictated the need to identify the center of gravity or central area of focus for the use of its weaker forces to maximize their effectiveness. The Red Army also sought to guard against dispersing its forces on the battlefield where they might be more easily destroyed.

The third and perhaps core component of a strategic guideline is the basis of preparations for military struggle (*junshi douzheng junbei de jidian*). This refers to the form of warfare (*zhanzheng xingtai*) and form or pattern of operations (*zuozhan xingtai, zuozhan yangshi*), both of which describe how future wars should be waged. During the civil war and into the early 1980s, the main debate over the "form of warfare" was how to combine mobile, positional, and guerrilla warfare and which form of warfare to prioritize or emphasize. Afterward, the focus turned to combined operations (*hetong zuozhan*) of the combat arms such as infantry and armor in the ground forces and then to various conceptualizations of joint operations (*lianhe zuozhan*) involving the combination of ground, air, and naval forces.

The fourth component of a strategic guideline is the basic guiding thought (*jiben zhidao sixiang*) for the use of military force. This refers to general operational principles to be applied in a conflict. Based on the main form of warfare, such principles were intended to describe how to conduct operations and thus should be viewed as providing guidance for the operational level of war. During the civil war, for example, mobile warfare was often paired with an emphasis on battles of quick decision. With the shift from defending against total wars of invasion to peacetime modernization and local wars in the late 1980s, strategic guiding thought (*zhanlue zhidao sixiang*) for the overall use of military force, especially in situations short of war such as a crisis, became a more prominent part of the strategic guidelines in addition to basic guiding thought for operations.

Several differences between the strategic guidelines during the civil war and after 1949 should be noted. The guidelines formulated during the civil war reflected changes in strategy in wartime and not in peacetime. Thus, numerous guidelines were issued or adjusted during the more than twenty years of the civil war from 1927 to 1949. By contrast, since 1949, the PRC has only issued nine strategic guidelines, or roughly one every eight years, less frequently than during the civil war. In addition, the guidelines developed during the civil war were generally determined by the party's top leaders, especially those on the Politburo or other leading bodies. After 1949, the guidelines were formulated by senior military officers serving on the Central Military Commission, with the approval or consent of the party's top leader.

ACTIVE DEFENSE

China's nine strategic guidelines after 1949 have all been described as embodying the principle of active defense (*jiji fangyu*). As a strategic concept, active defense provides guidance for how to conduct operations when facing a superior enemy, numerically or technologically, and thus when on the strategic defensive. The main challenge under these conditions is how to preserve one's forces and then how to gradually gain the initiative. Thus, active defense offers a vision for how to overcome weakness, not how to conduct operations when on the strategic offensive or when engaging an opponent from a position of overall superiority.

The term active defense was first used in a party document in December 1935 at the Wayaobu meeting. Mao was the primary author of the resolution that was approved, as it is included in his official documentary collection.[93] The resolution stated that the Red Army should oppose both "pure defense" (*danchun fangyu*) and "preemptive" (*xianfa zhidi*) actions. Given the Red Army's inferiority, either passive defense or preemptive strikes would risk destroying large numbers of CCP forces, especially when operating on interior lines or within the areas that the CCP controlled. Instead, the Red Army should conduct an "active defense" and "gain control by striking afterwards"[94] (*houfa zhiren*).†
In this way, active defense—defined as waiting for the enemy to strike and then counterattacking—formed the "correct principle for fighting on interior lines"

---

† A typical translation of "*houfa zhiren*" is "gaining mastery after the enemy has struck." Schram helpfully translates this term as "gaining control by striking last," which I have modified slightly. See Stuart R. Schram, ed., *Mao's Road to Power*, Vol. 5 (Toward the Second United Front, January 1935-July 1937) (Armonk, NY: M. E. Sharpe, 1997), p. 80.

when facing a stronger and more powerful opponent. These were the conditions that the Red Army faced for most of the civil war. These were also the conditions that China faced after 1949 when the United States and the Soviet Union were its main adversaries.

The thinking underpinning active defense, however, appeared before the Wayaobu meeting. In many ways, the initial operational principles for guerrilla warfare that Mao Zedong and Zhu De developed in the Jinggangshan base area contain the same idea. The slogan to describe the Red Army's approach at the time was "the enemy advances and we retreat, the enemy camps and we harass, the enemy tires and we attack, the enemy retreats and we pursue."[95] Likewise, during the encirclement campaigns in the 1930s (especially during the first three), the Red Army waited for the Nationalists to attack before striking. At the Zunyi meeting in January 1935, Mao argued that "offensive defense," based on mobile warfare, would have been the best strategy for the Red Army to have used to counter the Nationalists in the fifth encirclement campaign.

Mao provided a more complete definition of active defense in his December 1936 lecture on "Problems of Strategy in China's Revolutionary War." As discussed earlier, the lecture examined the strategic defensive and the strategy the Red Army should use when faced with its numerical and technological inferiority. Mao's answer was "active defense," which he defined as "offensive defense or defense through decisive engagements." Revisiting the debate over strategy in the fifth encirclement campaign and arguments at the Zunyi meeting, he contrasted active defense with "passive defense" or "purely defensive defense." Offensive actions at the campaign and tactical levels could be used to seize the initiative from an otherwise passive position in order to achieve the objective of strategic defense and ultimately the transition to a counteroffensive. Nevertheless, the main operational actions that Mao called for while on the strategic defensive were maneuver and retreat (to wear down an opponent) along with short and quick battles, with the objective of destroying the enemy's forces, not seizing or holding territory. Mobile warfare was the primary form of warfare, as it facilitated both retreats along with large maneuvers to win engagements by concentrating superior forces at a specific time and place. But the overall idea was how to use offensive actions to achieve defensive goals—in this case, the defense of the CCP's base areas against Nationalist offensives.

After 1949, China's nine strategic guidelines have been described as being rooted in active defense. The PLA today defines active defense as "using proactive offensive actions to defend against the attacking enemy."[96] The PLA definition further notes that active defense usually combines offensive operations on exterior lines as part of the protracted defense of interior lines. As will be seen in the following chapters, the meaning of active defense varies in the different strategic guidelines adopted by the PRC. Nevertheless, the main principle of waiting for the adversary to attack and then counterattacking remains a common thread, one that is also linked with the concept of a just war. Only in the early 2000s did greater discussion emerge over what might constitute a "first strike" that would prompt a counterattack. Strategists from AMS suggest that a "first shot" on the "plane of politics" in addition to an invasion or an attack could prompt a counterattack under the rubric of active defense, highlighting challenges from "national separatists."[97] Even in this context, however, the emphasis remained on counterattacking against an adversary's action that harmed China's core interests, especially Taiwan's potential pursuit of de jure independence.

The continued emphasis on active defense contains several implications for how to understand China's approach to military strategy. The first is the belief that the goals for which China prepares to use force are defensive ones, such as the defense of the homeland from invasion or the defense of what China views as long-standing territorial claims in disputes with neighboring states. The implication of references to active defense is that China pursues defensive goals, though that is not explicit. The second is the implicit assumption that China is the weaker party and therefore more vulnerable, which places a premium on using offensive actions to achieve defensive goals. The third is that China will not be the first to attack, but instead will focus on counterattacking once an attack on China occurs. Mao captured this idea in 1939 when he said that "we will not attack unless we are attacked. If we are attacked, we will certainly counterattack."[98] Although these ideas have characterized most of China's military strategies since 1949, changes in China's material power in the past decade raise serious questions about the meaning of active defense in the future because China will no longer be in a position of material or technological inferiority.

LURING THE ENEMY IN DEEP

Luring the enemy in deep is closely related to early formulations of active defense in the civil war. As a military concept, it was in fact articulated before active defense, although the two were intertwined in the 1930s.

Luring the enemy in deep was first introduced as part of the strategy for countering the Nationalists in the first encirclement campaign in October 1930. The concept is attributed to Mao, who said "the primary task for the Front Army is to lure the enemy deep into red areas to tire and annihilate the [Nationalists]."[99] In his subsequent analysis, Mao also credited luring the enemy in deep with the successes in the second and third encirclement campaigns. Nevertheless, as discussed earlier, luring in deep was less prominent in these campaigns, even though the Red Army attacked Nationalist forces within the territory of the Central Soviet. In the second campaign, the Red Army set an ambush for a Nationalist division attacking the soviet, while in the third campaign the Red Army used continuous maneuver without engagement to wear down the Nationalist forces.

When the concept of active defense was first introduced in December 1935, luring in deep played a central role in its description. Using luring the enemy in deep to create favorable conditions for an attack despite overall weakness was the core of active defense in 1935. Nevertheless, despite its role in the encirclement campaigns, luring the enemy in deep was used much less frequently after the Long March. By the late 1930s, the CCP had established base areas it could defend without luring enemy units into their territory. When attacked, the Red Army would simply avoid engagements if possible, even if the result was a reduction in the size of the base area. In addition, as discussed above, the approach was contested even at the time it was adopted in 1930, and opposition to it was partly responsible for the decision to remove Mao from responsibility for military affairs at the Ningdu Conference in 1932.

PEOPLE'S WAR

Perhaps no concept is more closely associated with China's military strategy during the civil war than people's war. The term has different meanings, only some of which bear directly on military strategy.[100] Most generally, it refers to the righteousness or justness of the goal being pursued, through armed conflict, on behalf of the "people." In China, the goal was socialist revolution (against the Nationalists) and national liberation (against the Japanese). In addition, it refers to a general political-military strategy for overcoming weakness in such conflicts by mobilizing and organizing "the masses" to increase the manpower and material support for the armed forces and broader political support for the party's objectives. In China, the peasantry was the target of such mobilization. Third, it refers to the military aspects of such conflicts, including the kinds of forces that would be developed as well as the way in which they would be used. People's war is often viewed as synonymous with guerrilla warfare, especially outside China. Although militia forces and guerrilla tactics were certainly a part of the civil war in China, they were only a part. As the CCP's military strategies in the civil war demonstrate, the primary military forces were regular main force units, not militia, and the dominant way of fighting was mobile warfare, not guerrilla warfare.

A further complication is the historical usage of the term "people's war" by the CCP. Ironically, during the civil war itself, CCP leaders did not widely or frequently use the term. In fact, although it is associated closely with Mao Zedong's military thought, he only first described it in April 1945 in a report to the Seventh Congress of the CCP.[101] Moreover, he did not use the term frequently afterwards, in the late 1940s, and it rarely appeared in the party's main newspaper, the *People's Daily*. Nevertheless, many of the ideas now associated with people's war, especially the centrality of mobilizing and organizing the masses, first appeared almost two decades earlier, even if they were not labeled as part of the concept. Mao's 1927 report on the peasant situation in Hunan, for example, identified their potential for political mobilization.[102] Mao's 1936 essay on strategy in China's revolutionary war contains most of the ideas associated with people's war but never uses the term.[103]

The basic idea of people's war is as follows. Wars of revolution or national liberation are just or righteous conflicts that pit a weaker party against a much stronger one. Such wars can only be won if the party can "mobilize, organize, direct, and arm" the people so that weakness can gradually be overcome, victories achieved on the battlefield, and the final political goals accomplished.[104] As Mao wrote in 1938, "The army and the people are the foundation of victory."[105] A modernized army would "drive [Japan] back across the Yalu River." At the same time, "the richest source of power in war lies in the masses."[106] Similarly, Mao maintained that the political mobilization of the people would "create a vast sea in which to drown the enemy, create the conditions that will compensate for the lack of weapons and other things, and create the prerequisites for overcoming every difficulty in the war."[107]

When mobilized, the people provided manpower, materiel, and financial resources that would otherwise not be available and would help to gradually shift the balance of forces for the revolutionary or national liberation movement. A mobilized populace can also engage in "struggle" in domains other than military affairs to help bring about victory.[108] On the military side, in addition to providing recruits for the regular units of the Red Army, the peasantry were organized into militia and self-defense corps assigned to specific areas and tasked with local defense, small-scale guerrilla operations, and support and logistics activities.[109] As the size of the PLA grew in the last phase of the civil war, the role of the militia and self-defense corps became more prominent in providing aid and support for the regular field armies.

In his lectures in the 1930s, Mao viewed wars of revolution or liberation as being protracted contests. Such conflicts were viewed as moving through three stages: the strategic defense when the enemy attacks, the strategic stalemate when the enemy sought to consolidate its gains, and the strategic offensive when China counterattacked. These wars would be protracted not just because of China's weakness, but also because time was needed to mobilize the population, develop a broad base of support among the people, organize them around the party's goals, wear down the enemy militarily, and gradually be in a position to engage in offensive military operations. For the purposes of revolution or national liberation, a long war held out a much greater prospect of victory than a short one, given the imperative and benefits of popular support that would need to be nurtured and cultivated over time.

Although guerrilla warfare is often viewed as synonymous with people's war, such a conclusion or view is incorrect. In Mao's writings and in the various stages of the Chinese civil war, guerrilla warfare would only be waged in areas occupied by the opponent, such as Nationalist-held areas in the mid-1930s. Elsewhere, the emphasis would be on mobile operations by regular forces. In the various phases of the Chinese civil war, guerrilla warfare was most prominent in the initial establishment of base areas in central China in the late 1920s and in operations behind Japanese lines after 1937. In other phases, such as the encirclement campaigns in the early 1930s, the establishment of base areas in north China in the late 1930s, and the operations against the Nationalists after 1945, mobile warfare with conventional units was the dominant and primary form of warfare. In other words, in the three stylized phases of a protracted war, guerrilla warfare was only prominent in the second phase, the strategic stalemate. Because the opponent had maximized the amount of territory it could hold in this phase, the opportunities for using guerrilla warfare increased to wear down the enemy while the people were mobilized and organized in the base areas beyond the enemy's control and behind enemy lines. By contrast, during the strategic defensive and strategic offensive, the main form of military operations was mobile warfare. Because of its emphasis on fluid fronts and mobility, mobile warfare is sometimes described as having guerrilla elements. Nevertheless, mobile warfare was based on the use of conventional forces in direct engagement and not irregulars.

The idea of a people's war, and the primacy of peasant mobilization for the CCP, had an important corollary for the development of the armed forces. The core idea was that the army belonged to the people and existed to liberate the people. A high level of "political consciousness" would boost morale and enhance effectiveness. To aid the broader mobilization of the people, the army also needed to be seen and to see itself as united with the people and not, in contrast to the rapacious warlord armies of the day, as exploiting them.[110] Party control of the armed forces, first established at the Gutian Conference in 1929, was central, in addition to regulations on behavior and discipline that were issued in the early 1930s.[111] In addition, the army was tasked with functions other than fighting to aid the party's broader political mobilization of the population. The army engaged in direct political work to facilitate the party's efforts to mobilize the masses, as well as in agricultural and other forms of production to ease the economic burden on the peasantry. These roles were especially prominent when seeking to establish and enlarge base areas while avoiding direct engagements with a much stronger enemy.

After 1949, the meaning of people's war changed. Inside China, the term only began to be used widely in 1958 during the Great Leap Forward and amid the "anti-dogmatism" movement to counter excessive reliance on Soviet ideas in military affairs (as discussed in the following chapter). In 1965, the concept was further popularized inside and outside China with the publication of an essay on the twentieth anniversary of Japan's surrender, signed by Lin Biao, entitled "Long Live People's War!"[112] Discussion of people's war then peaked during the radicalization of the Cultural Revolution. People's war was cast as an indigenous Chinese approach that reflected Mao's military genius as a model for others to follow, especially in Vietnam. Outside China, the term was associated with a strategy of continental defense in which China would trade time for space and leverage its large size and population to defeat an invasion or attack in a protracted war.[113] In the 1980s, foreign analysts would describe China's strategy as "people's war under modern conditions."[114] As subsequent chapters in this book will show, such a view of people's war is also inaccurate. It implies an exaggerated role for irregular forces, guerrilla warfare, and societal mobilization, and downplays the centrality of conventional forces and operations and the role of mobilization in directly supporting military operations by providing manpower for the PLA.

More generally, after 1949, people's war had other meanings, both of which resonated with the PLA's experience during the civil war. In practice, it contains the idea that China, as a newly independent but materially weak state, would need to continue to mobilize its population and resources to prevail in a major conflict, especially if attacked. Even after the end of the Cold War, continued references to people's war underscores the focus on societal mobilization to enhance China's strength.[115] Today, for example, the PLA defines people's war as "organizing and arming the broad masses of the people to carry out war to oppose class oppression or resist the invasion of foreign enemies."[116] A current example might be the emphasis on "military-civil integration" (*junmin ronghe*), which seeks to tap civilian expertise to develop new warfighting technologies.[117] People's war also has a clear political meaning or connotation—namely, that the PLA should never forget that it is a party army under the absolute control of the CCP.

ARMY BUILDING

Army building (*jundui jianshe*) refers to all efforts related to force modernization and development. In Chinese, "*jianshe*" means construction, building, or development. Accordingly, "*jundui jianshe*" is typically translated as "army building" or "army construction." It could also be translated as military building or military construction.

Since "*jianshe*" does not have an English equivalent, the term requires brief clarification. It first became widely used in the early to mid 1950s, when the party's main goal was "socialist modernization," which required building or constructing different parts of the party state. The military component of this effort was thus "army building." Economic development, for example, is sometimes described as "economic construction" (*jingji jianshe*). Today, the PLA defines army building as "a general designation of all activities to build armed forces [*zujian jundui*], maintain and improve the system of military power, and increase combat power."[118]

MILITARY STRUGGLE, PREPARATIONS FOR MILITARY STRUGGLE, AND COMBAT READINESS

Other commonly used terms involve military struggle and war preparations. These are not as closely tied to the civil war experience, except in the general sense of the CCP's struggle with the Nationalists for the control of China. Today, the PLA defines military struggle (*junshi douzheng*) as "the primary use of military means to carry out struggle," referring to the competition among states to achieve political or economic goals.[119] Military struggle, however, does not necessarily only refer to actual combat or military operations but also to the general deterrent and compellent roles of military force. The PLA definition thus notes that "war is the highest form of military struggle."

Accordingly, preparations for military struggle (*junshi douzheng zhunbei*) refer to all efforts to prepare an armed force to fight. The PLA defines preparations for military struggle as "preparations carried out to satisfy the requirements for military struggle."[120] The core is "war preparations," or "*zhanbei*," which might be better translated as "combat readiness." The PLA defines *zhanbei* as "the preparation and alertness of the armed forces in peacetime to respond in a timely manner to wars or sudden incidents."[121] It is described as "the regular basic work of the armed forces in peacetime."[122]

The PLA and Its Challenges in 1949

For more than twenty years before the PRC's founding in 1949, the Red Army and then the PLA had focused on ensuring the survival of the CCP and defeating the Nationalists so that it could seize power and build a new socialist state. After 1949, however, the PLA faced a series of daunting new tasks, which were intertwined with the development of the country's first national military strategy.

The first major task was how to shift from being a revolutionary army focused on seizing power to one that would be able to defend the sovereignty and territorial integrity of the newly established nation-state. Previously, by emphasizing its survival and maintaining its effective strength, the PLA would avoid combat engagements or even cede territory to be able to fight another day. Such an approach was appropriate during the civil war, when the CCP's armed forces were often significantly weaker than the Nationalists, but it was at odds with defending a nation-state.

The PRC's security environment in many ways greatly complicated the task of defending a new nation-state. First, the PRC faced a challenging geopolitical situation. China's sheer size along with the diversity of the terrain and climate within and along its borders would require an army that would be able to operate in different environments.[123] When the new state was founded, the CCP was not even in full control of the territory it claimed to govern. From 1949 to 1952, the PLA continued to consolidate the CCP's control of the country through "bandit suppression" campaigns against remnant Nationalist troops and local warlords in addition to mounting a campaign to seize and incorporate Tibet in 1951. The PLA would have to defend a long coastline and an even longer land border. China would become involved in territorial disputes with each of its neighbors on land and at sea, which created a series of ongoing disputes with the ability to erupt into armed conflict and, at times, distract that state from other security issues.[124]

Second, despite establishing a new state, the CCP had not completely defeated its adversary in the civil war. The bulk of the Nationalist force, including the government led by Chiang Kai-shek, retreated to Taiwan in late 1949.[125] Defeating the Nationalists on the island would require an invasion and amphibious assault—a formidable military task for any military, but especially challenging for a military such as the PLA that had not yet formed an air force or a navy and remained composed of primarily infantry units. The PLA's failed attempt in 1949 to seize Jinmen, an island only a mile off the coast of Fujian province, reflected the severity of this challenge.[126]

Third, within a year, the PRC found itself locked in confrontation with the world's most powerful country at the time, the United States. Given the CCP's early history of seeking to ensure the party's survival against the much stronger Nationalists, facing off against a stronger adversary was a familiar challenge. Now, however, the nation-state and not just the party was at risk. Moreover, China would not catch up anytime soon, as its economy remained based on agriculture and had only begun to industrialize in certain regions, such as the northeast. By the fall of 1950, a year after declaring the establishment of the PRC, China would intervene on the Korean Peninsula, engaging the United States on the battlefield to rescue North Korea and defend its northeastern border.[127]

The second major task was how to build an armed force that could meet the challenges of this new environment—ensure sovereignty and territorial integrity of the new state, conquer Taiwan and defeat the Nationalists, and defend China against a much more powerful adversary. How the PLA developed as a military in the civil war provided several legacies that would need to be overcome.

The first was a legacy of decentralized operations, command, and control. In the 1930s, the Red Army was organized into three main front armies that were only loosely commanded by the national party leadership but usually operated independently in their base areas. A similar pattern repeated itself when elements of the Eighth Route Army established base areas throughout northern China. In the civil war, the PLA was organized regionally, depending on a unit's area of operations. By the end of the war, there were four large field armies, which operated in different areas of the country. The party's central headquarters delegated a substantial amount of decision-making authority, especially at the level of operations and campaigns, to local commanders. This reflected the wide distances over which units were operating in different parts of the country, along with the center's lack of detailed knowledge of local circumstances and the challenges of maintaining communications. The center would provide general guidance for the goals to be achieved in different areas, but even the assessment and discussion of these goals would reflect a great deal of input from local commanders. After 1949, as this book argues, the party delegated substantial responsibility for military affairs to top military leaders. The party leadership's willingness to delegate such responsibility has its roots in the civil war.[128]

A second and closely related legacy was wide variation in how units were trained, organized, and equipped. As the PLA was composed of units that had been established at different times and in different parts of the country, the PLA had no standard table of equipment and organization used across all units. Typically, PLA soldiers were equipped with weapons they had acquired on the battlefield, either from defeated or surrendered Nationalist or Japanese units or captured from enemy armories. At the end of the civil war, PLA infantry units used rifles with more than a dozen different calibers.

Starting in 1945, the size of the PLA increased substantially. The size and scope of operations also increased from involving perhaps tens of thousands of soldiers to hundreds of thousands. This affected all aspects of force development, including operational doctrine, training, organization, logistics, supply, and command. Such efforts were perhaps most prominent in the northeast, where Lin Biao developed a large force that would eventually be known as the Fourth Field Army. The initial exploration of developing a large standing army, and the challenges of managing one, were explored during the final phase of the civil war and would be an important task that the leadership would take up after the PRC was established.[129] Creating a unified force with standardized organization, equipment, training, and procedures for managing the various challenges of defending a new country would be one of the main tasks for senior officers to address in the 1950s.

A third legacy, reflecting the weakness of the Chinese economy, was the technological weakness of the PLA. In 1949, the PLA had very few indigenous defense industries apart from munitions and light arms. China had no ability to manufacture the weapons it would need for a modern force, such as armored vehicles and airplanes.

Conclusion

When the People's Republic was established in 1949, the new leadership faced the daunting task of building a new state after more than twenty years of civil war with the Nationalists, along with Japanese occupation since 1931. As China's top leaders embarked on this endeavor, they would draft China's first national military strategy, which was adopted in 1956. The years of experience accumulated on the battlefield, and the PLA's main approaches to warfighting—how to combine mobile, positional, and guerrilla warfare—would cast a long shadow over the formulation of strategy until the adoption of the 1993 strategy. The concepts associated with strategy that were developed during this period—including the strategic guideline, active defense, and people's war—continue to frame how China conceives of military strategy today.

3

The 1956 Strategy: "Defending the Motherland"

In March 1956, the Central Military Commission of the Chinese Communist Party held an enlarged meeting that gathered together senior military officers. When the meeting concluded, the CMC issued China's first national military strategy, which outlined how to counter a US invasion through a strategy of forward defense. The strategy envisioned a transition from a military composed mostly of lightly armed infantry units to one based on partial mechanization able to conduct combined arms operations, supported by air and naval forces, to defeat the invasion.

The adoption of the 1956 strategic guideline is puzzling for several reasons. To start, the new strategy was issued during what Chinese leaders perceived to be a relatively stable security environment. Although China remained locked in a confrontation with the United States in East Asia, China did not expect a war to occur for at least a decade or more. Consistent with such perceptions, defense spending as a share of the national budget declined steadily during this period.

In addition, despite China's alliance with the Soviet Union, China did not seek to emulate the military strategy of its senior security partner. The 1956 strategic guideline was adopted during the height of Chinese-Soviet military cooperation, when thousands of Soviet military advisors and technical experts were assisting the PLA in its modernization effort. The Soviet Union also provided enough weapons and equipment to arm more than half of the PLA's infantry divisions, as well as blueprints, technologies, and factories for China's nascent defense industries. As such, China presents a "most likely" case for arguments about major military change based on the mechanism of emulation. Nevertheless, China did not emulate the Soviet strategy. Instead, China rejected the basic elements of the Soviet approach, including its emphasis on first strikes and preemption. By 1958, the CMC decided to downplay the Soviet model and only adopt selected components linked with weapons technologies and combined arms tactics.

As the first military strategy adopted after 1949, the 1956 strategic guideline represents a watershed in the PLA's history. The new strategy demonstrates that China's dedication to building a modern military began much earlier than is commonly believed in most studies of the PLA, which tends to view this period through the lens of Mao Zedong's "people's war."[1] The focus on combined arms operations, in fits and starts, continued into the Cultural Revolution, even after military ranks were abolished and Mao started to shift China's military strategy back to "luring the enemy in deep" from the civil war. Some of the core ideas of the 1956 strategy resurfaced when the PLA began to consider how best to counter the Soviet threat from the north in the late 1970s. Likewise, when drafting China's 1993 strategy, General Zhang Zhen used the 1956 strategy as a reference.[2] Thus, a complete understanding of China's approach to military strategy begins with the 1956 strategic guideline.

As the PRC's first military strategy, the external motivations for formulating it are likely overdetermined. China would need to adopt a military strategy at some point after 1949 and, furthermore, was locked in a hostile relationship with the United States. Nevertheless, within that context, the principal motivation was a perception of a significant shift in the operational conduct of warfare. During the early 1950s, China sought not only to absorb the lessons from World War II and the Korean War, but it also considered the implications of the nuclear revolution for conventional operations. Senior military officers also led the formulation of the 1956 strategy with little or no input from top party leaders. Such military-led change was possible because of the unprecedented unity within the CCP in the early to mid-1950s, which insulated the military from party politics and gave it substantial autonomy for managing military affairs.

This chapter unfolds as follows. The first section demonstrates that the strategy adopted in 1956 reflected a major change in China's approach to military strategy, especially when contrasted with the approaches used in various phases of the civil war discussed in the previous chapter. The next two sections highlight the factors that explain the adoption of the guideline: perceptions of a shift in the conduct of warfare, and party unity. The fourth section reviews the initial reforms implemented to reorganize the PLA in the early 1950s, while the fifth section examines the adoption of the new strategy in 1956. The sixth section considers the main alternative explanation: that China sought to copy or emulate the Soviet strategy. The last section reviews the adoption of a new strategic guideline in 1960, after Lin Biao assumed leadership of military affairs following the purge of Peng Dehuai at the Lushan Conference, to argue that it represents only a minor change to the 1956 strategy.

"Defending the Motherland"

The 1956 strategic guideline represents the first of three major changes in China's military strategy since 1949. Called the "strategic guideline for defending the motherland," it outlined a strategy of forward defense of China's coastal areas during the first six months of a US invasion. This strategy emphasized positional warfare and downplayed mobile and guerrilla warfare, which had been much more prominent in the civil war. Countering a US invasion would require the PLA to conduct combined arms operations, coordinating the actions of garrison and maneuver forces, along with air and naval forces, all under nuclear conditions.

OVERVIEW OF THE 1956 STRATEGY

In the 1956 strategic guideline, the "basis of preparations for military struggle" was a surprise attack by a technologically and materially stronger adversary: the United States. With the outbreak of the Korean War in 1950, the United States became China's primary adversary. After a stalemate was reached on the Korean Peninsula, China began to consider the possibility of a US amphibious assault against the mainland, most likely on the Liaodong or Shandong peninsulas in the northeast. However, neither senior military officers nor top party leaders believed that an attack was imminent. This defense planning scenario was first identified in 1952 during the Korean War and emphasized again in March 1955, based on Mao's assessment of growing US power in the region after it established a network of alliances and announced the doctrine of "massive retaliation" in 1954. Because the 1956 strategic guideline identified the United States as China's "strategic opponent," the new strategy focused on how to fight an adversary with technologically superior capabilities. The guideline also emphasized how to fight "under nuclear conditions," as it was almost universally assumed than any US attack would begin with the use of nuclear weapons.[3]

The 1956 strategy was a strategy of strategic defense. It described how China would respond once the United States had initiated a conflict and attacked Chinese territory. The core of the 1956 strategy was a forward defense of China's coastal areas, including potential invasion routes in the north, along with the defense of China's industrial and economic areas in and around Shanghai. The strategy stated that the PLA, if attacked, "must be able to respond immediately with a strong counterattack and stop the enemy's offensive in predetermined fortified areas." Peng summarized "the basic content of our army's strategic guideline of active defense" as "stabilize the front, smash the enemy's plan for rapid attack and victory, and compel the enemy to engage in protracted operations with our military so that we can gradually strip them of their strategic initiative and have it gradually transferred to our military—that is, transitioning from strategic defense to strategic offense."[4]

OPERATIONAL DOCTRINE

A key component of any strategic guideline is the identification of the "form of operations" that the PLA should be prepared to conduct in the future. The 1956 guideline departed from the PLA's past emphasis on using lightly armed infantry units to engage in mobile warfare on fluid fronts. Instead, according to Peng, the strategy "should be a fusion of positional and mobile warfare: that is, linking together mobile offensive warfare with positional defensive warfare."[5] This form of operations significantly downplayed mobile and guerrilla warfare that had been prominent in the Chinese civil war and marked a watershed in the PLA's approach to operations.

The "basic guiding thought for operations" is the way in which positional and mobile warfare would be combined. Garrison forces would defend permanent fortifications along the coast and on coastal islands to slow down the US attack and pin down US forces by holding their positions. Afterward, maneuver units would be deployed with the aim of destroying US forces.[6] The PLA would only engage in guerrilla operations in territory that was lost in the initial attack. The goal was to withstand an assault for three to six months, or even longer, denying the United States a quick victory, overextending its supply lines, and buying time for a full-scale mobilization to destroy and expel its forces.[7]

After the adoption of the 1956 strategic guideline, the PLA drafted combat regulations to describe how it would conduct combined arms operations. Starting in 1950, the PLA had used translated copies of Soviet army field manuals in its military academies and schools. The new strategy, however, called for developing China's own military science. In 1958, the CMC decided to draft combat regulations based on the PLA's own combat experience in addition to the practices of foreign militaries. The drafting of regulations began in late 1958. In May 1961, the CMC issued the first two sets of regulations: *General Combat Regulations for a Combined Army* (*hecheng jundui zhandou tiaoling gaize*) and *Infantry Combat Regulations* (*bubing zhandou tiaoling*). By 1965, regulations for the air force and navy as well as artillery, communications, chemical defense, engineering, and railway units were issued by the services and branches.[8] The regulations issued during this period subsequently became known as the "first generation" of combat regulations.[9]

FORCE STRUCTURE

The 1956 strategic guideline envisioned creating a combined force (*hecheng jundui*) of various services and branches. The strategy emphasized the development of the ground forces and the air force over the navy. The ground forces were seen as the bulwark of China's defense, while the air force would defend against the initial US bombing campaigns and protect the ground forces. Within the ground forces, the strategy sought to increase the proportion of artillery, as well as armored, anti-tank, and air defense units, along with improved mechanization. The navy was secondary, though still important, focusing on coastal defense (*jin'an fangyu*) through the development of torpedo boats and submarines.[10]

To implement the new strategy, the PLA's force structure changed significantly between 1950 and 1958. Personnel in the air force and navy grew to constitute 12.2 percent and 5.8 percent of the PLA, respectively. Likewise, personnel in artillery and armored units under the CMC constituted 4.8 and 2.3 percent of the force. Over the same time frame, the organization of infantry divisions also changed to reflect the shift to combined arms. The share of personnel in infantry units declined from 61.1 percent in 1950 to 42.3 percent in 1958, while troops in artillery units increased from 20.4 to 31.9 percent and engineering troops grew from 1.6 percent to 4.4 percent. In 1958, armored and chemical defense units, which did not exist in 1950, made up 4.7 and 1.2 percent.[11]

The 1956 guideline reaffirmed an earlier decision to cap the total size of the force at 3.5 million, down from over 6 million during the height of the Korean War. Downsizing was required to limit the burden of defense expenditure on the state as it embarked on the Second Five-Year Plan and to emphasize quality over quantity in the force itself. Between 1956 and 1958, the size of the force was further reduced to roughly 2.4 million. The proportion of the national budget devoted to defense shrunk from 34.2 percent to just over 12 percent.[12]

TRAINING

Consistent with the emphasis on combined arms operations, the PLA adjusted its approach to training. The PLA's first training program was drafted in 1957 and implemented in provisional form in January 1958. The *Liberation Army Daily* described the purpose of the program as "learning combat skills for modern conditions [to] deal with emergencies at any time." Consistent with the 1956 strategy, the new program offered a summary of Chinese views of modern warfare at the time and stated that future training should "continue to raise modern military skills and learn combined arms operations under nuclear, chemical, missile and other complicated conditions."[13]

Before and after the adoption of the 1956 guideline, the PLA established a professional military education system. One requirement of Peng's strategy was for skilled officers to command and direct combined arms operations along with technically proficient soldiers to operate the new types of weapons and equipment that would be used by individual units. In 1957, the PLA established the Advanced Military Academy (*gaodeng junshi xueyuan*) to train senior officers in the principles and techniques of modern command and the operational level of war. Other academies established during this period include the Military Academy, the Political Academy, and the Logistics Academy.[14] In March 1958, the Academy of Military Science (AMS) was founded, with Marshal Ye Jianying as its first president. The appointment of one of the ten great marshals from the revolutionary war as president underscored the importance that was attached to developing China's military science.

China also began to conduct large-scale military exercises involving different services and combat arms. Most of these were demonstration exercises to highlight various aspects of modern warfare and operations that China should be able to conduct. Before the guideline was established, the first such exercise, which simulated a campaign to counter an amphibious assault, was held on the Liaodong Peninsula. The exercises involved units from each of the services and a total of 68,000 soldiers.[15] Every year thereafter, the General Staff Department (GSD) organized combined arms exercises, including joint exercises with Soviet and North Korean forces in 1957 and a large-scale simulation of an amphibious landing in May 1959.[16]

World War II and the Korean War

In the early to mid-1950s, three events shaped China's perceptions of shifts in the operational conduct of warfare: World War II, the Korean War, and the nuclear revolution. As a late military modernizer, China's perspective of these events was shaped by the military it possessed at the end of the Chinese civil war. When the PRC was founded in 1949, the PLA included more than five million soldiers, almost all of which were light infantry. The PLA lacked services such as a navy and air force and only a small percentage of the ground forces were in combat arms such as artillery or armored units. The ground forces had no tradition of combined arms operations that required coordinating action among different combat arms. In the civil war, as discussed in chapter 2, command had also been decentralized. Commanders of the various field armies were given wide latitude when planning and conducting operations within their area of operations as well as for recruiting, organizing, and training their soldiers.

Given the PLA's limited capabilities and broad responsibility for defending the newly established state, it is perhaps not surprising that military leaders would study the prevailing conduct of warfare as they considered how to defend their new country. In a speech on November 2, 1950, Su Yu, the deputy chief of staff and a famous commander during the civil war, highlighted four characteristics of modern war, drawing heavily on World War II.* Importantly, Su's speech reflects views about the conduct of warfare before Chinese and US forces clashed on the Korean Peninsula only a few weeks later. Su highlighted the multiple dimensions of warfare on and under the sea, on land and underground, on the front line and in now-vulnerable rear areas. Warfare was a "competition of high technology" on the battlefield in which opponents would seek to use their most advanced weapons. Another key characteristic Su stressed was the fast pace of modern war, facilitated by mechanization, which increased the speed of operations and consumption of supplies. Finally, the speed of operations also underscored the importance of coordination among combat arms.[17] As Su told his audience, "According to these characteristics, we must grasp and master modernization."[18]

China's senior military officers gained additional insight into modern warfare by fighting the world's most advanced military on the Korean Peninsula. China's experience during the Korean War affirmed the assessment of shifts in the conduct of warfare as revealed in World War II. According to China's official history of the Korean War, the conflict "greatly pushed forward the development of China's military art and powerfully accelerated China's military transformation in the 1950s."[19] The transformations influenced by the Korean War highlighted by the study included: from only infantry operations to joint operations with multiple services and branches; from ground operations to three-dimensional (liti) operations (i.e., land, air, and sea); from mobile warfare to mobile warfare and positional warfare; and from front-line operations to total operations in the front and rear, among others.[20]

Yet these were not the only lessons that China drew from its experience on the Korean Peninsula. Although the war was fought to a stalemate along the thirty-eighth parallel, it revealed how destructive contemporary warfare could be, especially for the weaker side. Chinese casualty figures are only estimates, but ten Chinese soldiers probably perished for every one American soldier, and an equal number of American and Chinese soldiers were wounded.[21] In addition to the destructiveness of modern war, the PLA also learned that logistics and supply problems constrained the scope and extent of offensive operations that it could conduct. Because Chinese forces were not mechanized and traveled mostly on foot, they could not easily exploit any breakthroughs that occurred on the battlefield. Similarly, despite the efforts of railway and air defense troops to build, maintain, and defend supply lines, transportation and supply problems limited the PLA's ability to sustain offensive operations, as it would quickly exhaust its supplies.[22] As Peng Dehuai stated in December 1953,

---

* Su Yu participated in the Nanchang Uprising in 1927, led the most effective division in the New Fourth Army in south-central China in the 1930s, and engineered victories in many campaigns in the civil war (most notably in the HuaiHai Campaign).

"The experience of the Korean War proves that in modern war if there is no guarantee of ample supply of materiel from the rear, war is impossible to conduct."[23] Similarly, the lack of sufficient airpower and the inability to maintain even localized air superiority was seen as perhaps the greatest challenge faced by Chinese forces, as it played a key role in the high number of casualties and vulnerability of supply lines to disruption.[24]

Nevertheless, China during the Korean War developed methods for overcoming its own technological inferiority. First, although the United States was stronger, the PLA could win individual battles by attacking what were perceived as weak points that American forces could not address. These included the limited utility of airpower at night and a desire by American forces to maintain physical contact with rear areas, which led the PLA to conduct operations at night, engage in close-quarters combat, and seek to separate smaller units from larger ones.[25] Second, following the shift to negotiations and to defending the territory under its control, the PLA reduced to some degree its vulnerability to airpower and artillery through the use of extensive tunnels and defensive fortifications on the rough and hilly terrain around the thirty-eighth parallel.[26] These defensive systems would be used again as China prepared to counter a US invasion in the 1950s.

China paid more attention to the nuclear revolution after US Secretary of State John Foster Dulles articulated the doctrine of massive retaliation in 1954. Most Chinese generals believed that nuclear weapons would be used in strategic bombing campaigns at the start of a war. When combined with the advent of jet propulsion, Su Yu described future war in 1955 as starting with an "atomic blitz" (*yuanzi shanji*) in which aircraft would be used to bomb industrial centers, cities, and military targets.[27] Nuclear weapons also further increased the vulnerability of rear areas. Nevertheless, senior military officers such as Su Yu and Ye Jianying maintained that infantry units would remain central because nuclear weapons could not be used to occupy territory.[28] The advent of nuclear weapons also underscored the importance of airpower, to defend against nuclear strikes, and the importance of mechanization, to facilitate a rapid response capability and provide added protection of forces on the nuclear battlefield.[29]

Party Unity after Victory in the Revolution

Remarkable and perhaps unsurpassed unity within the CCP created favorable conditions for military-led change in the 1950s. As Frederick Teiwes has demonstrated, one indicator of this unity was the continuity of membership of the CCP's Central Committee, as all members elected in 1945 were reelected in 1956 (along with new members). Similarly, little change in the composition of the Politburo occurred.[30] Dramatic changes in the composition of either leadership body would have signaled much greater conflict within the party. Another indicator of unity is the relative absence of purges, in contrast to the Soviet system under Stalin and China during the Cultural Revolution. Only two senior party leaders were purged before the 1959 Lushan Conference: Gao Gang and Rao Shushi, in 1954. Moreover, their purge did not threaten unity within the party. Gao and Rao, who sought to remove Liu Shaoqi and Zhou Enlai as top leaders of the party and state bureaucracies, respectively, were widely seen as violating party norms. The leadership accepted their removal.[31]

Party unity during this period stemmed from several sources. Victory in the revolution, and the national unification that was achieved as a result, consolidated the authority of the revolution's leaders. Top party leaders shared a commitment to Marxist ideology and to socialist modernization through the Soviet model. The initial success during the period of consolidation after 1949 and then in the First Five-Year Plan starting in 1953 further bolstered unity. Finally, senior party leaders acknowledged Mao's unquestioned authority, which had been established in 1942.[32] In contrast to later periods, Mao observed the principles of collective leadership, delegated authority to the most competent party leaders regardless of their personal ties to him, and encouraged debate among the party on key issues.[33]

The unity within the party created conditions for senior military officers to initiate strategic change. Because the party was unified, top party leaders had no incentive to draw the PLA into intraparty politics. Likewise, with a unified party, the PLA was not tempted to inject itself into elite politics. Hence, senior military officers could focus on military affairs and were even encouraged by China's top party leaders. As Mao noted in September 1949, "Our people's armed forces must be maintained and developed. We must not only have a strong army, but also a strong air force and navy."[34]

To be sure, the PLA still played a political role during this period, but as an agent of the party. From 1949 to 1953, many PLA units administered the areas they had conquered in the civil war. As victory in the revolution occurred much faster than the CCP's top leaders had anticipated, the party lacked enough civilian cadres to administer the country and relied upon the military to undertake this task.[35] The PLA also engaged in military operations to eliminate all remaining armed opposition to CCP rule, including remnant Nationalist units and local warlords. Known as "bandit suppression" campaigns, they occurred throughout the country, but especially in the southwest and northwest.[36] By 1954, as the party-state had consolidated its authority through violent land reform in rural areas and mass campaigns in the cities, the PLA withdrew significantly from governance. Nevertheless, it continued to play a role in internal security, as the public security forces (*gong'an budui*) remained under the military during this period.[37]

Based on this unity, the top party leaders delegated substantial responsibility for military affairs to the PLA's high command. The process began in mid-1952, as the first Five-Year Plan was being drafted. Peng Dehuai, then the commander of Chinese forces in Korea, assumed responsibility for military affairs on behalf of the party. Zhou Enlai had shouldered this task since 1947, but now sought to turn his attention to government administration and economic development. After Peng returned to Beijing in April 1952 to be treated for a chronic disorder, the Politburo then decided that Peng should remain in Beijing to take charge of the CMC's daily affairs and run the CMC's general office.[38] After resting for several months, Peng formally assumed his new responsibilities on July 19, 1952. A CMC circular sent to all military units stated that "starting from today, every related document and telegram should all be copied and sent to Vice-Chairman Peng."[39]

The delegation of military affairs was reaffirmed when a new CMC was formed after the first National People's Congress was held in September 1954. Mao Zedong chaired this new CMC, while its members included Deng Xiaoping, along with the ten veterans of the civil war who would be given the rank of marshal the following year.[40] At its first meeting, the CMC affirmed the 1952 decision that Peng would be responsible for the CMC's daily affairs—effectively overseeing all aspects of military affairs.[41] Huang Kecheng, then a deputy chief of the general staff who worked directly with Peng, recalled later that Mao "formally gave all work of the armed forces [budui] to Peng to manage."[42] At the same time, "major issues would be decided by the CMC."

Two examples reflect the delegation of military affairs to Peng and the other veteran commanders in this period. The first is Mao's absence from all enlarged meetings of the CMC until June 1958. Official party history sources contain no references to Mao attending CMC meetings.[43] Peng would consult with Mao, but often after meetings were held. The second is Mao's own statements. In June 1958, for example, Mao acknowledged the delegation of responsibility to senior military officers, noting that "I have not interfered in military affairs for four years, which was all given [tuigei] to comrade Peng Dehuai."[44] Peng frequently consulted with Mao and other top party leaders on major decisions but the initiative for change emanated from Peng and his fellow officers.

Initial Reforms and the Development of a New Strategy

Before 1956, senior military officers implemented foundational reforms to the entire organization of the PLA. Although they preceded the formal adoption of China's first military strategy that would be issued a few years later, they were pursued for the same reason: to enable the PLA to wage modern warfare. Some included decisions on components of the strategy that would be formalized in the strategic guideline issued in 1956. The process by which these reforms were initiated also illustrates the delegation of responsibility for military affairs from the top party leadership to the senior military officers. Although Mao Zedong approved these reforms as chairman of the CMC, he did not intervene in the process by which they were determined.

THE FIVE-YEAR PLAN FOR MILITARY DEVELOPMENT

In mid-1952, the GSD drafted the PLA's first five-year plan. Called the *Outline of the Five-Year Plan for Military Development,* the document contained several decisions regarding China's military strategy that would become part of the 1956 strategic guideline, including the identification of China's main enemy, the "primary strategic direction" or center of gravity in a future war, and the force structure needed to defend China in such a conflict. The plan also contained what one senior general described as China's "blueprint" for the PLA's modernization.[45]

In early 1952, the top party leadership started to draft the first Five-Year Plan for the development of China's economy. Because economic development would need to be coordinated with national defense requirements, Zhou Enlai instructed the GSD to draft a five-year plan for the development of the armed forces.[46] In early April 1952, Su Yu, the deputy chief of the general staff, proposed that the CMC should first determine China's strategic guideline before drafting any development plans. Su's proposal, contained in a report submitted to the CMC, marks the first time that a senior military officer proposed formulating a national military strategy for the People's Republic.[47] Su urged that "[we] must first determine the overall strategic guideline for our country" so that "our overall national defense plans can be formulated according to the whole strategic guideline."[48] Without a strategy, Su feared, development plans would lack clear direction, be poorly coordinated and, ultimately, be ineffective. Su stressed the need to determine the enemy's primary and secondary directions of attack along with the PLA's operational plans for countering such attacks.[49] Although the CMC did not formulate a strategic guideline at this time, Su's report prompted a clarification of some of these "urgent strategic issues" that would become incorporated into the PLA's five-year plan.[50]

In May 1952, the GSD requested that all services, branches, and departments submit five-year plans. Lei Yingfu, Zhou Enlai's military secretary, who had just been appointed as deputy director of the GSD's operations department, authored a draft of the five-year plan, which was completed in early June. The draft included an assessment of the enemy, the objectives of the plan, the requirements of the plan, defense deployments, and authorized strength and equipment.[51] The GSD submitted the draft to Mao and other top party leaders on June 24 and it was approved in mid-July.

Although the five-year plan never addressed Su Yu's idea of using strategy to guide military planning, it did contain several components of the 1956 strategy. The first part of the plan was an assessment of China's external security

TABLE 3.1. Projected Force Deployment by Type and Region in 1952 (Percent of Total)

Theater	Infantry Divisions	Artillery Forces	Armored Forces	Air Force Units
Northern	54%	83%	90%	60%
Eastern	16%	10%	10%	17.3%
Central Southern	16%	3.3%	0%	16%
Southwestern	8%	3.3%	0%	4%
Northwestern	6%	0%	0%	2.7%

Note: In wartime, the number of divisions in the northern theater would increase to 70 percent of all divisions.

Source: Shou Xiaosong, ed., *Zhongguo renmin jiefangjun junshi*, Vol. 3, pp. 299-300.

environment. Unsurprisingly, given the ongoing war on the Korean Peninsula, the United States was identified as China's main adversary. The plan noted that "enemy countries" could attack China with between 4.5 and 6 million soldiers, presumably in a joint U.S.-Nationalist attack.[52] It identified north China as the main strategic direction, which was described as "an area to defend to the death and wage decisive battles."[53] North China represented the area north of the Longhai railroad that terminated at Lianyungang on the coast of Jiangsu province and included the Shandong and Liaodong peninsulas. East China was a secondary strategic direction and described as "an area that we must hold" (*jianshou de diqu*), especially the cities of Nanjing, Shanghai, Xuzhou, and Ningbo.[54] A third area of importance was southern China, with a focus on Hainan Island.

As shown in table 3.1, the proposed deployment of China's forces in the plan reflected the threat assessment. These deployments implied that China would not adopt a strategy of "luring the enemy in deep." Instead, it called for maintaining the ability to successfully destroy enemy units on the main battlefield—what the PLA describes as annihilation operations.[55] What the plan did not discuss, however, was how China would fight if invaded, a topic that the 1956 strategic guideline would address.

Regarding force structure, the plan emphasized the development of the ground forces and the air force over the navy and proposed maintaining a peacetime ground force of 100 divisions with approximately 1.57 million soldiers organized into 28 army headquarters (*junbu*).[56] In wartime, the plan called for expanding the ground forces to 300 divisions organized into 80 headquarters. The plan also called for raising 150 squadrons in the air force by 1957, with over 6,200 aircraft and 450,000 personnel. A major lesson drawn from China's experience in the Korean War was that China would always be in a passive position in future wars without the ability to seize local air superiority.[57] The navy's development, however, was limited to coastal defense (*jin'an fangyu*) and coastal fortifications. Nevertheless, the plan called for expanding the navy from 298 to 785 vessels and increasing the tonnage from 11.5 million tons to 25 million tons. The plan also outlined increasing the size of the branches, including artillery, armored, and engineering corps, as well as air defense troops.[58]

The plan called for establishing an indigenous defense industry to produce the weapons and equipment that China would need to arm this new force and supplement equipment being purchased from the Soviet Union. The plan envisioned China buying or producing enough weapons, artillery, and tanks for one hundred divisions along with light weapons for two hundred additional divisions.[59] Although China continued to seek arms from the Soviets, the plan expressed a clear preference to meet its requirements through domestic production. The plan also suggested that the development of civilian (*minyong*) industries should consider the requirements for producing weapons and ammunition for the force in wartime.[60]

As the Korean War continued, implementation of the five-year plan was limited in the first year to the development of a system of permanent fortifications and defensive works in coastal areas. The need for such fortifications was one lesson that Peng drew from World War II, especially the stubborn Finnish defense against the Soviet invasion.[61] On August 25, 1952, the CMC decided to build fortifications in five areas. As shown in map 3.1, the first three of these were in the northeast, which had been identified as the main strategic direction: the Liaodong Peninsula, the area from Qinhuang Island to Tanggu on the coast just northeast of Tianjin, and the Jiaodong Peninsula (which refers to main part of the Shandong Peninsula). The other two areas of focus were the Zhoushan Islands area near Shanghai, and Hainan Island.[62] In January 1953, the CMC approved a plan to build 184 defensive areas (*fangyu zhendi*) by 1956, which was later extended to 1957.[63] Starting in the fall of 1952, Peng began to conduct inspection tours of coastal areas to identify potential landing zones for an American attack and to issue instructions for the construction of fortifications. He began by visiting the Liaodong Peninsula in October 1952, as he feared that US forces might seek to launch an assault there to outflank the Chinese forces in Korea.

1953–1954 CONFERENCE OF SENIOR MILITARY CADRE

After the five-year plan was approved, the second phase of initial reforms occurred during a conference of senior military leaders in December 1953 and January 1954. Peng Dehuai used the conference to build consensus among the PLA leadership around the importance of modernization and how it would be achieved.

The spark for the conference was an urgent directive in July 1953 to reduce spending on defense. The state faced a budget crisis, with a deficit surpassing

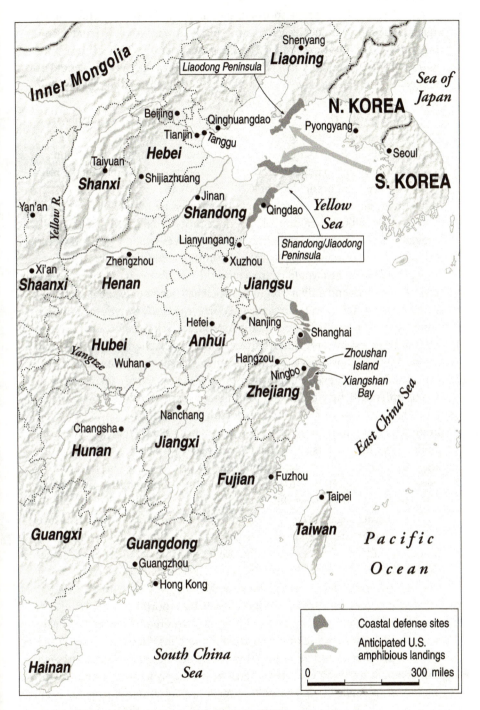

MAP 3.1. The northeastern strategic direction in the 1956 strategy

twelve percent. To close the shortfall, spending on government and military agencies had to be reduced significantly. The PLA was instructed that spending in 1953 could not exceed 1952 levels, placing severe constraints on the ambitions of the five-year plan. The plan had to be revised, as China could no longer afford to import the new weapons with which it was going to expand and equip the air force, navy, and combat arms.

How to pursue the PLA's modernization under these conditions became the central challenge facing China's senior military officers. In August and September 1953, Peng Dehuai convened several CMC meetings to formulate a response. The group debated how much to downsize the force and the roles of the services and branches. The CMC agreed on a general framework for modernization. First, the force should be reduced by 1.3 million within two years, to 3.5 million (including the public security force).[64] This reaffirmed a previous decision (taken before the budget cap was announced) and would consist mostly of demobilizing infantry units. Second, the growth of the services and branches would be frozen for the next five years. Third, the general departments and military regions, which had become "excessively large," would be streamlined and reorganized. Fourth, the CMC would study various systems (*zhidu*) such as conscription, ranks, and salaries to increase efficiency and effectiveness of command necessary for complex, modern operations.[65]

As the CMC's proposals would influence all aspects of army building at the organizational level, Peng proposed holding an army-wide meeting of senior officers. Peng would need to build consensus for his vision among a much broader group of the PLA's leadership beyond those on the CMC and in the GSD who had drafted the five-year plan in 1952. Peng identified the goals of the meeting as summarizing the past four years of military work and "discussing and resolving the guideline for army building in the future."[66] Peng's goal was ambitious—to transform the PLA into "a superior modernized revolutionary army in the world."[67]

The meeting began on December 7 and lasted for almost two months. More than 120 leaders from the general departments, military regions, services, branches, and academies participated. Reflecting the meeting's importance, the presidium included all members of the CMC except for Deng Xiaoping (who was not involved in military affairs at the time), as well as other leaders.[68] Most members of the CMC made speeches. In his report, Peng identified several obstacles to modernization that "cannot be ignored."[69] The first obstacle was a poor understanding of modern warfare and insufficient recognition of the changes that would be required to transform the PLA. Peng critiqued "some comrades" who viewed modernization simply as adding new equipment, such as tanks or planes, without major organizational change. Instead Peng viewed the changes as a shift "from only infantry to the coordination of various branches and services, from backwards weapons and equipment to modern equipment, from dispersed operations to centralized modern standardized operations." Peng stressed that these changes constituted "a big leap forward. It is a change in essence, not just simply an increase in quantity."[70]

The second obstacle concerned the PLA's organizational deficiencies. Peng noted that the PLA's "organization, personnel and systems . . . were not suited to the demands of building a modern military." A core problem was the decentralization of command during the civil war, where individual units used different kinds of weapons and adopted their own organizational practices regarding training, discipline, and so forth. Coordination among units from different areas was rare. Again, Peng criticized "some comrades" who "still lack sufficient understanding that the more modern a military is, the higher the demand for centralization and close cooperation."[71] Overstaffed and redundant organizations also hindered improving coordination and standardization.

When the conference concluded in January 1954, the PLA leadership reached consensus around how to pursue modernization. The meeting outlined the "general guideline and general mission" of building a "modernized revolutionary force" to safeguard China's socialist development and defend against "imperialist aggression."[72] As Peng said, a "modernized force must have modernized weapons and equipment" along with the transportation infrastructure to support such a force.[73] China should not rely on foreign imports to achieve these goals, but instead develop its own industrial base and, especially, heavy industries. Reducing defense spending and reducing the force to 3.5 million would free up resources for the nation's industrial development. The conference also affirmed the decision to halt the growth of the services and combat arms and instead focus on increasing the quality of the existing forces.

Beyond these general goals for the PLA's modernization, the conference also decided many policy issues. One decision, perhaps obvious, was to emphasize formal training and especially the training of officers. Training officers was described as "the core of the core of building a modernized force."[74] By 1957, the PLA established 106 comprehensive and specialized military academies.[75]

Another decision was to prioritize what Peng frequently described as "standardization" (*zhengguihua*). This meant using "formal standards in all aspects of the army" to overcome the decentralization of command and organization from the civil war.[76] Perhaps most important, standardization was necessary for "meeting the requirements for unified command and coordinated action in modern warfare," or how the PLA would need to fight in the future.[77] Other elements of standardization included unified systems, organization, training, and discipline.[78] Over the next year, the CMC would develop "the three great systems" (*sanda zhidu*) of conscription, salaries, and ranks that were issued in 1955 to replace the use of volunteers, rations, and informal ranks during the civil war.[79] The conference also determined the responsibilities and organization of the military regions, military districts, and military subdistricts along with the leading bodies of the services and branches and the authorized strength of operational units.[80]

A fourth decision was to strengthen the role of headquarters and other command units. Headquarters (*silingbu*) were deemed to be the body for organizing modern warfare and commanding the campaigns and battles of an integrated force with various services and branches.[81] Successful command required "sound, capable and effective command bodies [*jiguan*]."[82] As part of improving command, the CMC decided in late 1954 to establish twelve military regions, replacing a more cumbersome system of management and command from the civil war. Under the CMC's overall leadership, the military regions were responsible for the command of the main force units (then called the national defense army), while the provincial military districts and prefectural subdistricts would only command local forces.[83] The rationale was to reduce the layers of command and organize China's forces according to operational targets and directions, geographic conditions, transportation, and other factors. In China's main strategic direction in northern China, for example, the Shenyang, Beijing, and Jinan Military Regions were established to focus on defending the capital and key invasion routes.

From February 1954 to the end of 1955, the force was reduced to 3.5 million, or by more than twenty-one percent. Most of the reductions occurred in infantry units, increasing the proportion of the force in the services and branches.[84] New branches were also established, including railway, communications, and chemical defense troops. When combined with armor, artillery, and engineering units, the PLA now had seven branches (*bingzhong*). Another noteworthy development was the expansion of armored forces. Nevertheless, similar to the five-year plan adopted in 1952, the senior cadre conference did not contain a clear strategy outlining how these forces would be used. Instead, it focused on erecting the foundation for the organization and development of a modern force that could be used effectively once a strategy was adopted.

1955 LIAODONG PENINSULA EXERCISE

In November 1955, the PLA conducted its largest exercise since 1949 on the Liaodong Peninsula in Liaoning province. The exercise was based on how China would counter the primary threat China believed it faced—a US amphibious assault in the northeast—and highlighted the organizational reforms identified at the senior cadre meeting to enhance the PLA's ability to conduct modern-style operations. In other words, the exercise demonstrated how the PLA leadership viewed the conduct of warfare that would inform the new strategy adopted only a few months later.[85]

In July 1955, the CMC decided to hold a large-scale exercise on the Liaodong Peninsula. Ye Jianying, a vice-chairman of the CMC and acting director of the Training Supervision Department, served as the director (*daoyan*).[86] The exercise was a "demonstration exercise" (*shifanxing yanxi*) of an anti-landing campaign (*kangdenglu zhanyi*) to show how to respond to an amphibious and airborne assault that involved the use of nuclear and chemical weapons. Ye described the purpose as helping commanders and headquarters "to learn how to organize and command complex campaigns and battles under modern conditions."[87]

The Liaodong exercise would be the largest exercise that the PLA would hold until the "802" meeting in 1981. Reflecting one of the main threats to China identified in 1952, the opposing force in the exercise would seek to establish beachheads and seize ports in the Bohai Gulf to then attack Beijing and Shenyang.[88] The Chinese practiced how to counterattack with a coastal defense campaign using a group army composed of various branches (*zhubing-zhong jituanjun*). More than 68,000 troops from all three services participated, including soldiers from 32 regiments along with 262 aircraft and 18 ships.[89] Most of the CMC as well as top party leaders including Liu Shaoqi, Zhou Enlai, and Deng Xiaoping observed the exercise along with representatives from the Soviet Union, North Korea, Vietnam, and Mongolia.[90]

In discussing the exercise, senior military officers highlighted the importance of studying modern warfare, which would inform the strategy that would be adopted in a few months. In his evaluation of the exercise, Ye Jianying noted that nuclear and chemical weapons along with missiles and motorization "increased the suddenness and destructiveness of warfare" while also increasing the scale of wars that had become "more arduous and brutal." For Ye, the result of these changes was that "the organization and command of war is more complex and difficult."[91]

Peng Dehuai also observed that the exercise demonstrated the characteristics of modern warfare. At the closing ceremony, Peng criticized "some comrades" who relied only on past battlefield experience and did not embrace training. Peng warned that by "relying on past experience and not learning the knowledge of modern warfare, it is impossible to command a modern force to victory."[92] Peng stressed the centrality of coordinated action (*xietiao dong-zuo*) among the services and branches. "In modern warfare," he said, "no single branch can solve strategic and campaign tasks alone, and no single branch can replace another."[93] For Peng, "the coordinated action of the various branches is the most important issue in modern warfare."[94] The use of new technologies in warfare increased the speed and mobility of modern forces. As a result, in the battles and campaigns of modern war, "changes in circumstances will be quick and complex."[95] Without the strong coordination of operational actions, Peng asserted, "it will be difficult to achieve victory in battles or campaigns."[96]

At the tactical and operational level, improving coordination required mastering new skills, which the Liaodong exercise was intended to demonstrate.

Peng underscored that "modern warfare requires that the armed forces . . . be fluent in the tactical and technical performance of various weapons."[97] These skills formed the foundation of tactics and were necessary for achieving campaign plans based on tactical performance. Consistent with his focus on standardization, Peng also called for implementing military regulations, stating that "the implementation of common regulations is the key to moving toward the standardization of our military."[98] He stressed the need for combat regulations for all the branches, which would guide training in peacetime and serve as the basis for organizing and conducting battles in wartime.[99]

Adoption of the 1956 Strategic Guideline

The decision to formulate China's first strategic guideline occurred in the spring of 1955 and the CMC established the new strategy in March 1956. The decision to adopt the new strategy demonstrates how senior military officers led the process of strategic change.

DECISION TO ADOPT THE STRATEGIC GUIDELINE

After building consensus around modernization at the senior cadre conference and launching reforms to deepen standardization of the force, Peng Dehuai turned toward formulating China's first strategic guideline. Soviet advisors had urged Peng as early as July 1952 to draft an army-wide operations plan for a major war. At the time, however, Peng believed that it was necessary to first take initial steps toward modernizing the force, including absorbing the new equipment being acquired from the Soviet Union and developing the new services and branches. Only once progress had been made toward equipping the force, Peng believed, could an effective operations plan be drafted and implemented.

Mao provided an opening for Peng during his assessment of China's security environment at the CCP's National Congress in March 1955.[100] Overall, Mao was upbeat, observing that "international conditions" were favorable for China's socialist development, especially the strength of the socialist bloc. Nevertheless, the possibility of conflict with the United States could not be eliminated. China remained "surrounded by imperialist forces" and therefore "must prepare to deal with sudden incidents [*turan shibian*]."[101] Mao did not say that war was likely or even imminent, but he believed that if "the imperialists" did strike, it would start with a "surprise attack" (*turan de xiji*) and China should "avoid being caught unprepared."[102] Although this meeting focused almost exclusively on domestic issues, such as the First Five-Year Plan, Mao's comment reflected a call for vigilance after the 1954 Taiwan Straits crisis and the expansion of US alliances in the region.

Peng had also decided that the time had come for drafting an army-wide operations plan. Developing one, however, would also requiring determining China's strategic guideline. When chairing a working conference on war preparations (*zhanbei*) in early April, Peng stated that an operations plan for a major war should be drafted. Peng outlined his view on the relationship between positional and mobile warfare and guiding principles for operations. In April, the GSD drafted an outline of the plan, which Peng then presented to a meeting of the Central Committee Secretariat on April 29.[103] In his presentation, Peng said that "it was necessary first to resolve the question of the strategic guideline" to provide a framework for the operations plan.[104] In response, Mao reaffirmed that "our strategic guideline has always been active defense, our operations will be counter-attacks, and we will never be the first to initiate a war."[105] As Peng was also preparing to visit the Soviet Union the following month, Mao suggested that he discuss China's strategy and operational coordination with his Soviet counterparts.

In early June, progress toward developing the strategic guideline continued after Peng returned from Moscow. In a report on his trip to the party leadership, Peng requested permission to "write a document that set forth China's strategic guideline." He said that the document would then be discussed at an enlarged meeting of the CMC and distributed to "unify the thought of the whole army and the whole party."[106] Peng also made two other suggestions based on his trip. First, China needed to develop its own military science so that it would not have to rely on the Soviet Union and on Soviet approaches. Second, China should draft two versions of the operations plan: one in collaboration with Soviet advisors to reflect general principles and to be used as the basis for wartime coordination, and another that China would write by itself, based on China's strategic guideline and actual conditions.[107] On August 16, during a meeting to discuss the operations plan, Peng noted that many differences with the Soviets had been resolved because "our position and method suits our backwards situation, not because we are particularly smart."[108]

After the completion of the Liaodong anti-landing exercise in November 1955, the last step toward adopting the new strategy occurred in early December 1955. On December 1, the CMC sent a report to Mao suggesting that an enlarged meeting be held in early 1956 to discuss the strategic guideline as part of an army-wide discussion of strategy. According to the report, "Everyone's understanding and knowledge of this guideline is still not in agreement." Agreement was needed "so that everyone can comprehensively plan all work under unified operational guidance." Given the development of China's defense industries, as well as new services and branches, the report concluded that "the conditions are now relatively ripe to resolve this important issue."[109] Mao agreed and the drafting of the report began. Participants in the drafting included Peng's secretaries, Su Yu (now chief of the general staff), and Lei Yingfu (section chief in the operations department).[110]

PENG'S REPORT ON THE NEW STRATEGY

In March 1956, an enlarged meeting of the CMC was convened to adopt China's first military strategy. In addition to members of the CMC, the leaders of the general departments, services, branches, and all military districts—as well as the Soviet military advisor and his deputy—attended. Reflecting the importance of the task and the broader impact of military strategy on the economy, leading officials from the State Council and key line ministries such as finance and transportation also participated.[111]

When the meeting opened on March 6, Peng Dehuai introduced the new strategy on behalf of the CMC in a report entitled *On the Strategic Guideline for Defending the Motherland and National Defense Building*. The first section of the report, "On the Strategic Guideline," described the content of the new strategy, while the second section, "On National Defense Building," discussed its implementation.[112] Other members of the CMC who spoke at the meeting included Ye Jianying, Nie Rongzhen, Su Yu, and Huang Kecheng. When the meeting ended on March 15, participants agreed to adopt the strategy described in Peng's report. Although Mao did not attend the meeting, he reviewed and approved Peng's report in early April, which reflects the high level of delegation for overseeing military affairs from top party leaders to senior military officers.[113]

The new strategy focused on the single contingency of a major war with the United States. As Peng discussed at the meeting, his report focused on "the strategic guideline that our military should adopt when the enemy in the future engages in a large-scale and direct attack of our country." Specifically, the strategy covered "the initial or first stage of a war."[114] During this period, which would last roughly six months, the PLA's defense would deny the United States a quick victory and buy time for a nation-wide mobilization to wage a protracted war.

The core of the strategy was the idea of active defense. As Peng would later describe, "Our country should have a guideline of strategic defense."[115] However, "this kind of defense should not be passive defense but rather should be a strategic guideline of active defense."[116] Peng sought to adapt Mao's concept from the mid-1930s—when the Red Army fought for its survival against the much stronger Nationalists—to defend the sovereignty, territorial integrity, and security of the new state.

First, and most obviously, the proposed strategy was defensive. Put simply, China's material inferiority against the United States dictated a defensive posture. China had no choice but to try to counter an invasion—it had no ability to strike first, much less to take the fight to the enemy. A defensive posture was also consistent with China's identity as a socialist state (which would not engage in aggression against others) and its identification with a just war tradition that viewed the use of force as legitimate only for "righteous" reasons such as national defense.[117] In the mid-1950s, China also desired a peaceful environment for pursuing socialist modernization and sought to strengthen ties with nonaligned states, especially after the 1955 Bandung Conference, when China began to stress the Five Principles of Peaceful Coexistence.[118] China would undermine these goals, and its effort to portray the United States and imperialism as aggressive, if it adopted an offensive strategy.

Second, despite adopting a defensive posture, the strategy for defending the People's Republic would be an active one, not a passive one. Although this resonates with Mao's own definition, the emphasis on being active and not passive had new meaning. Given China's material and technological inferiority, the purpose of the strategy was to inflict sufficient casualties on the enemy to create conditions for the transition at the strategic level from defense to offense. In the event of an attack, China needed "to be able to respond immediately with a powerful counterattack."[119] Thus, defense would be strategically combined with active attacks in campaigns and at the tactical level. The purpose of these offensive actions was to weaken the enemy and allow China to transition from being in a passive position when first attacked to an active one.

Third, and perhaps most different from the 1930s, the new strategy required undertaking sufficient preparations to "actively take measures to prevent or postpone the outbreak of war."[120] Peng described such measures as "continuously strengthening our nation's military strength and expanding our nation's activity in the international united front."[121] In other words, the strategy was as much about deterrence as it was about victory. Although China's alliance with the Soviet Union and its efforts to build support among the nonaligned movement would also help to deter a conflict, the 1956 strategy emphasized the role of China's own efforts to continue to enhance its military power and combat readiness. As Peng told his colleagues, "We must actively carry out all preparations."[122] These included building a network of fortifications in important coastal regions, formulating campaign plans, ensuring that basic industries were dispersed and not heavily concentrated, educating urban residents on nuclear and chemical defense, and improving reconnaissance and air defense capabilities for detecting signs of an attack or the use of weapons of mass destruction.[123] This would ensure that "our military's forces on the front line and in depth can promptly enter into battle and the whole country can rapidly switch from a peacetime to a wartime posture."[124]

Taken together, Peng's interpretation of active defense provided China with a theory of victory. Once an invasion started, China would strive to "resist several continuous enemy offenses and limit their advance into predetermined areas."[125] Although the strategy assumed that an invasion could not be pre-vented and that the United States would seize some territory along the coast, it sought to deny a quick victory to the United States and force it to wage a protracted war.

An important innovation in the 1956 strategy was the primary form of operations that would be used. This was "combining positional defensive oper-ations by garrison forces with mobile offensive warfare by maneuver units."[126] The emphasis on positional warfare marked a clear departure from the PLA's dominant way of fighting from the civil war to the stalemate on the Korean Peninsula in 1951. As Peng observed, positional warfare was "rare in the history of our military."[127] Now tasked with defending national territory, the 1956 strat-egy stated that "we must do everything we can to hold key areas, islands and important cities along the coast."[128] Otherwise, if the PLA allowed the enemy to "drive straight in," China would have to return to the use of mobile warfare of the civil war and the country "would suffer great difficulties." Therefore, "to rely completely on mobile warfare to annihilate the enemy is extremely mistaken."[129] Guerrilla warfare no longer had "strategic status" and would only be used in areas temporarily occupied by the enemy.[130]

The concept of operations or the "basic guiding thought for operations" in the new strategy described how the combination of positional and mobile warfare would achieve the strategy's defensive goals. The strategy envisioned "using the ground forces as the main element, complemented by coordination with the air force and the navy, to annihilate the main force of the enemy's attack in the coastal areas of our national territory."[131] No more than one quar-ter of the ground forces would be designated as garrison units (*shoubei budui*) to defend selected coastal areas that would be heavily fortified to create a perim-eter defense (*huangxing fangyu*).[132] These units would be well equipped with large stockpiles of ammunition so that they could "tenaciously defend" these positions to "do all they can to pin down the enemy by holding fast to their positions and engaging in appropriate counterattack operations."[133] In this way, garrison units would "create conditions for maneuver units to annihilate the enemy."[134] Coastal islands in these same areas would also be fortified to slow down the tempo of the enemy's attack. If defenses were well prepared and troops were well trained, gar-rison forces would be able to "stop [*dangzhu*] several waves of surprise attacks."[135]

The remaining three-quarters of the ground forces would be designated as maneuver units (*jidong budui*). These units would be deployed in echelons, in-depth and dispersed so as not to be easily destroyed through strategic bomb-ing before the invasion. If garrison units were able to stop or slow down the offensive, the maneuver units would then be employed to annihilate enemy forces. The timing of their deployment, however, was critical and "must be selected cautiously."[136] If used too soon or too hastily, they could become vul-nerable or unable to destroy the US forces. To improve success, these units would endeavor to "use a covert and sudden attack to resolutely destroy the enemy."[137] Thus, the strategy called for coordination among the garrison and maneuver units, along with the services and branches that would participate in the defense.

The second half of the report discussed goals for military modernization, mobilization, and military scientific research. In terms of army building, the report affirmed earlier decisions to limit the size of the force to 3.5 million and envisioned shrinking the force to 2.4 million by the end of 1957. The report called for "giving particular attention" to the development of the air force and air defense forces. Secondary tasks would be focusing on submarines and torpedo boats in the navy and increasing the proportion of artillery, tank, chemical defense, and communications units in the ground forces, as well as overall levels of mechanization.[138] All these changes in force structure would be achieved by reducing the number of infantry units. Although wildly unrealistic in hindsight, the strategy hoped to be able to "reach a level of technological sophistication that approaches advanced countries" in ten years, by 1967.[139] More realistically, the report also called for building coastal defense installations as well as transportation networks that would connect them and the interior by 1962.[140] Emphasis would be placed on islands, ports, and transportation nodes, as well as political and economic centers in coastal areas, to create a defensive perimeter.[141] The construction of such fortifications would continue efforts, discussed earlier in this chapter, that had begun in 1952.

Regarding mobilization, the report emphasized enhancing China's preparations. As the strategy was premised on buying time for nation-wide mobilization, how to mobilize was an important topic to address. Key tasks included establishing mobilization offices and developing an overall mobilization plan by 1957. An important part of the plan would be to ensure sufficient manpower and supplies to expand the force and replenish units in the first six months of a war. This included plans for wartime expansion of the force, ensuring sufficient stocks of weapons, supplies, and the like.[142]

A final topic of discussion was developing China's own capacity for military science research. For Peng, "war in the future will be different from the past civil war and the War of Resistance against Japan, and will be different from the Soviet Patriotic War."[143] Peng noted "the wide application of the latest advances in science and technology to military affairs and the emergence of large numbers of weapons of mass destruction" in concluding that "the methods and forms of future wars will have many new characteristics."[144] Based on these changes, Peng called for "actively developing" China's own military science research institutes for researching strategy, campaigns, tactics, military history, and military technology.[145] According to Peng's official biography, the discussion of this topic at the meeting "was the first program for the army-wide development of military science."[146]

During this period, China determined the elements of its naval strategy. This subsequently became known as "near-coast defense" (*jin'an fangyu*), even though, ironically enough, this term was not used by the PLA at the time.[147] In addition to the general parameters contained in the strategic guideline, naval strategy was further detailed during the first conference of party representatives in the navy from June 9 to June 19. The resolution endorsed by the participants contained "the three obeys" (*fucong*): the navy must follow the guideline for national economic development by limiting the size of its force, must pursue its own development while giving priority to the air force and air defense force, and must focus its development on naval aviation, submarines, and torpedo boats.[148] Within these parameters, the navy was assigned two tasks. The first was to disrupt an amphibious assault and support all efforts to counter such an attack. The second was to patrol China's coast, especially to defend against Nationalist harassment and infiltration operations and to protect Chinese fishermen and shipping.[149] This strategy would continue until 1986, when "near-seas defense" was articulated as the strategic concept for China's naval strategy.

Was China Emulating the Soviet Model?

The initial reforms in the early to mid-1950s and the adoption of the 1956 strategic guideline should represent an "easy" case for arguments about emulation. China was a late military modernizer, allied with one of the two most powerful militaries in the international system. It had access not only to Soviet hardware such as weapons, equipment, and related technologies, but also to Soviet software such as operational doctrine, training regimens, and organizational practices. China and the Soviet Union also shared some similar strategic characteristics that might inform their choice of strategy—for example, strategic depth, and long histories as land powers. If emulation is going to explain change in military strategy anywhere, it should be able to explain China during the 1950s.

To be sure, the Soviet influence on the PLA cannot be dismissed. As Peng Dehuai's biographers note with candor not always found in other sources, "Soviet military and strategic thought had an influence on China's armed forces."[150] In terms of weapons and equipment, the Soviets sold China equipment for 60 infantry divisions as well as plans, machinery, and technology to jump-start the development of China's defense industries. Of the 156 factories that the Soviets provided to the Chinese, 44—or more than 30 percent—were for defense industries. Chinese soldiers wore Soviet-style uniforms and were issued Soviet-style decorations. Key Soviet field regulations were translated into Chinese and used in China's military academies and schools for most of the 1950s as teaching texts. Soviet advisors trained Chinese military personnel directly, especially in the navy and the air force but also in the service branches and combat arms. Overall, there were almost 600 military advisors and at least 7,000 technical experts in China in the 1950s.[151]

China clearly used the Soviet Union as a vehicle for studying the content and practice of modern warfare in the early 1950s. Nevertheless, the key question is whether China sought to emulate the Soviet model for waging modern war and its strategy in particular. Below I examine the potential for emulation at the strategic and operational levels of analysis, which provide only limited support for emulation. Despite the euphoria associated with learning from the Soviets in the early 1950s, by the middle of the decade Chinese strategists had focused on "how" to learn. The main reason for this shift was a recognition that the disparity in national conditions and warfighting history meant that not all things Soviet were necessarily appropriate for China. Chinese leaders also clearly recognized that they lacked the industrial base to field the type of mechanized force that the Soviets possessed.

Before proceeding, two other points should be noted. To start, China sought to learn about modern warfare from a number of countries, not just the Soviet Union. It translated American field manuals in addition to Soviet ones. This suggests that China was less interested in imitation or copying and more interested in understanding the characteristics of the type of war that they might need to fight. In January 1957, for example, Peng said that the PLA's regulations "should be based on China's own traditions and experiences, reference the Soviet experiences, and absorb the useful things from capitalist countries."[152] In April 1957, Peng urged the staff at the Advanced Military Academy to study "capitalist" countries as well. As Peng said, "Capitalist countries don't have anything advanced? I don't believe it. Then how did Hitler's army fight its way to the outskirts of Moscow? How did the American military fight its way to the banks of the Yalu River?"[153]

In addition, although the Soviet Union and China were treaty allies, the relationship was an unequal one. China was the junior partner who depended on what Moscow was willing to share, a dynamic which, over time, led China to question the merits of the Soviet approach. For instance, although the Soviets provided equipment and expertise, China had to pay for all of it. Most of the weapons that the Soviets provided were World War II–era and not the latest models in the Soviet arsenal.[154] Peng himself realized this after observing that the weapons used by the Soviets in a series of 1954 exercises were newer and better than those being sold to China.[155] The Soviets were selling surplus weapons to China to modernize their own force. When pressed, the Soviets were reluctant to sell current models.[156]

STRATEGIC EMULATION

Strong evidence against emulation can be found at the strategic level of analysis. As discussed above, the 1956 strategy was based on the strategic defensive—namely, absorbing a first strike before retaliating. When this strategy was conceived and adopted, however, Soviet strategic thought increasingly emphasized preemptive action and first strikes. China was fully aware of the shift in Soviet thinking and rejected it.[157]

The differences over strategy between China and the Soviet Union emerged most clearly when Peng Dehuai visited Moscow in May 1955 after attending the inaugural meeting of the Warsaw Pact in Poland. On May 22, he met with defense minister Georgy Zhukov to discuss military strategy and outlined China's plans for countering a potential invasion.[158] Peng informed Zhukov that China's strategy would be based on "active defense" and the principle of "gaining control by striking afterwards" (houfa zhiren).[159] Zhukov opposed China's approach. He told Peng that a nuclear attack would be decisive and that, in modern war, victory and defeat would be determined in only a few minutes.[160] For Zhukov, the advent of nuclear weapons represented a clear shift from conventional wars of the past, even World War II or Korea. With the first-strike advantages created by nuclear weapons, Zhukov believed that no country would be able to recover once attacked.

Peng challenged Zhukov's view. He stated that great powers such as China and the Soviet Union could undertake sufficient preparations to withstand a nuclear attack. Moreover, for Peng, the military advantages to be gained through a first strike were only temporary and would not offset the political cost of using such weapons. Peng noted how Germany and Japan were defeated despite striking first in World War II, and also argued that China won its past wars by emphasizing the strategic defensive, such as during the war against Japan and in the Chinese civil war.[161] Peng's views about nuclear weapons were not necessarily accurate. Nevertheless, China rejected the Soviet approach to military strategy, despite being one of the leading military powers in the system.

According to Wang Yazhi, Peng's military secretary, the exchange with Zhukov had a profound impact and helped to clarify Peng's approach to China's military strategy. It highlighted the differences in approach to strategy, which in turn would affect operational doctrine, force structure, and training. Peng questioned the utility and authoritativeness of Soviet military science, which up to that point had been embraced without much critical reflection. Peng also noted the Soviet tendency to emphasize achieving victory through superior technology and equipment, whereas the PLA had achieved victory by finding ways to use inferior equipment to defeat superior adversaries. Given China's technical and industrial inferiority versus the United States, the Soviet strategy was not particularly appealing (or feasible).[162] Thus, Peng's meeting with

Zhukov affirmed the importance of the strategic defensive and the concept of active defense, which Peng viewed as well suited to China's circumstances. It also reaffirmed his desire, expressed before his trip, that the CMC adopt a formal strategic guideline and, as contained in the 1956 report, that China develop its own military science.

Perhaps not unsurprisingly, available sources contain no references to Peng's consultations with Soviet advisors when drafting his 1956 report on the strategic guideline. The chief military advisor, General Petroshevskii, did attend the March 1956 CMC meeting and Peng shared a copy of the report with the advisors afterwards. Their disapproval, however, suggests that the strategy did not seek to emulate the Soviet approach to warfare. Indeed, they openly derided the concept of active defense in the 1956 guideline. The Soviet advisors maintained that "the offensive is the only military means for gaining victory."[163] The chief Soviet advisor at the Nanjing Military Academy even referred to active defense as "metaphysics" (*xing er shang xue*).[164]

OPERATIONAL AND ORGANIZATIONAL EMULATION

To be sure, the 1955 Liaodong Peninsula exercises reflected a Soviet approach to defensive warfare. According to Peng's secretary, "On a certain level it was an exercise in studying the Soviet army's field operations regulations."[165] Troops were organized into fronts (*fangmian jun*) and combined arms group armies (*jituan jun*), according to the Soviet force structure. The aim of the exercise was to halt the invasion at the beaches by using echeloned forces and reserve units.[166] Nevertheless, the operational principles contained in the 1956 guidelines did not envision defending China against an amphibious assault in this manner. Instead, it accepted that China could only engage US units once they had landed, defending fixed positions while using maneuver forces against the main direction of attack. In this way, it was decidedly non-Soviet. In fact, one of the main lessons of the exercise may well have been the inapplicability of the Soviet model to what China viewed as its main security threat. Such disagreements with the Soviets probably began much earlier. When Peng decided in August 1952 to construct a system of permanent coastal fortifications, Soviet advisors opposed the plan. Peng, however, "could not understand" the Soviet objection and continued to build the fortifications.[167]

Similarly, even before 1949 and certainly after Chinese troops joined the Korean War, the PLA had used translations of Soviet army field regulations. For instance, in Korea, the PLA used Soviet artillery regulations as it increased the proportion of artillery in infantry units.[168] Liu Bocheng himself supervised the translation of the 1954 Soviet army field regulations.[169] By mid-1956, however, Peng had concluded that China must draft its own operations regulations within three to five years.[170] In January 1957, he noted that "if we follow others, then we will always take a circuitous route."[171] In early 1958, he assigned this task to the newly established AMS. The move to draft China's own regulations gained momentum during a debate about "dogmatism" and "blind copying" of the Soviet system that occurred at an enlarged meeting of the CMC that lasted from late May until mid-July 1958. At the meeting, senior officers deemed to have been "dogmatists" were demoted, including Marshal Liu Bocheng, then president of the Military Academy in Nanjing, and Xiao Ke, head of the GSD's training department, among others.[172] The meeting resolved that China should draft its own combat regulations and, in so doing, "use China's experience as the basis" (*yi wo wei zhu*) and "use the Soviets as a reference." The primacy of the Soviet approach was rejected for several reasons, but the most important one was that it was ill suited to China's actual geographic, economic, and industrial conditions. It was, simply put, not a model that could be emulated because it would not enhance China's security.

Perhaps one of the strongest pieces of evidence that supports emulation is the decision in 1954 to adopt the Soviet general staff structure. In 1954 and 1955, general ordnance, training supervision, armed forces supervision, and finance departments were added to the existing general staff, political, logistics, and cadre departments. When this reorganization was complete, China's general staff was an exact replica of the Soviet Union's. Yet two years later, in 1957, the Soviet system was dismantled and the eight departments were consolidated into three (general staff, political, and logistics departments), a structure that would not change for four decades.[173] According to an authoritative history, the Soviet system was dismantled because "the division of labor was excessively detailed" and perhaps too rigid for a military organization such as the PLA with a relatively lean general staff structure when compared with the military regions and field armies.[174]

Similarly, China considered but ultimately rejected the new Soviet command structure adopted in 1954. In the Chinese civil war, the PLA developed a tradition of dual command, in which both a unit's commander and the top political officer possessed decision-making authority. In 1953, however, when considering how to revise regulations for political work, Peng contemplated instituting the "single command system" (*yi zhang zhi*), as used by the Soviets, in all battalions and companies.[175] This proposal immediately generated controversy because it threatened the position of political commissars and was seen as inconsistent with the PLA's "glorious tradition." When the CMC issued new political work regulations in 1954, the Soviet command system was not adopted and the dual command system was preserved.[176]

Finally, China moved away from using Soviet rules and regulations to govern routine and other activities. In the PLA, these rules are contained in the common regulations for service, drills, and discipline. Although the PLA had versions of these regulations before 1949, the 1953 revisions borrowed heavily from those used in the Soviet Union.[177] A year later, however, senior military officers acknowledged that the implementation of these regulations, especially those covering discipline, were at odds with the PLA's grassroots traditions and "internal democracy" and thus viewed as damaging the unity among officers and soldiers that characterized the PLA during the civil war. This is perhaps unsurprising, as the Soviet military was much more hierarchical than the PLA and depended upon strict punishments, such as confinement, to enforce discipline among the troops. By late 1956, after reading a report from the General Political Department (GPD) on the implementation of disciplinary regulations, Peng concluded that they were flawed, which affirmed the decision earlier in the year, discussed above, that China should draft its own regulations.[178] On August 1, 1957, the CMC issued new disciplinary regulations, which downplayed punishments and abolished the practice of confinement. On October 24, 1957, new regulations for routine tasks were also issued.[179]

The 1960 Strategy: "Resist in the North, Open in the South"

In February 1960, the CMC adopted a new strategic guideline. Although given a new label—"resist in the north, open in the south" (*beiding, nanfang*)—the content of China's military strategy remained largely the same. The 1960 guideline represents a minor change to the 1956 strategy, with some limited adjustments in the deployment of China's forces, but it did not alter operational doctrine, force structure, or training.

BACKGROUND TO THE 1960 STRATEGY

The 1960 strategic guideline was adopted following the political upheaval at the Lushan Conference in July 1959, which ended with the purge of Peng Dehuai. The meeting was originally convened to examine the economic policies of the Great Leap Forward, which were beginning to encounter difficulties.[180] Peng expressed his concerns in a private letter to Mao Zedong. Given criticisms that were already being raised at the meeting, Mao decided to attack Peng and quash all opposition by circulating Peng's letter and making it the focus of the meeting. In the weeks that followed, Peng was accused of "anti-party crimes" and pursuing a "bourgeois military line," which led to his removal from all party and military posts. Although other senior party members had reservations about the Great Leap Forward, Peng's purge did not reflect disunity in the party. Mao achieved this goal by building consensus for the action among the party leadership at the conference. Few openly opposed the move.

Lin Biao, then a member of the Politburo Standing Committee, replaced Peng as the first vice-chairman of the CMC and minister of defense. During the Chinese civil war, Lin commanded the Fourth Field Army that played a decisive role in key campaigns in Manchuria. At Lushan, Lin distinguished himself by his own criticism of Peng and support for Mao. As other senior officers associated with Peng were either transferred or demoted, a new CMC was formed in September 1959. Lin Biao assumed responsibility for daily affairs of the CMC. In addition, Luo Ruiqing, then minister of public security, replaced Huang Kecheng as chief of the general staff. Soon thereafter, the CMC created two new entities. The first was the "CMC office meeting" (*junwei bangong huiyi*).[181] Given Lin Biao's fragile health, this group would oversee the daily affairs of the CMC on Lin's behalf. Importantly, however, it reflected substantial delegation of executive power from Lin to his subordinates and empowered Luo Ruiqing, its secretary-general. The second was the "CMC strategy research small group" (*junwei zhanlue yanjiu xiaozu*), with Liu Bocheng as director and Xu Xiangqian and Luo Ruiqing as vice directors.[182]

OVERVIEW OF THE 1960 STRATEGY

On January 22, 1960, the newly constituted CMC held an enlarged meeting in Guangzhou to discuss the PLA's strategic guideline and national defense development that would last for one month. One reason for the meeting was the CMC strategy research group's study of how to defend against a surprise attack by the United States. This does not appear to reflect a change in China's security environment, as such a surprise attack was first raised by Mao in March 1955, but it likely highlighted concerns about advances in US nuclear weapons and ballistic missile programs.[183] Another reason, however, was to determine the basic principles for integrating army building with overall national economic development, most likely because of the economic crisis being created by the Great Leap Forward.[184] A final reason was political. As Peng Dehuai's biographer notes, when Peng was purged, his 1956 report on the strategic guideline "was negated" (*bei fouding*).[185] The PLA could not continue to use a strategy that had been developed by a disgraced leader and therefore needed to adopt a new strategy. As the PLA's new leader, Lin may also have wanted to have a strategy associated with his name. Thus, at the meeting, the CMC adopted a new strategic guideline under a "new spirit."[186]

Assessment of the 1960 strategic guideline is problematic for several reasons. No record exists of the speech in which Lin Biao introduced the new strategy, though all sources indicate that the strategic guideline was adjusted at this meeting.[187] In addition, no record exists of consultations between Lin and Mao over the content of the strategic guideline, or even Mao's approval of the new guideline.[188] Nevertheless, available sources suggest that the 1960 guideline differed only slightly from the 1956 one in several ways.

First, the primary change was a shift in the areas where China would engage in positional warfare. At the CMC meeting, Lin Biao stated that "[we] should use the Yangtze river as the dividing line." In the north, China "should be fully prepared and resolutely resist the invading enemy such that every inch of our territory must be defended." In the south, however, "[we] can consider allowing them to enter and subsequently attack them."[189] Specifically, China would continue to pursue positional defense north of Xiangshan Bay in Zhejiang province, just south of Ningbo.[190] South of this line, the PLA would use the principle of "luring the enemy in deep." Thus, the 1960 guideline became known as "resist in the north, open in the south."[191] In August 1960, the CMC clarified that it "would resolutely prevent the enemy from coming in from the north" and that the northeast and Shandong peninsula would be "defended to the death," repeating language from the 1956 strategy. An enlarged meeting of the CMC in January 1961 further limited the area where China would "open" itself to an adversary. The meeting affirmed that the north would be "defended to the death," the area south of the Yangtze River would be "defended tenaciously," and the PLA could "open" only in Guangdong and Guangxi.[192]

Lin's new slogan did not represent a major change from China's existing military strategy. The areas where Lin instructed the PLA to resist included the northern and eastern theaters that were identified as the primary and secondary strategic directions in 1952. Echoing the 1952 plan, Lin described the northern region as an area that China should "defend to the death."[193] In May 1960, for example, Lin conducted an inspection tour of the Jinan Military Region, which included the Shandong Peninsula, describing it as an area to be held "at all costs" through positional warfare.[194] Peng had also viewed the south as much less strategically important than the north, as more than seventy percent of the ground forces had already been deployed in the areas Lin sought to defend.[195] Nevertheless, during a tour of Fujian, Guangdong, and Hainan in September 1954, Peng instructed local commanders to establish fortifications in key areas to prevent the United States from "driving straight in" if it attacked.[196] Peng's secretaries speculate that these instructions formed the basis for the difference between Peng and Lin.[197] Regardless, Lin proposed shifting slightly more forces to the north.[198] He ordered the transfer of the Twelfth Army (*jun*) from Jinhua in Zhejiang province (south of Shanghai) to Subei in Jiangsu province (north of Shanghai). He also relocated the 127th Division on Hainan Island back to the mainland.[199] Nevertheless, these redeployments amounted to around only four divisions out of around one hundred on active duty at the time. Despite the new label, Lin's actions affirmed Peng's strategy much more than they challenged it.

In terms of the form of operations, the 1960 strategy slightly increased the relative importance of mobile and guerrilla warfare when compared with the 1956 strategic guideline. By clarifying that China should not engage in positional warfare south of the Yangtze (and later only in Guangdong or Guangxi), the 1960 strategy underscored a greater role for mobile and guerrilla warfare because a larger area might potentially be lost to the United States in an initial attack that occurred in the south. Nevertheless, the main strategic direction, where China expected an attack to occur, remained in the north and not in the south. Luring the enemy in deep was making a virtue of the necessity that the south was much harder to defend than the north.

Second, the PLA under Lin increased the relative emphasis on political work in training. During an enlarged meeting of the CMC in October 1960, Lin attacked Tan Zheng, director of the GPD, for not supporting Lin's own efforts to increase the emphasis on Mao's thought in political work.[200] Yet Lin remained committed to giving priority to the military component of training, stating that "60 to 70 and even 80 percent of [training time] should be spent on military training"—roughly the same percentages as under Peng.[201] Again, these efforts are perhaps best interpreted as an effort to distinguish Lin's leadership of the CMC from Peng's, even though the substance remained similar. According to one prominent strategist from AMS, the 1960 strategy contained only "limited adjustments and additions" (*jubu tiaozheng he buchong*) to the 1956 strategy.[202] The primary strategic direction, as well as the basis of preparations for military struggle and main form of operations, remained the same.[203]

INDICATORS OF STRATEGIC CHANGE

All the indicators of strategic change demonstrate that the strategic guideline adopted in 1960 represents only a minor change to the 1956 guideline. The 1960 guideline should be viewed as continuing the implementation of the 1956 strategy.

Discussion of an army-wide operations plan in 1961 demonstrates how little China's operational doctrine had changed under Lin Biao. The plan reflected continuity with Peng's approach more than two years after the Lushan Conference and was based on the worst-case assumption of a major war in which the adversary would strive for a quick resolution. The decisive counterattack would occur on Chinese territory. Strategic reserves would play a key role along with rapid mobilization.[204] An operations plans research small group (*zuozhan jihua yanjiu xiaozu*) formed in December 1960 discussed an army-wide operations plan from early to mid-July 1961 and then submitted a report to the Central Committee and CMC.[205]

The drafting of China's first generation of combat regulations offers another indicator of continuity with the 1956 guidelines. Although the first two regulations were issued in 1961, more than a year after Lin Biao replaced Peng, the framework for the content of the regulations remained unchanged.[206] No source indicates that the content or drafting process was significantly altered by either Peng's removal from office or the adoption of the 1960 strategic guideline. The content of the eighteen regulations that were published between 1961 and 1965 emphasized how to conduct combined arms operations, as Peng himself had envisioned.[207]

The 1960 strategic guideline did not call for a major change in either the PLA's force structure or in how units should be equipped. During an October 1960 enlarged meeting, the CMC drafted an eight-year plan for the PLA's organization and equipment. The plan reflects continuity with the 1956 strategy, which had envisioned equipping the force with modern weapons by 1967.[208] It called for strengthening China's defense industrial base while prioritizing the development of the air force over the navy. In the ground forces, the development of combat arms over light infantry units was prioritized.[209] In this spirit, Nie Rongzhen in February 1963 further outlined ambitious plans to modernize the PLA's outdated equipment and envisioned arming the PLA with a complete set of modern conventional weapons before 1970. He hoped to equip the force with sufficient artillery and tanks while making breakthroughs in nuclear and missile technology.[210] The allocation of resources among the different services also remained unchanged. Under the 1960 guideline, modernization efforts focused on increasing the air and naval forces within PLA. From 1958 to 1965, the navy's authorized personnel (*bianzhi*) increased by 51.6 percent, while the air force's increased by 41.8 percent.[211]

No new training program was issued after the adoption of the 1960 strategic guideline. One indicator of continuity in training comes from the curriculum of the Advanced Military Academy in Beijing. During this period, the bulk of the curriculum examined questions of strategy and operations, though political education was also included. The focus remained on training commanders serving in divisions as well as military region headquarters to command the services and combat arms.[212] In 1963, for example, the curriculum included the study of strategy, campaigns, service branches and combat arms, scenarios, campaign analysis, and foreign military studies. The emphasis on professional military training continued until late 1964, when Mao began intervening to change China's military strategy.[213]

The one significant change concerning training was an increase in the proportion of political training, mostly concerning the study of Mao Zedong's thought (*sixiang*) and, especially, his military writings (*junshi zhuzuo*). This shift, although small at first, would become more pronounced after 1964. In 1961, the CMC instructed cadres at the division level or above to spend one- to two-thirds of training studying Mao's writings.[214] At the same time, in response to the variety of threats that grew more acute in 1962, the CMC reoriented the training according to combat requirements, as discussed in more detail in the next chapter.[215]

Conclusion

The strategic guideline adopted in 1956 represents the first major change in China's military strategy. The content of the initial reforms that preceded the new strategy, as well as the strategy itself, all show that the new guideline was adopted to modernize the PLA so that it could face the type of war senior officers believed would occur in the future—one shaped by the lessons of World War II and to a lesser extent the Korean War. Remarkable unity in the party facilitated the adoption of the initial reforms and the 1956 guideline by insulating the PLA from intraparty politics. Left alone to plan how to defend China, senior military leaders, especially Peng Dehuai, sought to build a force that could wage modern, mechanized war against the strongest military in the world at the time.

4

The 1964 Strategy: "Luring the Enemy in Deep"

In June 1964, Mao Zedong intervened directly in military affairs and changed China's military strategy. He rejected the identification of the northeast as China's primary strategic direction where a US invasion might occur and the use of a forward defense to counter such an attack. Over the next twelve months, Mao would reorient China's military strategy around the concept of "luring the enemy in deep," in which territory would be yielded to an invader to defeat it in a protracted conflict through mobile and guerrilla warfare.

The adoption of the 1964 strategic guideline presents an anomaly. It represents the one instance when a top party leader initiated a change in military strategy. The other eight strategic guidelines adopted since 1949 were initiated by senior military officers. It also represents an example of a reverse or retrograde change in strategy, in which an older strategy replaces a current one. The 1964 strategy was not a major change based on a new vision of warfare or a minor change that adjusted elements of an existing strategy. Instead, as discussed in chapter 2, luring the enemy in deep was a concept of operations developed during the encirclement campaigns in the 1930s, when the Red Army sought to defend itself against a much stronger Nationalist force. Mao now sought to use this idea as the organizing principle for countering a US attack.

Mao's intervention to change China's military strategy is puzzling because China did not face an immediate or pressing external threat that would warrant such a dramatic reversal in how to defend China. China's security environment had deteriorated in 1962, producing a large-scale mobilization to defeat a feared Nationalist invasion in June and then a border war with India in October and November. Yet these threats had diminished by 1963 and had certainly dissipated by 1964. Although the United States was increasing the number of military advisors in South Vietnam, by mid-1964, there were still no indications that the war in Vietnam would expand beyond the seventeenth parallel toward China's border. Despite ideological tensions with the Soviets, China's northern border did not start to be militarized until the very end of 1965. Finally, China successfully tested its first atomic bomb a few months after Mao changed strategy, an event that should have significantly increased China's security and confidence about preventing an invasion.

The adoption of the 1964 strategy illustrates how party disunity and leadership splits can distort and politicize strategic decision-making. In the early 1960s, Mao became increasingly concerned about the threat of revisionism within the Chinese Communist Party, which would prevent the continuation and deepening of China's revolution. Mao pushed for a strategy of luring in deep not to enhance China's security, but instead as part of a broader attack on party leaders whom he viewed as revisionists, including the decision to industrialize China's hinterland by "developing the third line" (*sanxian jianshe*). These efforts would culminate with the launch of the Cultural Revolution two years later.

Understanding the origins of the 1964 strategic guideline is important for several reasons. One reason is that the strategy of luring the enemy in deep shaped China's military strategy for more than a decade. It would not be abandoned until September 1980, when the second major change in China's military strategy occurred. After the clash with the Soviet Union at Zhenbao Island in March 1969, China maintained this strategy of strategic retreat. By that point, too, the split within the CCP leadership and the PLA's leading role in maintaining law and order likely prevented the formulation of a new strategy. Another reason is that the origins of the 1964 guideline highlight that Mao himself never stated during this period (or before 1969) that China needed to prepare to fight "an early, major, nuclear war" (*zaoda, dada, da hezhanzheng*).[1] Although China acknowledged that a war with the United States would involve nuclear weapons, the phrase did not become commonly used until after China faced the Soviet threat in 1969. Finally, it offers a revisionist interpretation of Mao Zedong's own motivations. In most Chinese and Western histories of the period, Mao's approach to the third line and military strategy is portrayed as a response to growing external threats. This chapter suggests that internal threats, in the form of revisionism, were the decisive factor in Mao's calculus.

This chapter proceeds as follows. The first section examines the year of 1962, when China faced increased threats from many directions simultaneously. In response, China implemented its existing strategy of forward defense, mobilizing to counter a Nationalist invasion along the coast and then attacking Indian forces along the disputed border. The next section describes the content of the strategic guideline initiated in 1964, to show that it constituted a reverse or retrograde change to China's existing strategy. The third section outlines the political logic of Mao's intervention and how his concerns about revisionism within the CCP led him to call for the development of the third line and decentralization of economic policy under the guise of a general exhortation to prepare for war. The fourth section examines the process by which the 1964 strategy was changed, highlighting how Mao's concerns about revisionism and his desire to industrialize the hinterland also required a decentralized approach to military strategy under the idea of luring the enemy in deep. The final section examines briefly the continuity of this strategy after a Soviet invasion became the most pressing threat to China's security in 1969.

New Threats and Strategic Continuity in 1962

In early January 1960, the CMC assessed that China faced a relatively stable external security environment. Mao's own judgment was that neither a major war nor nuclear war was likely to occur. Similarly, in February 1960, Su Yu noted the weakness and vulnerabilities of the United States versus the socialist bloc.[2] Nevertheless, consistent with earlier assessments of the mid-1950s, Mao also believed that "so long as imperialism exists, the threat of war still exists."[3] Marshal Ye Jianying observed that China should continue to prepare for the worst and "focus on the most dangerous aspects."[4] Thus, China's military strategy remained the same as before, adopting a forward defensive posture to defend against a "surprise attack" (*turan xiji*).[5]

By mid-1962, however, China's external security environment had deteriorated. In June, China faced simultaneous threats from multiple directions, including across the Taiwan Strait and along the disputed boundary with India as well as from the Soviet Union adjacent to Xinjiang. Yet, facing these threats, China did not change its military strategy. Instead, Beijing moved to improve combat readiness (*zhanbei*), in which the force was reorganized, growing from roughly 3 million soldiers in 1961 to 4.47 million by early 1965.[6] China also responded to the most immediate and severe threat of the time, a potential Nationalist assault, by mobilizing forces and adopting a forward defensive posture to repel the invasion—actions consistent with its existing military strategy. The new threats that arose did not warrant a new military strategy. When Mao rejected the existing strategy in June 1964, he did so not to counter external threats and enhance China's security, but instead to pursue his domestic political agenda.

"THREATS IN ALL DIRECTIONS"

The context for the deterioration of China's security environment was the election of John F. Kennedy as president of the United States, the shift to "flexible response," and the expansion of the US military. As Zhou Enlai noted in February 1962, "The enemy is expanding its force and preparing for war [*kuojun beizhan*]."[7] Of particular concern was the "two-and-a-half" doctrine, which suggested that the United States was preparing to wage war in Asia and Europe simultaneously. In June 1962, Zhou stressed the threat posed by the growing presence of the United States, observing that "Southeast Asia is a strategic area and the place where American imperialism is competing for the long term."[8] China viewed the establishment of the US Military Assistance Command and the increase in US advisors in Vietnam by the end of 1962 as part of an effort to encircle China, but this reflected the continuation of hostility between the two countries from the 1950s and not a specific threat.[9]

The most direct threat to China was a Nationalist invasion, especially if supported by the United States. Sensing weakness on the mainland after the Great Leap, Chiang Kai-shek saw a window of opportunity to strike. In his 1962 Chinese New Year's speech, Chiang made bellicose statements about an imminent Nationalist return to the mainland.[10] In March, the Nationalist government issued a conscription mobilization decree to increase manpower, adopted a special budget for wartime mobilization efforts, and imposed a "return to the mainland" tax to help fund the effort.[11] By late May, China's leaders concluded that a Nationalist attack was likely. According to the CMC's strategy research small group, the Nationalists "will certainly seize the opportunity of our economic difficulties to come and attack us [*gao women*]" because it presented "an exceedingly rare good opportunity." The group concluded that "the probability of hostilities occurring was greatest along the southeast coast."[12] In early June, Zhou Enlai assessed the most likely scenario was the seizure of several beachheads on the Fujian and Zhejiang coasts that would be used as bases for surging forces and launching larger attacks on the mainland.[13]

As tensions grew across the Strait, China faced a second, albeit lesser, threat on its western flank in Central Asia adjacent to the Soviet Union. From late April to late May 1962, more than sixty thousand ethnic Kazakhs fled from Xinjiang to the Soviet Union, during which a large riot erupted in the city of Yili (Kulja) on May 29, 1962. China accused the Soviet Union of encouraging this exodus by issuing false citizenship papers to Xinjiang residents in the cities of Yili and Tacheng (Qoqek), spreading print and radio propaganda about opportunities in the Soviet Union, and opening gateways in the border fence to facilitate emigration. From China's perspective, the Soviet Union was seeking to destabilize a part of the country where the central government's authority was weak, while also exposing China's lack of border defenses and border control in the area. Although the "YiTa Incident" did not threaten to start a war or even a military clash, it underscored China's sense of insecurity in 1962.[14]

Finally, in the southwest, India began a "forward policy" of occupying disputed territory on the China-India border. Implementation of the policy started in the eastern sector around Tawang in February 1962 and in the western sector in the Chip Chap Valley in March 1962. In mid-April, China announced that it would resume patrols in the western sector, and the General Staff Department (GSD) ordered troops in Xinjiang to strengthen border defenses. By the end of May, the GSD issued a report on strengthening combat readiness along the border, and instructions regarding the deployment of forces, supplies, fortifications, and combat readiness training (*zhanbei xunlian*). Nevertheless, Mao Zedong and Zhou Enlai both indicated that a Nationalist attack posed the primary threat and ordered that China should fight only if attacked by India first.[15]

CHINA'S RESPONSE TO EXTERNAL THREATS

China responded to these threats in several different ways. Taken together, however, they did not prompt China to reevaluate the utility of its existing military strategy. Instead, China moved to enact its existing strategy.[16] China mobilized to counter a Nationalist invasion by preparing to execute a forward defense in the likely areas of attack.

Before the emergence of new threats in 1962, the PLA was implementing an eight-year organization and equipment plan (*zuzhi bianzhi jihua*) approved in October 1960. Consistent with the existing strategy, this plan marked the PLA's continued transformation from a light infantry force to a combined force composed of multiple services and branches. The plan focused on modestly expanding the size of operational and combat-duty troops; strengthening air, naval, and specialized units as the production of new equipment would permit; strengthening forces in border areas; and establishing engineering and research units. By September 1961, the PLA grew by approximately three hundred thousand to three million.[17] During this process, many shortcomings were identified, which suggested that further reorganization was needed. Areas identified for future reform included oversized departments (*jiguan*), a surplus of officers, understrength infantry units (especially those engaged in border and coastal defense), and the limited mobility of units below the division level.[18]

In February 1962, before the extent of the deterioration of China's security environment became clear, the CMC convened an army-wide meeting on organization and equipment to address these shortcomings. This meeting would last for several months. At the end of February, Zhou Enlai participated in the meeting and said that military work should emphasize "reorganizing the military, improving combat readiness [*zhengjun beizhan*]."[19] The meeting determined the principle of reorganization would be the "four lightens and four strengthens" (*si qing si zhong*). This slogan called for concentrating heavy weapons in units in the north and at the army level and above, while those in the south and at lower levels would be more lightly armed. Noncombat departments (*jiguan*) should be reduced while operational units (*liandui*) should be increased.[20]

The plan also sought to improve the mechanization of troops in the north and on coastal islands that would be the first line of defense in an invasion, while those in the south would remain equipped as light infantry units, owing to the tropical terrain that limited mobility of motorized vehicles.[21] Because of the challenges of arming the ground forces with new weapons, fifty-five percent of infantry divisions would be designated as full-strength combat-duty divisions to be equipped with the best equipment. By contrast, twenty-seven percent were designated as ordinary divisions that would engage in economic production for half the year, and eighteen percent as "small" divisions that would focus on training.[22]

China responded to the threat across the Strait with the largest mobilization of forces since the Korean War.[23] Consistent with a strategy of forward defense, the operational guideline for countering a Nationalist attack was to "resist [*ding*], do not let the enemy come."[24] At the end of May, Shandong, Zhejiang, Fujian, Jiangxi and Guangdong provinces were instructed to prepare for conflict. Along the southeast coast, thirty-three infantry divisions, ten artillery divisions, three tank regiments, and other forces were placed on high alert.[25] An additional one hundred thousand veterans were mobilized to supplement these forces and efforts were begun to mobilize an additional one hundred thousand militia members.[26] On June 10, 1962, the CMC issued "Instructions for Smashing Nationalist Raids in the Southeast Coastal Area," which implemented a widespread domestic mobilization in coastal provinces.[27] In June and July, seven combat-duty divisions, two railway corps divisions, and other specialized units from Liaoning, Hebei, Henan, and Guangzhou were deployed to Fujian while the air force placed almost seven hundred planes on alert status.[28] All told, the PLA mobilized approximately four hundred thousand soldiers and one thousand planes to repel an attack.[29]

The threat began to dissipate after a meeting between US and Chinese ambassadors in Warsaw on June 23. The United States indicated that Washington did not encourage Chiang's current efforts and would provide no military support to Taiwan in the event of a Nationalist assault.[30] Nevertheless, concerns about the security of China's coastal areas dominated PLA planning for the next few years. In October 1962, to emphasize its commitment to coastal defense, the Fuzhou Military District adjacent to Taiwan organized a large-scale, live-fire anti-landing exercise with approximately 36,500 soldiers.[31] In 1963 and 1964, the defense of coastal islands would become a focal point in PLA operations planning, as the islands constituted the outer limit of China's first line of defense against an attack.[32]

As tensions eased across the Strait in the summer of 1962, the situation on the China-India border deteriorated. In September, a stand-off in the eastern sector over an area named Chola (Dohla) precipitated an escalation of tensions. In mid-October, China decided to attack Indian units that had been deployed as part of the "forward policy" and attacked Indian forces in both sectors on October 20. After pausing to press India to hold talks, China attacked again in November, destroying the remainder of Indian forces in disputed areas before declaring a unilateral halt to hostilities and withdrawing to the line of actual control before the conflict started.[33]

By the end of 1962, China's security environment stabilized. The Nationalist invasion did not occur, while the PLA readily defeated Indian forces. Nevertheless, the size of the PLA grew significantly in 1963 and 1964. Although the 1962 reorganization plan called for maintaining the current size of the armed forces, the increase was consistent with growing threats and the need to increase combat duty units and address multiple threats simultaneously. In late 1961, the size of the force was approximately three million. Starting in 1963, it began to grow, reaching 4.47 million at the start of 1965.[34] Reflecting the focus on external threats, just over seventy-nine percent of the force consisted of combat troops (*zuozhan budui*), a share what would fall to just over fifty percent when the force expanded again after 1969 in the Cultural Revolution.[35]

"Luring the Enemy in Deep"

In June 1964, Mao Zedong rejected the existing military strategy of forward defense during a speech at the Ming Tombs outside Beijing. Instead, Mao envisioned luring the enemy in deep, allowing an adversary to occupy territory, and then defeating it through a protracted war that would leverage China's large territory and population.

Among all of China's military strategies since 1949, the 1964 strategic guideline represents an anomaly. First, it envisioned a return to a familiar way of warfighting, not a new vision of warfare, and thus did not require the PLA to pursue major organizational reforms. Second, the new strategy was not codified in a report drafted, discussed, and approved by China's senior military officers. Instead, it was based on the various remarks Mao had made over the following year. In 1980, Song Shilun, the president of the Academy of Military Science, lamented that only "fragments" of Mao's remarks on strategy from this period were available.[36]

The 1964 military strategy remained premised on countering a US invasion. Nevertheless, Mao changed the core components of the existing strategic guideline revised in 1960. The first was a change in the "primary strategic direction." China's existing strategy was premised on a US assault on the Shandong Peninsula. Nevertheless, Mao believed that the direction of attack was uncertain and could occur anywhere along the coast, from Tianjin down to Shanghai. Therefore, China could no longer rely on "resisting in the north, opening in the south," which had been premised on a forward defense of northern areas, especially the Shandong Peninsula. The broader implication was that China did not have a primary strategic direction around which to orient its military strategy and would need to prepare for an attack from multiple directions.

The second change followed from the absence of a primary strategic direction and concerned the "basic guiding thought for operations." The concept of operations from the civil war—luring the enemy in deep—replaced the emphasis on defending fixed positions. Luring the enemy in deep was a form of strategic retreat, in which an adversary would be allowed to gain a foothold on China's territory so that the PLA could then engage an enemy in a protracted war of attrition. In turn, mobile and guerrilla warfare replaced positional warfare as the main form of operations that the PLA should be able to conduct.

The 1964 strategy remained a strategy of strategic defense. The main objective of the 1964 strategy was to defeat an adversary through a protracted conflict on Chinese territory. Mao envisioned ceding territory to an invader, including major cities, so that it would extend its supply lines and be degraded through a protracted conflict, in which soldiers as well as civilians would be mobilized.[37] In other words, Mao envisioned that PLA main force units would remain the core fighting force, but that they would be supplemented by local armed forces and militia that would be able to conduct independent operations in different parts of the country. Guerrilla warfare would be waged in areas ceded to the adversary, while main force units would engage in mobile operations on fluid fronts in China's interior.

With the launch and upheaval of the Cultural Revolution in 1966, it is impossible to observe the implementation of the 1964 strategy. Thus, the main change examined in this chapter is Mao's rejection of the existing strategy for a variant of an older one, not the implementation of the new strategy. In general terms, the return to mobile warfare and luring the enemy in deep did not require the PLA to develop new operational doctrine. Instead, it only required the PLA to revive its "glorious traditions" from the civil war. No effort was made to draft new operational doctrine. The size of the force grew significantly, from 4.47 million in early 1965 as the strategy was changing to 6.31 million by 1969. Much of this growth occurred after the clash with the Soviet Union over Zhenbao Island in March 1969, though nineteen divisions were formed or reorganized between 1966 and 1968.[38] The PLA did not draft a new training program, though the training that did occur increasingly emphasized studying politics and not military affairs.

Mao pushed for the change in strategy to address the potential US threat to China only. Nevertheless, China continued to adhere to the 1964 strategic guideline after the Soviet threat replaced the American one in 1969. Whether or not it was an appropriate strategy for dealing with a ground invasion, the strategy could not be altered because of the deep divisions in the party and military leadership created by the Cultural Revolution.

The Political Logic of Mao's Intervention

Mao changed China's military strategy in 1964 to counter revisionism and internal threats to his revolution rather than external threats to China's security. In the aftermath of the Great Leap Forward, Mao became increasingly concerned about the potential for revisionism within the CCP, as the party leadership returned to conventional central planning practices and strengthened the role of the party's central bureaucracy. It was these practices that Mao had sought to circumvent when he launched the leap. To challenge these tendencies and to again decentralize decision-making, he called for "developing the third line," or the massive industrialization of China's southwestern hinterland that would consume just over half of all capital investment in the Third Five-Year Plan.[39] The change was so radical that Mao could only justify it by the need to prepare for war, which also dictated that he intervene to change China's military strategy as well as its economic policy.

The argument that Mao championed—developing the third line and changing China's military strategy in 1964 to counter internal threats and not external ones—is itself a revisionist interpretation of this period. Almost all scholarship and histories from inside and outside China highlight the deterioration of China's security environment as the reason why Mao pushed for development of the third line.[40] The only exception is an essay by a party historian, Li Xiangqian, that questions the role of the escalation of the war in Vietnam in Mao's decision to develop the third line and suggests that Mao may have also harbored domestic motives.[41]

GROWING CONCERNS ABOUT REVISIONISM

Revisionism refers to an unacceptable departure from orthodox Marxist-Leninist ideology that eventually leads to socialist degeneration. After the Great Leap Forward, Mao concluded that the greatest danger to China's revolution was not an external attack. Instead, the main threat was internal—the "restoration of capitalism" led by "revisionists" within the CCP. Mao's efforts to combat revisionism would culminate two years later with the launch of the Great Proletarian Cultural Revolution.[42] Mao targeted the CCP's senior leadership, most of whom were purged in 1966, as well as the vast, centralized bureaucracy that they had created to govern the country, which Mao hoped to rectify through a "mass insurgency" from below.[43] Mao's motives, of course, were mixed, as he sought to preserve both his own power within the CCP and the legacy of China's revolution, as he defined it. Nevertheless, he viewed threats to his power through an ideological lens, as ideological threats.

Mao's fear of revisionism within the CCP began in the aftermath of the Great Leap Forward. In launching the Great Leap, Mao aimed to circumvent the Soviet-style approach that China had used in the First Five-Year Plan to achieve rapid growth by applying well-honed techniques of mass mobilization to the economy.[44] In practice, the policies of the leap weakened the control of the central bureaucracy over the economy and empowered local party leaders, who had become responsible for achieving ambitious production goals. Farmers were organized into large communes in the countryside to dramatically increase surplus grain that could then be used to support investment in heavy industry. As Andrew Walder writes, the Great Leap was a "political campaign that cast economic policy in terms of political loyalty, equating it with class struggle."[45]

The Great Leap, however, was a great failure. Grain output fell from 200 million tons in 1958 to only 143 million tons in 1961. Only in 1966 would grain output surpass 200 million tons again.[46] Likewise, from 1960 to 1962, industrial output fell by fifty percent and only exceeded the level output from 1958 in 1965.[47] Tens of millions of Chinese citizens perished in famines throughout the country, with estimates ranging from 30 to 45 million deaths.[48]

As the calamity mounted at the end of 1960, the party started to take steps to stem the crisis and rebuild the economy. Taken together, these measures sought to reestablish the bureaucracy's control over the economy, taking it back from the party. In practice, retrenchment involved lowering production targets, terminating mass mobilization, dismantling communes, and increasing material incentives for farmers under the slogan (approved in January 1961) of "adjustment, consolidation, replenishment, improvement" and prioritizing agriculture over industry. The goal was to return the rural economy to how it had been organized before the start of the Great Leap.[49]

The economic and human devastation created by the Great Leap raised questions about the efficacy of Mao's leadership. By early 1962, top party leaders had begun to blame the party's policies, and thus Mao himself, for the catastrophe. To encourage support for the recovery effort and "unify thought," the party center in January 1962 convened an unprecedented meeting of over seven thousand cadres from the party center to the county and factory level.[50] Top party leaders criticized the party's role in the crisis. Liu Shaoqi, then the party's vice-chairman and Mao's successor, even suggested that the famine was "three tenths natural disaster, seven tenths man made calamity."[51] Mao could only view such a remark as a direct criticism.[52] In 1959 and 1960, Mao stated repeatedly that the "accomplishments" of the Great Leap could be counted on nine fingers while the "setbacks" could be counted on only one.[53] Liu publicly reversed this assessment, criticizing Mao before the largest meeting of party cadre ever held since 1949.

Mao did offer a rare, if vague, self-criticism at the conference. Nevertheless, the criticisms of the policies that produced the catastrophe, and blaming the party in addition to natural disasters, raised questions for Mao about the loyalty of the leaders in charge of day-to-day policymaking, like Liu Shaoqi and Deng Xiaoping (secretary-general of the Central Committee Secretariat), and their commitment to continuing Mao's revolution. At the end of 1958, Mao started to delegate responsibility for the party's daily affairs to Liu and Deng by deciding to move himself to the "second line," and stopped attending Politburo meetings on a regular basis. Mao was beginning to regret that decision.

In early 1962, Liu and Deng redoubled their efforts to rescue the economy by reestablishing central control. Economic recovery measures were put in place to restore balance between the rural and industrial economies, primarily by reducing investment in industry to increase support for agriculture. These measures included policies such as reducing the urban population, decreasing investment in capital projects, and continuing experiments with household farming methods like the household responsibility system, to create material incentives for increasing production. Liu and Deng also started to reexamine the cases of some cadres persecuted in the Anti-Rightist Movement in 1958, a topic that Mao had opposed when it was raised at the seven thousand cadres conference.[54] The Liu and Deng approach rolled back Mao's emphasis on decentralization and empowering localities, marking a return to the more centralized, bureaucratic, and technocratic approach to economic policy that Mao had rejected when he launched the leap.

By the summer of 1962, Mao was becoming alarmed. He was especially concerned with the household farming system, which set quotas for output and allowed farmers to keep any surplus production. At the same time, the party began to loosen restrictions on intellectuals in a bid to tap their expertise to aid the recovery.[55] In July, during a tense exchange with Liu Shaoqi, Mao accused Liu of abandoning the revolution, asking, "What will happen after I die?"[56] In August 1962, at the annual leadership retreat at Beidaihe, Mao revealed his reservations to a wider audience. He criticized what he viewed as excessive pessimism in assessments of the situation and noted the danger that household farming could increase class polarization. He also underscored the need to continue with the collectivization of agriculture and not reversing verdicts on those deemed as rightists, especially Peng Dehuai.[57]

Mao's concerns about revisionism and the importance of continuing class struggle featured prominently in the Tenth Plenum in September 1962. He laid down a marker in the plenum's communiqué, which he edited, noting that "class struggle cannot be avoided" because there were some people who "intend to depart from the socialist road and go along the capitalist road." Moreover, "this class struggle will inevitably be reflected in the party." Thus, the communiqué warned, "While struggling against class enemies at home and abroad, we must be vigilant and resolutely opposed to all types of opportunistic ideological tendencies within the party."[58] As party historians would later observe, Mao at the meeting outlined his "basic strategy" of "opposing revisionism and preventing revisionism" (*fanxiu fangxiu*) at home and abroad.[59] The imperative of continuing class struggle to prevent the "restoration of capitalism" would prompt Mao's decision to launch the Cultural Revolution four years later.[60]

Despite raising the question of class struggle, the economy remained fragile and the plenum agreed to continue with recovery measures. Although Mao emphasized class struggle, he was unable to pursue it at the expense of the economy. In April 1963, an enlarged meeting of the Politburo Standing Committee decided that "opposing revisionism" would focus on growing tensions with the Soviet Union over the direction of the worldwide communist movement. The party published nine open letters or polemics between September 1963 and July 1964 that denounced Soviet revisionism in its foreign and domestic policies and delegitimized its leadership. Many of the critiques of the Soviet Union, however, reflected Mao's concerns about the CCP's own trajectory. The Politburo Standing Committee also decided that "preventing revisionism" at home would start with the Socialist Education Movement.[61] The movement began with the "four cleans" (*siqing*) in the countryside and "five antis" (*wufan*) in the cities, and would continue until the start of the Cultural Revolution.[62]

By 1964, the trends that would push Mao to attack the CCP's leadership and launch the Cultural Revolution were present. The party's top leadership favored pragmatism over ideology. The central bureaucracy had regained authority over the vast majority of enterprises and the allocation of goods that it had lost during the Great Leap.[63] The State Council had returned to its size in 1956, before the start of the Great Leap.[64] Even the Socialist Education Movement emphasized strengthening party organization and combating corruption, not rooting out revisionism and engaging in class struggle.[65] As Walder writes, the ninth polemic against the Soviet Union published in July 1964 "expressed what was to be the ideological justification for the Cultural Revolution."[66] The document decried the domestic and foreign policies of "the revisionist Khrushchev clique" before asking whether "genuine proletarian revolutionaries" would maintain control of the party and the state in China. The selection of revolutionary successors, the letter concluded, was "a matter of life and death for our Party and our country."[67]

MAO ATTACKS ECONOMIC PLANNING

In mid-March 1964, Mao decided that he would now focus on revisionism inside China. His decision was announced at a Politburo Standing Committee meeting to discuss an upcoming central work conference. He informed his colleagues that "in the past year, my main efforts have been spent on the struggle with Khrushchev. Now I should turn back to domestic issues, connecting [*lianxi*] opposing revisionism and preventing revisionism internally."[68] Mao's decision to focus on domestic revisionism set the stage for a clash over economic policy, from which he had retreated in late 1958.

One main topic for the central work conference was the draft framework of the Third Five-Year Plan. The State Planning Commission began to work on the plan in late 1962 and emphasized the recovery of the economy. Li Fuchun, head of the State Planning Commission, proposed that the plan concentrate on agricultural output and the production of "food, clothing, and daily necessities" (*chi, chuan, yong*).[69] Basic industry and national defense would be secondary priorities. In the summer of 1963, Mao agreed with Li Fuchun's suggestion to postpone the start of the Third Five-Year Plan to give the economy more time to recover. The period from 1963 to 1965 would be a "transitional stage" between the second and third five-year plans, again with a focus on agriculture.[70] Bo Yibo, Li's deputy on the State Planning Commission, recalls that, during this transitional period, "agriculture was first, basic industry second, and national defense third."[71]

In early 1964, Li Fuchun's approach to the Third Five-Year Plan remained focused on these objectives. The draft framework circulated in April 1964 contained three main tasks to be accomplished. The first task was "greatly developing agriculture, basically resolving the people's issue of food, clothing and daily necessities." The second and third tasks were to "appropriately develop national defense, striving for breakthroughs in sophisticated technology," and to strengthen basic industry.[72] In other words, national defense and basic industrial development remained lower priorities and would only be pursued if they did not harm the recovery of the economy based on agriculture.[73] According to Bo Yibo, agriculture would be the "foundation" of "planning."[74]

Yet on the eve of the central work conference, Mao attacked the approach to economic policy that he had previously endorsed. Instead of supporting the emphasis on agriculture, he called for the industrialization of China's hinterland[75] or "developing the third line."* When Li Fuchun briefed Mao in early May, Mao responded that defense and heavy industries should receive greater attention, thereby negating the priorities in the draft framework of the plan. He said he "could not relax" if steel mills at Panzhihua (in Sichuan province) and Jiuquan (in Gansu province) were not built, asking "what should be done if a war erupts" and China lacked such industrial plants.[76] These projects had been initiated in 1958 and later postponed because of the economic crisis.[77] Mao also observed that "defense industries" should be a "fist" for the economy as well as agriculture, indicating he believed that they should play an equally

---

* The third line, sometimes translated as the "third front," refers to two parts of China's hinterland, the southwest (Yunan, Guizhou, Sichuan along with the western portions of Hunan and Hubei) and the northwest (Shaanxi, Gansu, Qinghai along with the western portions of Henan and Shanxi). The "first line" refers to coastal provinces, while the "second line" refers to central areas.

important role in the economy.[78] As Li Fuchun's biographers observe, Mao now viewed "the starting point for the Third Five-Year Plan as more about preparing for war."[79]

When the central work conference began, Mao attacked the framework for the Third Five-Year Plan before the party's top leadership. During a meeting of the Politburo Standing Committee on May 27, he argued that the plan paid insufficient attention to the development of China's "butt" (basic industry) and rear (*houfang*) or the "third line." Mao observed that "in the nuclear age, it is unacceptable to have no rear area."[80] He further suggested that, over the next six years, "a foundation should be established in the southwest" with industrial bases for metallurgy, national defense, oil, railroad, coal, and machinery.[81] The main reason for developing the third line was to "prepare for the enemy's invasion" (*fangbei diren de ruqin*).[82]

Mao's intervention was remarkable and must have surprised Li Fuchun and other top leaders. Available sources contain no instances of Mao ever referring to the third line before this meeting.[83] The immediate effect of his intervention was to transform the focus of the conference. The next day, May 28, Liu Shaoqi transmitted Mao's instructions on developing the third line to the work conference's leading small group, thereby altering the direction of the conference in a way that none of the participants had anticipated when it started.[84] Although Mao had avoided economic policy since the Great Leap, he had decided to reengage. His intervention could not be ignored.

On June 8, Mao participated in the central work conference for the first time, chairing an enlarged meeting of the Politburo Standing Committee. In various remarks at this session, he connected his concerns about revisionism with his critique of the Third Five-Year Plan and the need to develop the third line.[85] He criticized China's method of planning, which was "basically learned from the Soviet Union" and simply "using a calculator."[86] Mao thus implied that China's approach to planning, and those executing it, was revisionist. This method, he charged, was "not suited to reality" because it could not account for unexpected events that might arise, such as natural disasters or wars. Revealing his dissatisfaction, Mao asserted that "[we] must change the method of planning." He described such a task as a "revolution," as once the Soviet approach was adopted it was hard to change, and critiqued not only the content of the framework for the Third Five-Year Plan, but also the process by which it had been developed and thus the top party leaders who had formulated and approved it.[87]

Next, Mao highlighted how planning should be anchored in the need to prepare for war. Such arguments were a cudgel for attacking what he viewed as revisionism within the party, including the flaws in central planning and complacency among local cadre.[88] Mao reminded his colleagues that "as long as imperialism exists, there is a danger of war."[89] He said that every coastal province should have ordnance factories, as these provinces could not wait for the second and third lines to supply them once a war started. Mao also said that every province should have their own first, second and third lines and urged that "every province should have some military industries to produce their own rifles, sub-machine guns, light and heavy machine guns, mortars, bullets and explosives. As long as we have these, we can relax."[90]

At the same time, Mao viewed local cadres as complacent, not interested in preparing for the worst. He complained that "now localities do not engage in military affairs" and then called for developing local armed forces (*difang budui*) in first- and second-line provinces.[91] Otherwise, "as soon as something happens, you will be unprepared." Mao further chided the audience, stating that local cadre were less prepared than the Viet Cong, who were waging a guerrilla war in South Vietnam. He asked, "What happens when war erupts? When the enemy invades [*dajin*] our national territory? I dare to assert that it will not be like South Vietnam." For Mao, the core of the problem was that "party committees in all localities cannot care only about civil affairs and not military ones, only care about money and not care about guns."[92] Foreshadowing his emphasis on luring the enemy in deep, Mao noted that "as soon as fighting starts, prepare to smash [the enemy] to pieces, and prepare to abandon cities. Every province must have a solution."[93]

Mao's concerns about revisionism within the CCP motivated his criticism of planning and local cadre. When Liu Shaoqi raised the subject of revisionism occurring in China, Mao said "it had already appeared."[94] More ominously, again implicating local cadre, Mao warned that "a third of the power of the state is not in our hands, it is in the hands of the enemy."[95] He then issued what Bo Yibo recalled as a solemn appeal: "Pass on [this message] all the way down to the county level: what if a Khrushchev-like figure emerges? What if there is revisionism at the center in China? County party committees must resist a revisionist center."[96] Mao implied that localities must not only prepare to deal with an invasion, but also with a revisionist central leadership.

Deng Xiaoping later concluded that Mao's decision to overturn economic policy in 1964 marked the start of the Cultural Revolution. Deng recalled that after the "defeat" of the Great Leap, Mao "rarely inquired about the economy" and focused on class struggle. But in 1964, Mao "scolded" Li Fuchun, Li Xiannian and Bo Yibo when he asked "why China was not developing the third line." Deng noted that "China subsequently entered into a high tide of fervent development of the big and small third lines. I think the Cultural Revolution found its origin at that time."[97]

Adoption of the 1964 Strategic Guideline

At the end of the central work conference, Mao met with the Politburo Standing Committee and the first party secretaries of the CCP's regional bureaus at the Ming Tombs outside Beijing. As Liu Ruiqing recalled, Mao in his remarks "negated" the existing strategic guideline of "resist in the north, open in the south."[98] In its place, Mao called for a strategy based on preparing for an attack from any direction and abandoning a forward defense in favor of luring the enemy in deep. By increasing the importance of military affairs for local party committees, such a military strategy complemented Mao's plans to decentralize economic planning and combat revisionism within the party bureaucracy.

MAO REJECTS THE EXISTING MILITARY STRATEGY

Several features of Mao's speech highlight his domestic political motivations. To start, his concerns about the existing military strategy were not raised in a meeting of China's senior military officers, such as a CMC meeting, or even during an informal gathering of senior generals, such as Lin Biao and Luo Ruiqing. Lin Biao, the ranking party member in charge of the PLA, was only briefed on Mao's speech several weeks later.[99] Instead, Mao chose to challenge China's existing military strategy before central and regional party leaders with little or no direct involvement in high-level military affairs. The choice of venue alone indicates that his comments on strategy were designed to bolster his political agenda, not China's security. In addition, Mao's remarks did not focus exclusively or primarily on military strategy. Instead, the two topics of his speech were the need for local party committees to "grasp" military affairs, and the question of leadership succession within the party—two areas at the fore of his concerns about revisionism.

The first part of Mao's speech stressed again the need for local party committees to emphasize their work on military affairs. To do so, Mao questioned the primary strategic direction in the 1960 guideline. As noted earlier, he believed that local officials were lax and complacent. Identifying a general problem for local party leaders to solve would counter such complacency—in this case, their lack of preparations to conduct independent military operations in their areas if China was attacked. If China lacked a primary strategic direction and an attack could occur anywhere, then military affairs and preparing for war would be the responsibility of all local leaders, not just those in the likely area of a US attack in the north. The emphasis on independent operations also evoked the revolutionary spirit of the civil war, again reflecting Mao's concerns about revisionism.

Mao began by stating that "local party committees need to work on military affairs." For Mao, "just watching exercises is not enough." He then stated that all regions (*daqu*) and provinces "need to create a plan that includes working on the people's militia and repairing machinery and munitions factories." He placed the onus on provincial party committees, stating that they needed to "take an interest in the troops and militia within the provinces," and further chided provincial first party secretaries, who were also political commissars, for shirking their responsibilities and being "phony commissars."

Then Mao turned to the strategic guideline, which he said he "had thought about for long time." He first questioned the primary strategic direction in the 1960 strategy, which had been premised on an attack occurring in the northeast, especially the Shandong Peninsula. Mao began by stating that "in the past, we have discussed resisting in the north and opening in the south. My view is, not necessarily."[100] Mao then asked whether the enemy would "necessarily have to come from the northeast." After dismissing the possibility of an attack from the southwest through Guangxi, he then raised alternative directions of attack. As shown in map 4.1, these included landing at Tanggu in the Bohai Gulf to occupy Tianjin and Beijing; landing at Qingdao to occupy Tianjin or Xuzhou; landing at Lianyungang to advance onto Xuzhou, Kaifeng, and Zhengzhou; or landing at Shanghai to take Nanjing and Wuhan. His larger point was the danger of focusing on a singular strategic direction, as "it is possible that the enemy may come in from any of these places."

Mao then questioned the second component of the 1960 strategy, the basic guiding thought of "resisting" (*ding*) an invasion by defending fixed positions. Against invoking the revolutionary period, Mao said that "we can still use the old way of fighting," the combination of fighting and moving at the heart of mobile warfare. Invoking language from his 1936 lecture on military strategy in the revolution, he stated: "Fight if you can fight and win, and move when you cannot fight and win." More generally, he asserted that it would be unacceptable "to consider action based entirely on being able to resist the enemy." Thus, for Mao, "considerations must be based on the inability to resist the enemy. If you can't resist the enemy, it's better to go!" Any member of the audience would understand that Mao was signaling his preference for luring the enemy in deep and mobile warfare.

Mao used these critiques of the existing strategy to argue that each province, county, and prefecture should develop its own militia and local forces that would be able to conduct independent operations in a major war. If a war broke out, he instructed, "Do not rely on the central government; do not rely on only the few millions of the People's Liberation Army. In a country of this size, with a battlefront this long, it is insufficient to just rely on the People's Liberation Army." Again underscoring the need for self-reliance, local officials would be responsible for the defense of their own territory. Mao once more chastised them, stating that "there must be preparation. You people here only demand money, not guns." He also called on the provinces to build their

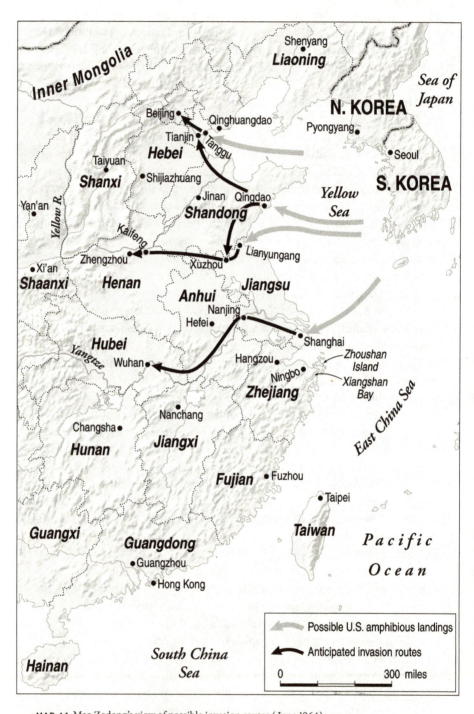

MAP 4.1. Mao Zedong's view of possible invasion routes (June 1964)

military factories. For Mao, "it will be too late to do so once the fighting starts and you are cut off."

The second part of Mao's speech focused on the need to select successors, foreshadowing the ninth open letter to the Soviet Union that would be published in July. Mao linked "preventing revisionism" with the questions of "selecting successors" in the party. He called for the need to select successors at all levels, including the center, provinces, prefectures, and counties—a task that he also assigned to party secretaries. He then outlined several ways to avoid revisionism in the next generation of leaders, such as practicing Marxism-Leninism, focusing on serving the majority of people and not a few, uniting with the majority of people, adopting a democratic work style, and conducting self-criticisms when making mistakes.[101]

Afterward, Mao continued to stress themes mentioned in his June 16 speech. On July 2, he broadened the scope of his concern to include the Soviet Union, though he would still focus primarily on the United States for the next few years. Mao noted that "you cannot only pay attention to the east and not the north, only to imperialism and not revisionism." He then emphasized again the need for all provinces to build their own munitions factories. Furthermore, "if problems arise," such as a war, "the provinces are in charge of themselves" and "cannot rely on the center and the CMC" because "the center cannot take care of this." Finally, Mao also underscored what appeared to be at least part of his motivation for using military preparations to counter revisionism: "If everything is prepared well, the enemy may not come, but if it is not prepared well, the enemy may come."[102]

On July 15, Mao again hinted at luring in deep as the basic guiding thought for operations. As he told Zhou Enlai, "Our way of fighting [dafa] is that if 'I' can defeat 'you,' then I will defeat you. When I cannot defeat you, then I won't allow you to defeat me. If the opportunity is not ripe, our main forces will not fight with you desperately, but will maintain their distance. Until the time when we can wipe you out, we will annihilate you. Little by little, you will be defeated."[103] Mao also said, "If Beijing is lost, it is not critical" and that party leaders "will go to caves in the mountains between Beijing and Taiyuan and struggle with the enemy there."[104] He stressed again the development of local forces and the importance of being able to conduct independent operations, suggesting that eleven or twelve divisions be sent to coastal and border provinces to develop and train militias to carry out these operations.[105] For Mao, in the upcoming war, "these divisions would form the backbone" of any resistance.[106]

USING THE THIRD LINE TO ATTACK CENTRAL PLANNING

As Mao rejected the existing military strategy, he continued his attack on China's central planning apparatus. After Mao's initial interventions in May 1964,

Li Fuchun began to study how to enact Mao's instructions for the third line. In the middle of June, teams from the State Planning Commission visited various locations that would become part of the third line. Nevertheless, putting Mao's ambitious plan into practice was challenging. For example, during the planning process, a dispute arose over where to site the Panzhihua steel mill. Local officials from the Southwest Bureau and the Sichuan party committee believed the proposed location was too remote and inhospitable, contradicting officials from the State Planning Commission seeking to enact Mao's wishes.[107]

By mid-August, Mao had become "greatly dissatisfied" with the pace of plans for developing the third line. He asked Li Fuchun, "Why is the third line construction so slow?"[108] Li replied as one might expect an economic planner to reply, stating that the conditions surrounding Panzhihua were complicated, that that China lacked funds, and that formulating an investment plan would require additional meetings and analysis. Although Li's response was reasonable, Mao blamed the State Planning Commission. He then charged that its methods of planning were "inappropriate" and that its work was "ineffective."[109] Mao's criticisms reflected his dissatisfaction with the Soviet-style planning process that it was designed to execute, and the party bureaucracy more generally.

At the annual Beidaihe leadership retreat in early August, criticism of the State Planning Commission mounted. Mao's surrogate on the commission, Deputy Director Chen Boda, attacked it for its "procrastinating and lax work style."[110] Chen echoed Mao by alleging that the commission's Soviet-style "management system helped revisionism grow."[111] Mao then instructed that Chen's views be distributed to all local party committees and be placed on the agenda for the upcoming central work conference in October. Mao included his own criticism of the commission, leaving no doubt about his intentions. He declared that "the method of planning work must change within the next two years. If they do not change, it would be better to eliminate the planning commission and replace it with another body."[112] At the end of the month, Mao even criticized the State Planning Commission for not "reporting their work" (*huibao gongzuo*) and "blocking" (*fengsuo*) him and Liu Shaoqi.[113] Given that many members of the State Planning Commission's leadership were also part of the Central Committee's Secretariat, Mao's claim was disingenuous, but it did reflect his dissatisfaction with the front-line leadership of the party.

In mid-August, the pace of efforts to develop the third line accelerated. Mao commented on a GSD report written in April 1964, which had outlined the high concentration of people, infrastructure, and industry in coastal provinces that would be vulnerable to an attack in a war.† Mao's comments led to the

---

† Many scholars view this report as the basis for Mao's desire to develop the third line in May. However, Mao only read the report in August. Moreover, this report identifies the vulnerability of China's economy in coastal areas and does not reference the concept of a third line.

formation of a leading small group, headed by Li Fuchun, to oversee drafting of plans for developing the third line. More broadly, Mao also began to push for decentralization in economic decision-making. In his study of China's economy during this period, Barry Naughton concludes that economic decentralization and the third line development were "complementary."[114] In September 1964, local governments were authorized to control output from smaller factories and to hire temporary workers, thereby allowing localities to "run truly autonomous industrial systems."[115] The role of the State Planning Commission was limited in favor of the empowering the provinces and multiprovince economic regions, who were encouraged to be more self-reliant and responsible for economic development within their own areas. Thus, the development of the third line, justified by an ambiguous threat, helped Mao to weaken a core pillar of the bureaucracy, which he associated with revisionism.

In December, Mao completed his attack on the State Planning Commission when he removed Li Fuchun, its director, from daily work. Mao had Yu Qiuli transferred from the Daqing oil field to serve as deputy director and party secretary of the State Planning Commission. Yu served as a political commissar in the First Field Army during the civil war and, in 1958, became minister of petroleum in charge of developing the Daqing oil field in Heilongjiang province. Yu formed a group within the State Planning Commission that became known as the "little planning commission" (*xiao jiwei*), which reported directly to Mao and subverted existing party channels. It oversaw the drafting of the Third Five-Year Plan that would be keyed to the third line development and an economy that would be geared to preparing for war.[116] Mao had regained control.

EXTERNAL THREATS?

The conventional explanation for Mao's desire to develop the third line, and to change China's military strategy in 1964, emphasizes external threats, especially the US escalation of the war in Vietnam. Nevertheless, although external security concerns may have been part of Mao's calculus, they offer a weak explanation for Mao's decisions regarding economic policy and military strategy for several reasons.

First, although China had experienced heightened insecurity in 1962, China's external environment had stabilized by 1963. After its defeat in 1962, India refrained from challenging China's control of the border. Following the aborted effort to attack the mainland in June 1962, the Nationalists focused on small-scale coastal raids, most of which were easily defeated.[117] Toward the south, the United States had escalated its commitment to defending South Vietnam since 1962, dispatching an increasing number of advisors. Yet there were no indications in the spring of 1964 that the United States was planning to escalate the war to include attacks on North Vietnam or the deployment of combat forces in South Vietnam.[118] Finally, after the 1962 YiTa Incident in Xinjiang revealed China's inability to secure its borders against the Soviet Union, China had begun to rectify its weak border defenses in the northwest.[119] Nevertheless, in early 1964, Moscow had not yet started to increase the number of forces along China's northern border; this would begin at the very end of 1965.[120] Moreover, throughout the first half of 1964, Beijing and Moscow held substantive negotiations on their disputed border, reaching a consensus on how to delimit the eastern sector.[121] Although Soviet-Chinese ties were poor, armed conflict was far from imminent. Chinese military planners studied how to improve border security, but primarily to rectify the lack of any defenses in the 1950s rather than to prepare to defend against a major attack.[122] Finally, when Mao pushed for the third line, China was on the cusp of exploding its first atomic device in October, a development that should have allayed concerns about growing external threats.

Second, Mao's push for the third line and rejection of the existing military strategy occurred three months before the Gulf of Tonkin Incident in early August 1964. Thus, US escalation of the war in Vietnam cannot explain the change in Mao's approach to either economic policy or military strategy.[123] A week before Mao rejected the existing strategy in June, he did not view a US attack as imminent, stating that "we are not the chief of staff of the United States. We do not know when he will fight."[124] Even the Gulf of Tonkin incident in early August did not alter Mao's assessment of the likelihood of a conflict with the United States. During a meeting with the Vietnamese leader Le Duan on August 13, for example, when commenting on the US bombing of North Vietnam after Tonkin, Mao observed that "America has not sent ground forces." He concluded that "it appears that America does not want to fight, you do not want to fight, we do not want to fight."[125]

Third, Mao appeared to reject the most likely way in which the United States and China might clash. In his June speech, he downplayed the possibility of a US attack in southern China along the border with Vietnam and said that "even if the enemy comes through Guangxi and Guangdong? He could fight into Yunnan, Guizhou and Sichuan, but he wouldn't obtain anything."[126] In both this speech and in remarks in November 1965, after the United States had escalated the war in South Vietnam, Mao continued to emphasize different points of attack along the coast. In other words, he did not propose reorienting China's strategy to address the most likely scenario and instead continued to underscore that the direction was unclear. External threats cannot account for this aspect of Mao's thinking, but internal threats and revisionism can. Focusing on wide possibilities along the coast allowed Mao to magnify the threat that China faced, justifying the development of the third line and the shift in strategy to luring the enemy in deep.

Fourth, when Mao discussed external threats in May and June 1964, he described them vaguely and without urgency. He did not appear to believe that China would be attacked immediately, except for a brief period in the spring of 1965, as discussed below.[127] Mao's statement in May 1964 to guard against a surprise attack repeated almost verbatim a similar remark from 1955.[128] Both remarks reflected ongoing hostility between the United States and China rather than an imminent threat. In early July 1964, Liu Shaoqi, summarizing Mao's remarks from the central work conference, did not convey any sense of urgency. Liu said that "we have not yet seen the sign of when the imperialists plan to attack, but we must prepare and every day be alert to the presence of the enemy."[129] Finally, in mid-July 1965, Luo Ruiqing summarized his understanding of Mao's comments on strategy as "thinking of things as if they were more difficult, and taking into consideration all possible difficulties."[130]

Fifth, the plans for developing the third line in the fall of 1964 did not reflect a sense of urgency that would be associated with an increased external threat. At this point, plans for the third line were as much about industrial development as specific defense industries and war preparations. The main projects Mao identified, for example, were steel mills, other basic industries, and railway networks. These projects were capital-intensive efforts with long lead times of seven to ten years, reinforcing the emphasis on industry over agriculture in economic policy and the general lack of urgency. If these projects were necessary for China to defend itself in the way Mao imagined, then their long lead times implied that a major war was not imminent. But these projects were necessary for weakening the party bureaucracy and enabling self-reliance.

U.S. ESCALATION IN VIETNAM

The escalation of the war in Vietnam in 1965 created an opportunity for China to reconsider US threats. The prospect of escalation provided an opportunity for Mao to reemphasize many of the ideas he had raised since June 1964, including his general exhortation of "preparing for the worst." Yet when the US threat abated in June 1965, he continued to press ahead with his new economic policy and military strategy, becoming much more explicit about the role of luring the enemy in deep. Mao's emphasis on luring in deep after the US threat receded is consistent with his domestic motivations to change China's military strategy in June 1964.

At the start of 1965, Chinese leaders did not perceive an increased threat from the United States. On January 9, during an interview with the American journalist Edgar Snow, Mao sounded relatively optimistic. In response to Snow's statement that a major war would not occur between China and the United States, Mao concurred, replying, "It may be that you are right."[131] He also noted Secretary of State Dean Rusk's comment that the United States would not escalate the war in South Vietnam to the North, thereby precluding the possibility of a direct US-China conflict.[132] At the same time, the CMC issued a directive instructing Chinese pilots to avoid direct engagements with aircraft from United States that entered into Chinese airspace.[133]

In February 1965, the Viet Cong attacked a US Army helicopter base at Pleiku in South Vietnam. The immediate US response was to conduct several bombing campaigns against the North. The strategic response was the decision to deploy combat forces, which began in early March, when two Marine battalions landed in Danang and would grow to over eighty thousand by June 1965.[134] Following the initial US deployment of combat troops, North Vietnam dispatched a delegation to Beijing to seek greater support from China. This request prompted China's top leaders to make a series of decisions about their involvement in the Vietnam War that offers an opportunity to examine how a significant increase in threat—the prospect that the war would escalate to China's border—influenced thinking on military strategy.

First, over the next few months, China agreed to provide Vietnam with military support. Although China did not provide the pilots that Vietnam requested, by June 1965 China began to dispatch air defense, engineering, logistics, and others troops to Vietnam. Between June 1965 and March 1968, China would send a total of 320,000 troops.[135]

Second, China decided to signal its resolve to the United States to deter any expansion of the war in Vietnam to China's border or within China. This started with "militant" articles in outlets like the *People's Daily*. In early April, while in Karachi, Zhou Enlai asked Pakistani President Ayub Khan to send a message to Washington. The essence of the message was that China would not initiate or provoke a conflict with the United States, but would fiercely resist "should the United States impose a war on China."[136] After Khan's trip to the United States was postponed in mid-April, China asked the British chargé d'affairs in Beijing to pass along the same message, which took place in Washington on June 2.[137] Mao also authorized a change in the rules of engagement after US intrusions in the airspace over Hainan Island on April 8 and 9, stating that China "should resolutely attack" such aircraft.[138] On April 12, the *People's Daily* carried a strongly worded editorial about the encounters consistent with this change.[139]

Third, Mao instructed that China undertake a domestic mobilization. As Mao had explained at the end of March, domestic mobilization "displays strength [*shiwei*] to the enemy, supports Vietnam, and promotes all aspects of our work."[140] Reflecting his preference for worst-case planning, Mao concluded that China "must prepare to fight this year, next year, the following year."[141] Even with the heightened level of threat and uncertainty about US escalation, Mao's comment that mobilization would help "all aspects of our work" also points to the domestic imperative behind his effort to change strategy. On April 12, a full meeting of the Politburo was held to discuss the mobilization. At the meeting, Deng Xiaoping stated that "the scope of the war could expand" to include Chinese territory along the border with Vietnam or even a larger scale limited war with the United States."[142] This period in early April likely represents the peak of Chinese concerns about US escalation. Nevertheless, China had not yet mobilized PLA units or localities to counter a potential US attack, unlike the preparations to counter a Nationalist attack in May and June 1962.

On April 12, the Central Committee issued instructions for strengthening war preparations. The document noted that the US expansion of the war in Vietnam "directly threatens our security" and that China "must prepare for the United States to bring the flames of war to our homeland." Reflecting the uncertainty over the future of the war that Deng had raised, the instructions also noted that China "must be prepared for a small, medium or even large war." They also highlighted China's vulnerability to aerial attacks and the need to defend major military facilities, industrial bases, transportation nodes, strategic areas (*yaodi*) and cities.[143] Ironically, the document echoed many of the reasons why Mao had pushed for the development of the third line a year earlier, when there was no imminent threat of the United States expanding the war.

Fourth, the PLA held an army-wide operations meeting, which lasted for about six weeks. In the early 1960s, the PLA convened such army-wide operations meetings every spring, in either March or April.[144] The purpose of this particular meeting was to discuss Mao's various instructions on military strategy since his June 1964 speech to "unify thinking" and then draft army-wide operations and combat readiness (*zhanbei*) plans.[145] As Luo Ruiqing recalled, "This operations meeting specifically discussed implementing the strategic guideline instructed by the chairman."[146] Although the discussion was no doubt colored by concerns about US escalation of the war in Vietnam, the meeting was not convened for this reason, and the question of how to respond to this contingency does not appear to have been its main focus. For example, when a document distributed during the meeting suggested that the United States would attack China through Guangxi province, which is adjacent to Vietnam, Luo criticized it for contradicting Mao's comment in June 1964 that the area of attack was uncertain and would not necessarily come from this direction.[147] The meeting also stated that although the PLA should be rooted in preparing for the worst case, China was not facing "imminent danger or in a desperate situation [*jiji kewei buke zhongri*]."[148]

In late April, senior military officers briefed Mao on the army-wide operations meeting. In his response, Mao emphasized themes that he had already introduced in 1964. On the one hand, he agreed with building three defensive layers and not allowing the "enemy" to "drive straight in," as in Germany's invasion of Russia. On the other hand, he also underscored the importance of not holding territory for "too long." For Mao, the only purpose of a fixed defense was to buy time to mobilize. Afterward, he said, "let him in, lure the enemy in deep and afterwards annihilate him." Mao also indicated that he did not believe that China faced an immediate threat from the United States. He described the United States as an "opportunist" and "not that adventurous," asserting that the United States had entered World War I and World War II only after other states had done most of the fighting.[149] The clear implication was that Mao did not believe a US attack on China was imminent.

The party leadership's instructions to the army-wide operations meeting were also consistent with Mao's views on strategy. On May 19, top party leaders attended the operations meeting, including Liu Shaoqi, Zhou Enlai, Zhu De, Lin Biao, and Deng Xiaoping. All issued instructions that did not reflect a concern about an immediate threat. The leaders noted that China should "prepare for an early war, a large-scale war and fighting enemies on all sides." Such preparations were viewed as key to delaying or even preventing a war because "as long as we are well prepared, enemies will not initiate conflicts easily." The leaders nevertheless cautioned against significantly increasing force levels, noting that "if we spend too many resources and too much effort on the military, national economic development will be affected."[150]

CONSOLIDATING LURING THE ENEMY IN DEEP

On June 7, the British chargé d'affairs in Beijing informed the foreign ministry that China's warning had been transmitted to Secretary of State Dean Rusk. Combined with US statements about limiting its combat operations to South Vietnam, the threat of expansion of the war in Vietnam had receded. Nevertheless, Mao continued to emphasize the change in China's military strategy he made a year earlier by underscoring the role of luring the enemy in deep over a fixed, forward defense.

The occasion for Mao's remarks was a debate over the appropriate force posture along the east coast during a meeting of party leaders in Hangzhou on June 16, 1965. The exchange itself indicated that the PLA had not yet "unified thought" on China's military strategy, despite Mao's previous instructions and remarks. Xu Shiyou, commander of the Nanjing Military Region, advocated for "completely resisting the enemy": defeating him on the coast and not allowing him to "come in."[151] Xu echoed the strategy of forward defense, which he had used to prepare to defend the region since the mid-1950s.[152] Mao responded by arguing for luring the enemy in deep, stating that "if you don't give the enemy a slight advantage, giving him a taste of victory, then that just won't do because he won't come in. He will only come in when you let him feel a taste of victory." He then suggested that China "prepare to give the enemy Shanghai, Suzhou, Nanjing, Huangshi, and Wuhan. This way our forces can spread out [*baikai*] and fight victoriously."[153]

Mao's remarks are revealing. First and foremost, by mid-June, the threat of conflict with the United States on China's border adjacent to Vietnam had abated. Zhou's warning to the United States had been delivered by the United Kingdom, allaying Chinese fears.[154] The United States indicated that it would not expand the war to North Vietnam or beyond. Mao emphasized luring the enemy in deep when the threat of conflict with the United States decreased. Moreover, he continued to push for luring in deep throughout the second half of 1965, which is consistent with the political logic outlined above but inconsistent with China's assessment of the situation it faced in Vietnam. Likewise, Mao's June remarks in Hangzhou contained no reference to the situation in Vietnam. Nor did Luo Ruiqing's summary of Mao's thinking on military strategy delivered a few weeks later.[155]

Second, Mao's emphasis on luring the enemy in deep revealed his desire for a decisive and total victory over the United States. Mao did not emphasize luring in deep because it provided a better way to defend China. He preferred luring in deep because it was the only way for China to fight a "war of annihilation" (jianmie zhan) that would produce a decisive victory, which would presumably enhance Mao's reputation at home and within the socialist bloc. Such an approach would also complement efforts to decentralize decision-making power and weaken the party's central bureaucracy. Mao believed that a protracted war inside China would create conditions for a decisive victory when compared with more limited operations to prevent the United States from seizing territory. As he noted, "I simply worry that the enemy won't come in and that he'll only fight a little on the border . . . the enemy can only be fought well when he is lured deep into home territory."[156] Later Mao was more explicit, noting that "you can't catch fish without bait."[157] He also partly contradicted himself by stating that if China prepared sufficiently for war, then the enemy would not attack. Nevertheless, he still preferred to prepare to fight a protracted war on Chinese territory that might hold the promise of a decisive victory versus more limited operations to prevent an enemy from seizing any territory.

Third, Mao preferred luring in deep because of the domestic political benefits for countering revisionism and continuing class struggle. For Mao, "if the enemy really will not come, that's actually a bad thing." He reasoned that, without an invasion, the masses would not gain any experience and "bad" elements in society would not be "differentiated [budao fenhua]," such as landlords, rich peasants, and counterrevolutionaries. Moreover, "the enemy will not be exposed"—by implication, Mao's domestic enemies and not China's foreign ones.[158]

The domestic political benefits of a strategy of luring the enemy in deep explains why strategic retreat was more important than stopping an invasion. Because preparing to lure the enemy in deep would further administrative decentralization from the center to localities, general war preparations would benefit Mao's goals of combating revisionism and promoting self-reliance. Decentralization would weaken the first-line leaders like Liu and Deng, whom Mao would attack directly when launching the Cultural Revolution a year later. For example, Mao called for including the "four bad elements" in any propaganda for war preparations, again indicating his concern with domestic class struggle and revisionism in his thinking about military strategy.

By the end of June 1965, the change in strategy was complete. On June 23, the Central Committee Secretariat asked Luo Ruiqing to give a speech summarizing Mao's comments and instructions on strategy over the past year.[159] The audience for the speech is unknown, but the role of the secretariat in asking Luo to deliver such a speech suggests that it was most likely for party leaders and not military ones.[160] As such, it suggests a desire to communicate Mao's ideas about military strategy within the party, not the PLA, and to integrate his disparate remarks on questions of strategy over the past year. That such a speech at all was necessary underscores the unconventional way in which the strategy was changed.

Luo started with Mao's speech at the Ming Tombs in June 1964 and ended with the June 1965 conversation between Mao and Xu Shiyou recounted above. In his own gloss, Luo stressed Mao's desire to focus on preparing to fight a "large-scale war" (dada), "quick war" (kuaida), and a war with nuclear weapons (da yuanzidan).[161] Invoking the spirit of the revolution, he also emphasized aspects of PLA operations during the civil war, such as people's war and concentrating superior forces to fight battles of annihilation. As Luo noted, "Guidelines, policies and principles that have been used effectively in the past must be continued." Yet, as Luo described, the focus of such preparations was to "prepare for the best and the worst" (zhunbei liangshou).[162]

On August 11, the Politburo Standing Committee held a meeting to discuss the new strategic guideline. Luo Ruiqing delivered a report on Lin Biao's instructions for implementing "Mao Zedong's strategic guideline of luring the enemy in deep."[163] At the meeting, Mao repeated that "we must lure the enemy in deep." Mao's reasoning was that "whoever lures the enemy in deep will annihilate the enemy." Moreover, if the enemy won some initial battles, they would be "jubilant," and more easily lured in deep. Mao repeated his view that the enemy needed to be "given a taste" of victory; otherwise it would not come in. He then called on the GSD to study what methods could be used bring the enemy in.[164]

Shortly thereafter, in early October 1965, Mao linked developing the third line with revisionism, specifically focusing on the "mini" third lines within coastal provinces. During a discussion of the Third Five-Year Plan and the third line with party leaders, Mao warned that "if revisionism appears within the party center, there should be a revolt [zaofan]." Furthermore, if the party center made major mistakes—"if a Khrushchev-like figure appears"—he underscored that "the mini third lines will be good for a revolt."[165] The link between combating revisionism and the self-reliance of localities, especially in military affairs, could not be clearer.

In November 1965, Mao repeated many of these themes. He stated that if war did occur, "[the provinces] cannot rely on the center and must be self-reliant." Furthermore, they must "resist the enemy for three months, then let the enemy come in, taste the sweetness, lure the enemy in deep, annihilate it, first annihilate a battalion, then a regiment and a division."[166] The following day, he repeated his view that "luring the enemy in deep is the best way to annihilate [the enemy]." He then outlined the different directions from which the United States might attack, including through the northeast, Tianjin, Qingdao, Lianyungang, and the Yangtze River.[167]

In January 1966, the GSD convened a small-scale operations meeting in Beijing. The purpose was to study how to implement Mao's instructions on strategy, along with revising and adjusting the five-year plan to develop fortifications (*shefang*).[168] The GSD outlined two layers into which the enemy could be lured. The first layer comprised Tianjin, Jinan, and Xuzhou along with the area around Shanghai, while the second layer included Beijing, Shijiazhuang, Zhengzhou, the northern foothills of the Dabie mountains, and the area east of Nanjing. The idea was to "greatly annihilate the enemy" in the plains of northern and central China, itself quite reminiscent of the operations in 1947 and 1948 in the Chinese civil war.[169]

The Soviet Threat and the Cultural Revolution

The intensification of the Soviet threat represented a key change in China's security environment. Starting in 1966, as Chinese-Soviet ties worsened, the number of Soviet divisions deployed along the border (and in Mongolia) began to increase. On March 2, 1969, PLA soldiers ambushed a Soviet patrol on the disputed Zhenbao (Damansky) Island in the Ussuri River, the first of three clashes that month. Afterward, Soviet forces began to probe different parts of the border with China, including a significant incursion in Xinjiang, and then leaked plans in August that it was considering a preemptive strike on China's nascent nuclear forces. China concluded that these actions constituted a precursor to an invasion, a belief bolstered by Moscow's 1968 intervention in Czechoslovakia and the Brezhnev doctrine of intervening in the affairs of socialist states.[170]

The threat of war with the Soviet Union created a new and pressing threat to China's security. In March 1969, Mao said China "must prepare for war," which was a major theme of the Ninth Party Congress convened the following month.[171] In 1970, Mao told the North Korean leader Kim Il Sung that the Soviet Union intended to occupy Chinese territory north of the Yellow River, a significant portion of the country.[172] Nevertheless, the new Soviet threat did not prompt China to change its military strategy. Instead, it doubled down on the approach of luring the enemy in deep from 1964. In April 1969, Mao said that, in a major war with the Soviets, China should "adopt the method [*zhanfa*] of luring the enemy in deep." Consistent with his earlier views, Mao stressed again that "I advocate giving up some places."[173] By August 1969, China began to reorient its defense planning around securing the regions adjacent to the Soviet Union or the "three norths." Part of these initial efforts included evacuation of key personnel from Beijing in the fall of 1969.[174]

China's main response to the Soviet threat was twofold. First, the size of the PLA increased significantly. During the year of 1969, the PLA grew to 6.31 million soldiers, exceeding its size at the height of the Korean War. The ground forces added three new army headquarters (*junbu*) and established or reconstituted thirty divisions. The air force added two army headquarters, eight air divisions, and two antiaircraft artillery divisions.[175] Forces were also added to the navy and specialized branches. Second, select units were redeployed from southern China near the border with North Vietnam to bolster the strategic reserve force in the center of the country that would be used in the case of a Soviet attack. In total, five armies (*jun*) along with four divisions of technical troops were moved.[176] In November 1969, for example, the Forty-Third Army then based in Guangxi province was transferred to Henan province.[177]

Even if China wanted to adopt a different strategy to counter the Soviet threat, however, the intensification and chaos of the Cultural Revolution and the split in the party leadership paralyzed the PLA. Although a detailed account of the PLA during the Cultural Revolution lies beyond the scope of this book, some of the main effects of party disunity on the PLA as a military organization and its operational readiness can summarized.[178]

First, many veteran commanders who held leadership positions in 1965 before the outbreak of the Cultural Revolution were persecuted, purged, or sidelined. These individuals served in the CMC, general departments, military regions, and military districts as well as in main force units. Thirty-seven of sixty-one PLA officers who were members or alternates of the Central Committee selected at the Eighth Party Congress in 1956 were "framed or persecuted."[179] Using a conservative methodology, a 1967 CIA study concluded that twenty-five to thirty percent of the PLA leadership had been removed, with much higher rates in the military regions and general departments.[180]

Second, the CMC became bloated as members of different factions were added to this body. The CMC selected in April 1969, for example, had forty-two members, ensuring that it would not be able to perform its task of overseeing military affairs. Such a large CMC was too unwieldy to be effective. During this period, executive bodies within the CMC also turned over several times.

Third, Mao decided to employ the PLA domestically in the Cultural Revolution. He began by asking the PLA in early 1967 to "support the left," which often placed local PLA units at odds with one or more rebel groups and only increased the violence that was breaking out. As violence peaked in mid-1967, Mao decided instead to use the PLA to implement a system of military control (*junguan*). Military control committees or groups were established and PLA officers were placed in key positions on revolutionary committees that were being formed to govern provinces and localities and often dominated these bodies. The PLA also assumed control of the basic institutions of local governance, such as grain storage, public security, and propaganda. Additionally, PLA units participated in industrial and agricultural production that had been disrupted by the ongoing upheaval. In total, between 1967 and 1972, more than 2.8 million soldiers were involved in these various domestic tasks, not traditional military duties.[181] The impact on operational readiness was clear. As one study concludes, more than seventy-three percent of combat units during this period "were engaged in activities of little or no military benefit."[182]

Fourth, military education and training largely stopped. At the start of the Cultural Revolution, Lin Biao's emphasis on "giving prominence to politics" dominated training in the PLA. According to one account, only one or two months within a twelve-month period were devoted to tactical military training, with the remainder being occupied by political training and activities within localities such as production or militia training.[183] One official history conludes that "military training paused [*tingdun*] for three years."[184] Following the intensification of the Soviet threat, training resumed but only partially. In the latter half of 1969, units focused on anti-tank tactics. In 1970, Mao instructed the PLA to engage in "camp and field training" (*yeying xunlian*) that would combine marches as long as one thousand kilometers with basic technical and tactical training.[185] Nevertheless, large-scale field exercises were not held, again at the expense of the PLA's readiness to meet the external threat China faced.

Conclusion

The strategic guideline adopted in 1964 represents an anomalous—yet fascinating—case of strategic change. It was an instance of what might be described as reverse or retrograde change, whereby an existing strategy was abandoned in favor of a previous one—in this case, the idea of "luring the enemy in deep," or strategic retreat. It was also the only change in strategy initiated not by senior military officers but instead by the top leader of the party, Mao Zedong. Although my argument cannot explain the direction or the mechanism of change, the case nevertheless illustrates how party disunity and leadership splits can distort strategic decision-making. In 1964, Mao pushed for a strategy of luring in deep not to enhance China's security but instead to attack party leaders whom he viewed as revisionists and a threat to China's revolution—efforts that would culminate with the launch of the Cultural Revolution two years later. Because of the party disunity of the Cultural Revolution, it would remain China's strategy until 1980, despite the threat of a Soviet invasion that emerged in 1969.

5

The 1980 Strategy: "Active Defense"

In September 1980, the General Staff Department (GSD) convened a month-long meeting of senior officers to discuss how to counter an attack by the Soviet Union. The meeting's purpose was to determine what principles should guide PLA operations during the initial phase of such a war. At the end of the meeting, the CMC approved a new strategic guideline known simply as "active defense." In contrast to the existing strategic guideline, which stressed luring the enemy in deep, the new strategy called for the PLA to resist a Soviet invasion and prevent a Soviet breakthrough using a forward defense anchored around positional warfare.

The adoption of the 1980 strategic guideline, which represents the second of the three major changes in China's military strategy, is puzzling. China had faced a clear military threat from the Soviet Union for over a decade. In 1966, the Soviet Union signed a defense treaty with Mongolia and began to increase the number of troops deployed along China's northern border. Following the March 1969 clash between Chinese and Soviet forces at Zhenbao (Damansky) Island, the Soviet threat continued to grow, with fifty divisions facing China by 1979. Nevertheless, despite this threat, China did not adopt a new military strategy until 1980. The onset of the Soviet military threat alone did not prompt China to change its military strategy.

Apart from the Soviet threat, two other factors are central to understanding when, why, and how China changed its military strategy in 1980. First, an important motivation was an assessment of a significant shift in the conduct of warfare that would characterize Soviet operations in an invasion of China. This assessment was based on observations of the 1973 Arab-Israeli War, in which clients of the United States and the Soviet Union employed advanced weapons in new ways. PLA strategists such as Su Yu and Song Shilun, among others, believed that a significant shift in the conduct of warfare had occurred that would place China in an even more disadvantageous position should conflict erupt with the Soviet Union. The content of the 1980 strategic guideline reflected an effort to counter a Soviet threat that would be characterized by new ways of warfare.

Second, a split at the highest levels of the CCP prevented the PLA from responding to the Soviet threat. Throughout the Cultural Revolution, the CCP elite was fractured, as different groups competed for power. After Mao Zedong's death in 1976, the party lacked a clear consensus on the structure of authority. Hua Guofeng, who was anointed as Mao's successor months before Mao's death, held the top positions in the party, state, and military. After Deng Xiaoping returned to work in 1977, he would spend the next few years displacing Hua and consolidating his position as China's paramount leader. After party unity was restored, the PLA was able to pursue a major change in strategy.

The adoption of the 1980 strategic guideline is illuminating for several reasons. Previously, Western analysts have often described China's strategy during this period as "people's war under modern conditions," which implies continuity with Maoist approaches.[1] Although some senior officers used this phrase in their speeches, it was not part of the formulation of the new strategy. Instead, it only reflected the view that any war with the Soviet Union on China's territory would be a protracted one, given the gap in Soviet and Chinese capabilities. The phrase did not describe how such a war would be waged or what forces would be required. Following the death of Mao, references to people's war also likely maintained superficial ideological continuity, despite the significant changes in operations in the new guideline that rejected Mao's idea of luring the enemy in deep.

The examination of the 1980 strategic guideline also clarifies the relationship between China's military strategy and the "strategic transformation" in army building that was announced along with the reduction of one million soldiers in 1985. The strategic transformation did not signal the adoption of a new military strategy. Instead, it refers to Deng Xiaoping's judgment that China would not face a total war for one or two decades and thus could shift from a "war footing" posture to peacetime military modernization. Moreover, the 1985 force reduction represents the continuation of downsizings in 1980 and 1982 to improve the quality and effectiveness of the force under the 1980 strategy. The strategic transformation did not outline what kind of wars the PLA should prepare to fight or how it should prepare to fight them.

This chapter unfolds in seven parts. The first section demonstrates that the strategic guideline adopted in 1980 represents a major change in China's military strategy. The next section shows that senior military officers perceived a significant shift in the conduct of warfare, which served as the external stimulus for the adoption of a new strategy in addition to the Soviet threat. As the third section demonstrates, however, the PLA's high command could only act on these shifts in the conduct of warfare once political unity after Mao's death had been restored following Deng's consolidation of political power in 1979 and 1980. The next two sections examine the adoption and implementation of the new strategy, while the final two sections review the 1985 downsizing and adoption of the 1988 strategic guideline.

"Active Defense"

The strategic guideline adopted during the September 1980 meeting of senior officers represents the second major change in China's military strategy since 1949. The 1980 guideline, known simply as "active defense," outlined a strategy to counter a Soviet invasion and prevent a strategic breakthrough. It represented a clear rejection of the existing strategy from the mid-1960s based on luring the enemy in deep and strategic retreat. Instead, similar to the 1956 strategy, the 1980 strategic guideline envisioned a forward defense that would be based on positional warfare and supplemented by small-scale mobile warfare. Such a strategy required that the PLA develop the ability to conduct combined arms operations to coordinate tank, artillery, and infantry units, deployed in a layered defensive network of fixed positions.

OVERVIEW OF THE 1980 STRATEGY

In the 1980 strategic guideline, the "basis of preparations for military struggle" was a surprise attack by the Soviet Union. The primary strategic direction was China's northern border, also known as the "three norths" or the area from Heilongjiang province in the east to Xinjiang in the west.[2] Following the 1969 clash with the Soviets over Zhenbao Island, the situation on China's northern border deteriorated, raising the prospect of a major war with Moscow.[3] Although the major Soviet attack that China's leaders had feared in the fall of 1969 did not occur, the Soviet military threat grew throughout the decade. By 1979, the number of Soviet divisions along China's northern border had increased from thirty-one to fifty.[4] Concerns about Soviet intentions intensified when Moscow signed a defense treaty with Vietnam in November 1978 and invaded Afghanistan in December 1979. Chinese strategists believed that a Soviet attack would involve tank columns conducting rapid, deep strikes, along with airborne operations in rear areas, to seek a swift and decisive victory.[5]

The 1980 strategy was a strategy of strategic defense. It described how China would respond once the Soviet Union had invaded. The core of the 1980 strategy was a forward defense of China's northern border, especially potential invasion routes through Zhangjiakou or Jiayuguan, to prevent any strategic breakthrough and buy time for a nationwide mobilization. Afterward, the strategy called for combining the defense of strategic interior lines with offensive campaigns and operations on exterior lines to create a stalemate. Finally, if the effective strength of the invading force was sufficiently weakened, the PLA would shift to a strategic counterattack.[6] Although the new strategy altered how China would respond to an invasion, it remained based on waging a protracted war with the Soviet Union. A forward defense, rather than retreat, was viewed as key to victory in such a conflict.

The 1980 strategy excluded preempting a Soviet attack. The PLA lacked any credible means to launch strikes beyond its borders. Consistent with the principle of "gaining control by striking afterwards" or counterattacking (*houfa zhiren*), China would use force only after a Soviet invasion had started. In the initial phase, the role of offensive operations would be limited to small-scale mobile operations from fixed positions, especially along Soviet flanks. Once a strategic stalemate had occurred, offensive operations would play a central role in expelling the invading force. The role of nuclear weapons, which China now possessed, was also limited to defensive uses. Despite the potential of using nuclear weapons as a form of "invasion insurance," China's strategy envisioned their use only in response to a nuclear attack on China, including the use of tactical nuclear weapons by the Soviets. Although China researched the neutron bomb in the early 1980s, it did not ultimately decide to develop and deploy such weapons, nor did it alter its approach to nuclear weapons under the 1980 strategic guideline.[7]

OPERATIONAL DOCTRINE

A key component of any strategic guideline is the identification of the "form of operations" that the PLA should be prepared to conduct in the future. In contrast to the centrality of mobile and guerrilla warfare in luring the enemy in deep, the 1980 strategy identified positional warfare as the main form of operations for the PLA or "positional warfare of fixed defense" (*jianshou fangyu de zhendizhan*).[8] By rejecting luring in deep as the basis for China's strategy, senior military officers downplayed the role of mobile warfare at the strategic level. Instead, the 1980 guideline envisioned creating a layered, in-depth network of defensive positions, each of which an invader would need to destroy.

The "basic guiding thought for operations" was the way in which positional, mobile, and guerrilla warfare would be combined. In the initial phase of a war, positional warfare would occur in forward areas between China's main population areas and its international frontiers. The new strategic guideline limited the role of mobile warfare to small and medium-sized offensive operations close to the defensive positions that the PLA would try to hold. Nevertheless, the main goal of the strategy was to resist a Soviet attack as long as possible, to create a stalemate and buy time to mobilize forces.[9] Guerrilla warfare would be limited to those areas that China would be unable to defend in the initial phase of a war, such as parts of Xinjiang.

Successful positional warfare required developing combined arms capabilities for both defensive and offensive operations. Although the 1956 strategic guideline envisioned creating such a capability, this goal was never achieved because of Mao's decision to pursue luring the enemy in deep and its emphasis on the dispersion of forces and independent operations. China's 1979 invasion of Vietnam revealed the PLA's inability to conduct combined arms operations, even though the war itself was not a primary factor in the adoption of the new strategy.[10] To develop such a capability, the PLA started to draft the "third generation" of combat regulations in 1982, which were finished in 1987.[11] Similarly, the drafting of the *Science of Campaigns Outline*, the PLA's first text on the operational level of war, restarted in the early 1980s and was published in 1987, along with the first edition of the *Science of Military Strategy*.[12]

FORCE STRUCTURE

The 1980 strategic guideline required China to develop a more nimble and effective force. When the strategy was adopted, the PLA had roughly six million soldiers. As early as 1975, Deng Xiaoping as chief of the general staff had criticized the PLA as "bloated" because of the rapid growth in the number of officers and noncombat troops in the late 1960s. Following the adoption of the 1980 strategic guideline, three major force reductions were undertaken to improve the flexibility of command and overall effectiveness of the force while also reducing the defense burden on a national economy now focused on reform and opening. The first two reductions occurred in 1980 and 1982, in which roughly two million soldiers were cut. Planning for the third reduction of one million troops began in early 1984 and was announced in June 1985, bringing the total size of the force to 3.2 million when it was completed in 1987.[13] The 1985 reduction was part of a much broader reorganization of the force, including the consolidation of eleven military regions into seven and the transformation of thirty-five armies into twenty-four combined arms group armies in addition to the reduction and streamlining of headquarters and command departments.[14]

Changes in force structure were also pursued to enhance the PLA's ability to conduct combined arms operations. One of the topics discussed at the 1980 seminar to adopt the new strategic guideline was the importance of creating a "combined force" (*hecheng jundui*) that would be able to conduct combined arms operations. The PLA decided to experiment with transforming armies into combined arms group armies composed of infantry, artillery, tank, rocket, and antiaircraft artillery units. These would be used as a mobile reserve force (*yubei dui*) that would be deployed in the direction of the Soviet attack to prevent a breakthrough. In early 1981, the CMC decided to form two units on a trial basis.[15] Pilot units were created in 1983 and by 1985 all armies (*jun*) had been converted into combined arms group armies as part of the 1985 force reduction.

TRAINING

All aspects of education and training changed under the 1980 strategic guideline. In October 1980, the general departments issued a sweeping plan to reopen and revitalize military academies, which had ceased to function effectively during the Cultural Revolution and were ill suited to training soldiers to conduct the complex military operations that the new strategy required.[16] In November 1980, the PLA held an army-wide training meeting, which identified "coordinated operations" (*xietong zuozhan*)— essentially combined arms operations—as the focus for future training of the force.[17] In February 1981, the GSD issued a new training program that provided a new framework for all aspects of training, with an emphasis on combined arms operations.[18]

Along with changes to education, the PLA increased the scope and tempo of military exercises. The renewed emphasis on exercises and training was symbolized by an exercise held in the Beijing Military Region in September 1981. Dubbed the "802" meeting, it represented the PLA's largest exercise since 1949 and involved more than 110,000 troops from eight divisions. The purpose was to explore defensive operations during the initial phase of a Soviet invasion and thereby "concretize the strategic guideline."[19] Afterward, other military regions as well as the services began to hold larger and more realistic exercises, in stark contrast to the 1970s, when small-scale exercises were held sporadically, if at all, reflecting a much higher degree of professionalism with the force.

The 1973 Arab-Israeli War and the Conduct of Warfare

Throughout the 1970s, China faced a clear and growing threat from the Soviets, but did not alter its military strategy of luring the enemy in deep for a decade. Nevertheless, by the mid-1970s, senior PLA officers began to reconsider China's approach for countering the Soviet threat and to advocate for changing China's military strategy. These assessments were based on shifts in the conduct of warfare that were seen as characterizing how the Soviets would fight, especially the increased speed and lethality of modern military operations involving armored forces and airpower.

SU YU'S CRITIQUES OF LURING THE ENEMY IN DEEP

Su Yu, the chief of staff from the 1950s, was the earliest and most prominent advocate for changing China's strategy. In 1972, after the death of Lin Biao, Su Yu had returned from working in the State Council on government affairs to serve as the commissar and party secretary of the Academy of Military Science (AMS). Su was worried. From his perspective, the PLA in the Cultural Revolution had failed to study how to fight future wars and ignored foreign technological developments that would influence warfighting. Instead, as Su's biography notes, "it was as if the abstract slogan of people's war could solve all problems."[20] In a series of reports to party and military leaders, Su assessed China's military strategy and critiqued the focus on luring the enemy in deep.

Su spent almost a year drafting his initial report on how China should fight a future war. Drafting was difficult, as he held many views that were "obviously different from dominant views within the party and army."[21] Entitled "Operational Guidance in Future Anti-Aggression Wars," Su submitted the report to Mao Zedong, Zhou Enlai, and Ye Jianying in February 1973.[22] A second report, "Several Issues in Future Anti-Aggression Wars," was given to top party leaders and the CMC in late December 1974 and subsequently distributed to all Politburo members in Beijing in January 1975.[23] Because these reports were authored by a senior officer with Su's prestige and authority on strategy, and distributed at the highest levels in the party and the PLA, they offer insight into changing views of the conduct of warfare.

The 1973 report contained the basic ideas that Su would develop throughout the rest of the decade. The clear implication is that the PLA's existing strategy was ill suited to the threat that China faced from the Soviet Union, which was characterized by vast armored forces with unprecedented firepower and mobility along with air power. Although Su Yu blamed Lin Biao for the PLA's current shortcomings, he was really critiquing Mao's 1964 strategic guideline, which Lin had implemented.[24] Su argued that China's troops were too dispersed, which would weaken their effectiveness, strength, and ability to conduct maneuver operations, placing China in a passive position.[25] More controversially, he questioned the primacy of mobile warfare by suggesting that some cities and key strategic points (*yaodian*) "must be resolutely defended tenaciously" and that even "some must be defended to the death [*sishou*]."[26] Su stressed that "there should be sufficient understanding" of the importance of positional defensive operations, which relied on fixed fortifications to blunt assaults.[27] He also challenged luring the enemy in deep by highlighting the importance of operations on open plains and around transportation nodes, rather than just retreating to mountainous areas. Specifically, he suggested that such operations would require an in-depth deployment of forces (*zongshen peizhi*) along with the construction of anti-tank obstacles and improved use of artillery to destroy invading armored forces. He also underscored the importance of denying the Soviets air control by strengthening China's air defenses.

By 1975, Su Yu believed a fundamental shift in the conduct of warfare had occurred. In a lecture on anti-tank warfare, Su stated that "future wars will be unlike those" against Japan, the Nationalists, or the United States.[28] He stressed that the Soviet Union's advanced weaponry, especially its tanks and armored vehicles, could not be destroyed using the PLA's traditional methods of "gouging eyes" (throwing grenades through sight openings) and "cutting ears" (crawling on tanks to remove the antenna).[29] Although not always explicit, Su's concern was not just with Soviet intentions, but rather the Soviet Union's advanced weaponry and new operational methods.

For military professionals around the world, the 1973 Arab-Israeli War marked a turning point in modern military operations. A key question is whether this conflict influenced China's assessments of the Soviet military threat, given the prominence of Soviet weaponry and tactics in the Egyptian and Syrian armed forces. When the 1973 Arab-Israeli War occurred, the PLA's research institutes were only beginning to resume normal operations.[30] Documents from the period are extremely limited. Nevertheless, available sources suggest that the war informed China's assessments of the Soviet threat.

In January 1974, the GSD dispatched a delegation to Egypt and Syria to study the conflict. The seven-person delegation was headed by Ma Suzheng, the deputy commander of the engineering corps, and spent two weeks in the region as guests of the Egyptian and Syrian militaries. When the delegation returned in February, Ma briefed the leadership of the general departments and authored a report on the war. He noted that anti-tank and antiair operations were the "main defining features of the conflict" and "the tactics of the two sides basically reflected the operational thought of the Soviet Union and United States."[31] Importantly, he stressed, "the experience and lessons of the October War were beneficial for our army's preparation for war against foreign aggression."[32] Ma's report, along with materials on the war from the Egyptian and Syrian militaries, were approved for wide distribution within the PLA, "attracting attention from leaders at all levels."[33]

Ma's report and related materials almost certainly informed Su Yu's analysis. Su's reports are consistent with the characteristics of this conflict, especially the focus on the speed and lethality of armored assaults, the role of anti-tank weapons, and the importance of achieving or denying air superiority. These same features of the 1973 war were highlighted in a 1975 article in the *Liberation Army Daily*, which also suggests that the lessons of the war were widely discussed within the PLA. The article notes that the war was characterized by the use of multiple offensives to achieve frontal breakthroughs, the role of large numbers of tanks in these offensives, the effectiveness of anti-tank weapons, the struggle for air superiority and the success of Egypt's air defenses, the use of US and Soviet weaponry, and the rapid consumption or expenditure of equipment.[34]

THE 1977 STRATEGIC GUIDELINE

Despite Su's reports, China did not change its military strategy. In fact, during a rare plenary meeting (*quanti huiyi*) of the CMC held in December 1977, the CMC instead affirmed and formalized Mao's strategy from the mid-1960s, calling it "active defense, luring the enemy in deep." This plenary meeting was the first meeting of the PLA high command after the death of Mao and arrest of the Gang of Four, following the election of a new CMC at the Eleventh Party Congress in August 1977. At the meeting, Ye Jianying, CMC vice-chairman in charge of daily affairs, called for "carrying out Chairman Mao's strategic thought and completing war preparations." Ye repeated the basic tenets of Mao's strategy, affirming that "the basic method is annihilating the enemy through movement [*zai yundong zhong*]," that the strategic guideline was "active defense, luring the enemy in deep," and to "be rooted in fighting an early, major and nuclear war."[35]

Nevertheless, some senior military officers did call for a change in strategy. At the 1977 plenary meeting, Song Shilun, the president of AMS, argued that luring the enemy in deep should be dropped as part of China's strategic guideline, stating it was "inadvisable."[36] In January 1978, Su Yu submitted a report to Xu Xiangqian, head of the CMC's strategy commission, that also rejected a strategy based on luring in deep and outlined a strategy of forward defense.[37] Su highlighted the importance of building fortifications, using strategic reserves to conduct counterattacks, and increasing the importance of positional warfare. His report, discussed in more detail below, was then circulated to the CMC vice-chairmen, including Deng Xiaoping, and within the GSD.

The 1977 plenary meeting most likely maintained luring the enemy in deep as a temporary measure. Senior military officers understood the need to rebuild an armed force that had been ravaged by the Cultural Revolution. Although Mao had changed China's strategy to luring in deep in 1964, it had never been adopted formally by the PLA. Thus, as Ye Jianying noted at the plenary meeting, one imperative for the PLA after the Cultural Revolution was "to unify operational thought," a prerequisite for consolidating and rebuilding the force as a whole.[38] By emphasizing Mao and the existing strategy, Ye invoked a leader whom all in the PLA could support and attributed the PLA's deficiencies to Lin Biao and the Gang of Four.[39] Similarly, as Deng said at the meeting, "without a clear strategic guideline, many matters cannot be handled well."[40] For these reasons, one general recalls that the 1977 strategic guideline "played an important role in promoting army-building and war preparations after the smashing of the Gang of Four."[41] Raising the question of changing military strategy so soon after Mao's death would have invited broader reexamination of his legacy that the party and the PLA were not yet ready to undertake, especially given the divisions among the top party leaders over the structure of authority. Mao also still enjoyed a great deal of admiration among the PLA's grassroots, who joined the force during the Cultural Revolution.

CONSENSUS BUILDS FOR CHANGE AMONG THE HIGH COMMAND

In early 1978, Su Yu continued his challenge of luring the enemy in deep. His 1978 report to Xu Xiangqian, discussed above, was entitled "Several Opinions on Strategy and Tactics in the Initial Phase of a War."[42] Su observed that "whether the initial phase of the war is fought well will have a significant relationship on the development of the entire course of the war."[43] He then stressed the importance of identifying key defensive points (*fangshou yaodian*) and increasing the size of the reserve forces in the center of the country. Again challenging the existing strategy, he believed that "the initial phase of future wars will be different when compared with many past wars."[44] For example, "the proportion of defensive positions [*zhendi shoubei*] should be increased and our army's positional warfare capability must be raised" to resist waves of armored and artillery attacks.[45] Foreshadowing a focus on combined arms, Su called for infantry, armored, engineering, and air forces as well as the militias to create a "tight anti-tank firepower network [*huowang*]" with long, medium and short ranges.[46]

In April 1978, Su Yu repeated similar themes in a lecture at AMS.[47] Given the speed and range of the Soviet Union's heavy weapons, Su concluded that "our operational methods, ways, and means must also change and even must be transformed."[48] The PLA needed to employ more troops in defensive operations, limit mobile operations at the start of the war to supporting defensive operations, and avoid decisive battles in which the poorly equipped PLA forces would suffer heavy losses. In the civil war, Su said, "we generally used mobile defense," but this required gradual retreats that would now require abandoning cities that he believed should be defended to the death, given their importance for China's ability to mobilize its population for a longer war. Su grounded his arguments in shifts in the conduct of warfare, and repeatedly referred to "the rapid development of modern science and technology and its extensive use in the military." For Su, this "inevitably will lead to changes and even a transformation in operational methods, raising a new series of problems for war preparations [*zhanzheng zhunbei*]."[49]

Su Yu's challenge to China's existing strategy gained much wider exposure in January 1979, when he was invited to lecture at the PLA's Military Academy and the CCP's Central Party School. He examined "solving operational problems under modern conditions," or how to deal with the Soviet threat based on the shifts in the conduct of warfare.[50] Importantly, he delivered his talk shortly before China's invasion of Vietnam the following month. Although China's poor performance in this conflict may have created an additional impetus for military reforms, Su's views on shifts in the conduct of warfare as a reason to change strategy were formed well before China's invasion and whatever lessons might have been learned on the battlefield.[51]

He began with the observation that advances in science and technology heralded a new stage in the development of weapons, equipment, and war-fighting methods. According to Su, "these changes challenge some of our army's traditional operational arts and urgently demand that our army develop our strategy and tactics." Otherwise, "as soon as the enemy launches a large-scale war of aggression, we may not be able to adapt to the requirements of the circumstances of the war and may even pay much too high a price."[52] The Soviet and US militaries were dominated by heavy weapons that were "armored, fast, powerful, and long range." For this reason, Su argued, "the destructive power and lethality of modern conventional weapons are unmatched in the past," and would play a key role in warfare especially in a war with its northern neighbor.[53] As he quipped, "Even if you make a lot of noise using bullets and grenades against tanks, you cannot destroy the tanks."[54]

For China, the main challenge in a war with the Soviet Union would be countering a surprise attack. Soviet military theory viewed the opening phase of the war as decisive, determining whether a rapid victory could be achieved.[55] Soviet advantages in weaponry would allow them to rapidly strike China's strategic political, economic, and military centers, and thus paralyze China's "defensive system" and destroy its ability to resist. The key issue was "resisting the first few waves of the enemy's strategic surprise attack" while maintaining the PLA's effective strength and avoiding concentrating forces and decisive battles.[56]

Su's answer, consistent with his previous writings, contradicted the existing strategy by emphasizing positional warfare over mobile warfare. As Su said, "An important difference with the past is that positional defensive warfare has clearly grown in importance."[57] Mobile warfare should be restricted to areas near fixed positions and medium-sized battles in prepared positions behind the front line. "Under modern warfare conditions," he said, "at the beginning of the war, the main feature of the form of operations will be positional operations [zhendi de zuozhan] and operations not far from these positions."[58] Although mobile warfare had been the mainstay of PLA offensive campaigns in the Korean War, he stated that it emphasized mobility without taking rear areas into consideration that would now be critical in mobilizing the nation. As Su noted, "In the past, we would attack if we could win, and flee if we could not, but now whether or not we can win or lose, there is a still a problem whether or not we can get away." Thus, "if we copy that way of fighting from the revolution, it would not be pragmatic."[59] Instead, "the situation of future wars of anti-aggression was different" because China would need to defend key forti-fications (*zhongdian shefang*) and garrison areas, including key cities, islands and coastal areas as well as other strategic areas.[60] Although some areas could be abandoned, others the PLA must "defend to the death." For Su, some cities not only needed to be held, but also could be used like Stalingrad as an opportunity to weaken the enemy.

Su Yu's speech received a great deal of publicity. A Xinhua reporter attended the meeting and introduced its basic ideas to a wider audience.[61] The GSD organized staff to listen to recordings of the lecture. By March, seventy percent of cadres in the GSD had heard the speech.[62] The lecture was published in an internal AMS journal, *Military Arts*, in March 1979 and then in the widely circulated *Liberation Army Daily* newspaper on May 15, 1979, sparking vigor-ous debate and discussion.[63] The CMC also instructed that Su's speech be distributed as required reading for all senior cadre in the army, which indicated high-level approval of the contents of his lecture.[64]

That summer and fall, many senior officers publicly endorsed Su's ideas and called for a new strategy. In October 1979, for example, Xu Xiangqian, one of the PLA's ten marshals, published a lengthy article on defense modern-ization in *Red Flag*, a publication under the Central Committee, that linked changes in the conduct of warfare with questions of strategy. Xu noted how the application of new technologies to military affairs was "causing great changes in weaponry and equipment." Furthermore, "these changes will inevitably lead to corresponding changes in operational methods." For Xu, "modern warfare is very different from any war in the past." In a war with the Soviet Union, for example, "the target of attack, scale of war, and even method of fighting are something we have not encountered before. We must study and solve a number of new prob-lems according to these new conditions." Rejecting Maoist ideas, Xu said that "if we view and command a modern war with the old vision of the 1930s and the 1940s, we are bound to be rebuffed and suffer great hardships in a future war."[65] The clear implication of Xu's remarks was that China needed a new strategy.

Over the following year, *Military Arts* published articles supporting Su's position, including many by senior officers.[66] In November 1979, for example, Yang Dezhi endorsed Su Yu's ideas about the importance of defensive opera-tions and positional warfare. Yang would replace Deng Xiaoping as chief of the general staff in March 1980. Yang observed that the CMC had already deter-mined China's strategic guideline, but acknowledged that issues remained regarding "how to better understand and implement the guideline"—a not so subtle way of saying that the guideline should be revised. More bluntly, he said the core issue was whether to "resist the enemy's strategic breakthrough" or "carry out luring the enemy in deep."[67] He then argued for emphasizing positional warfare and for improving coordination among the services and combat arms as the key to success.[68]

Many commentaries on Su's speech in *Military Arts* used the 1973 Arab-Israeli War as an important example. In a January 1980 speech at AMS, for example, Song Shilun repeatedly referred to the 1973 war when describing the characteristics of modern warfare, such as the high consumption of weaponry and the importance of strategic surprise.[69] Similarly, when commenting on how to revise a draft of the *Science of Campaigns* in August 1980, Song instructed that researchers at AMS should "appropriately borrow from the campaign operational experience of foreign armies, especially the operational experience of the Fourth Middle East War."[70] The *Science of Campaigns* was to serve as a guide for how to conduct campaigns and thus should "strive to reflect operational characteristics under modern conditions."[71]

The 1973 Arab-Israeli War had also become an important reference point for training. A report from the Shenyang Military Region in late 1978, for example, notes that the war was used as the main case study (*zhanli*) for anti-tank operations.[72] In 1979, the war featured prominently in anti-tank training in the Beijing Military Region.[73] In 1981, a study group at an army in the Nanjing Military Region was established to study surprise attacks in the opening phase of a war. The group used three books, including one entitled *The Fourth Middle East War*.[74] Most likely, similar study groups were formed in other military regions. Likewise, in 1985, AMS published a translation of a Japanese study of the Arab-Israeli wars. The preface written by AMS stated that "in the history of warfare to this day, the Fourth Middle East War is the one war that prominently reflects modern characteristics."[75]

The Deng-Hua Power Struggle and Restoration of Party Unity

Although senior PLA officers recognized by 1978 that China needed to change its military strategy, a new strategic guideline was not adopted until October 1980. The main obstacle was the disunity in the highest levels of the party, created by the politics of the Cultural Revolution, that continued even after the death of Mao Zedong in 1976. The restoration of party unity required that a new consensus be reached on the structure of power and authority within the party, which was achieved when Deng Xiaoping defeated Hua Guofeng in a struggle to become China's top leader.

FRAGMENTATION AT THE TOP

When Mao Zedong died in September 1976, four contending elite groups or factions existed. The "leftists" were radicals unleashed by Mao to rectify revisionism he believed had taken root in the party, who controlled propaganda and education, among other areas. The most prominent members of this group were the so-called "Gang of Four," although they had not always operated as a unitary group in the Cultural Revolution.[76] The "beneficiaries" were those party elites whose careers had prospered during the upheaval of the Cultural Revolution and found themselves in elevated positions of power after more senior leaders were persecuted. The veteran "survivors" included those older members of the party who largely avoided being purged, either because they had been protected by Mao or Zhou or because they successfully navigated the ever-changing politics of the time. Waiting in the wings, however, was a fourth group: the "victims" or members of the old guard who held senior positions before 1966 and had then been persecuted. These individuals were often associated with more pragmatic and less radical policies before the Cultural Revolution and had held important positions in the party, state, and military. They most likely resented the beneficiaries, who often occupied posts that they had vacated, but also possessed the bureaucratic skills and extensive connections within the party that would be needed to rebuild the country when the Cultural Revolution ended.[77]

To varying degrees, the Cultural Revolution created divisions within the party, state, and military. When Zhou Enlai died, the position of premier of the State Council became vacant for the first time since 1949. Mao appointed Hua Guofeng, a beneficiary, to replace Zhou because a leftist would have lacked support from other senior leaders. As first vice-premier throughout 1975, Deng Xiaoping would have been Zhou's logical successor. Deng, however, had fallen out of favor with Mao at the end of 1975 and would be stripped again of his positions in April 1976. When Hua became premier, he was also named as the first vice-chairman of the CCP, indicating that he had become Mao's chosen successor.[78]

When Mao died in September 1976, the positions of party chairman and CMC chairman became vacant. An alliance formed between veteran survivors, led by Ye Jianying, and the beneficiaries, such as Hua Guofeng. Following a series of moves by the Gang of Four to consolidate power immediately after Mao's death, the leading survivors and beneficiaries agreed to the arrest of the "gang" and their key supporters, thus rejecting a radical vision for the future of the party and eliminating one group contending for power.[79] The Politburo named Hua as the chairman of both the CCP and the CMC. Hua thus became the first political leader since 1949 to hold the top positions in the party, state, and military.

Hua's formal titles, however, exceeded his informal authority and status within the party. After the arrest of the Gang of Four, the Politburo Standing Committee had only two members: Hua (chair) and Ye Jianying (vice-chairman). A new Politburo Standing Committee would need to be formed, which required convening a party congress. When the Eleventh Party Congress was finally held in August 1977, almost a year later, new leadership bodies were formed but they reflected an unstable balance among beneficiaries, survivors, and victims. Hua remained chairman of the CCP and thus chairman of the Politburo Standing Committee. Wang Dongxing, another beneficiary who played an instrumental role in the arrest of the gang, was named as vice-chairman of the party in addition to running the powerful central office of the CCP. Two survivors joined the new Politburo Standing Committee: Ye Jianying, who had been in charge of the PLA's daily affairs, and Li Xiannian, one of Zhou Enlai's economic advisors. The final member, Deng Xiaoping, represented the aspirations of the many victims.

Deng's return to work in 1977 required delicate negotiations between the beneficiaries and veteran survivors. Wang Dongxing and Wu De, the mayor of Beijing and another beneficiary, opposed Deng's return. But many others supported it, especially given the need to address widely acknowledged problems in the military. Deng wrote in a disingenuous letter in May 1977 that he accepted Hua's leadership of the party.[80] In July 1977, Deng assumed all the positions he had held in 1975—vice-chairman of the party, vice-chairman of the CMC, vice-premier, and chief of the general staff. By resuming positions in all three pillars of power, Deng also posed a clear threat to Hua Guofeng. The disunity within the highest levels of the party was reflected in the official ranking of Politburo members: Hua a beneficiary ranked first, Ye a survivor second, and Deng a victim third.[81]

Although the top party leadership remained divided, the new CMC formed after the Eleventh Party Congress was more favorable to Deng than any other leader. Hua remained chairman, with Ye Jianying, Deng Xiaoping, Liu Bocheng, Xu Xiangqian, and Nie Rongzhen as vice-chairmen. All but Hua were military professionals who had been involved in the PLA's modernization since the 1950s. The nucleus of the new CMC was its standing committee (*changwei*), which had eight members and would serve as the CMC's principal decision-making body. Only one member of this committee, Wang Dongxing, had strong ties to Hua.[82] The new CMC also had forty-three additional members, including the leadership of the three general departments, services and branches, military regions, and other units under the CMC. Thus, the CMC, like the PLA itself, was both bloated and fragmented, unable to take quick or resolute decisions.

DENG'S CONSOLIDATION OF POWER

Starting August 1977, Deng waged a steady campaign to consolidate power within the CCP. Following the arrest of the Gang of Four, the struggle for power occurred mainly between the beneficiaries around Hua Guofeng and the return of victims around Deng. In addition, within the lower ranks of the party and military, many beneficiaries and leftists remained, both of which could be mobilized by top party leaders and underscored the fragility at the top of the party. In this contest, Hua had two advantages. He held the top positions in the three institutional pillars of power, while also having been blessed by Mao with legitimacy as the chairman's chosen successor.[83] Hua's status as Mao's successor, however, also linked him to any reevaluation of the Cultural Revolution, which would touch on Mao's responsibility for what had occurred.[84] Deng ranked lower in the party, state, and military hierarchies, but nevertheless held senior positions in each, along with years of experience at the highest levels of policymaking from the founding of the PRC, which Hua lacked. Deng was especially powerful within the PLA, not just because of his historical ties with many of the top leaders on the CMC, but also by serving as a vice-chairman of the CMC and as chief of the general staff. Deng represented the aspirations of many others, inside and outside the military, who had been persecuted by the leftists and resented the beneficiaries.

As new research on Chinese elite politics demonstrates, the contest between Deng and Hua did not reflect underlying differences over policy or ideology. Deng and Hua surprisingly agreed on many policy issues, especially economic ones.[85] Where they likely disagreed would concern the future of the party, the evaluation of the Cultural Revolution, and, most important, the structure of power at the top of the party.[86] The struggle between Hua and Deng will not be recounted in detail here.[87] For the purposes of explaining major change in China's military strategy, the most important element of the struggle was the outcome—namely, the consolidation of authority and restoration of unity within the party under one leader, Deng Xiaoping.

Deng consolidated power over the next year and a half, roughly in two phases. In the first phase, which culminated in the Third Plenum of the Eleventh Party Congress in December 1978, Hua Guofeng and other beneficiaries were significantly weakened. As Joseph Torigian shows in exciting new research, Deng exploited Hua's political vulnerability as Mao's successor by promoting a debate over "practice is the sole criterion for judging truth," which questioned the utility of Maoist ideas under the slogan of the "two whatevers."* As Torigian concludes, "Deng had artificially manufactured an ideological debate he could turn into a political debate."[88] By the fall of 1978, most provinces and key military units had all expressed support for Deng's position on "seeking truth."[89]

The turning point in Hua's weakening occurred at a central work conference that was held in November 1978. The purpose of the conference was to discuss economic policy that would be ratified at the Third Plenum the following month. Nevertheless, almost as soon as the conference started, participants quickly changed the agenda to discuss reversing the verdicts of victims of the

---

* They were: "Resolutely uphold whatever policy decisions Chairman Mao made, and unswervingly follow whatever instructions Chairman Mao gave."

Cultural Revolution as well as those who had been implicated in the April 5, 1976, "Tiananmen Incident" that Hua had so far refused to reverse.[90] Although not the first to speak out, the most senior member of the party to raise these issues early in the meeting was Chen Yun, who called for the rehabilitation of veteran party members who had been criticized (including himself).

Chen Yun insisted that the reversal of verdicts must be addressed before tackling policy issues such as the economy. In the end, Hua Guofeng acceded to the demands Chen and others raised on reversing verdicts and adding victim-ized revolutionaries to the Politburo.[91] Many of Hua's supporters, such as Wang Dongxing, Wu De, Chen Xilian, and Ji Dengkui, performed self-criticisms for maintaining "leftist" positions associated with the Cultural Revolution. When the Third Plenum was held in mid-December, it confirmed the reversal of verdicts, placing more supporters of Deng on the Politburo. Wang Dongxing was removed from his positions as party vice-chairman and as director of the Central Committee's general office. Chen Yun replaced Wang as party vice-chairman and also joined the Politburo Standing Committee.

By this time, Deng had begun to exercise the authority of a paramount leader. Deng altered work assignments for those on the Politburo and Politburo Standing Committee, actions normally reserved for the party chairman, such as Hua.[92] Even before the work conference had started, Deng oversaw the negotia-tions for the normalization of diplomatic relations with the United States and pushed for a punitive attack on Vietnam in February 1979 for Hanoi's alignment with Moscow and invasion of Cambodia.[93] Previously, only Mao (or Zhou with Mao's approval) would have handled high-level diplomatic negotiations or decisions regarding the use of force. Hua Guofeng played little or no role in these decisions.

After the Third Plenum, Deng continued to consolidate power in the party, state, and military. In November 1979, the Central Committee approved the CMC's establishment of an "office meeting" (bangong huiyi) that would be responsible for managing daily affairs.[94] This executive body was packed with Deng supporters.[95] In January 1980, more Deng loyalists were added to the CMC Standing Committee.[96] Between January and April 1980, the leadership of several military regions was reshuffled. Commanders in all but two of the eleven military regions were replaced. In many cases, the reshuffling occurred because existing commanders were tapped for promotion into higher positions.[97] Like other major leadership changes within the PLA's military regions, however, the rotation of commanders may have also been intended to prevent the "moun-taintops" or factions that arise when one commander serves in the same region for a long period of time. The reshuffling allowed for the promotion of younger commanders—a long-standing goal of Deng's. Many of those promoted had also been persecuted during the Cultural Revolution and none of them had strong ties with Hua Guofeng. Finally, the ability to execute the reshuffling was also a sign of Deng's consolidation of power within the PLA.[98] No evidence exists that Hua was involved in these changes.

Deng's consolidation of power within the military presaged his move against Hua Guofeng in the party and state bureaucracies. At the Fifth Plenum, in February 1980, four members of the Politburo Standing Committee close to Hua Guofeng were removed, while Zhao Ziyang and Hu Yaobang were added.[†] The balance on the standing committee now favored Deng. Hu Yaobang was named as general secretary of the CCP, which placed him in charge of party affairs. Zhao Ziyang assumed responsibility for the daily work of the State Council and would officially replace Hua Guofeng as premier in August.[99] Although Hua would remain party chairman and CMC chairman for a few more months, he had been effectively sidelined from the party and state bureaucracies. In December, at a series of Politburo meetings, Hua relinquished these last two positions, a decision that would be formalized at the Sixth Plenum in June 1981.[100]

Adoption of the 1980 Strategic Guideline

This restoration of party unity created conditions for changing China's military strategy. By the end of 1979, a consensus had emerged on the need to resist a Soviet invasion through a forward defense and not a strategic retreat. Now, the PLA's leadership could act on that consensus. The decision to formulate a new strategic guideline was made in the spring and summer of 1980 and the new strategy was adopted in October 1980. The decision to adopt the new strategy demonstrates how senior military officers led the process of strategic change.

THE DECISION TO CHANGE STRATEGY

The move to change strategy began when Deng Xiaoping decided to step down as chief of the general staff in early 1980 to focus on economic and party affairs. Yang Dezhi, the commander of the Kunming Military Region who had led Chinese forces on the Kunming front in China's 1979 invasion of Vietnam, replaced Deng. By this point, most members of the CMC along with the leadership of the three general departments could be described as "modernizers" focused on military affairs and not politics. Within the GSD, Yang Dezhi's deputies were Yang Yong, Zhang Zhen, Wu Xiuquan, He Zhengwen, Liu Huaqing, and Chi Haotian.

Yang's first task as chief of the general staff was to develop a plan to streamline and reorganize (*jingjian zhengbian*) the force. This had been raised at the

---

[†] They were those who issued self-criticisms in late 1978: Wang Dongxing, Wu De, Chen Xilian, and Ji Dengkui.

1975 enlarged meeting of the CMC, but only limited progress was achieved following Deng's removal from office in 1976 and continued divisions within the party and PLA. Although 800,000 troops had been cut by the end of 1976, mostly from the ground forces, the size of the PLA grew again in the late 1970s, reaching 6,024,000 in 1979.[101] Streamlining and reorganization became the focus of an enlarged meeting of the CMC held in March 1980, as discussed in more detail below.

Yang's second task was to formalize the consensus around China's military strategy, specifically the PLA's "operational guiding thought" during the initial phase of a war with the Soviet Union. The first downsizing would need to be informed by an overarching vision for how the PLA should be organized and the operations that it would be required to execute. More important, a gap formed between the emerging consensus following the open publication of Su Yu's 1979 lecture and the existing strategic guideline of "active defense, luring the enemy in deep." Su's emphasis on positional warfare contradicted the concept of strategic retreat in the existing strategy. If the PLA was going to emphasize positional warfare, the CMC would need to revise the strategic guideline. The speed with which Su's ideas were embraced by the high command after his 1979 speech and the gap with the existing guideline indicated the need to "unify thought" (*tongyi sixiang*) on strategy and operations.

Several military regions had already started to implement Su Yu's ideas even though the strategic guideline had not yet been changed. In October 1979, for example, the Shenyang Military Region conducted a division-level exercise of positional defensive operations under nuclear conditions that was consistent with a greater emphasis on defending fixed positions following an initial attack.[102] In March 1980, the Shenyang Military Region held a training session that used Su's speech as the basis for evaluating the region's objectives and training plans.[103] In March 1980, the GSD and Wuhan Military Region instructed the 127th Division to conduct pilot training to improve coordination (*xietong*) to strengthen positional defense against an attacking enemy—the very kind of operations that Su had urged the PLA to emphasize.[104]

Shortly after replacing Deng, Yang Dezhi chaired several meetings to discuss the international situation and the PLA's operational guiding thought in a war with the Soviet Union. Based on these discussions, Yang proposed to the CMC on May 3 that the GSD convene a seminar (*yanjiuban*) for senior officers on operations in the initial period of an "anti-aggression" war.[105] As he would later note, such a seminar for top officers was unprecedented.[106] The purpose of the meeting was to raise the "strategic awareness" (*zhanlue yishi*) of senior officers and discuss how to respond strategically to a Soviet attack.[107] The broader goal was to change the strategic guideline, as the PLA could not answer the question of how it should respond to a Soviet attack without describing what kind of military strategy China should have. To maintain secrecy, the seminar was codenamed the "801" meeting.[108]

The CMC agreed with Yang Dezhi's proposal and placed him in charge of a leading small group to organize the seminar. Zhang Zhen served as head of the group's office and was put in charge of day-to-day planning. Yang and his deputies agreed that the first issue to decide was the "correct expression" (*zhengque biaoshu*) of the strategic guideline "to unify the thinking of the whole army."[109] The purpose of the seminar would be to discuss how to change China's military strategy in the context of a war with the Soviet Union. In describing the work of the leading small group, for example, Zhang Zhen refers on multiple occasions to revising the guideline.[110]

In the beginning of June, Yang Dezhi and Yang Yong, the first deputy chief of the general staff, spent one month conducting an inspection tour of Inner Mongolia, the Hexi Corridor and Helan Mountains, all different areas that would be on the frontline in any war with the Soviets. The trip's purpose was to inspect the combat readiness training, defensive fortifications, and terrain where an invasion might occur. Underscoring the importance of the trip, they were accompanied by leaders of the Beijing and Lanzhou Military Regions.[111] As Yang Dezhi would say several months later, "We discovered many problems."[112] As shown in map 5.1, three potential Soviet invasion routes had been identified in the early 1970s.[113] The route from Erenhot to Beijing through Zhangjiakou was the shortest and most threatening.

In the middle of June, Zhang Zhen began to prepare a series of lectures that would form a core part of the seminar. These lectures involved leaders from fifteen units and departments to study how to employ the services and branches in the initial phase of a war. Topics included how a breakthrough in a campaign could evolve into a strategic breakthrough, the coordination among the services and branches, command automation, electronic countermeasures, air defenses, and wartime mobilization, among others. Lectures also covered the operational characteristics of World War II and "several wars that recently occurred in the world," presumably including the 1973 Arab-Israeli war.[114] To avoid "empty talk," all speakers held practice lectures (*shijiang*) that the small group supervised.[115]

By the middle of August, preparations for the seminar were complete. At some point during this process, the leading small group decided that the strategic guideline should be changed and that "luring the enemy in deep" should be removed as part of the formula or expression of the guideline. Zhang Zhen, for example, recalls discussions with Yang Dezhi and Yang Yong in which they agreed on how to change the guideline, though he does not state exactly when these conversations occurred.[116] The leading small group solicited the opinions on changing the strategic guideline from the CMC's strategy commission and

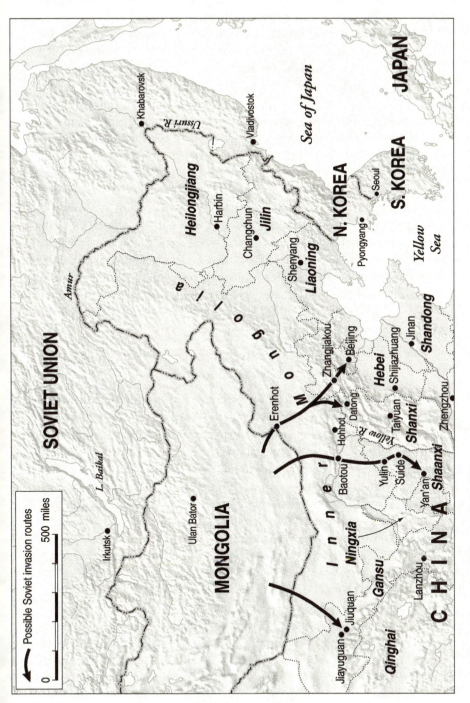

MAP 5.1. The northern strategic direction in the 1980 strategy

"relevant leading cadre."[117] According to Zhang Zhen, "Everyone favored [*qing-xiangyu*] making a partial adjustment to the strategic guideline."[118]

Between mid-August and the start of the seminar on September 17, the leading small group consulted with the old marshals and vice-chairmen of the CMC to seek their approval for the change in strategy. Nie Rongzhen, Ye Jian-ying, and Xu Xiangqian all agreed with the proposed revision of the guideline, pending CMC approval.[119] On September 30, the leading small group briefed Deng Xiaoping, who "clearly affirmed our views" and stated that he wanted to address the seminar.[120] The CMC approved the change in the guideline during the seminar.[121]

On September 9, Song Shilun, the president of AMS, sent a letter to Ye Jianying, one of the CMC's vice-chairmen. Song argued forcefully for dropping luring in deep from the strategic guideline because "it cannot be a strategic guideline to unify the overall war situation." Instead, it "can only be a kind of operational method under certain conditions, in certain strategic or campaign directions in a certain period of time."[122] The relationship between Song's letter and the deliberations of the leading small group is unclear.[123] Nevertheless, the old marshals endorsed Song's letter, and they agreed that luring the enemy in deep should be dropped from China's strategic guideline, as the leading small group had proposed.[124]

THE "801" MEETING

The army-wide senior officer's seminar on defensive operations, or the "801" meeting, began on September 17 and lasted for one month. More than one hundred senior officers gathered at the Jingxi Hotel in Beijing, including from the CMC, general departments, military regions, services, branches, and other departments.[125] The rostrum included the CMC secretary Geng Biao, Yang Dezhi, the GSD's leadership, and the CMC's advisors (*guwen*). The purpose of the meeting was to focus on global strategic trends, the assessment of a foreign invasion, the strategic guideline, operational guiding thought, and the PLA's strategic tasks (*zhanlue renwu*) in the initial phase of the war.[126]

In his opening remarks, Yang acknowledged how party disunity had ham-pered the development of military strategy. "Regarding operational thought," he said, "the interference and destruction of Lin Biao and the Gang of Four cannot be underestimated. Therefore, for a long period of time, conditions have not existed to unify operational thought."[127] Yang outlined the goals of the meetings as "studying and researching operational issues in the initial phase of an anti-aggression war, deepening understanding of the CMC's strategic guideline, unifying operational thought, and further implementing all combat readiness work [*zhanbei gongzuo*]."[128] Later in the seminar, Yang Dezhi gave another speech in which he outlined the central role that positional warfare should play in China's new strategy and operations for dealing with a Soviet invasion.[129]

At the time, open criticism of Mao, especially on military affairs, remained sensitive. When the seminar was held, the party had not yet reached its official judgment of Mao, which would be contained in the June 1981 resolution on party history. Toward this end, AMS under Song Shilun's direction attempted to gather all statements made by Mao on luring the enemy in deep. Song concluded that even when Mao had used the term, most of the time it was in the context of campaigns and tactics, not at the strategic level. The only time it was used at the strategic level, apart from in the mid-1960s, was during the Red Army period in the 1930s.[130] Therefore, Song and others argued that dropping luring the enemy in deep as a strategic concept was not inconsistent with much of what Mao had said, thereby creating ideological space for rejecting the existing strategy based on one of Mao's foundational ideas. Moreover, Song cleverly argued that the concept of active defense included the idea of luring the enemy in deep at the operational level.[131] These ideological gymnastics supported the abandonment of strategic retreat in favor of positional warfare.

At the conclusion of the seminar, Deng Xiaoping and Ye Jianying addressed the participants to endorse the change in strategy. In his straightforward style, Deng said, "For our future anti-aggression war, what guideline should we adopt after all? I approve these four characters—'active defense.'"[132] Ye Jianying concurred, "During this discussion everyone advocates for 'active defense' . . . I agree with everyone's opinion."[133] Yang Dezhi summarized what the meeting had accomplished. For him, it "basically unified understanding of the CMC's strategic guideline, further clarified strategic guiding thought and strategic tasks in initial phase of a future war, [improved] understanding of the situation of the services and branches, and strengthened the concept of combined operations [hecheng zuozhan]."[134] In other words, it changed China's military strategy.

Shifts in the conduct of warfare featured prominently in discussions at the seminar. According to one account, the participants concluded that "today's war is completely different from yesterday's war."[135] Moreover, "the adversary in future war was changing, weapons and equipment and ways of war [zhanzheng fangshi] were changing, making people dumbfounded."[136]

In his remarks at the end of the seminar, Ye Jianying underscored the role of shifts in the conduct of warfare. He told the participants that "our military thought must develop with changes in warfare." Specifically, "fighting conventional wars will be different than in the past." For Ye, "when a battle starts in the future, the enemy may come together from the sky, land and sea; the difference between front and rear is small. This will be an unprecedented three-dimensional war [liti zhan], combined war [hetong zhan], and total war [zongti zhan]." He then drew on the example of the 1973 Arab-Israeli War to illustrate how the conduct of warfare had changed and the challenge that now China faced:

When Egypt fought Israel in the Middle East war, in addition to air combat, it was mainly fighting tanks and tanks countering tanks. Ground operations had to deal with the enemy's airborne and helicopter landings. This is not the same as how we used to fight. As for us, many aspects are also different from the past, with more special forces and heavy weapons and equipment, which is not the same as the past millet plus rifles. As the force becomes more modern, it also relies more on logistics and the organization of logistics expands. These changes between the enemy and ourselves inevitably create new problems and characteristics in future wars.[137]

From an operational perspective, these shifts in the conduct of warfare indicated that the Soviet Union would be able to conduct deep and rapid strikes. If China did not try to stop, delay, or slow these strikes, the results would be devastating. Beijing, for example, was only about 380 miles from China's border with Mongolia. Moreover, strategic retreat would likely require relinquishing these urban areas without a fight. Top officers agreed that, under these conditions, failure to resist a Soviet attack would have dire consequences. The Soviets would either be able to achieve a rapid victory if not resisted or, in a larger war, it would be able to seize cities and other industrial areas that would not only weaken national morale but also degrade China's war potential and ability to mobilize to counterattack. Song Shilun went even further, noting that luring the enemy in deep was inconsistent with development in the types of wars since World War II. For Song, these included limited wars to seize some territory, proxy wars, and wars of quick decision (*suda sujue*). As Song wrote, "Luring the enemy in deep is not appropriate for all types of wars," as a strategic retreat in a limited war effectively allowed the enemy to achieve its war aims without fighting or paying a price.[138]

The 1980 strategic guideline is also associated with a shift in China's naval strategy from "near-coast defense" (or coastal defense) to "near-seas defense" (*jinhai fangyu*, or offshore defense). Under the former, the PLAN focused on deterring or preventing an amphibious assault and securing the Chinese coast. With the latter, however, the purpose was broader—to also defend the waters adjacent to China. Deng Xiaoping raised the prospect of such a change in April 1979, when, in a meeting with PLAN Commander Ye Fei, Deng stressed "near-seas operations."[139] In July 1979, Deng told the PLAN's party committee that "our strategy is near-seas operations [*jinhai zuozhan*]." Deng's main concern was countering the "powerful navy" of a hegemon, presumably the Soviet Union.[140] In this way, the extension of the PLAN's area of operations was consistent with pursuing a forward defense along the land border. When discussing the PLAN's streamlining and reorganization as part of the 1982 downsizing (discussed below), the CMC stated that the requirements of "near-seas defense" should guide the PLAN's reorganization, which perhaps marks the first time that the term describing the new strategy was used.[141]

In August 1982, Liu Huaqing, then a deputy chief of the general staff, replaced Ye Fei as PLAN commander. Beginning in 1983, Liu started to flesh out the content of near-seas defense as the PLAN's service strategy. The near seas are the seas adjacent to China's coast, including the Yellow, East China, and South China Seas and the waters east of Taiwan. In January 1986, the PLAN's party committee adopted a naval strategy under the slogan of "active defense, near-seas defense," demonstrating a clear link to the 1980 strategy.[142] The next month, Liu Huaqing and the PLAN commissar submitted a report to the CMC requesting permission to adopt a naval strategy of near-seas defense.[143] In Liu's vision, near-seas defense emphasized realizing Taiwan's unification, defending territorial sovereignty and maritime rights and interests, and deterring attacks from the sea. Key tasks in wartime would be coordinating with the army and air force to defend China against attacks from the sea and to protect sea-lines of communication. These tasks required being able to seize and retain command of the sea for a period of time, to control sea routes connected with the near seas, and even to be able to fight in adjacent waters.[144] As Bernard Cole has observed, much of what Liu outlined was aspirational at the time, but Liu's legacy played an important role in the 1990s and 2000s with the shift in China's overall military strategy from total wars to local wars.[145]

A RESPONSE TO POOR PERFORMANCE IN 1979?

Was the 1980 strategy adopted in response to the PLA's poor performance in its February 1979 invasion of Vietnam? China invaded Vietnam to punish Hanoi for its November 1978 defense treaty with the Soviet Union and then Vietnam's December 1978 invasion of Cambodia. China also sought to signal its resolve to resist the Soviet Union, who had deployed fifty divisions along China's northern border. China's military objective was to seize several provincial capitals and communications nodes, especially Lang Son, in order to demonstrate China's ability to occupy Hanoi. Afterward, China would withdraw.[146]

The invasion began on February 17, 1979. China mobilized between 330,000 and 400,000 soldiers from nine armies (*jun*) against 50,000 to 150,000 Vietnamese soldiers.[147] China did achieve its military objectives when it seized Lang Son on March 4 and then announced its intent to withdraw its forces, which was completed on March 16. Despite possessing a significant numerical advantage, China paid a high price for these limited gains, with 7,915 killed and another 23,298 wounded.[148] Moreover, Chinese forces advanced much more slowly than they had anticipated. Lang Son is only fifteen to twenty kilometers from the border but required sixteen days to capture. Thus, the invasion revealed significant deficiencies in the PLA's combat effectiveness when compared with its last major offensive operations in the Korean War against an even stronger adversary.[149] The reasons for the PLA's poor performance have been described elsewhere, but they include poor leadership and coordination at the tactical level created by the large numbers of new soldiers and cadres with little or no military training along with the organizational upheaval of expanding units to bring them to full strength in a short period of time.[150] More generally, the PLA's poor performance reflected the decline in readiness and training during the Cultural Revolution, when the PLA focused on garrison duties, local governance, and sideline production, as described in the previous chapter.

However, China's poor performance in the war was not a primary factor in the decision to adopt a new military strategy in October 1980. First, although the PLA high command may have hoped that sheer numerical superiority would have produced a rapid victory in 1979, they were well aware of the PLA's many problems. In June 1975, Deng had described the PLA as "swollen, scattered, arrogant, extravagant, and lazy."[151] In December 1977, the CMC affirmed Mao's "active defense, luring the enemy in deep" to stabilize the force internally in the aftermath of the Cultural Revolution while restarting military training. Even the invasion itself was postponed for a month after the PLA leadership conducted an inspection tour that uncovered significant deficiencies.[152] The commander of Chinese forces on the western front, Yang Dezhi, would even be promoted to replace Deng as the chief of staff a year later. Nevertheless, the force may have performed even more poorly than senior military officers had expected, and, in this way, the war may have further emphasized the importance of improving the quality of the force that was part of the 1980 strategy, especially the emphasis on military training.

Second, senior military officers advocated for China to change its military strategy well before the February 1979 invasion. As described earlier, Su Yu and Song Shilun both pushed to change China's strategy during and after the December 1977 CMC meeting that reaffirmed luring in deep. Su Yu's now famous lecture on how to deal with a Soviet invasion was delivered in early January 1979, a month before the invasion. More than any other single event, the content of Su's lecture played a clear and direct role in the content of the 1980 strategy. The lecture summarized arguments and ideas that he had developed over the past five years and was not a response to how the PLA might perform in the pending attack.

Third, available sources on the adoption of the 1980 strategy contain few references to the PLA's poor performance in 1979. The senior officer seminar in September and October 1980 focused on how to counter what was the greatest threat to China (a Soviet attack), how such an attack would occur, how China should respond, and whether luring the enemy in deep remained the best approach. The 1979 war may have been discussed, but does not appear to have been prominent. Planning and preparations for the meeting from May to August 1980 also contain no references to the war in available sources. The PLA did conduct a critical self-assessment of its performance, but it appears to have focused on tactical proficiency and political work.[153]

Finally, the 1979 invasion was not the type of conflict that might prompt the PLA to reconsider its approach to defending against an invasion by a much stronger enemy. From China's point of view, the 1979 invasion was a limited war, intended to teach Vietnam "a lesson." Many of the challenges the PLA encountered in the war were exacerbated by the requirements of conducting large-scale offensive operations that had not been executed for decades. The goal of the new strategy, however, was to slow or halt an invasion. If anything, Vietnam's defense against the invasion may have been more enlightening for the PLA as it considered the Soviet threat.

Implementation of the New Strategy

The PLA began to implement the new strategy almost immediately. New combat regulations and a campaign outline were drafted, three million troops were cut and the force reorganized, and military education and training were revitalized. The implementation of the 1980 strategic guideline not only underscores that it constituted a major change in China's military strategy, but also that the organizational changes to implement the strategy were consistent with the factors that prompted the change in the first place—a significant shift in the conduct of warfare, amid concerns about the Soviet threat.

OPERATIONAL DOCTRINE

Consistent with a major change in strategy, the PLA initiated substantial revisions to its operational doctrine. In 1982, the PLA began to draft the "third generation" of combat regulations. The previous generation of combat regulations had been issued on only a trial basis between 1975 and 1979 and had taken almost a decade to write due to the Cultural Revolution. As one Chinese military scholar describes, "The content of the [second generation] combat regulations 'gave prominence to politics.' "[154] The drafting of the third generation of combat regulations, therefore, constituted "a restoration period," given the absence of operational doctrine during the Cultural Revolution.[155] In an effort to improve standardization of operational doctrine, the CMC established a review group headed by Han Huaizhi, a deputy chief of staff, to examine the regulations for combined arms and infantry operations along with the *Science of Campaigns Outline* (*zhanyixue gangyao*) that AMS was drafting.[156]

More than thirty regulations were issued as part of the third generation of combat regulations. These included general regulations along with sixteen regulations for the ground forces, ten for the navy, five for the air force, and four for the rocket force. For the first time, they bore the signature of the CMC chairman, indicating the importance attached to their promulgation.[157] The *Liberation Army Daily* described the new regulations as "correctly implementing the CMC's strategic guideline of active defense" and "absorbing the experiences of recent local wars in the world and our counterattack in self-defense against Vietnam."[158] At the level of strategic guidance, an authoritative textbook notes that these regulations reflected the shift from luring in deep to active defense, or the 1980 strategic guideline.[159]

Importantly, following the lessons of the 1973 Arab-Israeli War, these new combat regulations were also the first to stress the operational level of war. New regulations were drafted for combined arms operations for ground forces and related branches and for the services. Infantry regulations were issued in 1985 and combined arms regulations were issued in 1987. As part of the combat regulations, the CMC also approved the promulgation of the PLA's first campaign-level document, the *Science of Campaigns Outline*.[160] One source describes this as "carrying legal status" (*daiyou faguixing*), placing it on par with the combat regulations.[161] Song Shilun began drafting the document in the early 1960s at AMS, as part of the 1956 strategic guideline, but it was delayed repeatedly by the Cultural Revolution. Although drafting restarted in 1976, Song appears to have jettisoned that draft after the Third Plenum, suggesting that it was too heavily influenced by the politics of the Cultural Revolution.[162] Song restarted the revision process again in August 1980, focusing specifically on basic campaign principles and, especially, combined arms operations.[163] He completed a preliminary draft in November 1981 and distributed it to units and military academies for comment. The CMC approved the campaign outline in 1986, which the GSD distributed in August 1987.[164]

Finally, the PLA published its first *Science of Military Strategy*. This book provided the first comprehensive account of China's military strategy and outlined in detail how China planned to resist a Soviet invasion.[165] Although the book was not published until 1987, drafting began in 1982, again supervised by Song Shilun at AMS.[166] Following the general spirit of the concept of active defense, the book divided a war with the Soviets into three phases that still reflected Mao's approach to total war. The first stage is the strategic defense, where the initial surprise attack by an opponent is countered using a combination of offensive and defensive operations to blunt the force of the attack. Positional warfare was key at this stage. The second stage is the strategic counterattack, where offensive operations are launched once the enemy's offensive has been stalled. The third and final stage is the strategic offensive once the enemy has been weakened and conditions have been created for a decisive battle to end the war.[167]

FORCE STRUCTURE

Implementation of the new strategy required a significant reduction in the size of the force. Reducing the size of the PLA had been featured prominently in the June 1975 enlarged meeting of the CMC that symbolized Deng's initial return to power before the end of the Cultural Revolution.[168] Yet, because of continuing party disunity, the 1975 downsizing fell far short of its original goal, cutting only thirteen percent of the force and not twenty-six, as originally planned.[169] Amid the struggle for power between Deng and Hua and China's 1979 invasion of Vietnam, the force grew again. By 1980, the PLA had more than six million soldiers, erasing all the gains of the previous downsizing.[170] Almost half of these soldiers were noncombat troops working in headquarters or logistic or support units, along with a surplus of officers.[171]

To create a more effective and modern force as envisioned in the new strategy, the PLA engaged in three force reductions, described as "streamlining and reorganizing" (*jingjian zhengbian*), in 1980, 1982, and 1985. By 1987, the size of the PLA had been halved, to roughly 3.2 million soldiers. As the 1985 downsizing is associated with Deng Xiaoping's assessment that the probability of a major war had declined significantly, enabling a "strategic transformation" from a war footing to peacetime modernization, it will be discussed separately. Nevertheless, it represents the continuation and culmination of efforts to reorganize the force that began in 1980.

Although the new strategy was a key element in the decision to reduce the force, other factors influenced the decision. Deng's reform and opening policy required reducing the defense burden on the budget. In 1979, defense expenditures accounted for 17.4 percent of government spending.[172] Economic reforms and the shift from plan to market would not succeed if defense spending was not also reduced.

The 1980 downsizing was first raised during a meeting of the CMC's standing committee in March 1980. As Deng stated, "One of our greatest problems is that the army is obese [*yongzhong*]." The bloated force not only put great pressure on the national budget, but also reduced effectiveness by preventing flexibility in command. In 1979, for example, the Ninety-Third Regiment had five deputy commanders and seven or eight deputy chiefs of staff.[173] Deng concluded that "it will be impossible to increase combat power efficiency without trimming the fat [*xiaozhong*]."[174] The CMC concurred, noting that "the current system of the military's structure and establishment [*tizhi bianzhi*] was not suited to the requirement of modern operations."[175] Therefore, "reforms must be carried out."[176]

Although planning for the 1980 downsizing started before the 1980 strategic guideline had been formally approved, its goals were consistent with the rationale for changing strategy. The main reason was to create a more capable and modern force, based on the view that China's current force and command structure was ill suited for fighting a more powerful adversary that could conduct rapid and deep strikes on Chinese territory.[177] By July 1980, the CMC approved the GSD's plan, which was published in August, and called for cutting 1.5 million soldiers by "streamlining administration [*jiguan*], decreasing the personnel quota, and reducing support and noncombat personnel."[178] The CMC instructed the GSD to start the downsizing in the fourth quarter of 1980 and basically complete it by the end of 1981. Noncombat personnel included internal security forces, railway and engineering troops, logistics and support units, communications units, and units in the three general departments and directly under the CMC. Combat units were also targeted by dividing infantry divisions into full-strength and reduced-strength units, which could be expanded in wartime. To promote modernization, the reduction in cadres also sought to promote talented younger officers.[179]

The 1980 reduction did not achieve its goal, but a significant reduction occurred in a short period of time. Overall, 830,000 soldiers were cut from the force, reducing it to 5,189,000.[180] Among the three general departments and other units under the CMC, 45,200 or 13.8 percent of personnel were cut. This included significant reductions to the GSD (46.45 percent), GPD (14.86 percent), and GLD (25 percent), as well as units such as AMS and the CMC's general office.[181] The ground forces shrunk by 17.6 percent, while the navy and the air force were cut by 8.5 and 6.4 percent, respectively.[182] Finally, the railway corps and engineering corps were cut by 48 percent (200,000) and 30 percent (156,000).[183] The PLA's share of the national budget fell from 17.4 percent in 1979 to 14.8 percent in 1981.

In late 1981, planning began for the second round of reforms, which mirrored structural reforms (*tizhi gaige*) of the party and state bureaucracies. The goal was to increase the efficiency and effectiveness of the organization while also mobilizing funds to pursue the "four modernizations" and economic development. In November 1981, the GSD requested permission from the CMC to form a "structural reform, downsizing and restructuring" leading small group, which was established in February 1982 and included leaders from all three general departments.[184] The CMC asked the GSD itself to develop a plan for reforming the three general departments to "destroy temples, move Buddhas, and reduce personnel."[185] This round of downsizing focused on the organization of combat forces to improve combined arms operations and operational effectiveness, such as the proportion of soldiers among the three services, the number of divisions in the ground forces, the establishment (*shezhi*) of the provincial and subprovincial military districts, the size of the academies, and the organization (*jianzhi*) of the engineering corps, among other topics.[186]

On September 16, 1982, the CMC announced the new force reduction plan. The main principles were "reforming the structure and organization, strengthening centralized and unified command, reducing numbers, raising quality, and improving combat effectiveness."[187] When completed at the end of 1983, the PLA was reduced by almost one million soldiers to 4,238,000, focusing on three areas.[188] First, the branches were reorganized. When the armored, artillery and engineering corps were formed in the early 1950s, they were placed directly under the CMC, not the GSD, to facilitate their development as new branches. However, this structure hindered the integration of the force and the development of combined arms operations. Thus, the armored, artillery, and engineering corps leadership offices were downsized and placed as departments under the GSD. Corresponding units in the military regions were downsized and placed under the headquarters of each military region and under army leadership.[189] Second, the three general departments were also reduced significantly, primarily by eliminating or merging bureaus and departments. The GSD shrunk by another 19.6 percent, while the GDP and GLD were cut a further 20.4 and 19.2 percent, respectively.[190] Third, the remainder of the railway corps was transferred to the Ministry of Railways, while the basic engineering units were transferred to local governments, civilianizing parts of the force.[191] Overall, the reductions included eliminating five military region-level units, twenty-one army-level units, and twenty-eight division-level units along with eight corps-level departments, four army-level departments, and 161 division-level departments.[192] Units within the headquarters, political departments and logistics departments of each military region were merged.[193] The military's share of the national budget fell to 10.6 percent by 1984.

Two other important changes to force structure occurred at this time. First, the CMC decided to reinstitute a system of military ranks within the PLA (that had been abolished in 1965). Although the process would not be completed until 1987, it was linked with planning for the 1982 downsizing.[194] Second, the PLA began to transform China's ground forces from armies (*jun*) to combined arms group armies (*hecheng jituanjun*). The CMC first discussed creating such units in 1980. In March 1981, Deng Xiaoping approved the creation of two experimental combined arms group armies, one each in the Beijing and Shenyang Military Regions.[195] Deng again expressed his support for the shift to combined arms at the "802" meeting in September 1981 discussed below, calling on the PLA to "strive to achieve the operational capability for combat arms coordination under modern conditions."[196] In September 1982, the Beijing and Shenyang Military Regions began to plan the formation of these experimental units, which began in 1983.[197] The two units chosen were the Thirty-Eighth Army in the Beijing Military Region and the Thirty-Ninth Army in the Shenyang Military Region.

In addition, the discussions held during this time proposed other potentially far-reaching reforms. Although they were not ultimately pursued, they reflect the focus on improving efficiency and effectiveness through reorganization of the PLA. The first was the creation of a joint logistics system (*lianqin*), while the second was the creation of a separate ground forces department.[198] The PLA eventually adopted these reforms in 2007 and 2016, respectively.

EDUCATION AND TRAINING

After the establishment of the new strategic guideline at the "801" meeting on strategy, the PLA immediately began to reform military education and training.

Military Education

Zhang Zhen, deputy chief of the general staff for training, led the effort within the GSD to overhaul training. Following an inspection tour of the Nanjing Military Region in May 1980, Zhang concluded that "the state of our army's academies and schools is very ill-suited to the requirements of national defense modernization and future anti-aggression wars."[199] Education and training had been one of the areas most seriously damaged during the Cultural Revolution. The content of the curriculum and the amount of time devoted to political education were vulnerable to changes in the prevailing political line. After the antidogmatism campaign in the 1950s, many officers did not want to be associated with academies. By 1969, the majority of academies were closed, effectively halting professional military training. Although they gradually reopened in the mid- to late 1970s, education emphasized political and not military learning.

After the adoption of the 1980 strategic guideline, the PLA launched three significant training reforms. To start, from October 20 to November 7, 1980, the PLA convened an army-wide meeting on military academies. The last such meeting had occurred sixteen years earlier, in 1964, just before the Cultural Revolution. More than 450 senior officers attended, including the deputy commanders and deputy commissars from the military regions, branches, and other units under the CMC, as well as the commandants and commissars of all 188 PLA academies.[200] The meeting examined how to adjust training tasks (*renwu*) and how to reorganize (*tiaozheng*) the military educational system to improve the PLA's ability to wage modern warfare. The meeting approved seven documents, which were then jointly issued army-wide by the three general departments. These documents formed a blueprint for comprehensive reforms and were described as "a strategic step for preparing to wage war."[201] To underscore the importance that the CMC now attached to military education within the PLA, education at the academies was formally incorporated into the promotion system for all officers.[202]

In addition, in November 1980, the PLA held an army-wide meeting on training. The meeting was held in Luoyang, Henan province, home to the 43rd Army in the Wuhan Military Region. In March 1980, the GSD tasked the 127th Division under the command of Zhang Wannian to conduct a pilot program on methods and training for coordinated operations.[203] The meeting's purpose was to examine the results of the pilot program to improve the ability of units within the PLA to conduct coordinated operations. Although the PLA had all the main combat arms of a modern force, such as tank and artillery units, it lacked the ability to coordinate their operations effectively. The 1979 invasion of Vietnam demonstrated that coordination was the "weak link."[204] As Zhang Zhen said at the meeting, "A high level of coordinated operations capability is an objective requirement of modern warfare." Moreover, such a capability was necessary "to raise our army's combat effectiveness and adapt to the requirements of future anti-aggression wars."[205] Zhang lamented that "some comrades" did not know how to deploy or utilize their troops and equipment.[206] The meeting discussed how to improve coordinated training through annual training plans.

Finally, the PLA issued a new training program. Drafting began in July 1980 and the GSD issued it army-wide in February 1981.[207] The goal was to increase the PLA's "operational capability under modern conditions." Furthermore, the program was drafted "according to the CMC's strategic guideline and operational guiding thought, and starting from the requirements of future anti-aggression wars."[208] Reflecting the desire to downplay politics, Zhang suggested that military affairs account for seventy percent of training under the program, while political education and culture compromise twenty and ten percent, respectively.[209] Following the November 1980 army-wide training meeting, the new training program emphasized combined arms operations at the campaign and tactical levels. Zhang again underscored that combined arms operations reflected the essence of modern warfare and the PLA's performance in Vietnam demonstrated its shortcomings in this area.[210]

These moves, however, only marked the start of an effort to reform education under the new strategy. Another army-wide conference on military academies was held in 1983 "to increase further self-defensive capabilities under modern warfare conditions."[211] Arguably the most important change occurred in April 1985, when the CMC decided to establish the PLA's National Defense University (NDU) by merging the Military Academy, the Political Academy, and the Logistics Academy. To underscore its importance, the CMC tasked Zhang Zhen with establishing the school. He became its first president when the NDU opened its doors in 1986. Unlike Lin Biao's creation of the Military and Political University in 1969, which was designed to weaken China's professional military training, the opening of the NDU in 1986 reflected an effort to improve the quality of education for China's senior officers. Within the PLA, it has roughly the same status as the Central Party School of the CCP as the highest-level training institute for senior officers.[212]

The "802" Meeting

After the change in military strategy, the GSD decided to hold several large-scale military exercises. These would focus on the different directions of a

Soviet invasion, including in north China, the northwest, and the Bohai Gulf. The first such exercise would be in north China, the most likely direction of attack, to explore how to organize and execute defensive operations.[213] Reflecting the link to the new strategy devised at the "801" meeting, the code name for the exercise was the "802" meeting. Zhang Zhen, then deputy chief of the general staff responsible for training, recalled that the exercise would "resolve the realization (*jutihua*) of the strategic guideline of 'active defense.'"[214]

The location chosen for the exercise was Zhangjiakou, an important transportation node northwest of Beijing. When held in September 1981, the "north China exercise" (*huabei yanxi*) became the largest field exercise held by the PLA since 1949. More than 110,000 troops participated, including 1,300 tanks and armored vehicles, 1,500 artillery pieces, and 285 airplanes.[215] The exercise, which lasted for five days, was premised on a campaign-level positional defensive operation that had been identified the year before as the core of the new strategy. The main components included an armored and airborne offensive along with positional defense, anti-airborne exercises and a campaign-level counterattack.[216] The exercise included every branch in the ground forces, paratroopers (then part of the PLAAF), and PLAAF units, "reflecting the characteristics of modern warfare."[217]

Before the exercise was held in September, two group training (*jixun*) activities were organized. All told, 247 senior officers from all eleven military regions as well as the services and branches participated. The group training combined detailed lectures on campaign theory focusing on a positional defensive campaign with a week-long scenario planning exercise in which the participants were divided into groups and asked to develop contingency plans "based on the CMC's strategic guideline and the tasks clarified by the 801 meeting."[218] Ye Jianying stated that the "'801' meeting last year unified the forces' strategic thought and determined 'active defense' as the strategic guideline. This year's '802' meeting will resolve the question of realizing [*jutihua*] the strategic guideline."[219]

When the field exercise began on September 14, 1981, it attracted a great deal of attention from senior leaders. Most of the Politburo, even Hua Guofeng, observed the exercise. Approximately thirty-two thousand people from party and state units also attended, as well as "responsible persons" from all provinces, cities, autonomous regions, and the local area.[220] Deng himself observed all five days of the event.[221] Afterward, Deng stated that the exercise "reflected relatively well the characteristics of modern warfare, explored coordinated operations of the various services and branches and improved . . . the actual combat level of the army."[222]

The final part of the exercise was a meeting to summarize what had been learned over the past several weeks. As Zhang Zhen recalls, the group training and field exercise helped to build consensus regarding how to implement the new strategic guideline. Most important, the participants agreed on maintaining the principle of "fortifying and garrisoning key points and building a great in-depth defensive system" to deal with various kinds of Soviet attacks.[223]

The exercise itself was clearly more aspirational than anything else. The forces participating in the exercise held at least two dress rehearsals (*yuyan*), the first in the middle of August and the second in early September.[224] Zhang Zhen states that organization and coordination among the units, and communications between ground and air forces, "was not done very well."[225] Nevertheless, this exercise created the model for smaller scale exercises that would occur in the first half of the 1980s.

After the "802" meeting, the pace of campaign-level exercises increased. In August 1982, the Lanzhou Military Region in Xinjiang organized a "three warfares" exercise, which included mobile and guerrilla warfare in addition to positional defensive warfare.[226] Given Xinjiang's distance from Beijing, geography, and limited forward-deployed forces, the CMC accepted that Xinjiang would have to conduct "independent operations," which increased the reliance on mobile and guerrilla operations. In 1983, the Second Artillery held its first campaign-level exercise simulating a nuclear counter-strike (as discussed in more detail in chapter 6).[227] In August 1984, the Lanzhou Military Region held a live-fire exercise with actual troops (*shibing shidan*) in Gansu at Jiayuguan (where the Great Wall ends), with a strengthened division conducting positional defensive operations.[228]

The 1985 Downsizing and "Strategic Transformation"

In June 1985, the CMC approved a plan to cut another one million soldiers from the force, after assessing that the threat of a total war had receded and the PLA could shift to peacetime modernization. The 1985 downsizing reflects the culmination of earlier efforts to streamline and reorganize and does not, by itself, constitute a change in military strategy.

DECISION TO DOWNSIZE

The decision to cut one million more from the force was the result of work that began in early 1984 to formulate and implement the next round of force reductions. When reviewing the 1982 downsizing plan in March 1982, Deng said that "this is not a plan that is relatively satisfactory." Deng viewed it as a first step, noting that "after it is finished, further plans can be studied."[229] As Yang Dezhi recalled, "After Chairman Deng read [the 1982 plan], he felt dissatisfied."[230] He Zhengwen, the deputy chief of staff in charge of downsizing, said Deng's comments made him "feel great pressure."[231] In February 1984, after the 1982 downsizing had been completed, Yang Dezhi tasked the streamlining and reorganization leading small group with developing plans for further downsizing. In April 1984, a CMC enlarged meeting approved a reorganization plan that the GSD drafted and instructed that it be developed further. The GSD completed a more detailed preliminary plan by the end of September, which included options for cutting three, five, or seven hundred thousand troops from the force.[232]

In October, the CMC convened a forum to discuss the goal of the downsizing plan. Earlier in the month, Deng reviewed the GSD plan and declared that all three options were "too small" and one million should be cut.[233] As Yang Dezhi said when the forum opened, "Recently, Chairman Deng made the decision to reduce the army by one million."[234] On November 1, Deng explained the decision. Deng repeated earlier assessments that war was not likely for at least ten years, including both a war between the United States and the Soviet Union (who were deterred from attacking each other) and a war involving China, which was now pursuring Deng's new "independent foreign policy of peace."[235] Therefore, Deng concluded, "we are able to develop in peace and can shift the focus of our work to development."[236] Even if war did erupt, Deng said, "we must also trim the fat." The PLA's senior leadership bodies were so bloated that they "fundamentally cannot command." Savings in personnel costs could be used "improve our weapons and equipment and even more importantly raise the quality of our force [*budui*]."[237] By streamlining the general departments, services and branches, and military regions, Deng said, "the efficiency of these institutions will certainly increase."[238]

Although the symposium reached agreement on the goal of cutting one million, the task facing the leading small group was how to achieve it. It would require disbanding combat units formed in the civil war and eliminating almost half of the military regions. The process would create winners and losers. To develop the final plan, the GSD convened forty-two meetings of its party committee and fourteen specialized meetings, including one with the leadership of the three general departments and another with the leadership of the military regions and services.[239] In March 1985, a CMC standing meeting (*changwu huiyi*) approved a revised plan.

From May 23 to June 6, 1985, the CMC held an enlarged meeting to review and approve the plan. At the start of the meeting, Yang Dezhi introduced the downsizing plan, which was then approved.[240] The meeting also approved the "strategic transformation in guiding thought of army building." Specifically, this was "shifting military work from a state of preparation for an imminent war based on an early, major and nuclear war to the path of peaceful development [*jianshe*]."[241] The PLA could now take full advantage of a peaceful environment to pursue modernization while not placing a burden on economic reforms.[242] Army building would focus on developing new weapons and equipment while raising the quality of personnel.[243]

At the end of the meeting, Deng provided a broader justification for the CMC's decisions. He repeated some of the same themes from his November 1984 speech, focusing on China's assessment of the international environment and China's new "independent" foreign policy. He declared that "we have changed our view that the danger of war is imminent." A world war was unlikely because the United States and the Soviet Union, with vast conventional and nuclear arsenals, were deterred from attacking each other, as neither "dares to go first."[244] More generally, the center of international competition had shifted to economics, in which science and technology would play a key role. Deng's assessment was also based on the "analysis of our peripheral environment," a reference to the view that a major war with the Soviet Union was also no longer likely. For this reason, China's foreign policy shifted from aligning with the United States "in one line" (*yitiaoxian*) against the Soviet Union to an "independent position" in a triangle with the two superpowers. Therefore, Deng said, "we can boldly and wholeheartedly pursue our four modernizations."[245] Economic growth would take priority over defense. He called for the PLA to be patient, noting that "only when we have a good economic foundation will it be possible for us to modernize the army's equipment."

On July 11, 1985, the CMC together with the State Council and Central Committee issued the plan, entitled the *Plan for the Reform, Streamlining, and Reorganization of the Military System* (*jundui tizhi gaige, jingjian zhengbian de fang'an*). The goal was to develop a force with streamlined administration, more flexible command, and greater combat power by reducing the number of personnel, eliminating the levels of bureaucracy, downgrading units, and closing some installations.[246] When the downsizing was completed in 1987, over a million soldiers—or, roughly, twenty-five percent of the force—had been cut. The total size of the PLA was now 3,235,000, falling to 3,199,000 by 1990.[247] By 1988, defense spending accounted for only 8.8 percent of the national budget, down from 17.4 in 1979 before the three rounds of downsizing had begun.

The 1985 downsizing occurred in two phases. The first phase focused on the three general departments, COSTIND, the services and branches, the military regions, and provincial-level military districts. Personnel in the general departments decreased by 46.5 percent, including the GSD (60 percent), GPD (30.4 percent) and GLD (52 percent).[248] Eleven military regions were merged into seven, reducing the number of personnel in subordinate offices and departments by 53 percent.[249] Within the services, the ground forces were cut by 23.2 percent, including 13.1 percent from the armies. Thirty-five armies were reorganized into twenty-four combined arms group armies, which eliminated eleven army headquarters and thirty-six divisions. Infantry troops were divided into mechanized infantry divisions and motorized infantry divisions in the north, motorized infantry divisions in the south, light motorized infantry divisions and infantry brigades in mountainous areas.[250] Likewise, the navy was reduced by 14.7 percent, with cuts coming from the headquarters and surface fleets, while the air force was reduced by 19.6 percent.

The second phase focused on military academies, support, logistics, and other units. The reconfiguration of military academies began in June 1986. The PLA's military, political, and logistics academies were combined to form the National Defense University. Along with redundant institutions in the military regions, the number of military academies were reduced from 117 to 103, and the within-quota personnel was reduced from 330,000 to 224,000.[251]

A NEW STRATEGY?

By changing the basic guiding thought for army building and describing it as a "strategic transformation," the 1985 downsizing has been described as a change in China's military strategy. Although it would have significant implications for strategy, it does not constitute a change in the strategic guideline and was not viewed within the PLA as a change in strategy.

First, as shown above, one motivation for the 1985 downsizing was to improve military effectiveness and command flexibility, as identified in the 1980 strategy—goals that motivated the 1980 and 1982 force reductions and reorganizations. These two downsizings, however, were not announced publicly. The 1985 one was publicized as part of China's new "independent" foreign policy, which avoided alignment with either the United States or the Soviet Union, but was the culmination of efforts since 1980 to reorganize the PLA.

Second, the primary judgment was that China would no longer need to prepare for a total war and could stand down from a war footing posture. Thus, this conclusion altered the assessment of China's security environment in the 1980 strategy regarding the intensity of the Soviet threat, especially in 1979 and 1980, even though the Soviet Union would remain China's main adversary until normalization in 1989. In this way, one of the main components of a strategic guideline was altered. Nevertheless, the 1985 meeting did not identify a new threat around which to orient China's military strategy. Instead, as one PLA scholar describes, it produced "heated debates" over the threats China faced and the wars it might need to fight.[252] The 1985 meeting only excluded one type of conflict, a total war or invasion of China, but did not identify a new one. Only in December 1988, more than three years after the 1985 meeting, would "local wars" (*jubu zhanzheng*) be identified as the main kind of conflict for which China should prepare to fight. If anything, the 1985 meeting produced a period of strategic drift and exploration.

Third, the CMC meeting did not alter other elements of the strategic guideline, including the "form of operations" or "basic guiding thought for operations." The reason, of course, is that the CMC focused on approving the reduction of one million soldiers and reorganization of the force, not the strategic guideline. Nevertheless, although the 1985 meeting included a key assessment that opened the possibility for focusing on local wars, authorizing such a shift was not the purpose of the meeting. Available sources indicate that changes in assessments of either the form of war or basic guiding thought for operations were not discussed in 1985.

Fourth, the 1985 meeting did not produce change in the indicators of a major change in military strategy. Although the drafting of the third generation of combat regulations was completed at the end of 1987, the drafting began in 1982 after the adoption of the 1980 strategy. Likewise, the *Science of Campaigns Outline* and *Science of Military Strategy*, which were also published in 1987, were drafted in the early 1980s and did not reflect the new assessment of the international situation. In terms of force structure, the content of the 1985 downsizing, especially the formation of the combined arms group armies, reflected ideas that had been developed to implement the 1980 strategy.

The 1988 Strategy: "Local Wars and Armed Conflicts"

The strategic guideline adopted in 1988 was a minor change to the 1980 one, identifying a general type of war for the PLA to prepare to fight and not a specific kind of war with a specific adversary. Nevertheless, the strategy did not describe how China should prepare to fight such wars, only that they should be the focus of planning.

BACKGROUND TO THE 1988 STRATEGY

Surprisingly little information is available regarding the 1988 strategic guideline. One reason is that it represented only a minor change in strategy. According to one AMS scholar, the 1988 guideline reflected the "completion of the adjustment of the military strategic guideline that began in the early 1980s."[253] Another reason is that the new guideline was adopted only a few months before the demonstrations in Tiananmen Square. After the massacre, the PLA turned inward, focusing on internal political education, as described in the next chapter.

The 1988 strategic guideline was the first strategy adopted after the 1985 CMC meeting that affirmed Deng's assessment about peace and development and the PLA's shift to peacetime modernization. If the PLA did not need to prepare to fight a total war of an invasion, then the most likely conflicts would be limited or local ones on China's periphery. The 1988 guideline thus reflected a central implication of the assessment of China's security environment reached in 1985. Nevertheless, the 1985 assessment only ruled out what kind of war China would need to fight and offered no guidance about the kind of wars

China would fight in the future, how they would be fought, or how the PLA should be structured and trained to fight them.[254]

To answer these questions, PLA strategists began to explore the future. The GSD convened a series of lectures (*jiangzuo*) from 1986 to 1988, which examined defense modernization and development strategy (1986), local wars and army building (1987), and strategic guidance for military struggle (1988).[255] Under Zhang Zhen's direction, the PLA's new NDU convened two major meetings on campaign theory and operational guiding thought in 1986 and 1988.[256] Finally, the PLA organized military exercises in different regions to explore the characteristics of local wars in different strategic directions. In 1987 and 1988, all military regions adjacent to an international boundary conducted exercises based on local conflicts and the particular features of their area, including the Jinan, Shenyang, Beijing, Lanzhou, Guangzhou, and Chengdu Military Regions.[257] Like the lectures, these exercises were exploratory and designed to help the PLA determine what kind of military strategy and campaign principles it should adopt in local wars it might face.

As with other strategic guidelines, the GSD, now under the leadership of Chi Haotian, appeared to play a key role in the adoption of the 1988 guideline. In December 1987, Chi Haotian declared that "our army in the new period urgently needs a clear and complete military strategy." He instructed the GSD to study high-level operational guidance to "explore our army's overall strategy, overall guideline, and overall requirements." The GSD party committee met in February 1988 and drafted a report entitled "Suggestions on Several Issues Regarding Our Army's Strategic Guidance Until the End of the Century." In consultation with the military regions, services, and other general departments, the report was revised ten times.[258] The GSD formally submitted its suggestions to the CMC on December 24, 1988, but it is unclear what role it played in the CMC enlarged meeting—which ended on December 20—when the 1988 guideline was adopted. The GSD report contained specific suggestions, but the original report is unavailable.

OVERVIEW OF THE 1988 STRATEGY

For the first time since 1949, the People's Republic in the late 1980s lacked a primary strategic adversary around which to orient its military strategy. The warming of ties with the Soviet Union after Gorbachev's 1986 speech at Vladivostok and the Soviet commitment to begin withdrawing troops deployed in the Russian Far East reflected a significant reduction in the threat China faced. China did not discount conflict with the Soviets entirely, but the warming of ties with Moscow, which led to the normalization of relations in May 1989, removed what had been the dominant threat to China's security since

1969. Instead, the overall goal of the 1988 strategic guideline was more general, identifying a kind of war and not an adversary as the focus of planning. Specifically, the 1988 guideline determined that the basis of preparations for military struggle was "dealing with local wars [*jubu zhanzheng*] and armed conflicts [*wuzhuang chongtu*] that might arise,"[259] especially those associated with China's outstanding sovereignty and territorial disputes.[260]

Despite the lack of a primary strategic adversary, the 1988 strategy placed greater emphasis on China's southern border and the South China Sea as the situation stabilized in the north. As the first strategy focused on a range of potential local wars and not a total war of invasion, the 1988 guideline was also the first to emphasize strategic guiding thought (*zhanlue zhidao sixiang*) as distinct from basic guiding thought for operations. The strategic guiding thought was "stabilize the northern line, strengthen the southern line, strengthen frontier defense, plan and manage the oceans" (*wending beixian, jiaqiang nanxian, qiangbian gufang, jinglue haiyang*).[261]

Because the strategic situation (*taishi*) in the north with the Soviet Union had stabilized, an opportunity existed to improve China's strategic situation in the south, where disputes remained.[262] These included land border disputes with India and Vietnam, as well as China's occupation of several reefs in the Spratly Islands. Throughout the 1980s, but especially from 1984 to 1986, a series of intense battles occurred over various hilltops on the disputed Chinese-Vietnamese border. In March 1988, Chinese and Vietnamese forces clashed violently in the Spratly Islands as China moved to occupy six reefs also claimed by Vietnam.[263] During 1986 and 1987, a tense standoff over an observation post on the Chinese-Indian border occurred at Sumdurong Chu, culminating with the mobilization of several divisions on both sides.[264] The confrontation was part of a much larger territorial dispute over 125,000 square kilometers between the two countries. Nevertheless, from a military perspective, defending China's interests in different territorial disputes on the Tibetan plateau, in jungles along the border with Vietnam, or in the South China Sea required different capabilities and concepts of operations.

The new strategic guideline was adopted at an enlarged meeting of the CMC held in December 1988 to plan military work for the coming year. The meeting also determined that improving combat effectiveness (*zhandouli*) would be the basic standard for assessing all military work.[265] Yang Shangkun, the vice-chairman and secretary of the CMC, broadly defined combat effectiveness to include the quality of military administration (*junzheng suzhi*), weapons and equipment, system and organization (*tizhi bianzhi*), strategy and tactics, and logistics and support. Deviations from strengthening combat effectiveness would mean that "army building was necessarily deviating from the correct direction."[266] The basic idea was to enhance China's overall deterrent power, also a new concept when compared with the previous emphasis on how to respond to an invasion.

INDICATORS OF STRATEGIC CHANGE

Various indicators of military change demonstrate that the 1988 strategic guideline continued the strategy adopted in 1980, but within the new context of local wars.

Based on available sources, the 1988 guideline contained no change to the basic guiding thought for operations. Therefore, it is not associated with any shift in the PLA's operational doctrine. In June 1988, the PLA had formally issued the "third generation" of combat regulations that it had begun drafting in 1982 and finished drafting in late 1987. When the new regulations were announced, they were described as "absorbing the operational experiences of recent local wars around the world and our counterattack in self-defense against Vietnam."[267] As the regulations focused on combined arms operations that had been reemphasized in the 1980 strategy, they were also described as "forming an important basis for combined training and operations in the new period."

Few changes in force structure also occurred. The PLA had just completed the 1985 downsizing in 1987. At the December 1988 enlarged meeting of the CMC, Yang Shangkun elaborated on the nature of the deterrent function of military power amid the competition among states for the strategic initiative. According to Yang, China's guideline for the development of weapons and equipment was to "maintain the principle of combining crack standing forces and reserve (*houbei*) forces, conventional forces and strategic nuclear deterrent forces ... and continuously raise the war fighting capability and integrated deterrent capability of our armed forces."[268] The focus on "integration" echoed the role of combined arms operations in the 1980 guidelines, but did not appear to contain a new vision for how China's forces should be structured.

The major change in China's approach to training during this period was the promulgation of a new training program in 1989 that was implemented in 1990. The program was divided into four parts, one each for the ground forces, navy, air force, and Second Artillery. According to the *Liberation Army Daily*, the drafting of the new training program began in 1988, after three years of work with three pilot units that developed new training guidelines at all levels from the soldier and platoon to the division.[269] This suggests that the new training program represented an effort to implement ideas that had been developed under the 1980 strategy. In particular, the new training program emphasized combined arms campaigns and tactics, the new group army-centric force structure, and the enhanced role of technical troops in the force. Again, however, this was not a major departure from what the PLA had been undertaking in the previous years.

Conclusion

The strategic guideline adopted in 1980 represents the second major change in China's military strategy. The content of the guideline, along with its implementation, demonstrate that the PLA's senior officers sought to prepare for a new kind of war with the Soviet Union. The 1973 Arab-Israeli War shaped how PLA officers believed a Soviet invasion would occur and how best to defend against such an attack. Nevertheless, the deep divisions within the party leadership created by the Cultural Revolution before and after 1973 prevented the PLA from formulating a new strategy to deal with the threat it faced. Once Deng Xiaoping defeated Hua Guofeng and restored party unity, the PLA was able to adopt a new military strategy.

In 1985, the CMC's announcement of the one-million-soldier downsizing was accompanied by a "strategic transformation in guiding thought for army building" to peacetime modernization. The main reason was Deng's assessment that the threat of a total war had receded. This assessment opened the door for changing the strategic guideline, but a new military strategy was not adopted at this time. After studying China's security environment for several years, the CMC in December 1988 adopted a new strategic guideline, in which the basis of preparations for military struggle was "dealing with local wars and military conflicts." This 1988 strategy for local wars, however, did not describe how such conflicts would be fought or what forces would be required. These questions would only be answered after the outbreak of the Gulf War, as described in the next chapter.

6

The 1993 Strategy: "Local Wars under High-Technology Conditions"

In December 1992, the PLA's high command convened a seminar to examine China's military strategy. By the end of the month, a new strategic guideline had been formulated, which the CMC adopted in early January 1993, known as "winning local wars under modern especially high-technology conditions." Unlike the 1956 and 1980 guidelines, the new strategy was not based on how to counter an invasion of Chinese territory. Instead, it emphasized how to wage wars over limited aims that would be characterized by new ways of fighting.

The strategic guideline adopted in January 1993 represents the third major change in China's military strategy since 1949. As with the 1956 and 1980 strategies, the adoption of the 1993 strategy is also puzzling. In the early 1990s, China's senior party and military leaders believed that China's regional security environment was the "best ever" since 1949, owing largely to the evaporation of the Soviet threat from the north and the end of the Cold War. Yet, despite the absence of a clear threat to China's homeland, the CMC adopted its most ambitious military strategy to date by seeking to develop the capability to conduct joint operations, in a wide range of contingencies, around its periphery.

Two factors are central to understanding when, why, and how China changed its military strategy in 1993. First, the Gulf War revealed that a significant shift in the conduct of warfare had occurred. Iraq's rapid defeat through the use of weapons such as precision-guided munitions had a profound impact on China's senior military officers. Although China had been tracking these shifts in warfare since the 1980s, including the 1982 Falklands War and 1986 US air strikes against Libya, the Gulf War underscored the need for a new strategy to ensure that the PLA would be prepared to fight as the conduct of warfare changed. Second, the PLA could not respond immediately to the Gulf War because of the divisions within the party leadership that emerged after the suppression of demonstrations in and around Tiananmen Square over whether and how to continue Deng Xiaoping's reforms. The PLA also became more politicized than at any time since the end of the Cultural Revolution. Only when unity was restored at the Fourteenth Party Congress in October 1992 was the PLA able to pursue a change in strategy.

The 1993 strategy is perhaps the most important strategic guideline that the CMC has adopted since 1956. It remains the basis of China's military strategy today, following adjustments in 2004 and 2014. Although the 1988 strategy signaled the turn to local wars, it did not outline how they would be fought. The 1993 strategy answered this question. It also affirmed the shift from the dominance of the ground forces to elevating the role of the other services, and from the modes of warfare used since the civil war—such as mobile warfare—to joint operations among the services.

This chapter unfolds in five parts. The first section demonstrates that the new strategic guideline established in January 1993 constitutes a major change in China's national military strategy. The next section shows that senior military officers identified the Gulf War as constituting a major shift in the conduct of warfare in the international system, which served as the external stimulus for initiating a change in military strategy. The third section reviews how disunity grew within the party leadership after Tiananmen and how the PLA became politicized before unity was restored at the Fourteenth Party Congress in October 1992. The last two sections discuss the adoption and initial implementation of the new strategy.

"Winning Local Wars under High-Technology Conditions"

The strategic guideline adopted in January 1993 at an enlarged meeting of the CMC represents the third major change in China's military strategy. The 1993 strategy, known as "winning local wars under modern especially high-technology conditions," was organized around different types of local or limited wars China might fight around its periphery. Joint operations replaced the trinity of positional, mobile, and guerrilla warfare, whose various combinations had constituted the PLA's approach to operations since its founding in 1927.

OVERVIEW OF THE 1993 STRATEGY

The biggest change in the new strategy concerned the "basis of preparations for military struggle." Unlike the 1956 and 1980 guidelines, the 1993 guideline was not based on countering an invasion of China by a superior adversary. When introducing the new strategy, Jiang Zemin, in his capacity as CMC chairman, explained that the PLA "must place the basis of preparations for future military struggles on winning local wars that may occur under modern technology, especially under high-technology conditions."[1] This judgment was premised on the conclusion that "as soon as a war breaks out, it is likely to be a high-technology confrontation."[2] The ability to use new technologies would determine whether or not a military could seize the initiative on the battlefield. Given these shifts in the conduct of warfare, if a state lacked appropriate capabilities, "it would always be in a passive position as soon as war erupted."[3] Because many countries were adjusting their own military strategies to incorporate new technologies, China would be left behind if it did not change its own strategy to keep pace with shifts in the conduct of warfare.

Unlike past strategic guidelines, the 1993 strategy did not initially identify a "primary strategic direction." Nevertheless, Jiang's speech noted that the "focal point of military struggle is to prevent a major incident of 'Taiwan independence' from occurring."[4] This required that the military support efforts by the party and the government to increase China's attractiveness to and influence over the island while also deterring a Taiwanese declaration of independence. Jiang called on the PLA to "prepare to deal with sudden incidents" (*zuohao yingbian zhunbei*), which would apply to a Taiwan contingency in addition to Hong Kong and China's outstanding territorial disputes. As the decade progressed, the "southeast" (Taiwan) would become China's main strategic direction.[5]

Jiang's speech summarized the content of the new strategic guideline. The goals of the strategy were to "defend national territorial sovereignty and maritime rights and interests, safeguard the reunification of the motherland and social stability, and provide strong security guarantees for reform and opening, and modernization."[6] The strategic guiding thought in the new guideline stressed how to achieve these goals: "Foster strengths and avoid weaknesses, be flexible in handling emergencies, deter wars, and win wars" (*yangchang biduan, linghuo yingbian, ezhi zhanzheng, daying zhanzheng*).[7] Thus, the new strategy contained an emerging emphasis on crisis management and strategic deterrence that would become more developed over the next decade. Jiang also noted that China's military strategy should "be subordinate to and serve the nation's development strategy, be rooted in winning a local war under modern especially high-technology conditions that might erupt, accelerate the quality building [*zhiliang jianshe*] of our army, and strive to raise our army's emergency combat capability."[8]

The sweeping nature of change envisioned by the new strategy should be emphasized. In 1994, CMC vice-chairman Liu Huaqing described the changes in China's approach to military strategy created by the advent of high-technology warfare. Liu stressed that "the new situation forces us to make breakthrough changes in the theory and practice of warfare." Furthermore, he identified the scope of the transformation as containing multiple changes, such as "from dealing with an all-round invasion of a major enemy in the past to dealing with various forms of struggle against multiple enemies, from protracted operations of resolute defense in the interior to wars of quick-decision based on maneuver operations (*jidong zuozhan*) in the near seas and border areas, from large-scale operations in pre-set battlefields and long-term preparations to limited operations with temporary deployments and rapid response, from ground warfare-based coordinated operations to joint operations of the three services with increased air and naval warfare."[9]

From China's perspective, the 1993 guideline remained conceived of as a strategy of strategic defense and based on active defense. However, the focus of what would be defended shifted from homeland territory to territorial disputes along China's periphery and Taiwan's unification. These more limited goals, when compared with defending against an invasion, increased the role of offensive capabilities. At the operational level, a single military campaign in a local war could have strategic effects, creating greater pressure than before for preemption, as well as the need to deter wars from arising or to contain them if they arose. At the strategic level, the scope of what might constitute a "first strike" appeared to expand over the decade. According to the 2001 edition of the *Science of Military Strategy*, "There is a difference between 'the first shot' politically and strategically and 'the first shot' tactically." Specifically, in the context of Taiwan, "once anyone violates the sovereignty and territorial integrity of another country, he will give the other party the right to 'shoot first' tactically."[10]

OPERATIONAL DOCTRINE

The 1993 strategy changed the "form of operations" that the PLA would be required to conduct. At least through the early 1980s, strategy focused on how to combine positional, mobile, and guerrilla forms of warfare to achieve military objectives. As past strategies were based on how to prevail after being attacked by a superior enemy, the prominence of these forms of warfare was understandable. After the 1980 strategic guideline emphasized combined arms operations within the ground forces, it is perhaps unsurprising that the 1993 guideline stressed joint operations (*lianhe zuozhan*) among the services as the basic form of operations that the PLA should now be able to conduct.[11] As positional, mobile, and guerrilla warfare were based on light infantry tactics, the emphasis on joint operations signaled a shift from emphasizing the ground forces alone to also integrating other services with the ground forces.

The "basic guiding thought for operations" explained how these joint operations would be conducted. The 1993 guideline embraced a new basic guiding principle for operations of "integrated operations, keypoint strikes" (*zhengti zuozhan, zhongdian daji*). In 1999, the PLA issued new operational doctrine that codified these changes in the form of operations regulations. The CMC issued seven campaign outlines (*zhanyi gangyao*), including the first-ever campaign outline for joint operations. The CMC also issued a new set of combat regulations, known as the "fourth generation" of combat regulations, which AMS started drafting in 1995. Reflecting the complexity of modern warfare, eighty-nine regulations were published, roughly three times more than the third generation of these regulations.[12]

FORCE STRUCTURE

Major changes in force structure quickly followed the adoption of the new strategic guideline. Almost all the changes were facilitated by two troop reductions designed to increase the quality of the force, streamline command, and strengthen the navy and the air force. In September 1997, the CMC announced that the force would be reduced by 500,000 personnel. Although the size of the air force and navy each declined by 11.4 and 12.6 percent, respectively, the army shrunk by 18.6 percent. Even though the army was the largest service, it, proportionally, took an even greater hit. Three headquarters were eliminated, a dozen divisions were deactivated, and another fourteen light infantry divisions were transferred to the People's Armed Police (PAP), China's paramilitary force then under the dual command of the CMC and Ministry of Public Security.[13] In 2003, the CMC announced that a further 200,000 personnel would be trimmed, again focusing on the ground forces.

In addition to these reductions, force structure was changed in other ways. In the 1997 reduction, roughly thirty divisions were reorganized into smaller brigades to increase the flexibility of the force. The PLA also stressed creating and improving "emergency mobile operations units" (*yingji jidong zuozhan budui*)[14] in each military region that could be deployed rapidly throughout the country.* To strengthen weapons design and procurement, the General Armaments Department was established in 1998. This was the first general department created since changes to China's general staff structure forty years earlier in 1958.

Throughout these changes, naval and air forces received extra resources to address potential conflicts on the periphery and the shift to joint operations and did not bear the brunt of downsizing and streamlining efforts. They were also the recipients of the bulk of new weapons systems that China purchased from Russia in the 1990s. The PLAN received *Kilo* submarines and *Sovremenny* destroyers, while the PLAAF acquired the Su-27 and Su-30 multi-role fighters as well as advanced surface-to-air missiles, such as the S-300.

---

* The secondary literature in English often refers to these as rapid reaction units.

TRAINING

The adoption of the 1993 strategy transformed the PLA's approach to military training. Jiang Zemin, using Deng Xiaoping's phrase from a 1975 speech, repeated that training "must be placed in a strategic position."[15] In December 1995, the GSD issued a new army-wide training program that included the ground forces, navy, air force, Second Artillery, COSTIND, and People's Armed Police.[16] Apart from the ground forces, past training programs had been issued by the individual services, branches, and combat arms, not by the GSD.

Training assumed such great importance under the new strategy that a second training program was promulgated in August 2001 and implemented in January 2002. The drafting of this program began in 1998 just as the PLA was completing the campaign outlines and combat regulations discussed above and emphasizing joint operations. One of the key changes was the identification of clear standards for the evaluation of training— hence the program was renamed as the military training and evaluation program (*junshi xunlian yu kaohe dagang*).[17]

Another component of military training is field exercises. In March 1996, during the crisis across the Taiwan Strait, the PLA conducted what it described as its first major joint exercise. Even before 1996, however, the training tempo began to increase just before the new guideline was adopted in 1993.[18] Throughout the decade, the scope and complexity of training increased. In 2001, for example, the PLA held a series of exercises on Dongshan Island off the southern coast of Fujian that matched the scale of the exercises in 1955 on the Liaodong Peninsula and in 1981 at Zhangjiakou, described in chapters 3 and 4, respectively.[19]

The Gulf War and the Conduct of Warfare

For China's senior military officers, the 1990–91 Gulf War represented a significant shift in the conduct of warfare. Although the PLA started to focus on local wars in 1988, it had not yet developed a clear strategy for how to fight such conflicts. The Gulf War, however, ignited a wholesale reconsideration of future warfare within the PLA. More than any other interstate conflict since 1949, the Gulf War for China (and many other states) symbolized a transformation in the conduct of warfare, which senior military officers started to describe as a "high-technology local war," and shaped the basis of preparations for military struggle in the 1993 strategy.[20]

THE CMC ASSESSES THE GULF WAR

Following Iraq's invasion of Kuwait in August 1990, the United States mobilized the international community to liberate the conquered state. Over the coming months, almost one million troops from allied countries deployed to the region. On January 17, 1991, Operation Desert Storm began with an air campaign that would last over a month. With more than 116,000 sorties, key targets included Iraqi main force units, air defenses, command and control nodes, and critical infrastructure. When the ground phase of the war began on February 24, it lasted for only one hundred hours. The outcome could only be described as lopsided. Forty-two Iraqi divisions were rendered ineffective, including 3,700 tanks, 2,400 armored vehicles and 2,600 artillery pieces. Although approximately 20,000 to 30,000 Iraq soldiers were killed, only 293 U.S. military personnel died.[21]

The speed of Iraq's defeat and the lopsided victory surprised many observers. In the fall and winter of 1990, for example, Chinese military analysts predicted that coalition forces would become bogged down in a protracted conflict against the battle-hardened Iraqi army and that air power would play only a marginal role in the war.[22] In early March 1991, just days after Gulf War ended, the CMC launched an army-wide effort to study all aspects of the conflict, including implications for shifts in the conduct of warfare and countermeasures that China should adopt. Although the PLA in January 1991 had just started to implement its Eighth Five-Year Plan, senior military officers had already concluded that the PLA's existing modernization plans would require substantial revisions. According to Admiral Liu Huaqing, vice-chairman and the ranking uniformed member of the CMC, "Our past considerations were correct, but a new situation has occurred."[23]

The scope of the CMC's effort to study the Gulf War was broad. The CMC tasked top-level units, including AMS, the GSD, and the General Logistics Department (GLD), with specific topics to research.[24] According to Liu Huaqing, the goal was "to answer and resolve new problems faced in national defense, army building, and command." The topics examined covered all aspects of the Gulf War, including military theory, strategic command, unit structure and organization, force deployment, tactics, command arrangements, employment of the services and branches, logistics and support, technology, and equipment. Another goal was to develop concrete proposals for how the PLA should respond to the changes lest China "suffer losses in future local wars and military conflicts." "We should have a plan," Liu said. "We should study how to give play to our strengths, overcome our shortcomings, and fight a future war."[25]

Between March and June 1991, the PLA leadership held a series of high-level meetings to study the Gulf War. In his capacity as CMC chairman, Jiang Zemin attended at least four of these sessions, underscoring the importance that the CMC and the party attached to the exercise.[†] Brief excerpts from

---

[†] Jiang's participation in these meetings may have also allowed him to build a relationship with the PLA. As minister of the electronics industry in the early 1980s, Jiang was familiar with and interested in technology.

Jiang's speeches at three of these meetings were subsequently published openly. The first meeting was held on March 12, 1991, when the GSD sponsored a symposium (*zuotanhui*) on the Gulf War to prepare for an army-wide seminar (*yantaohui*) of operations departments from key units. In early June, another round of meetings was held, examining the electronics industry and the war overall.

At the end of these meetings, the GSD submitted a report on the Gulf War to the CMC. The report discussed the characteristics of the conflict and suggested that the PLA should "learn from the experience and lessons of the Gulf War and strengthen the study of military strategy and other important problems."[26] This included operational methods for fighting a technologically superior adversary with China's current equipment and strengthening the quality of the PLA. Thus, two years before the new strategic guideline was adopted, the GSD's leadership linked the Gulf War with the need to reconsider China's national military strategy.

The PLA would spend the rest of the decade studying the Gulf War and its implications for shifts in the conduct of warfare. In 1992, Zhang Zhen, president of the PLA's National Defense University (NDU), urged students to "use the Gulf War to clarify what kind of war modern war will be."[27] During the process, senior military officers drew several preliminary conclusions that shaped the adoption of the 1993 strategy. One conclusion was that the transformation in warfighting revealed in the Gulf War revolved around the application of high technology on the battlefield. While conducting an inspection of the National University of Defense Technology in March 1991, Jiang Zemin noted, "As can be seen from the Gulf War, modern war is becoming high-tech war, becoming multi-dimensional warfare, including electronic warfare and missile warfare."[28] About ten days later, Liu Huaqing told PLA delegates to the National People's Congress that "the Gulf War was a high-technology local war . . . [that] shows that the development of high technology is the 'dragon's head' [*longtou*] of national defense and economic development."[29] When meeting with representatives from COSTIND in early June, Liu underscored that the Gulf War "was a war of the highest technological level and using the largest variety of new weapons since World War II."[30] As a result, "under modern conditions, military technology, especially new and high technology, is becoming increasingly important as a decisive factor for victory, and the difference in effectiveness is multiplying between old and new weapons."

Another conclusion was that the Gulf War, as a high-technology local war, reflected the kind of conflict that China would likely face in the future. In March 1991, Chief of the General Staff Chi Haotian described the Gulf War as "a representative example of a modern local war."[31] That same month, Zhang Zhen concluded that "the Gulf War has revealed some basic characteristics and operational patterns of high-technology conventional local wars."[32] Zhang then noted the range of issues to be studied: electronic warfare, air defense, troop mobility, air-sea coordination, patterns (*yangshi*) of operations, force structure (*bianzu*), logistics and support, and intelligence.[33]

A final conclusion was that China was woefully unprepared for a high-technology local war. China lacked the sophisticated technology that was seen as enhancing a state's military power and was, therefore, increasingly vulnerable. In March 1991, Jiang Zemin noted that "backwards technology means being in a passive position and taking a beating."[34] After reviewing the role of high technology in the war, Liu Huaqing told members of COSTIND in June 1991 that "we should face this reality squarely. In no way should we be satisfied with our present situation and hold an arbitrarily optimistic stance."[35] In June, Jiang Zemin noted that "we really do lag far behind in weapons and equipment, and in some areas, the gaps are increasing."[36]

China also lacked operational doctrine for employing advanced weapons on the battlefield. Although China had begun to emphasize the operational level of war in the late 1980s, its operational doctrine remained focused on countering a ground-based Soviet attack with an emphasis on defending fixed positions—more or less what Iraq had failed to do. Success required not just the acquisition of advanced military technologies, but also the ideas and concepts for using them. As Zhang Zhen told students at the PLA's NDU in 1992, "We must liberate ourselves from the Soviet army's approach to positional warfare emphasizing zones [*didai*] and echelons. The operational method of clinging to fixed positions is no longer relevant."[37]

These three conclusions indicated that the basis of preparations for military struggle had fundamentally changed, rendering China's existing strategy, based on the 1980 strategic guideline, obsolete. The PLA then embarked on a sustained effort to study the conflict to better understand the "characteristics and laws" of high-technology warfare. The lessons were summarized in the PLA's own official history of the Gulf War, which AMS published in 2000. This report draws extensively on US documents such as Pentagon reports on the war as well as on Chinese materials, including an earlier and more contemporaneous 1991 AMS assessment of the war.[38] Even though it was published well after the 1993 strategic guideline was issued, this history nevertheless demonstrates how the PLA believed that the Gulf War marked a significant shift in the conduct of warfare.

The AMS history concluded that the outbreak and result of the Gulf War challenged traditional warfighting concepts that had emerged after World War II. According to the authors, "The Gulf War has led to a worldwide military transformation characterized by the shift from mechanized warfare to information warfare."[39] War aims were now even more limited, not seeking the occupation of enemy territory or complete annihilation of an opposing force but instead the destruction of its comprehensive power (*zonghe liliang*). The main reason was the role of technology in warfighting, especially electronic and information technologies. The extensive use of "high-technology" weapons in the Gulf War caused "significant changes" in the course and outcome of wars, including operational thought, patterns (*yangshi*) and methods of operations as well as command and force structure. The study further noted that, in future wars, the distinction between offense and defense and front lines and rear areas would be blurred. Attacks would focus on destroying an opponent's operational system, marking a shift from concentrating troops and equipment to concentrating firepower and information. Such attacks would reflect a new approach to warfighting that combined precision-guided weapons, intelligence support systems, electronic warfare systems, and automated command systems. In terms of the form of war, the "obvious characteristic of the Gulf War" was the integration of land, air, sea, space, and electronic capabilities. Warfare had become a comprehensive contest (*quanmian jiaoliang*) of in-depth, multidimensional capabilities of the various services and weapons systems. Now, C4ISR had become a "force multiplier" for maintaining an integrated operations capability in modern warfare and the "nerve center" for the various services and weapons systems.[40]

Following its 1991 report on the Gulf War, the GSD continued to press for a reconsideration of China's military strategy. On January 6, 1992, the GSD convened a meeting of all departments and bureaus to assess China's security situation, during which Chi Haotian noted that such analysis was "related to the important matter of correctly determining military strategy."[41] Following the meeting, the GSD submitted a report with its assessment to the CMC. Unfortunately, no details regarding the report are available. Nevertheless, despite the recognition of the need to change, a new strategy would not be articulated until 1993. Disunity at the highest levels of the party prevented the CMC from acting on the reports submitted to it by the GSD.

The Collapse and Restoration of Party Unity after Tiananmen

Although senior military officers recognized immediately that the Gulf War marked a significant shift in the conduct of warfare, China did not adopt a new military strategy until 1993. Growing disunity at the highest levels of the party after the suppression of demonstrations in Tiananmen Square, along with the politicization of the PLA, prevented senior military officers from pursuing such a change.

PARTY DISUNITY AFTER TIANANMEN

The demonstrations and massacre in and around Tiananmen Square in 1989 created a rift at the highest levels of the party. Deng Xiaoping remained committed to reform, but was opposed by economic conservatives such as Chen Yun and ideological ones such as Deng Liqun, who blamed Deng's policies for the circumstances that had given rise to the protests.[42] Joseph Fewsmith concludes that "the depth of Party division created by Tiananmen was far greater than at the time of Hu Yaobang's ouster" as general secretary in January 1987.[43] These divisions prevented the party from reaching consensus on economic policy at party plenums from 1989 to 1991.

Although regarded as the "core" of the party leadership, Deng's authority, prestige, and position were diminished. The discontent that sparked the initial demonstrations suggested that Deng's reforms had moved too far and too fast. Zhao Ziyang, Deng's successor and general secretary, who had pursued a conciliatory approach to the demonstrations, was charged with "splitting the party" and stripped of all his positions.[44] Jiang Zemin, the party secretary of Shanghai, replaced Zhao as general secretary. Critiques of Zhao and of reform were also aimed at weakening Deng, since Zhao was Deng's protégé.[45] Later, Chen Yun would criticize Deng for being a "rightist" before Tiananmen (supporting liberal reforms) and a "leftist" afterward (pursuing the violent crackdown)—charges designed to weaken Deng politically by blaming him for the demonstrations and the poor handling of the situation.[46]

In a socialist state, no policy "line" is perhaps more important than economic policy, especially in China during the reform period. After June 1989, conservatives sought to use the Tiananmen demonstrations "as a pretext" for halting China's economic reforms.[47] In November 1989, the Fifth Plenum revealed deep divisions over economic policy. The meeting criticized Zhao Ziyang's management of the economy (and thus Deng's reform policies) and endorsed Chen Yun's more conservative economic ideas of retrenchment and balanced growth.[48] The next month, economic conservatives received another boost when Li Peng established a State Council Production Commission to strengthen the role of state planning in the economy.[49]

The rift over economic policy would continue throughout 1990. By the Seventh Plenum, the divisions were easy to observe.[50] The plenum's purpose was to review the Eighth Five-Year Plan. Although originally scheduled to occur in the fall of 1990, the plenum was delayed until December due to disagreements over economic policy. In a draft of the plan, Li Peng and Yao Yilin, another conservative, embraced Chen Yun's idea of "sustained, steady and coordinated development" as the guiding principle for economic policy, which Deng rejected. When the plenum was finally held, Richard Baum describes that "a standoff was in evidence."[51] The final document sought to balance Deng and

Chen's positions, but lacked substance and was "short on concrete program-matic guidelines or initiatives."[52] Its main purpose was to reveal a split among the top leadership.[53]

To build support for reform, in early January 1991 Deng traveled to Shang-hai, where he gave a series of talks. The talks were subsequently summarized in four commentaries published under the pseudonym Huangpu Ping ("Shang-hai commentator") in the pro-reform *Liberation Daily*, a local paper. Deng's daughter, Deng Nan, and then Shanghai party secretary Zhu Rongji super-vised the drafting of the commentaries.[54] Subsequently, provincial leaders from Guangdong, Tianjin, and elsewhere who supported the continuation of reform also penned similar pieces.[55]

Nevertheless, Deng's effort to restore consensus around reform failed. One reason is that conservatives controlled the party's propaganda and organization departments. In April 1991, a commentary in *Contemporary Trends*, a conser-vative journal, criticized Deng's talks and was then excerpted in the *People's Daily*. The commentary stressed the need to continue to oppose "bourgeois liberalization," which was linked with "capitalist" policies such as the ones Deng was seen as advocating.[56] Jiang Zemin's speech on the seventieth anniversary of the CCP on July 1 reflected the failure of Deng's effort. Although containing some references to Deng's ideas, the overall tone reflected conservative economic and ideological views, calling for the continuation of centralized planning and the centrality of state-owned enterprises, along with the need to combat "bourgeois liberalization," "peaceful evolution," class enemies, and hostile forces abroad and at home.[57]

The failed August 1991 coup in the Soviet Union heightened the leader-ship split. Conservatives intensified their attack on reform through critiques of "bourgeois liberalization" and "peaceful evolution." To counter the con-servatives, Deng instructed Jiang Zemin and Yang Shangkun (PRC president and first vice-chairman of the CMC) at the end of September to "resolutely persevere" with reform and opening.[58] The next month, Yang gave a speech that underscored the importance of the party's commitment to reform and opening. In response, noted ideological conservative Deng Liqun published a signed article in the *People's Daily* charging that China's "socialist cause would be ruined" if there was not a resolute struggle against liberalization and even linked reform and opening with Western "peaceful evolution."[59]

Amid the continuing struggle, the Eighth Plenum was postponed sev-eral times. When it was finally convened in late November 1991, little was achieved, as with the Seventh Plenum the year before, because of the split within the party's leadership. The Plenum's communiqué reflected a decision by party leaders to "postpone action on the most controversial agenda items."[60] These included ideology, economic policy, and personnel changes. Instead, the document focused mostly on guidelines for agricultural work, hardly the most contentious issue of the day. Although party leaders sought to prevent an open break, the outcome of the plenum nevertheless reflected a high level of disagreement and political deadlock.

POLITICIZATION OF THE PLA

Amid growing party disunity after Tiananmen, the PLA became much more politicized. The party launched an effort to strengthen control of the military and ensure its "absolute loyalty." Although Deng used units from all military regions in the crackdown to ensure that no senior commander could escape blame, the decision remained unpopular and divisive within the party and the military. Before the protests, intellectuals associated with Zhao Ziyang had called for separating the army from the party, which sharpened the importance of ensuring the PLA's loyalty.[61]

Measures to strengthen party control unfolded between mid-1989 and early 1990. The first step was to identify those officers and soldiers who displayed disloyalty during the crackdown. By the end of September, all "leading groups" at the division level and above had been investigated. Investigators found that 110 officers had committed serious breaches of discipline. Twenty-one senior officers were court-martialed for insubordination, including General Xu Qinxian, commander of the Thirty-Eighth Group Army, who refused to lead his troops into Beijing.[62] Approximately 1,400 soldiers were found guilty of abandoning their weapons and refusing to partake in the crackdown.[63]

Deng then moved to reorganize the CMC at the Fifth Plenum in November 1989. Because Zhao Ziyang was stripped of his party positions in June after the suppression, the CMC needed a new first vice-chairman. Deng had also previously announced his desire to relinquish the CMC chairmanship as part of his withdrawal from politics. To consolidate general secretary Jiang Zemin's new position as his successor, Deng tapped Jiang to become CMC chairman.[64] Yang Shangkun, who was already PRC president and executive vice-chairman of the CMC, became first vice-chairman, placing him in charge of the PLA's daily affairs. His half-brother, Yang Baibing, the director of the GPD and a member of the CMC, replaced him as CMC secretary-general, thus placing him in charge of personnel issues and the CMC's powerful general office.[65] Yang Baibing also joined the party secretariat. The Yang brothers, especially Yang Shangkun, were close associates of Deng from the civil war period and again during the 1960s, when Deng himself ran the party secretariat. Although Jiang held the title of chairman, power within the CMC was concentrated in the Yang brothers.[66]

The third step was a political education campaign throughout the PLA. Although propaganda to enforce the party's absolute control of the army began to appear soon after the crackdown, an army-wide political work conference in

December 1989 launched a campaign to strengthen party control. As Yang Baibing said at the conference, "to enhance the cadre's and soldier's political firmness and ensure that the barrel of the gun is held by politically reliable people is an issue of prime importance."[67] The conference produced a ten-point document that served as the basis of the campaign. The first three points were to ensure that the PLA would be "forever qualified politically," emphasize political work as "the lifeline" of the PLA, and maintain the party's absolute leadership over the army. [68]

In the first phase, through March 1990, the campaign targeted the leadership within the GSD, military regions, and other major units. More than fifteen thousand officers at the regimental level and above had attended courses linked with the campaign (presumably to "educate" others in their respective units).[69] After March 1990, attention turned toward lower levels, from the battalion to the company, focusing on enlisted personnel.[70] To gild this lily of political work, a "Learn from Lei Feng" campaign that started in December 1989 was intensified and featured prominently in the party's media outlets. By October 1990, every cadre at the regimental level or above had been investigated for their reliability.[71]

A fourth step in the effort to strengthen party control was to enhance the role of party committees within the PLA. Party committees (*dangwei*) serve as an institutional tool by which the party controls the PLA and is the real decision-making body in peacetime in many units.[72] For the first time, the PLA established party committees within companies. Previously, units at the company level and below had only party branches, not full-fledged committees.

The final element was the large-scale rotation and retirement of military officers in the seven military regions and other major units. One reason for the change was presumably to prevent the rise of local factions, mirroring similar PLA leadership reshufflings in 1973 and 1985. Another reason, however, was to reward those who supported the crackdown and punish those who did not. Commanders and commissars in six of seven of the military regions were rotated to different positions or retired. Within the military regions, more than half of the officers at the deputy commander level and above changed, with a special emphasis on commissars, enabling Yang Baibing to strengthen control over the political work system. Some leaders, especially those from the Beijing Military Region whose support for the military crackdown was only lukewarm, appeared to have been punished. Unlike previous high-level rotations, these were not discussed by the CMC as a whole and appear to have been decided by the Yangs, perhaps in partial consultation with Deng. Yang Baibing, not Jiang Zemin, personally handled these personnel changes by visiting many of the military regions. Normally, however, the CMC chairman, not the GPD head, would preside over high-level personnel changes.[73]

The PLA's politicization harmed military work in several ways. The indoctrination campaign consumed a great deal of time and energy in leading units for the better part of a year. Up to fifty percent of training time was devoted to political study.[74] The turmoil in the Soviet Union in 1991 only further reinforced the importance of ensuring the PLA's political reliability and party control.

Major training exercises also mostly stopped. In 1988 and 1989, many military regions held large-scale exercises to explore the kinds of threats that they would face following the shift to local wars, such as "West-88" in the Lanzhou Military Region and "South Sea-89" in the Guangzhou Military Region. The last such exercise, "Forward-89," occurred in December 1989 in the Shenyang Military Region, but was most likely planned before Tiananmen. In 1990, few field training exercises were held and none occurred above the level of a single group army. Although field training increased in 1991, region-level military exercises did not resume until 1993 (one exercise, "West-93") and not consistently until 1995, after the new strategy was adopted.[75]

In addition, broader modernization efforts stalled. Planning for the Eighth Five-Year Plan began in March 1990, just as the indoctrination campaign was escalating.[76] The PLA identified a number of deficiencies that would become even more apparent after the Gulf War: a bloated force, rigid command structures, outdated weaponry and equipment, a weak defense industrial base, and poor training.[77] When drafting the new five-year plan, however, many disagreements occurred, especially during a January 1991 enlarged meeting of the CMC convened to discuss the plan. As Liu Huaqing recalled, "When high-level cadres had varied opinions, it was very hard to proceed with practical work."[78]

One element of the PLA's Eighth Five-Year Plan included a reorganization and modest downsizing. Following the 1985 reduction of one million soldiers, the force had grown to 3.29 million.[79] In December 1991, the CMC decided to limit the force to three million while focusing on reforming high-level leading bodies, primarily to further define roles and responsibilities while reducing excessive division of labor and overlapping duties.[80] Liu Huaqing recalls obliquely that, in these reforms, "some measures were not implemented." The reason, he explained, was "because relatively big changes took place in the leading bodies of each unit." In addition, "some reforms that could be made were not actually carried out due to various restrictive factors."[81] It is not clear if Liu was referring to the 1990 leadership changes or those that would occur in late 1992 and early 1993 after the Fourteenth Party Congress. Regardless, it demonstrates how politicization after 1989 influenced the ability of the PLA to do military work.

Finally, the PLA high command itself became increasingly fractured. The focus on political education further elevated the role of the political work system and the Yang brothers. More operationally oriented officers began to object to the influence of the Yang brothers and their vision for the PLA.

Reports of divisions surfaced in the Hong Kong media in the summer of 1990 and would only grow over the next two years.[82] Many resented Yang Baibing in particular because he lacked any operational experience, even during the revolution; symbolized the elevation of the GPD over the GSD and defense ministry; and had been rapidly promoted by several levels from deputy commissar of the Beijing Military Region in 1982 to director of the GPD in 1987, joining the CMC in April 1988.[83]

THE PLA BACKS DENG

Deng's efforts to consolidate his reform and opening policies further politicized the PLA. His 1991 visit to Shanghai failed to build sufficient support for reform within the party. In mid-January 1992, Deng tried again, when he embarked on what became known as his "southern tour." Over the course of one month, he visited several towns in southern China, ending up in Shenzhen in Guangdong province, one of the first special economic zones established in the early 1980s and a symbol of reform and opening. Along the way, he visited factories and gave speeches extolling his vision of reform.

Unlike his 1991 trip to Shanghai, however, Deng began to turn the tide. In mid-February, the Politburo decided to communicate Deng's remarks orally to party members of ministerial rank and above (including at the army level and above). Later that month, the *People's Daily* published several articles in support of his reforms, even though conservatives continued to speak out in opposition.[84]

The turning point, however, was an enlarged Politburo meeting in early March 1992, when a decision was made to accelerate Deng's reform and opening policies. Shortly thereafter, the *People's Daily* published a detailed account of Deng's southern tour.[85] As Deng sought to build support for his economic policies, the PLA publicly signaled its support for him. At the end of March, at the National People's Congress, Yang Baibing announced that the PLA would "protect and escort" (*baojia huhang*) Deng's reform and opening policies. Yang's remarks were then distributed by Xinhua and carried in authoritative newspapers, such as the *People's Daily* and *Liberation Army Daily*. Yang was unequivocal about the military's role in the party's political debate, stating that "the PLA will unswervingly and persistently support, sustain, join and defend reform and opening, 'protecting and escorting' reform and opening and developing the economy."[86] Thus, the PLA inserted itself into the highest level of intraparty politics. As Fewsmith writes, "This military intervention in domestic politics was a clear indication of the degree of tension in the party."[87]

Yang Baibing's remarks were not isolated. Instead, they reflected an effort by the PLA leadership, or at least by the Yangs, to support Deng in his struggle with the economic and even ideological conservatives. In Shenzhen, for example, CMC vice-chairmen Yang Shangkun and Liu Huaqing accompanied Deng. Between the end of March and the Fourteenth Party Congress in October, the phrase "protect and escort" appeared on the pages of the *Liberation Army Daily* 308 times. On the sixty-fifth anniversary of the PLA's founding in July 1992, for example, Yang Baibing published a lengthy article on protecting and escorting reform.[88] The GPD also organized four groups of generals to tour Shenzhen in the spring of 1992, retracing some of Deng's steps earlier in the year and further indicating to Deng's opponents that they lacked the support of the military.[89]

UNITY RESTORED

Following the "southern tour," disunity among the top party leadership began to dissipate. Deng's willingness to call on the army for support no doubt helped to build consensus within the top leadership of the party.[90] At the Fourteenth Party Congress in October 1992, the party championed Deng's reform policies, which became the centerpiece of the work report delivered by Jiang Zemin. The congress not only endorsed his overall policy guideline, but also the creation of a "socialist market economy," which moved beyond his original formulation for reform in the early 1980s.[91] In stark contrast to the earlier plenums, the work report reflected the reestablishment of party unity on economic policy and a clear vision for the future.

Along with his ideological victory, Deng pushed for organizational changes at the highest levels of the party. On the Politburo Standing Committee, he maintained a balance between reformers and more conservative members such as Li Peng. Four of the seven members kept their positions (Jiang Zemin, Li Peng, Qiao Shi, and Li Ruihuan) while three were added (Zhu Rongji, Liu Huaqing, and Hu Jintao). Within the PLA, however, more drastic personnel changes occurred. Although Deng had relied on the Yang brothers to ensure the PLA's loyalty after Tiananmen and then to support consolidation of his reform policies, he severed their ties with the PLA. Yang Shangkun, then eighty-six, retired from all his posts. Yang Baibing, who may have been expecting to succeed his elder half-brother as the CMC first vice-chairman, was promoted to the Politburo but stripped of all his military positions.

In addition, an almost entirely new CMC was selected. The turnover of CMC membership contrasts with the greater continuity on the Politburo Standing Committee. The only holdover from the previous CMC was Liu Huaqing, who replaced Yang Shangkun as first vice-chairman. Zhang Zhen, then commandant of the PLA's NDU, was named as the second vice-chairman. Chi Haotian, the outgoing chief of the general staff, joined the CMC as defense minister. Zhang Wannian, Yu Yongbo, and Fu Quanyou, who would lead the GSD, GPD, and GLD, respectively, were the last three additions. They were viewed as members of the "third generation" of PLA leadership and would become the "core" after 1995. Major turnover also occurred in the leadership of the general departments, especially in the GPD, where only one deputy director would remain after the party congress.[92] According to one account, three hundred officers close to Yang Baibing were replaced, transferred, or demoted.[93]

Deng articulated the rationale for these leadership changes in a secret letter written on October 6, 1992. Deng suggested that Liu Huaqing and Zhang Zhen should manage the CMC's daily work under Jiang's leadership.[94] Deng also appeared to acknowledge the problems the Yang brothers had created for the military, stressing that "the army must remain united as one and the existence of factionalism or a 'mountain-stronghold mentality' can never be tolerated."[95] He further urged that the PLA must emphasize training and cultivating younger officers who would be able to lead the military in the future, and also said that the "picking of successors needs to be done by someone who is familiar with the military," indicating this was a professional task and not a political one.[96] Reconstituting the PLA's leadership would be an important task that Liu and Zhang would undertake before their retirement in 1997.

Adoption of the 1993 Strategic Guideline

The Fourteenth Party Congress in October 1992 marked the restoration of party unity. In the PLA, operationally focused commanders and not political commissars dominated the new CMC. One of its first tasks was to adopt a new military strategy, which it would complete in December 1992.

DRAFTING THE NEW STRATEGY

The CMC formulated the 1993 strategic guideline rapidly. Less than a month after the new CMC was formed, it announced a major reshuffling of key leadership positions in the military regions and other major units. These changes were undertaken to cleanse the senior ranks of leaders associated with the Yang brothers and promote members of the "third generation" of military leaders into more senior positions. During a speech outlining the rationale for these personnel changes on November 9, Jiang Zemin suggested that the PLA needed to address military strategy. According to Jiang, "The international situation is now changing rapidly. We must closely observe and grasp developments and changes in the situation, and correctly decide our military strategic guideline."[97] He further instructed that the new guideline be based on the concept of active defense and "attach great importance to the influence of high technology on the development of military affairs and building a quality army."[98] Earlier, during an army-wide meeting on military affairs at the end of 1990, Jiang stated that although "active defense" was the PLA's strategic guideline, it should be "carried forward and developed . . . following changes in the situation."[99] After the Gulf War and restoration of party unity, the situation had clearly changed.

Jiang's comment might suggest that top party leaders and not military ones pushed for adopting a new strategic guideline. Jiang, however, was likely drawing on his own participation in the PLA's discussions of the Gulf War in 1991, as well as the GSD's reports on reconsidering China's military strategy submitted to the CMC in both 1991 and 1992. As CMC chairman, Jiang would have almost certainly read these reports. Nevertheless, the CMC did not act on these reports at the time. One possibility is that it would have empowered the GSD at the expense of the GPD under Yang Baibing's leadership. Another is that the CMC may have been unable to reach agreement upon the reports, either because they would have likely empowered the GSD at the expense of the GPD or because the party leadership was distracted by its disunity. Nevertheless, Jiang's remark indicates that the top party leader agreed to a change proposed by senior military officers.

Afterward, the CMC moved quickly. Zhang Zhen assumed the overall leadership of the development of the new strategy, presumably because of his experience in the early 1980s in the GSD's operations department, as well as from his experience founding the PLA's NDU in the mid-1980s.[100] The CMC instructed the GSD, AMS, NDU, and CMC general office to draft documents and produce opinions on various aspects of the new guideline.[101] The CMC tasked Zhang Wannian in his capacity as chief of the general staff with drafting a report and providing suggestions for the new strategy. Zhang Wannian established an investigation group (*lunzheng xiaozu*), led by the operations department along with members from the GPD and GLD. Key members of the group were Xu Huizi, then head of the operations department, and Xiong Guangkai, from military intelligence, who was responsible for assessments of the international situation. The group focused on developing answers to four questions: "With whom will we fight? Where will we fight? What is the character (*xingzhi*) of the war that we will fight? How will we fight?"[102]

The CMC also decided to hold a small-scale symposium (*zuotanhui*) on military strategy in early December 1992. The purpose was to analyze "the international strategic situation and closely examine the regional security environment," which would be a key factor in formulating the new guideline.[103] The symposium opened on December 5, 1992. A report produced by Zhang Wannian's assessment group served as the basis for discussion. The meeting was originally envisioned as a "retreat" (*wuxuhui*), but the discussion was described as "heated." A range of issues were raised, including assessments of the international strategic situation and China's regional security environment, as well as the historical development of China's strategic guidelines, weapons, training, and personnel.[104]

At the end of two days, the group reached consensus on the "basic foundation and content" of the new strategy. The meeting reaffirmed Deng's 1985 judgment that total war was unlikely, that peace and development remained the "trend of the times," that the world was moving toward a multipolar structure, and that mutual interdependence would restrict the outbreak of war. Local conflicts, however, were unavoidable and would be the most likely situation for the PLA to confront. The basis of preparations for military struggle should be high-technology local wars. Given the prior assessments of the Gulf War, this is perhaps unsurprising.[105]

The focus on high-technology local wars, however, raised another question—namely, how to carry out "active defense" under these conditions. Participants agreed on the importance of traditional ideas such as "gaining control by striking afterwards" (*houfa zhiren*) and "being rooted in using inferior equipment to defeat an enemy."[106] Zhang Zhen also highlighted challenges that the PLA would need to resolve under "new conditions," including rapid reaction, flexibility, and effectively subduing the enemy (*youxiao zhidi*). To address these challenges, Zhang Wannian proposed that China must create "fists" (*quantou*) and "assassin's maces" (*shashoujian*). The "fists" would be units with strong mobile operational capabilities, especially naval, air, and conventional missile forces. According to Zhang Wannian, "As soon as an incident occurs, these forces can be sent rapidly to the theater, control the situation, and resolve problems." The "assassin's maces" referred to the development of advanced weapons that can be useful means for actually "subduing the enemy."[107]

After the meeting, Zhang Wannian's group spent the rest of December completing a report with recommendations for the new strategic guideline. The CMC also held several standing committee meetings to discuss issues relating to the new guideline.[108] On December 31, 1992, the report on the guideline was completed and sent to Jiang Zemin. This report formed the basis of the speech that Jiang delivered at an enlarged meeting of the CMC in January to formally adopt the new strategy.

As this account suggests, top military leaders and not political ones directed the drafting and formulation of the new strategy. The only top party leader involved was Jiang Zemin, but largely in his ex officio capacity as CMC chairman and he played only an indirect role. Although Jiang did not participate directly in the symposium in early December, he did review the materials from the meetings, including the transcripts of speeches and presentations, offering suggestions and changes.[109] He most likely did not attend the CMC's standing committee meetings, but likely did review their reports.

The CMC enlarged meeting opened on January 13 and would last for seven days. On the first day, Jiang, as CMC chairman, delivered a report on the new strategic guideline that linked clearly the new strategy with the Gulf War. He said that "the facts of the Gulf War demonstrate that, following the application of high technology in the military domain, the accuracy of weapons and the intensity of operations have reached unprecedented heights while the characteristics of suddenness, three-dimensionality, mobility, rapidity and deep strikes [in wars] are extremely prominent." Thus, "whoever has high-tech superiority clearly has the initiative on the battlefield."[110]

ALTERNATIVE EXPLANATIONS

Several alternative explanations cannot account for the decision to change the strategic guideline in early 1993. One would be that China faced a new or more pressing threat to its security, which in turn prompted China to reconsider its existing strategy and adopt a new one. Nevertheless, Jiang Zemin in his speech introducing the new strategic guideline stated unequivocally that "our . . . relations with peripheral countries are the best ever since the founding of the country."[111] Jiang was certainly referring to the dissipation of the Soviet threat on China's northern border. His remark also represented a conclusion that the current territorial disputes with India and Vietnam were not severe. Liu Huaqing, for example, concluded in 1990 these issues "should not be overestimated."[112] In other assessments between 1990 and 1992, Liu also noted how China's security environment had improved.[113] Since Chinese sources from this period do not refer to external threats as playing an important role in the strategic guideline, it offers a weak explanation for the decision to adopt a new strategy in 1993.

Another related explanation would focus on China's assessment of a growing threat from the United States. The collapse of bipolarity left the United States as the only remaining superpower in the world and thus a threatening country in general because of its unparalleled capabilities. It may have been perhaps especially threatening for China, with whom relations had deteriorated significantly after the massacre in Tiananmen Square in 1989. Such assessments would have been sharpened after the Gulf War, which displayed America's unrivaled military prowess.

After the 1995–96 Taiwan Straits crisis and especially after the 1999 Kosovo War, the US threat began to play a greater role in China's assessments of the international situation. Jiang Zemin's 1993 speech introducing the new strategic guideline, however, does not contain any direct references to the United States. The indirect references to "hegemony" and "power politics" did likely refer to the United States, but largely for ideological reasons, as China viewed the West as encouraging China's "peaceful evolution" to weaken the CCP. Jiang called for vigilance, noting that "world socialism is at a low ebb, and international hostile forces are increasing their infiltration of and subversive activities within socialist countries."[114]

Nevertheless, the overall assessment of the international situation in the report introducing the new guideline was relatively benign. First, China did not view the end of the Cold War as increasing the US threat. Instead, the judgment was that "the world is now becoming multipolar, mutual constraints are increasing in the international arena, and the forces for peace continue to grow."[115] Furthermore, Jiang's report suggested that the West was not too threatening, noting that "conflicts within and between Western countries are daily coming to light and becoming more intense, and the internal and external difficulties of these countries continue to grow."[116] China saw fewer constraints and more opportunities. Regarding threats, the report emphasized "ethnic, religious and territorial conflicts" suppressed during the Cold War, and global military competition in the area of high technology. Thus, at the time that the strategy was adopted, it did not reflect a judgment that the United States posed new or pressing threat to China.

An additional potential explanation would emphasize new missions that had arisen for the PLA, which required a new strategy to execute them. Specifically, the collapse of bipolarity reinforced the judgment that the kinds of wars it would most likely face in the future would be local wars on China's periphery and not total wars on Chinese homeland territory. The PLA, however, had reached this conclusion earlier, based on its assessment of the trend in US-USSR relations and the likelihood of a total war in the mid-1980s. Moreover, it had incorporated local wars into the strategic guideline adopted in December 1988. The essential contribution of the 1993 guideline was to describe how China believed that these wars would be fought, which the 1988 guideline did not address. The Gulf War provided clarity about how local wars would be fought.

A final alternative explanation would focus on emulation—specifically, that China sought to emulate the United States after the Gulf War by adopting its military strategy. As the 1990s progressed, the PLA's efforts to study the military experience and operational doctrines of the United States increased. The Gulf War was studied intensely as an example of a local high technology war, for example. Published US doctrine on joint operations was a key reference point for the PLA's own approach to the subject. Some of the changes in force structure, such as the shift from divisions to brigades among the ground forces, likely reflected the study of the United States and other advanced militaries.

Nevertheless, emulation is an inadequate explanation for the adoption of the 1993 guideline. To start, when the guideline was adopted, China's focus was on how to use its existing equipment to fight under high-technology conditions. The primary problem was how to fight under these conditions, not how to fight like the United States. In this way, the 1993 guideline reveals the limitation of arguments about emulation when applied to strategy in particular, versus the spread of specific kinds of military capabilities or organizational forms within military organizations. China's intensive study of the United States through the 1990s, especially toward the end of the decade, was also intended to identify weaknesses that could be exploited in addition to areas to copy. Finally, over the course of the 1990s, the PLA did pursue its own innovations. The most noteworthy would be the development of conventional ballistic missiles, especially short-range ones that have been deployed adjacent to Taiwan across the Strait.[117]

Implementation of the New Strategy

The PLA began to implement the new strategy soon after the enlarged meeting of the CMC in January 1993. Training was reformed, new operational doctrine was drafted and promulgated, and 700,000 soldiers were cut from the force. Taken together, the measures to implement the 1993 strategic guideline not only underscore that it constituted a major change in China's military strategy, but also that the organizational changes required by the new guideline were consistent with the factor that prompted the change in the guideline in the first place—a significant shift in the conduct of warfare, as revealed in the Gulf War.

THE JUNE 1993 CMC OPERATIONS MEETING

From June 8 to June 20, 1993, the CMC held an operations meeting to implement the new military strategy. Documentary sources on the meeting are limited but indicate that the purpose was to adjust operational tasks in various strategic directions and further clarify the basic principles for combat readiness and future operations. Participants included the leadership of the military regions and the services.[118]

At the meeting, CMC vice-chairman Liu Huaqing stressed the role of offensive operations in campaigns and battles to achieve strategically defensive goals. Liu first emphasized the importance of using military power to deter an adversary and avoid war to ensure China's development. Then, he underscored how the advent of high-technology warfare challenged the PLA's traditional approach to defense. According to Liu, the PLA in the past had emphasized a fixed defense (*jianshou fangyu*) to deal with an adversary's large-scale invasion. Now, citing several local wars such as the Gulf War, "the situation is no longer the same." He said the key in striving for the initiative "depends on whether you have an active sense of attack and whether you can organize strong offensive operations."[119] For Liu, one lesson of Iraq's defeat in the Gulf War was that a technologically inferior side who pursued a passive defense would lose the initiative. Weaker states like China "must rely on active offensive operations to seize the initiative."[120] He speculated that if Iraq had concentrated forces to launch assaults against the United States, presumably before all US forces had been deployed to the region, it might have altered the situation.[121] He also referred to China's own conflicts after 1949, such as the border war with India, to note that "without active offensive operations in campaigns and battles, the general goal of strategic defense cannot be realized."[122]

CMC vice-chairman Zhang Zhen addressed changes to the guiding thought for operations. Zhang introduced the concept of "integrated operations, key-point strikes" as operational guiding thought for campaigns. The concept was first raised during a series of meetings on campaigns that Zhang had organized at the PLA's NDU in the late 1980s, drawing partly on the study of American and Soviet doctrine. Zhang noted that the concept had received new attention, as it "accorded with developing trends in modern local wars."[123] Future wars would be "based on the joint operations of the various services and branches that is unprecedented for our army," underscoring that joint operations would become the main form of operations in the new strategy and key to the concept of "integrated operations."[124] He also noted that the advent of high-technology wars challenged the traditional Maoist principles of concentrating forces to fight battles of annihilation. For Zhang, the concentration of forces must focus on quality as well as quantity, while also being combined with the concentration of firepower (not soldiers). In the past, he observed, the PLA would concentrate forces through "advanced deployments" (*yuxian bushu*). Now, however, the PLA needed to use rapid mobility within operations to concentrate forces.[125]

Both Liu Huaqing and Zhang Zhen underscored that China's new approach to operations must satisfy several criteria. First, military actions would need to serve political goals and to be coordinated with economic and diplomatic elements of statecraft. Second, China had only limited funds with which to modernize its force, which meant that the study of operations should emphasize how to wage high-technology warfare from an inferior position, with the weapons and equipment that China possessed. The immediate task was to reform training and then rewrite China's operational doctrine. The meeting also reviewed and adjusted operational guidance for different strategic directions.

TRAINING

After adopting the new strategy, the PLA immediately began to reform training. Although improving training had been a key component of the PLA's Eighth Five-Year Plan, the GSD revamped the approach to training in line with the new strategy. In March 1993, CMC vice-chairman Zhang Zhen instructed that "the GSD should revise training plans for cadres and troops according to the military strategic guideline for the new period. Last year's arrangements for training should be adjusted and necessary reforms should be undertaken."[126] In response, the GSD submitted a report to the CMC outlining how training would be reformed, which was then distributed to all troops and the military academies. The report contained the basic principles and main missions for training and adjusted the 1993 army-wide training tasks published at the end of 1992. Reflecting the new strategy, the report shifted the basis of training from "dealing with general wars" to winning local high-technology wars.[127]

In June 1993, the GSD initiated training reform by issuing two notices, one on training and the other on military academies. When distributing the notices, Chief of the General Staff Zhang Wannian instructed that two key points should be highlighted: "the operational methods [*zhanfa*] and training methods [*xunfa*] for local wars under high-technology conditions."[128] Training reform would include the content and methods of training programs as well as support and management of training. Pilot units to carry out reforms were identified in each of the services.[129] Taken together, the "one document, two notices" formed the basis of changes in training to meet the requirements of the new strategy.[130]

In September 1993, the GSD organized a large group training (*jixun*) under the code name "934." This was the first army-wide training exercise undertaken to explore how to link training with the characteristics of the high-technology battlefield.[131] The 934 meeting itself was organized by the Jinan and Guangzhou Military Regions as well as the PLA Navy and PLA Air Force to explore pilot training outlines (*gangmu*) for amphibious landing, urban, mountain, and airborne operations.[132] Together, the "four kinds of outlines" covered the main contingencies China might face on its periphery, which had been identified in early 1992, when Beijing became more anxious about Hong Kong's return after Governor Chris Patten sought to pursue democratic reforms before the handover in 1997.[133] The meeting explored the organization and command, operational methods, and coordination among the services for these operations.[134]

Several thousand individuals participated, including the leaders from major units as well as personnel from key offices (*jiguan*) and the services. CMC vice-chairman Liu Huaqing attended the session along with most of the GSD's leadership.[135] Liu described the event as "a major act to implement the CMC's military strategic guideline for the new period."[136] The head of the GSD's training department recalled that the meeting "was another step towards studying and understanding the guideline. They helped establish the thinking that [for China] a war would have to be fought with the equipment in hand."[137] As Liu and Hua had emphasized, the PLA needed to determine how best to fight with the inferior equipment it possessed before new and more advanced equipment was acquired. The inclusion of the PLAN and PLAAF reflected the emphasis on coordination (*xietong*) in joint operations.

Over the next several years, the tempo of training increased. Areas of focus included night fighting, air defense, electronic warfare, maneuver operations (*jidong zuozhan*), and logistics and support, among other topics. The PLA also held some of its largest field exercises since 1949. In "Shensheng-94," the PLAN practiced how to blockade "a large island" (such as Taiwan), while in "Kongjian-94" the PLAAF established new guiding principles for conducting air strikes. Meanwhile, the Shenyang Military Region held an exercise for coordinating ground, air, and naval units to counter an air strike.[138] All these exercises were experimental, designed to explore how training exercises should be reformed. Nevertheless, they indicate how the focus on high-technology operations guided the planning and execution of training exercises after the new guideline was established.[139]

In 1995, the focus of training reform turned to "operational methods" (*zhanfa*). Zhang Wannian defined operational methods as "how wars should be fought."[140] In March 1995, the CMC approved a three-year plan for deepening research on operational methods, which was also linked to the development of operational doctrine, as discussed in the next section. The goal of this effort was to develop an "operational system" for the 1993 strategic guideline. Topics to be addressed included operational theory for local high-technology wars, operational guiding principles and countermeasures for each strategic and campaign direction, and concrete operational methods for divisions and regiments.[141]

In October 1995, the GSD organized a major meeting on operational methods in the Lanzhou Military Region under the code name "9510." Participants included officers in charge of training and experimental or pilot units at all major units, along with the Lanzhou Military Region and GSD leaders. The meeting's goal was to review the operational methods for fighting high-technology wars that had been developed in the past three years. Zhang Wannian stressed the need to incorporate science and technology into training, emphasizing information technology as being "of the utmost importance" and a force multiplier.[142] He also emphasized the need to link operational tasks with the study of operational methods for all strategic directions, underscoring the importance of joint operations. By this point, as Zhang had stated in June 1995, the PLA had concluded that "joint operations among the services had already become the basic pattern of operations [*zuozhan yangshi*] of local high-technology wars."[143]

Following these three years of study, the CMC issued a "new generation" training program in November 1995 that would provide an overarching framework for annual training directives. Reflecting the new strategy, the 1995 training program "revolved around winning local wars under modern high-technology conditions."[144] The new training program contained the first army-wide framework for the ground forces, navy, air force, Second Artillery, COSTIND, PAP.[145] In addition to improving knowledge of high technology and tech skills throughout the force, it emphasized more realistic combat training (*shizhan*) and countering high-technology surveillance and reconnaissance systems, electronic warfare equipment, and precision strike weapons, among other areas. The *Liberation Army Daily* stated that the new training program "symbolized another historic transformation in our army's military training" and that "the content of the various services and branches training underwent in-depth and systematic reform."[146]

Afterward, the pace of training increased. Events across the Taiwan Strait created an opportunity for training exercises. A series of exercises were held in 1995 and 1996, including a joint island landing campaign ("Lian"-96) as well as conventional missile exercises ("Shenjian"-95), culminating in the March 1996 exercise. In addition to the deterrent and signaling goals of these exercises, they also represented opportunities for the PLA to practice a nascent form of joint operations. In December 1997, the GSD convened an army-wide symposium (*zuotanhui*) to review training reforms since 1993. More important, the meeting decided several measures for further improving training, including deepening the focus on the "adversary's situation" (*diqing*) and new operational methods (*zhanfa*). The meeting also stressed the need to enhance the knowledge and role of high technology in training, and a more scientific approach to training methods.[147]

OPERATIONAL DOCTRINE

Following the study of operational methods, the PLA drafted and issued new operational doctrine. As described by Zhang Wannian, "Operations regulations . . . are the basic foundation for training and operations of the army. They relate directly to combat effectiveness."[148] To draft new operations regulations, the CMC established an army-wide commission to standardize operational concepts and the format of these regulations, thereby strengthening coordination among the services. Previously, individual units had drafted their own regulations, apparently without coordinating with each other.[149] As chief of the general staff, Zhang Wannian headed the commission, whose members included leaders from the three general departments. The commission's office was housed within the Department of Campaigns and Tactics at AMS.

At one of the commission's first meetings in August 1995, Zhang Wannian outlined the general principles for drafting new regulations. Most important, he linked the need for new regulations with the 1993 strategy. The strategic guideline, he said, "urgently demands that we draft regulations and earnestly summarize experiences from training and exercises in recent years."[150] Moreover, "the regulations must be suited to the requirements of local wars under modern especially high-technology conditions"—in other words, the basis of preparations for military struggle in the new strategy.[151] Zhang further noted that the regulations should be based on the "operational target" and "main operational directions in the future."[152] He also stressed the importance of finding ways to use the equipment that the PLA currently possessed to defeat a more capable adversary: a clear indication that China's operational doctrine would not emulate the United States and instead would need to identify countermeasures for defending against technologically more capable adversaries. Areas of initial focus included landing operations, urban warfare, mountain operations, airborne operations, sea and air blockade, island and reef operations, and night operations, all under high-technology conditions.[153]

In 1999, the drafting process was completed and the army-wide commission approved two sets of operations regulations that would be issued by the CMC. The number and scope of the new regulations eclipses all that the PLA had published before. The first set of regulations was seven campaign outlines (*zhanyi gangyao*) that replaced the single *Science of Campaigns Outline* published in 1987.[154] The most important outline was the *Joint Campaign Outline*, the PLA's first written doctrine on joint operations. The other campaign outlines covered the ground forces, navy, air force, missile force, logistics, and equipment and support. In 1997, an AMS and NDU research team drafted a document on the main points for the new campaign outlines, which concluded that "the campaigns that our army will conduct in the future will normally be joint campaigns."[155] Consistent with the 1993 guideline, the joint campaign outline affirmed the judgment that the PLA would need to fight local wars "under the conditions of the broad use of high-technology weapons and equipment."[156] The joint campaign outline identified the PLA's primary campaigns as island blockade, island assault, border area counterattack, counter–air raid, and anti-landing campaigns; it also described the basic methods for prosecuting them.[157] Reflecting these campaigns, the joint campaign outline described the operational tasks for the PLA as "[to] maintain unity of the motherland, defend the sovereignty of territorial waters and maritime rights and interests, defend the territorial sovereignty of border areas, defend important coastal areas, and defend the security of airspace over strategic areas."[158] The joint campaign outline also affirmed that the main battlefields would be coastal and border areas, especially the southeastern coastal area—or, in other words, a Taiwan contingency. The main challenge would be confronting a technologically superior adversary.[159]

The 1999 campaign outlines marked a clear break with Mao Zedong's "ten military principles," introduced in 1947. Conceived in the context of the civil war, Mao's principles provided mostly tactical guidance for light infantry forces and emphasized defeating an opponent through battles of annihilation and the concentration of superior forces.[160] Building on Zhang Zhen's 1993 proposal, the 1999 joint campaign outline identified the "basic guiding thought for campaigns" as "integrated operations, keypoint strikes."[161] The concept called for combining all available forces to destroy and paralyze an enemy's "operational system."[162] That is, the PLA would focus on destroying the enemy's fighting systems to paralyze its ability to fight, rather than simply destroying or annihilating an opponent's forces. In addition, ten new basic principles of campaigns were developed to replace Mao's principles. These include: know the enemy and know yourself, be fully prepared, be proactive, concentrate forces, in-depth strikes, take the enemy by surprise, unified coordination, continuous fighting, comprehensive support, and political superiority.[163]

The second set of regulations published in 1999 was combat regulations based on the campaign outlines. These focused on the operational and tactical level of military operations within each of the services. Eighty-nine such regulations were published. The primary document was the *General Combat Principles for a Combined Army* which replaced a document with the same title published in 1987. The core principle identified as the basic thought for tactics was "integrated and combined, in-depth and multi-layered, keypoint strikes" (*zhengti hetong, zongshen liti, zhongdian daji*).[164] The combat regulations were drafted to "uphold the military strategic guideline for the new period as the basis and emphasize reflecting the combat characteristics and laws of local wars under modern high-technology conditions."[165] The document on general principles provided a framework for combat regulations for combined arms operations for divisions, brigades, and regiments along with similar regulations for the navy, air force, Second Artillery, logistics, and equipment and support. A further eighty-three regulations were issued for specific services and branches, including twenty-seven for the ground forces, twenty-one for the navy, fourteen for the air force, four for the Second Artillery, nine for logistics, and eight for equipment and support.[166]

FORCE STRUCTURE AND THE NINTH FIVE-YEAR PLAN

The 1993 strategy was adopted in the middle of the Eighth Five-Year Plan. Thus, organizational reforms beyond training and operational doctrine could not be launched until the start of the Ninth Five-Year Plan in 1996. The development and execution of this plan demonstrates how the new strategic guideline was implemented throughout the PLA, consistent with the rationale for pursuing the new strategy. Two overarching concepts emerged from the planning process: the notion that the PLA was undergoing "two fundamental transformations," especially the emphasis on quality over quantity, and the idea of "strengthening the army through science and technology" (*keji qiangjun*). Organizationally, the most important component of the plan was the decision to reduce the force by five hundred thousand soldiers in order to increase the quality and operational effectiveness of the force.

In January 1995, the CMC established a leading small group to draft the Ninth Five-Year Plan for the PLA. Zhang Wannian, as chief of the general staff, headed the group and was charged with submitting it to the CMC standing committee by September 1995.[167] At the group's first meeting, Zhang clearly linked the content of the five-year plan with the new military strategy, noting that the plan "must revolve around thoroughly implementing the military strategic guideline of the new period."[168] Goals for the plan included making breakthroughs in some defense technologies and weapons programs, strengthening key units and readiness in the main directions of "military struggle," deepening reform and streamlining, and raising the quality of officers.[169] In a subsequent meeting in March 1995, Zhang stated that the plan must solve two problems: scale and funding. These two challenges were related, as the force would need to be downsized so that even more resources could be invested in the development of high-technology equipment. This was the "optimum" choice for the "preparations for military struggle."[170]

After the leading small group completed a draft plan in September 1995, the CMC standing committee discussed it seven times. In December 1995, the CMC held an enlarged meeting where Zhang Wannian introduced and summarized the plan.[171] The core of the plan subsequently became known as the "two fundamental transformations": the transformation from preparing to fight and win general local wars to local wars under high-technology conditions, and the transformation from focusing on quantity and mass in force development to quality and technology. Although the first transformation had already effectively been determined by the 1993 guideline, the second transformation reflected how the PLA would achieve the requirements of the new strategy. Zhang noted that the plan was designed to overcome gaps in China's force development described as the "three maladjustments" (sange bu shiying): the incompatibility with China's international status, the incompatibility with major trends in the development of military technology, and the incompatibility with the requirements of winning local wars under modern high-technology conditions.[172]

The Ninth Five-Year Plan for the military had several components. First, the force would be reduced from 3 million to 2.5 million soldiers. This downsizing included substantial changes in organization and force structure. Second, emergency mobile operations units would be given new equipment to ensure that they had an integrated operational capability. This reflected an effort to invest heavily in the modernization of a select number of units. Third, national defense scientific and technological research would be strengthened so that "assassin's maces" with a "strong deterrent capability" would be developed. Fourth, combat readiness in "the main direction of military struggle," presumably the southeast, would be strengthened. The plan also called for reforming the cadre system to improve the quality of officers, increasing standardization by strengthening laws and regulations, and deepening logistics and support reform.[173]

To achieve all these objectives, Zhang Wannian introduced the idea of "strengthening the army through science and technology" (*keji qiangjun*). For him, this was the crux of realizing the two fundamental transformations. The key points were strengthening national defense scientific research, improving weapons and equipment, raising the scientific and technological quality of officers and soldiers, establishing a scientific system and organization, and raising the level of scientific innovation capability and scientific management.[174]

At the same meeting, other leaders also linked the objectives of the five-year plan with the new military strategic guideline. For example, Jiang Zemin noted that "if we do not increase quality, we will not adapt to the development of the situation and have no way of completing the tasks of preparations for military struggle in the new period."[175] Regarding weapons development, the meeting determined that the PLA should focus on a rather ambitious program to develop capabilities for air defense, anti-submarine warfare, long-range strike, command and control, communications, intelligence and reconnaissance, electronic warfare, and precision-guided weapons.[176] In addition, as Liu Huaqing noted in his speech, the PLA should "create some 'assassin's maces' that will scare the enemy," which are also described as "new type" weapons.[177]

DOWNSIZING AND REORGANIZATION

One of the main goals of the Ninth Five-Year Plan was to reduce the size of the PLA while increasing its quality and combat effectiveness. The means for achieving this end was another effort at "streamlining and reorganization" (*jingjian zhengbian*). In so doing, the PLA believed that it was adapting itself to major changes that had occurred with the advent of high-technology warfare and implementation of the 1993 strategic guideline.

Although the Ninth Five-Year Plan started in January 1996, the decision to reduce the force by 500,000 was not announced until September 1997 at the Fifteenth Party Congress. Similar to the establishment of the five-year plan, a leading small group was established to plan for the downsizing and headed by Fu Quanyou, now the chief of the general staff.[178] On the basis of the leading group's work, Zhang Wannian and Chi Haotian, now vice-chairmen of the CMC, sent a report on the streamlining plan to Jiang Zemin in January 1998. The report stated that by the end of 1997, 240,000 troops had been reduced through the transfer of units (mostly infantry divisions) to the People's Armed Police.[179] These units were only lightly mechanized and did not have many subordinate combat arms, such as armored units. The remaining question, however, was how to identify the other 260,000 troops to be cut and how to reform the "system and establishment" (*tizhi bianzhi*).

In early February 1998, the CMC held a standing committee meeting to discuss the leading small group's report. Jiang Zemin outlined three principles to guide the streamlining and reorganization known as the "three benefits" (*san youyi yu*): 1) strengthening centralized, unified leadership; 2) education, training and management; and 3) future wars.[180] The CMC's principles for the downsizing were: "reduce numbers, raise quality, optimize the structure, rationalize relations."[181] In short, the goal was to combine the reduction in the overall size of the force with a major reorganization of the PLA.

At this time, debate within the PLA leadership focused on three major and potentially revolutionary changes. These included whether to create a separate department for the ground forces (*lujunbu*), whether to alter the function of the military regions so that they no longer exercised command over the ground forces, and whether to establish a general armaments department. These options were debated intensely for several months. Historically, ground force units were under the command of the military regions, which in turn were commanded by the CMC (through the GSD). Thus, advocates within the GSD wanted to remove one command layer by establishing a ground forces department and eliminating the command function of the military regions over the group armies. Others, however, maintained that this would create duplication if the military regions and ground forces department held the same rank (and presumably had some command responsibilities).[182]

The debate came to a head during a CMC standing committee meeting on March 29, 1998. Unusually, Jiang Zemin personally presided over the meeting. According to Zhang Wannian's biography, Jiang instructed that a general armaments department would be established, but a ground forces department would not be established and the function of the military regions would remain unchanged.

How to structure the command of the ground forces was not a new issue for the PLA. As early as 1982, some officers had suggested establishing a ground forces headquarters (*lujun silingbu*).[183] The fault lines of this debate are not entirely clear. Zhang Wannian's biographers describe him as opposing a fundamental alteration to the ground forces command structure and supporting keeping the military regions as command organizations. One concern was that the creation of a new department would potentially introduce another layer in the command structure and thereby subvert the streamlining effort. Another concern was that a single department would be unable to effectively oversee all the PLA's group armies, and that management would actually be weakened and not strengthened. Zhang also believed that the military regions could be used to strengthen the ability to conduct high-technology joint operations, presumably as war zones for joint operations. His reservations reflected a view that the PLA, since the civil war, had been well served by using military regions to command its forces, along with his own career within the ground forces.[184] Nevertheless, the consideration of such a potentially revolutionary change for the PLA reflected the willingness to engage in fundamental reforms if required by the new strategy.

Once Jiang Zemin had issued his instructions for the overall framework for the downsizing and streamlining, the GSD's leading small group began to draft a detailed plan. The plan was discussed during an enlarged meeting of the CMC on April 22 and approved two days later. On May 4, 1998, the CMC issued the plan for the downsizing, which would occur in three phases: in the second half of 1998, the streamlining of units and troops would occur, while the weapons and equipment and logistics units would be streamlined in the first half of 1999. In the second half of 1999, academies, training organs, and other units would be streamlined. The basic principle behind the downsizing was to reduce the size of the force while increasing overall quality. Improvements in quality and, thus, effectiveness would be achieved by reducing the number of administrative departments, general forces, and support units while strengthening key units. The goal was the same as in 1985: "Elite, integrated, efficient."[185]

In a speech that has never been openly published, Jiang linked the downsizing and reorganization with the goals of the 1993 strategic guideline. Jiang noted that future warfare would be "informatized" and an "exchange of knowledge," which would blur the links between weapons systems and operational units through use of information technology. As a result, these trends "require military organizations to transform accordingly," as the current method of organization was suited for the industrial age and not the information age.[186] The downsizing and reorganization should be "centered on implementing the military strategic guideline for the new period" and "fixed on winning local wars under modern especially high-technology conditions."[187]

The results of the downsizing were impressive and broad-based. First, flexibility and efficiency of command was increased by reducing redundancies created by leading bodies (*jiguan*) in high-level units. Multiple offices often had responsibility for the same issue, while many departments had similar functions.[188] The number of offices in the general departments, seven military regions, and the services was reduced by 11.5 percent. At the army level and above, a total of 1,500 offices were eliminated. Even deeper cuts occurred within the provincial-level military districts and the subprovincial-level military sub-districts, where the number of personnel was reduced by 20 percent.[189]

Second, in addition to streamlining command functions, the structure of the force was optimized. The goal was to make units smaller, lighter, and more diversified by reducing the number of ground forces. Overall, the size of the ground forces decreased by 18.6 percent. Some divisions and regiments were removed from the group armies and were repurposed as divisions within the People's Armed Police. Within the ground force, priority for new equipment was given to selected units. Although the overall size of the air force, navy, and Second Artillery also shrank, the cuts were not as deep. In the services, outdated equipment was retired, while aging ports and air fields were closed. The number of organizational units (*jianzhi danwei*) and command levels were reduced. The navy shrunk by 11.4 percent, the air force 12.6 percent, and the Second Artillery only 2.9 percent.[190]

Third, an entirely new system for weapons and equipment was established. A new general department was created—the General Armaments Department—to solve army-wide problems in the management of weapons and equipment. This was the first general department created since changes to China's general staff structure in 1958. Although China sought to fill key gaps in its order of battle by purchasing modern equipment from Russia, indigenous production remained the long-term goal and was implied by the 1993 guideline. Reportedly modeled on the French Directorate General of Armaments, the purpose of the new department was to strengthen central control over weapons research, development, and production. The GAD absorbed all military personnel from the organization it replaced, the Commission on Science, Technology, and Industry for National Defense (COSTIND) as well as its "most prestigious and profitable assets," including all test ranges, facilities, and research institutes for nuclear and conventional weapons.[191]

In 2003, the CMC announced that a further 200,000 personnel would be trimmed. Almost all of the cuts in this round came from the ground forces. Overall, 130,000 personnel were eliminated, along with another 60,000 who were cut from headquarters units in the military regions and military districts (which were army-dominated command structures). Almost all of these personnel were officers. When the reductions were completed in 2005, the army had shrunk by 1.5 percent while the air, navy, and missile forces grew by 3.8 percent.[192] In the 2003 reductions, more divisions were downsized to brigades or reorganized into other types of units, such as a motorized infantry unit into a mechanized or armored one. In addition, in some divisions, one of three infantry regiments were reorganized as an armored one.[193]

Conclusion

The strategic guideline adopted in 1993 represents the third major change in China's military strategy. The content of the guideline, along with its implementation, demonstrates that the PLA's senior officers sought to prepare for a new kind of war: "high-technology local wars." The 1991 Gulf War decisively shaped how PLA officers believed wars would be fought in the future.

Nevertheless, the PLA high command could not immediately adjust China's military strategy because of the divisions within the party and then the military after the crackdown in Tiananmen Square. Only after Deng Xiaoping rebuilt consensus around continuing with reform, and around his leadership, was the PLA able to adopt a new military strategy.

7

China's Military Strategies since 1993: "Informatization"

Since 1993, China has adjusted its military strategy twice: in 2004 and 2014. These strategic guidelines, however, represent minor and not major changes in China's military strategy. Nevertheless, they merit examination because they are the most recent guidelines that the CMC has adopted. The 2004 guideline remained focused on local wars but highlighted the role of "informatization" in warfare and marked a shift in the main form of operations from joint operations to "integrated joint operations." The 2014 guideline further emphasized informatization and remains focused on integrated joint operations.

The analysis in this chapter remains preliminary. Unlike the previous strategic guidelines, little documentary evidence is available with which to study the decision-making behind the adoption of the 2004 and 2014 guidelines. The senior military officers involved in formulating them have not yet written their memoirs or may even still be on active duty. Official collections of documents and official chronologies have not yet been compiled for senior military officers on the CMC when these adjustments were made.

This chapter proceeds as follows. The first section examines the 2004 strategic guideline, while the second section examines the 2014 strategic guideline. Each section describes the background to the adoption of these guidelines, their content, and the likely reasons for the change in strategy.

The 2004 Strategy: "Winning Local Wars under Informatized Conditions"

In June 2004, an enlarged meeting of the CMC adopted a new strategic guideline. Available sources suggest that the 2004 strategic guideline did not constitute a major change in China's military strategy. Instead, it reflected an adjustment to the 1993 strategy, highlighting the manifestation of high technology in warfare as "informatization" or the application of information technology to all aspects of military operations. As one authoritative source describes, the 2004 guideline "enriched and improved" (*chongshi wanshan*) the 1993 guideline—language indicating a limited adjustment in military strategy and not a major change.[1]

OVERVIEW OF THE 2004 STRATEGY

Limited information is available with which to assess the content of the 2004 guideline. No speech or document introducing it has been published.[2] Like the 1993 strategy, the 2004 guideline remained premised on fighting a local war on China's periphery, not a total war of invasion of Chinese territory. The main strategic direction remained the southeast, referring specifically to a war that might occur over Taiwan and one that could involve the United States. Authoritative doctrinal sources indicate that the PLA remained focused on the same main joint campaigns that were identified under the previous strategy, including island assault (Taiwan), island blockade (Taiwan), and border area counterattack (India) campaigns, among others.[3] The strategic guiding thought in the new guideline was "contain crises, control war situations, win wars" (*ezhi weiji, kongzhi zhanju, daying zhanzheng*).[4] In this way, it retained the emphasis in the 1993 strategy on deterrence as well as warfighting, while further stressing crisis prevention, management, and control.

The 2004 guideline was adopted at a June 2004 meeting of the CMC. The key change concerned the assessment of the basis of preparations for military struggle, as "informatized conditions" (*xinxihua tiaojian*) replaced "high-technology conditions" in the 1993 guideline.[5] At the meeting, Jiang Zemin stated that "we must clearly place the basis of preparations for military struggle on winning local wars under informatized conditions." This change reflected the CMC's judgment that "the basic characteristic of high-technology warfare is informatized warfare. Informatized warfare will become the basic form [*xingtai*] of 21st century warfare."[6] Jiang instructed that the PLA "must adapt to the transformation in the basis of preparations for military struggle, promote deeper development of a military transformation with Chinese characteristics, and realize the strategic goals of building an informatized force [*jundui*] and winning informatized wars."[7] In December 2004, the change in the strategic guideline was announced only indirectly to the public, when the 2004 defense white paper stated that the PLA "should be rooted in winning local wars under informatized conditions."[8]

"Informatization" is an awkward translation of the Chinese term "*xinxihua*." In China, informatization is a national-level concept used in civil as well as military affairs to describe the transition from the Industrial Age to the Information Age generated by the development, spread, and application of information technology. As Joe McReynolds and James Mulvenon explain, informatization "describes the process of moving toward greater collection, systematization, distribution, and utilization of information."[9] Thus, informatization affects and shapes all aspects of society, including the economy and governance, as well as warfare. In 2006, for example, China's State Council issued a *State Informatization Development Strategy* (*guojia xinxihua fazhan zhanlue*) to guide the overall development of informatization.[10] In 2008, the State Council established the Ministry of Industry and Information Technology (MIIT) to oversee and regulate the development of IT hardware and software as well as postal services and telecommunications.

Within the military sphere, informatization changes how military capabilities will be generated and how wars will be fought. Information itself is not only a new domain, but also what connects other domains such as the land, sea, and air with each other. Warfare "under informatized conditions" refers to the application of information technology to all aspects of military operations, including sensors and electronics on weapons systems and platforms, automated command and control systems, and nonlethal information operations (such as information, cyber, electronic, public opinion, psychological, and legal warfare).[11] The "informatization" of weapons makes them more precise and more lethal, and, when networked together, enables the unified, simultaneous command of disparate units and forces.[12] Command, control, communications, computers, intelligence, surveillance, and reconnaissance (C4ISR) systems gather and process large amounts of information to command "informatized" weapons, platforms, and units to increase the efficiency, flexibility, responsiveness, and effectiveness of military forces. Operations under informatized conditions occur at a high tempo, over a large physical area, in multiple domains simultaneously, and in all-weather conditions. Such operations are often described as "system of systems" confrontations, in contrast to more traditional confrontations between individual platforms or services. These systems of systems "are created through the integration of information flows that themselves are generated by the incorporation of information technology into every facet of military activities."[13]

Operational Doctrine

In the 2004 strategic guideline, the PLA altered its description of the main form of operations it would conduct. "Integrated joint operations" (*yitihua lianhe zuozhan*) replaced "joint operations" as the main form of operations. The new terminology first appeared in the 2004 white paper on national defense, which stated that the PLA "should adapt to the requirements of integrated joint operations."[14] Earlier, in February 2004, the GSD's annual training guidance emphasized training "according to the requirements of integrated joint operations."[15] The concept was featured in a speech by Hu Jintao at an enlarged meeting of the CMC in December 2005 and in the 2006 edition of the *Science of Campaigns*, an authoritative textbook published by the PLA's NDU.[16] As Hu Jintao summarized in June 2006, "Local wars under informatized conditions are a confrontation of systems of systems and the basic form of operations is integrated joint operations."[17]

The main difference between the 1993 and 2004 concepts of joint operations revolves around how units from the services interact with each other in a campaign. Some analysts described the new concept as "fully integrated" or "unified" joint operations and the old one as merely "coordinated" joint operations.[18] Under the rubric of the latter, the actions of different services would be coordinated to achieve the operational or campaign goal, usually by assigning discrete roles and missions to different units. Under the former, units from the services would not just be coordinated in their action, but fused or integrated together, which informatization writ large now enables. As Dean Cheng describes, "The PLA's conception of joint operations has shifted from multiple, individual services operating together in a coordinated fashion in the same physical space to unified operations under a single command-and-control network."[19]

Consistent with the adjustment in the main form of operations, the PLA also adjusted the basic guiding thought for operations. Some uncertainty exists, however, surrounding the new formulation. A 2006 textbook on campaigns from the PLA's NDU states that "integrated operations, subduing the enemy through precision strikes" (*zhengti zuozhan, jingda zhidi*) replaced "integrated operations, keypoint strikes" from the 1993 strategy.[20] But in a 2012 textbook on campaigns, the basic guiding thought was described as "information dominance, precision operations, destruction of systems, overall victory" (*xinxi zhudao, jingque zuozhan, tixi poji, zhengti zhisheng*).[21] A 2013 textbook on joint operations describes basic guiding thought in a similar way, replacing "destruction of systems" with "destroy strategic points" (*zhongda yaohai*).[22] Another 2013 textbook, on joint campaigns, offers a different formulation of "integrated operations, destruction of systems, asymmetrical operations, striving for quick decision" (*yitihua zuozhan, tixi poji, feiduicheng zuozhan, liqiu sujue*).[23]

The reason for the different formulations of the basic guiding thought for integrated joint operations is that the PLA never finalized the drafting of the fifth generation of operations regulations. Drafting began in 2004 and was completed in 2009. Some regulations were given to units on a trial basis in 2010, but the fifth generation of regulations were never promulgated. According to Yang

Zhiyuan, the general who was responsible for drafting operations regulations, these regulations include elements of informatization, including information warfare and electronic warfare.[24] Joint operations have received much greater prominence.[25] In addition to a revised joint campaign outline (*gangyao*), these regulations included eleven outlines on various aspects of joint operations along with campaign outlines for each of the services, the PAP, political work, counterterror operations, and the "three warfares" (public opinion, psychological, legal).[26] Eighty-six regulations were drafted for the services, PAP, logistics, and support.

Force Structure

In September 2004, just months after the 2004 guideline was adopted, a new CMC was formed. For the first time, its members included the commanders of each of the services as well as the Second Artillery, reflecting the growing importance that China's high command attached to joint operations. Previously, officers from the ground forces occupied most of the positions on the CMC, which, along with the persistence of the system of army-dominated military region command structures, posed a clear obstacle to effectively conducting joint operations.

Nevertheless, the services and subordinate branches were not substantially reorganized following the adjustment of the 2004 guideline. Instead, the services were recapitalized, a process that was most evident in the navy and the air force. In the navy, for example, the number of "new type" or modern destroyers and frigates increased from twenty-seven in 2007 to forty-nine in 2014.[27] Likewise, the number of "new-type" or modern submarines increased from twenty-one in 2007 to forty-five in 2014.[28] In the air force, the proportion of ground attack and support aircraft grew to almost fifty percent of the force, further reducing the almost exclusive reliance on interceptors with a limited territorial defense role.[29] The PLA also began to develop an integrated joint logistics system to replace the separate logistics branches within each service and branch.[30]

In addition, the PLA undertook smaller-scale reforms to promote informatization of the force. In 2005, the CMC promulgated an outline on army informatization building and planning (*quanjun xinxihua jianshe jihua*) to guide informatization through 2020. Headquarters regulations updated in 2006 also stressed the need for greater informatization. As early as 2003, the PLA established an army-wide informatization leading small group under the GSD.[31] Likewise, starting in the late 2000s, the PLA began to deploy an "integrated command platform" (*yitihua zhihui pingtai*) to improve the PLA's C4ISR capabilities at the operational level. The platform reportedly provides real-time information about the battlespace to improve the command of forces, along with intelligence, weather, and geospatial data.[32]

Training

A new military training and evaluation program was issued in July 2008 and took effect in January 2009. Drafting of the new program began after an army-wide training conference in June 2006 and was revised to adapt to the requirements of integrated joint operations and informatized conditions. It also sought to increase the overall amount of time devoted to training: night training, high-intensity training, and training to generate integrated operational capabilities.[33] The new training program sparked an increase in joint training exercises, usually at the brigade level and within a single military region.[34] In 2009, when the new training program was issued, the PLA began to develop joint campaign training exercises, which usually involved units from different military regions.[35] Perhaps the most noteworthy exercise was "Stride-2009," which involved four divisions from four different military regions. This was the first transregional exercise in PLA history, which involved the coordination of units from different military regions and not just the participation of units from different military regions. Also in 2009, the CMC tasked the Jinan Military Region with developing a theater-level joint training leadership organization to serve as a pilot project for coordinating and developing joint training at the military region level.[36]

ADOPTION OF THE 2004 STRATEGIC GUIDELINE

Despite being a minor change in China's military strategy, available sources suggest that the 2004 guideline was adopted for reasons consistent with the central argument of this book. PLA sources indicate a growing awareness of the centrality of information in "high technology" in the conduct of warfare as revealed in conflicts involving the United States. As an AMS textbook describes, "Several recent local wars, especially the 1999 Kosovo War and the 2003 Iraq War, gave us a glimpse of the vivid realities of local wars under informatized conditions, providing us with many lessons."[37]

The 1999 Kosovo War

On March 24, 1999, United States–led NATO forces launched a seventy-eight-day bombing campaign against Yugoslavia over Kosovo. China had opposed the war at the United Nations, making it a salient conflict for China politically as well as militarily. In addition, on May 7, 1999, five US JDAM bombs struck the Chinese embassy in Belgrade, killing three Chinese journalists and wounding twenty people.

Even before the embassy bombing, the air war sparked a significant debate within China over Deng Xiaoping's assessment that "peace and development" represented the "trend of the times." The core issue was whether China still enjoyed the time and security to focus on economic development that would allow the PLA to modernize under less constrained and urgent conditions. The debate concluded by reaffirming that peace and development would continue, along with a gradual shift toward multipolarization.[38] Nevertheless, "hegemonism" was seen as increasing, along with the frequency of military interventions. The Kosovo War also suggested a US willingness to intervene in a conflict over Taiwan and thus China's need to prepare to resist a "strong adversary." In this way, the air war in Kosovo had a greater impact on the PLA's threat perceptions than the 1995–96 Taiwan Straits crisis.[39]

The PLA high command studied the war closely. As an asymmetric conflict, it would hold important implications for China, which still viewed itself as relatively weak militarily. Even before the war ended, Chief of the General Staff Fu Quanyou ordered the GSD to "study the style and characteristics of the U.S. military operations."[40] On May 21, 1999, the GSD convened its first meeting on the war, which involved participants from nineteen units, and then submitted a preliminary report on the war to the CMC that emphasized the need to improve China's air defenses. In the middle of October 1999, AMS and the CMC general office dispatched a group of military experts to study how Yugoslavia had sought to counter NATO operations.[41]

Militarily, the PLA learned important lessons from the Kosovo War that would influence the adjustment to the 1993 strategic guideline in 2004. In July 1999, CMC vice-chairman Zhang Wannian concluded that the Kosovo War, along with the Gulf War, "raised a series of important questions for our country's national defense, army building, and preparations for military struggle."[42] In February 2000, Fu Quanyou foreshadowed the shift in the main form of operations from joint operations to integrated joint operations, describing the most important aspect of the war as "integrated joint operations of the services" focusing on land, sea, air, space, and electromagnetic operations.[43]

In March 2000, the PLA's NDU authored a detailed assessment of the war, which the GSD's training department then published. Regarding the conduct of warfare, the report concluded that "in modern wars, information superiority is the basic superiority. Whoever has information superiority . . . will be able to gain the initiative in war." The report described NATO as using advanced technologies to "carry out the total disruption, suppression and destruction of Yugoslavia's command center and telecommunications system." Moreover, NATO's sophisticated C4ISR allowed it "to gain total information dominance on the battlefield, creating the conditions for winning the war."[44] The combination of intelligence, electronic, psychological, network and other forms of information warfare were described as key to NATO's victory.[45] Specific capabilities emphasized included the persistent and continuous reconnaissance and all-spectrum jamming,[46] along with the use of satellites, reconnaissance aircraft, and early warning aircraft to gather intelligence,[47] and the use of "electromagnetic superiority" to jam Yugoslav communications and radars that enabled many "soft kills."[48]

The report's second main conclusion focused on the lethality of air strikes in modern warfare and the need for China to develop appropriate countermeasures. This, of course, reflected the fact that ground forces were not used and air strikes were the primary means of attack. Nevertheless, the NDU study highlighted the use of short-range and long-range airstrikes, precision strikes, and stealth aircraft.[49] Since a ground invasion of China was unlikely, air strikes were viewed as the most likely way in which Chinese territory would be attacked in the future. As the study concluded, "An air strike includes aerospace integration, long-range attack, ultra-long range attack, stealth strike, precision attack, speed, and flexible control characteristics. The powerful attack and rapid mobility capabilities of air power can conduct comprehensive in-depth 'non-contact' strikes against the enemy."[50] Of course, such air strikes were seen as the most likely way in which the United States, as a "strong enemy," might attack China, a concern elevated by the political-military context of the air war.[51]

After the 1999 Kosovo War, discussion within the PLA of informatized conditions and informatized warfare increased. By 2000, a consensus began to emerge around the importance of informatization. As Fu Quanyou said in September 2000, "Informatized war is gradually becoming the dominant form of warfare."[52] In a speech to an enlarged meeting of the CMC in December 2000, Jiang Zemin noted that "high-technology local wars since the Gulf War demonstrate that information technology plays an extremely important role in modern warfare. The main characteristic of high-technology war is informatization. The new military transformation is essentially a revolution in military informatization. Informatization is becoming a multiplier of the combat effectiveness of the armed forces."[53]

By 2002, the consensus that informatization is the core manifestation of high technology in local wars appeared to have been consolidated. In December 2002, Jiang Zemin drew attention to the importance of informatization in a speech at an enlarged meeting of the CMC.[54] Like Jiang's other speeches in his capacity as CMC chairman, it was likely drafted by CMC's general office or the GSD. Jiang stated that the growing role of high technology in warfare, described as a part of a "revolution" beginning in the 1980s, was entering a new phase due to the wars in Kosovo and Afghanistan. According to Jiang, "The new transformation in military affairs is entering into a new stage of qualitative changes and will likely develop into a profound military revolution that spreads around the globe and involves all military fields."[55] Jiang described informatization as "the core" of these changes and identified four trends. First, informatized weapons and equipment would determine the core of a military's combat capability. Second, the role of stand-off strikes, described as noncontact and nonlinear operations, would become more important. Such strikes would be used to target an opponent's C4ISR, air defense, and other systems. Third, "confrontations among systems will become the basic feature of battlefield confrontations." Fourth, space had become "the new strategic high ground."[56]

Jiang's speech portrayed informatization as a great challenge for China and the PLA. It was described as "an important manifestation of the pressure our country still faces from the economic and scientific superiority of developed countries," which complemented the political pressure they were able to exert. Furthermore, informatization of military affairs would likely "further widen the gap in military power between China and the major countries of the world and increase the potential threat to our country's military security."[57] In this way, Jiang's speech reflected China's identity as a late military modernizer, seeking to catch up with more advanced military powers.

Nevertheless, Jiang did not announce a change in the strategic guideline. Instead, he raised several issues for further discussion by the high command, which indicated that consensus around the importance of informatization had not yet produced a consensus regarding how China should adjust its military strategy. Addressing this directly, Jiang said "we should further deepen our research on strategic guiding thought and principles."[58] Specifically, he highlighted the need for greater study of strategic deterrence and joint operations. Regarding the latter, he said, "In 1993, we continued to emphasize the idea of coordinated operations, but now we should greatly strengthen the study of joint operations of the various services and branches in order to promote the development of the theory and practice of our joint operations."[59]

Why did the CMC not change the strategic guideline in 2002? Two reasons are likely. First, although the PLA acknowledged the growing importance of informatization in the conduct of warfare, exactly how it might shape future operations remained unclear because the lessons from Kosovo were limited to informatization in the context of air power. Although some of the US aircraft used in the Kosovo War were launched from carriers in the Adriatic Sea, the war did not involve the significant use of other naval forces, such as surface or submarine combatants, or any use of ground forces. US operations in Afghanistan were ongoing and by December 2002 it was increasingly likely that the United States was going to invade Iraq, which would reveal broader lessons.

The second reason may be related to Jiang's decision to retain the CMC chairmanship after Hu Jintao became general secretary of the CCP at the Sixteenth Party Congress in October 2002. By staying on the CMC, Jiang was following in the footsteps of Deng Xiaoping, who remained chairman of the CMC after relinquishing all of his other party posts at the Thirteenth Party Congress in 1987. Jiang may have sought to ensure a smooth transition to a new generation of leaders or to maintain his ability to influence the direction of the party's policies. He also developed an interest in military affairs during his thirteen years as general secretary, however, and may have wanted to consolidate his legacy in this area by presiding over the formal shift in the strategic guideline from high-technology conditions to informatized ones.

China's assessment of the Kosovo War provides little evidence for emulation as a driver of the 2004 strategy. The main conclusion was that air strikes were more powerful and destructive than previously imagined—enabled by informatization as well as by advances in weapons systems—and that China was quite vulnerable to such strikes. The PLA moved to develop countermeasures, not its own ability to conduct similar offensive air operations. As the NDU report concluded, the PLA "must strengthen research on counter-air raid operations."[60] This included a new variation of the "three attacks and three defenses." The three attacks were reconnaissance, jamming, and precision strikes, while the three defenses were early warning and counter-reconnaissance, mobility, and surface-to-air missile systems.[61] More generally, the role of information in NATO operations illustrated just how far China lagged behind the United States. The report also concluded that China needed to "greatly develop information systems and weapons and equipment for information operations to narrow the gap with developed countries." Although the PLA closely studied US operations in the war, it studied the Serbian response with equal care and attention.

The 2003 Iraq War

On March 20, 2003, the United States and the United Kingdom led a coalition of thirty states and 380,000 troops to invade Iraq and depose Saddam Hussein. By April 14, allied forces had captured Baghdad, concluding the high-intensity phase of the war. On May 1, US President George W. Bush declared the end of major military operations. If the Kosovo War highlighted the role of information in warfare, the invasion of Iraq demonstrated its broad application and effectiveness with greater and more diverse forces, across a much wider area.

The PLA watched the invasion of Iraq closely. Within nine months, PLA research institutes published three assessments of the war, analyzing its origins, the operations by each side, its main characteristics, and the implications for China. The first was a study from the PLA's NDU;[62] the second, a study from the PLA's Nanchang Ground Forces Academy;[63] and the third, a collection of essays from well-known strategists at AMS and NDU, which was published by AMS.[64] In the absence of sources that can directly reveal the views of senior military officers, these internal assessments serve as proxies for what the PLA viewed as the main characteristics of the war and shifts in the conduct of warfare that may have been revealed. Two of the reports were published with circulation restricted within the PLA (*junnei*) and so were likely read by senior officers or their staffs.

First, these assessments conclude that the Iraq War further demonstrated the trend toward informatization in warfare and the full integration of military operations in joint operations that informatization enables. The Nanchang Academy study concluded that the Iraq War "is the war with the highest level of informatization so far in the world today."[65] According to the AMS report, the invasion showed that "high-technology warfare advanced greatly toward informatized warfare."[66] The NDU study concluded that the "informatized weapons and equipment of the American military has made the form of war gradually move in the direction of informatization and has even begun to dominate the battlefield."[67] Informatization increased the effectiveness, lethality, and speed of military operations, in which fewer forces that are closely coordinated and integrated together achieve much greater effects. For the authors of the NDU study, "the amount of force that the United States used in this war was not even half as much as the first Gulf War, but in a smaller period of time [it] was able to occupy Iraq."[68]

Although each PLA study stressed slightly different elements of the invasion, several common themes in the discussions of the conduct of military operations and informatization can be identified. One theme was the deployment and use of informatized weapons systems and platforms. The Nanchang Academy study observed that more than sixty percent of naval weapons and systems and seventy percent of Air Force ones were informatized.[69] Special focus was given to the use of systems that could be employed beyond visual range, enabling "non-contact" operations or stand-off strikes. Another theme was the greatly expanded use of precision-guided munitions. All three studies noted that the use of precision-guided munitions grew from eight percent of all munitions expended in the 1990–1991 Gulf War to sixty-eight percent in the Iraq War.[70] A final theme was the use of extensive C4ISR systems to integrate these weapons and munitions controlled by the different services over a wide area. Units communicated with each other much more quickly and easily, while commanders possessed a high degree of battlespace or domain awareness within which to deploy these units.[71]

Second, high levels of informatization enabled the deep integration of forces to execute joint operations. In this way, all three studies foreshadowed the emphasis on "integrated joint operations" as the main form of operations in the 2004 strategy. The AMS report, for example, highlighted "the close coordination of services and branches, a unified entity [*hunruan yiti*] [in which] integrated joint operations were raised to an unprecedented level, fully displaying overall operational strength."[72] Examples included the coordination among ground units and between air and ground units, especially in the drive to Baghdad, in which precision air strikes were coordinated with armored and special forces on the ground.[73] One consequence of this integration was what the Nanchang Academy study called "precision strike joint operations," referring not to the use of precision-guided munitions but to the precision with which operations could be conducted when enabled by information superiority and robust C4ISR systems used by the United States and its allies.[74]

Third, the central role of information in military operations in the war underscored the importance of achieving information superiority in addition to air superiority. For PLA analysts, the Iraq War confirmed what the Kosovo War had suggested—that information dominance had become the key factor influencing its conduct and conclusion. Seizing information superiority was now a "primary task" in war.[75] The side that controlled information would have overwhelming advantages, while the side that lacked control would be rendered ineffective. All PLA studies of the war emphasized the efforts in the opening days to dismantle Iraq's command and control system, thereby limiting its ability to mount an effective defense while gaining information superiority.

Two other topics in these PLA assessments should be noted. First, air power was viewed as playing a decisive role in the war. Although none of the studies suggested that air power alone could produce victory, the lack of air power would have greatly complicated the operations. As the NDU study observed, "Defeat in the air can cause defeat on the land (or on the sea)."[76] Second, PLA analysts highlighted psychological warfare, such as efforts to sow divisions within the Iraqi leadership and split the Iraqi people from the leadership as well as weaken the morale of Iraqi forces. The Nanchang Academy study concluded that "along with the arrival of informatized war, it plays a more and more important role."[77]

The PLA's "New Historic Mission"

Shortly after replacing Jiang Zemin as CMC chairman, Hu Jintao introduced the idea of a "new historic mission" for the PLA at an enlarged meeting of the CMC in December 2004. This new mission centered around four main tasks that the PLA should carry out for the party.* Nevertheless, it should not be viewed (and is not viewed by the PLA) as a change in the strategic guideline. One goal was to explain expanding the roles of the PLA beyond warfighting into what was described as "non-war military operations" (*fei zhanzheng junshi xingdong*), such as disaster relief, to help the party maintain stability within China and overseas. Another goal was to highlight new domains in which the PLA would need to operate to defend China's interests, such as the maritime, outer space, and electromagnetic domains. The latter two had already been identified in the 2004 guideline as areas of importance, but received additional emphasis.

---

* Many English analyses describe this as the "new historic missions," but, as shown here, it includes one mission (*shiming*) with four subsidiary tasks (*renwu*).

The first two tasks in the PLA's new historic mission were linked squarely with the internal goal of enhancing regime security. The first task was "to provide an important powerful guarantee to consolidate the party's ruling status."[78] Although defense of the CCP and regime security have been a long-standing goal for China's armed forces, pre-dating even Deng Xiaoping's reforms, it was reemphasized by Hu because of the new challenges that the party faced as the transition from a planned economy to the market accelerated. China's leaders believe that political instability can not only disrupt economic growth, but also pose a clear challenge to the CCP's legitimacy. Likewise, the second task was "to provide a strong security guarantee for protecting the great period of strategic opportunity for national development."[79] This refers to territorial and boundary disputes with other countries in addition to independence movements in Taiwan, separatist movements within China in areas such as Xinjiang and Tibet, and the challenge of maintaining domestic stability amid a rise in mass incidents and public demonstrations. Although this task combined internal and external questions of sovereignty, both reflected how disruptions in any of these areas would upset social stability and challenge the party.

The third task in the PLA's new historic mission was most closely related to conventional military strategy. This was "to provide a powerful strategic support for safeguarding national interests," with a particular emphasis on the defense of China's growing interests in the maritime, space, and cyber domains.[80] If the first two tasks highlighted traditional concerns for the CCP with clear implications for regime stability, the space and cyber components of the third task overlapped with and further emphasized the core elements of informatization that had prompted the adjustment in military strategy earlier in 2004.

The fourth task also had a clear external orientation, but its purpose was not combat oriented. This task for the PLA was "to play an important role in maintaining world peace and promoting common development."[81] This reflected China's growing integration with other regions of the world, especially regions where it engaged in trade and investment, and the importance for China of contributing to maintaining stability in these regions.

When Hu Jintao introduced the concept of the PLA's new historic mission, he also outlined the capabilities that it should possess. During an enlarged meeting of the CMC in December 2005, he said that "we must ... continuously raise the ability to deal with multiple security threats to ensure that our army can deal with crises, maintain peace, contain wars, and win wars under different kinds of complicated situations."[82] During a 2006 meeting with PLA delegates to the NPC, Hu similarly instructed the PLA to "work hard to develop capabilities to deal with many kinds of security threats and complete diversified military tasks."[83]

The phrase "many kinds of security threats" refers to the goals that were part of the four tasks for the PLA's new historic mission in addition to conventional military ones. "Diversified military tasks" means using China's growing military capabilities in two different ways. The first highlights the conventional war-fighting capabilities that were part of the 2004 strategic guideline. The second, however, emphasizes noncombat operations to enhance regime security and promote economic development by maintaining stability at home and abroad. The types of noncombat operations most frequently discussed in authoritative sources are those that help the state maintain public order and, ultimately, defend the CCP.[84] Domestic noncombat operations can be grouped into three broad categories. The first is disaster relief, such as the operations that the PLA conducted after the 2008 Wenchuan earthquake in Sichuan. The second is maintaining social stability, including containing demonstrations, riots, uprisings, rebellions, and large-scale mass incidents that would upset social order, especially in China's ethnic minority regions. A third category includes counterterrorism, which primarily addresses domestic terrorism, such as the attacks against government officials in many areas of Xinjiang in the 1990s or the heightened concerns about terrorist attacks during the 2008 Olympics and the sixtieth anniversary of the People's Republic in October 2009.[85] What unites these types of operations with others such as border security and garrison operations is that they all stress bolstering regime security through maintaining social order and managing internal challenges to the CCP.[86]

However, not all of the new noncombat operations identified for China's armed forces are domestic. The two most frequently discussed international noncombat operations are peacekeeping and disaster relief. Peacekeeping is the only international noncombat operation that receives as much attention in Chinese writings as the domestic ones.[87] In addition to enhancing China's image in international society, these operations play an important role in maintaining a stable external environment that facilitates China's development and indirectly bolsters regime security and have also allowed select units to gain expeditionary military experience. Peacekeeping has attracted the most attention, and it is the one international noncombat operation where the PLA and PAP have accumulated the most experience.

The 2014 Strategy: "Winning Informatized Local Wars"

In the summer of 2014, the PLA's strategic guideline changed for a ninth time. Available sources suggest that the 2014 strategy did not constitute a major change in China's military strategy. Instead, it reflected an adjustment to the 2004 strategy by further emphasizing the role of informatization in warfare and justifying far-reaching organizational reforms that the PLA needed to undertake in order to effectively execute joint operations.

The change in the strategic guideline was not announced publicly. Nevertheless, new language in China's 2015 defense white paper, published in May

2015, indicated that the guideline had changed. As the white paper noted, China adjusts its strategy "according to the evolution of the form of war and the national security situation."[88] The white paper contained two new assessments that informed the change. The first was that further evolution in warfare required a change in the basis of preparations for military struggle for the PLA, noting that "the basis of preparations for military struggle will be placed on winning informatized local wars." This adjustment consisted of dropping only four characters from the 2004 strategy, changing from "winning local wars under the conditions of informatization" to "winning informatized local wars" (*daying xinxihua jubu zhanzheng*). As one AMS scholar describes, the removal of these characters indicates that "a qualitative change has occurred."[89]

The white paper's section on China's national security situation summarizes the assessment that the form of war has changed. Information, broadly defined, now plays a "leading role" in war and is no longer just an "important condition" of warfare.[90] According to the white paper, "The form of war is accelerating its transformation to informatization." These changes included "clear trends" toward the development and use of long-range, precision, smart, and unmanned weapons and equipment. Space and cyber domains are described as becoming the "commanding heights of strategic competition." These trends, which have been occurring over the past decade, require a change in the basis of preparations for military struggle that forms the foundation of any strategic guideline.

The 2014 strategy also contained new strategic guiding thought. The goals in the strategy emphasized balancing the defense of China's rights and interests with the maintenance of stability, "firmly safeguarding national territorial sovereignty, unification, and security," and supporting China's development.[91] Toward this end, the new strategic guiding thought was "emphasize farsighted planning and management, shape favorable situations, comprehensively manage crises, and resolutely deter wars and win wars" (*zhuzhong shenyuan jinglue, suzao youli taishi, zonghe guankong weiji, jianjue ezhi zhanzheng he daying zhanzheng*). This strategic guidance highlighted the shift from territorial defense to protecting China's developmental interests and coordinating military tools with economic and diplomatic ones to create a favorable environment for development. It also stressed preventing crises from erupting but controlling them if they did in addition to the importance of strategic deterrence in deterring wars.[92] Along these lines, important elements of the new strategy were "effectively controlling major crises, properly handling possible chain reactions."[93]

Importantly, however, the main form of operations in the strategy remained unchanged. That is, the main form of operations remained "integrated joint operations," as identified in the 2004 strategy. The white paper does call for the PLA to "create new basic operational thought" for integrated joint operations. Specifically, it suggests that the operational guiding thought is "information dominance, precision strikes on strategic points, joint operations to gain victory" (*xinxi zhudao, jingda yaohai, lianhe zhisheng*), but this seems similar to the guiding thought of the 2004 strategy. The PLA has not yet drafted new operations regulations as part of this change in strategy.

The second assessment is that China faces more pressing national security threats, especially in the maritime domain. The white paper stresses the role of "maritime military struggle" and "preparations for maritime military struggle." Previous strategic guidelines did not highlight specific domains, but nevertheless implied the dominance of ground warfare. One factor, clearly, is the intensification of disputes over territorial sovereignty and maritime jurisdiction in waters adjacent to China, or the near seas. The white paper concludes that the "maritime rights defense struggle will exist for a long time." The second factor is "the continuous expansion of China's national interests," in which overseas interests such as access to markets and open sea lines of communication "have become prominent." These are not new concerns for China, but they have become more prominent in Chinese assessments of their security environment compared with previous editions of the white paper.

Consistent with the increasing focus on the maritime domain, the white paper states publicly for the first time that the Chinese navy's strategic concept "will gradually shift from 'near-seas defense' [*jinhai fangyu*] to the combination of 'near-seas defense' and 'far-seas protection' [*yuanhai huwei*]."[94] Near-seas defense emphasizes defending China's immediate maritime interests, especially in territorial and jurisdictional disputes in the seas adjacent to the Chinese mainland. Far seas protection emphasizes safeguarding China's expanding interests overseas, such as the protection of sea lines of communication and Chinese businesses abroad.[95] The former requires an active posture, while the latter suggests a reactive one.[96]

The white paper does not identify the main strategic direction that defines the geographic focus of strategy. Nevertheless, the primary strategic direction appears to be the same, focusing on Taiwan and China's southeast, but may have been expanded to include the Western Pacific or what retired Lieutenant General Wang Hongguang describes as the "Taiwan Strait-Western Pacific" direction.[97] Whether the South China Sea has become part of the primary strategic direction remains unclear. While Wang notes such a link, he still writes that the "Taiwan Strait is the primary strategic campaign direction" and the "nose of the ox."[98]

Although the white paper confirms that the strategic guideline has been adjusted, it does not state when the decision was made. Historically, the CMC has adopted or adjusted the strategic guidelines at enlarged meetings. These meetings, however, are rarely publicized. In 2004, for example, the change in strategy was introduced during an enlarged meeting of the CMC that was held in June.[99] Yet the first public reference to the strategy did not occur until the publication of the 2004 defense white paper six months later. The meeting itself was never publicized. Likewise, speeches about a new strategic guideline are not openly published when the guideline is introduced and sometimes never openly published at all. Jiang Zemin's speech introducing the 1993 guideline, for example, was not released until 2006.

The CMC most likely decided to adjust the strategic guideline in the summer of 2014. The phrase "winning informatized local wars" has appeared in the *Liberation Army Daily* 94 times. But 81 of these references have occurred since mid-August 2014 (as of September 2018). The term first appeared in an August 21, 2014, article announcing a new GSD document on improving the level of realistic training.[100] Over this same period, 308 articles have appeared with the term "the military strategic guideline in the new situation" (*xin xingshi xia junshi zhanlue fangzhen*), which is an indirect reference to the 2014 strategy. The term first appeared in an article on the eighty-seventh anniversary of the PLA's founding published on August 2, 2014, suggesting that the change in strategy occurred sometime in July.[101] This term only appeared once before, in September 2010, and now appears in many official PLA documents to refer to the strategy adopted under Xi Jinping. Thus, the strategy may have been changed in July 2014. At an "important meeting" on July 7, 2014, Xi urged high-ranking cadre to "implement the military strategic guideline" by "promoting the requirements of the military strategic guideline in army building, reform, and preparations for military struggle."[102] Later, during a meeting with newly appointed officers at the army level (*junji*) in October 2014, he referred to the "military strategic guideline in the new situation" to urge the audience that "all construction work throughout the army must be carried out under the new strategic guideline and be subject to the requirements of serving the strategic guideline."[103]

The guideline was likely adjusted in the summer of 2014 to provide top-level support and justification for the organizational reforms of the PLA announced in November 2015. Broadly speaking, the reforms are designed to improve joint operations by dividing responsibility for commanding troops from managing the development and training of forces. Toward this end, the organizational changes are unprecedented: transforming seven military regions into five theater commands, breaking up the four general departments into fifteen smaller organizations directly under the CMC, elevating the Second Artillery from a branch to a service, creating a separate ground forces command, establishing a Strategic Support Force (SSF) with a focus on space and cyber, and cutting three hundred thousand troops from the armed forces.[104] Notably, the reforms contained changes that the PLA had considered in the past, such as the establishment of the ground forces command first raised in the early 1980s and again in the late 1990s. Other goals were to improve the process of force development and discipline.

The adjustment in military strategy and the PLA reforms were foreshadowed together at the Third Plenum of the Eighteenth Party Congress, which met in November 2013 and outlined an ambitious program for "deepening reform" in all areas of the party, state, and economy. In the past, any reorganization or downsizing of the PLA has occurred only several years after the adoption of a new strategy. This time, however, the intention to alter the military strategy and reorganize the PLA were announced simultaneously. This strongly suggests that the main reason for revising the strategic guideline was to provide an overarching framework for the reforms that would be undertaken.

When the plenum concluded, the Central Committee issued its "decision" outlining the reforms that would be pursued. The preamble to the section on national defense noted the need to "improve [*wanshan*] the military strategic guideline for the new period" or to adjust China's military strategy.[105] The decision then called for "reform of the military leadership system." The next month, in December 2013, Xi Jinping explained at an enlarged meeting of the CMC that, despite past efforts to reform the PLA, "deep-rooted contradictions were not resolved" and these "fundamentally restrict army building and preparations for military struggle." Xi stressed that the PLA's "leadership and management system is unscientific" and "the command system for joint operations is unsound."[106] Later in the speech, he noted that "we have extensively explored the command system for joint operations, but the problem has not been fundamentally resolved."[107] Thus, the purpose of changing strategy appears to be linked closely with the need to further reform the PLA. No significant shift in the conduct of warfare occurred from 2004 to 2014 to prompt adoption of a new strategy, nor did it contain a new vision of warfare. Nevertheless, the strategy did justify the reforms necessary for effectively conducting the integrated joint operations that had been identified in 2004.

The emphasis on the maritime domain also suggests that changes in China's security environment and threat perceptions were a secondary factor in the decision to adopt a new strategy in 2014. The maritime threats are not described as dominant, only "more prominent," and thus are secondary in importance when compared with pursuing the reforms outlined in the plenum. Looking forward, the focus on the maritime domain in the 2015 white paper suggests that threat perceptions are likely to play an even more important role in future changes in China's strategy, assuming that the reforms are successfully implemented.

Conclusion

China has adjusted the 1993 strategic guideline twice. Both the 2004 and 2014 strategies emphasize integrated joint operations as the main form of operations for the PLA to conduct in the future. Each guideline is described as "enriching and improving" the previous one, indicating that the PLA views these changes to strategy as minor, not major changes. In the 2004 strategy, however, the direction of change is consistent with the argument advanced in this book—shifts in the conduct of warfare. Although the organizational reforms pursued under the 2014 strategy are far-reaching, they are intended to enable the PLA to be better able to conduct joint operations, a goal first identified in the 1993 strategic guideline.

8

China's Nuclear Strategy since 1964

China's military strategy, which emphasizes conventional operations, has been dynamic, changing nine times since 1949. By contrast, China's nuclear strategy, based on achieving deterrence through assured retaliation, has remained largely unchanged since China exploded its first nuclear device in October 1964. China has also not sought to alter its nuclear strategy despite its vulnerability, at various times, to an invasion or nuclear first strike by the United States or the Soviet Union. In addition, no apparent relationship exists between China's conventional and nuclear strategies. Although China's nuclear strategy is consistent with the general principle of "active defense," planning for the use of nuclear weapons has been decoupled from the planning for the use of conventional forces. China's declaratory strategy and operational doctrine envision only using nuclear weapons in response to a nuclear attack, not in conventional conflicts. Why has China's nuclear strategy been constant while its conventional strategy has varied, often substantially? Why have China's conventional and nuclear strategies not been more closely integrated?

This chapter advances several arguments to answer these questions. First, unlike conventional military strategy, top party leaders never delegated authority over nuclear strategy to senior military officers. Nuclear strategy was viewed as a matter of supreme national policy that only the party's top leaders could determine, not the PLA leadership more broadly, including the Second Artillery or the General Staff Department (GSD). Top party leaders never delegated China's nuclear strategy to senior military officers, including decisions regarding force structure and force posture. Even after the Second Artillery began to develop into an operational branch in the late 1970s, it has acted primarily as the custodian of China's nuclear forces under the close supervision of the CMC, the party's decision-making body for military affairs. Second, because top party leaders never delegated nuclear strategy to senior military officers, the views of China's top party leaders on nuclear weapons, especially Mao Zedong, Zhou Enlai, and Deng Xiaoping, have had an especially powerful influence on China's nuclear strategy, even today. Their views, based on the limited utility of nuclear weapons, support maintaining a strategy of assured retaliation and not integrating nuclear strategy with conventional strategy or pursuing limited nuclear warfighting.

New sources permit the reconsideration of existing arguments about China's development of nuclear weapons advanced by John Lewis and Xue Litai in their landmark 1988 book, *China Builds the Bomb*.[1] First, China seriously considered pursuing the bomb earlier than Lewis and Xue claim. Lewis and Xue emphasize the role of the 1954–55 Taiwan Straits Crisis and the US shift to massive retaliation in China's January 1955 decision to build the bomb. Nevertheless, a consensus among China's top leaders to acquire nuclear weapons formed earlier, by the spring of 1952, directly in response to US nuclear threats during the Korean War. Moreover, the political decision to develop the bomb in 1955 did not reflect a response to intensified external threats but instead the view that, after discovering uranium in Guangxi in 1954, China could now launch such a project.

Second, Lewis and Xue's explanation of China's nuclear strategy is based on technological determinism. They argue that China's nuclear strategy was shaped critically by the technologies available to China and the capabilities that China could develop. As Lewis and Xue write, "China had no clearly articulated nuclear doctrine that would shape its early nuclear weapons procurement and deployment policies." Moreover, "technological imperatives began to drive the army's actual policy decisions."[2] Similarly, Lewis and another coauthor, Hua Di, conclude that "technology, not strategy, determined the pace and main direction of the ballistic missile program at least until the late 1970s."[3]

China's leaders, however, did not develop their nuclear strategy or force structure based on what was technically possible. Instead, their views of the utility of nuclear weapons shaped the parameters of the strategy of assured retaliation that they pursued. China's leaders viewed the role of nuclear weapons as limited to preventing nuclear coercion and deterring a nuclear attack on China. Such objectives required only a small force capable of launching a counterstrike because China's leaders did not envision either engaging in nuclear warfighting or using nuclear weapons to deter conventional threats. Choices made during the early years of China's nuclear program reflect these goals, such as focusing on missiles rather than gravity bombs, adopting a no-first-use policy, and giving the Second Artillery the sole mission of conducting a nuclear counterstrike. These early decisions, informed by Chinese leaders' views of nuclear strategy, continued to shape the parameters in which the Second Artillery started to develop operational doctrine for executing a counterstrike in the 1970s. More broadly, the strongest evidence against the claim that technology has determined China's nuclear strategy is its consistency over the past fifty years, when the availability of technology has changed dramatically.

This chapter proceeds as follows. The first section describes how China's nuclear strategy has remained largely constant since 1964, focused on deterring nuclear coercion or attack with the smallest possible force. The next section reviews the beliefs of China's top leaders regarding the utility of nuclear weapons, which not only influenced the strategy that was adopted but also the decision to decouple nuclear strategy from conventional strategy. The third section examines the development of China's nuclear forces and strategy, from the initial decision to pursue the bomb to the development of operational doctrine for China's rocket forces, to highlight the role of top party leaders in these decisions. The last section discusses the relationship between China's nuclear strategy and the strategic guidelines discussed elsewhere in this book.

China's Nuclear Strategy

Since testing its first atomic device in October 1964, China has pursued a nuclear strategy of assured retaliation. China seeks to prevent other states from using nuclear weapons to coerce or attack China by developing a secure second-strike capability. For many decades, China's nuclear strategy was based on the statements of China's leaders and internal doctrinal publications. In 2006, China's nuclear strategy was articulated publicly in a defense white paper.

LEADERSHIP VIEWS ON NUCLEAR STRATEGY

Across several generations, China's top party leaders embraced the notion of deterrence through assured retaliation. This was the belief that a small number of survivable weapons would be sufficient to impose unacceptable damage in a retaliatory strike and thus deter nuclear attack or coercion. These ideas were most forcefully articulated by Mao Zedong and Zhou Enlai in the 1960s and by Deng Xiaoping in the late 1970s to the early 1980s. Subsequent Chinese leaders have embraced the same nuclear strategy.[4]

The emphasis on building a small but survivable arsenal began with Mao Zedong. His ideas regarding the size of China's nuclear force along with a simple notion of what deters has endured for decades. In 1960, Mao suggested that a few weapons would be sufficient for deterrence, stating that "our country in the future may produce a few atomic bombs, but we by no means intend to use them. Although we do not intend to use them, why produce them? We will use them as a defensive weapon."[5] In 1961, Zhou Enlai concurred, noting that "only when [we] have missiles and nuclear weapons, can we prevent [others] from using them; if we do not have missiles and nuclear weapons, imperialists will use missiles and nuclear weapons [against us]."[6] A few months after China's first successful nuclear detonation, Mao observed in an interview with Edgar Snow, "We don't wish to have too many atom bombs ourselves. What would we do with so many? To have a few is just fine."[7]

This view of deterrence required only China's ability to retaliate after being attacked, not nuclear parity with an adversary. Given China's no-first-use pledge issued in 1964, assured retaliation required that China's forces be able to survive a first strike and then launch a retaliatory counterstrike. As Marshal Nie Rongzhen described in his memoir, China needed to develop nuclear weapons "to have the minimum means of counterattacking [*you qima de huanji shouduan*] when our country sustains an imperialist surprise attack with nuclear weapons."[8] As Deng told Chile's foreign minister in 1978, "We also want to build some nuclear weapons, but we are not preparing to make many. When we have the power [*liliang*] to counterattack [*huanji*], we won't continue to develop them."[9] Deng Xiaoping offered the most complete statement of Chinese leadership views about nuclear deterrence during a meeting with the Canadian Prime Minister in 1983:

> We have a few nuclear weapons. France also has a few. These weapons themselves are useful only for [creating] pressure. We have said many times that is the point of our few nuclear weapons! Only to show that we also have what they have. If they want to destroy us, they themselves will also suffer some retaliation. We have consistently said that we want to force the superpowers not to dare to use nuclear weapons. In the past, this was to deal with the Soviet Union, to force them not to use these weapons rashly. To have even only a few weapons after all is a kind of restraining power [*zhiyue liliang*].[10]

Deng's remarks suggest that the ability to inflict "some retaliation" is sufficient to deter an opponent, even a superpower.

Mao, Zhou, and Deng never openly discussed in any detail the operational requirements for China's nuclear forces. In 1970, for example, Zhou Enlai stated at a planning meeting of the National Defense Science and Technology Commission (NDSTC) that China did not intend to use nuclear weapons to intimidate others and thus did not need many weapons. Nevertheless, Zhou stated that China "must build a certain number of a certain quality and a certain variety."[11] In 1978, as China was developing its first intercontinental ballistic missile (ICBM), the Dongfeng-5 (DF-5), Deng outlined the general requirements for the development of China's nuclear forces. According to Deng, "Our strategic weapons should be updated [*gengxin*] and the guideline [for their development] is few but capable [*shao er jing*]. Few means numbers and capability should increase with each generation."[12]

Among the first two generations of Chinese leaders, General Zhang Aiping offered the most detailed description of China's view of the requirements of deterrence. Zhang played a leading role in China's strategic weapons program, in both the early 1960s and from the late 1970s to the early 1980s.[13] In 1980, Zhang noted, "As for strategic weapons . . . our task is to ensure a certain power to strike back. This of course is not in terms of a numerical comparison with the enemy and also not focusing first on precision. Instead, the key point is having nuclear weapons that are complete [*wanshan*] and can be used operationally." Furthermore, Zhang argued, "we must think of ways to strengthen the survivability of these weapons and shorten the preparation time so that when the enemy launches a surprise nuclear attack, the missiles that we do have can be preserved and then be used to carry out a counterattack, 'gaining control by striking afterwards' [*houfa zhiren*]. This requires that the weapons be reliable and that the preparation time be shorter. After these two problems are resolved, we can consider again precision."[14]

Zhang made his remarks just months after China had successfully tested the DF-5 and while it was in the final stages of developing its first submarine-launched ballistic missile (SLBM), the Julang-1 (JL-1). If his speech is viewed as an outline for China's future plans for the development of its nuclear force in the 1980s, when China faced an overwhelming conventional and nuclear threat from the Soviet Union, reliability and survivability were paramount. Consistent with Deng's perspective, having the capability to retaliate, even with only a few weapons, was viewed as sufficient for deterring a nuclear attack against China.

Available sources lack discussion of Chinese leadership views on why only a small number of nuclear warheads would be enough to impose unacceptable damage and deter potential adversaries from attacking China. Nevertheless, the consistency with which China's leaders focused on a small, retaliatory force implies that they viewed the threshold for such damage as low. In 1967, Mao reportedly told André Malraux, "When I have six atomic bombs, no one can bomb my cities. . . . The Americans will never use an atom bomb against me."[15] Deng expanded on this view in 1981, noting that "in the future, there may not be a nuclear war. We have [nuclear weapons] because they also have them. We will have more if they have more. Probably everyone will not dare to use them."[16]

In the post–Deng era, Chinese leaders' beliefs about deterrence have remained unchanged. Perhaps unsurprisingly, Jiang Zemin's views are remarkably similar to those of his predecessors. In the aftermath of the 1990–91 Gulf War, Jiang noted that China would maintain "a necessary deterrent capability [*weishe nengli*]," but would focus defense spending on conventional, not nuclear, forces, again implying a preference for a small and survivable nuclear force.[17] According to an authoritative book on Jiang's military thought, he held the same views regarding the sources of deterrence: "China developed strategic nuclear weapons, not to attack but for defense. . . . it is a kind of great deterrent toward nuclear weapons states and makes them not dare to act indiscriminately."[18] In 2002, he highlighted the broader and multifaceted Chinese concept of "strategic deterrence" (*zhanlue weishe*) for which he noted that "nuclear weapons were the core capability."[19]

Very few public statements by Hu Jintao and Xi Jinping on questions of nuclear strategy are available. Reporting of these statements, however, indicates that they are consistent with the views of previous leaders, focusing on the deterrent role of nuclear weapons. On the fortieth anniversary of the Second Artillery's founding in 2006, Hu Jintao stated that it "played an extremely important role in containing wars and crises, defending national security and maintaining world peace."[20] Likewise, during remarks at the meeting of the Eighth Party Congress of the Second Artillery in late 2012, Xi Jinping echoed Jiang by stating that the Second Artillery was "the core force [*hexin liliang*] of China's strategic deterrent."[21] Articles by high-ranking members of the Second Artillery on nuclear strategy refer to Hu Jintao and Xi Jinping's views in ways that are consistent with the views of previous leaders.[22]

OPERATIONAL DOCTRINE FOR CHINA'S NUCLEAR FORCES

The Second Artillery's operational doctrine demonstrates that China has pursued a consistent nuclear strategy based on assured retaliation. As the Second Artillery was formally established on July 1, 1966, only weeks before Mao called for "bombarding the headquarters" and launched the Cultural Revolution, the organization faced numerous challenges as it sought to become an operational unit for China's nuclear-armed missiles. During this period, China continued to develop bases for its existing missiles, the DF-2 and DF-3, but achieved little else.[23] At the end of the Cultural Revolution, the Second Artillery gained new leadership and clear guidance from Deng Xiaoping, which accelerated its development, including operational doctrine.

Statements made in the first few years after the Second Artillery's establishment reflect the adoption of a strategy of assured retaliation. Although the Second Artillery did not begin to draft its operational doctrine until the late 1970s, its original mission was to develop a retaliatory force. In July 1967, the CMC issued temporary regulations for the Second Artillery, stating that its task (*renwu*) was "building a nuclear counterattack force to realize active defense."[24] This remains the mission of China's nuclear forces today. When an old Deng ally Li Shuiqing was appointed as commander of the Second Artillery in 1977, he emphasized that the Second Artillery's operational principles should "let the troops know how to wage counter-strike operations [*fanji zuozhan*]," focusing, again, on this singular mission.[25] During a meeting on operations in 1978,

Li again stressed developing the Second Artillery as a "nuclear counterstrike force."[26] The meeting discussed how to implement the "guiding thought, guideline and principles, and main tasks [*renwu*] of strategic counter-attack."[27] In December 1979, the Second Artillery convened a meeting to study "operational employment" (*zuozhan yunyong*). The meeting's final report emphasized the "principles and guidelines for the Second Artillery's counterstrike operations."[28] The 1980 training program noted that command officers (*zhihui ganbu*) in the Second Artillery should focus on "command training for defense and counterstrike operations."[29]

China's approach to nuclear strategy was detailed in the 1987 *Science of Military Strategy*, the PLA's first comprehensive text on military strategy published after 1949. Reflecting the views of Mao, Zhou, and Deng, the book describes the primary purpose of nuclear weapons as deterring a nuclear attack against China.[30] The Second Artillery's mission is to possess "a type of deterrent and retaliatory capability" to counter "nuclear monopoly, nuclear blackmail, and nuclear threats."[31] A "nuclear counterstrike" (*he fanji*) is the only campaign described in the book in which nuclear weapons would be used: "If the enemy first uses nuclear weapons, we must resolutely implement a counterattack and carry out nuclear retaliation."[32] The 1987 *Science of Military Strategy* also identified the "basic guiding thought" (*jiben zhidao sixiang*) for "bringing into play the deterrent and retaliatory uses" of nuclear weapons.[33] The four principles are centralized control (*jizhong zhihui*), striking only after the enemy has struck (*houfa zhiren*), close defense (*yanmi fanghu*) and keypoint counterstrikes (*zhongdian fanji*).[34]

In 1996, the Second Artillery published its first document on strategy, the *Science of Second Artillery Strategy*. Although the text outlined China's strategy for the Second Artillery as an independent branch of the PLA, it closely approximated China's nuclear strategy at the time of its publication.[35] The book describes the service strategy for the Second Artillery as "emphasize deterrence, effective counterattack" (*zhongzai weishe, youxiao fanji*). Echoing the 1987 *Science of Military Strategy*, the purpose of nuclear weapons is to deter a nuclear attack against China and to prevent a conventional war from escalating to a nuclear war. The text describes three major actions. First, strategic defense refers to ensuring the survivability of the force. Second, strategic deterrence describes how to deter a nuclear attack or the nuclear escalation of a conventional war. And, third, strategic counterattack outlines how China will retaliate if attacked with nuclear weapons. Importantly, the book maintains the clear firebreak between the use of conventional and nuclear weapons. The *Science of Second Artillery Strategy* indicates that China will use nuclear weapons only after attacked first with nuclear weapons. It does not envision the use of nuclear weapons first in a major conventional conflict as a form of "invasion insurance."

Subsequent publications on China's military strategy and operational doctrine continue to describe the nuclear counterstrike campaign (*he fanji zhanyi*) as the only nuclear campaign for the Second Artillery. Various descriptions of this campaign are contained in the 2000 and 2006 editions of the National Defense University's (NDU) *Science of Campaigns*, the 2002 *Campaign Theory Study Guide,* and the 2001 and 2013 editions of the *Science of Military Strategy*, among others.[36] Limited circulation texts by the Second Artillery—such as doctrinal texts on campaign methods and tactics from the mid-1990s, along with the 2004 edition of the *Science of Second Artillery Campaigns*—also describe the nuclear counterstrike campaign as the only nuclear campaign for the Second Artillery.[37]

CHINA'S DECLARATORY STRATEGY

By the early 2000s, the Chinese government's official statements about nuclear strategy became clearer as well. An initial attempt at articulating a nuclear strategy was made in 2000, in China's second national defense white paper, but it amounted to a restatement of past policies. The most complete official explanation appeared in the 2006 defense white paper, which for the first time ever publicly articulated China's nuclear strategy. It stated that China pursues a "self-defensive nuclear strategy" (*ziwei fangyu he zhanlue*), which is the official government formulation. The two principles of this strategy are "counterattack in self-defense" (*ziwei fanji*) and "limited development" (*youxian fazhan*) of nuclear weapons. The 2006 white paper noted that China seeks to possess "a lean and effective nuclear force" (*jinggan youxiao he liliang*) as a "strategic deterrent" (*zhanlue weishe zuoyong*).[38] Subsequent white papers have repeated this formulation, along with China's no-first-use policy. The 2008 white paper, for example, stated the conditions under which China would use nuclear weapons. In peacetime, China's nuclear forces did not target any country. When China faced nuclear threats, however, it would place its forces on alert status. If China was attacked with nuclear weapons, it would "resolutely counterattack against the enemy" with nuclear weapons.[39]

Leadership Views on the Utility of Nuclear Weapons

Since 1949, China's top party leaders have emphasized that the main purpose of nuclear weapons is to prevent nuclear coercion and deter a nuclear attack. Senior Chinese leaders never viewed them as a means for fighting or winning wars. The atomic bomb was also seen as imparting other benefits, such as demonstrating China's status as a major power in the international community and serving as a source of national pride for the Chinese people.[40] These latter functions, however, are less central to understanding the consistency of China's nuclear strategy across several decades. As the 1996 *Science of Second Artillery Strategy* states unequivocally, the Second Artillery's strategy is "based on and even determined by the nuclear strategic thought of Mao Zedong and Deng Xiaoping."[41] These views are described below.

DETERRING NUCLEAR ATTACK

China's top leaders' notion of deterrence through assured retaliation discussed in the previous section reflects their view that the most important function of nuclear weapons is to deter nuclear attacks against China. Despite Mao Zedong's well-known denigration of nuclear weapons as "paper tigers," he valued such weapons for deterring their use against China by the United States and, later, the Soviet Union.[42] Mao was keenly aware of China's vulnerability to nuclear strikes and the need for a solution to this problem. In 1950, during the Korean War, he observed that "if the United States strikes with atomic bombs, we have none and can only allow it to strike. This is something that we cannot resolve."[43] Twenty years later, in 1970, he noted the deterrent role of nuclear weapons in the US-Soviet superpower competition. In meeting with a delegation from North Vietnam, he stated that "although the possibility of the major powers fighting a world war remains, everyone does not dare to start such a war only because they have nuclear weapons."[44] Mao clearly embraced the notion of mutual deterrence, which was reflected in the statement that China issued after its first test of a nuclear device in October 1964.

Zhou Enlai held similar views. In 1955, Zhou described how after World War I the possession of chemical weapons, another weapon of mass destruction, created a condition of mutual vulnerability and thus deterrence. Based on this, he concluded in 1955 that "now it is also possible to ban the use of atomic weapons," as the mutual possession of nuclear weapons would deter states from using them. Later, in 1961, he was more blunt, arguing, "If we don't have missiles, then the imperialists can use missiles [against us]."[45] Zhou's remark reflected the PLA's focus in the 1950s on preparing to fight a conventional war after the United States used nuclear weapons as part of an attack against China (as described in chapter 3).[46]

China's second generation of leaders, especially Deng Xiaoping, similarly emphasized the deterrent role of nuclear weapons. During a 1975 meeting with the prime minister of Guyana, Deng alluded to the deterrent function of these weapons, stating that "France has also built some [nuclear weapons]. We understand [why] France has built them. Britain has also made some, but not many. Our reason for building a few is that we will have them if others [*tamen*] have them. Nuclear weapons have only this function."[47] Although only by implication, he was referring to their deterrent role. Later that year, he likewise told officials from the Seventh Machine Industry (Aerospace), which was responsible for developing China's ballistic missiles, "We must have some deterrent force [*weishe liliang*] if they also have it. We are unable to do too much, but to have it is useful."[48]

Finally, China's other generations of leaders stressed the deterrent role of nuclear weapons. Jiang Zemin, for example, stated that "as long as there are nuclear weapons in the world and there is nuclear deterrence, we must maintain and develop a nuclear counterstrike force."[49] Elsewhere Jiang stated that "keypoint counterstrikes reflect the use of the concentration of forces in nuclear war. Our country's nuclear strength [*liliang*] is limited, only by concentrating nuclear firepower and executing keypoint counterstrikes against limited targets can it effectively achieve its strategic goal."[50] Although few primary source documents on Hu Jintao's approach to military affairs have been published, authoritative articles by senior military scholars have continued to stress this view of nuclear weapons since Hu became general secretary of the CCP in 2002.[51] According to Zhang Qihua, former director of the Second Artillery's equipment department, "Chairman Hu's important instructions were the continuation and development of the thought of the core three generations of leaders on the development of our country's strategic deterrent."[52] Authoritative books on Chinese strategy published after Xi Jinping became general secretary of the CCP and chairman of the CMC also indicate that nuclear weapons are intended primarily to deter nuclear attacks.[53]

PREVENTING NUCLEAR COERCION

China's top party leaders, especially the first generation, stressed another role of nuclear weapons: to resist and prevent nuclear coercion, when a nuclear weapons state threatens a state without nuclear weapons.[54] Ironically, one reason why Mao likely disparaged the atomic bomb as a "paper tiger" was instrumental—namely, to encourage the Chinese public not to be intimidated by such destructive weapons possessed by China's opponents.[55]

The need to prevent nuclear coercion is a theme that runs through Mao's limited references to nuclear weapons. During the first meeting of the National Defense Commission in 1954, for example, Mao noted, "Imperialists [i.e., the United States] assess that we only have a few things and then they come to bully us. They say, 'how many atomic bombs do you have?' "[56] When meeting with French parliamentarians in 1964 before China's first nuclear test, he argued, "With batches and batches of nuclear weapons in the United States and the Soviet Union, they often shake them in their hands to intimidate people."[57] Likewise, Marshal Nie Rongzhen, one of the key figures in China's nuclear weapons program, observed that "when the Chinese people have this weapon, [the United States'] nuclear blackmail toward the people of the world will be completely destroyed."[58]

Mao's focus on countering coercion reflects the initial decision to pursue nuclear weapons. In his famous 1956 speech "On the Ten Great Relationships," Mao noted that "we want to have not only more planes and heavy artillery, but also the atomic bomb. In today's world, if we don't want to be bullied, then we cannot do without this thing."[59] During a 1958 CMC meeting, he linked them with the ability to stand up to stronger states, noting that "[we] also want that atomic bomb. I hear that with such a big thing, if you don't have it, then others will say that you don't count. Fine, we should build a few."[60]

Although China's concern with countering nuclear coercion was perhaps most evident during the early Cold War, other generations of Chinese leaders have also emphasized this function of nuclear weapons. In 1975, for example, Deng Xiaoping told a delegation of foreign visitors that China does "not advocate nuclear proliferation at all, but we even more strongly oppose nuclear monopolies."[61] Similarly, Jiang Zemin observed that by acquiring the bomb in the 1960s, China "smashed the U.S.-Soviet nuclear monopoly and nuclear blackmail, making our country one of the world's few nuclear weapons states."[62]

AVOIDING NUCLEAR WARFIGHTING

China's top party leaders agreed that nuclear weapons lacked any meaningful warfighting utility. Mao Zedong, of course, stressed that only people and not weapons enabled countries to win wars. After the strikes on Hiroshima and Nagasaki, for example, he concluded that nuclear weapons could not resolve wars, in general, or force Japan to surrender, in particular. For Mao, "with only atomic bombs and without people's struggles, then atomic bombs are meaningless."[63] Indeed, Mao's writings on military affairs are replete with references to the superiority of people over weapons on the battlefield, a view that was central to the main strategic problem that the CCP encountered before and after 1949: defeating an adversary with superior weapons and equipment.

China's early leaders also viewed nuclear weapons as blunt instruments that were hard to employ on the battlefield. When Marshal Ye Jianying discussed the appearance of tactical nuclear weapons in a 1961 speech, for example, he noted "the use of atomic weapons is subject to certain conditions. They cannot be used to strike at any time or at any target as one pleases."[64] Ye further observed that terrain, climate, and battlefield developments all influenced whether they could be employed.

Mao and Zhou viewed conventional weapons, not nuclear weapons, as the source of victory in war. During a meeting of the National Defense Industry Commission (NDIC) in August 1961, Zhou highlighted the need to possess nuclear weapons to deter an "imperialist" attack with nuclear weapons.

But "for face to face struggles, [we] must still rely on conventional weapons and must grasp the development of conventional weapons."[65] The following month, in a lengthy conversation with British Field Marshal Bernard Montgomery, Mao said nuclear weapons "will not be used. If more are made, then nuclear war will not be fought." Instead, he underscored the importance of conventional weapons, observing that "if you want to fight, you still need to use conventional weapons to fight."[66] In January 1965, during an enlarged meeting of the Politburo Standing Committee, he noted that "we will only use conventional weapons to fight with them," referring to "imperialists" and "revisionists."[67]

Deng Xiaoping shared Mao, Zhou and Ye's views. By the mid-1970s, Deng Xiaoping had concluded that the United States and the Soviet Union were unlikely to fight a nuclear war, despite the development of nuclear warfighting doctrines in both countries. When meeting with the Mexican defense minister in 1978, Deng observed that "future wars will mainly be wars with conventional weapons and not atomic wars. The reason is that the destructive power of nuclear weapons is too great and the enemy will not easily use them." In Deng's view, wars were fought to control territory and extract resources, not to destroy another state's infrastructure completely. Thus, Deng concluded, "we will mainly develop conventional weapons."[68] In 1981, during a meeting with the Danish Prime Minister, Deng warned not to "ignore conventional war. Because with nuclear weapons, if you have them, I will have them. If you have more, I will have more and perhaps no one will dare to use them. Conventional war is possible."[69] Finally, as part of the 1985 CMC meeting on China's strategic transformation in force modernization, Deng expressed again his view that nuclear war was unlikely: because "the US and USSR today both have so many atomic bombs, so if war breaks out who will launch the first one if they fight a war—this is not an easy decision to make." Furthermore, he noted, "a future world war will not necessarily be a nuclear war. This is not only our view, but the Americans and Soviets also believe that in the future it is quite likely that conventional wars will be fought."[70]

The Development of China's Nuclear Strategy and Forces

China's top party leaders, not senior military officers, have dominated the development of China's nuclear strategy and forces. These leaders, especially Zhou Enlai, decided what kinds of weapons to develop, how many to develop, as well as basing modes and strategy. When the development of the Second Artillery as an independent branch of the PLA accelerated in the late 1970s, the CMC became much more directly involved in its development, but as the party's leading body for military affairs.

DECISION TO DEVELOP THE BOMB

China's top party leaders began to consider developing nuclear weapons while still fighting the Korean War. Key discussions about developing nuclear weapons were held in early to mid-1952. The political decision to move forward with a nuclear program was not made until January 1955, after discovering a domestic source of uranium.[71] China's leaders also wanted to be able to assemble a team of qualified scientists to develop nuclear weapons.

In June 1951, a Chinese graduate student in France, Yang Chengzong, received his PhD in radiology from the University of Paris under the supervision of Irene Joliot-Curie. As Yang was preparing to return to China, Irene arranged a meeting with her husband, Frederick Joliot-Curie, also a noted French physicist. Frederick asked him to pass along a message to Mao: "If you want to defend peace and oppose the atomic bomb, you must have the atomic bomb yourself." Furthermore, "the atomic bomb is not so terrible and the principles of the atomic bomb were not invented by Americans." To encourage China, Frederick told Yang that China had its own scientists, such as Qian Sanqiang, He Zehui, and Wang Dezhao.[72] After Yang returned to China, he joined the Institute of Modern Physics and told its director, Qian Sanqiang, about Joliot-Curie's message for Mao. In October 1951, Qian then asked another member of the institute, Ding Zan, to inform the central leadership.[73]

It is unclear when Mao and other leaders first received Joliot-Curie's message, but later they would refer to it frequently. Regardless, China began to explore developing the bomb in March 1952, when Zhou Enlai instructed two of his secretaries, Lei Yingfu and Wei Ming, to visit the noted Chinese scientist Zhu Kezhen.[74] The purpose of the meeting was to better understand "the technological prerequisites for the trial production of the atomic bomb and other sophisticated weapons."[75] Zhu told Lei and Wei that such an endeavor would be much more expensive than developing conventional weapons, require a group of talented personnel (including overseas Chinese with advanced technical training), and depend on imported materials and equipment. When Lei Yingfu reported back to Zhou, Lei said Zhu's "opinion is expert."[76]

In May 1952, Zhou Enlai met with members of the CMC to discuss the first five-year plan for military development. Other participants in the meeting included Zhu De, Nie Rongzhen, Peng Dehuai, and Su Yu.[77] They discussed the development of nuclear weapons but decided more research was needed to determine how to develop it and when to begin.[78] Zhou Enlai also understood the importance of identifying a domestic supply of uranium, which China had not yet discovered. In November 1952, Zhou Enlai read a report about a piece of uranium ore sent from the Anshan Iron Company, which he immediately shared with Mao and other party leaders. He also suggested inviting Soviet experts to jointly explore for uranium[79] and supported the development of the Institute of Modern Physics within the Chinese Academy of Science (CAS), which would be the center of China's technical and theoretical work.[80] The recollection of Guo Yinghui, another secretary for Zhou Enlai, describes how the development of nuclear weapons was discussed at the May 1952 meeting. Mao Zedong and Zhou Enlai "both believed that if China did not have the atomic bomb and other sophisticated weapons, others would not respect China."[81]

After the May 1952 meeting, senior Chinese leaders continued to discuss the need for China to acquire nuclear weapons and began to approach the Soviet Union for aid. Acting on Zhou Enlai's instructions, Qian Sanqiang asked to visit atomic physics research institutes and facilities when a delegation from CAS visited Moscow in March 1953.[82] While visiting the Moscow Institute of Physics, Qian asked his counterpart if the Soviet Union could provide assistance to build a cyclotron and experimental reactor.[83] In November 1953, Peng Dehuai expressed his desire for China to have all the weapons that the United States possessed, including nuclear weapons.[84] Peng continued to explore the process of building nuclear weapons, meeting with Qian in August 1954 before traveling to Moscow.[85] In September 1954, during a trip to Moscow with other senior Chinese leaders to observe the SNOWBALL nuclear exercise, Peng again explored the possibility of assistance to build a cyclotron and experimental reactor.[86]

The situation changed in the fall of 1954, when uranium was discovered in Guangxi. In February 1954, Zhou Enlai established an office in the Ministry of Geology responsible for developing China's uranium resources.[87] Surveys conducted between June and October yielded samples from Shanmuchong in Guangxi that suggested China would have a sufficient indigenous supply to support a nuclear weapons program.[88] Leading the effort was Liu Jie, the vice minister of geology, who recalls that the discovery in Guangxi was made in late August or early September.[89] The day after he reported the discovery to Zhou Enlai, Liu was instructed to fly to Beijing. In Mao's office in Zhongnanhai, Liu displayed the ore that had been found. He described Mao as "excited," stating that "our country has abundant resources and we must develop atomic energy." At the end of the meeting, Mao stated that "this must be dealt with well, it will determine our destiny."[90] Thus, by late August or early September 1954, the decision to pursue the bomb had been made informally.

Following the discovery of uranium, Mao Zedong and Zhou Enlai believed that China could now pursue the development of nuclear weapons. Mao himself directly raised the question during Nikita Khrushchev's visit to Beijing in October 1954 to celebrate the fifth anniversary of the founding of the PRC. Mao reportedly asked Khrushchev to "reveal to China the secret of the atomic bomb and to assist the PRC in launching the production of atomic bombs."[91] Peng Dehuai asked Li Fuchun, who was supervising negotiations over cooperation with the Soviet Union, to request aid with a reactor and accelerator during Khrushchev's visit.[92] According to Peng, they "must be built as soon as possible."[93] Later in October 1954, Mao told Indian Prime Minister Jawaharlal Nehru that "China now does not have an atomic bomb . . . we are beginning to study [it]."[94]

On January 14, 1955, Zhou Enlai convened a small meeting with two leading scientists, Li Siguang (also minister of geology) and Qian Sanqiang, along with economic planner Bo Yibo and vice minister of geology Liu Jie. They reviewed the technical requirements for developing nuclear weapons to prepare for a meeting of the Central Committee Secretariat. At the meeting, for example, Zhou reviewed the nuclear threats that China had faced during the Korean War as the main rationale for acquiring the bomb. To underscore the need for China to have nuclear weapons, Zhou quoted Joliot-Curie's 1951 message to Mao Zedong: "If you want to oppose the atomic bomb, you need to possess the atomic bomb."[95] With the discovery of uranium, Zhou concluded that "the situation had now changed. . . . It is time to consider the development of atomic energy."[96]

The next day, on January 15, an enlarged meeting of the Central Committee Secretariat convened to discuss whether to develop nuclear energy and pursue the bomb. The secretariat was the party's top leadership decision-making body, roughly equivalent to today's Politburo Standing Committee. At the time, no active duty military officers were members of the secretariat.[97] Other participants in the meeting included Peng Dehuai, Peng Zhen, Deng Xiaoping, Li Fuchun, Bo Yibo, and Liu Jie.[98] Out of the roughly ten participants, only one, Peng Dehuai, was a senior military officer. In other words, although Peng had favored the development of the bomb, the party's top leaders collectively made the decision to pursue it. Participants watched the demonstration of a Chinese-made Geiger counter from the Institute of Modern Physics with a piece of uranium from Guangxi. Qian Sanqiang, head of the institute, said that China's research on atomic energy had "started from scratch," but now, "after several years of effort, a foundation has been established," including forming a team of experts to work on the project.[99] The meeting ended with the "strategic decision" to develop nuclear weapons.[100]

Soon after the January 1955 meeting, steps were taken to create the necessary organizations to develop nuclear weapons. Top party leaders, especially Zhou Enlai, and not senior military officers, made all the key decisions. Zhou Enlai would play a dominant role in overseeing the development of China's strategic weapons from 1955 until his death. The first coordinating body for China's nuclear program was established in July 1955, and was composed of vice-premier Chen Yun, Marshal Nie Rongzhen, and economic planner Bo Yibo.[101] They were charged with overseeing all work for establishing China's nuclear industry and reported to Zhou, with Bo Yibo handling daily affairs. In early 1955, China signed several agreements with the Soviet Union in the areas of uranium mining and nuclear energy, which became the focus of the

Chen-Nie-Bo coordinating group. In December 1955, the State Council published a twelve-year plan for the development of China's nuclear industry, which was then included as a task in the 1956 twelve-year plan for the development of science and technology in China. In November 1956, a ministry to manage the development of China's nuclear industry was established and replaced the Chen-Nie-Bo group.[102]

DECISION TO CONTINUE WITH STRATEGIC WEAPONS DEVELOPMENT

In 1961, China's top party leaders confronted a critical decision about developing the bomb. In 1959 and 1960, the Soviet Union terminated all support for China's nuclear program. Although the role of Soviet nuclear assistance in China's strategic weapons program has probably been overstated, the withdrawal of advisors left China without much-needed equipment to continue specific parts of the projects, and without manuals and technical materials for the equipment that had been delivered.[103] The disastrous economic policies of the Great Leap Forward also sparked a devastating famine and the collapse of China's economy at precisely the time that a key decision about how to allocate resources for strategic weapons would need to be made. As discussed in chapter 4, in January 1961 the top party leadership began to focus on rehabilitating the economy through the policy of "adjustment, consolidation, replenishment, improvement."

Under these conditions, the NDIC held a work conference at the leadership retreat in Beidaihe from July 18 to August 12. The work conference covered many topics, such as reducing the number of workers in the defense industrial sector (consistent with efforts to reduce the urban population more generally). On July 27, the focus turned to the merits of emphasizing conventional versus "sophisticated" weapons and a debate arose over whether to "mount the horse" (shangma) or "dismount the horse" (xiama)—that is, whether to continue with the nuclear program or not.[104] Those in charge of economic planning opposed continuing with the program, while most of the senior military officers, including Nie Rongzhen, He Long, and Chen Yi, argued for continuing with the program.[105] Zhou Enlai called for continuing to produce conventional weapons, which he justified as the basis for developing "sophisticated" ones.[106] Zhou's remarks appeared to indicate that he favored prioritizing conventional weapons production over strategic weapons development.[107]

The discussion about whether to halt the nuclear program continued in the Politburo in August and September 1961. A majority favored continuing.[108] Nie Rongzhen even wrote a report to Mao in late August arguing for the program's continuation.[109] Nevertheless, Liu Shaoqi, vice-chairman of the CCP, instructed that the "basic condition of the nuclear industry" should be investigated before deciding.[110] Mao, Chen Yi and Nie Rongzhen agreed. Afterwards, Nie proposed that Zhang Aiping lead the investigation.[111] Zhang was a deputy chief of the general staff and deputy director of the NDSTC, among other posts related to weapons development.

To conduct his investigation, Zhang worked closely with key scientists, including Liu Xiyao, Liu Jie, and Zhu Guangya. He studied all aspects of the program and facilities in the Second Ministry of Machine Building, which was now responsible for China's nuclear weapons. In November 1961, Zhang submitted his report to Zhou Enlai, Deng Xiaoping, and the CMC. Zhang Aiping concluded that China would be able to test its first device in 1964. However, "the next year is the critical year, if organized well and grasped firmly."[112] Improved coordination among the units involved in the nuclear program would be required to achieve this goal. The program included fifty organizations with more than three thousand people.[113] Zhang stressed that success required the "vigorous support" of central departments, regional bureaus, provinces, and cities.[114] Deng Xiaoping forwarded the report to Mao, Liu Shaoqi, Zhou Enlai, and Peng Zhen.[115] Zhou Enlai and Peng Zhen both indicated agreement with Zhang's report, while members of the CMC expressed their approval.[116] This is believed to have ended the debate over whether or not to halt the program.[117]

Nevertheless, it is unclear whether Zhang's recommendations were implemented. Nie Rongzhen's secretary suggests that Mao may not have given his final blessing to continue with the program until June 1962.[118] After receiving a report that month on war preparations for a Nationalist attack, Mao said "the research and development of sophisticated weapons should continue, we cannot relax or stop [xiama]."[119] Whether other party leaders were waiting for Mao's final blessing or whether efforts to rehabilitate the economy after the Great Leap Forward had slowed progress of the nuclear program in the previous year, the program received renewed attention from the leadership at the Beidaihe retreat in August 1962.[120] If China had nuclear weapons, foreign minister Chen Yi said at the meeting, "it would be much easier for me to be foreign minister!"[121] Afterward, the Second Ministry of Machine Building (in charge of China's nuclear industry) prepared a report for Mao and the leadership, which reviewed the progress achieved so far and concluded that China would be able to conduct its first nuclear test by 1964 or in the first half of 1965, at the very latest.[122] The report became known as the "two-year plan."[123] The plan was refined in October 1962 to first test a device from a tower and then conduct an air-dropped test.[124]

To be able to test a bomb within two years, however, required the coordination of many departments beyond the Second Ministry. To achieve this goal, the Politburo decided to create a special coordinating body. When the Politburo discussed the nuclear program in early October, Liu Shaoqi stated that "the cooperation of all sides is very important, the center should create a commission to strengthen leadership in this area."[125] As head of the National

Defense Industry Office (NDIO), Luo Ruiqing was asked to propose a list of names for such a body, which he submitted on October 30, 1962.[126] In early November, Mao approved, urging them to "make a great effort to coordinate and complete this work."[127]

The Politburo established the Central Special Commission (*zhongyang zhuanmen weiyuanhui*), a body under the Central Committee of the CCP, on November 17, 1962. Reflecting the role of top party leaders, Zhou Enlai chaired the new commission, along with seven vice-premiers and seven members with ministerial rank. Although most of the members were from the state apparatus, military members included He Long (as NDIC director), Nie Rongzhen (as NDSTC director), Zhang Aiping (as NDSTC deputy director), and Luo Ruiqing (as NDIO director).[128] In March 1965, the scope of the Central Special Commission's (CSC) responsibility was expanded to include the development of China's ballistic missile program, and more members were added. The CSC played a key role in China's first test of an atomic device in October 1964, along with key decisions about what kind of nuclear forces to develop and how to develop them. The first few meetings of the CSC in November and December 1962 reviewed the Second Ministry's two-year plan and how to achieve a test by early 1965.

CHINA'S FIRST NUCLEAR TEST

In his capacity as CSC chairman, Zhou Enlai directly supervised the preparations for China's first nuclear test. In April 1964, the CSC established a command department (*zhihui bu*) headed by Zhang Aiping. From this point forward, Zhang's main task was to manage the preparations for the test of China's first device, reporting directly to Zhou.[129] In August 1964, Zhang, along with Liu Xiyao, vice minister of the Second Ministry, supervised a pretest (*yuyan*) of all components that would be used in the actual test. Zhou instructed Zhang to report the results of this test to him directly, using a special telephone line that had been established to link the test site with Zhou's office.[130]

Following the success of these pretests, Zhou convened the ninth meeting of the CSC. On September 16 and 17, the commission then debated the timing of the actual test. One group favored testing earlier, in October 1964, while another group favored testing later, in the spring of 1965.[131] He then reported the options to Liu Shaoqi and Mao Zedong, who would make the final decision. Mao favored testing sooner rather than later, stating that "since it will scare people, let's do it earlier."[132] Although the original plan called for testing in early October, the date was changed to mid-October so that it would not overlap with the presence of foreign dignitaries who would be visiting for China's national day.

Secrecy regarding the test offers another indication of party control over China's nuclear program. Zhou instructed that the timing of the test would only be known by members of the Politburo Standing Committee, the two vice-chairmen of the CMC, and Peng Zhen: a total of eight people. Zhou also devised code words to be used for the test. The bomb would be called "Miss Qiu" (*qiu xiaojie*), the testing tower as the "dressing table" (*shuzhuangtai*), and the fuse or detonator as the "braid" (*shubianzi*).[133] To maintain secrecy, Zhang Aiping communicated with Zhou Enlai through Zhang's assistant, Li Xuge. When an updated weather report threatened to disrupt the test, Zhang dispatched Li to Beijing to inform Zhou Enlai and propose delaying the test until a window of good weather between October 15 and 20. Zhou agreed and then sent the report to Mao Zedong, Liu Shaoqi, Lin Biao, Deng Xiaoping, Peng Zhen, He Long, Nie Rongzhen, and Luo Ruiqing to review; they approved the changes.[134] When the test occurred, Zhang reported the results directly to Zhou Enlai, using a direct phone link that had been established at China's testing facility in Lop Nor.

After the successful test of China's first atomic device, top party leaders continued to dominate the development of China's nuclear weapons. Soon after the first test, Zhou Enlai informed Zhang Aiping and Liu Xiyao that "the center" (*zhongyang*) had decided on the following plan for developing China's strategic weapons: to conduct an air-drop test in 1965, to test a missile with a nuclear warhead in 1966, and to test a hydrogen bomb in 1967.[135]

FORMULATION OF CHINA'S NUCLEAR POLICY

China's approach to nuclear weapons distinguishes between nuclear policy and nuclear strategy. China's nuclear policy (*he zhengce*) refers to national policy positions adopted after the successful test in October 1964. These policies established the parameters for China's nuclear strategy and force posture, which highlights the role of top party leaders in determining nuclear strategy. China's nuclear strategy (*he zhanlue*) refers to more specific operational questions and cannot violate the main tenets of the policy, such as not using nuclear weapons first. China's top party leaders, especially Mao and Zhou, determined China's nuclear policy, which remains influential today.

A statement issued after China successfully tested its first nuclear device introduced China's nuclear policy. Reflecting the dominant role of top party leaders, the document was entitled "Statement of the Government of the People's Republic of China."[136] Since 1949, the use of government statements (*zhengfu shengming*) to announce policy decisions is relatively rare, underscoring the authoritativeness of its content.[137] The key phrase was: "The Chinese government solemnly declares that China at any time and under any circumstances will not be the first to use nuclear weapons." The statement indicated that China had developed nuclear weapons for defensive purposes ("China's development of nuclear weapons is for defense and for protecting the Chinese people from U.S. threats to launch nuclear war"), and that China would not attack nonnuclear weapons states with nuclear weapons and would pursue complete disarmament.

China's nuclear policy has influenced the development of China's nuclear strategy in several ways. First, in the hierarchy of China's military science, military strategy is defined as serving broader national political goals. In the nuclear realm, China's nuclear policy outlines these political goals and defines the essential purposes of China's nuclear weapons. Moreover, changing these political goals lies beyond the purview of military leaders and is an issue reserved for top party leaders. Second, the party created clear guidelines for China's nuclear strategy. Put simply, the no-first-use pledge determined that China's nuclear forces would adopt a retaliatory posture (because China would not use nuclear weapons first) and would need to create a force that would be capable of surviving an initial nuclear attack to be able to retaliate. Not only does China's nuclear policy reflect the dominance of top party leaders in China's approach to nuclear weapons. Morever, it has also constrained China's subsequent nuclear strategy and force development. Third, the policy explains the overriding emphasis on survivability in China's force development, reflected first in the decision to base the bulk of China's nuclear forces in tunnels and silos, and then the desire to add mobile components, with road-mobile missile systems and submarine-launched ballistic missiles.

China's top party leaders formulated China's nuclear policy. On October 11, 1964, Zhou Enlai began to draft the statement that would be issued with China's first test. To discuss the content of the statement, he gathered officials from the MFA, CSC, and GSD. On October 13, Zhou supervised the drafting of the statement. Assisting him was Wu Lengxi (editor of the *People's Daily*), Qiao Guanhua (deputy minister of foreign affairs), and Yao Qin (deputy director of the propaganda department). Zhou described what he wanted the statement to cover and a draft was completed later that day. On October 14, Zhou submitted the draft to top party leaders for their approval, including Mao Zedong, Liu Shaoqi, Lin Biao, Deng Xiaoping, Peng Zhen, and He Long.[138]

The effect of China's nuclear policy is perhaps most evident in the 1996 *Science of Second Artillery Strategy*. Overall, the text mentions "no-first-use" eighteen times and China's "nuclear policy" twenty-six times. The terms are used to establish the parameters for the Second Artillery's use of nuclear weapons. The text states, for example, that "our country's policy of not using nuclear weapons first determines that the Second Artillery must adopt the principle of 'gaining control by striking afterwards' [*houfa zhiren*]."[139] Furthermore, "only after an enemy nuclear state attacks us can the Second Artillery resolutely conduct a nuclear counterattack according to the order of the Central Military Commission."[140] Likewise, the text notes that "the Second Artillery will strictly abide by our country's nuclear policy of no-first-use to develop and employ nuclear missile forces."[141] In short, China's nuclear policy influences and constrains the key elements of strategy: when China will use nuclear weapons and how it will do so.

FORCE STRUCTURE AND DEVELOPMENT

Before and after China's first test of an atomic device in 1964, top party leaders played a key role in determining the type of nuclear weapons that China should develop and how they would develop them. China's strategy and force posture were not dictated by technology. Instead, the goal of possessing a retaliatory force capable of deterring a nuclear attack guided the development of China's nuclear forces.

Even before the CSC was established, senior party leaders provided top-level guidance on the question of force structure. In July 1962, for example, the head of the Fifth Academy at the Ministry of Defense (responsible for missile design and development), Wang Binzhang, delivered a report to the Central Committee on a framework for developing missiles, including an intermediate range (*zhongcheng*) missile that would become the DF-3. Zhou Enlai and Deng Xiaoping approved Wang's report, which focused on lessons learned from the failed test of the DF-2 in March 1962 and other lessons from the DF-2 program for the development of the DF-3.[142]

When the CSC was established, it allowed top party leaders to continue to supervise the development of these weapons systems. After the first design for a nuclear device was developed in March 1963, for example, Zhou Enlai signaled the importance of focusing on weaponization and not just the initial test of an atomic device. Specifically, Zhou said that China "not only must explode a nuclear device, but must also resolve the question of weapons production."[143] A nuclear test by itself would have little deterrent effect. Instead, China would need a deliverable and thus usable nuclear weapon.

In December 1963 and January 1964, party leaders under Zhou Enlai made a series of important decisions about the development of China's nuclear forces. The impetus was twofold. First, in November 1963, scientists had successfully tested the explosive assembly and the initiator—crucial components in an atomic device. After this test, the last step was manufacturing the uranium core.[144] Thus, China had made an important "breakthrough" that increased confidence in a successful test. Second, in August 1963, the United States, the United Kingdom, and the Soviet Union signed a limited test-ban treaty that proscribed testing in the atmosphere, outer space, and underwater. China viewed this as part of an effort to prevent China from acquiring nuclear weapons, especially since it had planned its first test to be above ground.

At its seventh meeting in December 1963, the CSC decided what kind of nuclear weapons China should develop. As Zhou Enlai instructed, "The direction of research on nuclear weapons should prioritize missile warheads, while air-dropped bombs should be secondary."[145] China was perhaps choosing the more difficult path, as it had made only some progress on developing a medium-range missile, the DF-2. Nevertheless, as noted Chinese scholar and scientist Sun Xiangli has observed, the poor survivability and limited range of airplanes "made it difficult [for them] to play a strategic deterrent role."[146] Over the longer term, missiles would provide a more robust retaliatory deterrent than bombers. Later that month, Qian Xuesen submitted a report to the NDSTC on pathways for the development of missile technologies. When Nie Rongzhen approved the report in January 1964, he underscored the need for China to have a long-term plan for developing missiles.[147]

On January 29, 1964, Zhou Enlai prepared a report in the name of the CSC for Mao Zedong, suggesting that China must accelerate the development of its nuclear weapons. Zhou wanted to reduce the time between development and actually equipping the force with an operational weapon and be able to deploy China's first weapons within the timeframe of the Third Five-Year Plan (1966–70). Zhou then suggested that, after a successful nuclear test, China should immediately commence with research on a warhead and accelerate development of the DF-2 so that the force could be equipped with a nuclear-tipped missile as soon as possible.[148]

Mao and other top party leaders approved Zhou's report. Afterward, Zhou called on relevant departments to determine concrete development plans. Over the next year, each department outlined how they would achieve this goal. In July 1964, even before a successful nuclear test, Zhou dispatched his military secretary, Zhou Jiading, to the Second Ministry of Machine Building with instructions to accelerate miniaturization, which was required for a missile delivery system.[149] The Second Ministry indicated it would first focus on research necessary for the test of a nuclear-tipped missile with a fission bomb and then aim to conduct a test of a hydrogen bomb by 1968 that would serve as the foundation of the warheads for China's strategic missiles. The CSC approved the Second Ministry's plan in February 1965.[150]

At the same meeting in February 1965, the CSC made two other crucial decisions. The CSC decided to increase the range of the DF-2 by twenty percent and set 1975 as the deadline for China to develop an ICBM. In this way, top party leaders provided high-level guidance for the development of China's nuclear forces. An ICBM is the essential component of a retaliatory capability and clearly the desired goal.

In March 1965, the Seventh Ministry of Machine Building submitted a missile development plan to the CSC. The plan became known as "four bombs in eight years" because it outlined benchmarks for developing a series of liquid-fueled missiles of various ranges between 1965 and 1972: the DF-2 (medium range), DF-3 (intermediate range), DF-4 (long range), and DF-5 (intercontinental). Initial discussion of the plan began in 1963, before Zhou's 1964 report, as part of a review of the failure of the first DF-2 test launch in March 1962.[151] Given the CSC's requirement that China develop an ICBM by 1975, the main question in 1964 was how to achieve this goal and, specifically, whether China should first develop a long-range missile or move straight to developing an ICBM.

To decide this issue, the Seventh Ministry convened a meeting from February 18 to March 7 that involved more than two thousand researchers, management cadre, and production experts.[152] Zhou Enlai dispatched a team to participate, headed by Zhao Erlu, one of the deputy directors of the CSC's office.[153] Among other issues, debate revolved around whether to develop an experimental long-range missile as part of the effort to develop an ICBM, or whether to design a class of long-range missiles that would then be deployed along with an ICBM.[154] In the end, the participants decided to build a class of long-range missiles, the DF-4, which would be a two-stage design, using the DF-3 as the first stage. Doing so would not only give China experience designing a two-stage missile and allow for a long-range missile to be developed more quickly, but it would also cover targets between China's medium-range missiles and an ICBM.[155] Although technology was certainly a factor, it did not determine the choices made about China's nuclear strategy and force posture. Possessing an ICBM was the desired end goal and the only question was how to achieve it, either directly or by first mastering related technologies through the design and development of the DF-4. As early as 1961, Zhou Enlai had outlined such a phased development of missiles, from shorter-range to longer-range.[156]

On March 20, 1965, the CSC approved the plan to develop "four missiles in eight years." It affirmed the development schedule for the DF-2 with extended range and plans to develop the DF-3 that had been set in 1964.[157] In addition to the DF-2, the development plan outlined milestones for the other missiles that China planned to build. The plan called for conducting the first flight test of the DF-4 in 1969 and certifying the missile (*dingxing*) by 1971, and for the DF-5 to conduct its first flight test in 1971 and to be certified in 1973.[158] Of course, these goals were wildly optimistic. The DF-4 was not completed until 1980, while the first full-range test of the DF-5 occurred nine years behind schedule.[159]

CREATION OF THE SECOND ARTILLERY

Another example of the dominance of China's top party leaders in nuclear strategy is the decision to create the Second Artillery as an independent branch under the CMC to control China's nuclear weapons. At midnight on May 30, 1965, Zhou Enlai summoned Zhang Aiping for an urgent meeting. Zhou stated that the Central Committee and CMC had decided to create a leading body (*lingdao jiguan*) for China's missile forces (*daodan budui*). The time was right, as China was preparing to test a nuclear warhead mated to a missile for the first time.[160] Zhou asked Zhang to create the new unit. What is noteworthy about Zhou's request is that he was not even a CMC member. Instead, he was acting in his capacity as a member of the Politburo Standing Committee and CSC chair, with final authority over China's strategic weapons programs.

Zhang acted quickly to implement Zhou's request. On June 2, Zhang established a group that included the commander of the CMC's artillery corps, the deputy director of the NDSTC, and the heads of the GSD's operations and military affairs departments.[161] On June 15, Zhang submitted a preliminary report to Zhou Enlai and Luo Ruiqing, then chief of the general staff. Based on Zhang's report, the CMC in July 1965 instructed that the Artillery Corps under the CMC would be reorganized to focus on missiles as well as conventional artillery and then be split into two different units that would focus on missiles and conventional artillery, respectively.[162] Based on these instructions, the artillery forces under the CMC began to create new offices in its three general departments to focus on missiles.

In March 1966, for reasons unrelated to the creation of the Second Artillery, the CMC decided to disband the PLA's public security force (gong'an budui). At the time, reorganization of the artillery corps to include missile units was not proceeding as quickly as China's leaders had hoped.[163] Zhang Aiping decided that this presented an opportunity, whereby the leadership of the public security force could be combined with the departments of the artillery corps overseeing missiles. The new organization would be housed in the offices of the old public security force. The commander of the artillery corps, We Kehua, in consultation with Zhang, submitted a report to the GSD proposing the change. Zhang Aiping approved the report in his capacity as deputy chief of the general staff and then submitted it to the CMC, which approved it shortly thereafter.[164]

In his report, Zhang wanted to use two different names for China's missiles forces. Internally, the name would be the rocket artillery force (huojian paobing budui). Externally, it would be called the Second Artillery (di'er paobing). Zhou Enlai, however, suggested that just the name "Second Artillery" should be used.[165] Zhou stated that this name "differentiated it from the American's Strategic Air Force and was different than the Soviet Union's Strategic Rocket Corps. The name is roughly the same as rocket forces and will also maintain secrecy."[166] On June 6, 1966, the Central Committee and CMC decided to establish the Second Artillery based on units from the public security and artillery forces. On July 1, 1966, the Second Artillery was formally established.[167] Although Zhang Aiping played a key role in how the organization was formed, he did so under the direct instructions of China's top party leaders, who reviewed and approved his proposals. Although the CMC would come to play a much larger role in managing the development of the Second Artillery in the late 1970s, it did not play an important role in its establishment despite being a military unit under its command.

The decision to establish the Second Artillery as an independent branch directly under the CMC underscores the desire to centralize command of China's strategic weapons. At the time, other "specialized" units were also directly under the CMC, including the artillery and armored branches. As relatively new technologies for the PLA to master, their development also required close supervision. Over time, these branches were all eventually downgraded as units under the GSD and eventually incorporated into the combined arms group armies formed in the mid-1980s. The Second Artillery, however, remained as the only independent branch directly under the CMC—in effect, functioning like a service. In 2016, China's missile forces were formally established as a service (*junzhong*) and renamed the PLA Rocket Force.

ESTABLISHMENT OF THE SECOND ARTILLERY

After the Second Artillery's establishment, the CMC would play a more direct role in the organization's development. This reflected the chain of command, given that the Second Artillery was created as a unit directly under the CMC. It also still allowed for more direct influence of top party leaders over the organization, some of whom were on the CMC.

On July 12, 1967, the CMC issued temporary regulations for the Second Artillery that outlined its mission and organizational structure. The CMC's primary mission for the Second Artillery was "building a nuclear counterattack force to realize active defense."[168] Furthermore, the regulations underscored the Second Artillery's subordination to the CMC: "Its development, deployment, movements, and especially operations must all be under the centralized leadership of the CMC and it must extremely strictly and accurately follow the orders of the CMC."[169] On September 12, 1967, the CMC standing committee discussed the question of the Second Artillery's mission.[170] The CMC for the first time clearly outlined the development goal for the Second Artillery as "strict and pure, small but effective" (*yanmi jietun, duanxiao jinggan*).[171] The former referred to the quality and organization of the force, while the latter described the capabilities that China aspired to achieve.

The chaos of the Cultural Revolution also engulfed the Second Artillery. Even though established in July 1966, a commander and commissar were not appointed until almost a year later, in 1967, but the order was not disseminated and the designated commander, Xiang Shouzhi, was not informed. A month later, Xiang fell victim to factional politics and was persecuted, leaving the Second Artillery without a commander until 1968.[172] During this period, the organization focused primarily on the construction of several missile bases and associated infrastructure, but not operational doctrine. The Second Artillery's first detailed deliberation of a nuclear counterstrike operation occurred in October 1975, when the Second Artillery's new leadership held a meeting to examine operational employment, marking the first time that operational guiding thought and employment principles for the Second Artillery were discussed (almost a decade after it was established). The crux was that they be compatible with "active defense" so that the troops would know how to conduct "counterstrike operations" (*fanji zuozhan*).[173]

In October 1978, the Second Artillery held an operations meeting to discuss force development. Hua Guofeng, Deng Xiaoping, Ye Jianying and other members of the Central Committee and the CMC met with the participants to comment on the deliberations. During the meeting, Commander Li Shuiqing described the need to develop the Second Artillery into a "lean and effective nuclear counterstrike force."[174] Li's speech again underscored the emphasis on a counterstrike campaign and raised for the first time the concept of "lean and effective" that would later be adopted as the overall guiding principle for the development of China's nuclear forces. The meeting also produced a document on the general principles for the Second Artillery's operations.[175] In 1980, nuclear counterstrike operations were incorporated into the PLA's training program.[176]

In September 1980, the CMC established the basic operational principles for the Second Artillery. This occurred during the "801" meeting on strategy described in chapter 5. The Second Artillery's leadership was invited to participate, with He Jinheng, then a deputy commander and chief of staff, delivering a speech on how the Second Artillery would be used in a future war. Given the high degree of centralization and secrecy surrounding China's nuclear weapons, He's speech marked the first time that other senior officers in the PLA were introduced to how China's nuclear weapons would be used.[177] The CMC instructed that two principles should serve as the basis for the Second Artillery's operations in a way that was consistent with the concept of active defense and the no-first-use policy—"close defense" (*yanmi fanghu*) and "keypoint counterstrikes" (*zhongdian fanji*). At the meeting, Yang Dezhi, then chief of the general staff and a member of the CMC, stated that "the Second Artillery must be closely defended and, according to the order of the CMC, carry out keypoint counterstrikes."[178]

After the "801" meeting, the Second Artillery leadership acted quickly to flesh out the meaning of these principles. In October 1980, Li Shuiqing convened a third meeting to study the operational employment of the Second Artillery.[179] The participants emphasized increasing survivability, rapid reaction, and integrated operational capabilities.[180] In July 1981, the Second Artillery's leadership held a fourth meeting on operational employment, which discussed operational guiding thought. The Second Artillery then formally adopted "close defense, keypoint counterstrikes" as its operational principles, based on the strategic guideline of active defense and the "spirit" of the "801" meeting.[181] These principles remain the basis of China's nuclear operations to this day.[182]

In August 1983, the Second Artillery's first campaign-level exercise codified these operational principles and its nuclear counterstrike mission. Previously, select units had conducted launch exercises, but this marked the first time that the Second Artillery as an independent branch conducted a campaign-level exercise. Planning for the exercise began in February 1983, with CMC approval. The scenario was based on defending against a nuclear attack and launching a nuclear counterstrike after being attacked with nuclear weapons during an invasion by a "blue force" striving for "global hegemony."[183] According to He Jinheng, now commander of the Second Artillery, the exercise was undertaken "to deepen understanding of the operational principles of 'close defense' and 'keypoint counterstrikes.' "[184] To underscore survivability and rapid reaction, the exercise emphasized the organization, command, and coordination of protection and counterstrike operations at the start of a war.[185] The exercise was held in the northeast and involved two bases (*jidi*) and two launch contingents (*zhidui*). The PLA leadership, including CMC members Yang Shangkun and Yang Dezhi, attend the live-fire launches that were part of the exercise.[186] A group training event on campaign methods held alongside the exercise produced a draft document on campaign methods that was then revised into the first *Science of Second Artillery Campaigns*, which was published in 1985.[187]

During this period, only one core principle for the development of the Second Artillery was not directly given to the Second Artillery by the CMC. This was the concept of developing a "lean and effective" (*jinggan youxiao*) force. As noted earlier, Li Shuiqing first raised this formula during the 1978 operations meeting. He Jinheng further developed the idea in a 1984 article for the internal journal *Military Arts*.[188] After some debate, the standing committee of the Second Artillery adopted "lean and effective" as its overall development goal in December 1984.[189] Nevertheless, the phrase was adopted because it reflected the views of China's top party leaders regarding the mission of the CMC, especially the 1967 instruction to develop a "small but effective" force and Deng Xiaoping's 1978 instruction to develop a "few but capable" nuclear weapons.

DRAFTING OF A NUCLEAR STRATEGY OUTLINE

An attempt by the Second Artillery to draft a document on China's nuclear strategy in the late 1980s offers a rarely observed example of the CMC exercising its authority over the content of nuclear strategy and the lack of delegation in the area of strategy from top party leaders to senior military officers. Because the document was recalled in 1989 and never published, source materials on this episode remain incomplete. Nevertheless, it demonstrates that the Second

Artillery lacked the standing to issue documents or statements on China's nuclear strategy without the approval of China's top party leaders.

In March 1985, the Second Artillery published the first edition of the *Science of Second Artillery Campaigns*, a doctrinal text on how to conduct a nuclear counterstrike. During a meeting to review and revise a draft of the text, the participants concluded that such campaigns involved questions of national and military strategy. Li Lijing, a former base commander and then consultant to the Second Artillery headquarters, recalls that "because the rational basis and authoritative interpretation of China's nuclear strategy had not been finalized, the science of campaigns for China's strategic rocket forces could not be finalized." For example, "if a great power nuclear war were to start, it was unclear where China should strike and how much of the enemy's nuclear equivalent should be destroyed."[190]

After further investigation, Li Lijing discovered that no other department was researching nuclear strategy. Li then submitted a report to He Jinheng and Li Xuge, the commander and deputy commander of the Second Artillery, respectively, suggesting that a group be formed to study the issue. He and Li approved the establishment of a small research group, headed by Li Lijing and composed of members of the military studies department (*junshixue bu*) within the Second Artillery's headquarters.[191] Li Lijing suggested that the group research and write an authoritative document entitled *China's Nuclear Strategy* (*Zhongguo hezhanlue*) within two or three years. As one account notes, the project was "inspired by research on strategy throughout the army" in the mid-1980s following the shift to peacetime modernization in 1985.[192] According to one account, Li Lijing then discussed the project with a deputy chief of the general staff involved in an army-wide strategy small group. The GSD then entrusted (*zecheng*) the Second Artillery and AMS to work together and complete the project.[193]

The project's pace accelerated in 1987. Shen Kehui, head of the military studies department, recalls that the Second Artillery, along with AMS, NDU, COSTIND, and the Ministry of State Security, organized a series of seminars on "academic issues of strategy and nuclear strategy."[194] Roughly fifty to sixty people from twenty different units inside and outside the military participated. The topics covered included national security and nuclear strategy, general strategy and nuclear strategy, China's nuclear strategy, and the development strategy for China's missiles.[195] Following these discussions, Li Lijing's research group began to draft a document entitled *Nuclear Strategy Outline* (*he zhanlue gangyao*). After almost three years of work, the group completed a preliminary draft at the end of 1988. The outline was circulated as a "classified document" (*jimi wenjian*) within the Second Artillery as well as some of the PLA's academies and the GSD for feedback.[196]

Top party leaders, however, strongly criticized the circulation of the draft. According to a biography of Li Xuge, then the commander of the Second

Artillery, "nuclear strategy should be a matter for the headquarters and should not be carried out by the Second Artillery."[197] When the CMC learned of the document, the reaction was even stronger. Vice-chairman Liu Huaqing met with Liu Lifeng, then the Second Artillery's political commissar, and transmitted a message from Yang Shangkun, who at the time was the highest-ranking member of the CMC after Deng and PRC President.[198] Yang "severely criticized" the document and said "it should be killed." Yang ordered that all copies be recalled and that discussion of it be prohibited, as it "involved the highest secrets of the state, which would have serious consequences."[199]

The problem with the strategy outline was not its content, but, rather, the Second Artillery's lack of authority to write a document on China's nuclear strategy. Several sources indicate that the statements of China's leaders served as the basis for the strategy that was discussed in the draft. According to Li Lijing, for example, the draft was based on Deng's idea of "limited retaliation" (*youxian baofu*).[200] Shen Kehui likewise recalls that the outline was based on "related speeches by party and national leaders and our country's nuclear policy."[201] The problem was that the Second Artillery, as the custodian of China's nuclear missile forces, lacked the standing to write about much less formulate China's nuclear strategy. In his critique of the document's circulation, Yang Shangkun said that "the Second Artillery does not have the authority to do this, it cannot be permitted."[202]

In 1996, the Second Artillery published a textbook entitled the *Science of Second Artillery Strategy*. It was part of a three-volume series that examined campaign methods and tactics as well as strategy, as part of an effort to create an "operational theoretical system" for the Second Artillery. Yet even this volume was not a statement of China's national nuclear strategy but, instead, the Second Artillery's service strategy.[203] It underscores the subordination of the strategic actions of the Second Artillery to the nation's overall strategy. Importantly, unlike the previous document on strategy discussed above, the CMC approved (and likely supervised) the drafting of this volume as a military research project in the Eighth Five-Year Plan.[204]

FORCE POSTURE

China's force posture is consistent with the singular use of nuclear weapons to execute a retaliatory strike. Given the no-first-use policy, survivability has been a dominant driver of China's nuclear force posture. China has pursued survivability in several ways. First, leveraging China's sheer size, China's nuclear forces are dispersed throughout the country. When China began creating missile units, even before the Second Artillery's formal establishment, dispersion was a key principle. In the early 1960s, for example, China's first missile battalions were located in Xi'an, Shenyang, Beijing, and Jinan.[205] When plans to develop

ICBMs were discussed in the mid-1960s, Zhou Enlai planned to deploy some in mountains in the north and others in jungles in the south.[206] Today, the Second Artillery has six bases, each headquartered in a different province. Each base is composed of launch brigades that operate specific missile systems. China's ICBMs, the DF-5 and DF-31A, are similarly organized into ten launch brigades under five bases in six provinces.[207]

Second, most bases and launch brigades are part of tunnel networks, sometimes described as an "underground great wall" (*dixia changcheng*). As China learned in the Korean War, tunnels offered a relatively cheap solution for defending fixed targets. With a no-first-use policy, it was essential to use whatever means available to ensure that China's nuclear forces could survive a first strike. Amid growing tensions between China and the Soviet Union in 1969, reports emerged that Moscow was considering a "surgical strike" on China's nuclear forces. After reading reports on the subject in the Western media, Zhou Enlai summoned Ye Jianying to discuss the construction of missile locations (*zhendi*). Zhou stated that China had to accelerate the development of these facilities to create an operational capability. Once created, Zhou stated, "we won't fear others' threats or coercion. Plans to conduct a surgical strike will be wishful thinking. . . . We promised early on not to use nuclear weapons first, but as soon as we suffer a nuclear attack, we have the right to retaliation and self-defense."[208]

In the mid-1980s, as China was developing and deploying its first true ICBM, the DF-5, the Second Artillery began a large-scale construction project for the missile's launch brigades. The DF-5 itself was so large that it could only be based in silos. Initial plans called for the silos to be placed in mountainous and jungle areas, where the terrain would provide some natural concealment. Some DF-5 launch brigades would be located toward the north in Henan province and others toward the south in Hunan province. Deng Xiaoping approved the plans in the late 1970s, and construction began in the early 1980s and was not completed until 1995.[209]

Third, as China developed newer missiles, it emphasized increasing mobility to enhance survivability. In August 1978, Deng Xiaoping had called on the Second Artillery to "use missiles to fight guerrilla warfare" (*yong daodan da youjizhan*).[210] On land, China pursued mobility by creating missiles that could be more easily transported. This required reducing the weight of the missile so that it could be carried by a TEL (transporter-erector-launcher) and shifting from liquid to solid fuel to reduce time to launch. The first solid-fuel mobile missile was the DF-21, which was developed in the 1980s and first deployed in 1991. The first road-mobile ICBMs were the DF-31 and DF-31A, respectively, which began to be deployed in 2006. At sea, China has sought to develop SSBNs. Although China has pursued such ambitions since the late 1950s, they have yet to be fully realized. China's first SSBN, the *Xia* class, encountered so many technical problems that it never conducted a single deterrent patrol.[211] China deployed a newer design in the late 2000s, the Type-094 or *Jin* class SSBN. The missile for this submarine, the JL-2, remains under development and it is unclear when deterrent patrols will begin.

FORCE STRUCTURE

China's nuclear force structure is consistent with the singular focus on a nuclear counterstrike campaign in China's nuclear strategy. Early on, China's top party leaders decided to create a diversified nuclear force. This included short, medium, and intercontinental ballistic missiles capable of striking targets on China's periphery and beyond. China did not achieve a true intercontinental strike capability until the successful test of the DF-5 in May 1980. By that time, China had also successfully deployed shorter-range missiles, including the DF-3 (1971) and DF-4 (1980). In 1984, the CMC placed China's nuclear forces on alert status for the first time, signifying the establishment of a rudimentary retaliatory capability.[212]

Since then, China has continued to modernize its force. Although the number of ICBMs in the arsenal has increased significantly when compared with 1984, the overall size of the force remains small when compared with the world's two major nuclear powers, the United States and the Soviet Union/Russia. By 1991, China may have deployed only four DF-5s.[213] The initial design for the missile was being revised to produce to a longer-range and more accurate version, the DF-5A, which entered service in the 1990s. In 2000, the Department of Defense estimated that China had eighteen silos for the DF-5 and roughly twenty missiles.[214] During the 1999 military parade to celebrate the fiftieth anniversary of the PRC, China unveiled the DF-31 series of missiles, which began to be deployed in 2006. Unlike the DF-5, which was liquid-fueled and silo-based, the DF-31 was a three-stage, solid-fueled mobile missile. The longer-range variant, the DF-31A, is capable of striking most of the continental United States.

Today, the overall size of China's force posture remains consistent with a strategy of assured retaliation limited to deterring nuclear coercion and attack. China has roughly sixty ICBMs capable of striking the United States. As half of the DF-5 missiles have now been equipped with MIRVs, China can strike the United States with approximately eighty warheads.[215] China also has roughly sixty shorter-range missiles with single warheads, including the DF-21 and the DF-4.[216] The DF-26 introduced at the 2015 military parade was described as "dual capable" with conventional and nuclear variants but appears to have primarily a conventional, antiship role.[217]

Looking forward, the size of the force will almost certainly grow. China could equip the remainder of its DF-5s with MIRVs. China is also reportedly developing a new mobile ICBM, the DF-41, that may likely be able to carry

MIRVs. China may finally deploy its second-generation SSBN, the *Jin* class, each of which would carry twelve JL-2 missiles. Although, in part, these developments represent a desire to modernize the force and retire old systems such as the DF-3, DF-4, and JL-1, China also seeks to ensure its ability to retaliate as US missiles defense and conventional counterforce capabilities increase.

Nuclear Strategy and the Strategic Guidelines

The strategic guidelines discussed throughout this book emphasize conventional military operations. In the documents available on the various guidelines, nuclear strategy and the Second Artillery as a nuclear force are rarely mentioned. Nevertheless, the development and deployment of China's nuclear forces have been consistent with the basic principle in all the guidelines of "active defense." Although the concept has been interpreted differently at various times since 1949, it has been the basic organizing principle for all of the PRC's military strategies and has served as a general principle for China's nuclear strategy as well.

The prominence of nuclear issues in past strategic guidelines has varied. The 1956 strategic guideline was based on the assumption that the PLA would have to wage war "under nuclear conditions." Although the 1964 strategic guideline was later sometimes described as preparing to fight an "early, major, nuclear war," it did not contain specific guidance for how China's nuclear forces would be used. In fact, the emphasis on "luring the enemy in deep" into Chinese territory suggested that they would not be used. Moreover, although China had exploded its first nuclear device, it did not possess any reliable means of delivering nuclear weapons. Despite the lack of a reliable delivery system, the CMC's 1967 temporary regulations for the Second Artillery linked future nuclear operations with active defense. The regulations noted that the "Second Artillery is an important nuclear strike force to realize our country's strategic task [*renwu*] of active defense."[218] At around the same time, the CMC described the Second Artillery's mission as "developing a nuclear counterstrike force to realize active defense."[219]

Only with the 1980 guideline did nuclear strategy appear to be discussed in the context of China's national military strategy. At the "801" meeting described in chapter 5, China adopted a new strategic guideline to deal with the Soviet threat that emphasized active defense and abandoned luring the enemy in deep as a strategic concept. At the meeting, the CMC raised "close defense" and "keypoint counterstrikes" as the Second Artillery's operational principles, which were intended to be consistent with a retaliatory posture. He Jinheng, commander of the Second Artillery from 1982 to 1985, recalls that the development of the principle of "lean and effective" in the early 1980s was designed to carry out the strategic guideline of active defense.[220] His biography also notes that the concept of active defense shaped the drafting of the 1985 edition of the *Science of Second Artillery Campaigns*. Likewise, the Second Artillery's first campaign exercise in 1983 "used the strategic guideline of active defense as guidance."[221]

The relationship between the overall strategic guidelines and nuclear strategy is perhaps most clear in the 1993 strategic guideline. At this time, the Second Artillery's role in the PLA had expanded to include conventional missiles in addition to nuclear ones, which gave the Second Artillery a long-range conventional strike mission in addition to its nuclear deterrence and nuclear counterattack mission. Immediately after the adoption of the 1993 strategy, the Second Artillery held a meeting for all senior officers to "disseminate and study the spirt of the enlarged meeting of the CMC."[222] Thereafter, like other services in the PLA, the Second Artillery launched a series of training reforms to implement the new strategic guideline. Other recollections by senior officers in the Second Artillery link the organization's development in the 1990s to the 1993 strategy.[223] Reflecting the connection, Jiang Zemin penned an inscription when inspecting a Second Artillery unit in 1998: "Carry out the strategic guideline of active defense, build a lean and effective strategic rocket force."[224]

Doctrinal publications also highlight the relationship between the strategic guidelines and nuclear strategy. The 1996 *Science of Second Artillery Strategy* contains numerous references to the strategic guidelines as the basis for developing the Second Artillery's strategy. For example, the text describes the Second Artillery as "a strategic rocket force to carry out our country's active defense military strategy."[225] The Second Artillery's service strategy of "emphasizing deterrence, effective counterstrike" is "based on our country's nuclear policy and our army's active defense military strategy."[226] Moreover, the 1993 strategic guideline is "the basic guidance and foundation for the development and strategic employment of the Second Artillery."[227] In terms of strategic operations, the text contains a detailed discussion of how commanders should "obey the basic spirit of the military strategic guideline."[228] For example, "according to our country's active defense strategic guideline for the new period and nuclear policy, the ultimate goal of the Second Artillery's strategic deterrence is to make enemy nuclear states stop risking actions of nuclear threats and nuclear attacks."[229]

References to the strategic guidelines also appear in the 2004 *Science of Second Artillery Campaigns*. It states, for example, that "according to our country's strategic guideline of active defense, nuclear forces carry out counterstrike operations."[230] Furthermore, the book notes that "Second Artillery campaigns are part of a local war and are restricted by the military strategic guideline. Therefore, raising the issue of the guiding thought for Second Artillery campaigns must be based on the military strategic guideline and resolutely implement the requirements of the military strategic guideline."[231]

In sum, the PLA's strategic guidelines emphasize conventional operations. Most of these guidelines have been based on the general principle of active defense, which includes the idea of "gaining control by striking afterwards." The development of China's nuclear strategy and forces has been consistent with the guidelines at this most general level—that is, to focus on active defense by developing a retaliatory capability. However, as shown throughout this chapter, China's nuclear strategy has not changed with each new strategic guideline.

Conclusion

China's nuclear strategy is the exception that proves the rule. Since 1949, China's strategic guidelines, which emphasize conventional operations, have changed frequently. Senior military officers have pushed for changes in China's military strategy in response to significant shifts in the conduct of warfare in the international system. By contrast, China's strategy for the use of nuclear weapons has been roughly constant. China has developed nuclear forces to deter nuclear strikes and to prevent nuclear coercion. China has sought to achieve these goals through assured retaliation, or developing a retaliatory capability that can survive a first strike and inflict unacceptable damage on an adversary. China's nuclear strategy has remained constant because this aspect of military affairs has not been delegated by top party leaders to senior military officers. Since the decision to develop nuclear weapons in the early 1950s, the establishment of the Second Artillery in 1966, and its development since the 1970s, top party leaders have dominated decision-making for China's nuclear strategy. What has changed is how China implements this strategy.[232]

Conclusion

This study makes four contributions to understanding the process of change in China's military strategy. The first is to provide the first complete account of all the strategic guidelines issued since 1949. This is a crucial first step in any effort to explain changes in Chinese strategy and, more broadly, to understand the evolution of China's defense policies. Previously, neither Western nor Chinese studies of China's defense policies have offered a complete examination of the PRC's military strategies. Although Chinese scholarship on military strategy in the past decade does refer to the strategic guidelines, at most only a few of the guidelines that were adopted are discussed and they do not necessarily identify the same set of strategies. Due to the constraints imposed by limited access to relevant Chinese sources, most Western scholarship has inferred China's strategies not from the content of the strategic guidelines themselves, but from Chinese statements, press reports, and weapons development. China's strategy before the 1980s was often viewed simply as "people's war," then "people's war under modern conditions" in the 1980s, and, finally, variants of "local wars" since the 1990s. The one-million-man downsizing in 1985 was interpreted as a change in China's strategy when, in fact, it was not.

Second, this study demonstrates that three of the strategies that China has adopted since 1949 represent major changes in its military strategy. Major change consists of a new vision of warfare, which then prompts reforms in the areas of operational doctrine, force structure, and training in order to execute this vision. In 1956, China's first major change in military strategy emphasized positional warfare and fixed defenses to stop or blunt an American invasion. This was a clear departure from the dominance of mobile warfare that prevailed during much of the civil war and the Chinese offensives in the Korean War. In 1980, the PLA again emphasized positional warfare to counter a Soviet invasion. This strategy was a major departure from that of "luring the enemy in deep," adopted in 1964 and used throughout the Cultural Revolution, which emphasized ceding land to an invader, mobile warfare, and decentralized operations. In 1993, the third major change in China's military strategy shifted from how to defend China against an invasion to how to prevail in local wars over limited aims on its periphery, especially in territorial and sovereignty disputes.

Third, China has pursued major changes in its military strategy when a significant shift in the conduct of warfare has occurred in the international system—but only when the party leadership is united. A shift in the conduct of warfare creates a strong incentive for a state to adopt a new military strategy if the shift demonstrates that a gap exists between a state's current capabilities and the requirements of future wars. The effect of these shifts should be particularly salient for developing countries or late military modernizers such as China who are trying to improve their military capabilities. These states are already at a comparative disadvantage and need to monitor their capabilities closely relative to stronger states. In socialist states with party-armies and not national ones, the party is likely to grant substantial autonomy for the management of military affairs to senior military officers, who will adjust strategy in response to changes in their state's security environment. Because senior military officers are also party members, the party can delegate responsibility for military affairs without the fear of a coup or concerns that the military will pursue a strategy inconsistent with the party's political goals. Such delegation, however, is only possible when the party's political leadership is united over questions of the party's basic policies and the structure of authority within the party.

Shifts in the conduct of warfare and party unity feature prominently in the three major changes in China's military strategy since 1949. The 1956 strategy was adopted during a period of unprecedented unity within the CCP. Senior PLA officers, especially Su Yu and Peng Dehuai, initiated the change in strategy as the PLA absorbed the lessons of World War II and the Korean War, along with the nuclear revolution. The 1980 strategy was adopted after Deng Xiaoping consolidated his position as China's paramount leader and reestablished party unity following the leadership splits and general upheaval of the Cultural Revolution. Senior PLA officers, especially Su Yu, Song Shilun, Yang Dezhi, and Zhang Zhen, initiated and led the change in strategy in response to their assessment of the Soviet threat based on the tank and air operations in the 1973 Arab-Israeli War. The 1993 strategy was adopted after Deng restored party unity following the leadership split during and after the violent suppression of the 1989 demonstrations in Tiananmen Square. Senior PLA officers, especially Liu Huaqing, Chi Haotian, Zhang Zhen, and Zhang Wannian, initiated the change in strategy following the demonstration of new kinds of military operations in the 1990–91 Gulf War.

However, one change in China's military strategy, in 1964, cannot be explained by this argument. It represents the only instance where the top party leader—in this case, Mao Zedong—intervened in military affairs to change strategy. Otherwise, senior military officers have initiated all other changes in China's military strategy. The 1964 strategy did not contain a new vision of warfare, but called upon the PLA to return to an approach it had honed in the 1930s during the civil war—mobile warfare and luring the enemy in deep. Nevertheless, the case demonstrates how a split within the leadership and growing party disunity can distort or disrupt the process of strategic decision-making. Mao intervened not to enhance China's security, but as part of his attack on revisionists within the party leadership that would culminate in 1966 with the launch of the Cultural Revolution.

The book's final contribution is to explain why, in contrast to its conventional military strategy, China's nuclear strategy has remained constant over the same period of time. The reason is simple: China's top party leaders have never delegated responsibility for nuclear strategy to senior military officers. China's nuclear strategy is constrained by China's national nuclear policy, which remains the purview of top party leaders. Because nuclear strategy is subordinate to China's nuclear policy, it is an issue that can only be decided by the highest levels of the party. Unlike the strategy for conventional operations, senior military officers have never been empowered to initiate change in nuclear strategy.

Changes in China's Military Strategy and International Relations Theory

This book's findings contribute in several ways to the study of international relations. First, a focus on shifts in the conduct of warfare as a motivation for change in military strategy complements existing arguments in the literature on military doctrine and innovation about the external sources of military change. It identifies a new motivation for states to change their military strategy when they are not facing a pressing or immediate threat. Developing countries or late military modernizers such as China need to closely monitor their security environment and to husband scarce resources for defense (which could come at the expense of supporting continued economic growth). When a war occurs in the international system, such states are likely to assess its key features and implications for their own security. By contrast, other motivations identified in this literature, such as the onset of new missions for the use of a country's armed forces or emergence of new technologies that can be applied to warfighting, are less likely to prompt these states to change their military strategy. Focusing on the effects of significant shifts in the conduct of warfare thus enriches and broadens arguments about the external sources of change in military strategy. In the case of China, even when clear threats existed, such as the prospect of US or Soviet invasion, they were often only a necessary but not sufficient condition for pursuing a major change in strategy. Shifts in the conduct of warfare helped to clarify how to prepare for such threats.

Second, in the long-running debate over whether change in military organizations requires civilian intervention, China provides an important case of strategic change initiated by senior military officers without civilian intervention. Of the nine military strategies that China has adopted since 1949, eight of them were initiated and led by senior military officers, subject only to the approval of the top party leader, in his capacity as the chairman of the party's CMC. This includes not only the three major changes in strategy in 1956, 1980, and 1993, but also minor adjustments and refinements of strategy in 1960, 1988, 2004, and 2014, and one case of no change when luring the enemy in deep was affirmed in 1977. In fact, the only instance of direct civilian (party) intervention that produced a change in strategy—in 1964—was pursued not to jolt the generals from their own complacency, as has been the case in other states, but instead as part of Mao's response to revisionism within the party leadership.

One potential caveat or exception concerns the organizational reforms associated with the strategic guideline issued in 2014. These reforms occurred amid a much broader party effort to pursue institutional and economic reforms that were outlined at the Third Plenum in November 2013. Xi Jinping's intervention was likely essential for the military reforms to be launched. But whether, in his role as the top party leader, he pushed for these reforms against the wishes of the PLA high command remains unclear. As the reforms were designed to improve the PLA's ability to conduct joint operations (a PLA goal for two decades), the idea for such reforms was almost certainly not Xi's alone. Rather, it likely involved substantial input from those within the PLA who sought to bring about such changes, drawing on previous efforts to reorganize the PLA.

Third, more generally, the reason why the PLA was able to initiate major changes in China's military strategy without civilian intervention—the structure of civil-military relations—contributes to a growing emphasis on civil-military relations as an independent or explanatory variable in explaining state behavior. Historically, the study of civil-military relations has emphasized treating it as a dependent variable, with a focus on explaining whether and when the military intervenes in politics, especially coups.[1] New research, however, demonstrates the effects of different patterns or structures of civil-military relations on strategic assessment,[2] military effectiveness,[3] intervention,[4] and nuclear strategy.[5] More generally, a much broader body of scholarship asserting and debating the "democratic advantage" in war and on regime type and conflict is often based on assumptions about specific patterns of civil-military relations.[6] The role of party-military relations in enabling the PLA's senior officers to initiate strategic change demonstrates the effect of civil-military relations in a specific type of authoritarian state—socialist ones with Leninist systems—at the highest level of military affairs. Precisely because the PLA is a party-army under the CCP and not a national army, civilian intervention for strategic change was simply not necessary. As such, there may be a "Leninist advantage" in the ability of such states to change military strategy, despite the disadvantages centralization in such a system may pose at the tactical or operational levels of contemporary warfare.

Fourth, the role of party unity in enabling or facilitating strategic change in China expands the scope of arguments, often described as "neoclassical realism," that explore how domestic factors mediate the structural pressures of the international system.[7] Whatever the label, the case of strategic change in China indicates how such arguments might be applied in socialist states and not just Western democratic ones. Party unity, for example, reflects a kind of elite cohesion that Randall Schweller identifies as a source of underbalancing.[8] In socialist states, however, the key elite is the party elite. The question is not whether the party elite agrees upon the nature of external threats but instead whether it agrees upon the basic policies that the party should pursue and how authority should be structured within it. When the party elite does agree—when the party is united—then changes to military strategy initiated by senior military officers, as circumstances require, will be adopted.

Fifth, militaries as organizations are often portrayed as resistant to change. For this reason, scholars have argued that civilian intervention is necessary to produce change in strategy.[9] In the China case, however, the PLA has proven to be quite willing to pursue strategic change. In the area of nuclear strategy, moreover, it has been civilians rather than the military that has resisted change (to China's no-first-use policy). Of course, this does not mean that no resistance to change is present. In the 1950s, some parts of the PLA worried about excessive reliance on Soviet advice and doctrine, at the expense of the PLA's own warfighting experience and traditions. Even in the early 1980s, parts of the PLA, especially local units at the grassroots level, viewed the move away from Maoist ideals of the Cultural Revolution with suspicion. Since the early 1990s, the consistent loser in PLA reorganizations has been elements associated with the ground forces and the regional command structure. Nevertheless, the CMC has issued new strategies or adjusted old ones, as necessitated by changes in the external security environment, and, especially, by overall trends in the conduct of warfare. Moreover, the PLA has pursued ten force reductions since 1949, including three totaling one million soldiers since 1997, which would be a significant change for any organization and perhaps especially for a military. The PLA's identity as a party-army and not a national one likely explains why it has been less resistant to change—namely, because it identifies its purpose with the CCP's own goals. As a party institution, it is expected to change as circumstances require.

Sixth, contrary to the seminal work on civil-military relations by Samuel Huntington, professionalism can take root in militaries subject to extensive political control such as party-armies in socialist states. The PLA as a party-army and not a national one is a politicized force. Based on Huntington's argument, such a politicized force under "subjective control" is less likely to behave as a professional force.[10] Yet, at the strategic level, the PLA has generally demonstrated more professionalism than Huntington might expect, despite its loyalty to the party and not the state. The reason can be found in the structure of civil-military relations in socialist states. Despite the politicization of the armed forces, the tendency for the party to delegate military affairs to senior officers with minimal oversight also creates the autonomy that Huntington believed was necessary for professionalization through the idea of "objective" control. The catch, of course, is that the conditions that create autonomy for the PLA to perform as a professional military depend on party unity. When unity is present, professionalism can grow. When unity is absent, professionalism atrophies.

Finally, the pattern of change in China's military strategy illuminates the question of whether great powers can ascertain each other's intentions. The negative argument invokes a strand of structural realism that prizes uncertainty.[11] The evolution of China's military strategy, however, suggests that intentions may not be as uncertain as these arguments suggest, at least in the short to medium term. The content of China's strategic guidelines, if nothing else, reveals China's general military goals at different points in time. Although China does not engage in public diplomacy to propagate the guidelines, they are formulated under the general parameters of the party's policies and overall political goals. The integration of military strategy and the political objectives of China's grand strategy has been high. For this reason alone, in addition to the many other sources that one could consult to understand China's intentions beyond the military sphere, intentions are simply not as inscrutable as some scholars suggest. Likewise, if China's intentions change, such changes are likely to be observed in changes in China's military strategy, along with its operational doctrine, force structure, and training.

The Future of China's Military Strategy

Looking forward, a key question is when China might next change its military strategy. The history of the major changes contained in this book may help to illuminate when and why future changes in strategy are likely to occur.

Overall, until recently, the PLA's self-assessment of its capabilities suggests that it continues to play "catch up" with other major military powers, especially the United States. The PLA's analysis of its own performance can be quite critical and deficiencies have been identified in many areas.[12] Xi Jinping's repeated calls for the PLA to be "ready to fight and win wars" likely reflects a belief that the PLA is unable to do so. For this reason, the PLA will continue to monitor closely other wars that occur in the international system, especially those involving US forces or US allies who use American weaponry, tactics, and procedures. Of course, if relations with the United States were to deteriorate significantly and, from China's view, if the United States posed a greater threat to its security, then that threat would likely assume a more central role in China's military strategy and perhaps even lead to the adoption of a new strategic guideline focused on a single adversary akin to those before 1988. Events in 2018 suggest that such a deterioration may have begun. These include the start of a trade war aimed at the structure of China's economy, US concerns about Chinese "influence operations" within democratic societies in Asia and elsewhere, and increasing tension in East Asia's maritime disputes (especially in the South China Sea). The 2018 US *National Defense Strategy* described China as a "strategic competitor." If Chinese leaders conclude that Deng Xiaoping's assessment that peace and development no longer characterizes China's security environment, then a change in strategy—and possibly a major change—is much more likely. Even without a major deterioration in US-China relations, however, China will focus on the military operations of the United States simply because it possesses the most advanced military in the world whose operations could signal a shift in the conduct of warfare.

China's continued economic growth suggests that the goals of its military strategy could become more expansive than they have been in the past. For the PRC's first four decades, military strategy focused on the singular challenge of countering an invasion of Chinese territory—how to defeat an amphibious assault by the United States and then how to defeat a Soviet ground invasion from the north. However, for the past thirty years, the PLA has not faced a threat of invasion, and instead China has focused its military strategy on local conflicts over limited aims along its periphery. Along with the growth of the Chinese economy, however, China's interests have expanded beyond East Asia, symbolized by the establishment of China's first overseas base in Djibouti in 2017. Thus, new interests overseas, and the missions they may create for the PLA, may come to play a greater role in China's military strategy going forward. They clearly played a role in the highlighting of the maritime domain in the 2014 strategy, though it is unclear if they will be sufficient to produce a major change in China's military strategy. For the short to medium term, the main issues over which China has envisioned using force in the past three decades remain, such as Taiwan, the China-India border, and maritime disputes in the South China Sea. As long as these remain unresolved, they will likely occupy the bulk of strategic planning and be the central focus of China's military strategy. Nevertheless, the role of new missions, and their potential to spark change in China's military strategy, should be closely followed.

Although on the basis of per capita income, China remains a relatively poor country, it also now possesses an advanced industrial base. Through the Made in China 2025 program announced in 2015, China is actively seeking to be a leader in the development of various advanced technologies. Many of these, such as artificial intelligence, quantum computing, and robotics, have potential military applications whose development could enable China to develop new ways of warfighting that, in turn, could spark a change in military strategy to employ these new capabilities. In the past, China changed its strategy in response to changes in the conduct of warfare as practiced by other states. In the future, however, it may be able to produce military innovations that shape how others view the conduct of warfare and may change its strategy accordingly.

Whether China can pursue either a major or minor change in its military strategy will depend on the continued unity of the CCP's leadership over basic policies and the structure of authority. Although periods of party disunity may be hard to predict, one important consequence of such periods is that they can prevent the adoption of a new military strategy. Since becoming general secretary in late 2012, Xi Jinping has embarked on an ambitious plan to reconstitute the CCP, using anticorruption drives as the main tool to enforce discipline. So far, the party leadership has remained united and a major split in the leadership has not developed. Nevertheless, the sheer number of people ensnared in these campaigns, including some very senior party and military leaders like former Politburo Standing Committee member Zhou Yongkang or retired CMC vice-chairmen Xu Caihou and Guo Boxiong, suggests the potential for cleavages within the party elite that could erupt into an open split—if, for example, economic growth slows even more quickly than currently planned. Regardless of the trigger, however, disunity among the party leadership will likely prevent a change in strategy from occurring, even if a transformation in China's security environment presents a compelling reason to do so. Party unity remains a key precondition for the PLA to pursue either major or minor changes in its military strategy.

NOTES

Introduction

1. On the literature on military change and innovation, see Adam Grissom, "The Future of Military Innovation Studies," *Journal of Strategic Studies*, Vol. 29, No. 5 (2006), pp. 905–934; Theo Farrell and Terry Terriff, "The Sources of Military Change," in Theo Farrell and Terry Terriff, eds., *The Sources of Military Change: Culture, Politics, Technology* (Boulder, CO: Lynne Rienner, 2002), pp. 3–20; Tai Ming Cheung, Thomas G. Mahnken, and Andrew L. Ross, "Frameworks for Analyzing Chinese Defense and Military Innovation," in Tai Ming Cheung, ed., *Forging China's Military Might: A New Framework* (Baltimore: Johns Hopkins University Press, 2014), pp. 15–46.

2. See, for example, Stephen Peter Rosen, *Winning the Next War: Innovation and the Modern Military* (Ithaca, NY: Cornell University Press, 1991); Williamson Murray and Allan R. Millet, eds., *Military Innovation in the Interwar Period* (New York: Cambridge University Press, 1996); Barry Posen, *The Sources of Military Doctrine: France, Britain, and Germany Between the World Wars* (Ithaca, NY: Cornell University Press, 1984); Harvey M. Sapolsky, Benjamin H. Friedman and Brendan Rittenhouse Green, eds., *US Military Innovation Since the Cold War: Creation Without Destruction* (New York: Routledge, 2009).

3. On Japan, see Leonard A. Humphreys, *The Way of the Heavenly Sword: The Japanese Army in the 1920s* (Stanford, CA: Stanford University Press, 1995).

4. On the Soviet Union, see Kimberly Marten Zisk, *Engaging the Enemy: Organization Theory and Soviet Military Innovation, 1955–1991* (Princeton, NJ: Princeton University Press, 1993); Harriet Fast Scott and William F. Scott, *Soviet Military Doctrine: Continuity, Formulation and Dissemination* (Boulder, CO: Westview, 1988).

5. Here I distinguish studies of the PLA as an actor from other security-related topics, especially those that examine China's use of force. On China's use of force, for example, see Allen S. Whiting, "China's Use of Force, 1950–96, and Taiwan," *International Security*, Vol. 26, No. 2 (Fall 2001), pp. 103–131; M. Taylor Fravel, *Strong Borders, Secure Nation: Cooperation and Conflict in China's Territorial Disputes* (Princeton: Princeton University Press, 2008); Andrew Scobell, *China's Use of Military Force: Beyond the Great Wall and the Long March* (New York: Cambridge University Press, 2003); Thomas J. Christensen, "Windows and War: Trend Analysis and Beijing's Use of Force," in Alastair Iain Johnston and Robert S. Ross, eds., *New Directions in the Study of China's Foreign Policy* (Stanford, CA: Stanford University Press, 2006), pp. 50–85.

6. Such overviews include Ji You, *The Armed Forces of China* (London: I. B. Tauris, 1999); David Shambaugh, *Modernizing China's Military: Progress, Problems, and Prospects* (Berkeley, CA: University of California Press, 2002); Ellis Joffe, *The Chinese Army after Mao* (Cambridge, MA: Harvard University Press, 1987); John Gittings, *The Role of the Chinese Army* (London: Oxford University Press, 1967); Harlan W. Jencks, *From Muskets to Missiles: Politics and Professionalism in the Chinese army, 1945–1981* (Boulder, CO: Westview, 1982).

7. Godwin's articles and book chapters are too numerous to cite. See, for example, Paul H. B. Godwin, "From Continent to Periphery: PLA Doctrine, Strategy, and Capabilities towards

2000," *China Quarterly*, No. 146 (1996), pp. 464-487; Paul H. B. Godwin, "Chinese Military Strategy Revised: Local and Limited War," *Annals of the American Academy of Political and Social Science*, Vol. 519, No. January (1992), pp. 191-201; Paul H. B. Godwin, "Changing Concepts of Doctrine, Strategy, and Operations in the Chinese People's Liberation Army, 1978-1987," *China Quarterly*, No. 112 (1987), pp. 572-590.

8. A few partial exceptions include Paul H. B. Godwin, "Change and Continuity in Chinese Military Doctrine: 1949-1999," in Mark A. Ryan, David M. Finkelstein, and Michael A. McDevitt, eds., *Chinese Warfighting: The PLA Experience Since 1949* (Armonk, NY: M. E. Sharpe, 2003), pp. 23-55; Nan Li, "The Evolution of China's Naval Strategy and Capabilities: From 'Near Coast' and 'Near Seas' to 'Far Seas,'" *Asian Security*, Vol. 5, No. 2 (2009), pp. 144-169; Ka Po Ng, *Interpreting China's Military Power* (New York: Routledge, 2005).

9. Works that have used these materials include Li, "The Evolution of China's Naval Strategy and Capabilities"; Nan Li, "Organizational Changes of the PLA, 1985-1997," *China Quarterly*, No. 158 (1999), pp. 314-349; Nan Li, "The PLA's Evolving Warfighting Doctrine, Strategy, and Tactics, 1985-1995: A Chinese Perspective," *China Quarterly*, No. 146 (1996), pp. 443-463; Nan Li, "Changing Functions of the Party and Political Work System in the PLA and Civil-Military Relations in China," *Armed Forces and Society*, Vol. 19, No. 3 (1993), pp. 393-409; Ng, *Interpreting China's Military Power*.

10. David M. Finkelstein, "China's National Military Strategy: An Overview of the 'Military Strategic Guidelines'", in Andrew Scobell and Roy Kamphausen, eds., *Right Sizing the People's Liberation Army: Exploring the Contours of China's Military* (Carlisle, PA: Strategic Studies Institute, Army War College, 2007), pp. 69-104; M. Taylor Fravel, "The Evolution of China's Military Strategy: Comparing the 1987 and 1999 Editions of *Zhanlue Xue*," in David M. Finkelstein and James Mulvenon, eds., *The Revolution in Doctrinal Affairs: Emerging Trends in the Operational Art of the Chinese People's Liberation Army* (Alexandria, VA: Center for Naval Analyses, 2005), pp. 79-100.

11. Even one recent history of the PLA drawing extensively on Chinese sources contains almost no mention of the strategic guidelines. See Xiaobing Li, *A History of the Modern Chinese Army* (Lexington: University of Kentucky Press, 2007).

12. Su Yu, *Su Yu wenxuan* [Su Yu's Selected Works], Vol. 3 (Beijing: Junshi kexue chubanshe, 2004), p. 611.

13. See Marshal Ye Jianying's 1959 speech on military science in Ye Jianying, *Ye Jianying junshi wenxuan* [Ye Jianying's Selected Works on Military Affairs] (Beijing: Jiefangjun chubanshe, 1997), p. 395.

14. See, for example, Shambaugh, *Modernizing China's Military*, p. 60.

Chapter 1. Explaining Major Change in Military Strategy

1. On grand strategy, see Barry Posen, *The Sources of Military Doctrine: France, Britain, and Germany Between the World Wars* (Ithaca, NY: Cornell University Press, 1984); Colin Dueck, *Reluctant Crusaders: Power, Culture, and Change in America's Grand Strategy* (Princeton, NJ: Princeton University Press, 2006); Robert J. Art, *A Grand Strategy for America* (Ithaca, NY: Cornell University Press, 2003).

2. John I. Alger, *Definitions and Doctrine of the Military Art* (Wayne, NJ: Avery, 1985); John M. Collins, *Military Strategy: Principles, Practices, and Historical Perspectives* (Dulles, VA: Potomac, 2001).

3. See, for example, Harvey M. Sapolsky, *The Polaris System Development: Bureaucratic and Programmatic Success in Government* (Cambridge, MA: Harvard University Press, 1972); Andrew J. Bacevich, *The Pentomic Era: The US Army between Korea and Vietnam* (Washington, DC: National Defense University Press, 1986); Stephen Peter Rosen, *Winning the Next War: Innovation and the*

Modern Military (Ithaca, NY: Cornell University Press, 1991); Owen Reid Cote, "The Politics of Innovative Military Doctrine: The US Navy and Fleet Ballistic Missiles," PhD dissertation, Department of Political Science, Massachusetts Institute of Technology, 1996.

4. Posen, *The Sources of Military Doctrine*, pp. 14–15; Ariel Levite, *Offense and Defense in Israeli Military Doctrine* (Boulder, CO: Westview, 1989); Jack L. Snyder, *The Ideology of the Offensive: Military Decision Making and the Disasters of 1914* (Ithaca, NY: Cornell University Press, 1984).

5. Posen, *The Sources of Military Doctrine*, p. 13; Jack Snyder, "Civil-Military Relations and the Cult of the Offensive, 1914 and 1984," *International Security*, Vol. 9, No. 1 (Summer 1984), p. 27; Kimberly Marten Zisk, *Engaging the Enemy: Organization Theory and Soviet Military Innovation, 1955–1991* (Princeton, NJ: Princeton University Press, 1993), p. 4, fn. 5. Some works do not even define the term. See, for example, Deborah D. Avant, *Political Institutions and Military Change: Lessons from Peripheral Wars* (Ithaca, NY: Cornell University Press, 1994); Rosen, *Winning the Next War*.

6. See, for example, *Department of Defense Dictionary of Military and Associated Terms*, Joint Publication 1–02 (2006), p. 168.

7. On the Soviet concept of doctrine, see Willard C. Frank and Philip S. Gillette, eds., *Soviet Military Doctrine from Lenin to Gorbachev, 1915–1991* (Westport, CT: Greenwood, 1992); Harriet Fast Scott and William F. Scott, *Soviet Military Doctrine: Continuity, Formulation and Dissemination* (Boulder, CO: Westview, 1988). Chinese sources usually translate "doctrine" in the US context as "operational theory" (*zuozhan lilun*).

8. Suzanne Nielsen, *An Army Transformed: The US Army's Post-Vietnam Recovery and the Dynamics of Change in Military Organizations* (Carlisle, PA: Army War College: Strategic Studies Institute, 2010), p. 14.

9. Ibid., pp. 3, 19.

10. Rosen, *Winning the Next War*, p. 5; Adam Grissom, "The Future of Military Innovation Studies," *Journal of Strategic Studies*, Vol. 29, No. 5 (2006), pp. 905–934. Also, see Emily O. Goldman and Leslie C. Eliason, eds., *The Diffusion of Military Technology and Ideas* (Palo Alto, CA: Stanford University Press, 2003); Williamson Murray and Allan R. Millet, eds., *Military Innovation in the Interwar Period* (New York: Cambridge University Press, 1996), pp. 1–5. These various definitions build on the broader scholarship on innovation and organizational change. See Everett M. Rogers, *Diffusion of Innovations*, 5th ed. (New York: Free Press, 2003); James Q. Wilson, *Bureaucracy: What Government Agencies Do and Why They Do It* (New York: Basic, 1989).

11. This definition of innovation is often used to describe changes within service branches, such as the establishment of new combat arms.

12. Rosen, *Winning the Next War*, pp. 7–9.

13. Posen, *The Sources of Military Doctrine*, pp. 59–79.

14. Zisk, *Engaging the Enemy*, p. 4.

15. Gary Goertz and Paul F. Diehl, "Enduring Rivalries: Theoretical Constructs and Empirical Patterns," *International Studies Quarterly*, Vol. 37, No. 2 (June 1993), pp. 147–171; William R. Thomson, "Identifying Rivals and Rivalries in World Politics," *International Studies Quarterly*, Vol. 45, No. 4 (December 2001), pp. 557–586.

16. Zisk, *Engaging the Enemy*, pp. 47–81. What is less clear in Zisk's account, however, is whether states are responding to a change in their opponents' strategy or to some other factor, such as new capabilities that an opponent deploys to implement its existing strategy.

17. Harvey M. Sapolsky, Benjamin H. Friedman and Brendan Rittenhouse Green, eds., *US Military Innovation Since the Cold War: Creation Without Destruction* (New York: Routledge, 2009), pp. 8–9.

18. William Reynolds Braisted, *The United States Navy in the Pacific, 1897–1909* (Austin: University of Texas Press, 1958); Rosen, *Winning the Next War*, pp. 64–67.

19. See, for example, Posen, *The Sources of Military Doctrine*, pp. 179–219.

20. Ibid., pp. 59–79; Rosen, *Winning the Next War*, p. 57.

21. Rosen, *Winning the Next War*, pp. 68–75.

22. Timothy Hoyt draws attention to regional powers that have been able to develop military innovations, primarily by developing new technologies. See Timothy D. Hoyt, "Revolution and Counter-Revolution: The Role of the Periphery in Technological and Conceptual Innovation," in Emily O. Goldman and Leslie C. Eliason, eds., *The Diffusion of Military Technology and Ideas* (Palo Alto, CA: Stanford University Press, 2003), pp. 179–204.

23. Posen, for example, suggests that a client state's use of new technology could promote innovation. See Posen, *The Sources of Military Doctrine*, p. 59. Such assessments could also be revealed in other ways, such as through war-gaming and simulations.

24. Michael Horowitz, *The Diffusion of Military Power: Causes and Consequences for International Politics* (Princeton, NJ: Princeton University Press, 2010), pp. 8, 24. Horowtiz examines the diffusion of military innovations, especially weapons systems, which start with the "debut" or demonstration of the innovation.

25. Martin Van Creveld, *Military Lessons of the Yom Kippur War: Historical Perspectives* (Beverly Hills, CA: Sage, 1975).

26. Jonathan M. House, *Combined Arms Warfare in the Twentieth Century* (Lawrence: University of Kansas Press, 2001), pp. 269–279.

27. For example, although the final years of fighting in World War I highlighted the importance of combined arms operations, states in the interwar period sought to incorporate this change in different ways. See ibid.

28. Timothy L. Thomas, John A. Tokar and Robert Tomes, "Kosovo and the Current Myth of Information Superiority," *Parameters*, Vol. 30, No. 1 (Spring 2000), pp. 13–29.

29. See Posen, *The Sources of Military Doctrine*; Snyder, *The Ideology of the Offensive*.

30. Elizabeth Kier, *Imagining War: French and British Military Doctrine Between the Wars* (Princeton, NJ: Princeton University Press, 1997).

31. Austin Long, *The Soul of Armies: Counterinsurgency Doctrine and Military Culture in the US and UK* (Ithaca, NY: Cornell University Press, 2016).

32. Posen, *The Sources of Military Doctrine*, pp. 69–70.

33. Ibid., pp. 210–213.

34. Avant, *Political Institutions and Military Change*.

35. Rosen, *Winning the Next War*; Zisk, *Engaging the Enemy*; Avant, *Political Institutions and Military Change*.

36. See, for example, the introductions in John A. Nagl, *Learning to Eat Soup with a Knife: Counterinsurgency Lessons from Malaya and Vietnam* (Chicago: University of Chicago Press, 2005); Sapolsky, Friedman and Green, eds., *US Military Innovation Since the Cold War*.

37. Posen, *The Sources of Military Doctrine*, pp. 74–77.

38. On effectiveness, see Suzanne Nielsen, "Civil-Military Relations Theory and Military Effectiveness," *Public Administration and Management*, Vol. 10, No. 2 (2003), pp. 61–84.

39. Peter Feaver, "Civil-Military Relations," *Annual Review of Political Science*, No. 2 (1999), pp. 211–241; Michael C. Desch, *Civilian Control of the Military: The Changing Security Environment* (Baltimore: Johns Hopkins University Press, 1999); Nielsen, "Civil-Military Relations Theory and Military Effectiveness."

40. Among others, see Caitlin Talmadge, *The Dictator's Army: Battlefield Effectiveness in Authoritarian Regimes* (Ithaca, NY: Cornell University Press, 2015).

41. Posen, *The Sources of Military Doctrine*; Snyder, *The Ideology of the Offensive*.

42. Avant, *Political Institutions and Military Change*.

43. Kier, *Imagining War*.

44. Zisk, *Engaging the Enemy*.

45. Samuel P. Huntington, *The Soldier and the State: The Theory and Politics of Civil-Military Relations* (Cambridge, MA: Belknap Press of Harvard University Press, 1957).

46. James C. Mulvenon, "China: Conditional Compliance," in Muthiah Alagappa, ed., *Coercion and Governance in Asia: The Declining Political Role of the Military* (Stanford, CA: Stanford University Press, 2001), p. 317.

47. A recent database of coups since 1950 does not record any coups in socialist states. See Jonathan Powell and Clayton Thyne, "Global Instances of Coups from 1950-Present," *Journal of Peace Research*, Vol. 48, No. 2 (2011), pp. 249-259.

48. Roman Kolkowicz, *The Soviet Military and the Communist Party* (Princeton, NJ: Princeton University Press, 1967); Timothy J. Colton, *Commissars, Commanders, and Civilian Authority: The Structure of Soviet Military Politics* (Cambridge, MA: Harvard University Press, 1979); William Odom, "The Party-Military Connection: A Critique," in Dale R. Herspring and Ivan Volgyes, eds., *Civil-Military Relations in Communist Systems* (Boulder, CO: Westview, 1978), pp. 27–52; Amos Perlmutter and William M. Leogrande, "The Party in Uniform: Toward a Theory of Civil-Military Relations in Communist Political Systems," *American Political Science Review*, Vol. 76, No. 4 (1982), pp. 778–789.

49. Perlmutter and Leogrande, "The Party in Uniform."

50. Odom, "The Party-Military Connection," p. 41. One implication of my argument is that any offensive bias reflected in strategy should be a function of the party's goals, not the military's own preferences.

51. I thank Barry Posen for suggesting this phrase.

52. Risa Brooks, *Shaping Strategy: The Civil-Military Politics of Strategic Assessment* (Princeton, NJ: Princeton University Press, 2008). Brooks's concept of strategic assessment includes the integration of a state's goals with its military capabilities, along with the assessment of an opponent's capabilities, in the context of decisions to go to war.

53. The difference with Brooks is that political dominance in socialist states creates autonomy for the armed forces. Brooks argues that military dominance is required for autonomy.

54. This suggests that party unity is the key to explaining underbalancing in socialist states. On underbalancing, see Randall Schweller, *Unanswered Threats: Political Constraints on the Balance of Power* (Princeton, NJ: Princeton University Press, 2006).

55. Kenneth N. Waltz, *Theory of International Politics* (New York: McGraw-Hill, 1979), p. 127.

56. Sociological approaches and John Meyer's work on institutional isomorphism along with transnational norms offer other mechanisms by which one state may imitate or emulate. See, for example, Theo Farrell, "Transnational Norms and Military Development: Constructing Ireland's Professional Army," *European Journal of International Relations*, Vol. 7, No. 1 (2001), pp. 63–102.

57. Waltz might respond that the behavior of developing countries or late military modernizers lies beyond the scope of his claim, which is focused on "contending states" or the existing great powers. In practice, however, scholars have applied this argument to secondary states. See Joao Resende-Santos, *Neorealism, States, and the Modern Mass Army* (New York: Cambridge University Pres, 2007).

58. For more detailed treatments, see ibid; Barry Posen, "Nationalism, the Mass Army, and Military Power," *International Security*, Vol. 18, No. 2 (1993), pp. 80–124; Jeffrey W. Taliaferro, "State Building for Future War: Neoclassical Realism and the Resource Extractive State," *Security Studies*, Vol. 15, No. 3 (July 2006), pp. 464–495.

59. On the variety of state responses to innovations in military technology, see Horowitz, *The Diffusion of Military Power*; Goldman and Eliason, eds., *The Diffusion of Military Technology and Ideas*.

60. Stephen Biddle, *Military Power: Explaining Victory and Defeat in Modern Battle* (Princeton, NJ: Princeton University Press, 2004), pp. 28–51.

61. Resende-Santos, *Neorealism, States and the Modern Mass Army*; Posen, "Nationalism, the Mass Army, and Military Power."

62. For example, a state's ability to wage war at the operational level and how they have sought to conduct combined arms operations has varied widely within the parameters of the modern system. See Robert Michael Citino, *Blitzkrieg to Desert Storm: The Evolution of Operational Warfare* (Lawrence: University Press of Kansas, 2004); House, *Combined Arms Warfare in the Twentieth Century*.

63. Resende-Santos, *Neorealism, States, and the Modern Mass Army*, p. 11.

64. Goldman and Eliason, eds., *The Diffusion of Military Technology and Ideas*; Horowitz, *The Diffusion of Military Power*.

65. Alexander L. George and Andrew Bennett, *Case Studies and Theory Development in the Social Sciences* (Cambridge, MA: MIT Press, 2005).

66. On process tracing, see ibid., pp. 205–232; Stephen Van Evera, *Guide to Methods for Students of Political Science* (Ithaca, NY: Cornell University Press, 1997), pp. 64–67; Henry E. Brady and David Collier, *Rethinking Social Inquiry: Diverse Tools, Shared Standards* (Lanham, MD.: Rowman & Littlefield, 2004), pp. 207–220; Andrew Bennett and Jeffrey T. Checkel, eds., *Process Tracing in the Social Sciences: From Metaphor to Analytic Tool* (New York: Cambridge University Press, 2014).

67. Zisk, *Engaging the Enemy*.

68. Deng Xiaoping, *Deng Xiaoping lun guofang he jundui jianshe* [Deng Xiaoping on National Defense and Army Building] (Beijing: Junshi kexue chubanshe, 1992), p. 26.

69. On the strategic guidelines, see David M. Finkelstein, "China's National Military Strategy: An Overview of the 'Military Strategic Guidelines,'" in Andrew Scobell and Roy Kamphausen, eds., *Right Sizing the People's Liberation Army: Exploring the Contours of China's Military* (Carlisle, PA: Strategic Studies Institute, Army War College, 2007), pp. 69–140; M. Taylor Fravel, "The Evolution of China's Military Strategy: Comparing the 1987 and 1999 Editions of *Zhanlue Xue*," in David M. Finkelstein and James Mulvenon, eds., *The Revolution in Doctrinal Affairs: Emerging Trends in the Operational Art of the Chinese People's Liberation Army* (Alexandria, VA: Center for Naval Analyses, 2005), pp. 79–100.

70. Junshi kexue yuan, ed., *Zhongguo renmin jiefangjun junyu* [Military Terminology of the Chinese People's Liberation Army], 2011 ed. (Beijing: Junshi kexue chubanshe, 2011), p. 50.

71. The US military defines strategy as "a prudent idea or set of ideas for employing the instruments of national power in a synchronized and integrated fashion to achieve theater, national, and/or multinational objectives." See *Department of Defense Dictionary of Military and Associated Terms*, p. 518.

72. Junshi kexue yuan, ed., *Zhongguo renmin jiefangjun junyu*, p. 51.

73. Wang Wenrong, ed., *Zhanlue xue* [The Science of Military Strategy] (Beijing: Guofang daxue chubanshe, 1999), p. 136.

74. Junshi kexue yuan, ed., *Zhongguo renmin jiefangjun junyu*, p. 51.

75. Wang Wenrong, ed., *Zhanlue xue*, pp. 136–139; Gao Rui, ed., *Zhanlue xue* [The Science of Military Strategy] (Beijing: Junshi kexue chubanshe, 1987), pp. 81–85; Peng Guangqian and Yao Youzhi, eds., *Zhanlue xue* [The Science of Military Strategy] (Beijing: Junshi kexue chubanshe, 2001), pp. 182–186; Fan Zhenjiang and Ma Baoan, eds., *Junshi zhanlue lun* [On Military Strategy] (Beijing: Guofang daxue chubanshe, 2007), pp. 149–150.

76. See Song Shilun, *Song Shilun junshi wenxuan: 1958–1989* [Song Shilun's Selected Works on Military Affairs: 1958–1989] (Beijing: Junshi kexue chubanshe, 2007), pp. 242–245.

77. Jiang Zemin, *Jiang Zemin wenxuan* [Jiang Zemin's Selected Works], Vol. 3 (Beijing: Renmin chubanshe, 2006), p. 608; *2004 nian Zhongguo de guofang* [China's National Defense in 2004] (Beijing: Guowuyuan xinwen bangongshi, 2004).

78. John L. Romjue, *From Active Defense to AirLand Battle: The Development of Army Doctrine, 1973–1982* (Fort Monroe, VA: Historical Office, US Army Training and Doctrine Command, 1984).

79. Colonel Alexander Alderson, "The Validity of British Army Counterinsurgency Doctrine After the War in Iraq 2003–2009," PhD dissertation, Cranfield University, Defence Academy College of Management and Technology, 2009, p. 93.

80. Yuan Wei and Zhang Zhuo, eds., *Zhongguo junxiao fazhan shi* [History of the Development of China's Military Academies] (Beijing: Guofang daxue chubanshe, 2001).

81. Patrick J. Garrity, *Why the Gulf War Still Matters: Foreign Perspectives on the War and the Future of International Security*, (Los Alamos: Center for National Security Studies, 1993).

82. On military operations in World War II, see Williamson Murray and Allan R. Millet, *A War To Be Won: Fighting the Second World War* (Cambridge, MA: Belknap Press of Harvard University Press, 2000).

83. Conventional operations in counterinsurgency wars may yield lessons about changes in warfare, but such lessons are likely to be limited to a service or combat arm.

84. Biddle, *Military Power*; Citino, *Blitzkrieg to Desert Storm*; House, *Combined Arms Warfare in the Twentieth Century*; Trevor N. Dupuy, *Elusive Victory: The Arab-Israeli Wars, 1947–1974* (New York: Harper & Row, 1978); Stephen Biddle, "Victory Misunderstood: What the Gulf War Tells Us about the Future of Conflict," *International Security*, Vol. 21, No. 2 (Autumn 1996), pp. 139–179; Geoffrey Parker, ed., *The Cambridge History of Warfare* (New York: Cambridge University Press, 2005); Trevor N. Dupuy, *The Evolution of Weapons and Warfare* (Indianapolis: Bobbs-Merrill, 1980); Max Hastings and Simon Jenkins, *The Battle for the Falklands* (New York: Norton, 1983); James F. Dunnigan, *How to Make War: A Comprehensive Guide to Modern Warfare in the Twenty-first Century*, 4th ed. (New York: William Morrow, 2003).

85. For recent studies of factional politics in China, see Jing Huang, *Factionalism in Communist Chinese Politics* (New York: Cambridge University Press, 2000); Victor Shih, *Factions and Finance in China: Elite Conflict and Inflation* (Cambridge: Cambridge University Press, 2008).

86. A related indicator of disunity might be the size of the top leader's faction within the Central Committee compared with a potential challenger or successor. For analysis of factions, see Victor Shih, Wei Shan, and Mingxing Liu, "Gauging the Elite Political Equilibrum in the CCP: A Quantitative Approach Using Biographical Data," *China Quarterly*, No. 201 (March 2010), pp. 29–103.

87. On the Chinese political system, see Kenneth Lieberthal, *Governing China: From Revolution Through Reform*, 2nd. ed. (New York: W. W. Norton, 2004).

88. Richard Baum, *Burying Mao: Chinese Politics in the Age of Deng Xiaoping* (Princeton, NJ: Princeton University Press, 1994); Joseph Fewsmith, *China Since Tiananmen: The Politics of Transition* (Cambridge: Cambridge University Press, 2001).

Chaper 2. The CCP's Military Strategies before 1949

1. As Lyman Van Slyke notes, in Chinese, the word guerrilla combines the characters for "moving" and "hitting." See Lyman P. Van Slyke, "The Battle of the Hundred Regiments: Problems of Coordination and Control during the Sino-Japanese War," *Modern Asian Studies*, Vol. 30, No. 4 (1996), p. 983.

2. Participants included Zhou Enlai, Zhu De, He Long, Nie Rongzhen, and Liu Bocheng, among others.

3. Guofang daxue zhanshi jianbian bianxiezu, ed., *Zhongguo renmin jiefangjun zhanshi jianbian* [A Brief History of the Chinese People's Liberation Army], 2001 revised ed. (Beijing: Jiefangjun chubanshe, 2003), pp. 9–12.

4. Ibid., p. 17.

5. Yuan Wei, ed., *Zhongguo zhanzheng fazhan shi* [A History of the Development of War in China] (Beijing: Renmin chubanshe, 2001), pp. 842–847.

6. See Stephen C. Averill, *Revolution in the Highlands: China's Jinggangshan Base* (Lanham, MD: Rowman & Littlefield, 2006).

7. Guofang daxue zhanshi jianbian bianxiezu, ed., *Zhongguo renmin jiefangjun zhanshi jianbian*, pp. 58–66; Yuan Wei, ed., *Zhongguo zhanzheng fazhan shi*, pp. 837–851.

8. For brief biographies of PLA commanders during this period, see William W. Whitson and Zhenxia Huang, *The Chinese High Command: A History of Communist Military Politics, 1927–71* (New York: Praeger, 1973), pp. 224–74.

9. Ibid.

10. Guofang daxue zhanshi jianbian bianxiezu, ed., *Zhongguo renmin jiefangjun zhanshi jianbian*, p. 58.

11. Ibid.

12. On the campaign, see Whitson and Huang, *The Chinese High Command*, pp. 268–279; Edward L. Dreyer, *China at War, 1901–1949* (New York: Routledge, 1995), pp. 160–162; Guofang daxue zhanshi jianbian bianxiezu, ed., *Zhongguo renmin jiefangjun zhanshi jianbian*, pp. 68–70.

13. Dreyer, *China at War*, pp. 162–164; Guofang daxue zhanshi jianbian bianxiezu, ed., *Zhongguo renmin jiefangjun zhanshi jianbian*, pp. 70–73.

14. Dreyer, *China at War*, p. 164.

15. On the campaign, see Whitson and Huang, *The Chinese High Command*, pp. 270–272; Dreyer, *China at War*, pp. 162–164; Guofang daxue zhanshi jianbian bianxiezu, ed., *Zhongguo renmin jiefangjun zhanshi jianbian*, pp. 70–73.

16. Dreyer, *China at War*, p. 165; Guofang daxue zhanshi jianbian bianxiezu, ed., *Zhongguo renmin jiefangjun zhanshi jianbian*, p. 74.

17. William Wei, *Counterrevolution in China: The Nationalists in Jiangxi during the Soviet Period* (Ann Arbor: University of Michigan Press, 1985), pp. 46–47.

18. On the campaign, see Whitson and Huang, *The Chinese High Command*, pp. 272–274; Dreyer, *China at War*, pp. 165–168; Guofang daxue zhanshi jianbian bianxiezu, ed., *Zhongguo renmin jiefangjun zhanshi jianbian*, pp. 73–75.

19. Yuan Wei, ed., *Zhongguo zhanzheng fazhan shi*, p. 854.

20. Tony Saich, ed., *The Rise to Power of the Chinese Communist Party: Documents and Analysis* (New York: Routledge, 2015), p. 563.

21. Zhongyang dang'an guan, ed., *Zhonggong zhongyang wenjian xuanji* [Selected Documents of the Central Committee of the Chinese Communist Party], Vol. 8 (Beijing: Zhongyang dangxiao chubanshe, 1991), p. 236.

22. Stuart R. Schram, ed., *Mao's Road to Power*, Vol. 4 (The Rise and Fall of the Chinese Soviet Republic, 1931–1934) (Armonk, NY: M. E. Sharpe, 1997), pp. li–lxiii.

23. Pang Xianzhi, ed., *Mao Zedong nianpu, 1893–1949 (shang)* [A Chronicle of Mao Zedong's Life, 1893–1949 (Part One)] (Beijing: Zhongyang wenxian chubanshe, 2013), p. 389.

24. Mao Zedong, *Mao Zedong xuanji* [Mao Zedong's Selected Works], Vol. 1., 2nd ed. (Beijing: Renmin chubanshe, 1991), p. 203.

25. Dreyer, *China at War*, p. 187.

26. Whitson and Huang, *The Chinese High Command*, pp. 275–277; Dreyer, *China at War*, pp. 187–189; Guofang daxue zhanshi jianbian bianxiezu, ed., *Zhongguo renmin jiefangjun zhanshi jianbian*, pp. 101–103.

27. For a detailed account, see Wei, *Counterrevolution in China*, pp. 101–125.

28. Ibid., p. 106.

29. Guofang daxue zhanshi jianbian bianxiezu, ed., *Zhongguo renmin jiefangjun zhanshi jianbian*, pp. 105–106.

30. Dreyer, *China at War*, p. 194.

31. On the campaign, see Whitson and Huang, *The Chinese High Command*, pp. 278–281; Dreyer, *China at War*, pp. 190–194; Guofang daxue zhanshi jianbian bianxiezu, ed., *Zhongguo renmin jiefangjun zhanshi jianbian*, pp. 104–109.

32. For a recent analysis of the long march, see Shuyun Sun, *The Long March: The True History of Communist China's Founding Myth* (New York: Anchor Books, 2008).

33. The only account of Mao's speech comes from his chronology. Pang Xianzhi, ed., *Mao Zedong nianpu, 1893–1949 (shang)*, p. 442. Mao's ideas appear to have been incorporated into the resolution from the meeting. See Zhongyang dang'an guan, ed., *Zhonggong zhongyang wenjian xuanji* [Selected Documents of the Central Committee of the Chinese Communist Party], Vol. 10 (1934–1935) (Beijing: Zhongyang dangxiao chubanshe, 1991), p. 454.

34. Mao Zedong, *Mao Zedong xuanji*, Vol. 1, pp. 170–244.

35. Ibid., pp. 189, 190.

36. Ibid., p. 197.

37. Ibid., p. 230.

38. Ibid., p. 196.

39. Ibid., p. 230.

40. Mao Zedong, *Mao Zedong junshi wenxuan* [Mao Zedong's Selected Works on Military Affairs], Vol. 1, (Beijing: Junshi kexue chubanshe, 1993), pp. 413–421.

41. Ibid., p. 413.

42. Ibid.

43. By the end of 1936, or in one year, the CCP hoped to increase the Red Army to 200,000, including increasing forces in Shaanxi to 50,000.

44. Guofang daxue zhanshi jianbian bianxiezu, ed., *Zhongguo renmin jiefangjun zhanshi jianbian*, p. 254.

45. For official overviews, see ibid; Shou Xiaosong, ed., *Zhongguo renmin jiefangjun de 80 nian: 1927–2007* [Eighty Years of the Chinese People's Liberation Army: 1927–2007] (Beijing: Junshi kexue chubanshe, 2007), pp. 114–116.

46. Guofang daxue zhanshi jianbian bianxiezu, ed., *Zhongguo renmin jiefangjun zhanshi jianbian*, p. 254; Shou Xiaosong, ed., *Zhongguo renmin jiefangjun de 80 nian*, p. 115.

47. Shou Xiaosong, ed., *Zhongguo renmin jiefangjun de 80 nian*, p. 115. Also, see Chen Furong and Zeng Luping, "Luochuan huiyi junshi fenqi tansuo" [An Exploration of the Military Differences at the Luochuan Meeting], *Yan'an daxue xuebao (shehui kexue ban)*, Vol. 28, No. 5 (2006), pp. 13–15.

48. Mao Zedong, *Mao Zedong junshi wenxuan* [Mao Zedong's Selected Works on Military Affairs], Vol. 2, (Beijing: Junshi kexue chubanshe, 1993), pp. 44–45, 53–54.

49. Shou Xiaosong, ed., *Zhongguo renmin jiefangjun de 80 nian*, p. 115.

50. Mao Zedong, *Mao Zedong wenji* [Mao Zedong's Collected Works], Vol. 2 (Beijing: Renmin chubanshe, 1993), p. 441.

51. These essays include "Problems of Strategy in the Guerrilla War Against Japan" and "On Protracted War." See Mao Zedong, *Mao Zedong xuanji* [Mao Zedong's Selected Works], Vol. 2, 2nd ed. (Beijing: Renmin chubanshe, 1991), pp. 404–438, 439–518.

52. Guofang daxue zhanshi jianbian bianxiezu, ed., *Zhongguo renmin jiefangjun zhanshi jianbian*, p. 357.

53. Dreyer, *China at War*, p. 252.

54. Ibid., p. 253.

55. Lyman P. Van Slyke, "The Chinese Communist Movement During the Sino-Japanese War, 1937–1945," *The Nationalist Era in China, 1927–1949* (Ithaca, NY: Cornell University Press, 1991), p. 189.

56. Whitson and Huang, *The Chinese High Command*, p. 68.

57. For a complete account of the various motivations, see Van Slyke, "The Battle of the Hundred Regiments," pp. 979–1005.

58. The Eighth Route Army used 105 regiments in the offensive, hence the name.

59. Guofang daxue zhanshi jianbian bianxiezu, ed., *Zhongguo renmin jiefangjun zhanshi jianbian*, p. 365.

60. Whitson and Huang, *The Chinese High Command*, p. 71; Van Slyke, "The Battle of the Hundred Regiments," p. 1000.

61. Dreyer, *China at War*, p. 253.

62. Van Slyke, "The Chinese Communist Movement During the Sino-Japanese War," p. 189.

63. Ibid., p. 277.

64. Ibid.

65. Guofang daxue zhanshi jianbian bianxiezu, ed., *Zhongguo renmin jiefangjun zhanshi jianbian*, pp. 517–518.

66. Liu Shaoqi, *Liu Shaoqi xuanji* [Liu Shaoqi's Selected Works], Vol. 1 (Beijing: Renmin chubanshe, 1981), p. 372.

67. Steven I. Levine, *Anvil of Victory: The Communist Revolution in Manchuria, 1945–1948* (New York: Columbia University Press, 1987).

68. For a detailed discussion, see Christopher R. Lew, *The Third Chinese Revolutionary Civil War, 1945–49: An Analysis of Communist Strategy and Leadership* (New York: Routledge, 2009), pp. 20–34.

69. Guofang daxue zhanshi jianbian bianxiezu, ed., *Zhongguo renmin jiefangjun zhanshi jianbian*, pp. 517–518.

70. Mao Zedong, *Mao Zedong xuanji* [Mao Zedong's Selected Works], 2nd ed., Vol. 4 (Beijing: Renmin chubanshe, 1991), p. 1187.

71. Ibid., p. 1372.

72. Mao Zedong, *Mao Zedong junshi wenxuan* [Mao Zedong's Selected Works on Military Affairs], Vol. 3 (Beijing: Junshi kexue chubanshe, 1993), pp. 482–485.

73. Lew, *The Third Chinese Revolutionary Civil War*, pp. 62–66.

74. Guofang daxue zhanshi jianbian bianxiezu, ed., *Zhongguo renmin jiefangjun zhanshi jianbian*, pp. 558–559.

75. Dreyer, *China at War*, p. 253.

76. Zhongyang dang'an guan, ed., *Zhonggong zhongyang wenjian xuanji* [Selected Documents of the Central Committee of the Chinese Communist Party], Vol. 16 (1946–1947) (Beijing: Zhongyang dangxiao chubanshe, 1991), pp. 475–476.

77. Mao Zedong, *Mao Zedong xuanji*, Vol. 4, pp. 1229–1234.

78. Odd Arne Westad, *Decisive Encounters: The Chinese Civil War, 1946–1950* (Stanford, Calif.: Stanford University Press, 2003), pp. 168–172; Guofang daxue zhanshi jianbian bianxiezu, ed., *Zhongguo renmin jiefangjun zhanshi jianbian*, pp. 561–574; Lew, *The Third Chinese Revolutionary Civil War*, pp. 75–85.

79. Guofang daxue zhanshi jianbian bianxiezu, ed., *Zhongguo renmin jiefangjun zhanshi jianbian*, pp. 595–596.

80. Westad, *Decisive Encounters*, pp. 192–199; Guofang daxue zhanshi jianbian bianxiezu, ed., *Zhongguo renmin jiefangjun zhanshi jianbian*, pp. 596–602; Lew, *The Third Chinese Revolutionary Civil War*, pp. 108–114.

81. Guofang daxue zhanshi jianbian bianxiezu, ed., *Zhongguo renmin jiefangjun zhanshi jianbian*, pp. 602–603; Lew, *The Third Chinese Revolutionary Civil War*, p. 116.

82. Westad, *Decisive Encounters*, pp. 199–211; Guofang daxue zhanshi jianbian bianxiezu, ed., *Zhongguo renmin jiefangjun zhanshi jianbian*, pp. 602–607; Lew, *The Third Chinese Revolutionary Civil War*, pp. 114–123.

83. Guofang daxue zhanshi jianbian bianxiezu, ed., *Zhongguo renmin jiefangjun zhanshi jianbian*, pp. 607–611; Lew, *The Third Chinese Revolutionary Civil War*, pp. 123–129.

84. In July 1933, Zhou Enlai described the contents of a telegram from the party leadership as containing a "strategic guideline" for military operations in the Central Soviet. See Zhou Enlai, *Zhou Enlai junshi wenxuan* [Zhou Enlai's Selected Works on Military Affairs], Vol. 1 (Beijing: Renmin chubanshe, 1997), p. 302.

85. Zhongyang dang'an guan, ed., *Zhonggong zhongyang wenjian xuanji*, Vol. 10 (1934–1935), pp. 441–444.

86. Ibid., pp. 441–442.

87. Ibid., p. 460.

88. Zhongyang dang'an guan, ed., *Zhonggong zhongyang wenjian xuanji*, Vol. 10 (1934–1935), p. 589.

89. Guofang daxue zhanshi jianbian bianxiezu, ed., *Zhongguo renmin jiefangjun zhanshi jianbian*, p. 341. This was "consolidate the south, fight in the east, develop the north."

90. Ibid., p. 342.

91. Peng Dehuai, *Peng Dehuai junshi wenxuan* [Peng Dehuai's Selected Works on Military Affairs] (Beijing: Zhongyang wenxian chubanshe, 1988), p. 587.

92. Wang Wenrong, ed., *Zhanlue xue* [The Science of Military Strategy] (Beijing: Guofang daxue chubanshe, 1999), pp. 136–139; Gao Rui, ed., *Zhanlue xue* [The Science of Military Strategy] (Beijing: Junshi kexue chubanshe, 1987), pp. 81–85; Peng Guangqian and Yao Youzhi, eds., *Zhanlue xue* [The Science of Military Strategy] (Beijing: Junshi kexue chubanshe, 2001), pp. 182–186; Fan Zhenjiang and Ma Baoan, eds., *Junshi zhanlue lun* [On Military Strategy] (Beijing: Guofang daxue chubanshe, 2007), pp. 149–150.

93. Mao Zedong, *Mao Zedong wenji* [Mao Zedong's Collected Works], Vol. 1 (Beijing: Renmin chubanshe, 1993), pp. 376–382.

94. Ibid., p. 379.

95. Mao Zedong, *Mao Zedong wenji*, Vol. 1, p. 56. Although the phrase appears in Mao's collected works, Zhu De was the military commander and likely devised this approach. See Lei Mou, "Youji zhanzheng 'shiliu zikuai' de xingcheng yu fazhan" [The Origins and Development of the 'Sixteen Characters' of Guerrilla Warfare], *Guangming ribao*, December 13, 2017, p. 11. PLA sources attribute it jointly to Mao and Zhu. See Shou Xiaosong, ed., *Zhongguo renmin jiefangjun de 80 nian*, p. 27.

96. Junshi kexue yuan, ed., *Zhongguo renmin jiefangjun junyu* [Military Terminology of the Chinese People's Liberation Army], 2011 ed. (Beijing: Junshi kexue chubanshe, 2011), p. 52.

97. Peng Guangqian and Yao Youzhi, eds., *Zhanlue xue*, pp. 453–454.

98. Mao Zedong, *Mao Zedong wenji*, Vol. 2, p. 152.

99. Mao Zedong, *Mao Zedong junshi wenji* [Mao Zedong's Collected Works on Military Affairs], Vol. 1 (Beijing: Junshi kexue chubanshe, 1993), p. 181.

100. This typology below is loosely based on Alexander Chieh-cheng Huang, "Transformation and Refinement of Chinese Military Doctrine: Reflection and Critique on the PLA's View," in James Mulvenon and Andrew N. D. Yang, eds., *Seeking Truth From Facts: A Retrospective on Chinese Military Studies in the Post-Mao Era* (Santa Monica, CA: RAND, 2001), p. 132.

101. Mao Zedong, *Mao Zedong xuanji* [Mao Zedong's Selected Works], 2nd ed., Vol. 3, (Beijing: Renmin chubanshe, 1991), pp. 1038–1041.

102. Ibid., pp. 12–44.

103. Ibid., pp. 170–244.

104. Saich, ed., *The Rise to Power of the Chinese Communist Party*, p. 560.

105. Mao Zedong, *Mao Zedong xuanji*, Vol. 2, p. 477.

106. Ibid., p. 511.

107. Ibid., p. 480.

108. For a recent summary of people's war from AMS, see Yuan Dejin, *Mao Zedong junshi sixiang jiaocheng* [Lectures on Mao Zedong's Military Thought] (Beijing: Junshi kexue chubanshe, 2000), pp. 135–158.

109. Suzanne Pepper, *Civil War in China: The Political Struggle, 1945–1949* (Lanhan, MD: Rowman & Littlefield, 1999), p. 292.

110. William Wei, "Power Grows Out of the Barrel of a Gun: Mao and Red Army," in David A. Graff and Robin Higham, eds., *A Military History of China* (Lexington: University Press of Kentucky, 2012), pp. 234–236.

111. Ibid., p. 234.

112. Lin Piao, "Long Live the Victory of People's War," *Peking Review*, No. 36 (September 3 1965), pp. 9–20.

113. Ralph L. Powell, "Maoist Military Doctrines," *Asian Survey*, Vol. 8, No. 4 (April 1968), pp. 239–262.

114. See, for example, Harlan W. Jencks, "People's War under Modern Conditions: Wishful Thinking, National Suicide, or Effective Deterrent?," *China Quarterly*, No. 98 (June 1984), pp. 305–319.

115. Dennis Blasko, "The Evolution of Core Concepts: People's War, Active Defense, and Offshore Defense," in Roy Kamphausen, David Lai and Travis Tanner, eds., *Assessing the People's Liberation Army in the Hu Jintao Era* (Carlisle, PA: Strategic Studies Institute, Army War College, 2014), pp. 81–128.

116. Junshi kexue yuan, ed., *Zhongguo renmin jiefangjun junyu*, p. 47.

117. Dennis Blasko, "China's Evolving Approach to Strategic Deterrence," in Joe McReynolds, ed., *China's Evolving Military Strategy* (Washington, DC: Jamestown Foundation, 2016), p. 349.

118. Junshi kexue yuan, ed., *Zhongguo renmin jiefangjun junyu*, p. 8.

119. Ibid., p. 5.

120. Ibid.

121. Ibid., p. 190.

122. Ibid.

123. On China's geopolitical environment, see Andrew J. Nathan and Robert S. Ross, *The Great Wall and the Empty Fortress: China's Search for Security* (New York: W. W. Norton, 1997).

124. On China's many territorial disputes, see M. Taylor Fravel, *Strong Borders, Secure Nation: Cooperation and Conflict in China's Territorial Disputes* (Princeton, NJ: Princeton University Press, 2008).

125. On China and Taiwan, see Steven M. Goldstein, *Chin and Taiwan* (Cambridge: Polity, 2015).

126. He Di, "The Last Campaign to Unify China: The CCP's Unrealized Plan to Liberate Taiwan, 1949–1950," in Mark A. Ryan, David M. Finkelstein and Michael A. McDevitt, eds., *Chinese Warfighting: The PLA Experience Since 1949* (Armonk, NY: M. E. Sharpe, 2003), pp. 73–90.

127. On China's entry into the Korean War, see Allen S. Whiting, *China Crosses the Yalu: The Decision to Enter the Korean War* (New York: Macmillan, 1960); Chen Jian, *China's Road to the Korean War: The Making of the Sino-American Confrontation* (New York: Columbia University Press, 1994); Thomas J. Christensen, *Worse Than a Monolith: Alliance Politics and*

Problems of Coercive Diplomacy in Asia (Princeton, NJ: Princeton University Press, 2011), pp. 28–108.

128. On delegation, see Whitson and Huang, *The Chinese High Command*, p. 466.

129. On PLA's development under Lin Biao in the northeast, see Harold M. Tanner, *Where Chiang Kai-shek Lost China: The Liao-Shen Campaign, 1948* (Bloomington: Indian University Press, 2015); Chen Li, "From Burma Road to 38th Parallel: The Chinese Forces' Adaptation in War, 1942–1953," PhD thesis, Faculty of Asian and Middle Eastern Studies, Cambridge University, 2012.

Chapter 3. The 1956 Strategy

1. See, for example, David Shambaugh, *Modernizing China's Military: Progress, Problems, and Prospects* (Berkeley, CA: University of California Press, 2002), p. 60; Ka Po Ng, *Interpreting China's Military Power* (New York: Routledge, 2005), pp. 58–59.

2. Zhang Zhen, *Zhang Zhen huiyilu (xia)* [Zhang Zhen's Memoirs] (Beijing: Jiefangjun chubanshe, 2003), p. 364. Zhang Zhen served as a vice-chairman of the CMC from 1992 to 1997.

3. Peng Dehuai, *Peng Dehuai junshi wenxuan* [Peng Dehuai's Selected Works on Military Affairs] (Beijing: Zhongyang wenxian chubanshe, 1988), p. 601.

4. Wang Yan, ed., *Peng Dehuai zhuan* [Peng Dehuai's Biography] (Beijing: Dangdai Zhongguo chubanshe, 1993), p. 537.

5. Ibid., p. 538.

6. Yin Qiming and Cheng Yaguang, *Diyi ren guofang buzhang* [First Minister of Defense] (Guangzhou: Guangdong jiaoyu chubanshe, 1997), p. 46; Yu Huamin and Hu Zhefeng, *Zhongguo junshi sixiang shi* [History of Chinese Military Thought] (Kaifeng: Henan daxue chubanshe: 1999), p. 180.

7. Peng Dehuai, *Peng Dehuai junshi wenxuan*, pp. 584–601.

8. Jiang Jiantian, "Wojun zhandou tiaoling tixi de xingcheng" [Formation of Our Army's Combat Regulations System], *Jiefangjun bao*, July 16, 2000. Unless otherwise noted, all articles from the *Liberation Army Daily* (*jiefangjun bao*) newspaper come from the EastView database of this newspaper.

9. Zhou Jun and Zhou Zaohe, "Renmin jiefangjun diyidai zhandou tiaoling xingcheng chutan" [Preliminary Exploration of the Formation of the PLA's First Generation Combat Regulations], *Junshi lishi*, No. 1 (1996), pp. 25–27; Ren Jian, *Zuozhan tiaoling gailun* [An Introduction to Operations Regulations] (Beijing: Junshi kexue chubanshe, 2016), pp. 38–43.

10. A related component of the force structure was the establishment of reserve forces and development of a wartime mobilization plan. Because Peng sought to reduce the size of the standing army, he wanted a sufficient reserve force that could be mobilized if China was attacked.

11. All figures are from Shou Xiaosong, ed., *Zhongguo renmin jiefangjun de 80 nian: 1927–2007* [Eighty Years of the Chinese People's Liberation Army: 1927–2007] (Beijing: Junshi kexue chubanshe, 2007), p. 339.

12. Ibid., p. 338.

13. "Xunlian zongjianbu banfa xin de xunlian dagang" [Training Supervision Department Issues New Training Program], *Jiefangjun bao*, January 16, 1958.

14. Ma Xiaotian and Zhao Keming, eds., *Zhongguo renmin jiefangjun guofang daxue shi: Di'er juan (1950–1985)* [History of the Chinese People's Liberation Army's National Defense University: Volume 2 (1950-1985)] (Beijing: Guofang daxue chubanshe, 2007).

15. Jin Ye, "Yi Liaodong bandao kangdenglu zhanyi yanxi" [Recalling the Liaodong Peninsula Anti-Landing Campaign Exercise], in Xu Huizi, ed., *Zongcan moubu: Huiyi shiliao* [General Staff Department: Recollections and Historical Materials], (Beijing: Jiefangjun chubanshe, 1995), pp. 456–462.

16. Shou Xiaosong, ed., *Zhongguo renmin jiefangjun de 80 nian*, p. 345.

17. Su Yu, *Su Yu wenxuan* [Su Yu's Selected Works], Vol. 3 (Beijing: Junshi kexue chubanshe, 2004), p. 57.

18. Ibid., p. 58.

19. Qi Dexue, ed., *KangMei yuanChao zhanzheng shi* [History of the War to Resist America and Aid Korea], Vol. 3 (Beijing: Junshi kexue chubanshe, 2000), p. 555. Also, see Chen Li, "From Civil War Victor to Cold War Guard: Positional Warfare in Korea and the Transformation of the Chinese People's Liberation Army, 1951-1953," *Journal of Strategic Studies*, Vol. 38, No. 1-2 (2015), pp. 138-214.

20. Qi Dexue, ed., *KangMei yuanChao zhanzheng shi*, Vol. 3, p. 555. Also, see Li, "From Civil War Victor to Cold War Guard," pp. 183-214.

21. This is based on the estimate that roughly 400,000 Chinese soldiers were killed compared with approximately 37,000 American soldiers. On estimates of Chinese casualties, see Michael Clodfelter, *Warfare and Armed Conflicts: A Statistical Refernce to Casualty and Other Figures, 1500-2000* (Jefferson, NC: MacFarland, 2002), p. 173.

22. Qi Dexue, ed., *KangMei yuanChao zhanzheng shi*, Vol. 3, p. 552.

23. Peng Dehuai, *Peng Dehuai junshi wenxuan*, p. 492.

24. On the role of airpower, see Zhang Zhen, *Zhang Zhen huiyilu (shang)* [Zhang Zhen's Memoirs] (Beijing: Jiefangjun chubanshe, 2003); Xu Yan, *Di yi ci jiaoliang: KangMei yuanChao zhanzheng de lishi huigu yu fansi* [First Contest: Reviewing and Rethinking the War to Resist America and Aid Korea] (Beijing: Zhongguo guangbo dianshi chubanshe, 1998); Shou Xiaosong, ed., *Zhongguo renmin jiefangjun de 80 nian*, pp. 306-329.

25. Qi Dexue, ed., *KangMei yuanChao zhanzheng shi*, Vol. 3, p. 552.

26. Ibid.

27. Su Yu, *Su Yu wenxuan*, Vol. 3, p. 151.

28. Ye Jianying, *Ye Jianying junshi wenxuan* [Ye Jianying's Selected Works on Military Affairs] (Beijing: Jiefangjun chubanshe, 1997), pp. 244-265; Su Yu, *Su Yu wenxuan*, Vol. 3, pp. 164-171.

29. On implications of the nuclear revolution, see, for example, Su Yu, *Su Yu wenxuan*, Vol. 3, pp. 164-171.

30. Frederick C. Teiwes, "The Establishment and Consolidation of the New Regime," in Roderick MacFarquhar, ed., *The Politics of China: The Eras of Mao and Deng* (Cambridge: Cambridge University Press, 1997), p. 8.

31. Ibid., pp. 45-50.

32. In addition to Teiwes, see Avery Goldstein, *From Bandwagon to Balance-of-Power Politics: Structural Constraints and Politics in China, 1949-1978* (Stanford, CA: Stanford University Press, 1991).

33. This paragraph draws on Teiwes, "The Establishment and Consolidation of the New Regime," pp. 5-15.

34. Mao Zedong, *Mao Zedong wenji* [Mao Zedong's Collected Works], Vol. 5 (Beijing: Renmin chubanshe, 1996), p. 345.

35. Teiwes, "The Establishment and Consolidation of the New Regime," pp. 28-42.

36. Han Huaizhi and Tan Jingqiao, eds., *Dangdai Zhongguo jundui de junshi gongzuo (shang)* [Military Work of Contemporary China's Armed Forces, Part 1] (Beijing: Zhongguo shehui kexue chubanshe, 1989), pp. 276-319.

37. For an excellent history of the public security force, see Xuezhi Guo, *China's Security State: Philosophy, Evolution, and Politics* (New York: Cambridge University Press, 2012).

38. Wang Yan, ed., *Peng Dehuai zhuan*, pp. 494-495.

39. Wang Yan, ed., *Peng Dehuai nianpu* [A Chronicle of Peng Dehuai's Life] (Beijing: Renmin chubanshe, 1998), p. 530.

40. The other members were Zhu De, Peng Dehuai, Lin Biao, Liu Bocheng, He Long, Chen Yi, Luo Ronghuan, Xu Xiangqian, Nie Rongzhen, and Ye Jianying. On the CMC during this period, see Nan Li, "The Central Military Commission and Military Policy in China," in James Mulvenon and Andrew N. D. Yang, eds., *The People's Liberation Army as Organization: V 1.0., Reference Volume* (Santa Monica, CA: RAND, 2002), pp. 45–94; David Shambaugh, "Building the Party-State in China, 1949–1965: Bringing the Soldier Back In," in Timothy Cheek and Tony Saich, eds., *New Perspectives on State Socialism in China* (Armonk, NY: M. E. Sharpe, 1997), pp. 125–150. From 1949 to 1954, the CMC was known as the "People's Revolution Military Commission of the Central People's Government" because it included some non-CCP members (mostly former KMT generals). In September 1954, this body was renamed the National Defense Commission of the PRC, a government entity, and a new CMC was established under the CCP's Central Committee, which included only CCP members.

41. Wang Yan, ed., *Peng Dehuai nianpu*, p. 577.

42. Huang Kecheng, "Huiyi wushi niandai zai junwei, zongcan gongzuo de qingkuang" [Remembering Work Situations from the 1950s in the CMC and GSD], in Xu Huizi, ed., *Zongcan moubu: Huiyi shiliao* [General Staff Department: Recollections and Historical Materials] (Beijing: Jiefangjun chubanshe, 1995), p. 328.

43. This is based on my reading of available accounts of enlarged meetings of the CMC during this period. Mao may have stopped attending these meetings as early as 1952.

44. Huang Kecheng, "Huiyi wushi niandai zai junwei, zongcan gongzuo de qingkuang," p. 328.

45. Zhang Zhen, *Zhang Zhen huiyilu (shang)*, p. 473. Zhang Zhen was head of the GSD's operations department.

46. Ibid., p. 474.

47. Su Yu, *Su Yu wenxuan*, Vol. 3, pp. 71–75.

48. Ibid., p. 75.

49. Ibid., p. 73.

50. Zhu Ying, ed., *Su Yu zhuan* [Su Yu's Biography] (Beijing: Dangdai Zhongguo chubanshe, 2000), pp. 868–869.

51. Zhang Zhen, *Zhang Zhen huiyilu (shang)*, p. 476. The plan was never published openly.

52. Shou Xiaosong, ed., *Zhongguo renmin jiefangjun junshi* [A Military History of the Chinese People's Liberation Army], Vol. 4 (Beijing: Junshi kexue chubanshe, 2011), p. 296. On joint a US-Nationalist attack, see Zhang Zhen, *Zhang Zhen huiyilu (shang)*, p. 475.

53. Shou Xiaosong, ed., *Zhongguo renmin jiefangjun junshi*, Vol. 4, pp., 296, 299.

54. Ibid., p. 299.

55. Zhang Zhen, *Zhang Zhen huiyilu (shang)*, p. 476.

56. This refers only to infantry units and excludes the artillery, armored, engineering and public security troops. The original decision in 1951 to shrink the force was taken after the initiation of peace talks in the Korea War. See Shou Xiaosong, ed., *Zhongguo renmin jiefangjun junshi*, Vol. 4, p. 286.

57. Zhang Zhen, *Zhang Zhen huiyilu (shang)*, p. 476.

58. Shou Xiaosong, ed., *Zhongguo renmin jiefangjun junshi*, Vol. 4, pp. 297–299.

59. Zhang Zhen, *Zhang Zhen huiyilu (shang)*, p. 476. Each division was composed of three infantry regiments, an artillery regiment, a tank regiment, an anti-tank battalion, and an anti-aircraft battalion. See Shou Xiaosong, ed., *Zhongguo renmin jiefangjun junshi*, Vol. 4, p. 297.

60. Zhang Zhen, *Zhang Zhen huiyilu (shang)*, pp. 476–477.

61. Yin Qiming and Cheng Yaguang, *Diyi ren guofang buzhang*, p. 140.

62. Ibid., p. 141.

63. Shou Xiaosong, ed., *Zhongguo renmin jiefangjun junshi*, Vol. 4, p. 336.

64. Wang Yan, ed., *Peng Dehuai nianpu*, p. 557.

65. Ibid., p. 558.

66. Ibid., p. 560.

67. Peng Dehuai, *Peng Dehuai junshi wenxuan*, p. 476.

68. Wang Yan, ed., *Peng Dehuai nianpu*, p. 563. They included Huang Kecheng, Lin Biao, Chen Yi, and Gao Gang.

69. Peng Dehuai, *Peng Dehuai junshi wenxuan*, p. 474.

70. Ibid., p. 470. Peng also criticized "some comrades . . . who are too excited and impatient for success."

71. Ibid., p. 472.

72. Ibid., p. 498.

73. Ibid.

74. Shou Xiaosong, ed., *Zhongguo renmin jiefangjun de 80 nian*, p. 331.

75. Shou Xiaosong, ed., *Zhongguo renmin jiefangjun junshi* [A Military History of the Chinese People's Liberation Army], Vol. 5 (Beijing: Junshi kexue chubanshe, 2011), p. 116.

76. Peng Dehuai, *Peng Dehuai junshi wenxuan*, p. 500.

77. Ibid., p. 501.

78. Ibid., p. 500.

79. Shou Xiaosong, ed., *Zhongguo renmin jiefangjun junshi*, Vol. 5, pp. 43–60.

80. Xie Guojun, ed., *Junqi piaopiao* [The Army's Flag Fluttering] (Beijing: Jiefangjun chubanshe, 1999), p. 175; Shou Xiaosong, ed., *Zhongguo renmin jiefangjun junshi*, Vol. 5, pp. 5, 10.

81. Xie Guojun, ed., *Junqi piaopiao*, p. 175.

82. Ibid.

83. Shou Xiaosong, ed., *Zhongguo renmin jiefangjun de 80 nian*, p. 338; Nie Rongzhen, *Nie Rongzhen junshi wenxuan* [Nie Rongzhen's Selected Works on Military Affairs] (Beijing: Jiefangjun chubanshe, 1992), p. 381.

84. Shou Xiaosong, ed., *Zhongguo renmin jiefangjun de 80 nian*, p. 338.

85. On these points, see Ye Jianying, *Ye Jianying junshi wenxuan*, pp. 269–270.

86. Liu Jixian, ed., *Ye Jianying nianpu* [A Chronicle of Ye Jianying's Life], Vol. 2 (Beijing: Zhongyang wenxian chubanshe, 2007), p. 818.

87. Ye Jianying, *Ye Jianying junshi wenxuan*, p. 268.

88. Shou Xiaosong, ed., *Zhongguo renmin jiefangjun junshi*, Vol. 5, pp. 70–71.

89. Ibid., p. 71.

90. Jin Ye, "Yi Liaodong bandao kangdenglu zhanyi yanxi," p. 453.

91. Ye Jianying, *Ye Jianying junshi wenxuan*, p. 271.

92. Peng Dehuai, *Peng Dehuai junshi wenxuan*, p. 528.

93. Ibid., p. 531.

94. Ibid., p. 530.

95. Ibid.

96. Ibid., p. 531.

97. Ibid., p. 532.

98. Ibid.

99. Ibid., pp. 532-533.

100. Although a conference (*huiyi*) of party representatives, it should not be confused with a party congress (*dahui*) or the National People's Congress. This conference was convened to discuss the First Five-Year Plan and the purge of Gao Gang and Rao Shushi, and to create a central control commission.

101. Mao Zedong, *Jianguo yilai Mao Zedong junshi wengao* [Mao Zedong's Military Manuscripts Since the Founding of the Nation], Vol. 2 (Beijing: Junshi kexue chubanshe, 2010), p. 265.

102. Ibid.

103. Yin Qiming and Cheng Yaguang, *Diyi ren guofang buzhang*, p. 43.

104. Wang Yan, ed., *Peng Dehuai zhuan*, p. 535. Also, see Chen Haoliang, "Peng Dehuai dui xin Zhongguo jiji fangyu zhanlue fangzhen xingcheng de gongxian" [Peng Dehuai's Contribution to the Formation of New China's Strategic Guideline of Active Defense], *Junshi lishi*, No. 2 (2003), p. 44.

105. Quoted in Yin Qiming and Cheng Yaguang, *Diyi ren guofang buzhang*, p. 43. Also, see Pang Xianzhi and Feng Hui, eds., *Mao Zedong nianpu, 1949–1976* [A Chronicle of Mao Zedong's Life, 1949–1976], Vol. 2 (Beijing: Zhongyang wenxian chubanshe, 2013), p. 368.

106. Wang Yazhi, *Peng Dehuai junshi canmou de huiyi: 1950 niandai ZhongSu junshi guanxi jianzheng* [The Recollection of Peng Dehuai's Militiary Staff Officer: Witnessing Sino-Soviet Military Relations in the 1950s] (Shanghai: Fudan daxue chubanshe, 2009), p. 142.

107. Ibid.

108. Ibid.

109. Mao Zedong, *Jianguo yilai Mao Zedong junshi wengao*, Vol. 2, p. 292.

110. Zheng Wenhan, *Mishu rijili de Peng laozong* [Leader Peng in his Secretary's Diary] (Beijing: Junshi kexue chubanshe, 1998), pp. 69, 71, 76, 80. Su Yu's chronology, compiled by his secretary, Zhu Ying, suggests that Su's ideas and suggestions on strategy formed the basis of the strategic guideline. See Zhu Ying and Wen Jinghu, *Su Yu nianpu* [A Chronicle of Su Yu's Life] (Beijing: Dangdai Zhongguo chubanshe, 2006), pp. 593–594.

111. Shou Xiaosong, ed., *Zhongguo renmin jiefangjun junshi*, Vol. 5, p. 106.

112. Peng's report has not been openly published, but it has been described and excerpted in several sources. See Wang Yan, ed., *Peng Dehuai zhuan*, pp. 536–538; Yin Qiming and Cheng Yaguang, *Diyi ren guofang buzhang*, pp. 40–47; Wang Yazhi, *Peng Dehuai junshi canmou de huiyi*, pp. 142–144; Shou Xiaosong, ed., *Zhongguo renmin jiefangjun junshi*, Vol. 5, pp. 105–113. Peng described the essence of the strategy in a 1957 speech to the National Defense Commission on army building. See Peng Dehuai, *Peng Dehuai junshi wenxuan*, pp. 584–601. Finally, the guideline is summarized in detail in Xu Shiyou, *Xu Shiyou junshi wenxuan* [Xu Shiyou's Selected Works on Military Affairs] (Beijing: Junshi kexue chubanshe, 2013), pp. 390–420.

113. Mao Zedong, *Jianguo yilai Mao Zedong junshi wengao*, Vol. 2, p. 303.

114. Yin Qiming and Cheng Yaguang, *Diyi ren guofang buzhang*, p. 45.

115. Peng Dehuai, *Peng Dehuai junshi wenxuan*, p. 587.

116. Ibid.

117. Ibid., pp. 587–588.

118. On the Bandung Conference, see John W. Garver, *China's Quest: The History of the Foreign Relations of the People's Republic* (New York: Oxford University Press, 2016), pp. 92–112.

119. Quoted in Wang Yan, ed., *Peng Dehuai zhuan*, p. 537.

120. Peng Dehuai, *Peng Dehuai junshi wenxuan*, p. 588.

121. Quoted in Wang Yan, ed., *Peng Dehuai zhuan*, p. 537.

122. Quoted in ibid., p. 538.

123. Peng Dehuai, *Peng Dehuai junshi wenxuan*, pp. 588–589; Shou Xiaosong, ed., *Zhongguo renmin jiefangjun junshi*, Vol. 5, p. 108. Also, Xu Shiyou, *Xu Shiyou junshi wenxuan*, p. 393.

124. Peng Dehuai, *Peng Dehuai junshi wenxuan*, p. 589.

125. Ibid., p. 590.

126. Xu Shiyou, *Xu Shiyou junshi wenxuan*, p. 394.

127. Yin Qiming and Cheng Yaguang, *Diyi ren guofang buzhang*, p. 46.

128. Xu Shiyou, *Xu Shiyou junshi wenxuan*, p. 395.

129. Ibid.

130. Ibid., p. 399.

131. Quoted in ibid., p. 403.

132. Yin Qiming and Cheng Yaguang, *Diyi ren guofang buzhang*, pp. 46–47.

133. Xu Shiyou, *Xu Shiyou junshi wenxuan*, p. 398; Shou Xiaosong, ed., *Zhongguo renmin jiefangjun junshi*, Vol. 5, p. 109.

134. Xu Shiyou, *Xu Shiyou junshi wenxuan*, p. 398.

135. Shou Xiaosong, ed., *Zhongguo renmin jiefangjun junshi*, Vol. 5, p. 109.

136. Yin Qiming and Cheng Yaguang, *Diyi ren guofang buzhang*, p. 47.

137. Peng Dehuai, *Peng Dehuai junshi wenxuan*, p. 591.

138. Yin Qiming and Cheng Yaguang, *Diyi ren guofang buzhang*, p. 47.

139. Ibid.

140. Ibid.

141. Shou Xiaosong, ed., *Zhongguo renmin jiefangjun junshi*, Vol. 5, p. 109.

142. Wang Yan, ed., *Peng Dehuai zhuan*, p. 538; Shou Xiaosong, ed., *Zhongguo renmin jiefangjun junshi*, Vol. 5, pp. 111–112; Yin Qiming and Cheng Yaguang, *Diyi ren guofang buzhang*, pp. 47–48.

143. Yin Qiming and Cheng Yaguang, *Diyi ren guofang buzhang*, p. 47.

144. Peng Dehuai, *Peng Dehuai junshi wenxuan*, p. 599.

145. Yin Qiming and Cheng Yaguang, *Diyi ren guofang buzhang*, p. 48.

146. Wang Yan, ed., *Peng Dehuai zhuan*, p. 538.

147. According to one authoritative source, "the first time that a strategic concept was used to formulate completely [China's] naval strategic thought" was with the articulation of "near-seas defense" (*jinhai fangyu*) in the 1980s. See Qin Tian and Huo Xiaoyong, eds., *Zhonghua haiquan shilun* [A History of Chinese Sea Power] (Beijing: Guofang daxue chubanshe, 2000), p. 300.

148. Fang Gongli, Yang Xuejun and Xiang Wei, *Zhongguo renmin jiefangjun haijun 60 nian* [60 Years of the Chinese PLA Navy] (Qingdao: Qingdao chubanshe: 2009), p. 106. For a description of this meeting, see Xiao Jinguang, *Xiao Jinguang huiyilu (xuji)* [Xiao Jinguang's Memoirs (sequel)] (Beijing: Jiefangjun chubanshe, 1989), pp. 135–145. Xiao Jinguang was commander of the navy.

149. Fang Gongli, Yang Xuejun and Xiang Wei, *Zhongguo renmin jiefangjun haijun 60 nian*, p. 107.

150. Yin Qiming and Cheng Yaguang, *Diyi ren guofang buzhang*, p. 78.

151. Wang Yazhi, *Peng Dehuai junshi canmou de huiyi*, p. 115; Shen Zhihua, *Sulian zhuanjia zai Zhongguo* [Soviet Experts in China] (Beijing: Zhongguo guoji guangbo chubanshe 2003), pp. 407–408.

152. Wang Yan, ed., *Peng Dehuai nianpu*, p. 637.

153. Wang Yazhi, *Peng Dehuai junshi canmou de huiyi*, p. 140.

154. Yin Qiming and Cheng Yaguang, *Diyi ren guofang buzhang*, p. 82.

155. Ibid.

156. When Peng visited Moscow in September 1952, for example, the Soviets suggested that China purchase the T-4 bomber, which was based on the B-29 design, even though B-29s had been shot down in Korea by Soviet Mig-15s. The Soviets had already begun to manufacture the jet-propelled Tu-16 bomber, but they refused to sell this model. Ibid., p. 87.

157. Of course, China lacked the means to implement the Soviet strategy, especially nuclear weapons. Nevertheless, this demonstrates the limits of arguments about emulation, which are perhaps more applicable to states with similar material resources.

158. On these meetings, see Wang Yan, ed., *Peng Dehuai zhuan*, pp. 535–536; Yin Qiming and Cheng Yaguang, *Diyi ren guofang buzhang*, pp. 43–44; Wang Yazhi, *Peng Dehuai junshi canmou de huiyi*, pp. 130–131.

159. Liu Xiao, *Chu shi Sulian ba nian* [Eight Years as Ambassador to the Soviet Union] (Beijing: Zhonggong dangshi ziliao chubanshe, 1986), p. 13.

160. Wang Yazhi, *Peng Dehuai junshi canmou de huiyi*, p. 130.

161. Ibid., p. 131.

162. Ibid.

163. Yin Qiming and Cheng Yaguang, *Diyi ren guofang buzhang*, p. 78.

164. Ibid.

165. Wang Yazhi, *Peng Dehuai junshi canmou de huiyi*, p. 82. For a description of the Soviet approach, see David M. Glantz, *The Military Strategy of the Soviet Union: A History* (London: Frank Cass, 1992).

166. Jin Ye, "Yi Liaodong bandao kangdenglu zhanyi yanxi."

167. Yin Qiming and Cheng Yaguang, *Diyi ren guofang buzhang*, p. 78.

168. Wang Yazhi, *Peng Dehuai junshi canmou de huiyi*, p. 125.

169. Liu Bocheng studied at the Frunze Military Academy in Russia in 1927 and played a central role in translating Soviet military documents. As commander of the Second Field Army during the Chinese civil war, Liu is viewed as one of the PLA's great generals. On Liu's role as a translator, see Chen Shiping and Cheng Ying, *Junshi fanyijia Liu Bocheng* [Expert Military Translator Liu Bocheng] (Taiyuan: Shuhai chubanshe, 1988).

170. Wang Yan, ed., *Peng Dehuai nianpu*, p. 628.

171. Ibid., p. 637.

172. Su Yu was transferred to the newly established AMS.

173. The GLD absorbed the general finance and ordnance departments while the GPD absorbed the general cadre department. The training and armed forces supervision departments were abolished.

174. Shou Xiaosong, ed., *Zhongguo renmin jiefangjun de 80 nian*, p. 336.

175. Wang Yan, ed., *Peng Dehuai zhuan*, p. 544.

176. In practice, especially among higher units, these positions were held by the same individual. Peng Dehuai was both commander and political commissar of Chinese forces in Korea.

177. Yin Qiming and Cheng Yaguang, *Diyi ren guofang buzhang*, p. 93.

178. Wang Yazhi, *Peng Dehuai junshi canmou de huiyi*, p. 207.

179. Ibid., p. 210.

180. On the plenum and Peng's dismissal, see Frederick C. Teiwes and Warren Sun, *China's Road to Disaster: Mao, Central Politicians, and Provincial Leaders in the Unfolding of the Great Leap Forward, 1955–1959* (Armonk, NY: M. E. Sharpe, 1999), pp. 202–214; Frederick C. Teiwes, *Politics and Purges in China: Rectification and the Decline of Party Norms, 1950–1965* (Armonk, NY: M. E. Sharpe, 1979), pp. 384–411; Roderick MacFarquhar, *The Origins of the Cultural Revolution, Vol. 2* (New York: Columbia University Press, 1983), pp. 187–254.

181. Despite its name, the "office" was a coordinating committee. See Fu Xuezheng, "Zai zhongyang junwei bangongting gongzuo de rizi" [Working in the Central Mililitary Commission's Office], *Dangshi tiandi*, No. 1 (2006), pp. 18–16.

182. Shou Xiaosong, ed., *Zhongguo renmin jiefangjun junshi*, Vol. 5, p. 202.

183. Ibid., p. 206.

184. Ibid., pp. 202–204.

185. Wang Yan, ed., *Peng Dehuai zhuan*, p. 539.

186. Ma Xiaotian and Zhao Keming, eds., *Zhongguo renmin jiefangjun guofang daxue shi*, p. 241.

187. Even excerpts from Lin's selected works published in Hong Kong and the recollections of his secretary do not indicate that Lin delivered a report on the adjustment in strategy. Instead, it would appear that the change occurred in the context of the discussions at the CMC meeting. See Li De and She Yun, eds., *Lin Biao yuanshuai wenji (xia)* [Marshal Lin Biao's Selected Works] (Xianggang: Fenghuang shupin, 2013), p. 227.

188. One recollection suggests that even Luo Ruiqing did not support the new slogan for China's strategy. According to Li Tianyou, Luo approved Li's request to strengthen fortifications on Hainan Island, which would have been an area to be "opened" under Lin's guidelines. See Liu

Tianye, Xia Daoyuan, and Fan Shu, *Li Tianyou jiangjun zhuan* [General Li Tianyou's Biography] (Beijing: Jiefangjun chubanshe), pp. 355–356.

189. Li De and She Yun, eds., *Lin Biao yuanshuai wenji (xia)*, p. 227.

190. Li De and Shu Yun, *Wo gei Lin Biao yuanshuai dang mishu, 1959–1964* [I Served as Marshal Lin Biao's Secretary, 1959–1964] (Hong Kong: Fenghuang shupin, 2014), p. 16. Other sources indicate that the initial dividing point in the 1960 strategy was Lianyungang in Jiangsu province north of Shanghai. See Shou Xiaosong, ed. *Zhanlue xue* [The Science of Military Strategy] (Beijing: Junshi kexue chubanshe, 2013), p. 45.

191. For one detailed account, see Hu Zhefeng, "Jianguo yilai ruogan junshi zhanlue fangzhen tansuo" [Exploration and Analysis of Several Military Strategic Guidelines Since the Founding of the Nation], *Dangdai Zhongguo shi yanjiu*, No. 4 (2000), p. 24.

192. Jiang Nan and Ding Wei, "Lengzhan shiqi Zhonguo fanqinlue zhanzheng zhanlue zhidao de bianqe" [Evolution of China's Strategic Guidance in Anti-aggression Wars during the Cold War], *Junshi lishi*, No. 1 (2013), p. 16.

193. Li De and Shu Yun, *Wo gei Lin Biao yuanshuai dang mishu*, p. 16.

194. Ibid., p. 47.

195. See table 1.1 above.

196. Wang Yan, ed., *Peng Dehuai nianpu*, pp. 603–606.

197. Zheng Wenhan, *Mishu rijili de Peng laozong*, p. 47.

198. Yin Qiming and Cheng Yaguang, *Diyi ren guofang buzhang*, p. 187.

199. Ibid.

200. Guofang daxue dangshi dangjian zhengzhi gongzuo jiaoyan shi, ed., *Zhonghua renmin jiefangjun zhengzhi gongzuo shi: Shehui zhuyi shiqi* [History of Political Work in the PLA: The Socialist Period] (Beijing: Guofang daxue chubanshe, 1989), pp. 162–173; Frederick C. Teiwes and Warren Sun, *The Tragedy of Lin Biao: Riding the Tiger During the Cultural Revolution* (Honolulu: University of Hawaii Press, 1996), pp. 188–191.

201. Teiwes and Sun, *The Tragedy of Lin Biao*, p. 191.

202. Li Deyi, "Mao Zedong jiji fangyu zhanlue sixiang de lishi fazhan yu sikao" [The Historical Development of and Reflections on Mao Zedong's Strategic Thinking about Active Defense], *Junshi lishi*, No. 4 (2002), p. 52.

203. Peng Guangqian, *Zhongguo junshi zhanlue wenti yanjiu* [Research on Issues in China's Military Strategy] (Beijing: Jiefangjun chubanshe, 2006), p. 91.

204. Zhang Zishen, ed., *Yang Chengwu nianpu* [A Chronicle of Yang Chengwu's Life] (Beijing: Jiefangjun chubanshe, 2014), pp. 353, 357; Huang Yao, ed., *Luo Ronghuan nianpu* [A Chronicle of Luo Ronghuan's Life] (Beijing: Renmin chubanshe, 2002), pp. 849–850.

205. Liu Jixian, ed., *Ye Jianying nianpu*, Vol. 2, p. 883.

206. Jiang Jiantian, "Wojun zhandou tiaoling tixi de xingcheng"; Ye Jianying, *Ye Jianying junshi wenxuan*, pp. 380–385, 426–435, 446–455, 494–502; Ren Jian, *Zuozhan tiaoling gailun*, pp. 38–43.

207. Ren Jian, *Zuozhan tiaoling gailun*, p. 44.

208. Shou Xiaosong, ed., *Zhongguo renmin jiefangjun de 80 nian*, p. 378; Wang Yan, ed., *Peng Dehuai zhuan*, p. 538.

209. Shou Xiaosong, ed., *Zhongguo renmin jiefangjun junshi*, Vol. 5, pp. 204–205.

210. Zhou Junlun, ed., *Nie Rongzhen nianpu*, p. 922.

211. Shou Xiaosong, ed., *Zhongguo renmin jiefangjun de 80 nian*, p. 379.

212. Ma Xiaotian and Zhao Keming, eds., *Zhongguo renmin jiefangjun guofang daxue shi*, p. 273.

213. Ibid., p. 290.

214. Shou Xiaosong, ed., *Zhongguo renmin jiefangjun de 80 nian*, p. 382.

215. Ibid., p. 383.

Chapter 4. The 1964 Strategy

1. Chinese military scholar Yuan Dejin has shown how no documents exist to support the claim that Mao issued such instructions on October 22, 1964. Yuan Dejin, "Mao Zedong yu 'zaoda, dada, da hezhanzheng' sixiang de tichu" [Mao Zedong and the Proposition of 'Fighting an Early, Major, Nuclear War'], *Junshi lishi*, No. 5 (2010), pp. 1–6.

2. Su Yu, *Su Yu wenxuan* [Su Yu's Selected Works], Vol. 3 (Beijing: Junshi kexue chubanshe, 2004), pp. 404–405.

3. Shou Xiaosong, ed., *Zhongguo renmin jiefangjun junshi* [A Military History of the Chinese People's Liberation Army], Vol. 5 (Beijing: Junshi kexue chubanshe, 2011), p. 201.

4. Liu Jixian, ed., *Ye Jianying nianpu* [A Chronicle of Ye Jianying's Life], Vol. 2 (Beijing: Zhongyang wenxian chubanshe, 2007), pp. 437–438.

5. Shou Xiaosong, ed., *Zhongguo renmin jiefangjun junshi*, Vol. 5, p. 202.

6. Ibid., p. 306.

7. Zhou Enlai, *Zhou Enlai junshi wenxuan* [Zhou Enlai's Selected Works on Military Affairs], Vol. 4, (Beijing: Renmin chubanshe, 1997), p. 426.

8. Ibid., p. 434.

9. Shou Xiaosong, ed., *Zhongguo renmin jiefangjun junshi*, Vol. 5, p. 294.

10. "Chiang Urges Early Action," *New York Times*, March 30, 1962, p. 2.

11. Melvin Gurtov and Byong-Moo Hwang, *China Under Threat: The Politics of Strategy and Diplomacy* (Baltimore: Johns Hopkins University Press, 1980), pp. 127–128; Allen S. Whiting, *The Chinese Calculus of Deterrence: India and Indochina* (Ann Arbor: University of Michigan Press, 1975), pp. 62–72.

12. Wang Shangrong, "Xin Zhongguo jiansheng hou jici zhongda zhanzheng" [Several Major Wars After the Emergence of New China], in Zhu Yuanshi, ed., *Gongheguo yaoshi koushushi* [An Oral History of the Republic's Important Events], (Changsha: Henan renmin chubanshe, 1999), pp. 277–278.

13. Zhou Enlai, *Zhou Enlai junshi wenxuan*, Vol. 4, pp. 434–435.

14. M. Taylor Fravel, *Strong Borders, Secure Nation: Cooperation and Conflict in China's Territorial Disputes* (Princeton, NJ: Princeton University Press, 2008), pp. 101–105.

15. Junshi lilun jiaoyanshi, *Zhongguo renmin jiefangjun 1950–1979 zhanshi jiangyi* [Teaching Materials on the War History of the Chinese People's Liberation Army 1950–1979] (n.p.: n.p., 1987), p. 60.

16. China sought to resolve border disputes with many neighbors at this time. See Fravel, *Strong Borders, Secure Nation*, pp. 70–125.

17. Shou Xiaosong, ed., *Zhongguo renmin jiefangjun junshi*, Vol. 5, pp. 297–298.

18. Ibid., p. 298.

19. Zhou Enlai, *Zhou Enlai junshi wenxuan*, Vol. 4, p. 426. Zhou did not play a leading role at the meeting, but his participation underscored the importance of the task, given that the economic crisis created by the leap limited the resources available to the PLA.

20. Shou Xiaosong, ed., *Zhongguo renmin jiefangjun junshi*, Vol. 5, p. 299.

21. Ibid., p. 298.

22. Ibid., p. 301; Mao Zedong, *Jianguo yilai Mao Zedong junshi wengao* [Mao Zedong's Military Manuscripts Since the Founding of the Nation], Vol. 3 (Beijing: Junshi kexue chubanshe, 2010), p. 144.

23. For a discussion of Chinese decision-making during this period, see Yang Qiliang, *Wang Shangrong jiangjun* [General Wang Shangrong] (Beijing: Dangdai Zhongguo chubanshe, 2000), pp. 484–492.

24. Shou Xiaosong, ed., *Zhongguo renmin jiefangjun junshi*, Vol. 5, p. 314. According to one source, combat-duty units initially deployed several hundred kilometers away from the coast,

but were then instructed to move as close as possible to the coast. See Junshi lilun jiaoyanshi, *Zhongguo renmin jiefangjun 1950–1979 zhanshi jiangyi*, p. 61.

25. Shou Xiaosong, ed., *Zhongguo renmin jiefangjun junshi*, Vol. 5, p. 316; Wang Shangrong, "Xin zhongguo," p. 278.

26. Junshi lilun jiaoyanshi, *Zhongguo renmin jiefangjun 1950–1979 zhanshi jiangyi*, p. 61.

27. Yang Qiliang, *Wang Shangrong*, p. 486.

28. Shou Xiaosong, ed., *Zhongguo renmin jiefangjun junshi*, Vol. 5, p. 316; Junshi lilun jiao-yanshi, *Zhongguo renmin jiefangjun 1950–1979 zhanshi jiangyi*, p. 61.

29. Junshi lilun jiaoyanshi, *Zhongguo renmin jiefangjun 1950–1979 zhanshi jiangyi*, p. 62.

30. Wang Bingnan, *ZhongMei huitan jiunian huigu* [Reflections on Nine Years of Chinese-American Talks] (Beijing: Shijie zhishi chubanshe, 1985), pp. 85–90.

31. Shou Xiaosong, ed., *Zhongguo renmin jiefangjun junshi*, Vol. 5, p. 323.

32. Ibid., pp. 323–329; Zhang Zishen, ed., *Yang Chengwu nianpu* [A Chronicle of Yang Cheng-wu's Life] (Beijing: Jiefangjun chubanshe, 2014), pp. 356, 371, 373–374; Liu Yongzhi, ed., *Zongcan moubu dashiji* [A Chronology of the General Staff Department] (Beijing: Lantian chubanshe, 2009), pp. 459, 481.

33. On China's decision-making in the war with India, see Fravel, *Strong Borders, Secure Nation*, pp. 173–219; John W. Garver, "China's Decision for War with India in 1962," in Alastair Iain Johnston and Robert S. Ross, eds., *New Directions in the Study of China's Foreign Policy* (Stanford, CA: Stanford University Press, 2006), pp. 86–130.

34. Shou Xiaosong, ed., *Zhongguo renmin jiefangjun junshi*, Vol. 5, p. 306. This figure includes public security forces along with railway and engineering corps.

35. Ibid; Jiang Tiejun, ed., *Dang de guofang jundui gaige sixiang yanjiu* [A Study of the Party's Thought on National Defense and Army Reform] (Beijing: Junshi kexue chubanshe, 2015), p. 68.

36. Song Shilun, *Song Shilun junshi wenxuan: 1958–1989* [Song Shilun's Selected Works on Military Affairs: 1958–1989] (Beijing: Junshi kexue chubanshe, 2007), p. 244.

37. Han Huaizhi, *Han Huaizhi lun junshi* [Han Huaizhi on Military Affairs] (Beijing: Jiefangjun chubanshe, 2012), pp. 202–206.

38. Shou Xiaosong, ed., *Zhongguo renmin jiefangjun junshi* [A Military History of the Chinese People's Liberation Army], Vol. 6 (Beijing: Junshi kexue chubanshe, 2011), pp. 47, 114.

39. Barry Naughton, "The Third Front: Defense Industrialization in the Chinese Interior," *China Quarterly*, No. 115 (Autumn 1988), p. 365.

40. Shou Xiaosong, ed., *Zhongguo renmin jiefangjun junshi*, Vol. 5, pp. 392–393. This includes Chinese and Western scholarship on the third line. See, for example, Chen Donglin, *Sanxian jianshe: Beizhan shiqi de xibu kaifa* [Construction of the Third Line: Western Development in a Period of Preparing for War] (Beijing: Zhonggong zhongyang dangxiao chubanshe, 2004), pp. 74–93; Lorenz M. Luthi, "The Vietnam War and China's Third-Line Defense Planning before the Cultural Revolution, 1964–1966," *Journal of Cold War Studies*, Vol. 10, No. 1 (2008), pp. 26–51.

41. Li Xiangqian, "1964 nian: Yuenan zhanzheng shengji yu Zhongguo jingji zhengzhi de biandong" [The Year of 1964: The Escalation of the Vietnam War and the Fluctuations in China's Economics and Politics], in Zhang Baijia and Niu Jun, eds., *Lengzhan yu Zhongguo* [The Cold War and China], (Beijing: Shijie zhishi chubanshe, 2002), pp. 319–340. Li focuses mostly on the decision to push for developing the third line, not the change in the strategic guideline. I also stress the domestic factor even more than Li does.

42. On the origins of the Cultural Revolution, see, among others, Roderick MacFarquhar, *The Origins of the Cultural Revolution,* Vol. 3 (New York: Columbia University Press, 1997); Kenneth Lieberthal, "The Great Leap Forward and the Split in the Yenan Leadership," in John King Fairbank and Roderick MacFarquhar, eds., *The Cambridge History of China*, Vol. 14 (Cambridge: Cambridge University Press, 1987), pp. 293–359; Harry Harding, "The Chinese State in Crisis," in Roderick

MacFarquhar and John K. Fairbank, eds., *The Cambridge History of China, Vol. 15, Part 2* (Cambridge: Cambridge University Press, 1991), pp. 107–217; Andrew G. Walder, *China Under Mao: A Revolution Derailed* (Cambridge, MA: Harvard University Press, 2015), pp. 180–199.

43. Walder, *China Under Mao*, p. 201. Also, see Roderick MacFarquhar and Michael Schoenhals, *Mao's Last Revolution* (Cambridge, MA: Belknap Press of Harvard University Press, 2006).

44. For overviews of the Great Leap Forward, see Walder, *China Under Mao*, pp. 152–179; Carl Riskin, *China's Political Economy: The Quest for Development since 1949* (New York: Oxford University Press, 1987), pp. 81–147; Frederick C. Teiwes and Warren Sun, *China's Road to Disaster: Mao, Central Politicians, and Provincial Leaders in the Unfolding of the Great Leap Forward, 1955–1959* (Armonk, NY: M. E. Sharpe, 1999); Lieberthal, "Great Leap Forward," pp. 293–359; Roderick MacFarquhar, *The Origins of the Cultural Revolution*, Vol. 2 (New York: Columbia University Press, 1983).

45. Walder, *China Under Mao*, p. 155.

46. Ibid., p. 171.

47. Ibid., p. 177.

48. Jisheng Yang, *Tombstone: The Great Chinese Famine, 1958–1962* (New York: Farrar, Straus & Giroux, 2013), p. 1. Yang's estimate is thirty-six million.

49. MacFarquhar, *The Origins of the Cultural Revolution*, Vol. 3, p. 66.

50. For a detailed account of the conference, see ibid., pp. 137–181.

51. Liu Shaoqi, *Liu Shaoqi xuanji* [Liu Shaoqi's Selected Works], Vol. 2 (Beijing: Renmin chubanshe, 1981), p. 421.

52. Walder, *China Under Mao*, pp. 182–183; MacFarquhar, *The Origins of the Cultural Revolution*, Vol. 3, pp. 145–158.

53. Pang Xianzhi and Feng Hui, eds., *Mao Zedong nianpu, 1949–1976* [A Chronicle of Mao Zedong's Life, 1949–1976], Vol. 4 (Beijing: Zhongyang wenxian chubanshe, 2013), pp. 97, 198, 352, 511.

54. Walder, *China Under Mao*, p. 184; Yang, *Tombstone*, p. 506.

55. Walder, *China Under Mao*, pp. 185–188.

56. Wang Guangmei and Liu Yuan, *Ni suo buzhidao de Liu Shaoqi* [The Liu Shaoqi You Do Not Know] (Zhengzhou: Henan renmin chubanshe, 2000), p. 90.

57. MacFarquhar, *The Origins of the Cultural Revolution*, Vol. 3, pp. 274–283.

58. Pang Xianzhi and Jin Chongji, *Mao Zedong zhuan, 1949–1976* [Mao Zedong's Bioagraphy 1949–1976] (Beijing: Zhongyang wenxian chubanshe, 2003), p. 1259–1960.

59. Ibid., p. 1260.

60. Walder, *China Under Mao*, pp. 180–199.

61. Wu Lengxi, *Shinian lunzhan: 1956–1966 ZhongSu guanxi huiyilu* [Ten Years of Polemics: A Recollection of Chinese-Soviet Relations from 1956 to 1966] (Beijing: Zhongyang wenxian chubanshe, 1999), pp. 561–562.

62. Ibid. Nevertheless, the movement never fulfilled Mao's objective of pursuing class struggle and instead focused mostly on countering corruption among local cadre.

63. Riskin, *China's Political Economy*, p. 158.

64. Harry Harding, *Organizing China: The Problem of Bureaucracy, 1949–1976* (Stanford, CA: Stanford University Press, 1981), p. 197.

65. MacFarquhar, *The Origins of the Cultural Revolution*, Vol. 3, pp. 334–348.

66. Walder, *China Under Mao*, p. 195.

67. Ibid.

68. Wu Lengxi, *Shinian lunzhan*, p. 733. Also, Pang Xianzhi and Feng Hui, eds., *Mao Zedong nianpu, 1949–1976* [A Chronicle of Mao Zedong's Life, 1949–1976], Vol. 5 (Beijing: Zhongyang wenxian chubanshe, 2013), p. 324. On the importance of this statement, see Li Xiangqian, "1964 nian," p. 336.

69. According to Bo Yibo, "food" referred to grain, "clothing" referred to textiles as well as vinyl, nylon, and plastic products, and "daily necessities" referred to ordinary household furniture, woks, cooking utensils, and thermoses. See Bo Yibo, *Ruogan zhongda juece yu shijian de huigu* [Reviewing Several Major Decisions and Events] (Beijing: Zhonggong zhongyang dangshi chubanshe, 1993), p. 1194.

70. Pang Xianzhi and Feng Hui, eds., *Mao Zedong nianpu, 1949–1976*, Vol. 5, p. 236.

71. Bo Yibo, *Ruogan zhongda juece yu shijian de huigu*, p. 1194.

72. Fan Weizhong and Jin Chongji, *Li Fuchun zhuan* [Li Fuchun's Biography] (Beijing: Zhongyang wenxian chubanshe, 2001), p. 629.

73. Bo Yibo, *Ruogan zhongda juece yu shijian de huigu*, p. 1196; Fan Weizhong and Jin Chongji, *Li Fuchun zhuan*, p. 629.

74. Bo Yibo, *Ruogan zhongda juece yu shijian de huigu*, p. 1196.

75. Jin Chongji, ed., *Zhou Enlai zhuan* [Zhou Enlai's Biography], Vol. 4 (Beijing: Zhongyang wenxian chubanshe, 1998), p. 1968. Also, see Naughton, "The Third Front," pp. 351–386.

76. Pang Xianzhi and Feng Hui, eds., *Mao Zedong nianpu, 1949–1976*, Vol. 5, pp. 348–349.

77. Chen Donglin, *Sanxian jianshe*, p. 255.

78. Pang Xianzhi and Feng Hui, eds., *Mao Zedong nianpu, 1949–1976*, Vol. 5, p. 348.

79. Fan Weizhong and Jin Chongji, *Li Fuchun zhuan*, p. 631.

80. Pang Xianzhi and Feng Hui, eds., *Mao Zedong nianpu, 1949–1976*, Vol. 5, pp. 354–355.

81. Ibid.

82. Jin Chongji, ed., *Zhou Enlai zhuan*, Vol. 4, p. 1768.

83. For example, Mao's official chronology contains no reference to the third line before this date.

84. Chen Donglin, *Sanxian jianshe*, p. 50.

85. No complete transcript of this meeting is available. Mao's remarks appear in various sources, including Pang Xianzhi and Feng Hui, eds., *Mao Zedong nianpu, 1949–1976*, Vol. 5, pp. 357–369; Bo Yibo, *Ruogan zhongda juece yu shijian de huigu* pp. 1199–1200; Mao Zedong, *Jianguo yilai Mao Zedong junshi wengao*, Vol. 3, pp. 225–226; Mao Zedong, "Zai zhongyang gongzuo huiyi de jianghua (June 6, 1964)" [Speech at the Central Work Conference], in Song Yongyi, ed., *The Database for the History of Contemporary Chinese Political Movements, 1949-* (Harvard University: Fairbank Center for Chinese Studies, 2013). As the compilers of Mao's chronology note, Bo Yibo's memoir incorrectly states that the meeting was held on June 6 and not June 8. This may be because one of the partial transcripts is dated June 6, even though there is no record of Mao attending any meeting that day.

86. Mao Zedong, "Zai zhongyang gongzuo huiyi de jianghua." Also, see Bo Yibo, *Ruogan zhongda juece yu shijian de huigu*, pp. 1199–1200.

87. Chen Donglin, *Sanxian jianshe*, p. 53.

88. This evokes Tom Christensen's argument in which leaders exaggerate an external threat to mobilize support for changes in grand strategy. In this case, Mao exaggerated external threats to justify changes in domestic policy. See Thomas J. Christensen, *Useful Adversaries: Grand Strategy, Domestic Mobilization, and Sino-American Conflict, 1947–1958* (Princeton, NJ: Princeton University Press, 1996).

89. Mao Zedong, "Zai zhongyang gongzuo huiyi de jianghua"; Bo Yibo, *Ruogan zhongda juece yu shijian de huigu*, pp. 1199–1200.

90. Mao Zedong, *Jianguo yilai Mao Zedong junshi wengao*, Vol. 3, p. 225.

91. Ibid.

92. Mao Zedong, "Zai zhongyang gongzuo huiyi de jianghua." Also, see Mao Zedong, *Jianguo yilai Mao Zedong junshi wengao*, Vol. 3, pp. 225–226.

93. Mao Zedong, *Jianguo yilai Mao Zedong junshi wengao*, Vol. 3, p. 225.

94. Bo Yibo, *Ruogan zhongda juece yu shijian de huigu*, p. 1148; Pang Xianzhi and Feng Hui, eds., *Mao Zedong nianpu, 1949–1976*, Vol. 5, p. 358.

95. Pang Xianzhi and Feng Hui, eds., *Mao Zedong nianpu, 1949–1976*, Vol. 5, p. 358.

96. Mao Zedong, "Zai zhongyang changwei shang de jianghua." Also, Pang Xianzhi and Feng Hui, eds., *Mao Zedong nianpu, 1949–1976*, Vol. 5, p. 359.

97. This is based on the recollection of Mei Xing, a senior member of the Central Committee Secretariat staff, as reported in Chen Donglin, *Sanxian jianshe*, p. 66.

98. Quoted in Huang Yao and Zhang Mingzhe, eds., *Luo Ruiqing zhuan* [Luo Ruiqing's Biography] (Beijing: Dangdai Zhongguo chubanshe, 1996), p. 472.

99. Lin was briefed on July 10 and 11. See Huang Yao, "1965 nian zhongyang junwei zuozhan huiyi fengbo de lailong qumai" [The Origin and Development of the Storm at the 1965 CMC Operations Meeting], *Dangdai Zhongguo yanjiu*, Vol. 22, No. 1 (2015), p. 90. The delay in notifying Lin of Mao's rejection of Lin's formulation of the strategic guideline may be an underappreciated factor in tensions that would grow between Lin and Luo Ruiqing over the coming year. Although Lin was the CCP's highest ranking military leader as first vice-chairman of the CMC and defense minister, even he was not consulted by Mao before Mao intervened to change the strategy.

100. "Mao Zedong zai Shisanling shuiku de jianghua" [Mao Zedong's Speech at the Ming Tombs' Reservoir], June 16, 1964, from the Fujian Provincial Archive. Unless otherwise noted, all quotes from the speech are taken from this document. I'm grateful to Andrew Kennedy for sharing it with me. For Kennedy's account of the speech, see Andrew Kennedy, *The International Ambitions of Mao and Nehru: National Efficacy Beliefs and the Making of Foreign Policy* (New York: Cambridge University Press, 2011), pp. 117–118. Military portions of the speech are excerpted in Mao Zedong, *Jianguo yilai Mao Zedong junshi wengao*, Vol. 3, pp. 227–228. For another version of the speech, see Mao Zedong, "Zai shisanling guanyu difang dangwei zhua junshi he peiyang jiebanren de jianghua." [Speech at the Ming Tombs on Local Party Committees' Grasping Military Affairs and Cultivating Successors], in Song Yongyi, ed., *The Database for the History of Contemporary Chinese Political Movements, 1949–* (Harvard University: Fairbank Center for Chinese Studies, 2013).

101. Longer versions of the section on the speech on successors can be found in *Jianguo yilai Mao Zedong wengao*. [Mao Zedong's Manuscripts Since the Founding of the Nation], Vol. 11 (Beijing: Zhongyang wenxian chubanshe, 1993), p. 85–88; Mao Zedong, "Zai shisanling guanyu difang dangwei zhua junshi he peiyang jiebanren de jianghua."

102. Pang Xianzhi and Feng Hui, eds., *Mao Zedong nianpu, 1949–1976*, Vol. 5, p. 369. Also, Mao Zedong, *Jianguo yilai Mao Zedong junshi wengao*, Vol. 3, pp. 251–252. Liu Shaoqi also underscored the focus "on preparing for the worst."

103. Mao Zedong, *Jianguo yilai Mao Zedong junshi wengao*, Vol. 3, pp. 251–252.

104. Ibid.

105. Ibid., p. 251.

106. Ibid.

107. Fan Weizhong and Jin Chongji, *Li Fuchun zhuan*, p. 636.

108. Ibid.

109. Ibid.

110. Ibid., p. 639.

111. Quoted in Chen Donglin, *Sanxian jianshe*, p. 63.

112. Quoted in Pang Xianzhi and Feng Hui, eds., *Mao Zedong nianpu, 1949–1976*, Vol. 5, p. 397.

113. Ibid., p. 402.

114. Barry Naughton, "Industrial Policy During the Cultural Revolution: Military Preparation, Decentralization, and Leaps Forward," in Christine Wong, William A. Joseph, and David

Zweig, eds., *New Perspectives on the Cultural Revolution* (Cambridge, MA Harvard University Press, 1991), p. 165.

115. Ibid., pp. 164–166.

116. Chen Donglin, *Sanxian jianshe*, pp. 59–73.

117. For an account of coastal raids, see Shou Xiaosong, ed., *Zhongguo renmin jiefangjun junshi*, Vol. 5, pp. 315–328.

118. Graham A. Cosmas, *MACV: The Joint Command in the Years of Escalation, 1962–1967* (Washington, DC: Center of Military History, United States Army, 2006), pp. 117–178.

119. Fravel, *Strong Borders, Secure Nation*, pp. 101–105.

120. Office of National Estimates, *The Soviet Military Buildup Along the Chinese Border*, SM-7-68 [Top Secret] (Central Intelligence Agency, 1968); Central Intelligence Agency, *Military Forces Along the Sino-Soviet Border*, SM-70-5 [Top Secret] (Central Intelligence Agency, 1970).

121. On these talks, see Fravel, *Strong Borders, Secure Nation*, pp. 119–123.

122. Huang Yao and Zhang Mingzhe, eds., *Luo Ruiqing zhuan*, p. 385; Zhang Zishen, ed., *Yang Chengwu nianpu*, pp. 386–387.

123. On this point, see Li Xiangqian, "1964 nian," p. 324.

124. Mao Zedong, "Zai zhongyang gongzuo huiyi de jianghua."

125. Pang Xianzhi and Feng Hui, eds., *Mao Zedong nianpu, 1949–1976*, Vol. 5, p. 385.

126. "Mao Zedong zai Shisanling shuiku de jianghua," (Fujian Provincial Archive).

127. On the lack of urgency in Mao's assessments, see Li Xiangqian, "1964 nian," pp. 327, 332.

128. Mao Zedong, *Jianguo yilai Mao Zedong junshi wengao* [Mao Zedong's Military Manuscripts Since the Founding of the Nation], Vol. 2 (Beijing: Junshi kexue chubanshe, 2010), p. 265. See Chapter 3.

129. Liu Chongwen and Chen Shaochou, eds., *Liu Shaoqi nianpu, 1898–1969 (xia)* [A Chronicle of Liu Shaoqi's Life, 1898–1969] (Beijing: Zhongyang wenxian chubanshe, 1996), p. 594

130. Pang Xianzhi and Feng Hui, eds., *Mao Zedong nianpu, 1949–1976*, Vol. 5, p. 375.

131. Mao Zedong, *Jianguo yilai Mao Zedong junshi wengao*, Vol. 3, p. 284.

132. Ibid., p. 285.

133. Qiang Zhai, *China and the Vietnam Wars, 1950–1975* (Chapel Hill: University of North Carolina Press, 2000), p. 143.

134. http://www.history.com/topics/vietnam-war/vietnam-war-history.

135. Zhai, *China and the Vietnam Wars, 1950–1975*, pp. 133–139.

136. For the complete statement, see Zhai Qiang, *CWIHP Bulletin*, Issues 6–7 (Winter 1994/1996), p. 235. On this episode, see James G. Hershberg and Jian Chen, "Informing the Enemy: Sino-American "Signaling" in the Vietnam War, 1965," in Priscilla Roberts, ed., *Behind the Bamboo Curtain: China, Vietnam, and the World Beyond Asia* (Stanford, CA: Stanford University Press, 2006), pp. 193–258.

137. Ibid., pp. 226–227, 231.

138. Mao Zedong, *Jianguo yilai Mao Zedong junshi wengao*, Vol. 3, p. 306. Some sources indicate that China attacked US aircraft, but the first Chinese attack did not occur until September near Haikou. See Xiaoming Zhang, "Air Combat for the People's Republic: The People's Liberation Army Air Force in Action, 1949–1969," in Mark A. Ryan, David M. Finkelstein, and Michael A. McDevitt, eds., *Chinese Warfighting: The PLA Experience Since 1949* (Armonk, NY: M. E. Sharpe, 2003), p. 291.

139. "Zhongguo linkong burong qinfan!" [China's Airspace is Inviolable!], *Jiefangjun Bao*, April 12, 1965.

140. Pang Xianzhi and Feng Hui, eds., *Mao Zedong nianpu, 1949–1976*, Vol. 5, p. 487.

141. Ibid.

142. Yang Shengqun and Yan Jianqi, eds., *Deng Xiaoping nianpu (1904–1974)* [A Chronicle of Deng Xiaoping's Life (1904–1974)] (Beijing: Zhongyang wenxian chubanshe, 2009), p. 1856.

143. Zhongyang wenxian yanjiu shi, ed., *Jianguo yilai zhongyao wenxian xuanbian* [Selection of Important Documents Since the Founding of the Country], Vol. 20 (Beijing: Zhongyang wenxian chubanshe, 1998), pp. 141–145.

144. Similar army-wide operations meetings were held in March 1963, March 1964, and April 1966. Although the April 1965 operations meeting discussed Vietnam, the convening of the meeting itself was not unusual. See Zhang Zishen, ed., *Yang Chengwu nianpu*, pp. 274, 395, 430.

145. Ibid., p. 418.

146. Quoted in Huang Yao, "1965 nian zhongyang junwei zuozhan huiyi fengbo de lailong qumai," p. 93. Also, see Deng Xiaoping, *Deng Xiaoping junshi wenxuan* [Deng Xiaoping's Selected Works on Military Affairs], Vol. 2 (Beijing: Junshi kexue chubanshe, 2004), p. 345; Zhang Zishen, ed., *Yang Chengwu nianpu*, p. 418.

147. Huang Yao, "1965 nian zhongyang junwei zuozhan huiyi fengbo de lailong qumai," p. 92. Also, Pang Xianzhi and Feng Hui, eds., *Mao Zedong nianpu, 1949–1976*, Vol. 5, p. 538.

148. Shou Xiaosong, ed., *Zhongguo renmin jiefangjun junshi*, Vol. 5, p. 394.

149. This paragraph draws on Pang Xianzhi and Feng Hui, eds., *Mao Zedong nianpu, 1949–1976*, Vol. 5, p. 492.

150. Mao Zedong, *Jianguo yilai Mao Zedong junshi wengao*, Vol. 3, p. 311.

151. Ibid., p. 314. Also, see Luo Ruiqing, "Luo Ruiqing chuanda Mao Zedong zhishi (June 23, 1965)" [Luo Ruiqing Transmits Mao's Instructions], in Song Yongyi, ed., *The Database for the History of Contemporary Chinese Political Movements, 1949-* (Harvard University: Fairbank Center for Chinese Studies, 2013).

152. Xu Shiyou, *Xu Shiyou junshi wenxuan* [Xu Shiyou's Selected Works on Military Affairs] (Beijing: Junshi kexue chubanshe, 2013), pp. 390–420.

153. Quoted in Luo Ruiqing, "Luo Ruiqing chuanda Mao Zedong zhishi." Mao thus appears to contradict his earlier statement about preventing an enemy from driving straight in.

154. Hershberg and Chen, "Informing the Enemy," p. 234.

155. Luo Ruiqing, "Luo Ruiqing chuanda Mao Zedong zhishi."

156. Quoted in ibid.

157. Quoted in ibid.

158. Quoted in ibid.

159. Ibid.

160. The PLA leadership itself had been holding meetings on Mao's remarks since the summer of 1964, so they did not need to receive such a summary.

161. Luo was describing the characteristics of wars that China needed to prepare to fight, which would be large, occur quickly, and include nuclear weapons (used by the United States). This may be the first reference to what would be known was preparing to fight "an early, major, nuclear war."

162. Luo Ruiqing, "Luo Ruiqing chuanda Mao Zedong zhishi."

163. Pang Xianzhi and Feng Hui, eds., *Mao Zedong nianpu, 1949–1976*, Vol. 5, p. 520.

164. Ibid.

165. Ibid., p. 534.

166. Ibid., p. 538.

167. Ibid.

168. Liu Yongzhi, ed., *Zongcan moubu dashiji*, p. 539. See also Zhang Zishen, ed., *Yang Chengwu nianpu*, pp. 428, 429.

169. Yuan Dejin, "Mao Zedong yu xin Zhongguo junshi zhanlue fangzhen de queli he tiaozheng jiqi qishi" [Mao Zedong and the Establishment and Adjustment of New China's Military Strategic Guideline and Its Implications], *Junshi lishi yanjiu*, No. 1 (2010), p. 25.

170. On the March clash and its aftermath, see M. Taylor Fravel, *Strong Borders, Secure Nation: Cooperation and Conflict in China's Territorial Disputes* (Princeton, NJ: Princeton University Press,

2008), pp. 201–219; John Wilson Lewis and Litai Xue, *Imagined Enemies: China Prepares for Uncertain War* (Stanford, CA: Stanford University Press, 2006), pp. 44–76.

171. Shou Xiaosong, ed., *Zhongguo renmin jiefangjun junshi* [A Military History of the Chinese People's Liberation Army], Vol. 6 (Beijing: Junshi kexue chubanshe, 2011), p. 104

172. Yuan Dejin and Wang Jianfei, "Xin Zhongguo chengli yilai junshi zhanlue fangzhen de lishi yanbian ji qishi" [The Evolution of Military Strategic Guidelines Since the Establishment of New China and Its Implications], *Junshi lishi*, No. 6 (2007), p. 3.

173. Shou Xiaosong, ed., *Zhongguo renmin jiefangjun junshi*, p. 104.

174. Liu Zhinan, "1969 nian, Zhongguo zhanbei yu dui MeiSu guanxi de yanjiu he tiaozheng" [China's War Preparations and the Story of the Readjustment of Relations with the United States and Soviet Union in 1969], *Dangdai Zhongguo shi yanjiu*, No. 3 (1999), pp. 41–50.

175. Shou Xiaosong, ed., *Zhongguo renmin jiefangjun junshi*, Vol. 6, pp. 114–115.

176. Ibid., p. 113.

177. Guo Xiangjie, ed. *Zhang Wannian zhuan (shang)* [Zhang Wannian's Biography] (Beijing: Jiefangjun chubanshe, 2011), p. 304

178. On the PLA in the Cultural Revolution see, Li Ke and Hao Shengzhang, *Wenhua dageming zhong de renmin jiefangjun* [The People's Liberation Army During the Cultural Revolution] (Beijing: Zhonggong dangshi ziliao chubanshe, 1989); Andrew Scobell, *China's Use of Military Force: Beyond the Great Wall and the Long March* (Cambridge: Cambridge University Press, 2003), pp. 94–118.

179. Li Ke and Hao Shengzhang, *Wenhua dageming zhong de renmin jiefangjun* [The People's Liberation Army During the Cultural Revolution] (Beijing: Zhonggong dangshi ziliao chubanshe, 1989), p. 63.

180. Directorate of Intelligence, *The PLA and the "Cultural Revolution,"* POLO XXV, Central Intelligence Agency, October 28, 1967, p. 167.

181. Shou Xiaosong, ed., *Zhongguo renmin jiefangjun junshi*, Vol. 6, p. 18.

182. Edward C. O'Dowd, *Chinese Military Strategy in the Third Indochina War: The Last Maoist War* (New York: Routledge, 2007), p. 28.

183. Li Ke and Hao Shengzhang, *Wenhua dageming zhong de renmin Jiefangjun*, pp. 260–261.

184. Shou Xiaosong, ed., *Zhongguo renmin jiefangjun junshi*, Vol. 6, p. 120.

185. Ibid., pp. 116–117, 120–123.

Chapter 5. The 1980 Strategy

1. See, for example, Ellis Joffe, *The Chinese Army after Mao* (Cambridge, MA: Harvard University Press, 1987), pp. 70–93; Harlan W. Jencks, "People's War under Modern Conditions: Wishful Thinking, National Suicide, or Effective Deterrent?," *China Quarterly*, No. 98 (June 1984), pp. 305–319; Paul H. B. Godwin, "People's War Revised: Military Docrine, Strategy and Operations," in Charles D. Lovejoy and Bruce W. Watson, eds., *China's Military Reforms: International and Domestic Implications* (Boulder, CO: Westview, 1984), pp. 1–13; David Shambaugh, *Modernizing China's Military: Progress, Problems, and Prospects* (Berkeley, CA: University of California Press, 2002), p. 62.

2. This area includes northeastern China (*dongbei*), north China (*huabei*) and northwestern China (*xibei*).

3. M. Taylor Fravel, *Strong Borders, Secure Nation: Cooperation and Conflict in China's Territorial Disputes* (Princeton, NJ: Princeton University Press, 2008), pp. 201–219; John Wilson Lewis and Litai Xue, *Imagined Enemies: China Prepares for Uncertain War* (Stanford, CA: Stanford University Press, 2006), pp. 44–76.

4. Fravel, *Strong Borders, Secure Nation*, p. 205.

5. Sources for the guideline include Xu Yan, *Zhongguo guofang daolun* [Introduction to China's National Defense] (Beijing: Guofang daxue chubanshe, 2006), pp. 304–305, 351–352; Junshi kexue yuan junshi lishi yanjiu suo, *Zhongguo renmin jiefangjun gaige fazhan 30 nian* [Thirty Years of the Reform and Development of the Chinese People's Liberation Army] (Beijing: Junshi kexue chubanshe, 2008), pp. 20–21; Zhang Weiming, *Huabei dayanxi: Zhongguo zuida junshi yanxi jishi* [North China Exercise: The Record of China's Largest Military Exercise] (Beijing: Jiefangjun chubanshe, 2008), pp. 18–20, 35–39; Xie Hainan, Yang Zufa and Yang Jianhua, *Yang Dezhi yi sheng* [Yang Dezhi's Life] (Beijing: Zhonggong dangshi chubanshe, 2011), pp. 313–315. Shou Xiaosong, ed., *Zhongguo renmin jiefangjun de 80 nian: 1927-2007* [Eighty Years of the Chinese People's Liberation Army: 1927-2007] (Beijing: Junshi kexue chubanshe, 2007), pp. 455–457. For the most detailed exposition, see Han Huaizhi, *Han Huaizhi lun junshi* [Han Huaizhi on Military Affairs] (Beijing: Jiefangjun chubanshe, 2012), pp. 293–301.

6. Xu Yan, *Zhongguo guofang daolun*, p. 304.

7. Jonathan Ray, *Red China's "Capitalist Bomb": Inside the Chinese Neutron Bomb Program* (Washington, DC: Center for the Study of Chinese Military Affairs, Institute for National Strategic Studies, National Defense University, 2015).

8. Junshi kexue yuan junshi lishi yanjiu suo, *Zhongguo renmin jiefangjun gaige fazhan 30 nian*, p. 21; Xu Yan, *Zhongguo guofang daolun*, p. 304.

9. Xu Yan, *Zhongguo guofang daolun*, pp. 304–305.

10. Many articles in *Junshi Xueshu* in the early 1980s examined operations in Vietnam. See Junshi xueshu zazhishe, ed., *Junshi xueshu lunwen xuan (xia)* [Collection of Essays from Military Arts] (Beijing: Junshi kexue chubanshe, 1984); Junshi xueshu zazhishe, ed., *Junshi xueshu lunwen xuan (shang)* [Collection of Essays from Military Arts] (Beijing: Junshi kexue chubanshe, 1984). For a detailed account of the war, see Harlan W. Jencks, "China's 'Punitive' War Against Vietnam," *Asian Survey*, Vol. 19, No. 8 (August 1979), pp. 801–815; King C. Chen, *China's War with Vietnam, 1979: Issues, Decisions, and Implications* (Stanford, CA.: Hoover Institution, 1986); Edward C. O'Dowd, *Chinese Military Strategy in the Third Indochina War: The Last Maoist War* (New York: Routledge, 2007); Xiaoming Zhang, *Deng Xiaoping's Long War: The Military Conflict between China and Vietnam, 1979–1991* (Chapel Hill: University of North Carolina Press, 2015).

11. Yang Zhiyuan, "Wojun bianxiu zuozhan tiaoling de chuangxin fazhan ji qishi" [The Innovative Development and Implications of Our Army's Compilation and Revision of Operations Regulations], *Zhongguo junshi kexue*, No. 6 (2009), p. 113.

12. Gao Rui, ed., *Zhanlue xue* [The Science of Military Strategy] (Beijing: Junshi kexue chubanshe, 1987); Song Shilun, *Song Shilun junshi wenxuan: 1958-1989* [Song Shilun's Selected Works on Military Affairs: 1958-1989] (Beijing: Junshi kexue chubanshe, 2007), pp. 558–559; Yang Zhiyuan, "Wojun bianxiu zuozhan tiaoling de chuangxin fazhan ji qishi," p. 113.

13. Xu Yan, *Zhongguo guofang daolun*, pp. 323–324.

14. For details of both reductions, see Ding Wei and Wei Xu, "20 shiji 80 niandai renmin jiefangjun tizhi gaige, jingjian zhengbian de huigu yu sikao" [Review and Reflections on the Streamlining and Reorganization of the PLA in the Eighties of the 20th Cenutry], *Junshi lishi*, No. 6 (2014), pp. 52–57; Nan Li, "Organizational Changes of the PLA, 1985–1997," *China Quarterly*, No. 158 (1999), pp. 314–349.

15. Deng Xiaoping, *Deng Xiaoping junshi wenxuan* [Deng Xiaoping's Selected Works on Military Affairs], Vol. 3 (Beijng: Junshi kexue chubanshe, 2004), p. 178.

16. Yuan Wei and Zhang Zhuo, eds., *Zhongguo junxiao fazhan shi* [History of the Development of China's Military Academies] (Beijing: Guofang daxue chubanshe, 2001), p. 825.

17. Zhang Zhen, *Zhang Zhen junshi wenxuan* [Zhang Zhen's Selected Works on Military Affairs], Vol. 2 (Beijing: Jiefangjun chubanshe, 2005), p. 217; Guo Xiangjie, ed., *Zhang Wannian zhuan (xia)* [Zhang Wannian's Biography] (Beijing: Jiefangjun chubanshe, 2011), p. 399.

18. "Zong canmoubu pizhun banfa xunlian dagang," [GSD Approves and Issues Training Program], *Jiefangjun bao*, February 8, 1981. Drafting may have been finished in 1980. See Liu Yongzhi, ed., *Zongcan moubu dashiji* [A Chronology of the General Staff Department] (Beijing: Lantian chubanshe, 2009), p. 739.

19. Zhang Zhen, *Zhang Zhen huiyilu (xia)* [Zhang Zhen's Memoirs] (Beijing: Jiefangjun chubanshe, 2003), p. 212.

20. Zhu Ying, ed., *Su Yu zhuan* [Su Yu's Biography] (Beijing: Dangdai Zhongguo chubanshe, 2000), p. 1000.

21. Ibid.

22. Su Yu, *Su Yu wenxuan* [Su Yu's Selected Works], Vol. 3 (Beijing: Junshi kexue chubanshe, 2004), pp. 529–531.

23. Ibid., pp. 563–567.

24. Su often went to great pains to link his own ideas with Mao's slogans.

25. Su Yu, *Su Yu wenxuan*, Vol. 3, pp. 529–531.

26. Ibid., p. 529.

27. Ibid. Su did not completely reject mobile warfare. In a 1974 report, he underscored its importance in ultimately defeating an invading force. See ibid., pp. 563–567.

28. Ibid., p. 568.

29. Ibid., pp. 568–572.

30. AMS only began to resume research activities in 1972.

31. Ma Suzheng, *Bashi huimou* [Reflecting on Eighty Years] (Beijing: Changzheng chubanshe, 2008), p. 146.

32. Ibid.

33. Ibid.

34. Liang Ying, "Luetan di sici zhongdong zhanzheng de tedian " [Brief Discussion of the Fourth Middle East War], *Jiefangjun bao*, December 15, 1975.

35. Ye Jianying, *Ye Jianying junshi wenxuan* [Ye Jianying's Selected Works on Military Affairs] (Beijing: Jiefangjun chubanshe, 1997), pp. 681, 682. Ye's speech mistakenly states that Mao first raised luring in deep in 1962.

36. Mu Junjie, ed., *Song Shilun zhuan* [Song Shilun's Biography] (Beijing: Junshi kexue chubanshe, 2007), p. 601.

37. Su Yu, *Su Yu wenxuan*, Vol. 3, pp. 626–631.

38. Ye Jianying, *Ye Jianying junshi wenxuan*, p. 1960.

39. The irony that Lin himself criticized Peng at the Lushan Conference for pursuing passive defenses should not be overlooked.

40. Deng Xiaoping, *Deng Xiaoping lun guofang he jundui jianshe* [Deng Xiaoping on National Defense and Army Building] (Beijing: Junshi kexue chubanshe, 1992), p. 26.

41. Zhang Zhen, *Zhang Zhen huiyilu (xia)*, p. 194.

42. Su Yu, *Su Yu wenxuan*, Vol. 3, pp. 626–631.

43. Ibid., p. 626.

44. Ibid., p. 627.

45. Ibid.

46. Ibid., p. 629.

47. Ibid., pp. 640–653.

48. Ibid., p. 642.

49. Ibid., p. 654. Also, see ibid., p. 641.

50. Ibid., pp. 670–695.

51. Another motive for the attack may have been to demonstrate how China was unprepared for modern combat.

52. Su Yu, *Su Yu wenxuan*, Vol. 3, p. 672.

53. Ibid., p. 673.

54. Ibid., p. 674.

55. Su Yu was most likely referring to *The Initial Period of War* by S. P. Ivanov, which was published in 1974.

56. Su Yu, *Su Yu wenxuan*, Vol. 3, p. 678.

57. Ibid., p. 682.

58. Ibid., p. 679.

59. Ibid., p. 680.

60. Ibid., p. 682.

61. Zhu Ying, ed., *Su Yu zhuan*, pp. 1035–1036.

62. Ibid., p. 1035.

63. Ibid., pp. 1035–1036.

64. Junshi kexue yuan lishi yanjiusuo, *Zhongguo renmin jiefangjun gaige fazhan 30 nian* [30 Years of Reform and Development of the Chinese People's Liberation Army] (Beijing: Junshi kexue chubanshe, 2008), p. 19.

65. Xu Xiangqian, *Xu Xiangqian junshi wenxuan* [Xu Xiangqian's Selected Works on Military Affairs] (Beijing: Jiefangjun chubanshe, 1993), pp. 276, 279.

66. Those writing in support of Su's ideas included Yang Dezhi (Commander, Kunming MR); Song Shilun (President, AMS); Wang Bicheng (Commander, Wuhan MR); Zhang Ming; Tan Shanhe (Commander, Engineering Corps); Zhang Feng (Deputy Commander, Jinan MR); and Han Huaizhi (Assistant Chief of Staff). See Junshi xueshu zazhishe, ed., *Junshi xueshu lunwen xuan (xia)*; Junshi xueshu zazhishe, ed., *Junshi xueshu lunwen xuan (shang)*.

67. Yang Dezhi, "Weilai fanqinlue zhanzheng chuqi zuozhan de jige wenti" [Several Questions on Operations During the Initial Phase of a Future Anti-agression War], in Junshi xueshu zazhi she, ed., *Junshi xueshu lunwen xuan (xia)* [Collection of Essays from Military Arts] (Beijing: Junshi kexue chubanshe, 1984), p. 30.

68. Ibid., p. 38.

69. Song Shilun, *Song Shilun junshi wenxuan*, p. 191.

70. Ibid., p. 240.

71. Ibid., p. 233.

72. Sun Xuemin, "Moushi renzhen yanjiu da tanke xunlian jiaoxuefa" [A Certain Division Seriously Studies Teaching Methods for Fighting Tanks], *Jiefangjun bao*, September 13, 1978.

73. Yao Youzhi, Zhao Tianyou and Wu Yiheng, "Tuchu da tanke xunlian, zheng dang da tanke nengshou" [Give Prominence to Training Fighting Tanks, Strive to Become Masters at Fighting Tanks], *Jiefangjun bao*, March 1, 1979.

74. The other two were *The Initial Period of War* and *Military Strategy*. Huang Jiansheng and Qi Donghui, "Nanjing budui moujun juban zhanzheng chuqi fan tuxi yanjiu ban" [A Certain Army in Nanjing Holds a Study Group on Countering a Surprise Attack in the Initial Period of a War], *Jiefangjun Bao*, July 5, 1981.

75. Junshi kexue yuan waijun junshi yanjiu bu (trans), *ZhongDong zhanzheng quanshi* [A Complete History of the Wars in the Middle East] (Beijing: Junshi kexue chubanshe, 1985).

76. Roderick MacFarquhar and Michael Schoenhals, *Mao's Last Revolution* (Cambridge, MA: Belknap Press of Harvard University Press, 2006). The Gang of Four was Jiang Qing, Wang Hongwen, Yao Wenyuan, and Zhang Chunqiao.

77. On elite divisions after the Cultural Revolution, Frederick C. Teiwes and Warren Sun, *The End of the Maoist Era: Chinese Politics During the Twilight of the Cultural Revolution, 1972–1976* (Armonk, NY: M. E. Sharpe, 2007), pp. 12–14; Richard Baum, *Burying Mao: Chinese Politics in the Age of Deng Xiaoping* (Princeton, NJ: Princeton University Press, 1994), pp. 27–29; Roderick

MacFarquhar, "The Succession to Mao and the End of Maoism, 1969–82," in Roderick MacFar-quhar, ed., *The Politics of China* (New York: Cambridge University Press, 1993), pp. 278–279.

78. Teiwes and Sun, *The End of the Maoist Era*, p. 489.

79. Ibid., pp. 536–595.

80. Ezra F. Vogel, *Deng Xiaoping and the Transformation of China* (Cambridge, MA: Belknap Press of Harvard University Press, 2011), p. 196. On Deng's return, see also Joseph Torigian, "Prestige, Manipulation, and Coercion: Elite Power Struggles and the Fate of Three Revolutions," PhD dissertation, Department of Political Science, Massachusetts Institute of Technology, 2016.

81. MacFarquhar, "The Succession to Mao and the End of Maoism," p. 315.

82. Wei Guoqing (Director, GPD), Zhang Yanfa (Commander, Air Force), Su Yu, Luo Ruiq-ing, Li Xiannian, Chen Xilian (Beijing MR), and Su Zhenhua (PLAN Commissar). In late 1978, Chen would be tainted by his association with Hua.

83. Nevertheless, Hua did not gain these positions through ordinary party procedures.

84. Vogel, *Deng Xiaoping and the Transformation of China*, p. 170; Teiwes and Sun, *The End of the Maoist Era*, p. 489.

85. Teiwes and Sun, *The End of the Maoist Era*.

86. Frederick C. Teiwes and Warren Sun, "China's New Economic Policy Under Hua Guofeng: Pary Consensus and Party Myths," *China Journal* No. 66 (2011), pp. 1–23; Torigian, "Prestige, Manipulation, and Coercion."

87. For a superb account, see Torigian, "Prestige, Manipulation, and Coercion."

88. Torigian, "Prestige, Manipulation, and Coercion," p. 398.

89. Ibid., pp. 282–457.

90. The Tiananmen Incident refers to the suppression of spontaneous demonstrations that occurred in Tiananmen Square to memorialize Zhou Enlai. The demonstrations were labeled as "counterrevolutionary." Deng, who was then being criticized by Mao and the Gang of Four for rightist deviations, was blamed. See Frederick C. Teiwes and Warren Sun, "The First Tiananmen Incident Revisited: Elite Politics and Crisis Management at the End of the Maoist Era," *Pacific Affairs*, Vol. 77, No. 2 (2004), pp. 211–235.

91. Vogel, *Deng Xiaoping and the Transformation of China*, p. 236; Torigian, "Prestige, Manipu-lation, and Coercion," p. 351.

92. Vogel, *Deng Xiaoping and the Transformation of China*, p. 196.

93. On Deng's decision to attack Vietnam, see Zhang, *Deng Xiaoping's Long War*, pp. 40–66.

94. Fu Xuezheng, "Zai zhongyang junwei bangongting gongzuo de rizi" [Working in the Central Mililitary Commission's Office], *Dangshi tiandi*, No. 1 (2006), p. 14.

95. Geng Biao, Wei Guoqing, Yang Yong (deputy chief of general staff), Wang Ping (com-missar, GLD), Wang Shangrong (deputy chief of the general staff), Liang Biye (deputy director, GPD), Hong Xuezhi (Defense Industry Office), and Xiao Hongda (director, CMC general office). See Xu Ping, "Zhongyang junwei sanshe bangong huiyi" [The Three Office Meetings Established by the CMC], *Wenshi jinghua*, No. 2 (2005), p. 64.

96. Yang Dezhi, Xu Shiyou, Han Xianchu, Yang Yong, and Wang Ping. See Xu Ping, "Jianguo-hou zhongyang junwei renyuan goucheng de bianhua" [The Changing Compostion of the CMC After the Founding of the Country], *Dangshi bolan*, No. 9 (2002), p. 48.

97. In the Kunming MR, Zhang Zhixiu replaced Yang Dezhi as commander so that Yang could become chief of the general staff. In the Guangzhou MR, Wu Kehua replaced Xu Shiyou as commander, who joined the CMC. In the Wuhan MR, Zhang Caiqian replaced Wang Bisheng as commander (whose health was poor) so that Wang could join AMS. In the Jinan MR, Rao Shoukun replaced Zeng Siyu as commander, as Zeng was on the verge of retirement. In the Lanzhou MR, Du Yide replaced Han Xianchu as commander of the Lanzhou MR, who remained on the CMC. Finally, for political reasons, in the Beijing MR, Qin Jiwei replaced Chen Xilian as

commander, who would no longer be active in the PLA because of his ties to Hua Guofeng. In addition, new first political commissars were appointed in the Shenyang, Guangdong, Wuhan, and Kunming MRs.

98. For details on the transfers, see T'ieh Chien, "Reshuffle of Regional Military Commanders in Communist China," *Issues and Studies*, Vol. 16, No. 3 (1980), pp. 1–4; Gerald Segal and Tony Saich, "Quarterly Chronicle and Documentation," *China Quarterly*, No. 83 (1980), p. 616; Gerald Segal and Tony Saich, "Quarterly Chronicle and Documentation," *China Quarterly*, No. 82 (June 1980), pp. 381–382. For analysis of reasons behind the transfers, see Chien, "Reshuffle of Regional Military Commanders in Communist China."

99. Vogel, *Deng Xiaoping and the Transformation of China*, p. 363.

100. Hua would become CCP vice-chairman and was never stripped of party membership. See Liu Jixian, ed., *Ye Jianying nianpu* [A Chronicle of Ye Jianying's Life], Vol. 2 (Beijing: Zhong-yang wenxian chubanshe, 2007), p. 1193. As Torigian shows, Hua may have possessed some latent influence among younger soldiers who joined the party or PLA during the Cultural Revolution. See Torigian, "Prestige, Manipulation, and Coercion."

101. Jiang Tiejun, ed., *Dang de guofang jundui gaige sixiang yanjiu* [A Study of the Party's Thought on National Defense and Army Reform] (Beijing: Junshi kexue chubanshe, 2015), p. 58.

102. Junshi kexue yuan lishi yanjiusuo, *Zhongguo renmin jiefangjun gaige fazhan 30 nian*, p. 25; Shenyang junqu zhengzhibu yanjiu shi, ed., *Shenyang junqu dashiji, 1945–1985* (n.p.: n.p., 1985), pp. 213–214.

103. Shenyang junqu zhengzhibu yanjiu shi, ed., *Shenyang junqu dashiji, 1945–1985*, p. 218.

104. Guo Xiangjie, ed., *Zhang Wannian zhuan (shang)* [Zhang Wannian's Biography] (Beijing: Jiefangjun chubanshe, 2011), p. 399.

105. Xie Hainan, Yang Zufa and Yang Jianhua, *Yang Dezhi yi sheng*, p. 313.

106. Ibid.

107. Zhang Zhen, *Zhang Zhen huiyilu (xia)*, p. 193.

108. Ibid.

109. Ibid., p. 194.

110. Ibid., pp. 193,198.

111. Xie Hainan, Yang Zufa and Yang Jianhua, *Yang Dezhi yi sheng*, p. 312.

112. Ibid., p. 314.

113. Li Yuan, *Li Yuan huiyilu* [Li Yuan's Memoir] (Beijing: Jiefangjun chubanshe, 2009), p. 364.

114. Zhang Zhen, *Zhang Zhen huiyilu (xia)*, p. 200.

115. Ibid.; Yang Dezhi, "Xinshiqi zongcanmoubu di junshi gongzuo" [The General Staff Department's Military Work in the New Period], in Xu Huizi, ed., *Zongcan moubu: Huiyi shiliao* [General Staff Department: Recollections and Historical Materials] (Beijing: Jiefangjun chubanshe, 1995), p. 655.

116. Zhang Zhen, *Zhang Zhen huiyilu (xia)*, p. 198.

117. Ibid.

118. Ibid., p. 197.

119. Ibid., p. 199.

120. Ibid.

121. Yang Dezhi, "Xinshiqi zongcanmoubu di junshi gongzuo," p. 656.

122. Song Shilun, *Song Shilun junshi wenxuan*, pp. 242–245.

123. The letter is not mentioned in Yang Dezhi's biography or Zhang Zhen's memoir.

124. Mu Junjie, ed., *Song Shilun zhuan*, p. 602.

125. Zhang Zhen, *Zhang Zhen huiyilu (xia)*, p. 201; Xie Hainan, Yang Zufa and Yang Jianhua, *Yang Dezhi yi sheng*, p. 314.

126. Liu Yongzhi, ed., *Zongcan moubu dashiji*, p. 739.

127. Xie Hainan, Yang Zufa and Yang Jianhua, *Yang Dezhi yi sheng*, p. 313.

128. Ibid., p. 314.

129. Ibid., p. 315.

130. Song Shilun, *Song Shilun junshi wenxuan*, p. 244; Zhang Weiming, *Huabei dayanxi*, p. 38.

131. Song Shilun, *Song Shilun junshi wenxuan*, p. 244.

132. Deng Xiaoping, *Deng Xiaoping junshi wenxuan*, Vol. 3, p. 177.

133. Ye Jianying, *Ye Jianying junshi wenxuan*, p. 719.

134. Xie Hainan, Yang Zufa and Yang Jianhua, *Yang Dezhi yi sheng*, p. 314.

135. Zhang Weiming, *Huabei dayanxi*, p. 36.

136. Ibid.

137. Ye Jianying, *Ye Jianying junshi wenxuan*, p. 422.

138. Song Shilun, *Song Shilun junshi wenxuan*, p. 244. Also, see Zhang Zhen, *Zhang Zhen huiyilu (xia)*, pp. 197–198.

139. Shi Jiazhu and Cui Changfa, "60 nian renmin haijun jianshe zhidao sixiang de fengfu he fazhan" [The Enrichment and Development of Guiding Thought on Navy Building in the Past 60 Years], *Junshi lishi*, No. 3 (2009), p. 24. For an excellent overview of China's naval strategies since 1949, see Nan Li, "The Evolution of China's Naval Strategy and Capabilities: From 'Near Coast' and 'Near Seas' to 'Far Seas,'" *Asian Security*, Vol. 5, No. 2 (2009), pp. 144–169.

140. Deng Xiaoping, *Deng Xiaoping lun guofang he jundui jianshe*, p. 57.

141. Wu Dianqing, *Haijun: Zongshu dashiji* [Navy: Summary and Chronology] (Beijing: Jiefangjun chubanshe, 2006), p. 175.

142. Liu Huaqing, *Liu Huaqing huiyilu* [Liu Huaqing's Memoirs] (Beijing: Jiefangjun chubanshe, 2004), p. 436. On the link to the 1980 strategic guideline, see Wu Dianqing, *Haijun*, pp. 171, 188–189.

143. For a detailed summary of the report, see Jiang Weimin, ed., *Liu Huaqing nianpu* [A Chronicle of Liu Huaqing's Life], Vol. 2 (Beijing: Jiefangjun chubanshe, 2016), p. 688–692. It is unclear, however, when the CMC approved the report.

144. Liu Huaqing, *Liu Huaqing huiyilu*, p. 438.

145. Bernard D. Cole, "The PLA Navy and 'Active Defense,'" in Stephen J. Flanagan and Michael E. Marti, eds., *The People's Liberation Army and China in Transition* (Washington, DC: National Defense University Press, 2003), pp. 129–138.

146. O'Dowd, *Chinese Military Strategy*, pp. 45–55; Zhang, *Deng Xiaoping's Long War*, pp. 67–77.

147. On various estimates, see O'Dowd, *Chinese Military Strategy*, p. 3; Chen, *China's War with Vietnam, 1979*, pp. 88, 103.

148. Zhang, *Deng Xiaoping's Long War*, p. 119.

149. The one caveat would be that China's best units had remained deployed in the north to defend against the Soviet threat.

150. O'Dowd, *Chinese Military Strategy*, pp. 28–30, 111–121; Zhang, *Deng Xiaoping's Long War*, pp. 134–137.

151. Deng Xiaoping, *Deng Xiaoping junshi wenxuan*, Vol. 3, p. 28.

152. Zhang, *Deng Xiaoping's Long War*, p. 59.

153. The sources used by Zhang and O'Dowd contain these assessments.

154. Yang Zhiyuan, "Wojun bianxiu zuozhan tiaoling de chuangxin fazhan ji qishi," p. 113.

155. Ibid. On the challenges of developing operational doctrine during this period, see Chen Li, "Operational Idealism: Doctrine Development of the Chinese People's Liberation Army under Soviet Threat, 1969–1989," *Journal of Strategic Studies*, Vol. 40, No. 5 (2017), pp. 663–695.

156. Yang Zhiyuan, "Wojun bianxiu zuozhan tiaoling de chuangxin fazhan ji qishi," pp. 113–114.

157. Ibid., p. 113.

158. Zou Baoyi and Liu Jinsheng, "Xinyidai hecheng jundui douzheng tiaoling kaishi shixing" [Use of New Generation Combined Army Combat Regulations Has Begun], *Jiefangjun bao*, June 7, 1988.

159. Ren Jian, *Zuozhan tiaoling gailun* [An Introduction to Operations Regulations] (Beijing: Junshi kexue chubanshe, 2016), p. 47.

160. Liu Yixin, Wu Xiang and Xie Wenxin, eds., *Xiandai zhanzheng yu lujun* [Modern Warfare and the Ground Forces] (Beijing: Jiefangjun chubanshe, 2005), p. 479.

161. Ren Jian, *Zuozhan tiaoling gailun*, p. 47.

162. Mu Junjie, ed., *Song Shilun zhuan*, p. 516.

163. Song Shilun, *Song Shilun junshi wenxuan*, pp. 291–292.

164. Mu Junjie, ed., *Song Shilun zhuan*, p. 518.

165. Gao Rui, ed., *Zhanlue xue*.

166. Song Shilun, *Song Shilun junshi wenxuan*, p. 417.

167. M. Taylor Fravel, "The Evolution of China's Military Strategy: Comparing the 1987 and 1999 Editions of *Zhanlue Xue*," in David M. Finkelstein and James Mulvenon, eds., *The Revolution in Doctrinal Affairs: Emerging Trends in the Operational Art of the Chinese People's Liberation Army* (Alexandria, VA: Center for Naval Analyses, 2005) p. 89.

168. On Deng's return to power in 1975, see Teiwes and Sun, *The End of the Maoist Era*, pp. 178–304; Vogel, *Deng Xiaoping and the Transformation of China*, pp. 91–157.

169. Jiang Tiejun, ed., *Dang de guofang jundui gaige sixiang yanjiu*, p. 58.

170. Ibid.

171. Ibid., p. 68.

172. All figures for China's defense expenditure and national budget come from China Data Online, http://www.chinadataonline.org.

173. He Qizong, Ren Haiquan and Jiang Qianlin, "Deng Xiaoping yu jundui gaige" [Deng Xiaoping and Military Reform], *Junshi lishi*, No. 4 (2014), p. 2.

174. Deng Xiaoping, *Deng Xiaoping junshi wenxuan*, Vol. 3, p. 169.

175. Junshi kexue yuan lishi yanjiusuo, *Zhongguo renmin jiefangjun gaige fazhan 30 nian*, p. 25.

176. Ibid.

177. Deng Xiaoping, *Deng Xiaoping junshi wenxuan*, Vol. 3, p. 168.

178. Junshi kexue yuan lishi yanjiusuo, *Zhongguo renmin jiefangjun gaige fazhan 30 nian*, p. 26; Yang Dezhi, "Xinshiqi zongcanmoubu de junshi gongzuo," p. 651; Ding Wei and Wei Xu, "20 shiji 80 niandai renmin jiefangjun tizhi gaige, jingjian zhengbian de huigu yu sikao," p. 53.

179. Junshi kexue yuan lishi yanjiusuo, *Zhongguo renmin jiefangjun gaige fazhan 30 nian*, pp. 26–27.

180. Jiang Tiejun, ed., *Dang de guofang jundui gaige sixiang yanjiu*, p. 59.

181. Junshi kexue yuan lishi yanjiusuo, *Zhongguo renmin jiefangjun gaige fazhan 30 nian*, p. 28; Ding Wei and Wei Xu, "20 shiji 80 niandai renmin jiefangjun tizhi gaige, jingjian zhengbian de huigu yu sikao," p. 57.

182. Junshi kexue yuan lishi yanjiusuo, *Zhongguo renmin jiefangjun gaige fazhan 30 nian*, p. 28; Ding Wei and Wei Xu, "20 shiji 80 niandai renmin jiefangjun tizhi gaige, jingjian zhengbian de huigu yu sikao," p. 57.

183. Junshi kexue yuan lishi yanjiusuo, *Zhongguo renmin jiefangjun gaige fazhan 30 nian*, pp. 34–36.

184. Yang Dezhi, "Xinshiqi zongcanmoubu de junshi gongzuo," p. 652.

185. Ibid.

186. Ibid.

187. Liu Yongzhi, ed., *Zongcan moubu dashiji*, p. 785.

188. Hong Baoshou, "Zhongguo renmin jiefangjun 70 nianlai gaige fazhan de huigu yu sikao" [Reviewing and Reflecting on the Reform and Development of the Chinese People's Liberation

Army over 70 years], *Zhongguo junshi kexue*, No. 3 (1999), p. 23. Other sources claim that 1.2 million were cut, bringing the size of the force to just over 4 million. See Ding Wei and Wei Xu, "20 shiji 80 niandai renmin jiefangjun tizhi gaige, jingjian zhengbian de huigu yu sikao," p. 54.

189. Junshi kexue yuan lishi yanjiusuo, *Zhongguo renmin jiefangjun gaige fazhan 30 nian*, p. 28; Ding Wei and Wei Xu, "20 shiji 80 niandai renmin jiefangjun tizhi gaige, jingjian zhengbian de huigu yu sikao," p. 54.

190. Ding Wei and Wei Xu, "20 shiji 80 niandai renmin jiefangjun tizhi gaige, jingjian zhengbian de huigu yu sikao," p. 57.

191. By 1980, the railway corps had 416,000 troops organized into three command headquarters, fifteen divisions, three independent regiments, two academies, and one research institute. By the late 1970s, the engineering corps had 496,000 troops organized into ten army-level command headquarters, thirty-two division-level contingents, and five division-level academies. In 1981, the engineering corps fell to 340,000. See Junshi kexue yuan lishi yanjiusuo, *Zhongguo renmin jiefangjun gaige fazhan 30 nian*, pp. 34–36.

192. Ding Wei and Wei Xu, "20 shiji 80 niandai renmin jiefangjun tizhi gaige, jingjian zhengbian de huigu yu sikao," p. 54.

193. Junshi kexue yuan lishi yanjiusuo, *Zhongguo renmin jiefangjun gaige fazhan 30 nian*, pp. 28–29.

194. Yang Shangkun, *Yang Shangkun huiyilu* [Yang Shangkun's Memoirs] (Beijing: Zhongyang wenxian chubanshe, 2001), p. 360.

195. Deng Xiaoping, *Deng Xiaoping junshi wenxuan*, Vol. 3, p. 186.

196. Junshi kexue yuan lishi yanjiusuo, *Zhongguo renmin jiefangjun gaige fazhan 30 nian*, p. 92.

197. Ibid., p. 93; Lujun di sanshiba jituanjun junshi bianshen weiyuanhui, *Lujun di sanshiba jituanjun junshi* [A History of the Thirty-Eighth Group Army] (Beijing: Jiefangjun wenyi chubanshe, 1993), p. 664.

198. Ding Wei and Wei Xu, "20 shiji 80 niandai renmin jiefangjun tizhi gaige, jingjian zhengbian de huigu yu sikao," p. 55.

199. Zhang Zhen, *Zhang Zhen huiyilu (xia)*, p. 251.

200. Yuan Wei and Zhang Zhuo, eds., *Zhongguo junxiao fazhan shi*, p. 825.

201. Ibid., p. 826.

202. Shou Xiaosong, ed., *Zhongguo renmin jiefangjun de 80 nian*, p. 411.

203. Guo Xiangjie, ed., *Zhang Wannian zhuan*, p. 399. Zhang Wannian would become chief of the general staff in 1992 and vice-chairman of the CMC from 1995 to 2002.

204. Ibid.

205. Zhang Zhen, *Zhang Zhen junshi wenxuan*, Vol. 2, p. 217.

206. Ibid.

207. Zhang Zhen, *Zhang Zhen huiyilu (shang)* [Zhang Zhen's Memoirs] (Beijing: Jiefangjun chubanshe, 2003), p. 244. The PLA's second training program had been issued in 1978. However, the purpose of this program was "primarily to restore the normal training order" that had been disrupted by the Cultural Revolution. See Liu Fengan, "Goujian xinxihua tiaojianxia junshi xunlian xin tixi" [Establishing a New System for Military Training Under Informatized Conditions], *Jiefangjun Bao*, August 1, 2008, p. 3.

208. "Zong canmoubu pizhun banfa xunlian dagang."

209. Zhang Zhen, *Zhang Zhen junshi wenxuan*, Vol. 2, p. 199.

210. Ibid., p. 195.

211. Yuan Wei and Zhang Zhuo, eds., *Zhongguo junxiao fazhan shi*, p. 876.

212. Li Dianren, ed., *Guofang daxue 80 nian dashi jiyao* [Record of Important Events in Eighty Years of the National Defense University] (Beijing: Guofang daxue chubanshe, 2007).

213. Zhang Zhen, *Zhang Zhen huiyilu (xia)*, p. 206.

214. Ibid., p. 212.

215. Junshi kexue yuan lishi yanjiusuo, *Zhongguo renmin jiefangjun gaige fazhan 30 nian*, p. 43.

216. Ibid. For a detailed discussion, albeit from the "reportage literature," see Zhang Weiming, *Huabei dayanxi: Zhongguo zuida junshi yanxi jishi* [North China Exercise: The Record of China's Largest Military Exercise] (Beijing: Jiefangjun chubanshe, 2007).

217. Xie Hainan, Yang Zufa and Yang Jianhua, *Yang Dezhi yi sheng*, p. 322.

218. Zhang Zhen, *Zhang Zhen huiyilu (xia)*, p. 210.

219. Xie Hainan, Yang Zufa and Yang Jianhua, *Yang Dezhi yi sheng*, p. 321.

220. Zhang Zhen, *Zhang Zhen huiyilu (xia)*, p. 210.

221. Ibid., p. 211.

222. Deng Xiaoping, *Deng Xiaoping junshi wenxuan*, Vol. 3, p. 205.

223. Zhang Zhen, *Zhang Zhen huiyilu (xia)*, p. 212; Xie Hainan, Yang Zufa and Yang Jianhua, *Yang Dezhi yi sheng*, p. 322.

224. Zhang Zhen, *Zhang Zhen huiyilu (xia)*, p. 208; Xie Hainan, Yang Zufa and Yang Jianhua, *Yang Dezhi yi sheng*, p. 321.

225. Zhang Zhen, *Zhang Zhen huiyilu (xia)*, p. 213.

226. Junshi kexue yuan lishi yanjiusuo, *Zhongguo renmin jiefangjun gaige fazhan 30 nian*, p. 42.

227. Ibid., p. 43.

228. Zhang Zhen, *Zhang Zhen huiyilu (xia)*, p. 213; Junshi kexue yuan lishi yanjiusuo, *Zhongguo renmin jiefangjun gaige fazhan 30 nian*, p. 43.

229. Leng Rong and Wang Zuoling, eds., *Deng Xiaoping nianpu, 1975–1997* [A Chronicle of Deng Xiaoping's Life, 1975–1997], Vol. 2 (Beijing: Zhongyang wenxian chubanshe, 2004), p. 802.

230. Yang Dezhi, "Xinshiqi zongcanmoubu de junshi gongzuo," p. 654.

231. He Zhengwen, "Caijun baiwan jiqi qianqianhouhou" [The Whole Story of Reducing One Million], in Xu Huizi, ed., *Zongcan moubu: Huiyi shiliao* [General Staff Department: Recollections and Historical Materials], (Beijing: Jiefangjun chubanshe, 1995), p. 726.

232. Zong Wen, "Baiwan da caijun: Deng Xiaoping de qiangjun zhilu" [Great One Million Downsizing: Deng Xiaoping's Road to a Strong Army], *Wenshi bolan*, No. 10 (2015), p. 6; Xie Hainan, Yang Zufa and Yang Jianhua, *Yang Dezhi yi sheng*, pp. 343–344.

233. Zong Wen, "Baiwan da caijun," p. 6.

234. Xie Hainan, Yang Zufa and Yang Jianhua, *Yang Dezhi yi sheng*, p. 344.

235. Deng Xiaoping, *Deng Xiaoping junshi wenxuan*, Vol. 3, p. 265.

236. Ibid., p. 266.

237. Ibid.

238. Ibid., p. 267.

239. Yang Dezhi, "Xinshiqi zongcanmoubu de junshi gongzuo," p. 653.

240. Xie Hainan, Yang Zufa and Yang Jianhua, *Yang Dezhi yi sheng*, pp. 345–346.

241. Ibid, p. 346.

242. Shou Xiaosong, ed., *Zhongguo renmin jiefangjun de 80 nian*, p. 460; Junshi kexue yuan lishi yanjiusuo, *Zhongguo renmin jiefangjun gaige fazhan 30 nian*, p. 43.

243. Shou Xiaosong, ed., *Zhongguo renmin jiefangjun de 80 nian*, p. 460; Junshi kexue yuan lishi yanjiusuo, *Zhongguo renmin jiefangjun gaige fazhan 30 nian*, p. 43.

244. Deng Xiaoping, *Deng Xiaoping junshi wenxuan*, Vol. 3, p. 273.

245. Ibid., p. 274.

246. Pan Hong, "1985 nian baiwan dacaijun" [The One Million Downsizing in 1985], *Bainian chao*, No. 12 (2015), p. 44; Ding Wei and Wei Xu, "20 shiji 80 niandai renmin jiefangjun tizhi gaige, jingjian zhengbian de huigu yu sikao," p. 55.

247. Hong Baoshou, "Zhongguo renmin jiefangjun 70 nianlai gaige fazhan de huigu yu sikao," p. 23.

248. Ding Wei and Wei Xu, "20 shiji 80 niandai renmin jiefangjun tizhi gaige, jingjian zhengbian de huigu yu sikao," p. 55.

249. Ibid. Specifically, the Lanzhou MR absorbed the Urumqi MR, the Chengdu MR absorbed the Kunming MR, the Nanjing MR absorbed the Fuzhou MR, the Jinan MR and Guangzhou MRs absorbed parts of the Wuhan MR, and the Beijing MR and Shenyang MR stayed the same.

250. Ibid.

251. Ibid.

252. Yao Yunzhu, "The Evolution of Military Doctrine of the Chinese PLA from 1985 to 1995," *Korean Journal of Defense Analysis*, Vol. 7, No. 2 (1995), p. 57. On these debates, see Nan Li, "The PLA's Evolving Warfighting Doctrine, Strategy and Tactics, 1985–95: A Chinese Perspective," *China Quarterly*, No. 146 (1996), pp. 443–463.

253. Huang Yingxu, "Zhongguo jiji fangyu zhanlue fangzhen de queli yu tiaozheng" [The Establishment and Adjustment of China's Strategic Guideline of Active Defense], *Zhongguo junshi kexue*, Vol. 15, No. 1 (2002), p. 63.

254. Noted AMS strategist Mi Zhenyu outlined many of the issues a new strategy would need to address in a 1988 article in *Military Arts*. See Mi Zhenyu, *Zhanzheng yu zhanlue lilun tanyan* [Exploration of War and Strategic Theory] (Beijing: Jiefangjun chubanshe, 2003), pp. 269–286.

255. Qi Changming, "Jiaqiang zhanlue yanjiu, shenhua jundui gaige" [Deepen Military Reform, Strengthen Research on Strategy], *Jiefangjun Bao*, May 8, 1988; Gu Boliang and Liu Guohua, "Wojun zhanyi xunlian chengji xianzu" [Results of Our Army's Campaign Training], *Jiefangjun Bao*, December 26, 1988.

256. Zhang Zhen, *Zhang Zhen huiyilu (shang)*, p. 332.

257. Han Huaizhi, *Han Huaizhi lun junshi*, pp. 636–637; Gu Boliang and Liu Guohua, "Wojun zhanyi xunlian chengji xianzu."

258. Kong Fanjun, *Chi Haotian zhuan* [Chi Haotian's Biography] (Beijing: Jiefangjun chubanshe, 2009), p. 324.

259. Chen Zhou, "Shilun Zhongguo weihu heping yu fazhan de fangyuxing guofang zhengce" [An Analysis of China's Defensive National Defense Policy for Maintaining Peace and Development], *Zhongguo junshi kexue*, Vol. 20, No. 6 (2007), p. 2; Bi Wenbo, "Lun Zhongguo xinshiqi junshi zhanlue siwei (shang)" [On China's Military Strategic Thought in the New Period], *Junshi lishi yanjiu*, No. 2 (2004), p. 45.

260. Zhang Yining, Cai Renzhao and Sun Kejia, "Gaige kaifang sanshi nian Zhongguo junshi zhanlue de chuangxin fazhan" [Innovative Development of China's Military Strategy in Thirty Years of Reform and Opening], *Xuexi shibao*, December 9, 2008, p. 7.

261. Chen Zhou, "Zhuanjia jiedu Zhongguo de junshi zhanlue baipishu" [Expert Unpacks the White Paper China's Military Strategy], *Guofang* No. 6 (2015), p. 18; Zhang Yang, ed., *Jiakuai tuijin guofang he jundui xiandaihua* [Accelerate and Promote National Defense and Armed Forces Modernization] (Beijing: Renmin chubanshe, 2015), p. 93. The reference to "plan and manage the oceans" was included following China's occupation of six disputed reefs in the South China Sea earlier that year, in March 1988, and the need to defend its new possessions.

262. Li Deyi, "Mao Zedong jiji fangyu zhanlue sixiang de lishi fazhan yu sikao" [The Historical Development of and Reflections on Mao Zedong's Strategic Thinking about Active Defense], *Junshi lishi*, No. 4 (2002), p. 52; Peng Guangqian, *Zhongguo junshi zhanlue wenti yanjiu* [Research on Issues in China's Military Strategy] (Beijing: Jiefangjun chubanshe, 2006), pp. 96–97.

263. On these conflicts, see Fravel, *Strong Borders, Secure Nation*, pp. 267–299; Zhang, *Deng Xiaoping's Long War*, pp. 141–168.

264. Fravel, *Strong Borders, Secure Nation*, pp. 199–201.

265. Bi Wenbo, "Lun Zhongguo xinshiqi junshi zhanlue siwei (shang)," p. 45.

266. Yang Shangkun, *Yang Shangkun huiyilu*, pp. 366–367.

267. Zou Baoyi and Liu Jinsheng, "Xinyidai hecheng jundui douzheng tiaoling kaishi shixing."

268. Yang Shangkun, *Yang Shangkun huiyilu*, pp. 366–367.

269. Su Ruozhou, "Quanjun jinnian an xin xunlian dagang shixun" [This Year the Entire Army Will Train According to the New Training Program], *Jiefangjun bao*, February 15, 1990.

Chapter 6. The 1993 Strategy

1. Jiang Zemin, *Jiang Zemin wenxuan* [Jiang Zemin's Selected Works], Vol. 1 (Beijing: Renmin chubanshe, 2006), p. 285.

2. Ibid., p. 286.

3. Ibid., p. 285.

4. Ibid., p. 289.

5. Ren Jian, *Zuozhan tiaoling gailun* [An Introduction to Operations Regulations] (Beijing: Junshi kexue chubanshe, 2016), p. 47.

6. Jiang Zemin, *Jiang Zemin wenxuan*, Vol. 1, p. 290.

7. Ibid. On strategic guiding thought, see Ren Jian, *Zuozhan tiaoling gailun*, p. 49.

8. Jiang Zemin, *Jiang Zemin wenxuan*, Vol. 1, p. 290.

9. Liu Huaqing, *Liu Huaqing huiyilu* [Liu Huaqing's Memoirs] (Beijing: Jiefangjun chubanshe, 2004), p. 645.

10. Peng Guangqian and Yao Youzhi, eds., *Zhanlue xue* [The Science of Military Strategy] (Beijing: Junshi kexue chubanshe, 2001), pp. 453–454.

11. Dai Yifang, ed., *Junshi xue yanjiu huigu yu zhanwang* [Reflections and Prospects for Military Studies] (Beijing: Junshi kexue chubanshe, 1995), pp. 76–83.

12. This paragraph draws on Yang Zhiyuan, "Wojun bianxiu zuozhan tiaoling de chuangxin fazhan ji qishi" [The Innovative Development and Implications of Our Army's Compilation and Revision of Operations Regulations], *Zhongguo junshi kexue*, No. 6 (2009), pp. 112–118.

13. Dennis Blasko, *The Chinese Army Today: Tradition and Transformation for the 21st Century* (New York: Routledge, 2006), p. 22.

14. Jiang Zemin, *Lun guofang yu jundui jianshe* [On National Defense and Army Building] (Beijing: Jiefangjun chubanshe, 2002), p. 424.

15. Ibid., p. 78.

16. Zhang Jian and Ren Yanjun, "Xinyidai junshi xunlian dagang banfa" [New Generation Training Program Issued], *Jiefangjun Bao*, December 12, 1995.

17. Dong Wenjiu and Su Ruozhou, "Xin de junshi xunlian yu kaohe dagang pinfa" [Promulgation of the New Military Training and Evaluation Program], *Jiefangjun bao*, August 10, 2001.

18. On training in the 1990s and beyond, see Blasko, *The Chinese Army Today*, pp. 144–170; David Shambaugh, *Modernizing China's Military: Progress, Problems, and Prospects* (Berkeley, CA: University of California Press, 2002), pp. 94–107.

19. Blasko, *The Chinese Army Today*, pp. 152–153.

20. For previous analysis of Chinese views of the Gulf War, see Harlan W. Jencks, "Chinese Evaluations of 'Desert Storm': Implications for PRC Security," *Journal of East Asian Affairs*, Vol. 6, No. 2 (1992), pp. 447–477; Paul H. B. Godwin, "From Continent to Periphery: PLA Doctrine, Strategy, and Capabilities towards 2000," *China Quarterly*, No. 146 (1996), pp. 464–487; Dean Cheng, "Chinese Lessons from the Gulf Wars," in Andrew Scobell, David Lai and Roy Kamphausen, eds., *Chinese Lessons from Other Peoples' Wars* (Carlisle, PA: Strategic Studies Institute, Army War College, 2011), pp. 153–200; Shambaugh, *Modernizing China's Military*, pp. 71–77.

21. "The Operation Desert Shield/Desert Storm Timeline," US Department of Defense, August 8, 2000, http://archive.defense.gov/news/newsarticle.aspx?id=45404.

22. Jencks, "Chinese Evaluations of 'Desert Storm,'" pp. 447–477.

23. Liu Huaqing, *Liu Huaqing junshi wenxuan* [Liu Huaqing's Selected Works on Military Affairs], Vol. 2, (Beijing: Jiefangjun chubanshe, 2008), p. 127.

24. Ibid., p. 129. The GSD had already sent researchers to the Persian Gulf to assess the situation first-hand (thought it is not known where they went).

25. Ibid., p. 128.

26. Kong Fanjun, *Chi Haotian zhuan* [Chi Haotian's Biography] (Beijing: Jiefangjun chubanshe, 2009), p. 326.

27. Zhang Zhen, *Zhang Zhen junshi wenxuan* [Zhang Zhen's Selected Works on Military Affairs], Vol. 2 (Beijing: Jiefangjun chubanshe, 2005), p. 521.

28. Jiang Zemin, *Lun guofang yu jundui jianshe*, p. 32.

29. Liu Huaqing, *Liu Huaqing junshi wenxuan*, Vol. 2, p. 139.

30. Liu Huaqing, *Liu Huaqing huiyilu*, p. 610.

31. Chi Haotian, *Chi Haotian junshi wenxuan* [Chi Haotian's Selected Works on Military Affairs] (Beijing: Jiefangjun chubanshe, 2009), p. 282.

32. Zhang Zhen, *Zhang Zhen junshi wenxuan*, Vol. 2, p. 469.

33. Ibid., p. 470.

34. Jiang Zemin, *Lun guofang yu jundui jianshe*, p. 32.

35. Liu Huaqing, *Liu Huaqing huiyilu*, p. 610.

36. Jiang Zemin, *Jiang Zemin wenxuan*, Vol. 1, p. 145.

37. Zhang Zhen, *Zhang Zhen junshi wenxuan*, Vol. 2, p. 521.

38. Junshi kexue yuan lishi yanjiu bu, *Haiwan zhanzheng quanshi* [A Complete History of the Gulf War] (Beijing: Junshi kexue chubanshe, 2000). For the 1991 study, see Liu Yichang, Wang Wenchang, and Wang Xianchen, eds., *Haiwan zhanzheng* [The Gulf War] (Beijing: Junshi kexue chubanshe, 1991).

39. Junshi kexue yuan lishi yanjiu bu, *Haiwan zhanzheng quanshi*, p. 512.

40. Ibid., p. 466.

41. Kong Fanjun, *Chi Haotian zhuan*, p. 327.

42. Joseph Fewsmith, *China Since Tiananmen: The Politics of Transition* (Cambridge: Cambridge University Press, 2001), pp. 21–74.

43. Ibid., p. 33.

44. On Zhao's role and the decision-making behind the implementation of martial law in 1989, see Joseph Torigian, "Prestige, Manipulation, and Coercion: Elite Power Struggles and the Fate of Three Revolutions," PhD dissertation, Department of Political Science, Massachusetts Institute of Technology, 2016.

45. Joseph Fewsmith, "Reaction, Resurgence, and Succession: Chinese Politics Since Tiananmen," in Roderick MacFarquhar, ed., *The Politics of China: Sixty Years of The People's Republic of China* (New York: Cambridge University Press, 2011), p. 468.

46. Richard Baum, *Burying Mao: Chinese Politics in the Age of Deng Xiaoping* (Princeton, NJ: Princeton University Press, 1994), p. 319.

47. Ibid., p. 294.

48. Ibid., pp. 302–303.

49. Fewsmith, *China Since Tiananmen*, pp. 37–38.

50. Ibid., pp. 38–40; Baum, *Burying Mao*, p. 322.

51. Baum, *Burying Mao*, p. 322.

52. Ibid.

53. Ibid.

54. Fewsmith, *China Since Tiananmen*, pp. 44–45.

55. Ibid., pp. 45–46.

56. Ibid., pp. 55–56.

57. Ibid., pp. 57–58.

58. Baum, *Burying Mao*, p. 334; Fewsmith, *China Since Tiananmen*, p. 53.

59. Baum, *Burying Mao*, p. 334.

60. Ibid., p. 338.

61. Shambaugh, *Modernizing China's Military*, pp. 26–27.

62. David Shambaugh, "The Soldier and the State in China: The Political Work System in the People's Liberation Army," *China Quarterly*, No. 127 (1991), p. 552.

63. Ibid.

64. Yang Shangkun reportedly opposed the move, perhaps harboring ambitions of becoming chairman himself. See Baum, *Burying Mao*, p. 301.

65. Michael D. Swaine, *The Military & Political Succession in China: Leadership, Institutions, Beliefs* (Santa Monica, CA: RAND, 1992), p. 63.

66. Liu Huaqing, a proponent of military modernization, was also named as a vice-chairman, providing a modicum of balance against the Yangs.

67. Robert F. Ash, "Quarterly Documentation," *China Quarterly*, No. 131 (September 1992), p. 900.

68. Ibid., pp. 879–885. Also, see Shou Xiaosong, ed., *Zhongguo renmin jiefangjun bashi nian dashiji* [A Chronology of Eighty Years of the Chinese People's Liberation Army] (Beijing: Junshi kexue chubanshe, 2007), p. 482.

69. For a definitive account of the campaign, see Shambaugh, "The Soldier and the State in China," p. 559.

70. Ibid., pp. 558–559.

71. Ibid., p. 565.

72. Shambaugh, *Modernizing China's Military*, p. 29.

73. Swaine, *The Military & Political Succession in China*, p. 145.

74. Baum, *Burying Mao*, p. 306.

75. Dennis J. Blasko, Philip T. Klapakis and John F. Corbett, "Training Tomorrow's PLA: A Mixed Bag of Tricks," *China Quarterly*, No. 146 (1996), pp. 488–524.

76. For a detailed account for the planning of the Eighth Five-Year plan for the military, see Liu Huaqing, *Liu Huaqing huiyilu*, pp. 580–590; Kong Fanjun, *Chi Haotian zhuan*, pp. 342–346.

77. Liu Huaqing, *Liu Huaqing huiyilu*, pp. 580–589.

78. Ibid., p. 589.

79. Yuan Dejin, "30 nian Zhongguo jundui gaige lunlue" [30 Years of China's Military Reforms], *Junshi lishi yanjiu*, No. 4 (2008), p. 4.

80. Kong Fanjun, *Chi Haotian zhuan*, pp. 342–343. One of the important reforms was creating the Branch Department (*bingzhong bu*) by merging the artillery, armor, engineering, chemical defense, and army aviation branch departments.

81. Liu Huaqing, *Liu Huaqing huiyilu*, p. 589.

82. Shambaugh, "The Soldier and the State in China," p. 564.

83. Military elders who opposed the Yangs include Yang Dezhi, Chen Xilian, Geng Biao, Wu Xiuquan, Yang Chengwu, Zhang Aiping, and Hong Xuezhi, among others. Active-duty leaders who pushed for Yang Baibing's removal include Qin Jiwei (defense minister), Zhang Zhen (NDU president), and Chi Haotian (chief of the general staff). Li Feng, "Military Elders and Generals in Active Service Took Joint Action to Write a Letter to Deng Xiaoping Demanding the Ouster of the Yang Brothers from Office," *Ching Chi Jih Pao*, October 21, 1992, Foreign Broadcast Information Service (FBIS) #HK2110060592; Lo Ping, "The Inside Story of the Reduction of Yang Baibing's Military Power," *Cheng Ming*, No. 181, November 1992, pp. 6–8, FBIS #HK0411121992.

84. Fewsmith, *China Since Tiananmen*, p. 58.

85. Ibid., pp. 59–60.

86. Lu Tianyi, "Jundui yao dui gaige kaifang fazhan jingji 'baojia huhang'" [The Military Must 'Protect and Escort' Reform and Opening and Developing the Economy], *Jiefangjun Bao*, March 22, 1992.

87. Fewsmith, *China Since Tiananmen*, p. 60.

88. Yang Baibing, "Jianfuqi wei guojia gaige he jianshe baojia huhang de chonggao shiming" [Shoulder the Lofty Goal of Protecting and Escorting National Reform and Development], *Jiefangjun Bao*, July 29, 1992.

89. "Central Military Commission Organizes Visit to Shenzhen, Zhuhai for Senior Military Officers," *Ming Pao*, March 11, 1992, p. 2, in FBIS #HK1103074792.

90. For details, see Baum, *Burying Mao*; Fewsmith, *China Since Tiananmen*.

91. Fewsmith, *China Since Tiananmen*, p. 66.

92. Yu Yongbo became GPD director, while Zhou Wenyuan became deputy commissar of the Shenyang Military Region and Li Jinai became deputy commissar of COSTIND.

93. Willy Wo-Lap Lam, *China after Deng Xiaoping: The Power Struggle in Beijing since Tiananmen* (Hong Kong: P A Professional Consultants, 1995), pp. 213–214.

94. Liu Huaqing, *Liu Huaqing huiyilu*, p. 630.

95. Jiang Zemin, *Jiang Zemin wenxuan*, Vol. 1, p. 489.

96. Guo Xiangjie, ed., *Zhang Wannian zhuan (xia)* [Zhang Wannian's Biography] (Beijing: Jiefangjun chubanshe, 2011), pp. 4–5.

97. Jiang Zemin, *Lun guofang yu jundui jianshe*, p. 74.

98. As paraphrased in Wu Quanxu, *Kuayue shiji de biange: Qinli junshi xunlian lingyu guanche xin shiqi junshi zhanlue fangzhen shi er nian* [Change across the Century: Twelve Years of Personal Experience Implementing the Military Strategic Guideline in Military Training] (Beijing: Junshi kexue chubanshe, 2005), pp. 9–10.

99. Jiang Zemin, *Lun guofang yu jundui jianshe*, p. 21.

100. When the seminar was held, Liu Huaqing did not participate because he was conducting an inspection tour in Guangxi with Premier Li Peng. See Jiang Weimin, ed., *Liu Huaqing nianpu* [A Chronicle of Liu Huaqing's Life], Vol. 2 (Beijing: Jiefangjun chubanshe, 2016), pp. 1003–1006.

101. Guo Xiangjie, ed., *Zhang Wannian zhuan*, p. 60.

102. Ibid., p. 62.

103. Zhang Zhen, *Zhang Zhen huiyilu (shang)* [Zhang Zhen's Memoirs] (Beijing: Jiefangjun chubanshe, 2003), p. 361.

104. Guo Xiangjie, ed., *Zhang Wannian zhuan*, p. 62.

105. Ibid., p. 63.

106. Zhang Wannian, *Zhang Wannian junshi wenxuan* [Zhang Wannian's Selected Works on Military Affairs] (Beijing: Jiefangjun chubanshe, 2008), p. 365.

107. Ibid.

108. Zhang Zhen, *Zhang Zhen huiyilu (shang)*, p. 362; Jiang Weimin, ed., *Liu Huaqing nianpu*, Vol. 2, pp. 1008–1009.

109. Zhang Zhen, *Zhang Zhen huiyilu (shang)*, p. 364.

110. Jiang Zemin, *Jiang Zemin wenxuan*, Vol. 1, p. 285.

111. Ibid., p. 279.

112. Jiang Weimin, ed., *Liu Huaqing nianpu*, Vol. 2, p. 865.

113. Ibid., pp. 893, 957, 1009.

114. Jiang Zemin, *Jiang Zemin wenxuan*, Vol. 1, p. 280.

115. Ibid., p. 279.

116. Ibid.

117. On the development of China's conventional ballistic missiles, see Christopher P. Twomey, "The People's Liberation Army's Selective Learning: Lessons of the Iran-Iraq 'War of the Cities'

Missile Duels and Uses of Missiles in Other Conflicts," in Andrew Scobell, David Lai, and Roy Kamphausen, eds., *Chinese Lessons from Other Peoples' Wars* (Carlisle, PA: Army War College: Strategic Studies Institute, 2011), pp. 115–152; Michael S. Chase and Andrew Erickson, "The Conventional Missile Capabilities of China's Second Artillery Force: Cornerstone of Deterrence and Warfighting," *Asian Security*, Vol. 8, No. 2 (2012), pp. 115–137.

118. Liu Huaqing, *Liu Huaqing huiyilu*, p. 635.

119. Ibid., p. 638.

120. Ibid.

121. Ibid.

122. Ibid.

123. Zhang Zhen, *Zhang Zhen junshi wenxuan*, Vol. 2, p. 546.

124. Ibid., p. 547.

125. Ibid., p. 548.

126. Quoted in Wu Quanxu, *Kuayue shiji de biange*, p. 13.

127. Ibid., p. 14; Guo Xiangjie, ed., *Zhang Wannian zhuan*, p. 87.

128. Guo Xiangjie, ed., *Zhang Wannian zhuan*, p. 89.

129. Ibid., p. 88.

130. Wu Quanxu, *Kuayue shiji de biange*, p. 17.

131. Zhao Xuepeng, "'Sizhong gangmu' jixun chuixiang xunlian chongfenghao" ["Four Kinds of Outlines" Group Training Sounded the Bugle Call for Training], *Jiefangjun bao*, October 8, 2008, p. 21.

132. Guo Xiangjie, ed., *Zhang Wannian zhuan*, p. 88.

133. Wu Quanxu, *Kuayue shijie de biange*, p. 19.

134. Guo Xiangjie, ed., *Zhang Wannian zhuan*, p. 89.

135. Ibid., p. 88.

136. Quoted in Wu Quanxu, *Kuayue shiji de biange*, p. 22.

137. Ibid., p. 23.

138. Guo Xiangjie, ed., *Zhang Wannian zhuan*, pp. 92–93.

139. On exercises during this period, see Blasko, Klapakis and Corbett, "Training Tomorrow's PLA."

140. Guo Xiangjie, ed., *Zhang Wannian zhuan*, p. 95.

141. Ibid., pp. 94–95.

142. Zhang Wannian, *Zhang Wannian junshi wenxuan*, p. 515.

143. Ibid., p. 505.

144. Wu Quanxu, *Kuayue shiji de biange*, p. 19.

145. Zhang Jian and Ren Yanjun, "Xinyidai junshi xunlian dagang banfa."

146. Ibid.

147. For a review of the meeting, see Wu Quanxu, *Kuayue shiji de biange*, pp. 61–69.

148. Zhang Wannian, *Zhang Wannian junshi wenxuan*, p. 506.

149. On the PLA's operations regulations, see Yang Zhiyuan, "Wojun bianxiu zuozhan tiaoling de chuangxin fazhan ji qishi"; Wang An, ed., *Jundui tiaoling tiaoli jiaocheng* [Lectures on Military Regulations and Rules] (Beijing: Junshi kexue chubanshe, 1999), pp. 124–138.

150. Zhang Wannian, *Zhang Wannian junshi wenxuan*, pp. 506–508.

151. Ibid., p. 506.

152. Ibid., pp. 50–507.

153. Ibid., p. 507.

154. Yang Zhiyuan, "Wojun bianxiu zuozhan tiaoling de chuangxin fazhan ji qishi," pp. 112–118.

155. Wang An, ed., *Jundui tiaoling tiaoli jiaocheng*, pp. 126–127.

156. Ibid., p. 130.

157. Ibid., p. 127. For detailed descriptions of these campaigns, see Wang Houqing and Zhang Xingye, eds., *Zhanyi xue* [The Science of Campaigns] (Beijing: Guofang daxue chubanshe, 2000); Xue Xinglin, ed., *Zhanyi lilun xuexi zhinan* [Campaign Theory Study Guide] (Beijing: Guofang daxue chubanshe, 2002). For English summaries, see Blasko, *The Chinese Army Today*; Roger Cliff, *China's Military Power: Assessing Current and Future Capabilities* (New York: Cambridge University Press, 2015), pp. 17–25.

158. Wang An, ed., *Jundui tiaoling tiaoli jiaocheng*, p. 129.

159. Ibid., pp. 129–130.

160. These principles focused on operations and come from a 1947 speech. See Mao Zedong, *Mao Zedong xuanji* [Mao Zedong's Selected Works], 2nd ed., Vol. 4, (Beijing: Renmin chubanshe, 1991), pp. 1247–1248.

161. Xu Guocheng, Feng Liang and Zhou Zhenduo, eds., *Lianhe zhanyi yanjiu* [A Study of Joint Campaigns] (Jinan: Huanghe chubanshe, 2004), p. 25. Also, see Wang An, ed., *Jundui tiaoling tiaoli jiaocheng*, p. 127.

162. See Wang Houqing and Zhang Xingye, eds., *Zhanyi xue*, pp. 1010–114; Xue Xinglin, ed., *Zhanyi lilun xuexi zhinan*, pp. 28–29. For a review of these principles in English, see Blasko, *The Chinese Army Today*, pp. 105–116.

163. Blasko, *The Chinese Army Today*, pp. 98–104. For a similar list of principles at the tactical level, see Hao Zizhou and Huo Gaozhen, eds., *Zhanshuxue jiaocheng* [Lectures on the Science of Tactics] (Beijing: Junshi kexue chubanshe, 2000), pp. 184–215.

164. Hao Zizhou and Gaozhen, eds., *Zhanshuxue jiaocheng*, p. 134.

165. Wang An, ed., *Jundui tiaoling tiaoli jiaocheng*, p. 136.

166. Ren Jian, *Zuozhan tiaoling gailun*, p. 51. Also, see Wang An, ed., *Jundui tiaoling tiaoli jiaocheng*, p. 137; Hao Zizhou and Gaozhen, eds., *Zhanshuxue jiaocheng*, pp. 134–136.

167. This demonstrates the growing institutionalization of the PLA. Liu Huaqing, as a CMC vice-chairmen, led the drafting of the PLA's Eighth Five-Year Plan.

168. Zhang Wannian, *Zhang Wannian junshi wenxuan*, p. 490.

169. Ibid., p. 492.

170. Guo Xiangjie, ed., *Zhang Wannian zhuan*, p. 80.

171. Ibid., p. 81.

172. Ibid., p. 82.

173. Zhang Wannian, *Zhang Wannian junshi wenxuan*, pp. 517–522.

174. Guo Xiangjie, ed., *Zhang Wannian zhuan*, p. 83.

175. Jiang Zemin, *Lun guofang yu jundui jianshe*, p. 194.

176. Liu Huaqing, *Liu Huaqing junshi wenxuan*, Vol. 2, pp. 448–449.

177. Ibid.

178. Guo Xiangjie, ed., *Zhang Wannian zhuan*, pp. 135–136.

179. After Tiananmen, the CMC decided to strengthen the PAP so that it would serve as the first responder for social disorder. On the evolution of the PAP, see Murray Scot Tanner, "The Institutional Lessons of Disaster: Reorganizing The People's Armed Police After Tiananmen," in James Mulvenon and Andrew N. D. Yang, eds., *The People's Liberation Army as Organization: V 1.0., Reference Volume* (Santa Monica, CA: RAND, 2002).

180. Guo Xiangjie, ed., *Zhang Wannian zhuan*, p. 137.

181. Ibid.

182. Ibid., p. 138.

183. Ding Wei and Wei Xu, "20 shiji 80 niandai renmin jiefangjun tizhi gaige, jingjian zhengbian de huigu yu sikao" [Review and Reflections on the Streamlining and Reorganization of the PLA in the Eighties of the 20th Cenutry], *Junshi lishi*, No. 6 (2014), p. 55.

184. Guo Xiangjie, ed., *Zhang Wannian zhuan*, pp. 138–140.

185. Junshi kexue yuan lishi yanjiusuo, *Zhongguo renmin jiefangjun gaige fazhan 30 nian* [30 Years of Reform and Development of the Chinese People's Liberation Army] (Beijing: Junshi kexue chubanshe, 2008), p.207.

186. Jiang Zemin, *Lun guofang yu jundui jianshe*, p. 299.

187. Ibid., p. 301.

188. Guo Xiangjie, ed., *Zhang Wannian zhuan*, p. 151.

189. Junshi kexue yuan lishi yanjiusuo, *Zhongguo renmin jiefangjun gaige fazhan 30 nian*, p. 211.

190. Ibid.

191. Harlan W. Jencks, "The General Armament Department," in James Mulvenon and Andrew N. D. Yang, eds., *The People's Liberation Army as Organization: Reference Volume v1.0* (Santa Monica, CA: RAND, 2002), pp. 273–308.

192. *2006 nian Zhongguo de guofang* [China's National Defense in 2006] (Beijing: Guowuyuan xinwen bangongshi, 2006).

193. Blasko, *The Chinese Army Today*, p. 22.

Chapter 7. China's Military Strategies since 1993

1. Jiang Tiejun, ed., *Dang de guofang jundui gaige sixiang yanjiu* [A Study of the Party's Thought on National Defense and Army Reform] (Beijing: Junshi kexue chubanshe, 2015), p. 129.

2. Jiang Zemin gave a speech introducing the new guideline at a meeting of the CMC in June 2004, but that speech was not included in his selected works. See Jiang Zemin, *Jiang Zemin wenxuan* [Jiang Zemin's Selected Works], Vol. 3 (Beijing: Renmin chubanshe, 2006), p. 608; Shou Xiaosong, ed., *Zhanlue xue* [The Science of Military Strategy] (Beijing: Junshi kexue chubanshe, 2013), p. 47.

3. Li Yousheng, ed., *Lianhe zhanyi xue jiaocheng* [Lectures on the Science of Joint Campaigns] (Beijing: Junshi kexue chubanshe, 2012), pp. 201–203.

4. Wen Bin, "Dingzhun junshi douzheng jidian" [Pinpointing the Basis of Preparations for Military Struggle], *Xuexi shibao*, June 1, 2015, p. A7.

5. Jiang Zemin, *Jiang Zemin wenxuan*, Vol. 3, p. 608. *"Xinxihua"* is also sometimes translated as "informationization."

6. Ibid.

7. Ibid.

8. *2004 nian Zhongguo de guofang* [China's National Defense in 2004] (Beijing: Guowuyuan xinwen bangongshi, 2004).

9. Joe McReynolds and James Mulvenon, "The Role of Informatization in the People's Liberation Army under Hu Jintao," in Roy Kamphausen, David Lai, and Travis Tanner, eds., *Assessing the People's Liberation Army in the Hu Jintao Era* (Carlisle, PA: Strategic Studies Institute, Army War College, 2014), p. 211.

10. Ibid., p. 230.

11. Dennis J. Blasko, "Integrating the Services and Harnessing the Military Area Commands," *Journal of Strategic Studies*, Vol. 39, No. 5–16 (2016), p. 12. Some of these operations, however, could be lethal in their second-order effects.

12. Dean Cheng, "The PLA's Wartime Structure," in Kevin Pollpeter and Kenneth W. Allen, eds., *The PLA as Organization 2.0* (Vienna, VA: Defense Group, 2015), p. 461.

13. Ibid., p. 462. For detailed studies of the topic, see Jeff Engstrom, *Systems Confrontation and System Destruction Warfare: How the Chinese People's Liberation Army Seeks to Wage Modern Warfare* (Santa Monica, CA: RAND, 2018); Kevin McCauley, *PLA System of Systems Operations: Enabling Joint Operations* (Washington, DC: Jamestown Foundation, 2017).

14. *2004 nian Zhongguo de guofang*.

15. Wu Jianhua and Su Ruozhou, "Zongcan bushu quanjun xinniandu junshi xunlian gongzuo" [General Staff Department arranges army-wide annual training work], *Jiefangjun bao*, February 1, 2004.

16. Zong zhengzhi bu, *Shuli he luoshi kexue fazhanguan lilun xuexi duben* [A Reader for Establishing and Implementing the Theory of Scientific Development] (Beijing: Jiefangjun chubanshe, 2006), pp. 203–214; Zhang Yuliang, ed., *Zhanyi xue* [The Science of Campaigns] (Beijing: Guofang daxue chubanshe, 2006).

17. Hu Jintao, *Hu Jintao wenxuan* [Hu Jintao's Selected Works], Vol. 1 (Beijing: Renmin chubanshe, 2016), p. 453. For a thoughtful study of China's approach to joint operations, see Joel Wuthnow, "A Brave New World for Chinese Joint Operations," *Journal of Strategic Studies* Vol. 40, Nos. 1–2 (2017), pp. 169–195.

18. Dean Cheng, *Cyber Dragon: Inside China's Information Warfare and Cyber Operations* (Santa Babara, CA: Praeger, 2016), p. 85.

19. Ibid., p. 79.

20. Zhang Yuliang, ed., *Zhanyi xue.*

21. Qiao Jie, ed., *Zhanyi xue jiaocheng* [Lectures on the Science of Campaigns] (Beijing: Junshi kexue chubanshe, 2012), p. 172.

22. Tan Yadong, ed., *Lianhe zuozhan jiaocheng* [Lectures on Joint Operations] (Beijing: Junshi kexue chubanshe, 2013), p. 68.

23. Li Yousheng, ed., *Lianhe zhanyi xue jiaocheng*, pp. 87–89.

24. Yang Zhiyuan, "Wojun bianxiu zuozhan tiaoling de chuangxin fazhan ji qishi" [The Innovative Development and Implications of Our Army's Compilation and Revision of Operations Regulations], *Zhongguo junshi kexue*, No. 6 (2009), p. 113.

25. Ibid., p. 115.

26. Ren Jian, *Zuozhan tiaoling gailun* [An Introduction to Operations Regulations] (Beijing: Junshi kexue chubanshe, 2016), p. 53.

27. National Institute for Defense Studies, *NIDS China Security Report 2016: The Expanding Scope of PLA Activities and the PLA Strategy* (Tokyo: National Institute for Defense Studies, 2016), p. 14.

28. Ibid., p. 15.

29. Ibid., p. 27.

30. Abraham Denmark, "PLA Logistics 2004–11: Lessons Learned in the Field," in Roy Kamphausen, David Lai, and Travis Tanner, eds., *Learning by Doing: The PLA Trains at Home and Abroad* (Carlise, PA: Army War College: Strategic Studies Institute, 2012), pp. 297–336; Susan Puska, "Taming the Hydra: Trends in China's Military Logistics Since 2000," in Roy Kamphausen, David Lai, and Andrew Scobell, eds., *The PLA at Home and Abroad: Assessing the Operational Capabilities of China's Military* (Carlisle, PA: Army War College, Strategic Studies Institute, 2010), pp. 553–636.

31. McReynolds and Mulvenon, "The Role of Informatization in the People's Liberation Army under Hu Jintao," pp. 228–229.

32. On the system and its use in exercises, see Wanda Ayuso and Lonnie Henley, "Aspiring to Jointness: PLA Training, Exercises, and Doctrine, 2008–2012," in Roy Kamphausen, David Lai, and Travis Tanner, eds., *Assessing the People's Liberation Army in the Hu Jintao Era* (Carlisle, PA: Strategic Studies Institute, Army War College, 2014), p. 183.

33. Wu Tianmin, "Goujian xinxihua tiaojianxia junshi xunlian tixi" [Building a Training System Under Informatized Conditions], *Jiefangjun bao*, August 1, 2008.

34. For a list and description of these exercises, see McCauley, *PLA System of Systems Operations*, pp. 50–57.

35. For a list and description of these exercises, see ibid., pp. 58–65.

36. Huang Chao, "Wei renzhen guanche Hu Jintao guanyu jiaqiang lianhe xunlian zhongyao zhishi" [Earnestly Carry Out Hu Jintao's Important Instructions on Joint Training], *Jiefangjun bao*, February 25, 2009.

37. Qiao Jie, ed., *Zhanyi xue jiaocheng*, pp. 30–31.

38. On the debate, see David M. Finkelstein, *China Reconsiders Its National Security: "The Great Peace and Development Debate of 1999"* (Arlington, VA: CNA, 2000).

39. On the influence of the Kosovo War, see Fiona S. Cunningham, "Maximizing Leverage: Explaining China's Strategic Force Postures in Limited Wars," PhD dissertation, Department of Political Science, Massachusetts Institute of Technology, 2018.

40. Wang Xuedong, *Fu Quanyou zhuan (xia)* [Fu Quanyou's Biography] (Beijing: Jiefangjun chubanshe, 2015), p. 207.

41. Ibid., p. 209.

42. Zhang Wannian, *Zhang Wannian junshi wenxuan* [Zhang Wannian's Selected Works on Military Affairs] (Beijing: Jiefangjun chubanshe, 2008), p. 704.

43. Wang Xuedong, *Fu Quanyou zhuan*, p. 717. Also, see Fu Quanyou, *Fu Quanyou junshi wenxuan* [Fu Quanyou's Selected Works on Military Affairs] (Beijing: Jiefangjun chubanshe, 2015), p. 740.

44. Huang Bin, ed., *Kesuowo zhanzheng yanjiu* [A Study of the Kosovo War] (Beijing: Jiefangjun chubanshe, 2000), p. 98.

45. Ibid., pp. 78–89.

46. Ibid., pp. 98–100.

47. These include the E-8C "Growler," U-2S, RC-135, EC-130, E-2C and E-3.

48. Huang Bin, ed., *Kesuowo zhanzheng yanjiu*, p. 80.

49. Ibid., p. 150.

50. Ibid.

51. Fu Quanyou also emphasized US "total air attack warfare" (*quankong xizhan*). See, Wang Xuedong, *Fu Quanyou zhuan*, p. 303.

52. Fu Quanyou, *Fu Quanyou junshi wenxuan*, p. 740.

53. Jiang Zemin, *Jiang Zemin wenxuan*, Vol. 3, p. 162.

54. Ibid., pp. 576–599.

55. Ibid., p. 578.

56. Ibid., pp. 579–581.

57. Ibid., p. 582.

58. Ibid., p. 585.

59. Ibid.

60. Huang Bin, ed., *Kesuowo zhanzheng yanjiu*, p. 150.

61. Ibid., pp. 162–164; Wang Xuedong, *Fu Quanyou zhuan*, p. 303.

62. Ma Yongming, Liu Xiaoli and Xiao Yunhua, eds., *Yilake zhanzheng yanjiu* [A Study of the Iraq War] (Beijing: Junshi kexue chubanshe, 2003).

63. Chen Dongxiang, ed., *Pingdian Yilake zhanzheng* [Evaluating the Iraq War] (Beijing: Junshi kexue chubanshe, 2003).

64. He Zhu, *Zhuanjia pingshuo Yilake zhanzheng* [Experts Evaluate the Iraq War] (Beijing: Junshi kexue chubanshe, 2004).

65. Chen Dongxiang, ed., *Pingdian Yilake zhanzheng*, p. 1.

66. He Zhu, *Zhuanjia pingshuo Yilake zhanzheng*, p. 89.

67. Ma Yongming, Liu Xiaoli and Xiao Yunhua, eds., *Yilake zhanzheng yanjiu*, p. 143.

68. Ibid., p. 150.

69. Chen Dongxiang, ed., *Pingdian Yilake zhanzheng*, p. 175.

70. Ibid; He Zhu, *Zhuanjia pingshuo Yilake zhanzheng*, p. 83.

71. Ma Yongming, Liu Xiaoli and Xiao Yunhua, eds., *Yilake zhanzheng yanjiu*, pp. 153–154.

72. He Zhu, *Zhuanjia pingshuo Yilake zhanzheng*, p. 83.

73. Chen Dongxiang, ed., *Pingdian Yilake zhanzheng*, p. 172.

74. Ibid., pp. 319–326; Ma Yongming, Liu Xiaoli and Xiao Yunhua, eds., *Yilake zhanzheng yanjiu*, pp. 153–155.

75. Chen Dongxiang, ed., *Pingdian Yilake zhanzheng*, p. 320.

76. Ma Yongming, Liu Xiaoli and Xiao Yunhua, eds., *Yilake zhanzheng yanjiu*, p. 167.

77. Chen Dongxiang, ed., *Pingdian Yilake zhanzheng*, p. 192.

78. Zong zhengzhi bu, *Shuli he luoshi kexue fazhanguan lilun xuexi duben*, p. 77. This speech is also reprinted in Hu Jintao, *Hu Jintao wenxuan*, Vol. 1, pp. 256–262.

79. Zong zhengzhi bu, *Shuli he luoshi kexue fazhanguan lilun xuexi duben*, p. 78.

80. Ibid., p. 79.

81. Ibid., p. 80.

82. Ibid., p. 196.

83. Ibid., p. 253.

84. The Chinese definition of nonwar military operations include some operations that would be classified as combat operations, such as sea lane security.

85. For a review of authoritative sources discussing different kinds of nonwar operations, see M. Taylor Fravel, "Economic Growth, Regime Insecurity, and Military Strategy: Explaining the Rise of Noncombat Operations in China," *Asian Security*, Vol. 7, No. 3 (2011), p. 191.

86. Tan Wenhu, "Duoyanghua junshi renwu qianyin junshi xunlian chuangxin" [Diversified Military Tasks Draw Innovations in Military Training], *Jiefangjun bao*, July 1, 2008, p. 12.

87. Fravel, "Economic Growth, Regime Insecurity, and Military Strategy," p. 191.

88. *Zhongguo de junshi zhanlue*, [China's Military Strategy] (Beijing: Guowuyuan xinwen bangongshi, 2015). This section draws on M. Taylor Fravel, "China's New Military Strategy: 'Winning Informationized Local Wars,'" *China Brief*, Vol. 15, No. 13 (2015), pp. 3–6. Discussion of the 2014 guideline in Chinese sources is limited. See Luo Derong, "Jundui jianshe yu junshi douzheng junbei de xingdong gangling: Dui xin xingshi xia junshi zhanlue fangzhen de jidian renshi" [Action Plan for Army Building and Preparations for Military Struggle: Several Points on the Military Strategic Guideline in the New Situation], *Zhongguo junshi kexue*, No. 1 (2017), pp. 88–96; Junshi kexue yuan Mao Zeodong junshi sixiang yanjiusuo, "Qiangguo qiangjun zhanlue xianxing—Shenru xuexi guanche Xi zhuxi xin xingshi xia junshi zhanlue fangzhen zhong-yao lunshu" [Strong Nation, Strong Army, Strategy First: Thoroughly Study and Implement Chairman Xi's Important Expositions on the Military Strategic Guideline in the New Period], *Jiefangjun bao*, September 2, 2016.

89. "Yao dao haishang zhanzheng? Zhongguo yingzuo haishang junshi douzheng zhunbei [Fight a War at Sea? China Should Prepare for Maritime Military Struggle]," *Huanqiu shibao*, May 26, 2015, http://mil.huanqiu.com/strategysituation/2015-05/6526726_2.html.

90. Wen Bin, "Dingzhun junshi douzheng jidian" [Pinpointing the Basis of Preparations for Military Struggle], *Xuexi shibao*, June 1, 2015, p. A7.

91. *Zhongguo de junshi zhanlue*.

92. *Zhongguo de junshi zhanlue*; Chen Zhou, "Zhuanjia jiedu Zhongguo de junshi zhanlue baipishu" [Expert Unpacks the White Paper China's Military Strategy], *Guofang*, No. 6 (2015), p. 18.

93. *Zhongguo de junshi zhanlue*.

94. The English version of the white paper uses the terms "offshore waters defense" and "open seas protection," respectively.

95. Within the PLA, each service has its own strategic concept in addition to the strategic guideline for China's armed forces.

96. Interview, Nanjing, December 2017.

97. Wang Hongguang, "Cong lishi kan jinri Zhongguo de zhanlue fangxiang" [Looking at China's Strategic Directions Today from a Historical Perspective], *Tongzhou gongjin*, No. 3 (March 2015), p. 48. General Wang is the former deputy commander of the Nanjing Military Region, now retired.

98. Ibid., p. 49.50.

99. Jiang Zemin, *Jiang Zemin wenxuan*, Vol. 3, pp. 576–599.

100. Liang Pengfei, "Zongcan zongzheng yinfa 'guanyu tigao junshi xunlian shizhan shuiping de yijian xuexi xuanchuan tigang'" [GSD and GPD Issues Study and Publicity Outline for "The Opinion on Improving the Realistic Combat Level of Military Training"], *Jiefangjun bao*, August 21, 2014, p. 1.

101. Wang Tubin and Luo Zheng, "Guofangbu juxing shengda zhaodaihui relie qingzhu jianjun 87 zhounian" [The Ministry of Defense Holds Grand Reception to Celebrate 87th Anniversary of Founding the Army], *Jiefangjun bao*, August 2, 2014.

102. Xi Jinping, *Xi Jinping guofang he jundui jianshe zhongyao lunshu xuanbian (er)* [A Selection of Xi Jinping's Important Expositions on National Defense and Army Building (2)] (Beijing: Jiefangjun chubanshe, 2015), pp. 62–63.

103. Ibid., p. 80.

104. Blasko, "Integrating the Services and Harnessing the Military Area Commands"; Joel Wuthnow and Philip C. Saunders, *Chinese Military Reform in the Age of Xi Jinping: Drivers, Challenges, and Implications* (Washington, DC: National Defense University Press, 2017).

105. "*Zhonggong zhongyang guanyu quanmian shenhua gaige ruogan zhongda wenti de jueding*" [Decision of the Central Committee of the Communist Party of China on Some Major Issues Concerning Comprehensively Deepening Reform], November 13, 2013, http://www.gov.cn/jrzg/2013-11/15/content_2528179.htm.

106. Xi Jinping, *Xi Jinping guofang he jundui jianshe zhongyao lunshu xuanbian* [A Selection of Xi Jinping's Important Expositions on National Defense and Army Building] (Beijing: Jiefangjun chubanshe, 2014), p. 220.

107. Ibid., p. 223.

Chapter 8. China's Nuclear Strategy since 1964

1. John Wilson Lewis and Litai Xue, *China Builds the Bomb* (Stanford, CA: Stanford University ᵗ988).

⌐. 210.

Lewis and Hua Di, "China's Ballistic Missile Programs: Technologies, Strate-
ᵗ Security, Vol. 17, No. 2 (1992), p. 20.

Taylor Fravel and Evan S. Medeiros, "China's Search for Assured
Nuclear Strategy and Force Structure," *International Secu-

[Mao Zedong's Selected Works on Diplomacy]

Selected Works on Culture] (Bei-

orks], Vol. 7, (Beijing: Xinhua

noirs] (Beijing: Jiefangjun chuban-
y of activities contains any reference
rs to have made it when China debated
w).

9. Leng Rong and Wang Zuoling, eds., *Deng Xiaoping nianpu, 1975–1997* [A Chronicle of Deng Xiaoping's Life, 1975–1997], Vol. 1 (Beijing: Zhongyang wenxian chubanshe, 2004), p. 404.

10. Zhongyang junwei bangongting, ed., *Deng Xiaoping guanyu xin shiqi jundui jianshe lunshu xuanbian* [Deng Xiaoping's Selected Expositions on Army Building in the New Period] (Beijing: Bayi chubanshe, 1993), pp. 44–45.

11. Zhou Enlai, *Zhou Enlai wenhua wenxuan*, p. 661.

12. Zhongyang junwei bangongting, ed., *Deng Xiaoping guanyu xin shiqi jundui jianshe lunshu xuanbian*, p. 99.

13. On Zhang's role, see Dong Fanghe, *Zhang Aiping zhuan* [Zhang Aiping's Biography] (Beijing: Renmin chubanshe, 2000); Lu Qiming and Fan Minruo, *Zhang Aiping yu liangdan yixing* [Zhang Aiping and the Two Bombs, One Satellite] (Beijing: Zhongyang wenxian chubanshe, 2011); Zhang Sheng, *Cong zhanzheng zhong zoulai: Liangdai junren de duihua* [Coming From War: A Dialogue of Two Generations of Soldiers] (Beijing: Zhongguo qingnian chubanshe, 2008). Zhang Sheng is Zhang Aiping's son.

14. Zhang Aiping, *Zhang Aiping junshi wenxuan* [Zhang Aiping's Selected Works on Military Affairs] (1994), p. 392. Zhang was defense minister from 1982 to 1988.

15. Richard M. Nixon, *RN: The Memoirs of Richard Nixon* (New York: Grosset & Dunlap, 1978), p. 557.

16. Leng Rong and Wang Zuoling, eds., *Deng Xiaoping nianpu, 1975–1997*, Vol. 1, pp. 779–780.

17. Jiang Zemin, *Jiang Zemin wenxuan* [Jiang Zemin's Selected Works], Vol. 1, (Beijing: Renmin chubanshe, 2006), p. 156.

18. Jiang, paraphrased in Shan Xiufa, ed., *Jiang Zemin guofang he jundui jianshe sixiang yanjiu* [Research on Jiang's Zemin's Thought on National Defense and Army Building] (Beijing: Junshi kexue chubanshe, 2004), p. 342.

19. Jiang Zemin, *Jiang Zemin wenxuan* [Jiang Zemin's Selected Works], Vol. 3 (Beijing: Renmin chubanshe, 2006), p. 585. On China's concept of strategic deterrence, see Peng Guangqian and Yao Youzhi, eds., *Zhanlue xue* [The Science of Military Strategy] (Beijing: Junshi kexue chubanshe, 2001), pp. 230–245.

20. *Renmin Ribao*, June 29, 2006, p. 1

21. *Renmin Ribao*, December 6, 2012, p. 1

22. See Li Tilin, "Gaige kaifang yilai Zhongguo hezhanlue lilun de fazhan" [The Development of China's Nuclear Strategy Theory since Reform and Opening], *Zhongguo junshi kexue*, No. 6 (2008), pp. 37–44; Jing Zhiyuan and Peng Zhiyuan, "Huiguo di'er paobing zai gaige kaifang zhong jiakuai jianshe fazhan de guanghui licheng" [Recalling the Brilliant Process of the Accelerated Building and Development of the Second Artillery during Reform and Opening], in Di'er paobing zhengzhibu, ed., *Huihuang niandai: Huigu zai gaige kaifang zhong fazhan qianjin de di'er paobing* [Glorious Ag Reviewing the Development and Progress of the Second Artillery During Reform and Openi (Beijing: Zhongyang wenxian chubanshe, 2008).

23. On this period, Wu Lie, *Zhengrong suiyue* [Memorable Years] (Beijing: Zhonyang chubanshe, 1999), pp. 350–369; Wu Lie, "Erpao lingdao jiguan jiannan yansheng" [Th Birth of the Second Artillery's Leadership Structure], in Di'er paobing zhengzhibu, *heguo yiqi chengzhang: Wo zai zhanlue daodan budui de nanwang jiyi* [Growing the Republic: My Unforgettable Memories in the Strategic Rocket Forces], (Bei wenxian chubanshe, 2009), pp. 192–195; Liao Chengmei, "Fengyun shinian Years of the Storms of War Preparations], in Di'er paobing zhengzhibu, e *chengzhang: Wo zai zhanlue daodan budui de nanwang jiyi* [Growing Tog lic: My Unforgettable Memories in the Strategic Rocket Forces], (Beiji chubanshe, 2009), pp. 196–201.

24. Wu Lie, *Zhengrong suiyue*, p. 358.

25. Li Shuiqing, "Gaige, cong zheli qibu" [Reform, Started From Here], in Di'er paobing zhengzhibu, ed., *Huihuang niandai*, p. 29.

26. He Jinheng, " 'Jinggan youxiao' zongti jianshe mubiao de queli" [The Establishment of the Overall Development Goal of 'Lean and Effective'], in Di'er paobing zhengzhibu, ed., *Huihuang niandai*, p. 43.

27. Li Shuiqing, *Cong hongxiaogui dao huojian siling: Li Shuiqing's huiyilu* [From Little Red Devil to Rocket Commander: Li Shuiqing's Memoir] (Beijing: Jiefangjun chubanshe, 2009), p. 513.

28. Li Shuiqing, "Gaige, cong zheli qibu," p. 30. The text of the report is unavailable.

29. Ibid., p. 25.

30. Gao Rui, ed., *Zhanlue xue* [The Science of Military Strategy] (Beijing: Junshi kexue chubanshe, 1987). On the drafting, see Song Shilun, *Song Shilun junshi wenxuan: 1958–1989* [Song Shilun's Selected Works on Military Affairs: 1958-1989] (Beijing: Junshi kexue chubanshe, 2007), p. 352.

31. Gao Rui, ed., *Zhanlue xue*, p. 114.

32. Ibid., p. 235. Also, see ibid., p. 115. One passage refers to an aspiration for a launch on warning or launch under attack capability. See ibid., p. 136.

33. Ibid., p. 115.

34. On the importance of these guiding principles, see Alastair Iain Johnston, "Comments" (prepared for RAND-CNA conference on the PLA, December 2002). "*Yanmi fanghu*" may also be translated as "strict protection."

35. Di'er paobing silingbu, ed., *Di'er paobing zhanlue xue* [The Science of Second Artillery Strategy] (Beijing: Lantian chubanshe, 1996).

36. Gao Rui, ed., *Zhanlue xue*; Peng Guangqian and Yao Youzhi, eds., *Zhanlue xue*; Shou Xiaosong, ed., *Zhanlue xue* [The Science of Military Strategy] (Beijing: Junshi kexue chubanshe, 2013); Wang Houqing and Zhang Xingye, eds., *Zhanyi xue* [The Science of Campaigns] (Beijing: Guofang daxue chubanshe, 2000); Zhang Yuliang, ed., *Zhanyi xue* [The Science of Campaigns] (Beijing: Guofang daxue chubanshe, 2006).

37. Yu Xijun, ed., *Di'er paobing zhanyi xue* [The Science of Second Artillery Campaigns] (Beijing: Jiefangjun chubanshe, 2004); Di'er paobing silingbu, ed., *Di'er paobing zhanyi fa* [Second Artillery Campaign Methods] (Beijing: Lantian chubanshe, 1996); Di'er paobing silingbu, ed., *Di'er paobing zhanshu xue* [The Science of Second Artillery Tactics] (Beijing: Lantian chubanshe, 1996); Di'er paobing silingbu, ed., *Di'er paobing zhanlue xue*.

38. These sentences use the official English version of the 2006 white paper. The corresponding terms from the Chinese version are also included, as the translations in the English version do not fully capture the essence of some of the Chinese words.

39. *2008 nian Zhongguo de guofang* [China's National Defense in 2006] (Beijing: Guowuyuan xinwen bangongshi, 2008).

40. For a Chinese analysis of the views of China's leaders, see Sun Xiangli, *He shidai de zhanlue xuanze: Zhongguo hezhanlue wenti yanjiu* [Strategic Choices of the Nuclear Era: Research on Issues in China's Nuclear Strategy] (Beijing: Chinese Academy of Engineering Physics, 2013). For an abridged English translation, see Xiangli Sun, "The Development of Nuclear Weapons in China," in Bin Li and Zhao Tong, eds., *Understanding Chinese Nuclear Thinking* (Washington, DC: Carnegie Endowment for International Peace, 2016), pp. 79–102.

41. Di'er paobing silingbu, ed., *Di'er paobing zhanlue xue*, p. 9.

42. Mao Zedong, *Mao Zedong wenji*, Vol. 7, p. 328. For a concise summary of Chinese leadership views on nuclear strategy, see Yao Yunzhu, "Chinese Nuclear Policy and the Future of Minimum Deterrence," in Christopher P. Twomey, ed., *Perspectives on Sino-American Strategic Nuclear Issues* (New York: Palgrave Macmillan, 2008), pp. 111–124. For a detailed analysis of Mao's approach to nuclear weapons, see Cai Lijuan, *Mao Zedong de hezhanlue sixiang yanjiu* [Mao Zedong's Nuclear

Strategic Thought], Institute of International Studies, Tsinghua University, 2002. On Chinese thinking on nuclear weapons during the late 1940s and 1950s, see Alice Langley Hsieh, *Communist China's Strategy in the Nuclear Era* (Englewood Cliffs, NJ: Prentice-Hall, 1962); Mark A. Ryan, *Chinese Attitudes Toward Nuclear Weapons: China and the United States During the Korean War* (Armonk, NY: M. E. Sharpe, 1989). On China and the broader nuclear order, see Nicola Horsburgh, *China and Global Nuclear Order: From Estrangement to Active Engagement* (New York: Oxford University Press, 2015).

43. Quoted in Yin Xiong and Huang Xuemei, *Shijie yuanzidan fengyulu* [The Stormy Record of the Atom Bomb in the World] (Beijing: Xinhua chubanshe, 1999), p. 258.

44. *Mao Zedong yu Zhongguo yuanzineng shiye* [Mao Zedong and China's nuclear energy industry] (Beijing: Yuanzineng chubanshe, 1993), p. 13, quoted in Cai, *Mao Zedong de hezhanlue sixiang yanjiu*, p. 18.

45. Zhou Enlai, *Zhou Enlai junshi wenxuan* [Zhou Enlai's Selected Works on Military Affairs], Vol. 4, (Beijing: Renmin chubanshe, 1997), p. 422.

46. Ye Jianying, *Ye Jianying junshi wenxuan* [Ye Jianying's Selected Works on Military Affairs] (Beijing: Jiefangjun chubanshe, 1997), pp. 244-251.

47. Deng Xiaoping, *Deng Xiaoping junshi wenxuan* [Deng Xiaoping's Selected Works on Military Affairs], Vol. 3, (Beijing: Junshi kexue chubanshe, 2004), p. 16. In this context, "they" refers to other nuclear weapons states, especially the United States and the Soviet Union.

48. Leng Rong and Wang Zuoling, eds., *Deng Xiaoping nianpu, 1975-1997*, Vol. 1, p. 351.

49. Li Tilin, "Gaige kaifang yilai Zhongguo hezhanlue lilun de fazhan," p. 41.

50. Ibid., p. 42.

51. Jing Zhiyuan and Peng Zhiyuan, "Huiguo di'er paobing zai gaige kaifang zhong jiakuai jianshe fazhan de guanghui licheng," pp. 1-22. Jing and Peng were the commander and political commissar, respectively, of the Second Artillery. See also Zhou Kekuan, "Xin shiqi heweishe lilun yu shixian de xin fazhan" [New Developments in the Theory and Practice of Nuclear Deterrence in the New Period], *Zhongguo junshi kexue*, No. 1 (2009), pp. 16-20.

52. Zhang Qihua, "Huihuang suiyue zhu changjian" [Glorious Times Casting a Long Sword], in Di'er paobing zhengzhibu, ed., *Huihuang niandai*, p. 522.

53. Zhang Yang, ed., *Jiakuai tuijin guofang he jundui xiandaihua* [Accelerate and Promote National Defense and Armed Forces Modernization] (Beijing: Renmin chubanshe, 2015); Shou Xiaosong, ed., *Zhanlue xue*.

54. Based on Mao's concern with blackmail, one prominent Chinese scholar has argued that China's deterrent is best characterized as "counter nuclear coercion [*fan he weiya*]." See Li Bin, "Zhongguo hezhanlue bianxi" [Analysis of China's Nuclear Strategy], *Shijie jingji yu zhengzhi*, No. 9 (2006), pp. 16-22.

55. Ryan, *Chinese Attitudes Toward Nuclear Weapons*, p. 17; Ralph L. Powell, "Great Powers and Atomic Bombs Are 'Paper Tigers,'" *China Quarterly*, No. 23 (1965), pp. 55-63.

56. Mao Zedong, *Mao Zedong junshi wenji* [Mao Zedong's Collected Works on Military Affairs], Vol. 6 (Beijing: Junshi kexue chubanshe, 1993), p. 359.

57. Mao Zedong, *Mao Zedong wenji* [Mao Zedong's Collected Works], Vol. 8 (Beijing: Xinhua chubanshe, 1999), p. 370.

58. Nie Rongzhen, *Nie Rongzhen junshi wenxuan* [Nie Rongzhen's Selected Works on Military Affairs] (Beijing: Jiefangjun chubanshe, 1992), p. 498.

59. Mao Zedong, *Mao Zedong wenji*, Vol. 7, p. 27.

60. Mao Zedong, *Mao Zedong wenji* [Mao Zedong's Collected Works], Vol. 6 (Beijing: Xinhua chubanshe, 1999), p. 374.

61. Leng Rong and Wang Zuoling, eds., *Deng Xiaoping nianpu, 1975-1997*, Vol. 1, p. 92.

62. Jiang Zemin, *Jiang Zemin wenxuan* [Jiang Zemin's Selected Works], Vol. 2 (Beijing: Renmin chubanshe, 2006), p. 269.

63. Mao Zedong, *Mao Zedong xuanji* [Mao Zedong's Selected Works], 2nd ed., Vol. 4 (Beijing: Renmin chubanshe, 1991), pp. 1133–1134.

64. Ye Jianying, *Ye Jianying junshi wenxuan*, p. 490.

65. Jin Chongji, ed., *Zhou Enlai zhuan* [Zhou Enlai's Biography], Vol. 4 (Beijing: Zhongyang wenxian chubanshe, 1998), p. 1745; Zhou Enlai, *Zhou Enlai wenhua wenxuan*, p. 575.

66. Pang Xianzhi and Feng Hui, eds., *Mao Zedong nianpu, 1949–1976* [A Chronicle of Mao Zedong's Life, 1949–1976], Vol. 5 (Beijing: Zhongyang wenxian chubanshe, 2013), p. 27.

67. Ibid., p. 473.

68. Leng Rong and Wang Zuoling, eds., *Deng Xiaoping nianpu, 1975–1997*, Vol. 1, p. 308.

69. Zhongyang junwei bangongting, ed., *Deng Xiaoping guanyu xin shiqi jundui jianshe lunshu xuanbian*, p. 44.

70. Deng Xiaoping, *Deng Xiaoping junshi wenxuan* [Deng Xiaoping's Selected Works on Military Affairs], Vol. 2, (Beijing: Junshi kexue chubanshe, 2004), p. 273. See also Leng Rong and Wang Zuoling, eds., *Deng Xiaoping nianpu, 1975–1997*, Vol. 1, p. 101.

71. Guo Yingui, "Zhou Enlai yu Zhongguo de hewuqi" [Zhou Enlai and China's Nuclear Weapons], in Li Qi, ed., *Zai Zhou Enlai shenbian de rizi: Xihuating gongzuo renyuan de huiyi* [Days At Zhou Enlai's Side: Recollections of the Staff Members of West Flower Hall], (Beijing: Zhongyang wenxian chubanshe, 1998), p. 273.

72. This is based on Yang Chengzong's oral history. See Yang Chengzong, "Wo wei Yuliao Juli chuanhua gei Mao zhuxi" [I Gave Chairman Mao a Message from Joliot-Curie], *Bainian chao*, No. 2 (2012), pp. 25–30.

73. Ge Nengquan, ed., *Qian Sanqiang nianpu* [A Chronicle of Qian Sanqiang's Life] (Jinan: Shandong youyi chubanshe, 2002), p. 89.

74. Lei was Zhou's military secretary, while Wei Ming was Zhou's culture and science secretary.

75. This is based on Lei Yingfu's recollecion, reproduced in Qian Sanqiang's official chronology, along with an article by the Chinese historian of science Fan Hongye. See Ge Nengquan, ed., *Qian Sanqiang nianpu*, p. 95; Fan Hongye, "Yuanzidan de gushi: Ying cong 1952 nian qi" [The Story of the Atomic Bomb: It Should Start in 1952], *Zhonghua dushu bao*, December 15, 2004.

76. Ge Nengquan, ed., *Qian Sanqiang nianpu*, p. 95. Zhang Zuowen suggests that the meeting with Zhao Kejin occurred after the May 1952 CMC meeting. It possible that two meetings occurred.

77. Peng Dehuai zhuanji zu, *Peng Dehuai quanzhuan* [Peng Dehuai's Complete Biography] (Beijing: Zhongguo dabaike quanshu chubanshe, 2009), pp. 1073; Zhang Zuowen, "Zhou Enlai yu daodan hewuqi" [Zhou Enlai and Missile Nuclear Weapons], in Li Qi, ed., *Zai Zhou Enlai shenbian de rizi: Xihuating gongzuo renyuan de huiyi* [Days At Zhou Enlai's Side: Recollections of the Staff Members of West Flower Hall] (Beijing: Zhongyang wenxian chubanshe, 1998), pp. 657–658.

78. Ge Nengquan, ed., *Qian Sanqiang nianpu*, p. 94. Also, see Guo Yingui, "Zhou Enlai yu Zhongguo de hewuqi," p. 273.

79. Zhang Zuowen, "Zhou Enlai yu daodan hewuqi," pp. 657–658.

80. Guo Yingui, "Zhou Enlai yu Zhongguo de hewuqi," p. 273.

81. Ibid.

82. Zhang Zuowen, "Zhou Enlai yu daodan hewuqi," p. 658.

83. Ge Nengquan, ed., *Qian Sanqiang nianpu*, p. 102.

84. Wang Yan, ed., *Peng Dehuai nianpu* [A Chronicle of Peng Dehuai's Life] (Beijing: Renmin chubanshe, 1998), p. 563.

85. Ibid., p. 575.

86. Ge Nengquan, ed., *Qian Sanqiang nianpu*, p. 112; Wang Yan, ed., *Peng Dehuai nianpu*, p. 577. Peng would repeat his request during his next visit to Moscow in May 1955.

87. Zhang Zuowen, "Zhou Enlai yu daodan hewuqi," p. 658.

88. Ibid.

89. Peng Jichao, "Mao Zedong yu liangdan yixing" [Mao Zedong and Two Bombs and One Satellite], *Shenjian*, No. 3 (2013).

90. Ibid. Also, see 'Jam-dpal-rgya-mtsho, *Li Jue zhuan* [Li Jue's Biography] (Zhongguo Zangxue chubanshe: 2004), p. 435.

91. Mao quoted in Roland Timerbaev, "How the Soviet Union Helped China Develop the A-bomb," *Digest of Yaderny Kontrol (Nuclear Control)* No. 8 (Summer-Fall 1998), p. 44.

92. Ge Nengquan, ed., *Qian Sanqiang nianpu*, p. 113.

93. Ibid.

94. Mao Zedong, *Mao Zedong wenji* [Mao Zedong's Collected Works], Vol. 6 (Beijing: Renmin chubanshe, 1996), p. 367.

95. Quoted in Sun Xiangli, *He shidai de zhanlue xuanze*, p. 5.

96. Quoted in ibid., p. 6.

97. Members of the Central Committee Secretariat included Mao, Zhou, Zhu De, and Liu Shaoqi.

98. Li Ping and Ma Zhisun, eds., *Zhou Enlai nianpu, 1949–1976* [A Chronicle of Zhou Enlai's Life, 1949–1976], Vol. 2 (Beijing: Zhongyang wenxian chubanshe, 1997), p. 441.

99. Ge Nengquan, ed., *Qian Sanqiang nianpu*, p. 115.

100. Pang Xianzhi and Feng Hui, eds., *Mao Zedong nianpu, 1949–1976* [A Chronicle of Mao Zedong's Life, 1949–1976], Vol. 2 (Beijing: Zhongyang wenxian chubanshe, 2013), p. 338.

101. Nie Rongzhen was the senior military officer for weapons development.

102. This section draws on China's official history of its nuclear program. See Li Jue, et al., eds., *Dangdai Zhongguo he gongye* [Contemporary China's Nuclear Industry] (Beijing: Dangdai Zhongguo chubanshe, 1987).

103. On Soviet technology transfers, see Yanqiong Liu and Jifeng Liu, "Analysis of Soviet Technology Transfer in the Development of China's Nuclear Programs," *Comparative Technology Transfer and Society*, Vol. 7, No. 1 (April 2009), pp. 66–110.

104. Zhang Aiping, *Zhang Aiping junshi wenxuan*, p. 238. Although characterized as a debate over whether or not to continue the program, the debate was wide-ranging, including whether to prioritize conventional weapons and reduce the pace of work on strategic weapons. See Zhang Xianmin and Zhou Junlun, "1961 nian liangdan 'shangma' 'xiama" zhizheng" [The Dispute in 1961 over "Mounting" or "Dismounting" the Two Bombs], *Lilun shiye*, No. 12 (2016), pp. 55–58.

105. Lu Qiming and Fan Minruo, *Zhang Aiping yu liangdan yixing*, p. 66; Nie Rongzhen, *Nie Rongzhen huiyilu*, p. 814. For a detailed review of the discussions at the meeting, see Zhang Xianmin and Zhou Junlun, "1961 nian liangdan "shangma" "xiama" zhizheng," pp. 54–59.

106. Li Ping and Ma Zhisun, eds., *Zhou Enlai nianpu, 1949–1976*, Vol. 2, p. 426.

107. Zhou Enlai, *Zhou Enlai junshi wenxuan*, Vol. 4, p. 422.

108. When the Politburo discussion occurred is unclear. According to Zhang Aiping's biographer it was in August or September. See Lu Qiming and Fan Minruo, *Zhang Aiping yu liangdan yixing*, pp. 66–68. Nie Rongzhen's biography does not mention a Politburo meeting.

109. Nie Rongzhen, *Nie Rongzhen junshi wenxuan*, pp. 488–495.

110. Lu Qiming and Fan Minruo, *Zhang Aiping yu liangdan yixing*, p. 67. Lewis and Xue state that Mao sided with Nie, favoring moving forward with the bomb during the debate in the summer of 1961. However, they incorrectly attributed a statement Mao made in June 1962 in support of the nuclear program to 1961.

111. Ibid.

112. Zhang Aiping, *Zhang Aiping junshi wenxuan*, p. 239.

113. For a copy of the report, see ibid., pp. 238–245.

114. Ibid., p. 245.

115. Ibid., p. 238; Lu Qiming and Fan Minruo, *Zhang Aiping yu liangdan yixing*, p. 76.

116. Lu Qiming and Fan Minruo, *Zhang Aiping yu liangdan yixing*, p. 76.

117. Ibid., 59.

118. Zhang Xianmin and Zhou Junlun, "1961 nian liangdan 'shangma' 'xiama' zhizheng," p. 59.

119. Pang Xianzhi and Feng Hui, eds., *Mao Zedong nianpu, 1949–1976*, Vol. 5, p. 105.

120. Xi Qixin, *Zhu Guangya zhuan* [Zhu Guangya's Biography] (Beijing: Renmin chubanshe, 2015), p. 320.

121. Huang Yao and Zhang Mingzhe, eds., *Luo Ruiqing zhuan* [Luo Ruiqing's Biography] (Beijing: Dangdai Zhongguo chubanshe, 1996), p. 412.

122. According to one source, Zhou Enlai instructed the Second Ministry to be able to test a bomb within this time frame. See 'Jam-dpal-rgya-mtsho, *Li Jue zhuan*, p. 357.

123. Huang Yao and Zhang Mingzhe, eds., *Luo Ruiqing zhuan*, p. 412.

124. Ibid.

125. Ibid., p. 413.

126. For a copy of the report, see Luo Ruiqing, *Luo Ruiqing junshi wenxuan* [Luo Ruiqing's Selected Works on Military Affairs] (Beijing: Dangdai Zhongguo chubanshe, 2006), pp. 618–620.

127. Pang Xianzhi and Feng Hui, eds., *Mao Zedong nianpu, 1949–1976*, Vol. 5, p. 167.

128. He, Nie, and Zhang were all involved in supervising China's weapons programs, while Luo was running military affairs as chief of the general staff. All were members of the CMC.

129. Lu Qiming and Fan Minruo, *Zhang Aiping yu liangdan yixing*, p. 121.

130. Ibid., p. 179.

131. Ibid., p. 186.

132. Quoted in ibid., p. 187.

133. Ibid., p. 189.

134. Ibid.

135. Ibid., pp. 229–230.

136. *Renmin ribao*, October 17, 1964, p. 1.

137. Government statements jointly issued with another state are more common.

138. Jin Chongji, ed., *Zhou Enlai zhuan*, Vol. 4, pp. 1758–1762; Li Ping and Ma Zhisun, eds., *Zhou Enlai nianpu, 1949–1976*, Vol. 2, pp. 675–676.

139. Di'er paobing silingbu, ed., *Di'er paobing zhanlue xue*, p. 10.

140. Ibid.

141. Ibid., p. 23. References to China's no-first-use policy can also be found in the 2004 *Science of Second Artillery Campaigns*. See Yu Xijun, ed., *Di'er paobing zhanyi xue*, pp. 59, 60, 282, 298, 305, 356. The book also suggests changing China's nuclear policy (p. 294), but this nevertheless highlights the constraint of policy on strategy. Despite debate over changing China's no-first-use policy in the 2000s, it was not changed. See Fravel and Medeiros, "China's Search for Assured Retaliation," p. 80.

142. The DF-2 was China's first intermediate range ballistic missile with a range of 1050 kilometers, based on the Soviet R-5. The DF-3 was China's first intermediate range ballistic missile based on a Chinese design, with a range of 2650 kilometers. See Lewis and Di, "China's Ballistic Missile Programs," pp. 9–10.

143. Jin Chongji, ed., *Zhou Enlai zhuan*, Vol. 4, p. 1753.

144. Lewis and Xue, *China Builds the Bomb*, pp. 159–160.

145. Jin Chongji, ed., *Zhou Enlai zhuan*, Vol. 4, p. 1753; Liu Xiyao, "Woguo 'liangdan' yanzhi juece guocheng zhuiji" [Immediate Record of the Decision-making Process for Our Country's Research on "Two Bombs"], *Yanhuang chunqiu*, No. 5 (1996), p. 7.

146. Sun Xiangli, *He shidai de zhanlue xuanze*, p. 23.

147. Zhou Junlun, ed., *Nie Rongzhen nianpu* [A Chronicle of Nie Rongzhen's Life] (Beijing: Renmin chubanshe, 1999), p. 921; Zhang Xianmin, ed., *Qian Xuesen nianpu* [A Chronicle of Qian Xuesen's Life], Vol. 1 (Beijing: Zhongyang wenxian chubanshe, 2015).

148. No copy of the report is available. But it is summarized by one of Zhou Enlai's secretaries, Zhang Zuowen. See Zhang Zuowen, "Zhou Enlai yu daodan hewuqi," pp. 663–664. Due to its limited range, the DF-2 represented a stopgap measure, but reflected China's desire to deploy a deliverable nuclear weapon, however inadequate.

149. Liu Xiyao, "Woguo 'liangdan' yanzhi juece guocheng zhuiji," p. 7.

150. Zhang Zuowen, "Zhou Enlai yu daodan hewuqi," p. 664.

151. The DF-2 was the first missile that China attempted to design indigenously, albeit based on some designs provided by the Soviet Union.

152. Zhang Xianmin, ed., *Qian Xuesen nianpu*, Vol. 1, p. 309.

153. Xu Xuesong, "Zhongguo ludi didi zhanlue daodan fazhan de lishi huigu yu jingyan qishi" [Historical Review and Implications of the Development of China's Land-based Surface-to-Surface Strategic Missiles], *Junshi lishi*, No. 2 (2017), p. 25; Xie Guang, ed., *Dangdai Zhongguo de guofang keji gongye* [Contemporary China's Defense Science and Technology Industry], Vol. 1 (Beijing: Dangdai Zhongguo chubanshe, 1992), p. 83.

154. Liu Jiyuan, ed., *Zhongguo hangtian shiye fazhan de zhexue sixiang* [The Philosophy of the Development of China's Aerospace Industry] (Beijing: Beijing daxue chubanshe, 2013), p. 33.

155. "Zhongguo Dongfeng sihao daodan yanzhi shi: Jiaqiang Zhongguo de zhanlue he liliang [The Development History of China's Dongfeng-4: Strengthening China's Strategic Nuclear Power]," May 28, 2015, http://military.china.com/history4/62/20150528/19760409_all.html and ibid.

156. Li Ping and Ma Zhisun, eds., *Zhou Enlai nianpu, 1949–1976*, Vol. 2, p. 426.

157. Liu Jiyuan, ed., *Zhongguo hangtian shiye fazhan de zhexue sixiang*, p. 30.

158. Ibid., pp. 33, 35.

159. Xu Xuesong, "Zhongguo ludi didi zhanlue daodan fazhan de lishi huigu yu jingyan qishi," p. 27.

160. Lu Qiming and Fan Minruo, *Zhang Aiping yu liangdan yixing*, pp. 267–8; Dong Fanghe, *Zhang Aiping zhuan*, pp. 805–6.

161. At the time, China's artillery forces were a branch directly under the CMC.

162. Dong Fanghe, *Zhang Aiping zhuan*, p. 812.

163. Xiang Shouzhi, *Xiang Shouzhi huiyilu* [Xiang Shouzhi's Memoirs] (Beijing: Jiefangjun chubanshe, 2006), p. 331; Dong Fanghe, *Zhang Aiping zhuan*, p. 813.

164. Xiang Shouzhi, *Xiang Shouzhi huiyilu*, p. 331; Dong Fanghe, *Zhang Aiping zhuan*, p. 812.

165. Lu Qiming and Fan Minruo, *Zhang Aiping yu liangdan yixing*, p. 273; Dong Fanghe, *Zhang Aiping zhuan*, p. 813.

166. Quoted in Wu Lie, *Zhengrong suiyue*, p. 354.

167. Lu Qiming and Fan Minruo, *Zhang Aiping yu liangdan yixing*, p. 273.

168. Wu Lie, *Zhengrong suiyue*, p. 358.

169. Ibid., p. 357.

170. Liu Jixian, ed., *Ye Jianying nianpu* [A Chronicle of Ye Jianying's Life], Vol. 2 (Beijing: Zhongyang wenxian chubanshe, 2007), p. 970.

171. He Jinheng, " 'Jinggan youxiao' zongti jianshe mubiao de queli," p. 43.

172. Xiang Shouzhi, *Xiang Shouzhi huiyilu*, pp. 330–341.

173. Li Shuiqing, "Gaige, cong zheli qibu," p. 31.

174. He Jinheng, " 'Jinggan youxiao' zongti jianshe mubiao de queli," p. 43.

175. Han Chengchen, "He Jinheng," in Di'er paobing zhengzhibu, ed., *Di'er paobing gaoji jiangling zhuan* [Biographies of the Second Artillery's Senior Generals], (n.p.: Di'er paobing zhengzhibu, 2006), p. 359.

176. Li Shuiqing, "Gaige, cong zheli qibu," p. 31.

177. Ibid.

178. Quoted in Zhang Aiping, ed., *Zhongguo renmin jiefangjun (xia)* [The Chinese People's Liberation Army], Vol. 2 (Beijing: Dangdai Zhongguo chubanshe, 1994), p. 121.

179. Wang Huanping, "Li Shuiqing," in Di'er paobing zhengzhibu, ed., *Di'er paobing gaoji jiangling zhuan* [Biographies of the Second Artillery's Senior Generals], (n.p.: Di'er paobing zhengzhibu, 2006), p. 240; Han Chengchen, "He Jinheng," p. 361.

180. Li Shuiqing, "Gaige, cong zheli qibu," p. 31.

181. Zhang Aiping, ed., *Zhongguo renmin jiefangjun (xia)*, Vol. 2, p. 121.

182. Yu Xijun, ed., *Di'er paobing zhanyi xue*, p. 303; Shou Xiaosong, ed., *Zhanlue xue*, p. 175.

183. For a detailed description of the scenario, see Yang Wenting, "Dongfeng di yi zhi: Ji yici fangwei zuozhan yanxi" [The First East Wind: Remembering One Defensive Combat Exercise], in Di'er paobing zhengzhibu, ed., *Huihuang niandai*, pp. 107–113.

184. Han Chengchen, "He Jinheng," p. 365.

185. Ibid.

186. Liu Lifeng zhuan bianxiezu, "Liu Lifeng," in Di'er paobing zhengzhibu, ed., *Di'er paobing gaoji jiangling zhuan* [Biographies of the Second Artillery's Senior Generals], (n.p.: Di'er paobing zhengzhibu, 2006), p. 413.

187. See Shen Kehui, "Erpao junshi lilun yanjiu de tansuo" [Exploring the Second Artillery's Research on Military Theory], in Di'er paobing zhengzhibu, ed., *Huihuang niandai*, p. 140. Another edition was published in 2004.

188. He Jinheng, " 'Jinggan youxiao' zongti jianshe mubiao de queli," p. 45.

189. Ibid.

190. Xu Jian, *Niaokan diqiu: Zhongguo zhanlue daodan zhendi gongcheng jishi* [A Bird's-Eye View of the Earth: The Record of the Engineering of China's Strategic Missile Bases] (Beijing: Zuojia chubanshe, 1997), p. 363.

191. Shen Kehui, "Erpao junshi lilun yanjiu de tansuo," p. 141.

192. Dai Yifang, ed., *Junshi xue yanjiu huigu yu zhanwang* [Reflections and Prospects for Military Studies] (Beijing: Junshi kexue chubanshe, 1995), p. 360.

193. Xu Jian, *Niaokan diqiu*, p. 363.

194. Shen Kehui, "Erpao junshi lilun yanjiu de tansuo," p. 142.

195. Ibid.

196. Xu Jian, *Niaokan diqiu*, p. 364; Xu Jian, "Li Xuge" [Li Xuge], in Di'er paobing zhengzhibu, ed., *Di'er paobing gaoji jiangling zhuan* [Biographies of the Second Artillery's Senior Generals], (n.p.: Di'er paobing zhengzhibu, 2006), p. 489.

197. Xu Jian, "Li Xuge," p. 489.

198. Ibid. Liu Huaqing's chronology notes a meeting with Liu Lifeng to discuss "secrecy" (*baomi gongzuo*). See Jiang Weimin, ed., *Liu Huaqing nianpu* [A Chronicle of Liu Huaqing's Life], Vol. 2 (Beijing: Jiefangjun chubanshe, 2016), p. 812.

199. "Zhuan ji: Yige kangzhan laobing de zishu [Record: A War of Resistance Veteran's Own Words]," Gushan qiaofu de boke, February 26, 2011, http://blog.sina.com.cn/s/blog_5edd0ba60100pcra.html (accessed July 2, 2015). On the CMC's criticism, see also Xu

Jian, "Li Xuge," p. 489. For an indirect but clear reference to this criticism, see Xu Jian, *Niaokan diqiu*, p. 364.

200. Xu Jian, *Niaokan diqiu*, p. 364.

201. Shen Kehui, "Erpao junshi lilun yanjiu de tansuo," p. 141.

202. "Zhuan ji: Yige kangzhan laobing de zishu."

203. Di'er paobing silingbu, ed., *Di'er paobing zhanlue xue*, p. 1.

204. Dai Yifang, ed., *Junshi xue yanjiu huigu yu zhanwang*, p. 361.

205. Li Ke and Hao Shengzhang, *Wenhua dageming zhong de renmin jiefangjun* [The People's Liberation Army during the Cultural Revolution] (Beijing: Zhonggong dangshi ziliao chubanshe, 1989), p. 358.

206. Xu Jian, *Niaokan diqiu*, p. 14.

207. Fiona S. Cunningham and M. Taylor Fravel, "Assuring Assured Retaliation: China's Nuclear Posture and U.S.-China Strategic Stability," *International Security* Vol. 40, No. 2 (Fall 2015), pp. 42–44.

208. Xu Jian, *Niaokan diqiu*, pp. 13–14.

209. For a detailed account of the project, see ibid.

210. Xu Jian, "Li Xuge," p. 486.

211. Hans M. Kristensen and Robert S. Norris, "Chinese Nuclear Forces, 2015," *Bulletin of the Atomic Scientists*, Vol. 71, No. 4 (2015), p. 82.

212. Di'er paobing silingbu, ed., *Di'er paobing zhanlue xue*, p. 3.

213. Lewis and Di, "China's Ballistic Missile Programs," p. 19.

214. Office of the Secretary of Defense, *Military Power of the People's Republic of China 2000* (Department of Defense, 2000); National Air and Space Intelligence Center, *Ballistic and Cruise Missile Threat*, (Wright-Patterson Air Force Base, 2009), p. 21.

215. Hans M. Kristensen and Robert S. Norris, "Chinese Nuclear Forces, 2018," *Bulletin of the Atomic Scientists*, Vol. 74, No. 4 (2018), p. 290. This includes warheads on the DF-5A, DF-5B, DF-31, and DF-31A. The number is likely to increase when more information becomes available about the DF-31AG and when the new DF-41 is deployed. It remains unclear whether China's SSBNs with the JL-2 conduct deterrent patrols.

216. Ibid.

217. Ibid., pp. 291–292. See also Wang Changqin and Fang Guangming, "Women weishenme fazhan dongfeng-26 dadao daodan" [Why We Had to Develop the Dongfeng-26 Ballistic Missile], *Zhongguo qingnian bao*, November 30, 2015, p. 9.

218. Wu Lie, *Zhengrong suiyue*, p. 357.

219. Ibid., p. 358.

220. He Jinheng, "'Jinggan youxiao' zongti jianshe mubiao de queli," pp. 44, 46.

221. Yang Wenting, "Dongfeng di yi zhi," p. 108.

222. Xu Bin, "Erpao junshi xunlian gaige de zuyi" [The Path of Training Reforms in the Second Artillery], in Di'er paobing zhengzhibu, ed., *Huihuang niandai*, pp. 430–431.

223. Yu Xijun, "Xinshiji xinjieduan zhanlue daodan budui zuozhan lilun de chuangxin yu xin fazhan" [Innovations and New Developments in the Operational Theory of the Strategic Rocket Forces at the New Stage of the New Century], in Di'er paobing zhengzhibu, ed., *Huihuang niandai*, pp. 441–446.

224. Zhao Qiuling and Zhang Guang, "Yongbu tingbu de ziwo chaoyue" [Never Stop Transcending Onseself], in Di'er paobing zhengzhibu, ed., *Huihuang niandai*, p. 361.

225. Di'er paobing silingbu, ed., *Di'er paobing zhanlue xue*, p. 1.

226. Ibid., p. 9.

227. Ibid., p. 25.

228. Ibid., p. 58.

229. Ibid., p. 114.

230. Yu Xijun, ed., *Di'er paobing zhanyi xue*, p. 93.

231. Ibid., p. 122.

232. Cunningham and Fravel, "Assuring Assured Retaliation."

Conclusion

1. For a review, see Peter Feaver, "Civil-Military Relations," *Annual Review of Political Science*, No. 2 (1999), pp. 211–241.

2. Risa Brooks, *Shaping Strategy: The Civil-Military Politics of Strategic Assessment* (Princeton, NJ: Princeton University Press, 2008).

3. Suzanne Nielsen, "Civil-Military Relations Theory and Military Effectiveness," *Public Administration and Management*, Vol. 10, No. 2 (2003); Caitlin Talmadge, *The Dictator's Army: Battlefield Effectiveness in Authoritarian Regimes* (Ithaca, NY: Cornell University Press, 2015).

4. Stefano Recchia, *Reassuring the Reluctant Warriors: US Civil-Military Relations and Multi-lateral Intervention* (Ithaca, NY: Cornell University Press, 2016).

5. Vipin Narang, *Nuclear Strategy in the Modern Era: Regional Powers and International Conflict* (Princeton, NJ: Princeton University Press, 2014).

6. Dan Reiter and Allan Stam, *Democracies at War* (Princeton, NJ: Princeton University Press, 2002); Risa Brooks, "Making Military Might: Why Do States Fail and Succeed?," *Intenational Security*, Vol. 28, No. 2 (2003), pp. 1491–191. On regime-type and performance, see Jessica Weeks, *Dictators at War and Peace* (Ithaca, NY: Cornell University Press, 2014).

7. Randall Schweller, "The Progressiveness of Neoclassical Realism," in Colin Elman and Miriam Fendius Elman, eds., *Progress in International Relations Theory: Appraising the Field* (Cambridge: MIT Press, 2003), pp. 311–347; Stephen E. Lobell, Norrin M. Ripsman, and Jeffrey W. Taliaferro, eds., *Neoclassical Realism, the State, and Foreign Policy* (New York: Cambridge University Press, 2009).

8. Randall Schweller, *Unanswered Threats: Political Constraints on the Balance of Power* (Princeton, NJ: Princeton University Press, 2006).

9. Barry Posen, *The Sources of Military Doctrine: France, Britain, and Germany Between the World Wars* (Ithaca, NY: Cornell University Press, 1984).

10. Samuel P. Huntington, *The Soldier and the State: The Theory and Politics of Civil-Military Relations* (Cambridge, MA: Belknap Press of Harvard University Press, 1957).

11. Sebastian Rosato, "The Inscrutable Intentions of Great Powers," *International Security*, Vol. 39, No. 3 (2014/15), pp. 48–88; John J. Mearsheimer, *The Tragedy of Great Power Politics* (New York: W. W. Norton, 2001).

12. See, for example, Michael Chase, et al., *China's Incomplete Military Transformation: Assessing the Weaknesses of the People's Liberation Army (PLA)* (Santa Monica, CA: RAND, 2015).

BIBLIOGRAPHY

Chinese Language Sources

CHRONOLOGIES, DOCUMENTS, AND DOCUMENTARY COLLECTIONS

2004 nian Zhongguo de guofang. [China's National Defense in 2004]. Beijing: Guowuyuan xinwen bangongshi, 2004.

2006 nian Zhongguo de guofang. [China's National Defense in 2006]. Beijing: Guowuyuan xinwen bangongshi, 2006.

2008 nian Zhongguo de guofang. [China's National Defense in 2006]. Beijing: Guowuyuan xinwen bangongshi, 2008.

Chi Haotian. *Chi Haotian junshi wenxuan* [Chi Haotian's Selected Works on Military Affairs]. Beijing: Jiefangjun chubanshe, 2009.

Deng Xiaoping. *Deng Xiaoping lun guofang he jundui jianshe* [Deng Xiaoping on National Defense and Army Building]. Beijing: Junshi kexue chubanshe, 1992.

———. *Deng Xiaoping junshi wenxuan* [Deng Xiaoping's Selected Works on Military Affairs]. 3 Vols. Beijing: Junshi kexue chubanshe, 2004.

Fu Quanyou. *Fu Quanyou junshi wenxuan* [Fu Quanyou's Selected Works on Military Affairs]. Beijing: Jiefangjun chubanshe, 2015.

Ge Nengquan, ed. *Qian Sanqiang nianpu* [A Chronicle of Qian Sanqiang's Life]. 2 Vols. Jinan: Shandong youyi chubanshe, 2002.

Han Huaizhi. *Han Huaizhi lun junshi* [Han Huaizhi on Military Affairs]. Beijing: Jiefangjun chubanshe, 2012.

Hu Jintao. *Hu Jintao wenxuan* [Hu Jintao's Selected Works]. 3 Vols. Beijing: Renmin chubanshe, 2016.

Huang Yao, ed. *Luo Ronghuan nianpu* [A Chronicle of Luo Ronghuan's Life]. Beijing: Renmin chubanshe, 2002.

Jiang Weimin, ed. *Liu Huaqing nianpu* [A Chronicle of Liu Huaqing's Life]. 3 Vols. Beijing: Jiefangjun chubanshe, 2016.

Jiang Zemin. *Lun guofang yu jundui jianshe* [On National Defense and Army Building]. Beijing: Jiefangjun chubanshe, 2002.

———. *Jiang Zemin wenxuan* [Jiang Zemin's Selected Works]. 3 Vols. Beijing: Renmin chubanshe, 2006.

Leng Rong, and Wang Zuoling, eds. *Deng Xiaoping nianpu, 1975–1997* [A Chronicle of Deng Xiaoping's Life, 1975–1997]. 2 Vols. Beijing: Zhongyang wenxian chubanshe, 2004.

Li De, and She Yun, eds. *Lin Biao yuanshuai wenji (shang, xia)* [Marshal Lin Biao's Selected Works]. Xianggang: Fenghuang shupin, 2013.

Li Ping, and Ma Zhisun, eds. *Zhou Enlai nianpu, 1949–1976* [A Chronicle of Zhou Enlai's Life, 1949–1976]. 3 Vols. Beijing: Zhongyang wenxian chubanshe, 1997.

Liu Chongwen, and Chen Shaochou, eds. *Liu Shaoqi nianpu, 1898–1969* [A Chronicle of Liu Shaoqi's Life, 1898–1969]. Beijing: Zhongyang wenxian chubanshe, 1996.

Liu Huaqing. *Liu Huaqing junshi wenxuan* [Liu Huaqing's Selected Works on Military Affairs]. 2 Vols. Beijing: Jiefangjun chubanshe, 2008.

Liu Jixian, ed. *Ye Jianying nianpu* [A Chronicle of Ye Jianying's Life]. 2 Vols. Beijing: Zhongyang wenxian chubanshe, 2007.

Liu Shaoqi. *Liu Shaoqi xuanji* [Liu Shaoqi's Selected Works]. 2 Vols. Beijing: Renmin chubanshe, 1981.

Liu Yongzhi, ed. *Zongcan moubu dashiji* [A Chronology of the General Staff Department]. Beijing: Lantian chubanshe, 2009.

Luo Ruiqing. *Luo Ruiqing junshi wenxuan* [Luo Ruiqing's Selected Works on Military Affairs]. Beijing: Dangdai Zhongguo chubanshe, 2006.

——. "Luo Ruiqing chuanda Mao Zedong zhishi (June 23, 1965)" [Luo Ruiqing Transmits Mao's Instructions]. In Song Yongyi, ed., *The Database for the History of Contemporary Chinese Political Movements, 1949-* Harvard University: Fairbank Center for Chinese Studies, 2013.

Mao Zedong. *Jianguo yilai Mao Zedong junshi wengao* [Mao Zedong's Military Manuscripts Since the Founding of the Nation]. 3 Vols. Beijing: Junshi kexue chubanshe, 2010.

——. *Jianguo yilai Mao Zedong wengao.* [Mao Zedong's Manuscripts Since the Founding of the Nation]. 13 Vols. Beijing: Zhongyang wenxian chubanshe, 1993.

——. *Mao Zedong junshi wenji* [Mao Zedong's Collected Works on Military Affairs]. 6 Vols. Beijing: Junshi kexue chubanshe, 1993.

——. *Mao Zedong waijiao wenxuan* [Mao Zedong's Selected Works on Diplomacy]. Beijing: Shijie zhishi chubanshe, 1994.

——. *Mao Zedong wenji* [Mao Zedong's Collected Works]. 8 Vols. Beijing: Renmin chubanshe, 1993.

——. *Mao Zedong xuanji* [Mao Zedong's Selected Works]. 4 Vols. Beijing: Renmin chubanshe, 1991.

——. "Zai shisanling guanyu difang dangwei zhua junshi he peiyang jiebanren de jianghua (June 16, 1964)" [Speech at the Ming Tombs on Local Party Committees' Grasping Military Affairs and Cultivating Successors]. In Song Yongyi, ed., *The Database for the History of Contemporary Chinese Political Movements, 1949-* Harvard University: Fairbank Center for Chinese Studies, 2013.

——. "Zai zhongyang changwei shang de jianghua (June 8, 1964)" [Speech at the Politburo Standing Committee]. In Song Yongyi, ed., *The Database for the History of Contemporary Chinese Political Movements, 1949-* Harvard University: Fairbank Center for Chinese Studies, 2013.

——. "Zai zhongyang gongzuo huiyi de jianghua (June 6, 1964)" [Speech at the Central Work Conference]. In Song Yongyi, ed., *The Database for the History of Contemporary Chinese Political Movements, 1949-* Harvard University: Fairbank Center for Chinese Studies, 2013.

Nie Rongzhen. *Nie Rongzhen junshi wenxuan* [Nie Rongzhen's Selected Works on Military Affairs]. Beijing: Jiefangjun chubanshe, 1992.

Pang Xianzhi, ed. *Mao Zedong nianpu, 1893–1949 (shang, zhong, xia)* [A Chronicle of Mao Zedong's Life, 1893–1949]. Beijing: Zhongyang wenxian chubanshe, 2013.

Pang Xianzhi, and Feng Hui, eds. *Mao Zedong nianpu, 1949–1976* [A Chronicle of Mao Zedong's Life, 1949–1976]. 6 Vols. Beijing: Zhongyang wenxian chubanshe, 2013.

Shenyang junqu zhengzhibu yanjiu shi, ed. *Shenyang junqu dashiji, 1945–1985.* n.p.: n.p., 1985.

Shou Xiaosong, ed. *Zhongguo renmin jiefangjun bashi nian dashiji* [A Chronology of Eighty Years of the Chinese People's Liberation Army]. Beijing: Junshi kexue chubanshe, 2007.

Song Shilun. *Song Shilun junshi wenxuan: 1958–1989* [Song Shilun's Selected Works on Military Affairs: 1958–1989]. Beijing: Junshi kexue chubanshe, 2007.

Su Yu. *Su Yu wenxuan* [Su Yu's Selected Works]. 3 Vols. Beijing: Junshi kexue chubanshe, 2004.

Wang Yan, ed. *Peng Dehuai nianpu* [A Chronicle of Peng Dehuai's Life]. Beijing: Renmin chubanshe, 1998.

Xi Jinping. *Xi Jinping guofang he jundui jianshe zhongyao lunshu xuanbian* [A Selection of Xi Jinping's Important Expositions on National Defense and Army Building]. Beijing: Jiefangjun chubanshe, 2014.

———. *Xi Jinping guofang he jundui jianshe zhongyao lunshu xuanbian* (er) [A Selection of Xi Jinping's Important Expositions on National Defense and Army Building (2)]. Beijing: Jiefangjun chubanshe, 2015.

Xu Shiyou. *Xu Shiyou junshi wenxuan* [Xu Shiyou's Selected Works on Military Affairs]. Beijing: Junshi kexue chubanshe, 2013.

Xu Xiangqian. *Xu Xiangqian junshi wenxuan* [Xu Xiangqian's Selected Works on Military Affairs]. Beijing: Jiefangjun chubanshe, 1993.

Yang Shengqun, and Yan Jianqi, eds. *Deng Xiaoping nianpu (1904–1974)* [A Chronicle of Deng Xiaoping's Life (1904–1974)]. 3 Vols. Beijing: Zhongyang wenxian chubanshe, 2009.

Ye Jianying. *Ye Jianying junshi wenxuan* [Ye Jianying's Selected Works on Military Affairs]. Beijing: Jiefangjun chubanshe, 1997.

Zhang Aiping. *Zhang Aiping junshi wenxuan* [Zhang Aiping's Selected Works on Military Affairs]. Beijing: Changzheng chubanshe, 1994.

Zhang Wannian. *Zhang Wannian junshi wenxuan* [Zhang Wannian's Selected Works on Military Affairs]. Beijing: Jiefangjun chubanshe, 2008.

Zhang Xianmin, ed. *Qian Xuesen nianpu* [A Chronicle of Qian Xuesen's Life]. 2 Vols. Beijing: Zhongyang wenxian chubanshe, 2015.

Zhang Zhen. *Zhang Zhen junshi wenxuan* [Zhang Zhen's Selected Works on Military Affairs]. 2 Vols. Beijing: Jiefangjun chubanshe, 2005.

Zhang Zishen, ed. *Yang Chengwu nianpu* [A Chronicle of Yang Chengwu's Life]. Beijing: Jiefangjun chubanshe, 2014.

Zhongyang dang'an guan, ed. *Zhonggong zhongyang wenjian xuanji* [Selected Documents of the Central Committee of the Chinese Communist Party]. 18 Vols. Beijing: Zhongyang dangxiao chubanshe, 1991.

Zhongyang junwei bangongting, ed. *Deng Xiaoping guanyu xin shiqi jundui jianshe lunshu xuanbian* [Deng Xiaoping's Selected Expositions on Army Building in the New Period]. Beijing: Bayi chubanshe, 1993.

Zhongyang wenxian yanjiu shi, ed. *Jianguo yilai zhongyao wenxian xuanbian* [Selection of Important Documents Since the Founding of the Country]. 20 Vols. Beijing: Zhongyang wenxian chubanshe, 1998.

Zhou Enlai. *Zhou Enlai junshi wenxuan* [Zhou Enlai's Selected Works on Military Affairs]. 4 Vols. Beijing: Renmin chubanshe, 1997.

———. *Zhou Enlai wenhua wenxuan* [Zhou Enlai's Selected Works on Culture]. Beijing: Zhongyang wenxian chubanshe, 1998.

Zhou Junlun, ed. *Nie Rongzhen nianpu* [A Chronicle of Nie Rongzhen's Life]. Beijing: Renmin chubanshe, 1999.

Zhu Ying, and Wen Jinghu. *Su Yu nianpu* [A Chronicle of Su Yu's Life]. Beijing: Dangdai Zhongguo chubanshe, 2006.

Zong zhengzhi bu. Shuli he luoshi kexue fazhanguan lilun xuexi duben [A Reader for Establishing and Implementing the Theory of Scientific Development]. Beijing: Jiefangjun chubanshe, 2006.

BIOGRAPHIES, MEMOIRS, AND RECOLLECTIONS

HHND = Di'er paobing zhengzhibu, ed., *Huihuang niandai: Huigu zai gaige kaifang zhong fazhan qianji de di'er paobing* [Glorious Age: Reviewing the Development and Progress of the Second Artillery During Reform and Opening]. Beijing: Zhongyang wenxian chubanshe, 2008.

Bo Yibo. *Ruogan zhongda juece yu shijian de huigu* [Reviewing Several Major Decisions and Events]. Beijing: Zhonggong zhongyang dangshi chubanshe, 1993.

Chen Shiping, and Cheng Ying. *Junshi fanyijia Liu Bocheng* [Expert Military Translator Liu Bocheng]. Taiyuan: Shuhai chubanshe, 1988.

Dong Fanghe. *Zhang Aiping zhuan* [Zhang Aiping's Biography]. Beijing: Renmin chubanshe, 2000.

Fan Weizhong, and Jin Chongji. *Li Fuchun zhuan* [Li Fuchun's Biography]. Beijing: Zhongyang wenxian chubanshe, 2001.

Guo Xiangjie, ed. *Zhang Wannian zhuan (shang, xia)* [Zhang Wannian's Biography]. Beijing: Jiefangjun chubanshe, 2011.

Guo Yingui. "Zhou Enlai yu Zhongguo de hewuqi" [Zhou Enlai and China's Nuclear Weapons]. In Li Qi, ed., *Zai Zhou Enlai shenbian de rizi: Xihuating gongzuo renyuan de huiyi* [Days At Zhou Enlai's Side: Recollections of the Staff Members of West Flower Hall]. Beijing: Zhongyang wenxian chubanshe, 1998.

Han Chengchen. "He Jinheng." In Di'er paobing zhengzhibu, ed., *Di'er paobing gaoji jiangling zhuan* [Biographies of the Second Artillery's Senior Generals]. n.p.: Di'er paobing zhengzhibu, 2006.

He Jinheng. " 'Jinggan youxiao' zongti jianshe mubiao de queli" [The Establishment of the Overall Development Goal of 'Lean and Effective']. In *HHND*.

He Zhengwen. "Caijun baiwan jiqi qianqianhouhou" [The Whole Story of Reducing One Million]. In Xu Huizi, ed., *Zongcan moubu: Huiyi shiliao* [General Staff Department: Recollections and Historical Materials]. Beijing: Jiefangjun chubanshe, 1995.

Huang Kecheng. "Huiyi wushi niandai zai junwei, zongcan gongzuo de qingkuang" [Remembering Work Situations from the 1950s in the CMC and GSD]. In Xu Huizi, ed., *Zongcan moubu: Huiyi shiliao* [General Staff Department: Recollections and Historical Materials]. Beijing: Jiefangjun chubanshe, 1995.

Huang Yao, and Zhang Mingzhe, eds. *Luo Ruiqing zhuan* [Luo Ruiqing's Biography]. Beijing: Dangdai Zhongguo chubanshe, 1996.

Jin Chongji, ed. *Zhou Enlai zhuan* [Zhou Enlai's Biography]. 4 Vols. Beijing: Zhongyang wenxian chubanshe, 1998.

Jin Ye. "Yi Liaodong bandao kangdenglu zhanyi yanxi" [Recalling the Liaodong Peninsula Anti-Landing Campaign Exercise]. In Xu Huizi, ed., *Zongcan moubu: Huiyi shiliao* [General Staff Department: Recollections and Historical Materials]. Beijing: Jiefangjun chubanshe, 1995.

Jing Zhiyuan, and Peng Zhiyuan. "Huiguo di'er paobing zai gaige kaifang zhong jiakuai jianshe fazhan de guanghui licheng" [Recalling the Brilliant Process of the Accelerated Building and Development of the Second Artillery during Reform and Opening]. In *HHND*.

Kong Fanjun. *Chi Haotian zhuan* [Chi Haotian's Biography]. Beijing: Jiefangjun chubanshe, 2009.

Li De, and Shu Yun. *Wo gei Lin Biao yuanshuai dang mishu, 1959–1964* [I Served as Marshal Lin Biao's Secretary, 1959–1964]. Hong Kong: Fenghuang shupin, 2014.

Li Yuan. *Li Yuan huiyilu* [Li Yuan's Memoir]. Beijing: Jiefangjun chubanshe, 2009.

Li Shuiqing. "Gaige, cong zheli qibu" [Reform, Started From Here]. In *HHND*.

———. *Cong hongxiaogui dao huojian siling: Li Shuiqing's huiyilu* [From Little Red Devil to Rocket Commander: Li Shuiqing's Memoir]. Beijing: Jiefangjun chubanshe, 2009.

Liao Chengmei. "Fengyun shinian hua zhanbei" [Ten Years of the Storms of War Preparations]. In Di'er paobing zhengzhibu, ed., *Yu gongheguo yiqi chengzhang: Wo zai zhanlue daodan budui de nanwang jiyi* [Growing Together with the Republic: My Unforgettable Memories in the Strategic Rocket Forces]. Beijing: Zhongyang wenxian chubanshe, 2009.

Liu Huaqing. *Liu Huaqing huiyilu* [Liu Huaqing's Memoirs]. Beijing: Jiefangjun chubanshe, 2004.

Liu Lifeng zhuan bianxiezu. "Liu Lifeng." In Di'er paobing zhengzhibu, ed., *Di'er paobing gaoji jiangling zhuan* [Biographies of the Second Artillery's Senior Generals]. n.p.: Di'er paobing zhengzhibu, 2006.

Liu Tianye, Xia Daoyuan, and Fan Shu. *Li Tianyou jiangjun zhuan* [General Li Tianyou's Biography]. Beijing: Jiefangjun chubanshe.

Liu Xiao. *Chu shi Sulian ba nian* [Eight Years as Ambassador to the Soviet Union]. Beijing: Zhonggong dangshi ziliao chubanshe, 1986.

Ma Suzheng. *Bashi huimou* [Reflecting on Eighty Years]. Beijing: Changzheng chubanshe, 2008.

Mu Junjie, ed. *Song Shilun zhuan* [Song Shilun's Biography]. Beijing: Junshi kexue chubanshe, 2007.

Nie Rongzhen. *Nie Rongzhen huiyilu* [Nie Rongzhen's Memoirs]. Beijing: Jiefangjun chubanshe, 1986.

Pang Xianzhi, and Jin Chongji. *Mao Zedong zhuan, 1949–1976* [Mao Zedong's Biography, 1949–1976]. Beijing: Zhongyang wenxian chubanshe, 2003.

Peng Dehuai. *Peng Dehuai junshi wenxuan* [Peng Dehuai's Selected Works on Military Affairs]. Beijing: Zhongyang wenxian chubanshe, 1988.

Peng Dehuai zhuanji zu. *Peng Dehuai quanzhuan* [Peng Dehuai's Complete Biography]. Beijing: Zhongguo dabaike quanshu chubanshe, 2009.

Shen Kehui. "Erpao junshi lilun yanjiu de tansuo" [Exploring the Second Artillery's Research on Military Theory]. In *HHND*.

Wang Bingnan. *ZhongMei huitan jiunian huigu* [Reflections on Nine Years of Chinese-American Talks]. Beijing: Shijie zhishi chubanshe, 1985.

Wang Huanping. "Li Shuiqing." In Di'er paobing zhengzhibu, ed., *Di'er paobing gaoji jiangling zhuan* [Biographies of the Second Artillery's Senior Generals]. n.p.: Di'er paobing zhengzhibu, 2006.

Wang Shangrong. "Xin Zhongguo jiansheng hou jici zhongda zhanzheng" [Several Major Wars After the Emergence of New China]. In Zhu Yuanshi, ed., *Gongheguo yaoshi koushushi* [An Oral History of the Republic's Important Events]. Changsha: Henan renmin chubanshe, 1999.

Wang Xuedong. *Fu Quanyou zhuan (shang, xia)* [Fu Quanyou's Biography]. Beijing: Jiefangjun chubanshe, 2015.

Wang Yan, ed. *Peng Dehuai zhuan* [Peng Dehuai's Biography]. Beijing: Dangdai Zhongguo chubanshe, 1993.

Wang Yazhi. *Peng Dehuai junshi canmou de huiyi: 1950 niandai ZhongSu junshi guanxi jianzheng* [The Recollection of Peng Dehuai's Militiary Staff Officer: Witnessing Sino-Soviet Military Relations in the 1950s]. Shanghai: Fudan daxue chubanshe, 2009.

Wu Lengxi. *Shinian lunzhan: 1956–1966 ZhongSu guanxi huiyilu* [Ten Years of Polemics: A Recollection of Chinese-Soviet Relations from 1956 to 1966]. Beijing: Zhongyang wenxian chubanshe, 1999.

Wu Lie. *Zhengrong suiyue* [Memorable Years]. Beijing: Zhonyang wenxian chubanshe, 1999.

———. "Erpao lingdao jiguan jiannan yansheng" [The Difficult Birth of the Second Artillery's Leadership Structure]. In Di'er paobing zhengzhibu, ed., *Yu gongheguo yiqi chengzhang: Wo zai zhanlue daodan budui de nanwang jiyi* [Growing Together with the Republic: My Unforgettable Memories in the Strategic Rocket Forces]. Beijing: Zhongyang wenxian chubanshe, 2009.

Wu Quanxu. *Kuayue shiji de biange: Qinli junshi xunlian lingyu guanche xin shiqi junshi zhanlue fangzhen shi er nian* [Change across the Century: Twelve Years of Personal Experience Implementing the Military Strategic Guideline in Military Training]. Beijing: Junshi kexue chubanshe, 2005.

Xi Qixin. *Zhu Guangya zhuan* [Zhu Guangya's Biography]. Beijing: Renmin chubanshe, 2015.

Xiang Shouzhi. *Xiang Shouzhi huiyilu* [Xiang Shouzhi's Memoirs]. Beijing: Jiefangjun chubanshe, 2006.

Xiao Jinguang. *Xiao Jinguang huiyilu (xuji)* [Xiao Jinguang's Memoirs (sequel)]. Beijing: Jiefangjun chubanshe, 1989.

Xie Hainan, Yang Zufa, and Yang Jianhua. *Yang Dezhi yi sheng* [Yang Dezhi's Life]. Beijing: Zhonggong dangshi chubanshe, 2011.

Xu Bin. "Erpao junshi xunlian gaige de zuyi" [The Path of Training Reforms in the Second Artillery]. In *HHND*.

Xu Jian. "Li Xuge" [Li Xuge]. In Di'er paobing zhengzhibu, ed., *Di'er paobing gaoji jiangling zhuan* [Biographies of the Second Artillery's Senior Generals]. n.p.: Di'er paobing zhengzhibu, 2006.

Yang Dezhi. "Xinshiqi zongcanmoubu di junshi gongzuo" [The General Staff Department's Military Work in the New Period]. In Xu Huizi, ed., *Zongcan moubu: Huiyi shiliao* [General Staff Department: Recollections and Historical Materials]. Beijing: Jiefangjun chubanshe, 1995.

Yang Qiliang. *Wang Shangrong jiangjun* [General Wang Shangrong]. Beijing: Dangdai Zhongguo chubanshe, 2000.

Yang Shangkun. *Yang Shangkun huiyilu* [Yang Shangkun's Memoirs]. Beijing: Zhongyang wenxian chubanshe, 2001.

Yang Wenting. "Dongfeng di yi zhi: Ji yici fangwei zuozhan yanxi" [The First East Wind: Remembering One Defensive Combat Exercise]. In *HHND*.

Yin Qiming, and Cheng Yaguang. *Diyi ren guofang buzhang* [First Minister of Defense]. Guangzhou: Guangdong jiaoyu chubanshe, 1997.

Yu Xijun. "Xinshiji xinjieduan zhanlue daodan budui zuozhan lilun de chuangxin yu xin fazhan" [Innovations and New Developments in the Operational Theory of the Strategic Rocket Forces at the New Stage of the New Century]. In *HHND*.

Zhang Qihua. "Huihuang suiyue zhu changjian" [Glorious Times Casting a Long Sword]. In *HHND*.

Zhang Zhen. *Zhang Zhen huiyilu (shang, xia)* [Zhang Zhen's Memoirs]. Beijing: Jiefangjun chubanshe, 2003.

Zhang Zuowen. "Zhou Enlai yu daodan hewuqi" [Zhou Enlai and Missile Nuclear Weapons]. In Li Qi, ed., *Zai Zhou Enlai shenbian de rizi: Xihuating gongzuo renyuan de huiyi* [Days at Zhou Enlai's Side: Recollections of the Staff Members of West Flower Hall]. Beijing: Zhongyang wenxian chubanshe, 1998.

Zhao Qiuling, and Zhang Guang. "Yongbu tingbu de ziwo chaoyue" [Never Stop Transcending Onseself]. In *HHND*.

Zhu Ying, ed. *Su Yu zhuan* [Su Yu's Biography]. Beijing: Dangdai Zhongguo chubanshe, 2000.

'Jam-dpal-rgya-mtsho. *Li Jue zhuan* [Li Jue's Biography]. Zhongguo Zangxue chubanshe: 2004.

DOCTRINAL SOURCES

Di'er paobing silingbu, ed. *Di'er paobing zhanlue xue* [The Science of Second Artillery Strategy]. Beijing: Lantian chubanshe, 1996.

———. *Di'er paobing zhanshu xue* [The Science of Second Artillery Tactics]. Beijing: Lantian chubanshe, 1996.

———. *Di'er paobing zhanyi fa* [Second Artillery Campaign Methods]. Beijing: Lantian chubanshe, 1996.

Fan Zhenjiang, and Ma Baoan, eds. *Junshi zhanlue lun* [On Military Strategy]. Beijing: Guofang daxue chubanshe, 2007.

Gao Rui, ed. *Zhanlue xue* [The Science of Military Strategy]. Beijing: Junshi kexue chubanshe, 1987.

Hao Zizhou, and Huo Gaozhen, eds. *Zhanshuxue jiaocheng* [Lectures on the Science of Tactics]. Beijing: Junshi kexue chubanshe, 2000.

Junshi kexue yuan, ed. *Zhongguo renmin jiefangjun junyu* [Military Terminology of the Chinese People's Liberation Army]. 2011 ed. Beijing: Junshi kexue chubanshe, 2011.

Li Yousheng, ed. *Lianhe zhanyi xue jiaocheng* [Lectures on the Science of Joint Campaigns]. Beijing: Junshi kexue chubanshe, 2012.

Peng Guangqian, and Yao Youzhi, eds. *Zhanlue xue* [The Science of Military Strategy]. Beijing: Junshi kexue chubanshe, 2001.

Qiao Jie, ed. *Zhanyi xue jiaocheng* [Lectures on the Science of Campaigns]. Beijing: Junshi kexue chubanshe, 2012.

Shou Xiaosong, ed. *Zhanlue Xue* [The Science of Military Strategy]. Beijing: Junshi kexue chubanshe, 2013.

Tan Yadong, ed. *Lianhe zuozhan jiaocheng* [Lectures on Joint Operations]. Beijing: Junshi kexue chubanshe, 2013.

Wang An, ed. *Jundui tiaoling tiaoli jiaocheng* [Lectures on Military Regulations and Rules]. Beijing: Junshi kexue chubanshe, 1999.

Wang Houqing, and Zhang Xingye, eds. *Zhanyi xue* [The Science of Military Campaigns]. Beijing: Guofang daxue chubanshe, 2000.

Wang Wenrong, ed. *Zhanlue xue* [The Science of Military Strategy]. Beijing: Guofang daxue chubanshe, 1999.

Xu Guocheng, Feng Liang, and Zhou Zhenduo, eds. *Lianhe zhanyi yanjiu* [A Study of Joint Campaigns]. Jinan: Huanghe chubanshe, 2004.

Xue Xinglin, ed. *Zhanyi lilun xuexi zhinan* [Campaign Theory Study Guide]. Beijing: Guofang daxue chubanshe, 2002.

Yu Xijun, ed. *Di'er paobing zhanyi xue* [The Science of Second Artillery Campaigns]. Beijing: Jiefangjun chubanshe, 2004.

Yuan Dejin. *Mao Zedong junshi sixiang jiaocheng* [Lectures on Mao Zedong's Military Thought]. Beijing: Junshi kexue chubanshe, 2000.

Zhang Yuliang, ed. *Zhanyi xue* [The Science of Campaigns]. Beijing: Guofang daxue chubanshe, 2006.

BOOKS AND ARTICLES

Bi Wenbo. "Lun Zhongguo xinshiqi junshi zhanlue siwei (shang)" [On China's Military Strategic Thought in the New Period]. *Junshi lishi yanjiu*, No. 2 (2004): 43–56.

Chen Donglin. *Sanxian jianshe: Beizhan shiqi de xibu kaifa* [Construction of the Third Line: Western Development in a Period of Preparing for War]. Beijing: Zhonggong zhongyang dangxiao chubanshe, 2004.

Chen Dongxiang, ed. *Pingdian Yilake zhanzheng* [Evaluating the Iraq War]. Beijing: Junshi kexue chubanshe, 2003.

Chen Furong, and Zeng Luping. "Luochuan huiyi junshi fenqi tansuo" [An Exploration of the Military Differences at the Luochuan Meeting]. *Yan'an daxue xuebao (shehui kexue ban)*, Vol. 28, No. 5 (2006): 13–15.

Chen Haoliang. "Peng Dehuai dui xin Zhongguo jiji fangyu zhanlue fangzhen xingcheng de gongxian" [Peng Dehuai's Contribution to the Formation of New China's Strategic Guideline of Active Defense]. *Junshi lishi*, No. 2 (2003): 43–45.

Chen Zhou. "Shilun Zhongguo weihu heping yu fazhan de fangyuxing guofang zhengce" [An Analysis of China's Defensive National Defense Policy for Maintaining Peace and Development]. *Zhongguo junshi kexue*, Vol. 20, No. 6 (2007): 1–10.

———. "Zhuanjia jiedu Zhongguo de junshi zhanlue baipishu" [Expert unpacks the White Paper China's Military Strategy]. *Guofang* No. 6 (2015): 16–20.

Dai Yifang, ed. *Junshi xue yanjiu huigu yu zhanwang* [Reflections and Prospects for Military Studies]. Beijing: Junshi kexue chubanshe, 1995.

Ding Wei, and Wei Xu. "20 shiji 80 niandai renmin jiefangjun tizhi gaige, jingjian zhengbian de huigu yu sikao" [Review and Reflections on the Streamlining and Reorganization of the PLA in the Eighties of the 20th Cenutry]. *Junshi lishi*, No. 6 (2014): 52–57.

Dong Wenjiu, and Su Ruozhou. "Xin de junshi xunlian yu kaohe dagang pinfa" [Promulgation of the New Military Training and Evaluation Program]. *Jiefangjun bao*, August 10, 2001.

Fan Hongye. "Yuanzidan de gushi: Ying cong 1952 nian qi" [The Story of the Atomic Bomb: It Should Start in 1952]. *Zhonghua dushu bao*, December 15, 2004.

Fang Gongli, Yang Xuejun, and Xiang Wei. *Zhongguo renmin jiefangjun haijun 60 nian* [60 Years of the Chinese PLA Navy]. Qingdao: Qingdao chubanshe: 2009.

Fu Xuezheng. "Zai zhongyang junwei bangongting gongzuo de rizi" [Working in the Central Mililitary Commission's Office]. *Dangshi tiandi*, No. 1 (2006): 8–16.

Gu Boliang, and Liu Guohua. "Wojun zhanyi xunlian chengji xianzu" [Results of Our Army's Campaign Training]. *Jiefangjun Bao*, December 26, 1988.

Guofang daxue dangshi dangjian zhengzhi gongzuo jiaoyan shi, ed. *Zhonghua renmin jiefangjun zhengzhi gongzuo shi: Shehui zhuyi shiqi* [History of Political Work in the PLA: The Socialist Period]. Beijing: Guofang daxue chubanshe, 1989.

Guofang daxue zhanshi jianbian bianxiezu, ed. *Zhongguo renmin jiefangjun zhanshi jianbian* [A Brief History of the Chinese People's Liberation Army]. 2001 revised ed. Beijing: Jiefangjun chubanshe, 2003.

Han Huaizhi, and Tan Jingqiao, eds. *Dangdai Zhongguo jundui de junshi gongzuo (shang)* [Military Work of Contemporary China's Armed Forces, Part 1]. Beijing: Zhongguo shehui kexue chubanshe, 1989.

He Qizong, Ren Haiquan, and Jiang Qianlin. "Deng Xiaoping yu jundui gaige" [Deng Xiaoping and Military Reform]. *Junshi lishi*, No. 4 (2014): 1–8.

He Zhu. *Zhuanjia pingshuo Yilake zhanzheng* [Experts Evaluate the Iraq War]. Beijing: Junshi kexue chubanshe, 2004.

Hong Baoshou. "Zhongguo renmin jiefangjun 70 nianlai gaige fazhan de huigu yu sikao" [Reviewing and Reflecting on the Reform and Development of the Chinese People's Liberation Army over 70 years]. *Zhongguo junshi kexue*, No. 3 (1999): 22–29.

Hu Zhefeng. "Jianguo yilai ruogan junshi zhanlue fangzhen tansuo" [Exploration and Analysis of Several Military Strategic Guidelines Since the Founding of the Nation]. *Dangdai Zhongguo shi yanjiu*, No. 4 (2000): 21–32.

Huang Bin, ed. *Kesuowo zhanzheng yanjiu* [A Study of the Kosovo War]. Beijing: Jiefangjun chubanshe, 2000.

Huang Chao. "Wei renzhen guanche Hu Jintao guanyu jiaqiang lianhe xunlian zhongyao zhishi" [Earnestly Carry Out Hu Jintao's Important Instructions on Joint Training]. *Jiefangjun bao*, February 25, 2009.

Huang Jiansheng, and Qi Donghui. "Nanjing budui moujun juban zhanzheng chuqi fan tuxi yanjiu ban" [A Certain Army in Nanjing Holds a Study Group on Countering a Surprise Attack in the Initial Period of a War]. *Jiefangjun Bao,* July 5, 1981.

Huang Yao. "1965 nian zhongyang junwei zuozhan huiyi fengbo de lailong qumai" [The Origin and Development of the Storm at the 1965 CMC Operations Meeting]. *Dangdai Zhongguo yanjiu*, Vol. 22, No. 1 (2015): 88–99.

Huang Yingxu. "Zhongguo jiji fangyu zhanlue fangzhen de queli yu tiaozheng" [The Estabishment and Adjustment of China's Strategic Guideline of Active Defense]. *Zhongguo junshi kexue*, Vol. 15, No. 1 (2002): 57–64.

Jiang Jiantian. "Wojun zhandou tiaoling tixi de xingcheng" [Formation of Our Army's Combat Regulations System]. *Jiefangjun bao*, July 16, 2000.

Jiang Nan, and Ding Wei. "Lengzhan shiqi Zhonguo fanqinlue zhanzheng zhanlue zhidao de biange" [Evolution of China's Strategic Guidance in Anti-aggression Wars during the Cold War]. *Junshi lishi*, No. 1 (2013): 15–18.

Jiang Tiejun, ed. *Dang de guofang jundui gaige sixiang yanjiu* [A Study of the Party's Thought on National Defense and Army Reform]. Beijing: Junshi kexue chubanshe, 2015.

Junshi kexue yuan junshi lishi yanjiu suo. *Zhongguo renmin jiefangjun gaige fazhan 30 nian* [Thirty Years of the Reform and Development of the Chinese People's Liberation Army]. Beijing: Junshi kexue chubanshe, 2008.

Junshi kexue yuan lishi yanjiu bu. *Haiwan zhanzheng quanshi* [A Complete History of the Gulf War]. Beijing: Junshi kexue chubanshe, 2000.

Junshi kexue yuan lishi yanjiusuo. *Zhongguo renmin jiefangjun gaige fazhan 30 nian* [30 Years of Reform and Development of the Chinese People's Liberation Army]. Beijing: Junshi kexue chubanshe, 2008.

Junshi kexue yuan Mao Zeodong junshi sixiang yanjiusuo. "Qiangguo qiangjun zhanlue xianxing—Shenru xuexi guanche Xi zhuxi xin xingshi xia junshi zhanlue fangzhen zhongyao lunshu" [Strong Nation, Strong Army, Strategy First: Thoroughly Study and Implement Chairman Xi's Important Expositions on the Military Strategic Guideline in the New Period]. *Jiefangjun bao*, September 2, 2016.

Junshi kexue yuan waijun junshi yanjiu bu (trans). *ZhongDong zhanzheng quanshi* [A Complete History of the Wars in the Middle East]. Beijing: Junshi kexue chubanshe, 1985.

Junshi lilun jiaoyanshi. *Zhongguo renmin jiefangjun 1950–1979 zhanshi jiangyi* [Teaching Materials on the War History of the Chinese People's Liberation Army 1950–1979]. n.p.: n.p, 1987.

Junshi xueshu zazhishe, ed. *Junshi xueshu lunwen xuan (shang, xia)* [Selection of Essays from Military Arts]. Beijing: Junshi kexue chubanshe, 1984.

Lei Mou. "Youji zhanzheng 'shiliu zikuai' de xingcheng yu fazhan" [The Origins and Development of the 'Sixteen Characters' of Guerrilla Warfare]. *Guangming ribao*, December 13, 2017.

Li Bin. "Zhongguo hezhanlue bianxi" [Analysis of China's Nuclear Strategy]. *Shijie jingji yu zhengzhi*, No. 9 (2006): 16–22.

Li Deyi. "Mao Zedong jiji fangyu zhanlue sixiang de lishi fazhan yu sikao" [The Historical Development of and Reflections on Mao Zedong's Strategic Thinking about Active Defense]. *Junshi lishi*, No. 4 (2002): 49–54.

Li Dianren, ed. *Guofang daxue 80 nian dashi jiyao* [Record of Important Events in Eighty Years of the National Defense University]. Beijing: Guofang daxue chubanshe, 2007.

Li Jue, et al., eds. *Dangdai Zhongguo he gongye* [Contemporary China's Nuclear Industry]. Beijing: Dangdai Zhongguo chubanshe, 1987.

Li Ke, and Hao Shengzhang. *Wenhua dageming zhong de renmin jiefangjun* [The People's Liberation Army During the Cultural Revolution]. Beijing: Zhonggong dangshi ziliao chubanshe, 1989.

Li Tilin. "Gaige kaifang yilai Zhongguo hezhanlue lilun de fazhan" [The Development of China's Nuclear Strategy Theory since Reform and Opening]. *Zhongguo junshi kexue*, No. 6 (2008): 37–44.

Li Xiangqian. "1964 nian: Yuenan zhanzheng shengji yu Zhongguo jingji zhengzhi de biandong" [The Year of 1964: The Escalation of the Vietnam War and the Fluctuations in China's Economics and Politics]. In Zhang Baijia and Niu Jun, eds., *Lengzhan yu Zhongguo* [The Cold War and China]. Beijing: Shijie zhishi chubanshe, 2002.

Liang Pengfei. "Zongcan zongzheng yinfa 'guanyu tigao junshi xunlian shizhan shuiping de yijian xuexi xuanchuan tigang'" [GSD and GPD Issues Study and Publicity Outline for "The Opinion on Improving the Realistic Combat Level of Military Training"]. *Jiefangjun bao*, August 21, 2014.

Liang Ying. "Luetan di sici zhongdong zhanzheng de tedian" [Brief Discussion of the 4th Middle East War]. *Jiefangjun bao*, December 15, 1975.

Liu Fengan. "Goujian xinxihua tiaojianxia junshi xunlian xin tixi" [Establishing a New System for Military Training Under Informatized Conditions]. *Jiefangjun Bao*, August 1, 2008, 3.

Liu Jiyuan, ed. *Zhongguo hangtian shiye fazhan de zhexue sixiang* [The Philosophy of the Development of China's Aerospace Industry]. Beijing: Beijing daxue chubanshe, 2013.

Liu Xiyao. "Woguo 'liangdan' yanzhi juece guocheng zhuiji" [Immediate Record of the Decision-Making Process for Our Country's Research on "Two Bombs"]. *Yanhuang chunqiu*, No. 5 (1996): 1–9.

Liu Yichang, Wang Wenchang, and Wang Xianchen, eds. *Haiwan zhanzheng* [The Gulf War]. Beijing: Junshi kexue chubanshe, 1991.

Liu Yixin, Wu Xiang, and Xie Wenxin, eds. *Xiandai zhanzheng yu lujun* [Modern Warfare and the Ground Forces]. Beijing: Jiefangjun chubanshe, 2005.

Lu Qiming, and Fan Minruo. *Zhang Aiping yu liangdan yixing* [Zhang Aiping and the Two Bombs, One Satellite]. Beijing: Zhongyang wenxian chubanshe, 2011.

Lu Tianyi. "Jundui yao dui gaige kaifang fazhan jingji 'baojia huhang'" [The Military Must "Protect and Escort" Reform and Opening and Developing the Economy]. *Jiefangjun Bao*, March 22, 1992.

Lujun di sanshiba jituanjun junshi bianshen weiyuanhui. *Lujun di sanshiba jituanjun junshi* [A History of the Thirty-Eighth Group Army]. Beijing: Jiefangjun wenyi chubanshe, 1993.

Luo Derong. "Jundui jianshe yu junshi douzheng junbei de xingdong gangling: Dui xin xingshi xia junshi zhanlue fangzhen de jidian renshi" [Action Plan for Army Building and Preparations for Military Struggle: Several Points on the Military Strategic Guideline in the New Situation]. *Zhongguo junshi kexue*, No. 1 (2017): 88–96.

Ma Xiaotian, and Zhao Keming, eds. *Zhongguo renmin jiefangjun guofang daxue shi: Di'er juan (1950–1985)* [History of the Chinese People's Liberation Army's National Defense University: Volume 2 (1950-1985)]. Beijing: Guofang daxue chubanshe, 2007.

Ma Yongming, Liu Xiaoli, and Xiao Yunhua, eds. *Yilake zhanzheng yanjiu* [A Study of the Iraq War]. Beijing: Junshi kexue chubanshe, 2003.

Mi Zhenyu. *Zhanzheng yu zhanlue lilun tanyan* [Exploration of War and Strategic Theory]. Beijing: Jiefangjun chubanshe, 2003.

Pan Hong. "1985 nian baiwan dacaijun" [The One Million Downsizing in 1985]. *Bainian chao*, No. 12 (2015): 40–46.

Peng Guangqian. *Zhongguo junshi zhanlue wenti yanjiu* [Research on Issues in China's Military Strategy]. Beijing: Jiefangjun chubanshe, 2006.

Peng Jichao. "Mao Zedong yu liangdan yixing" [Mao Zedong and Two Bombs and One Satellite]. *Shenjian*, No. 3 (2013): 4–26.

Qi Changming. "Jiaqiang zhanlue yanjiu, shenhua jundui gaige" [Deepen Military Reform, Strengthen Research on Strategy]. *Jiefangjun Bao*, May 8, 1988.

Qi Dexue, ed. *KangMei yuanChao zhanzheng shi* [History of the War to Resist America and Aid Korea]. 3 Vols. Beijing: Junshi kexue chubanshe, 2000.

Qin Tian, and Huo Xiaoyong, eds. *Zhonghua haiquan shilun* [A History of Chinese Sea Power]. Beijing: Guofang daxue chubanshe, 2000.

Ren Jian. *Zuozhan tiaoling gailun* [An Introduction to Operations Regulations]. Beijing: Junshi kexue chubanshe, 2016.

Shan Xiufa, ed. *Jiang Zemin guofang he jundui jianshe sixiang yanjiu* [Research on Jiang's Zemin's Thought on National Defense and Army Building]. Beijing: Junshi kexue chubanshe, 2004.

Shen Zhihua. *Sulian zhuanjia zai Zhongguo* [Soviet Experts in China]. Beijing: Zhongguo guoji guangbo chubanshe 2003.

Shi Jiazhu and Cui Changfa. "60 nian renmin haijun jianshe zhidao sixiang de fengfu he fazhan" [The Enrichment and Development of Guiding Thought on Navy Building in the Past 60 Years]. *Junshi lishi*, No. 3 (2009): 22–26.

Shou Xiaosong, ed. *Zhongguo renmin jiefangjun de 80 nian: 1927–2007* [Eighty Years of the Chinese People's Liberation Army: 1927–2007]. Beijing: Junshi kexue chubanshe, 2007.

Shou Xiaosong, ed. *Zhongguo renmin jiefangjun junshi* [A Military History of the Chinese People's Liberation Army]. 6 Vols. Beijing: Junshi kexue chubanshe, 2011.

Su Ruozhou. "Quanjun jinnian an xin xunlian dagang shixun" [This Year the Entire Army Will Train According to the New Training Program]. *Jiefangjun bao*, February 15, 1990.

Sun Xiangli. *He shidai de zhanlue xuanze: Zhongguo he zhanlue wenti yanjiu* [Strategic Choices of the Nuclear Era: Research on Issues in China's Nuclear Strategy]. Beijing: Chinese Academy of Engineering Physics, 2013.

Sun Xuemin. "Moushi renzhen yanjiu da tanke xunlian jiaoxuefa" [A Certain Division Seriously Studies Teaching Methods For Fighting Tanks]. *Jiefangjun bao*, September 13, 1978.

Tan Wenhu. "Duoyanghua junshi renwu qianyin junshi xunlian chuangxin" [Diversified Military Tasks Draw Innovations in Military Training]. *Jiefangjun bao*, July 1, 2008.

Wang Changqin, and Fang Guangming. "Women weishenme fazhan dongfeng-26 dadao dao-dan" [Why We Had to Develop the Dongfeng-26 Ballistic Missile]. *Zhongguo qingnian bao*, November 30, 2015, p. 9.

Wang Guangmei, and Liu Yuan. *Ni suo buzhidao de Liu Shaoqi* [The Liu Shaoqi You Do Not Know]. Zhengzhou: Henan renmin chubanshe, 2000.

Wang Hongguang. "Cong lishi kan jinri Zhongguo de zhanlue fangxiang" [Looking at China's Strategic Directions Today from a Historical Perspective]. *Tongzhou gongjin*, No. 3 (March 2015): 44–50.

Wang Tubin, and Luo Zheng. "Guofangbu juxing shengda zhaodaihui relie qingzhu jianjun 87 zhounian" [The Ministry of Defense Holds Grand Reception to Celebrate 87th Anniversary of Founding the Army]. *Jiefangjun bao*, August 2, 2014.

Wen Bin. "Dingzhun junshi douzheng jidian" [Pinpointing the Basis of Preparations for Military Struggle]. *Xuexi shibao*, June 1, 2015.

Wu Dianqing. *Haijun: Zongshu dashiji* [Navy: Summary and Chronology]. Beijing: Jiefangjun chubanshe, 2006.

Wu Jianhua, and Su Ruozhou. "Zongcan bushu quanjun xinniandu junshi xunlian gongzuo" [General Staff Department Arranges Army-wide Annual Training Work]. *Jiefangjun bao*, February 1, 2004.

Wu Tianmin. "Goujian xinxihua tiaojianxia junshi xunlian tixi" [Building a Training System Under Informatized Conditions]. *Jiefangjun bao*, August 1, 2008.

Xie Guang, ed. *Dangdai Zhongguo de guofang keji gongye* [Contemporary China's Defense Science and Technology Industry]. Vol. 1. Beijing: Dangdai Zhongguo chubanshe, 1992.

Xie Guojun, ed. *Junqi piaopiao* [The Army's Flag Fluttering]. Beijing: Jiefangjun chubanshe, 1999.

Xu Jian. *Niaokan diqiu: Zhongguo zhanlue daodan zhendi gongcheng jishi* [A Bird's-Eye View of the Earth: The Record of the Engineering of China's Strategic Missile Bases]. Beijing: Zuojia chubanshe, 1997.

Xu Ping. "Jianguohou zhongyang junwei renyuan goucheng de bianhua" [The Changing Composition of the CMC After the Founding of the Country]. *Dangshi bolan*, No. 9 (2002): 45–55.

———. "Zhongyang junwei sanshe bangong huiyi" [The Three Office Meetings Established by the CMC]. *Wenshi jinghua*, No. 2 (2005): 61–64.

Xu Xuesong. "Zhongguo ludi didi zhanlue daodan fazhan de lishi huigu yu jingyan qishi" [Historical Review and Implications of the Development of China's Land-based Surface-to-Surface Strategic Missiles]. *Junshi lishi*, No. 2 (2017): 21–27.

Xu Yan. *Di yi ci jiaoliang: KangMei yuanChao zhanzheng de lishi huigu yu fansi* [First Contest: Reviewing and Rethinking the War to Resist America and Aid Korea]. Beijing: Zhongguo guangbo dianshi chubanshe, 1998.

———. *Zhongguo guofang daolun* [Introduction to China's National Defense]. Beijing: Guofang daxue chubanshe, 2006.

"Xunlian zongjianbu banfa xin de xunlian dagang." [Training Supervision Department Issues New Training Program]. *Jiefangjun bao*, January 16, 1958.

Yang Baibing. "Jianfuqi wei guojia gaige he jianshe baojia huhang de chonggao shiming" [Shoulder the Lofty Goal of Protecting and Escorting National Reform and Development]. *Jiefangjun Bao*, July 29, 1992.

Yang Chengzong. "Wo wei Yuliao Juli chuanhua gei Mao zhuxi" [I Gave Chairman Mao a Message from Joliot-Curie]. *Bainian chao*, No. 2 (2012): 25–30.

Yang Dezhi. "Weilai fanqinlue zhanzheng chuqi zuozhan de jige wenti" [Several Questions on Operations During the Initial Phase of a Future Anti-aggression War]. In Junshi xueshu zazhi she, ed., *Junshi xueshu lunwen xuan (xia)* [Selection of Essays from Military Arts]. Beijing: Junshi kexue chubanshe, 1984.

Yang Zhiyuan. "Wojun bianxiu zuozhan tiaoling de chuangxin fazhan ji qishi" [The Innovative Development and Implications of Our Army's Compilation and Revision of Operations Regulations]. *Zhongguo junshi kexue*, No. 6 (2009): 112–118.

Yao Youzhi, Zhao Tianyou, and Wu Yiheng. "Tuchu da tanke xunlian, zheng dang da tanke nengshou" [Give Prominence to Training Fighting Tanks, Strive to Become Masters at Fighting Tanks]. *Jiefangjun bao*, March 1, 1979.

Yin Xiong, and Huang Xuemei. *Shijie yuanzidan fengyulu* [The Stormy Record of the Atom Bomb in the World]. Beijing: Xinhua chubanshe, 1999.

Yu Huamin, and Hu Zhefeng. *Zhongguo junshi sixiang shi* [History of Chinese Military Thought]. Kaifeng: Henan daxue chubanshe, 1999.

Yuan Dejin. "30 nian Zhongguo jundui gaige lunlue" [30 Years of China's Military Reforms]. *Junshi lishi yanjiu*, No. 4 (2008): 1–11.

———. "Mao Zedong yu 'zaoda, dada, da hezhanzheng' sixiang de tichu" [Mao Zedong and the Proposition of 'Fighting an Early, Major, Nuclear War.'" *Junshi lishi*, No. 5 (2010): 1–6.

———. "Mao Zedong yu xin Zhongguo junshi zhanlue fangzhen de queli he tiaozheng jiqi qishi" [Mao Zedong and the Establishment and Adjustment of New China's Military Strategic Guideline and Its Implications]. *Junshi lishi yanjiu*, No. 1 (2010): 22–27.

Yuan Wei, ed. *Zhongguo zhanzheng fazhan shi* [A History of the Development of War in China]. Beijing: Renmin chubanshe, 2001.

Yuan Wei, and Zhang Zhuo, eds. *Zhongguo junxiao fazhan shi* [History of the Development of China's Military Academies]. Beijing: Guofang daxue chubanshe, 2001.

Zhang Aiping, ed. *Zhongguo renmin jiefangjun (shang, xia)* [The Chinese People's Liberation Army]. Beijing: Dangdai Zhongguo chubanshe, 1994.

Zhang Jian, and Ren Yanjun. "Xinyidai junshi xunlian dagang banfa" [New Generation Training Program Issued]. *Jiefangjun Bao*, December 12, 1995.

Zhang Sheng. *Cong zhanzheng zhong zoulai: Liangdai junren de duihua* [Coming From War: A Dialogue of Two Generations of Soldiers]. Beijing: Zhongguo qingnian chubanshe, 2008.

Zhang Weiming. *Huabei dayanxi: Zhongguo zuida junshi yanxi jishi* [North China Exercise: The Record of China's Largest Military Exercise]. Beijing: Jiefangjun chubanshe, 2008.

Zhang Xianmin, and Zhou Junlun. "1961 nian liangdan 'shangma' 'xiama' zhizheng" [The Dispute in 1961 over "Mounting" or "Dismounting" the Two Bombs]. *Lilun shiye*, No. 12 (2016): 54–59.

Zhang Yang, ed. *Jiakuai tuijin guofang he jundui xiandaihua* [Accelerate and Promote National Defense and Armed Forces Modernization]. Beijing: Renmin chubanshe, 2015.

Zhang Yining, Cai Renzhao, and Sun Kejia. "Gaige kaifang sanshi nian Zhongguo junshi zhanlue de chuangxin fazhan" [Innovative Development of China's Military Strategy in Thirty Years of Reform and Opening]. *Xuexi shibao*, December 9, 2008.

Zhao Xuepeng. " 'Sizhong gangmu' jixun chuixiang xunlian chongfenghao" ["Four Kinds of Outlines" Group Training Sounded the Bugle Call for Training]. *Jiefangjun bao*, October, 8, 2008.

Zheng Wenhan. *Mishu rijili de Peng laozong* [Leader Peng in His Secretary's Diary]. Beijing: Junshi kexue chubanshe, 1998.

Zhongguo de junshi zhanlue. [China's Military Strategy]. Beijing: Guowuyuan xinwen bangongshi, 2015.

" 'Zhongguo linkong burong qinfan!' " [China's Airspace is Inviolable!]. *Jiefangjun Bao*, April 12, 1965.

Zhou Jun, and Zhou Zaohe. "Renmin jiefangjun diyidai zhandou tiaoling xingcheng chutan" [Prelimarinary Exploration of the Formation of the PLA's First Generation Combat Regulations]. *Junshi lishi*, No. 1 (1996): 25–27.

Zhou Kekuan. "Xin shiqi heweishe lilun yu shixian de xin fazhan" [New Developments in the Theory and Practice of Nuclear Deterrence in the New Period]. *Zhongguo junshi kexue*, No. 1 (2009): 16–20.

"Zong canmoubu pizhun banfa xunlian dagang." [GSD Approves and Issues Training Program]. *Jiefangjun bao*, February 8, 1981.

Zong Wen. "Baiwan da caijun: Deng Xiaoping de qiangjun zhilu" [Great One Million Downsizing: Deng Xiaoping's Road to a Strong Army]. *Wenshi bolan*, No. 10 (2015): 5–11.

Zou Baoyi, and Liu Jinsheng. "Xinyidai hecheng jundui douzheng tiaoling kaishi shixing" [Use of New Generation Combined Army Combat Regulations Has Begun]. *Jiefangjun bao*, June 7, 1988.

English Sources

Alger, John I. *Definitions and Doctrine of the Military Art*. Wayne, NJ: Avery Publishing Group, 1985.

Art, Robert J. *A Grand Strategy for America*. Ithaca, NY: Cornell University Press, 2003.

Ash, Robert F. "Quarterly Documentation." *China Quarterly*, No. 131 (September 1992): 864–907.

Avant, Deborah D. *Political Institutions and Military Change: Lessons from Peripheral Wars*. Ithaca, NY: Cornell University Press, 1994.

Averill, Stephen C. *Revolution in the Highlands: China's Jinggangshan Base*. Lanham, MD: Rowman & Littlefield, 2006.

Ayuso, Wanda, and Lonnie Henley. "Aspiring to Jointness: PLA Training, Exercises, and Doctrine, 2008–2012." In Roy Kamphausen, David Lai and Travis Tanner, eds., *Assessing the People's Liberation Army in the Hu Jintao Era*. Carlisle, PA: Strategic Studies Institute, , Army War College, 2014.

Bacevich, Andrew J. *The Pentomic Era: The US Army between Korea and Vietnam*. Washington, DC: National Defense University Press, 1986.

Baum, Richard. *Burying Mao: Chinese Politics in the Age of Deng Xiaoping*. Princeton, NJ: Princeton University Press, 1994.

Bennett, Andrew, and Jeffrey T. Checkel, eds. *Process Tracing in the Social Sciences: From Metaphor to Analytic Tool*. New York: Cambridge University Press, 2014.

Biddle, Stephen. "Victory Misunderstood: What the Gulf War Tells Us about the Future of Conflict." *International Security*, Vol. 21, No. 2 (Autumn 1996): 139–179.

———. *Military Power: Explaining Victory and Defeat in Modern Battle*. Princeton, NJ: Princeton University Press, 2004.

Blasko, Dennis J. *The Chinese Army Today: Tradition and Transformation for the 21st Century*. New York: Routledge, 2006.

———. "The Evolution of Core Concepts: People's War, Active Defense, and Offshore Defense." In Roy Kamphausen, David Lai and Travis Tanner, eds., *Assessing the People's Liberation Army in the Hu Jintao Era*. Carlisle, PA: Strategic Studies Institute, Army War College, 2014.

———. "China's Evolving Approach to Strategic Deterrence." In Joe McReynolds, ed., *China's Evolving Military Strategy*. Washington, DC: Jamestown Foundation, 2016.

———. "Integrating the Services and Harnessing the Military Area Commands." *Journal of Strategic Studies*, Vol. 39, Nos. 5–16 (2016): 685–708.

Blasko, Dennis J., Philip T. Klapakis, and John F. Corbett. "Training Tomorrow's PLA: A Mixed Bag of Tricks." *China Quarterly*, No. 146 (1996): 488–524.

Brady, Henry E., and David Collier. *Rethinking Social Inquiry: Diverse Tools, Shared Standards*. Lanham, MD: Rowman & Littlefield, 2004.

Braisted, William Reynolds. *The United States Navy in the Pacific, 1897–1909*. Austin: University of Texas Press, 1958.

Brooks, Risa. "Making Military Might: Why Do States Fail and Succeed?" *International Security*, Vol. 28, No. 2 (2003): 149–191.

———. *Shaping Strategy: The Civil-Military Politics of Strategic Assessment*. Princeton, NJ: Princeton University Press, 2008.

Central Intelligence Agency. *Military Forces Along the Sino-Soviet Border*, SM-70-5 [Top Secret]. Central Intelligence Agency, 1970.

Chase, Michael S., and Andrew Erickson. "The Conventional Missile Capabilities of China's Second Artillery Force: Cornerstone of Deterrence and Warfighting." *Asian Security*, Vol. 8, No. 2 (2012): 115–137.

Chase, Michael S. et. al. *China's Incomplete Military Transformation: Assessing the Weaknesses of the People's Liberation Army (PLA)*. Santa Monica, CA: RAND, 2015.

Chen, Jian. *China's Road to the Korean War: The Making of the Sino-American Confrontation*. New York: Columbia University Press, 1994.

Chen, King C. *China's War with Vietnam, 1979: Issues, Decisions, and Implications*. Stanford, CA: Hoover Institution Press, 1986.

Cheng, Dean. "Chinese Lessons from the Gulf Wars." In Andrew Scobell, David Lai and Roy Kamphausen, eds., *Chinese Lessons from Other Peoples' Wars*. Carlisle, PA: Strategic Studies Institute, Army War College, 2011.

———. "The PLA's Wartime Structure." In Kevin Pollpeter and Kenneth W. Allen, eds., *The PLA as Organization 2.0*. Vienna, VA: Defense Group, 2015.

———. *Cyber Dragon: Inside China's Information Warfare and Cyber Operations*. Santa Barbara, CA: Praeger, 2016.

Cheung, Tai Ming, Thomas G. Mahnken, and Andrew L. Ross. "Frameworks for Analyzing Chinese Defense and Military Innovation." In Tai Ming Cheung, ed., *Forging China's Military Might: A New Framework*. Baltimore: Johns Hopkins University Press, 2014.

Chien, T'ieh. "Reshuffle of Regional Military Commanders in Communist China." *Issues and Studies*, Vol. 16, No. 3 (1980): 1–4.

Christensen, Thomas J. *Useful Adversaries: Grand Strategy, Domestic Mobilization, and Sino-American Conflict, 1947–1958*. Princeton, NJ: Princeton University Press, 1996.

———. "Windows and War: Trend Analysis and Beijing's Use of Force." In Alastair Iain Johnston and Robert S. Ross, eds., *New Directions in the Study of China's Foreign Policy*. Stanford, CA: Stanford University Press, 2006.

———. *Worse Than a Monolith: Alliance Politics and Problems of Coercive Diplomacy in Asia*. Princeton, NJ: Princeton University Press, 2011.

Citino, Robert Michael. *Blitzkrieg to Desert Storm: The Evolution of Operational Warfare*. Lawrence: University Press of Kansas, 2004.

Cliff, Roger. *China's Military Power: Assessing Current and Future Capabilities*. New York: Cambridge University Press, 2015.

Clodfelter, Michael. *Warfare and Armed Conflicts: A Statistical Reference to Casualty and Other Figures, 1500–2000*. Jefferson, NC: MacFarland, 2002.

Cole, Bernard D. "The PLA Navy and 'Active Defense.' " In Stephen J. Flanagan and Michael E.Marti, eds., *The People's Liberation Army and China in Transition*. Washington, DC: National Defense University Press, 2003.

Collins, John M. *Military Strategy: Principles, Practices, and Historical Perspectives*. Dulles, VA: Potomac, 2001.

Colton, Timothy J. *Commissars, Commanders, and Civilian Authority: The Structure of Soviet Military Politics*. Cambridge, MA: Harvard University Press, 1979.

Cosmas, Graham A. *MACV: The Joint Command in the Years of Escalation, 1962–1967*. Washington, DC: Center of Military History, United States Army, 2006.

Cote, Owen Reid. "The Politics of Innovative Military Doctrine: The U.S. Navy and Fleet Ballistic Missiles." Ph.D. dissertation, Dept. of Political Science, Massachusetts Institute of Technology, 1996.

Cunningham, Fiona S. "Maximizing Leverage: Explaining China's Strategic Force Postures in Limited Wars," Ph.D. dissertation, Dept. of Political Science, Massachusetts Institute of Technology, 2018.

Cunningham, Fiona S., and M. Taylor Fravel. "Assuring Assured Retaliation: China's Nuclear Posture and U.S.-China Strategic Stability." *International Security*, Vol. 40, No. 2 (Fall 2015): 7–50.

Denmark, Abraham. "PLA Logistics 2004–11: Lessons Learned in the Field." In Roy Kamphausen, David Lai, and Travis Tanner, eds., *Learning by Doing: The PLA Trains at Home and Abroad*. Carlisle, PA: Army War College, Strategic Studies Institute, 2012.

Department of Defense Dictionary of Military and Associated Terms. Joint Publication 1–02. 2006.

Desch, Michael C. *Civilian Control of the Military: The Changing Security Environment*. Baltimore: Johns Hopkins University Press, 1999.

Directorate of Intelligence, *The PLA and the "Cultural Revolution."* POLO XXV, Central Intelligence Agency, October 28, 1967.

Dreyer, Edward L. *China at War, 1901–1949*. New York: Routledge, 1995.

Dueck, Colin. *Reluctant Crusaders: Power, Culture and Change in America's Grand Strategy*. Princeton, NJ: Princeton University Press, 2006.

Dunnigan, James F. *How to Make War: A Comprehensive Guide to Modern Warfare in the Twenty-first Century*. New York: William Morrow, 2003.

Dupuy, Trevor N. *Elusive Victory: The Arab-Israeli Wars, 1947–1974*. New York: Harper & Row, 1978.

———. *The Evolution of Weapons and Warfare*. Indianapolis: Bobbs-Merrill, 1980.

Engstrom, Jeff. *Systems Confrontation and System Destruction Warfare: How the Chinese People's Liberation Army Seeks to Wage Modern Warfare*. Santa Monica, CA: RAND, 2018.

Farrell, Theo. "Transnational Norms and Military Development: Constructing Ireland's Professional Army." *European Journal of International Relations*, Vol. 7, No. 1 (2001): 63–102.

Farrell, Theo, and Terry Terriff. "The Sources of Military Change." In Theo Farrell and Terry Terriff, eds., *The Sources of Military Change: Culture, Politics, Technology*. Boulder, CO: Lynne Rienner, 2002.

Feaver, Peter. "Civil-Military Relations." *Annual Review of Political Science*, No. 2 (1999): 211–241.

Fewsmith, Joseph. *China since Tiananmen: The Politics of Transition*. Cambridge: Cambridge University Press, 2001.

————. "Reaction, Resurgence, and Succession: Chinese Politics Since Tiananmen." In Roderick MacFarquhar, ed., *The Politics of China: Sixty Years of The People's Republic of China.* New York: Cambridge University Press, 2011.

Finkelstein, David M. *China Reconsiders Its National Security: "The Great Peace and Development Debate of 1999."* Arlington, VA: CNA, 2000.

————. "China's National Military Strategy: An Overview of the 'Military Strategic Guidelines.'" In Andrew Scobell and Roy Kamphausen, eds., *Right Sizing the People's Liberation Army: Exploring the Contours of China's Military* Carlisle, PA: Strategic Studies Institute, Army War College, 2007.

Frank, Willard C., and Philip S. Gillette, eds. *Soviet Military Doctrine from Lenin to Gorbachev, 1915–1991.* Westport, CT: Greenwood, 1992.

Fravel, M. Taylor. "The Evolution of China's Military Strategy: Comparing the 1987 and 1999 Editions of *Zhanlue Xue.*" In David M. Finkelstein and James Mulvenon, eds., *The Revolution in Doctrinal Affairs: Emerging Trends in the Operational Art of the Chinese People's Liberation Army.* Alexandria, VA: Center for Naval Analyses, 2005.

————. *Strong Borders, Secure Nation: Cooperation and Conflict in China's Territorial Disputes.* Princeton, NJ: Princeton University Press, 2008.

————. "Economic Growth, Regime Insecurity, and Military Strategy: Explaining the Rise of Noncombat Operations in China." *Asian Security*, Vol. 7, No. 3 (2011): 177–200.

————. "China's New Military Strategy: 'Winning Informationized Local Wars.'" *China Brief*, Vol. 15, No. 13 (2015): 3–6.

Fravel, M. Taylor, and Evan S. Medeiros. "China's Search for Assured Retaliation: The Evolution of Chinese Nuclear Strategy and Force Structure." *International Security*, Vol. 35, No. 2 (Fall 2010): 48–87.

Garrity, Patrick J. *Why the Gulf War Still Matters: Foreign Perspectives on the War and the Future of International Security.* Los Alamos: Center for National Security Studies, 1993.

Garver, John W. "China's Decision for War with India in 1962." In Alastair Iain Johnston and Robert S. Ross, eds., *New Directions in the Study of China's Foreign Policy.* Stanford, CA: Stanford University Press, 2006.

————. *China's Quest: The History of the Foreign Relations of the People's Republic.* New York: Oxford University Press, 2016.

George, Alexander L., and Andrew Bennett. *Case Studies and Theory Development in the Social Sciences.* Cambridge, MA: MIT Press, 2005.

Gittings, John. *The Role of the Chinese Army.* London: Oxford University Press, 1967.

Glantz, David M. *The Military Strategy of the Soviet Union: A History.* London: Frank Cass, 1992.

Godwin, Paul H. B. "People's War Revised: Military Doctrine, Strategy and Operations." In Charles D. Lovejoy and Bruce W. Watson, eds., *China's Military Reforms: International and Domestic Implications.* Boulder, CO: Westview, 1984.

————. "Changing Concepts of Doctrine, Strategy, and Operations in the Chinese People's Liberation Army, 1978–1987." *China Quarterly*, No. 112 (1987): 572–590.

————. "Chinese Military Strategy Revised: Local and Limited War." *Annals of the American Academy of Political and Social Science*, Vol. 519, No. January (1992): 191–201.

————. "From Continent to Periphery: PLA Doctrine, Strategy, and Capabilities towards 2000." *China Quarterly*, No. 146 (1996): 464–487.

————. "Change and Continuity in Chinese Military Doctrine: 1949–1999." In Mark A. Ryan, David M. Finkelstein, and Michael A. McDevitt, eds., *Chinese Warfighting: The PLA Experience since 1949.* Armonk, NY: M. E. Sharpe, 2003.

Goertz, Gary, and Paul F. Diehl. "Enduring Rivalries: Theoretical Constructs and Empirical Patterns." *International Studies Quarterly*, Vol. 37, No. 2 (June 1993): 147–171.

Goldman, Emily O., and Leslie C. Eliason, eds. *The Diffusion of Military Technology and Ideas.* Palo Alto, CA: Stanford University Press, 2003.

Goldstein, Avery. *From Bandwagon to Balance-of-Power Politics: Structural Constraints and Politics in China, 1949–1978.* Stanford, CA: Stanford University Press, 1991.

Goldstein, Steven M. *China and Taiwan.* Cambridge: Polity, 2015.

Grissom, Adam. "The Future of Military Innovation Studies." *Journal of Strategic Studies,* Vol. 29, No. 5 (2006): 905–934.

Guo, Xuezhi. *China's Security State: Philosophy, Evolution, and Politics.* New York: Cambridge University Press, 2012.

Gurtov, Melvin, and Byong-Moo Hwang. *China under Threat: The Politics of Strategy and Diplomacy.* Baltimore: Johns Hopkins University Press, 1980.

Harding, Harry. *Organizing China: The Problem of Bureaucracy, 1949–1976.* Stanford, CA: Stanford University Press, 1981.

———. "The Chinese State in Crisis." In Roderick MacFarquhar and John K. Fairbank, eds., *The Cambridge History of China, Vol. 15, Part 2.* Cambridge: Cambridge University Press, 1991.

Hastings, Max, and Simon Jenkins. *The Battle for the Falklands.* New York: Norton, 1983.

He, Di. "The Last Campaign to Unify China: The CCP's Unrealized Plan to Liberate Taiwan, 1949–1950." In Mark A. Ryan, David M. Finkelstein, and Michael A. McDevitt, eds., *Chinese Warfighting: The PLA Experience Since 1949.* Armonk, NY: M. E. Sharpe, 2003.

Hershberg, James G., and Jian Chen. "Informing the Enemy: Sino-American 'Signaling' in the Vietnam War, 1965." In Priscilla Roberts, ed., *Behind the Bamboo Curtain: China, Vietnam, and the World Beyond Asia.* Stanford, CA: Stanford University Press, 2006.

Horowitz, Michael. *The Diffusion of Military Power: Causes and Consequences for International Politics.* Princeton, NJ: Princeton University Press, 2010.

Horsburgh, Nicola. *China and Global Nuclear Order: From Estrangement to Active Engagement.* New York: Oxford University Press, 2015.

House, Jonathan M.. *Combined Arms Warfare in the Twentieth Century.* Lawrence: University of Kansas Press, 2001.

Hoyt, Timothy D. "Revolution and Counter-Revolution: The Role of the Periphery in Technological and Conceptual Innovation." In Emily O. Goldman and Leslie C. Eliason, eds., *The Diffusion of Military Technology and Ideas.* Palo Alto, CA: Stanford University Press, 2003.

Hsieh, Alice Langley. *Communist China's Strategy in the Nuclear Era.* Englewood Cliffs, NJ: Prentice-Hall, 1962.

Huang, Alexander Chieh-cheng. "Transformation and Refinement of Chinese Military Doctrine: Reflection and Critique on the PLA's View." In James Mulvenon and Andrew N. D. Yang, eds., *Seeking Truth from Facts: A Retrospective on Chinese Military Studies in the Post-Mao Era.* Santa Monica: RAND, 2001.

Huang, Jing. *Factionalism in Communist Chinese Politics.* New York: Cambridge University Press, 2000.

Humphreys, Leonard A. *The Way of the Heavenly Sword: The Japanese Army in the 1920's.* Stanford, CA: Stanford University Press, 1995.

Huntington, Samuel P. *The Soldier and the State: The Theory and Politics of Civil-Military Relations.* Cambridge, MA: Belknap Press of Harvard University Press, 1957.

Jencks, Harlan W. "China's 'Punitive' War Against Vietnam." *Asian Survey,* Vol. 19, No. 8 (August 1979): 801–815.

———. *From Muskets to Missiles: Politics and Professionalism in the Chinese Army, 1945–1981.* Boulder CO: Westview, 1982.

———. "People's War under Modern Conditions: Wishful Thinking, National Suicide, or Effective Deterrent?." *China Quarterly,* No. 98 (June 1984): 305–319.

———. "Chinese Evaluations of 'Desert Storm': Implications for PRC Security." *Journal of East Asian Affairs*, Vol. 6, No. 2 (1992): 447–477.

———. "The General Armament Department." In James Mulvenon and Andrew N. D. Yang, eds., *The People's Liberation Army as Organization: Reference Volume v1.0*. Santa Monica: RAND, 2002.

Joffe, Ellis. *The Chinese Army after Mao*. Cambridge, MA: Harvard University Press, 1987.

Kennedy, Andrew. *The International Ambitions of Mao and Nehru: National Efficacy Beliefs and the Making of Foreign Policy*. New York: Cambridge University Press, 2011.

Kier, Elizabeth. *Imagining War: French and British Military Doctrine between the Wars*. Princeton, NJ: Princeton University Press, 1997.

Kolkowicz, Roman. *The Soviet Military and the Communist Party*. Princeton, NJ: Princeton University Press, 1967.

Kristensen, Hans M., and Robert S. Norris. "Chinese Nuclear Forces, 2015." *Bulletin of the Atomic Scientists*, Vol. 71, No. 4 (2015): 77–84.

———. "Chinese Nuclear Forces, 2018." *Bulletin of the Atomic Scientists*, Vol. 74, No. 4 (2018): 289–295.

Lam, Willy Wo-Lap. *China after Deng Xiaoping: The Power Struggle in Beijing since Tiananmen*. Hong Kong: P A Professional Consultants, 1995.

Levine, Steven I. *Anvil of Victory: The Communist Revolution in Manchuria, 1945–1948*. New York: Columbia University Press, 1987.

Levite, Ariel. *Offense and Defense in Israeli Military Doctrine*. Boulder, CO: Westview, 1989.

Lew, Christopher R. *The Third Chinese Revolutionary Civil War, 1945–49: An Analysis of Communist Strategy and Leadership*. New York: Routledge, 2009.

Lewis, John Wilson, and Hua Di. "China's Ballistic Missile Programs: Technologies, Strategies, Goals." *Intenational Security*, Vol. 17, No. 2 (1992): 5–40.

Lewis, John Wilson, and Litai Xue. *China Builds the Bomb*. Stanford, CA: Stanford University Press, 1988.

———. *Imagined Enemies: China Prepares for Uncertain War*. Stanford, CA: Stanford University Press, 2006.

Li, Chen. "From Burma Road to 38th Parallel: The Chinese Forces' Adaptation in War, 1942–1953," Ph.D. thesis, Faculty of Asian and Middle Eastern Studies, Cambridge University, 2012.

———. "From Civil War Victor to Cold War Guard: Positional Warfare in Korea and the Transformation of the Chinese People's Liberation Army, 1951–1953." *Journal of Strategic Studies*, Vol. 38, No. 1–2 (2015): 183–214.

———. "Operational Idealism: Doctrine Development of the Chinese People's Liberation Army under Soviet Threat, 1969–1989." *Journal of Strategic Studies*, Vol. 40, No. 5 (2017): 663–695.

Li, Nan. "Changing Functions of the Party and Political Work System in the PLA and Civil-Military Relations in China." *Armed Forces and Society*, Vol. 19, No. 3 (1993): 393–409.

———. "The PLA's Evolving Warfighting Doctrine, Strategy and Tactics, 1985–95: A Chinese Perspective." *China Quarterly*, No. 146 (1996): 443–463.

———. "Organizational Changes of the PLA, 1985–1997." *China Quarterly*, No. 158 (1999): 314–349.

———. "The Central Military Commission and Military Policy in China." In James Mulvenon and Andrew N. D. Yang, eds., *The People's Liberation Army as Organization: V 1.0., Reference Volume*. Santa Monica, CA: RAND, 2002.

———. "The Evolution of China's Naval Strategy and Capabilities: From 'Near Coast' and 'Near Seas' to 'Far Seas.'" *Asian Security*, Vol. 5, No. 2 (2009): 144–169.

Li, Xiaobing. *A History of the Modern Chinese Army*. Lexington: University of Kentucky Press, 2007.

Lieberthal, Kenneth. "The Great Leap Forward and the Split in the Yenan Leadership." In John King Fairbank and Roderick MacFarquhar, eds., *The Cambridge History of China, Vol. 14.* Cambridge: Cambridge University Press, 1987.

———. *Governing China: From Revolution through Reform.* New York: W. W. Norton, 2004.

Liu, Yanqiong, and Jifeng Liu. "Analysis of Soviet Technology Transfer in the Development of China's Nuclear Programs." *Comparative Technology Transfer and Society*, Vol. 7, No. 1 (April 2009): 66–110.

Lobell, Stephen E., Norrin M. Ripsman, and Jeffrey W. Taliaferro, eds. *Neoclassical Realism, the State, and Foreign Policy.* New York: Cambridge University Press, 2009.

Long, Austin. *The Soul of Armies: Counterinsurgency Doctrine and Military Culture in the US and UK.* Ithaca: Cornell University Press, 2016.

Luthi, Lorenz M. "The Vietnam War and China's Third-Line Defense Planning before the Cultural Revolution, 1964–1966." *Journal of Cold War Studies*, Vol. 10, No. 1 (2008): 26–51.

MacFarquhar, Roderick. *The Origins of the Cultural Revolution, Vol. 2.* New York: Columbia University Press, 1983.

———. "The Succession to Mao and the End of Maoism, 1969–82." In Roderick MacFarquhar, ed., *The Politics of China.* New York: Cambridge University Press, 1993.

———. *The Origins of the Cultural Revolution, Vol. 3.* New York: Columbia University Press, 1997.

MacFarquhar, Roderick, and Michael Schoenhals. *Mao's Last Revolution.* Cambridge, MA: Belknap Press of Harvard University Press, 2006.

McCauley, Kevin. *PLA System of Systems Operations: Enabling Joint Operations.* Washington, DC: Jamestown Foundation, 2017.

McReynolds, Joe, and James Mulvenon. "The Role of Informatization in the People's Liberation Army under Hu Jintao." In Roy Kamphausen, David Lai and Travis Tanner, eds., *Assessing the People's Liberation Army in the Hu Jintao Era* Carlisle, PA: Strategic Studies Institute, Army War College, 2014.

Mearsheimer, John J. *The Tragedy of Great Power Politics.* New York: W. W. Norton, 2001.

Mulvenon, James C. "China: Conditional Compliance." In Muthiah Alagappa, ed., *Coercion and Governance in Asia: The Declining Political Role of the Military* Stanford, CA: Stanford University Press, 2001.

Murray, Williamson, and Allan R. Millet, eds. *Military Innovation in the Interwar Period.* New York: Cambridge University Press, 1996.

———. *A War To Be Won: Fighting the Second World War.* Cambridge, MA: Belknap Press of Harvard University Press, 2000.

Nagl, John A. *Learning to Eat Soup with a Knife: Counterinsurgency Lessons from Malaya and Vietnam.* Chicago: University of Chicago Press, 2005.

Narang, Vipin. *Nuclear Strategy in the Modern Era: Regional Powers and International Conflict.* Princeton, NJ: Princeton University Press, 2014.

Nathan, Andrew J., and Robert S. Ross. *The Great Wall and the Empty Fortress: China's Search for Security.* New York: W.W. Norton, 1997.

National Air and Space Intelligence Center. *Ballistic and Cruise Missile Threat.* Wright-Patterson Air Force Base, 2009.

National Institute for Defense Studies. *NIDS China Security Report 2016: The Expanding Scope of PLA Activities and the PLA Strategy.* Tokyo: National Institute for Defense Studies, 2016.

Naughton, Barry. "The Third Front: Defense Industrialization in the Chinese Interior." *China Quarterly*, No. 115 (Autumn 1988): 351–386.

———. "Industrial Policy During the Cultural Revolution: Military Preparation, Decentralization, and Leaps Forward." In Christine Wong, William A. Joseph. and David Zweig, eds., *New Perspectives on the Cultural Revolution* Cambridge, MA: Harvard University Press, 1991.

Ng, Ka Po. *Interpreting China's Military Power*. New York: Routledge, 2005.

Nielsen, Suzanne. "Civil-Military Relations Theory and Military Effectiveness." *Public Administration and Management*, Vol. 10, No. 2 (2003): 61–84.

———. *An Army Transformed: The U.S. Army's Post-Vietnam Recovery and the Dynamics of Change in Military Organizations*. Carlisle, PA: Army War College, Strategic Studies Institute, 2010.

Nixon, Richard M. *RN: The Memoirs of Richard Nixon*. New York: Grosset & Dunlap, 1978.

O'Dowd, Edward C. *Chinese Military Strategy in the Third Indochina War: The Last Maoist War*. New York: Routledge, 2007.

Odom, William. "The Party-Military Connection: A Critique." In Dale R. Herspring and Ivan Volgyes, eds., *Civil-Military Relations in Communist Systems*. Boulder, CO: Westview, 1978.

Office of National Estimates. *The Soviet Military Buildup Along the Chinese Border*, SM-7-68 [Top Secret]. Central Intelligence Agency, 1968.

Office of the Secretary of Defense. *Military Power of the People's Republic of China 2000*. Department of Defense, 2000.

Parker, Geoffrey, ed. *The Cambridge History of Warfare*. New York: Cambridge University Press, 2005.

Pepper, Suzanne. *Civil War in China: The Political Struggle, 1945–1949*. Lanham, MD: Rowman & Littlefield, 1999.

Perlmutter, Amos, and William M. Leogrande. "The Party in Uniform: Toward a Theory of Civil-Military Relations in Communist Political Systems." *American Political Science Review*, Vol. 76, No. 4 (1982): 778–789.

Piao, Lin. "Long Live the Victory of People's War." *Peking Review*, No. 36 (September 3, 1965): 9–20.

Posen, Barry. *The Sources of Military Doctrine: France, Britain, and Germany between the World Wars*. Ithaca: Cornell University Press, 1984.

———. "Nationalism, the Mass Army and Military Power." *International Security*, Vol. 18, No. 2 (1993): 80–124.

Powell, Jonathan, and Clayton Thyne. "Global Instances of Coups from 1950-Present." *Journal of Peace Research*, Vol. 48, No. 2 (2011): 249–259.

Powell, Ralph L. "Great Powers and Atomic Bombs Are 'Paper Tigers.'" *China Quarterly*, No. 23 (1965): 55–63.

———. "Maoist Military Doctrines." *Asian Survey*, Vol. 8, No. 4 (April 1968): 239–262.

Puska, Susan. "Taming the Hydra: Trends in China's Military Logistics Since 2000." In Roy Kamphausen, David Lai, and Andrew Scobell, eds., *The PLA at Home and Abroad: Assessing the Operational Capabilities of China's Military*. Carlisle, PA: Army War College, Strategic Studies Institute, 2010.

Ray, Jonathan. *Red China's "Capitalist Bomb": Inside the Chinese Neutron Bomb Program*. Washington, DC: Center for the Study of Chinese Military Affairs, Institute for National Strategic Studies, National Defense University, 2015.

Recchia, Stefano. *Reassuring the Reluctant Warriors: U.S. Civil-Military Relations and Multilateral Intervention*. Ithaca: Cornell University Press, 2016.

Reiter, Dan, and Allan Stam. *Democracies at War*. Princeton, NJ: Princeton University Press, 2002.

Resende-Santos, Joao. *Neorealism, States and the Modern Mass Army*. New York: Cambridge University Pres, 2007.

Riskin, Carl. *China's Political Economy: The Quest for Development since 1949*. New York: Oxford University Press, 1987.

Rogers, Everett M. *Diffusion of Innovations*. New York: Free Press, 2003.

Romjue, John L. *From Active Defense to AirLand Battle: The Development of Army Doctrine, 1973–1982*. Fort Monroe, VA: Historical Office, US Army Training and Doctrine Command, 1984.

Rosato, Sebastian. "The Inscrutable Intentions of Great Powers." *International Security*, Vol. 39, No. 3 (2014/15): 48–88.

Rosen, Stephen Peter. *Winning the Next War: Innovation and the Modern Military*. Ithaca, NY: Cornell University Press, 1991.

Ryan, Mark A. *Chinese Attitudes toward Nuclear Weapons: China and the United States During the Korean War*. Armonk, NY: M. E. Sharpe, 1989.

Saich, Tony, ed. *The Rise to Power of the Chinese Communist Party: Documents and Analysis*. New York: Routledge, 2015.

Sapolsky, Harvey M. *The Polaris System Development: Bureaucratic and Programmatic Success in Government*. Cambridge, MA: Harvard University Press, 1972.

Sapolsky, Harvey M., Benjamin H. Friedman, and Brendan Rittenhouse Green, eds. *US Military Innovation since the Cold War: Creation without Destruction*. New York: Routledge, 2009.

Schram, Stuart R., ed. *Mao's Road to Power, Vol. 4 (The Rise and Fall of the Chinese Soviet Republic, 1931–1934)*. Armonk, NY: M. E. Sharpe, 1997.

———. ed. *Mao's Road to Power, Vol. 5 (Toward the Second United Front, January 1935–July 1937)*. Armonk, NY: M. E. Sharpe, 1997.

Schweller, Randall. "The Progressiveness of Neoclassical Realism." In Colin Elman and Miriam Fendius Elman, eds., *Progress in International Relations Theory: Appraising the Field*. Cambridge, MA: MIT Press, 2003.

———. *Unanswered Threats: Political Constraints on the Balance of Power*. Princeton, NJ: Princeton University Press, 2006.

Scobell, Andrew. *China's Use of Military Force: Beyond the Great Wall and the Long March*. New York: Cambridge University Press, 2003.

Scott, Harriet Fast, and William F. Scott. *Soviet Military Doctrine: Continuity, Formulation and Dissemination*. Boulder, CO: Westview, 1988.

Segal, Gerald, and Tony Saich. "Quarterly Chronicle and Documentation." *China Quarterly*, No. 82 (June 1980): 369–394.

———. "Quarterly Chronicle and Documentation." *China Quarterly*, No. 83 (1980): 598–637.

Shambaugh, David. "The Soldier and the State in China: The Political Work System in the People's Liberation Army." *China Quarterly*, No. 127 (1991): 527–568.

———. "Building the Party-State in China, 1949–1965: Bringing the Soldier Back In." In Timothy Cheek and Tony Saich, eds., *New Perspectives on State Socialism in China*. Armonk, NY.: M. E. Sharpe, 1997.

———. *Modernizing China's Military: Progress, Problems, and Prospects*. Berkeley, CA: University of California Press, 2002.

Shih, Victor. *Factions and Finance in China: Elite Conflict and Inflation*. Cambridge: Cambridge University Press, 2008.

Shih, Victor, Wei Shan, and Mingxing Liu. "Guaging the Elite Political Equilibirum in the CCP: A Quantitative Approach Using Biographical Data." *China Quarterly*, No. 201 (March 2010): 79–103.

Snyder, Jack. "Civil-Military Relations and the Cult of the Offensive, 1914 and 1984." *International Security*, Vol. 9, No. 1 (Summer 1984): 108–146.

Snyder, Jack L. *The Ideology of the Offensive: Military Decision Making and the Disasters of 1914*. Ithaca, NY: Cornell University Press, 1984.

Sun, Shuyun. *The Long March: The True History of Communist China's Founding Myth*. New York: Anchor, 2008.

Sun, Xiangli. "The Development of Nuclear Weapons in China." In Bin Li and Zhao Tong, eds., *Understanding Chinese Nuclear Thinking*. Washington, DC: Carnegie Endowment for International Peace, 2016.

Swaine, Michael D. *The Military & Political Succession in China: Leadership, Institutions, Beliefs.* Santa Monica, CA: RAND, 1992.

Taliaferro, Jeffrey W. "State Building for Future War: Neoclassical Realism and the Resource Extractive State." *Security Studies*, Vol. 15, No. 3 (July 2006): 464–495.

Talmadge, Caitlin. *The Dictator's Army: Battlefield Effectiveness in Authoritarian Regimes.* Ithaca, NY: Cornell University Press, 2015.

Tanner, Harold M. *Where Chiang Kai-shek Lost China: The Liao-Shen Campaign, 1948.* Bloomington: Indiana University Press, 2015.

Tanner, Murray Scot. "The Institutional Lessons of Disaster: Reorganizing the People's Armed Police after Tiananmen." In James Mulvenon and Andrew N. D. Yang, eds., *The People's Liberation Army as Organization: V 1.0., Reference Volume.* Santa Monica, CA: RAND, 2002.

Teiwes, Frederick C. *Politics and Purges in China: Rectification and the Decline of Party Norms, 1950–1965.* Armonk, NY: M. E. Sharpe, 1979.

———. "The Establishment and Consolidation of the New Regime." In Roderick MacFarquhar, ed., *The Politics of China: The Eras of Mao and Deng.* Cambridge: Cambridge University Press, 1997.

Teiwes, Frederick C., and Warren Sun. *The Tragedy of Lin Biao: Riding the Tiger during the Cultural Revolution.* Honolulu: University of Hawaii Press, 1996.

———. *China's Road to Disaster: Mao, Central Politicians and Provincial Leaders in the Unfolding of the Great Leap Forward, 1955–1959.* Armonk, NY: M. E. Sharpe, 1999.

———. "The First Tiananmen Incident Revisited: Elite Politics and Crisis Management at the End of the Maoist Era." *Pacific Affairs*, Vol. 77, No. 2 (2004): 211–235.

———. *The End of the Maoist Era: Chinese Politics during the Twilight of the Cultural Revolution, 1972–1976.* Armonk, NY: M. E. Sharpe, 2007.

———. "China's New Economic Policy Under Hua Guofeng: Pary Consensus and Party Myths." *China Journal* No. 66 (2011): 1–23.

Thomas, Timothy L., John A. Tokar, and Robert Tomes. "Kosovo and the Current Myth of Information Superiority." *Parameters*, Vol. 30, No. 1 (Spring 2000): 13–29.

Thomson, William R. "Identifying Rivals and Rivalries in World Politics." *International Studies Quarterly*, Vol. 45, No. 4 (December 2001): 557–586.

Timerbaev, Roland. "How the Soviet Union Helped China Develop the A-bomb." *Digest of Yaderny Kontrol (Nuclear Control)*, No. 8 (Summer–Fall 1998): 44–49.

Torigian, Joseph. "Prestige, Manipulation, and Coercion: Elite Power Struggles and the Fate of Three Revolutions," PhD dissertation, Department of Political Science, Massachusetts Institute of Technology, 2016.

Twomey, Christopher P. "The People's Liberation Army's Selective Learning: Lessons of the Iran-Iraq 'War of the Cities' Missile Duels and Uses of Missiles in Other Conflicts." In Andrew Scobell, David Lai, and Roy Kamphausen, eds., *Chinese Lessons from Other Peoples' Wars.* Carlisle, PA: Army War College, Strategic Studies Institute, 2011.

Van Creveld, Martin. *Military Lessons of the Yom Kippur War: Historical Perspectives.* Beverly Hills, CA: Sage, 1975.

Van Evera, Stephen. *Guide to Methods for Students of Political Science.* Ithaca, NY: Cornell University Press, 1997.

Van Slyke, Lyman P. "The Chinese Communist Movement During the Sino-Japanese War, 1937–1945." In *The Nationalist Era in China, 1927–1949.* Ithaca, NY: Cornell University Press, 1991.

———. "The Battle of the Hundred Regiments: Problems of Coordination and Control during the Sino-Japanese War." *Modern Asian Studies*, Vol. 30, No. 4 (1996): 919–1005.

Vogel, Ezra F. *Deng Xiaoping and the Transformation of China.* Cambridge, MA: Belknap Press of Harvard University Press, 2011.

Walder, Andrew G. *China Under Mao: A Revolution Derailed*. Cambridge, MA: Harvard University Press, 2015.

Waltz, Kenneth N. *Theory of International Politics*. New York: McGraw-Hill, 1979.

Weeks, Jessica. *Dictators at War and Peace*. Ithaca, NY: Cornell University Press, 2014.

Wei, William. *Counterrevolution in China: The Nationalists in Jiangxi during the Soviet Period*. Ann Arbor: University of Michigan Press, 1985.

———. "Power Grows Out of the Barrel of a Gun: Mao and Red Army." In David A. Graff and Robin Higham, eds., *A Military History of China*. Lexington: University Press of Kentucky, 2012.

Westad, Odd Arne. *Decisive Encounters: The Chinese Civil War, 1946–1950*. Stanford, CA: Stanford University Press, 2003.

Whiting, Allen S. *China Crosses the Yalu: The Decision to Enter the Korean War*. New York: Macmillan, 1960.

———. *The Chinese Calculus of Deterrence: India and Indochina*. Ann Arbor: University of Michigan Press, 1975.

———. "China's Use of Force, 1950–96, and Taiwan." *International Security*, Vol. 26, No. 2 (Fall 2001): 103–131.

Whitson, William W., and Zhenxia Huang. *The Chinese High Command: A History of Communist Military Politics, 1927–71*. New York: Praeger, 1973.

Wilson, James Q. *Bureaucracy: What Government Agencies Do and Why They Do It*. New York: Basic, 1989.

Wuthnow, Joel. "A Brave New World for Chinese Joint Operations." *Journal of Strategic Studies*, Vol. 40, Nos. 1–2 (2017): 169–195.

Wuthnow, Joel, and Philip C. Saunders. *Chinese Military Reform in the Age of Xi Jinping: Drivers, Challenges, and Implications*. Washington, DC: National Defense University Press, 2017.

Yang, Jisheng. *Tombstone: The Great Chinese Famine, 1958–1962*. New York: Farrar, Straus & Giroux, 2013.

Yao, Yunzhu. "The Evolution of Military Doctrine of the Chinese PLA from 1985 to 1995." *Korean Journal of Defense Analysis*, Vol. 7, No. 2 (1995): 57–80.

———. "Chinese Nuclear Policy and the Future of Minimum Deterrence." In Christopher P. Twomey, ed., *Perspectives on Sino-American Strategic Nuclear Issues*. New York: Palgrave Macmillan, 2008.

You, Ji. *The Armed Forces of China*. London: I. B. Tauris, 1999.

Zhai, Qiang. *China and the Vietnam Wars, 1950–1975*. Chapel Hill: University of North Carolina Press, 2000.

Zhang, Xiaoming. "Air Combat for the People's Republic: The People's Liberation Army Air Force in Action, 1949–1969." In Mark A. Ryan, David M. Finkelstein and Michael A. McDevitt, eds., *Chinese Warfighting: The PLA Experience since 1949*. Armonk, NY: M. E. Sharpe, 2003.

———. *Deng Xiaoping's Long War: The Military Conflict between China and Vietnam, 1979–1991*. Chapel Hill: University of North Carolina Press, 2015.

Zisk, Kimberly Marten. *Engaging the Enemy: Organization Theory and Soviet Military Innovation, 1955–1991*. Princeton, NJ: Princeton University Press, 1993.

INDEX

NOTE: **BOLD** PAGE NUMBERS INDICATE ILLUSTRATIONS.

"two-and-a-half doctrine," 110
"three alls" campaign, Japanese, 53
"three attacks and three defenses," 226
three-dimensional war *(liti zhan),* 78, 161, 202
Five Principles of Peaceful Coexistence, 93
"ten military principles," Mao's, 209–10
"801" meeting, 157–58, 160–63, 170, 172
"802" meeting, training exercise, 89, 144, 169, 171–73
"934" training exercise, 206
1956 strategic guideline, **34,** 74–77, 270; active defense and, 74, 92, 99; adoption of, 5–6, 90–92; and autonomy of military leadership, 81–82; CMC and formulation of, 72–73, 92; combined arms operations in, 72–77; and conduct of warfare, 5–6, 73, 77–78, 88, 271; defensive posture in, 92–93; deterrence and, 8, 93; force structure in, 75–76, 83; and guerrilla warfare, 94; Korean War and, 74; Mao and, 91, 109; "massive retaliation" doctrine and, 74, 79, 237; and modernization, 90; motivations for formulating, 72; and "nuclear conditions," 73–74, 77, 79, 89, 98; operational doctrine in, 75; party unity and, 106; Peng Dehuai and, 5–6, 74–75, 90–94, 271; and positional warfare as form of operations in, 74–75, 78, 93–94, 103, 270; publication of, 30; reforms prior to, 81–82; and Soviets as advisors, 90; strategic direction, primary, in, 82–84, **85;** Su Yu and, 82–83, 91–92; training provisions in, 76–77; and US as threat, 74–75, **92**
1960 strategic guideline, **34;** CMC and formulation of, 101–2; combat regulations and, 104–5; economic policy and, 102; guerrilla warfare in, 103–4; lack of documentation for, 102–3; Mao's rejection of, 122–25; as minor change, 104–6; mobile warfare in, 103–4; modernization and, 105; party disunity and purge and, 101–2;

political training emphasized in, 104, 105–6; positional warfare in, 103; and regulations, 104–5; strategic direction, primary, in, 103–4, 122, 123; and US as threat, 102
1964 strategic guideline, **34;** Cultural Revolution and implementation of, 114; and external threats (Soviets, India, US), 109–11, 127–29; and "luring the enemy in deep," 6, 113–14, 145–47, 271; and Mao's direct intervention, 107–9, 115, 272; as minor change, 107; Nationalist threat and, 107–12; and party disunity, 137–38; positional warfare in, 114; as retrograde change, 107–9, 137–38; strategic direction, primary, in, 113–14, 122, 131
1977 strategic guidelines, **34, 147**
1980 strategic guideline, **35;** "801" meeting and, 157–58, 160–63, 170, 172; "802" meeting training exercise and, 144, 169, 171–73; active defense and, 139–44, 166; basis of preparations in, 141, 190; and combined operations, 6, **35,** 141–44, 165–66, 171, 180, 185; and conduct of warfare, 6–7, 139–41, 144–51, 161–62, 165; defensive posture and, 141–42; downsizing as strategic change in, 173–76; force structure in, 143–44, 167–70; forward defense in, 139, 141–42, 156; implementation of, 165; "luring the enemy in deep" abandoned in, 148, 150–51, 157–58, 160, 161; as major shift, 181; modernization and, 156–57, 168; nuclear strategy, 142, 267–69; operational doctrine and form of operations in, 142–43, 165–66; positional warfare in, 139, 141–43, 149–50, 270–71; and Soviet threat, 6, 139, 141, 144, **159, 171–72;** strategic direction, primary, in, 141, 144, **159, 171–72;** Su Yu's lectures as influence on, 146, 148–50, 157, 164; training in, 144, 170–73

1988 strategic guideline, **35**; force structure in, 180; GSD and adoption of, 178; local wars as focus in, 176–81, 183; as minor change, 177, 180; operational doctrine in, 180; training in, 180–81

1993 strategic guideline, **35**; and absence of clear threat, 182; active defense and, 185, 199–201; basis of preparations for military struggle in, 183–84, 187, 201; CMC and, 182–84, 199–208; combat readiness or war preparation *(zhanbei)*, 204; combat regulations in, 208–10; and conduct of warfare, 7, 182–83, 187–91, 204; and deterrence, 184, 218, 225, 231; downsizing and reorganization in, 212–15; and external security threats, 182, 202; and first-strike or preemption, 185; force structure in, 186, 203–4, 210–12, 214–15; formulation and adoption of, 199–204; and ground forces, 183, 213; and Gulf War as strategic lesson, 7, 182, 187–91, 199–208, 215–16, 271; and high technology local wars, 7, 183–85, 201–2, 203, 215; implementation of, 204–11; and informatized warfare, 214; and Jiang Zemin, 199, 200, 201–2, 233–34; joint operations *(lainhe zuozhan)* in, 7, **35**, 182, 183, 185–86, 187, 203, 205–8, 209; and local wars as emphasis, 182–85, 203–11, 214–15, 271; operational doctrine in, 185–86, 208–10; party disunity and politicization of the PLA as obstacle to change, 191–98; and party unity, 272; strategic direction, primary, in, 184, 204, 211; training in, 187, 205–8; US as threat, 202–3

2004 strategic guideline, **35**; 2014 strategic guideline as extension of, 230, 234; basis of preparations for military struggle in, 218; CMC and formulation of, 217–19; and conduct of warfare, 7, 222, 234; as extension of 1993 guideline, 234; force structure in, 221; and Gulf War as strategic lesson, 8; and "informatized conditions" for war, 217–21, 224; and Iraq War (2003) as strategic lesson, 226–28; joint operations in, 8–9, **35**, 219–21, 222, 223, 225, 227–28; and Kosovo War as strategic lesson, 222–26; local wars and, 217, 218–20; as minor change, 218, 234; and new historic mission, 28, 228–30; operational doctrine in, 219–21; publication of, 30; strategic direction, primary, in, 218, 232

2014 strategic guideline, **35**; basis of preparations for military struggle in, 230–31; CMC and formulation of, 217–19; and conduct of warfare, 234–35; developmental interest as emphasis in, 231; as extension of 2004 strategic guideline, 230, 234; formulation of, 217–19; and "informatized local wars," 217, 230–34; and joint operations, 231–32, 234–35, 273; and maritime domain as emphasis, 231–32, 234, 276; as minor change, 234; reorganization in, 273

Academy of Military Science (AMS), 29, 77, 100, 113, 145, 148, 151, 161, 165, 168, 186, 188, 200, 208, 223, 263

active defense *(jiji fangyu)*, 5; 1956 strategic guideline and, 74, 92, 99; 1980 strategic guideline and, 139–44, 166; 1993 strategic guideline and, 185, 199–201; and Civil War encirclement campaigns, 61–64; and conduct of warfare, 161–62, 166; and defensive posture, 63; defined and described, 61–63; Deng Xiaoping and, 1, 161; and guerrilla warfare, 62; and high-technology, local wars, 201; and "luring the enemy in deep," 62–64, 147, 157, 161, 164, 167; Mao and, 62, 91, 147, 161; and mobile warfare, 62; and naval strategy, 162–63; and nuclear strategy, 98, 236, 241, 260–62, 267–69; Peng Dehuai and, 92–94, 98; in *Science of Military Strategy*, 166; Soviet criticisms of, 98–99; strategic guidelines and emphasis on, **34–35**, 58, 61–62, 269

active offense, 46–47, 62, 204–5

Advanced Military Academy, 77, 97, 105

Afghanistan, 31, 33, 141, 224, 225

agriculture, 6, 69, 116–17, 119–20, 129

air force (People Liberation Army Air Force, PLAAF): 1956 strategic guideline and, 75–76, 83, 95; increased emphasis and expenditures on, 75–76, 83, 186; lack of, 77; military exercises and, 172, 206–7; modernization and expansion of, 221

ambush. *See* "luring the enemy in deep"

amphibious assault forces: counter assault exercises, 77, 88–90, 162, 206, 276; and near-coast defense, 96; and near-seas defense, 162; and Taiwan as Nationalist stronghold, 69, 74

AMS. *See* Academy of Military Science (AMS)

annihilation of enemy forces, 41–42, 83, 133–34, 135, 190–91, 205, 209

anticorruption campaigns, 277

Arab-Israeli War (1967), 33
Arab-Israeli War (1973): as client war demonstrating Soviet threat, 33, 139, 144, 146, 181, 271; and combat regulations, 166; and conduct of warfare, 6, 14, 33, 146, 161–62; as strategic lesson, 139–47, 151, 158, 161–62; training and, 137, 151, 158
army building *(jundui jianshe)*, 67–68
atomic weapons. *See* nuclear weapons
autonomy, military: as internal motive for strategic change, 15–16, 18; Mao's direct intervention in military affairs, 107–9, 115; and military-led change, 17, 73, 81–82; of party-armies, 4–6, 9, 19–20, 271; of the PLA, 5–6, 19–20, 275
Autumn Harvest Uprisings, 42–43
Avant, Deborah, 17, 18
Ayub Khan, Muhammad, 130

Bandung Conference (1955), 93
base areas: CCP and, 43–45, **44**
basis of preparations for military struggle, 28, 60; in 1960 strategic guideline, 104; in 1980 strategic guideline, 141, 190; in 1988 strategic guideline, 179, 181; in 1993 strategic guideline, 183–84, 187, 201; in 2004 strategic guideline, 218; in 2014 strategic guideline, 230–31; as component of strategic guidelines, **34–35**, 60, 74; and informatized *vs.* high technology emphasis, 218, 231; and shift in conduct of warfare, 190
"Battle of One Hundred Regiments," 53
Baum, Richard, 192
Beidaihe leadership retreat, annual, 117, 126, 251, 252
Biddle, Stephen, 23
biographies as primary sources, 37
border security: India and border disputes, 107, 108, 109, 110–13; and limited wars over territory, 162; YiTa Incident in Xinjiang, 109–10, 128
Bo Yibo, 119, 121, 250
Brezhnev doctrine, 135
Brooks, Risa, 21
bureaucracy, centralization and coordination of, 89–90, 168–69; linked to revisionism, 134–35; Mao's preference for decentralized, local controls, 116, 117, 120–27

Cambodia, 155, 163
campaign outlines, 165, 166, 186, 187, 209–10, 221
Campaign Theory Study Guide, 243

CCP. *See* Chinese Communist Party (CCP)
centralization and coordination of bureaucracy, 89–90, 168–69; linked to revisionism, 134–35; Mao's preference for decentralized, local controls, 116, 117, 120–27
Central Military Commission (CMC): and 1956 strategic guideline, 72–73, 92; and 1960 strategic guideline, 101–2; and 1993 strategic guideline, 182–84, 199–208; 2004/2014 strategic guidelines and, 217–19; and adoption of strategic guidelines, 28–29, 92, 217–19; and CCP authority over PLA, 28; and combat regulations, 75, 100–101, 165–66, 183–84, 208–9, 260; and combined arms operations, 143–44, 182, 183, 208–9; composition of, 136; and definition of strategic guidelines, 3; Deng Xiaoping and, 153–57, 175, 177, 194; and downsizing of PLA, 157, 162–63, 168–69, 173–77, 181, 186, 196, 204, 212–15; and emphasis on military training, 170–71; and formulation of strategic guidelines, 58–59, 90–92, 99, 101–3, 105, 110, 112, 139, 147, 150, 157–58, 160–64, 177–79, 181, 182, 232–33, 273–74; and Gulf War as strategic lesson, 187–91, 201–2; Hua Guofeng and, 152, 156; Hu Jintao's leadership of, 228–29; Jiang Zemin's leadership of, 194, 195, 199–202, 212–14, 219, 224–26; and joint operations, 183–84, 205, 206, 222; and Kosovo War as strategic lesson, 223; Lin Biao's leadership and, 102–4; Mao's leadership and, 81–82, 90, 152; membership and factions within, 136–37, 147, 153, 167, 194, 198–99, 221; and military modernization, 86–88, 156, 247; and Ninth Five-Year plan for PLA, 211–12; Peng Dehuai, 81, 85–87, 90–92, 102; and reliance on guidelines, 1; and supervision of nuclear forces (Second Artillery), 236–37, 241, 245–47, 252, 258–62, 264, 266–67; Yang brothers and, 194, 195, 199
Central Special Commission (CSC), 253, 255–59
C4ISR systems, 191, 219, 221, 223, 225, 227–28
chemical weapons, 75–76, 89, 93, 95, 244
Chen Boda, 126
Cheng, Dean, 220
Chen-Nie-Bo group, 250–51
Chen Yi, 251–52
Chen Yun, 155, 192, 250, 251–52
Chiang Kai-shek, 42, 45–46, 48, 51, 54–55, 69, 110, 112

Chi Haotian, 156, 178, 189, 191, 198, 212
China Builds the Bomb (Lewis and Xue), 237
Chinese Communist Party (CCP): and adoption of strategic guidelines, 90, 271; anticorruption campaign and unity in, 277; armed force structure and organization, 40–42; authority over PLA, 1, 27, 69, 274 (*See also* autonomy, military; Central Military Commission (CMC)); Central Committee and leadership of, 36; Central Special Commission created, 253; Civil War strategies and (*See* Civil War (1927–1949)); Deng Xiaoping and consolidation of power within, 151–56; disunity within, 5–7, 6, 36, 108, 118, 140, 193, 229; and leadership succession, 79–80, 140, 152–56, 193, 225, 245; and Mao as strategist, 54–55; and military autonomy (*See* autonomy, military); and Nationalists as threat, 54–55; party unity and strategic change, 4–6, 73, 79–80, 271, 277; revisionism within, 108–9, 115–16, 118, 121; role of CMC in strategic policy, 28–29; Sino-Japanese War strategy, 40, 41, 50–53, 59; strategic guidelines and policy making, 28–29; Xi's anticorruption campaigns, 277
civil-military relations: civilian intervention as mechanism for change, 16–19, 273–74; in socialist states, 19–22
Civil War (1927–1949), 53–58; and active defense, 61–64; armed force structure and organization under CCP, 40–42; CCP victory in, 56–58, 69, 80; decisive battles of (map), 57; encirclement campaigns, 40, 43–50; and guerrilla warfare, 39, 41, 64–66; Long March and, 44; Mao as military leader during, 42–43, 49–50, 54–56; and mobile, conventional warfare, 39–41, 54–55, 58, 64; and offensive strategy, 55–56, 58; strategic lessons of, 98; and strategic retreat, 41–42, 49–50, 55; strategies deployed during, 5; urban uprisings and insurrections, 40, 42–43
client wars, 4, 9, 14, 32–33, 139–40. *See also specific, e.g.,* Kosovo War
CMC. *See* Central Military Commission (CMC)
coastal defense, 76, 83–84, 89, 93–95, 99, 112, 162, 209
Cold War, 27, 67, 182, 203, 246
Cole, Bernard, 163
combat readiness or war preparation *(zhanbei),* 7, 68, 93, 109–11, 131, 137, 158,

211–12; "801" meeting and, 160–61; 1993 strategic guideline and, 204; concerns regarding, 275–76; decline during the Cultural Revolution, 7, 164 (*See also* training)
combat regulations: 1960 strategic guideline and, 104–5; 1993 strategic guideline and, 208–10; CMC and, 75, 90, 100, 104–5, 143, 165–66, 177, 180, 210; and combined arms operations, 105, 166, 180, 208–10; emulation of Soviet model, 96–97, 100–101; for infantry, 75, 99, 165–66
combined arms group armies, **35,** 99, 143–44, 169, 175, 177, 260
combined arms operations, 33; in 1956 strategic guideline, 72–77; in 1980 strategic guideline, 6, **35,** 141–44, 165–66, 171, 180, 185; in 1988 strategic guideline, 180; in 1999 strategic guideline, 210; across military regions, 222; air force and, 172, 206–7; CMC and emphasis on, 143–44, 182, 183, 208–9; combat regulations and, 105, 166, 180, 208–10; as coordinated operations, 144, 170–72, 185, 225; downsizing and, 168–69, 175, 177; and force structure, 75–76, 143–44; and form of warfare, 60; ground forces and, 77, 166, 169, 185, 187; infantry and, 33, 60, 75, 78, 111, 141–44, 148, 185; informatized war and unified command-and-control network, 220; and joint operations, 225. *See also* combined arms group armies
combined operations *(lainhe zuozhan),* 60
combined war *(hetong zhan),* 161
Commission on Science, Technology, and Industry for National Defense (COSTIND), 187, 189, 207, 215, 263
competition, among states, 275–76; high-technology and, 78; and international system, 23; as motivation for strategic change, 14–15
conduct of warfare, shifts in: 1956 strategic guideline and, 5–6, 73, 77–78, 88, 271; 1980 strategic guideline and, 6–7, 139–41, 144–51, 161–62, 165; 1993 strategic guideline and, 7, 182–83, 187–91, 204; 2004 strategic guideline and, 7, 222, 234; 2014 strategic guideline and, 234–35; active defense as response to, 161–62, 166; and Arab-Israeli War (1973), 6, 14, 33, 139–47, 161–62; in Gulf War, 33, 182–83, 187–91, 201–4, 215–16, 223–24, 240, 271; in international system as motivation for strategic change, 9; mechanization of warfare, 33;

and party unity, **25**; and strategic change, 272–73; strategic change motivated by, 7, 9, 24–26, **25**, 32–33, 73, 277; and strategic changes, 271; and Su Yu's critiques of "luring the enemy in deep," 139–40; technology and, 78, 149–50 (*See also* high-technology); during WWII and Korean War, 77–78

Conference of Senior Military Cadre (1953–1954), 84–88

conscription, 16, 86, 87, 110

COSTIND. *See* Commission for Science, Technology, and Industry for National Defense

counterinsurgency wars, 33

counterterrorism efforts, 230

CSC (Central Special Commission). *See* Central Special Commission (CSC)

Cultural Revolution, 22; and decline in combat readiness, 7, 164; and divisions within party leadership, 22, 151–52; and implementation of 1964 strategic guideline, 114; and military training, 144; and origins in Mao's intervention in economic development, 121–22; party disunity and, 36; PLA and, 7, 260, 271, 274; revisionism and, 115; Soviet threat and, 135–37

Cultural Revolution Group, 36

Czechoslovakia, 135

"Dealing with local wars and military conflicts." *See* 1988 strategic guideline

decentralization, 69–70, 112, 122–27, 133–34; and "luring the enemy in deep," 109, 133–34; and Mao's emphasis on local control, 122–23

"Defending the Motherland." *See* 1956 strategic guideline

defense budgets, 3, 72, 76, 84–85, 87, 167, 175, 240

defense industries, 72, 84, 96, 105, 196, 246, 251; economic development and, 119–20; lack of, 70, 72, 84, 246; and strategic planning, 92

Deng Liqun, 192, 193

Deng Nan, 193

Deng Xiaoping: consolidation of power within CCP, 153–56; and diplomatic relationship with US, 155; and disunity after Tiananmen Square demonstrations, 192; and efforts to build support to reform, 192–94, 197–98; and leadership after Mao's death, 140; and modernization, 140; nuclear strategy and, 8, 175, 237–42,

244–47, 250–52, 254, 261–62, 264, 265, 271; and party unity, 36; PLA support for leadership of, 197–98; power struggle with Hua Guofeng, 140, 151–56, 167, 181; rehabilitation and influence of, 7, 140, 153

deployment of forces, by theater (1952), **83**

deterrence, 211, 240; 1988 strategic guideline and, 179–80; 1993 strategic guideline and, 184, 218, 225, 231; and assured retaliation, 236, 238–45, 268; conventional missiles and, 257, 265–66, 268; Mao's views on nuclear, 108, 237, 238–39, 240, 242, 244, 246–47; and military struggle, 68; nuclear strategy and, 8, 236, 238–45, 256, 268; and strategic guideline and, 8, 93

diffusion and strategic change, 22–24

Ding Zan, 248

disaster relief missions of PLA, 28, 228, 230

disunity, party. *See under* party unity

doctrine and military strategy, 11

downsizing: and reorganization of PLA, 157, 162–63, 168–69, 173–77, 181, 186, 196, 204, 212–15; as strategic decision, 173–76, 270

Dryer, Edward, 48

Dulles, John Foster, 79

economic development, 3, 5–6, 67–68, 81–83, 96, 101–2; First Five-Year Plan, 80–84, 86, 88, 90, 115–16; Second Five-Year Plan, 76; Third Five-Year Plan, 115, 119–20, 127, 134–35, 257; Eighth Five-Year Plan, 188, 192, 196, 205, 210, 257; Ninth Five-Year Plan, 210–12; and central control, 117; defense budgets and, 3, 72, 76, 84–85, 87, 119–20, 167, 175, 205, 240; Great Leap Forward, 5, 115–17; and industrial modernization, 69, 277; Mao and engagement in, 120; Mao's "class struggle" and, 117–18; and military preparedness, 119–21; party disunity and, 192–94; and party unity, 277; and revisionism, 115–16, 117–19; trade wars and, 276

education, military. *See* training

Eighth Five Year Plan, 188, 192, 196, 205, 210, 257

Eighth Route Army, 51, 52–53

emergency mobile operations units, 185

emulation, 96–101; as motive for strategic change, 15, 22–24, 72–73, 203–4; operational and organizational, 99–101; and resource limitations, 23; of Soviet Union, 72–73, 99–101; of US, 97, 203–4, 226 "encirclement and suppression" campaigns, 40, 43–46

exercises: "802" meeting, 89, 144, 169, 171–73; "934" group training, 206; 1980 strategic guideline and emphasis on, 144; joint with Soviet and North Korean forces, 77; Liaodong Peninsula, 77, 88–90, 99, 187; and "new generation" training program, 207–8; in north China, 171–72 (*See also* "802" meeting, training exercise *under this heading*); "Shensheng-94," 207; "Stride-2009," 222

Falklands War (1982), 33, 182–83

Fewsmith, Joseph, 192, 197

Finkelstein, David, 2

First Five-Year Plan, 80–81, 88, 90, 115–16; for military development, 82–84, 86, 248

First Front Army, 45n

first strikes and preemption. *See* preemption or first strikes

Five Principles of Peaceful Coexistence, 93

force deployment in 1952, **83**

force structure, 1, 31; 1956 strategic guideline and, 75–76, 83; 1980 strategic guideline and, 143–44, 167–70; 1993 strategic guideline and, 186, 203–4, 210–12, 214–15; 2004 strategic guideline and, 221; of CCP forces during civil war, 40; and combined army, 75–76; as component of strategic guidelines, **34–35**; and informatization, 221; local forces, in civil war, 40–41

form of operations: in 1956 strategic guideline, 74–75, 78, 93–94, 103, 270; as component of strategic guidelines, **34–35**

form of warfare, 41, 50, 60, 62, 66, 191, 224, 227, 231; as component of guidelines, 28; large-scale war (*dada*), 6, 132, 134; Mao's Ming Tombs speech (1964) and, 134; nuclear (*da yuanzidan*), 134; as part of strategic guidelines, 60; quick war (*kuaida*), 134. *See also specific, e.g.,* mobile warfare, positional warfare, and guerrilla warfare

fortifications, permanent defensive, 75, 79, 83–84, 93, 95, 99, 103, 135, 145, 147, 158

forward defense, 74, 107–9, 111–13, 162; in 1956 strategic guideline, 147; in 1980 strategic guideline, 139, 141–42, 156; rejected by Mao, 113–14, 122, 132

The Fourth Middle East War, 151

Fu Quanyou, 198, 212, 223, 224

GAD. *See* General Armaments Department

"gain control by striking afterwards" (*houfa zhiren*) principle, 61, 98, 142, 201, 240, 255, 269

Gang of Four, 7, 147–48, 151–53, 160, 309n76

Gao Gang, 80

garrison units, 94

General Armaments Department (GAD), **35**, 186, 215

General Logistics Department (GLD), 168, 169, 175, 188, 198–99

General Principles for Combined Operations, 210

General Staff Department (GSD), 126, 197, 198, 200; and "801" meeting, 160; 1956 strategic guideline and, 82, 86, 91; 1980 strategic guideline and, 139, 144; 1993 strategic guideline and, 187, 189, 191, 200, 205–8; "9510" meeting on high-technology, 207; and active defense, 139; and adoption of strategic guidelines, 178; and Arab-Israeli War as strategic lesson, 146, 166; Chi Haotian as leader of, 178, 189, 191; and downsizing and reorganization, 168–69, 213; and First Five-Year Plan, 82; and formulation of strategic guidelines, 82, 86, 91, 178, 191, 214, 263–64; and Gulf War as strategic lesson, 188–89; and Indian border conflict, 111; and informatization, 221; and Kosovo War as strategic lesson, 223; and "luring the enemy in deep," 134–35, 158–59; membership and leadership of, 156–57, 178, 195, 198, 206, 223; nuclear oversight and policy responsibilities, 236, 255, 259–60; and operational methods, 207–8; Su Yu's speech disseminated by, 150; and training, 144, 157–58, 170–76, 178, 187, 189, 205–8, 220, 221, 233

GLD. *See* General Logistics Department (GLD)

Godwin, Paul, 2

Great Leap Forward, 5, 115–17

ground forces, 60, 75–77, 83, 94–95, 103, 105, 172, 203; in 1993 strategic guideline, 183, 213; and combined arms operations, 166, 169, 185, 187; growth in response Soviet threat, 136, 157; and joint operations, 221; Mao on Vietnam and deployment of, 128; modernization of, 112; reductions in, 166, 175, 186, 214–15, 233; regulations for, 166, 207–9; under a separate headquarters, 169, 213, 233

GSD. *See* General Staff Department (GSD)

guerrilla warfare, 5, 39; and active defense, 62; defined and described, 41; Mao as proponent of, 43; and mobile guerrilla warfare, 52; people's war as distinct from, 42, 66; Red Army strategies, 40–43; and Sino-Japanese war, 52; as temporary measure, 43

Gulf of Tonkin Incident, 128

Gulf War (1990–1991): 1993 strategic guideline and, 7, 199–204, 215, 271; 2004 strategic guideline and, 8; and conduct of warfare, 33, 182–83, 187–91, 201–4, 215–16, 223–24, 240, 271; and informatization of warfare, 227–28; and precision-guided munitions, 14, 182, 227; and role of technology, 182–83, 187–91, 223–24, 227

Guo Boxiong, 277

Gutian Conference (1929), 66

Hainan Island, 58, 83, 84, 103, 130

Han Huaizhi, 165

He Jinheng, 261, 262, 263–64, 267

He Long, 45n, 51, 251, 253, 254, 255

He Zehui, 248

He Zhengwen, 156, 173

high-technology: 1956 strategic guideline and, 95; 1993 strategic guideline and, 7, 183–85, 201–2, 203, 215; "9510" meeting on, 207; and active defense, 201; and changes in conduct of war, 150; China as innovator in, 277; China as technologically inferior, 79; competition, 78; emulation and adoption of, 22–24; Gulf War and, 14, 182–83, 187–91, 223–24, 227; informatized warfare and, 218, 231; and local wars, 7, 183–85, 187–89, 196, 203–11, 214–15, 224; and modernization, 27, 70; and protracted war, 184–85; shift of emphasis to "informatized" war, 218; and strategic change, 14, 272–73; Su Yu on conduct of warfare and, 78

Horowitz, Michael, 14, 24

Hua Di, 237

Hua Guofeng, 172, 261; as Mao's successor, 36, 140; power struggle with Deng Xiaoping, 140, 151–56, 167, 181; and succession of leadership, 36, 140

HuaiHai Campaign, 56–58

Huang Kecheng, 81, 92, 102

Huang Ping (Deng's pseudonym), 193

Hu Jintao, 36, 198, 220, 225; and "new historic mission," 228–29; nuclear strategy and, 241, 245

humanitarian missions of PLA, 28, 228, 230

Huntington, Samuel, 19, 21, 275

Hu Yaobang, 36, 156, 192

ICBMs (intercontinental ballistic missiles), 239, 257–58, 264–67

India: border dispute with, 107, 108, 109, 110–13

Indo-Pakistani War (1971), 33

industrialization: defense industry, 70, 72, 84, 246; and development of "third line," 6, 108–9, 115, 119–21

infantry, 31, 40–41, 70, 77, 111–12, 209; and active defense, 141; combat regulations issued for, 75, 99, 165–66; and combined arms operations, 33, 60, 75, 78, 111, 141–44, 148, 185; modernization and decline in emphasis on, 72, 75, 105; and nuclear strategy, 79; reductions in, 76, 86, 88, 95, 111, 168, 175–76, 186, 212, 215; and Soviet model, 96

information technology, 27. See also high-technology

informatization, 7–8, 227; 1993 strategic guideline and, 214; 2004 strategic guideline and, 217–21, 224; 2014 strategic guideline and, 217, 230–34; Iraq War (2003) and, 226–28; Jiang Zemin as proponent of, 224–25; joint operations and, 217, 220, 221, 225–28; Kosovo War as strategic lesson in, 223; local wars under informatized conditions, 7, 35, 217, 218–20, 222, 224, 230–34; and precision-guided munitions, 227; and quick decision wars, 220; use of term and concept (xinxihua), 219; xinxihua, meaning and use of term, 219

innovation, 12–13, 277

international relations theory, 272–75

invasion, threat of, 60, 161; "801" meeting and, 160–61, 172; "802" meeting and, 171–73; and active defense, 62–63, 92–94, 98, 141; air attacks and, 224; and development of the third line, 120; and fixed defense, 204; and forward defense, 74, 107, 139, 141–42, 147, 156; mobilization and, 112; Nationalists and, 69, 107, 108, 109–11, 113; nuclear deterrence and, 107–8, 242; "people's war" and, 67; positional warfare and fixed defense, 35, 131–32, 142, 148–49, 160–61, 204, 270; routes of, 88, 124, 141–42, 158 (See also strategic direction, primary); shift of emphasis to local wars rather than, 178–79, 182–85, 218, 271; Soviet Union and, 1, 6, 109, 138–42,

invasion (*continued*)
144, 156, 158, 166, 171–72, 176, 181, 270–71 (*See also* Zhenbao (Damansky) Island); Taiwan and, 27, **35**, 69, 109, 184, 204, 208, 232 (*See also* Nationalists *under this heading*); US and, 13–14, **34**, 69, 74, 88–90, 94, 99, 107, 113–14, 131–32, 224, 236, 270, 276
Iraq War (2003), 33, 222; strategic lessons from, 226–28

Japan: invasion of Manchuria, 41, 48; "three alls" campaign, 53. *See also* Sino-Japanese War (1937–1945)
Jiang Zemin, 30, 36, 183–84, 187–90, 212–14, 218; and 1993 strategic guideline, 199, 200, 201–2, 233–34; and 2004 strategic guideline, 218, 224–25; as Deng Xiaoping's successor, 194–95; and informatization, 224–25; nuclear, 245, 246, 268
jianshe (construction, building, or development), 67–68
Jinmen Island, 69
Joint Campaign Outline (1999), 209, 221
joint operations *(lainhe zuozhan)*, 60, 78; in 1993 strategic guideline, 7, **35**, 182, 183, 185–86, 187, 203, 205–8, 209; in 2004 strategic guideline, 8–9, **35**, 219–21, 222, 223, 225, 227–28; in 2014 strategic guideline, 231–32, 234–35, 273; centralization and coordination of, 89–90; CMC and, 183–84, 205, 206, 222; doctrine for, 205–8; informatization and, 217, 220, 221, 225–28; and leadership training, 222; regulations for, 209–10, 221
Joliot-Curie, Frederick, 248
Joliot-Curie, Irene, 248
"just" war, concept of, 63–65

Kennedy, John F., 109
Khrushchev, Nikita, 118, 121, 249–50
Kier, Elizabeth, 16, 18
Kim Il Sung, 135
Korea, 69, 135
Korean War (1950–53), 33; 1956 strategic guideline and, 83; and development of strategic guidelines, 78; strategic lessons from, 78–80
Kosovo War (1999), 15, 33; strategic lessons from, 222–26; US bombing of embassy, 222

Lebanon War (1982), 33
Le Duan, 128
Lei Feng, 195

Lei Yingfu, 82, 91–92, 248
Leogrande, William, 19–20
Lewis, John, 237
Liaodong Peninsula exercise, 77, 88–90, 99, 187
LiaoShen campaigns, 56, 58
Liberation Army Daily (newspaper), 30, 76, 146, 150, 166, 180, 197–98, 208, 233
Li Fuchun, 119–21, 125–27, 250–51
Li Lijing, 263
Li Nan, 2
Lin Biao, 36, 70, 73, 102–5, 122, 132, 134, 145, 147, 160, 254, 255; as commander during civil war, 56–58; and military training, 137, 171; and "people's war," 67
Li Peng, 192, 198
Li Ruihuan, 198
Li Shuiqing, 241, 261–62
Li Siguang, 250
Liu Bocheng, 56, 99–100, 102, 153
Liu Huaqing, 156, 163, 184–85, 188–90, 196, 198–99, 202, 204–5, 206, 212, 264, 271
Liu Jie, 249–50, 252
Liu Jiejun, 250
Liu Lifeng, 264
Liu Shaoqi, 36, 54, 59, 89, 116–17, 120, 121, 126, 129, 132, 251–55; attempt to remove from party leadership, 80; on famine, 116; purge of, 80
Liu Xiyao, 252, 253, 254
Li Xiangqian, 115
Li Xiannian, 121, 153
Li Xuge, 254, 263–64
local wars, 7–8, 196, 270–71; 1980 strategic guideline and, 166; 1988 strategic guideline and, 176–81, 183; 1993 strategic guideline and, 182–85, 203–11, 214–15, 271; 2004 strategic guideline and, 217, 218–20; 2014 strategic guideline and informatized, 217, 230–34; and active defense, 185, 201; and Arab-Israeli War as strategic lesson, 166; Gulf War as, 187–89; and high-technology, 7, 183–85, 187–89, 196, 203–11, 214–15, 224; under informatized conditions, 7, **35**, 217, 218–20, 222, 224, 230–34; and Iraq War as strategic lesson, 222, 226–28; and Kosovo as strategic lesson, 222–26; Liu Huaqing and shift of emphasis to, 163; and nuclear strategy, 268; shift of emphasis to, **35**, 60, 163
Long, Austin, 16
"Long Live People's War!" (Lin), 67
Long March, 40, 48, 59, 64; and CCP base areas (1934–1936), map of, **44**

Luo Ruiqing, 102, 122, 129, 131, 134, 253, 254, 259; and NDIO, 253; speech summarizing Mao's instructions, 129, 133, 134

"luring the enemy in deep," 5; in 1964 strategic guideline, 6, 113–14, 145–47, 271; abandonment of, 140, 147–48, 150–51, 160, 161–62, 164; and active defense, 64, 161, 167; defined and described, 63–64; domestic political benefits of, 133–34; Mao as proponent of, 46, 50, 108, 121, 123, 131–35, 161; shift from, 158, 160–61, 271; Song Shilun's critiques of, 147, 160–62, 164; Su Yu's critiques of, 145–47; as tactic rather than strategy, 161; and war of annihilation, 133

Lushan Conference, 73, 80, 101–2, 104

Malraux, Andrew, 240

maneuver units, 94–95

Mao Zedong: 1956 strategic guideline and, 91; 1960 strategic guideline and, 122–23; 1964 strategic guideline and, 107–9, 115, 272; 1999 and break with Mao's ten principles, 209; and active defense, 62, 91, 147, 161; as author of strategic guidelines, 61; and concerns about revisionism, 6, 120–21, 125, 133–34; death of, 140–41, 147–48, 151–52; and decentralization (localization), 69–70, 109, 112, 122–27, 133–34; Deng Xiaoping and, 8, 116–17; direct intervention in military affairs, 107–9, 115–21, 125–26; economic policy, 6, 118–21; and encirclement campaigns during Civil War, 43, 45, 49–50; Great Leap and leadership challenges, 115–17; and guerrilla ethic, 43; and Hua Guofeng as premier, 152; as leader of the Red Army, 42–43; "luring the enemy in deep" strategy preferred by, 46, 50, 108, 121, 123, 131–35, 161; as military strategist, 42–43, 49–50, 67; and negotiations with Nationalists, 54; on nuclear weapons and strategy, 8, 237, 238–39, 245–46, 249, 252, 253; and "offensive defense," 49–50; and Peng Dehuai, 81, 101–2, 117; political logic of intervention in Military affairs, 115–21; and Soviet threat, 135–37; strategic direction, critique of emphasis on, 50, 107, 113, 122–23, 124, 128, 135; and strategic guidelines, 27, 29; as strategist, 47, 52, 55–56, 125, 209; successors chosen by, 36, 118, 125, 140, 152, 154; "ten military principles" of, 209–10; and "third line," 6, 108–9, 115, 119–21, 125–29, 131, 134; and US as threat, 127–32, 128, 133

maritime area as strategic direction, 231–32, 234, 276

massive retaliation, doctrine of, 74, 79, 237

Ma Suzheng, 146

McReynolds, Joe, 219

memoirs as primary sources, 37–38

methodology and sources, 2–3, 26–27, 37–48

Military Arts (journal), 150–51, 262

military publications as primary sources, 37

military regions, as organizational structure, 86–88, 143, 155, 169, 174–76, 195, 199, 213–15, 233

military strategic guidelines. *See* strategic guidelines *(zhanlue fangzhen)*

military strategy: defined, 10–11

military struggle *(junshi douzheng)*, 68. *See also* basis of preparations

militias and self-defense corps, 40–42, 52, 54, 64–65, 112, 114, 123

Ming Tombs speech (Mao, 1964), 134

Ministry of Industry and Information Technology (MIIT), 219

missions or objectives, military: as motives for strategic change, 13–14, 272–73; non-combat or humanitarian, 28, 228–30

"Miss Qiu" (atomic bomb), 254

mobile warfare, 5, 39; during civil war, 55; defined and described, 41; Mao and preference for, 123; Mao on, 50; and Red Army, 45

mobilization, 95, 104; in 1956 strategic guideline and, 95; domestic, 130–31; of economy, 116; Mao and domestic, 130–31; and nuclear survivability, 264–65; and "people's war," 42, 64–67

modernization: and decline in emphasis on infantry, 72, 75, 105

modernization, military: and army building, 67–68; and central coordination, 89–90; and diffusion, 22–24; and emulation, 22–23; and First Five-Year Plan, 82; and industrialized economy, 69, 277; lack of resources as obstacle, 205; and mechanization of warfare, 33; military science research and, 95; of military technology, 27, 70 (*See also* high-technology); and organizational changes, 86–87, 89; peacetime and, 93, 177; and "people's war," 3; politicization as obstacle to, 196; resources and, 23; and Soviet model, 72–73, 126; and standardization *(zhengguihua)*, 87–88; strategic guideline and, 1–3

Montgomery, Bernard, 247
motivations for strategic changes, 5, 12–16, 24–26
Mulvedon, James, 219

Nanching Ground Forces Academy study of Iraq War, 226–28
Nanjing Uprising (1927), 40, 42, 78n
National Army (Nationalist), 46, 48. *See also* Nationalists
National Defense Industry Commission (NDIC), 246
National Defense Industry Office (NDIO), 252–53
National Defense Science and Technology Commission (NDSTC), 239
Nationalists: 1964 strategic guideline and, 107–12; Civil War, 40; factionalism within, 46; as invasion threat, 69, 107–12; and Mao as strategist, 54–55; and mobile, 54–55; as ongoing threat, 96; as threat after Japanese surrender, 54
National Revolutionary Army search, 40
Naughton, Barry, 127
navy (PLAN): 1956 strategic guideline and, 75–76, 83–84, 95–96; 1980 strategic guideline and, 162–63; 1993 strategic guideline and, 186–87; 2004 strategic guideline and, 232; amphibious assault forces, 69, 77, 96, 162, 206; modernization and expansion of, 221; as nonexistent, 77
NDIC (National Defense Industry Commission), 246
NDSTC (National Defense Science and Technology Commission), 239
near-coast defense, 96, 162
near-seas defense, 96, 162–63, 232
neoclassical realism, 274
New Fourth Army, 51–53, 59, 78n
Nielsen, Suzanne, 11
Nie Rongzhen, 92, 105, 153, 160, 239, 245, 248, 251
Ninth Five Year Plan, 210–12
"no-first-use" policy, nuclear, 98, 255–56
North Korea, 135; joint exercises with, 77
nuclear strategy: in 1956 strategic guideline, 73–74, 77, 79, 89, 98; in 1980 strategic guideline, 142, 267–69; 2006 white paper and, 238, 243; and active defense, 236, 241, 261–62, 267–68; CMC and draft of strategy document, 262–64; as consistent, 236, 269; as decoupled from conventional strategy, 236–38, 267–69; Deng Xiaoping and, 8, 175, 237–42, 244–47,

250–52, 254, 261–62, 264, 265, 271; deterrence and (*See* deterrence); force posture and, 264–66; force structure and development, 256–58, 266–67; French influence on, 248; leadership views and articulation of, 238–41; Mao and, 8, 108, 237, 238–39, 240, 242, 244–47, 253; operational doctrine for, 241–43; and preemptive first strike, 98, 255–56; in *Science of Military Strategy* (1987), 242; in *Science of Second Artillery Strategy*, 242; and Second Artillery's role, 258–62, 264; self-defense and, 243; survivability, 240, 242, 255, 261–62, 264–66; training exercises for counterstrikes, 261–62; US and nuclear coercion, 245–46; Zhou Enlai and, 238–39, 244, 247–56
nuclear weapons, 27; air-dropped as delivery system, 252, 254, 256–57; and ballistic missiles, 253; for conventional operations, 5; as deterrent (*See* deterrence); and doctrine of massive retaliation, 79; economic resources for development of, 240, 251, 252; fission technology, 257; hydrogen technology, 254, 257; ICBMs as delivery system, 239, 257–58, 264–67; and international status, 243; leadership views of, 243–47; Mao on development of, 237, 245–46, 249, 252, 253; "Miss Qiu" code name, 254; as "paper tigers," 237, 244–45; Peng Dehuai's perspective on, 98, 248–50; research and development of, 142, 248–53; and Soviet expertise, 248–49; tests, 252–54, 256; top party leaders and direct oversight of, 238–41, 250–51, 254–56, 264; training and, 241; uranium as resource for development of, 248–50

Odem, William, 20
"offensive defense": Mao as proponent of, 49–50, 61–62. *See also* active defense (*jiji fangyu*)
official histories as primary sources, 37
"On the Ten Great Relationships" (Mao), 246
operational doctrine, 1, 30–31, 112; as component of guidelines, 34–35; emulation of Soviet model, 99–101; Mao and, 49–50; Peng Dehuai's operations plan, 91
operational principles, general: as component of strategic guidelines, 60–61
operational targets, 28, 60; as component of strategic guidelines, 34–35

operations regulations, 31, **34–35**, 185–86, 208–9, 220–21, 232; Soviet model for, 99. *See also* combat regulations

organizational bias, military, 15–16

organizational culture, 16

Pakistan, 33, 130

party-armies: autonomy of, 4, 9, 19–20, 271, 275; and ideological or policy responsibility, 21; strategic change and, 274–75

party unity, 33–36; and 1956 strategic guideline, 106; and 1960 strategic guideline, 101–2; and 1980 strategic guideline, 141; after Mao's death, 140, 151–56; after revolution, 79–81; consensus and strategic change, 7, 18–19, 33, 36, 148, 181; Cultural Revolution and disunity, 36, 140, 151–52; Deng-Hua power struggle and, 140, 151–56, 167, 181; Deng Xiaoping and restoration of, 198–99, 271; Deng Xiaoping's consolidation of power and, 151–56; disunity, 5–7, 6, 36, 108, 118, 140, 193, 229; external threats and, 22; leadership succession and factionalism, 36, 140, 151–56; and military change, 19–22; military retirements and, 195; purges, 33, 73, 79–80, 115, 136, 152; and shift in conduct of warfare, **25**; and strategic change, 4–6, 7, 21, 73, 80, 137–38, 181, 273–74, 277; Tiananmen Square demonstrations and collapse of, 191–94; Xi Jinping's anticorruption campaigns and, 277

peacekeeping, as mission of PLA, 230

Peng Dehuai, 5–6, 29–30, 52–53, 59, 74, 106; and 1953–1954 conference of senior military cadre, 84–87; and 1956 strategic guideline, 5–6, 90–94, 271; and active defense, 93–94; as commander in Korea, 78–79, 81, 84; and conference of senior military cadre, 84–88; on Liaodong Peninsula exercise, 89; on logistics and modern warfare, 78–79; Mao and, 81, 101–2, 117; and mobile guerrilla warfare, 52; and nuclear weapons development, 98, 248–50; and offensive against Japanese, 53; and permanent fortifications and defenses, 84, 99; purge of, 73, 101–2; responsibility for military affairs delegated to, 81; and Soviet Union, 91, 96, 98–100, 249–50; on strategic guidelines, 59, 91

Peng Zhen, 255

People's Armed Police, 186, 187, 212, 214–15

People's Liberation Army (PLA): base areas and Long March (1934–1936), map, **44**; CCP and authority over, 1, 27, 69, 274 (*See also* autonomy, military; Central Military Commission (CMC)); civil war and strategy development, 39; Cultural Revolution and, 7, 260, 271, 274; Deng Xiaoping's leadership supported by, 197–98; downsizing and reorganization of, 157, 162–63, 168–69, 173–77, 181, 186, 196, 204, 212–15; and dual command structure, 100; and emulation of Soviet organization and operations, 99–100; force structure and size, 39, 43–45, 55, 70, 77 (*See also* downsizing *under this heading*); and informatization, 221; joint logistics system created by, 221; modernization of, 221; new historic mission of, 28, 228–30; Ninth Five-Year Plan for, 211–12; noncombat (humanitarian relief) missions of, 28, 228, 230; as party army, 2, 67, 275; political roles of, 80, 137; politicization of, 191, 194–97; poor performance during Vietnam invasion, 163–65; Rocket Force as part of, 260; shift from revolutionary to national defense, 68–69

People's Republic of China, map, *xvi–xvii*, **25**

"people's war," 5, 71; defined and described, 64–67; and guerrilla warfare, 42, 66; Mao's, 73, 134; and strategic guidelines, 3, 5, 140, 270

Perlmutter, Amos, 19–20

Petroshevskii, General, 99

Ping Jin Campaign, 58

PLA. *See* People's Liberation Army (PLA)

PLAAF. *See* air force (People's Liberation Army Air Force PLAAF)

PLAN (People's Liberation Army Navy). *See* navy

PLARF (People's Liberation Army Rocket Force). *See* Second Artillery

Politburo: composition of, 36, 79, 152–53, 155, 198, 250; Deng Xiaoping's leadership and, 155–56, 172, 198; Mao and, 117, 118; members and leadership of, 199; and military strategy, 50–52, 59, 145, 152, 172; and nuclear strategy, 250–54; and party unity, 79–80; and Peng Dehuai's military leadership, 81, 102; and revisionism, 118

positional defensive warfare, **34**, 41, 48, 75, 94, 103, 145, 149, 157, 172–73

positional warfare *(zhendi zhan)* (form of operations), 41, 49, 166, 270–71; in 1956 strategic guideline, 74, 78, 94, 103, 270; in 1964 strategic guideline, 114; in 1980 strategic guideline, 139, 141–43, 149–50,

positional warfare (*continued*)
270–71; as alternative to strategic retreat, 161; as Soviet approach, 190; Su Yu and, 147, 148, 149, 157; Yang Dezhi and, 150, 160–61

precision-guided munitions, 7, 14, 15, 182, 212, 227–28

preemption or first strikes, 5; active offense, 46–47, 62, 204–5; China and rejection of, 5; Mao's opposition to, 61; and "no-first-use" nuclear policy, 98, 255–56; and Red Army, 47; Soviet Union and, 5, 98

"Problems of Strategy in China's Revolutionary War" (Mao, lecture, 1939), 49, 62

protracted war, 1, 42; and guerrilla warfare, 66; high-technology and, 184–85; and "luring the enemy in deep," 107, 113–14, 133; Mao and expectation of, 49–50, 65, 67; and potential conflict with Soviet Union, 140, 142; and potential conflict with US, 92, 133; Sino-Japanese war as, 51–52, 56; and wars of revolution, 65; wars of revolution or liberation as, 65

purges, 33, 73, 79–80, 115, 136, 152, 277

Qian Sanqiang, 248–50, 249
Qian Xuesen, 257
Qiao Guanhua, 198, 255
Qiao Shi, 198
quick-decision warfare, 41, 49–50, 60, 162, 185, 220

Rao Shushi, 80
rapid reaction units, 185
reactive innovation, 12–13
Red Army: First Front Army, 45n; force strength and numbers, 41, 44–45, 46, 47; and guerrilla warfare, 40–43; and "luring the enemy in deep," 45–47; and mobile warfare, 45; as People's Liberation Army (*See* People's Liberation Army (PLA)); and preemptive strikes, 47; resource limitations and strategies of, 40, 42, 48; and rural base areas, 43; strategies during the Civil War, 40–43; troop sizes, 52

regulations. *See* combat regulations; operations regulations

reinforcements: as targets, 47

research and development, military research, 95

Resende-Santos, Joao, 23

"resisting the enemy beyond the gates," 47, 50

"resist in the north, open in the south." *See* 1960 strategic guideline

retreat, strategic, 48, 50, 162, seee also "luring the enemy in deep"

revisionism: Cultural Revolution and, 115; decentralization and, 134–35; defined and described, 115; and factionalism after Mao's death, 151–52; Great Leap and, 115–16; Mao and attacks on, 6; Mao and revisionism as internal threat, 108; Mao's interventions in military affairs as response to, 115–21; and Mao's rejection of 1960 strategic guideline, 122–25; and party succession, 125; and political logic of Mao's intervention in military affairs, 115–21

rocket artillery force. *See* Second Artillery

Rosen, Stephen Peter, 14

Rusk, Dean, 129–30, 132

Science of Campaigns Outline, 143, 151, 165–66, 177, 209, 220, 243

Science of Military Strategy: 1987 edition, 143, 166, 177, 185, 242–43; 2001 edition, 185, 243; 2013 edition, 243

Science of Second Artillery Campaigns, 243, 262, 263, 267–68

Science of Second Artillery Strategy, 242–44, 255, 262–63, 262–64, 267–68

Second Artillery, 180, 187, 207, 210, 215, 221, 233, 236–38; establishment of, 34, 260–62, 269; and force structure, 34; and nuclear counter-strike exercises, 173, 241–42; and strategic guidelines, 268

Second Five-Year Plan, 76

Selected Works (Jiang Zemin), 30

Shen Kehui, 263, 264

"Shensheng-94" exercises, 207

Sino-Japanese War (1937–1945), 40, 71; CCP as inferior force during, 41; CCP strategy during, 40, 50–53, 59; Civil War as concurrent with, 59, 64–65; guerrilla warfare and, 66; Japan's surrender, 53–54; strategic lessons from, 54–55, 98; "three alls" retaliatory campaign, 53

Snow, Edgar, 129, 239

Socialist Education Movement, 118

The Soldier and the State (Huntington), 19

Song Shilun, 29, 113, 140, 151, 271; and abandonment of "luring the enemy in deep," 147, 160, 161–62, 164; and *Science of Military Strategy,* 164, 166

sources, Chinese primary, 3, 26–27; published strategic guidelines, 29–30

Soviet Union: as ally, 5; and Arab-Israeli War as client war, 33, 139, 144, 146, 181,

271; and clash over Zhenbao (Damansky) Island, 6, 27, 108, 114, 135, 139, 141; Cultural Revolution and, 135–37; emulation of, 72–73, 96–97, 100–101; as equipment or expertise source, 96–97, 248–49; Mao and threat from, 135–37; military exercises with, 77; as military rival, 6; military strategies rejected by China, 5, 98–99; modernization and co-operation with, 72–73, 126; normalization of relations with, 178–79; as nuclear power, 178–79, 246; and preemption or first strikes, 5, 98; and reactive innovation, 13; and revisionism, 118–19; as threat to China, 6, 109–11, 135–37, 139, 157; training advisors from, 96–97; as treaty ally, 97; and Vietnam, 155, 163; and Xinjiang incursions, 141, 143; YiTa incident and, 109–10, 128
space-based platforms, 7
Spratly Islands, 179
SSF. *See* Strategic Support Force (SSF)
standardization *(zhengguihua)*, 70, 87–88, 90, 165, 208, 211–12
strategic change: civilian intervention as motivation for, 273–74; identifying major, 30–32; indicators of (identification of), **34–35**; mechanisms of, 16–26; military autonomy and, 15–18, 73, 81–82; as military-led, 5–6; party armies and, 274–75
strategic direction, primary, 28, 178; in 1956 guideline, 82–84, **85**; in 1960 guideline, 103–4, 122, 123; in 1964 guideline, 113–14, 122, 131; in 1980 guideline, 141, 144, **159**, **171–72**; in 1993 guideline, 184, 204, 211; in 2004 guideline, 218, 232; as absent or de-emphasized, 113–14; as component of strategic guidelines, **34–35**, 60; and expected threats, 99; Mao's critique of, 50, 107, 113, 122–23, **124**, 128, 135; surprise attacks and uncertainty of, 113
strategic guidelines *(zhanlue fangzhen)*, 1; changes as military-led, 5–6, 24–25, 271; communication and implementation of, 29–30; described and defined, 27–30, 58–61; and identification of strategic opponent, 27; and operational targets, 27; publication of, 29–30. *See also list by year at beginning of alphabetic index*
strategic opponent *(zhanlue duishou)*, 28, 60, 74
Strategic Support Force (SSF), 229, 233
submarines, 31, 76, 95, 186, 221; submarine-based ballistic missiles (SSBNs), 240, 255

Sun Xiangli, 257
supply lines, 70, 75, 78–79, 114
surveillance and reconnaissance, 7
Su Yu, 77–79, 109, 139–40, 248, 271; and 1956 strategic guideline, 82–83, 91–92; critique of "luring the enemy in deep" strategy, 145–50, 157, 164; lectures as influence on 1980 strategic guideline, 146, 148–50, 157, 164; on nuclear war, 79

Taiwan: and 2004 strategic guideline and, 218; independence of, 63, 184, 229; Nationalist retreat to, 69; and preemptive first strike, 185; as threat, 27, **35**, 69, 109, 184, 204, 208, 232; and unification, 163, 185; US as ally of, 112, 216, 223
Taiwan Straits crisis (1954–55), 90, 237
Taiwan Straits crisis (1995–96), 202, 208, 223
Tan Zheng, 104
technology, military. *See* high technology
Teiwes, Frederick, 79
"ten military principles," Mao's, 209–10
terrorism, 230
Theory of International Politics (Waltz), 14–15
Third Five-Year Plan, 115, 119–20, 127, 134–35, 257
"third line" *(sanxian)*: development of, 6, 108–9, 115, 119–21, 134–35; Mao and, 6, 108–9, 115, 119–21, 125–29, 131, 134; and rejection of central planning, 125–27
"three alls" campaign, Japanese, 53
"three attacks and three defenses," 226
three-dimensional war *(liti zhan)*, 78, 161, 202
Tiananmen Square, 7, 36, 155, 177, 183, 202, 310n90; and party disunity, 191–94, 216, 271; politicization of PLA after, 194–97
Torigian, Joseph, 154
total wars, 60, 140, 161–63, 166, 173, 176–77, 181, 201, 203, 218
training, 1, 31–32; in 1988 strategic guideline, 180–81; Arab-Israeli War (1973) and, 137; and combined arms operations, 171; as component of strategic guidelines, **34–35**; Cultural Revolution's impact on, 137, 170; curriculum, military education, 32; and GSD, 144, 157–58, 170–76, 178, 187, 189, 205–8, 220, 221, 233; for high-technology warfare, 207–8; joint leadership training, 222; lectures, 158, 172, 178; operational methods emphasized in, 207; political work as military training, 104–6, 114, 137, 195–97; Soviet advisors and, 96–97; standardization *(zhengguihua)* and, 70

troop reductions. *See* downsizing
tunnel networks, 79, 255, 265
"two-and-a-half doctrine," 110

Union of Soviet Socialist Republics (USSR).
    See Soviet Union
United States: and air-war capability, 224;
    as ally of Taiwan, 112, 223; bombing of
    Chinese embassy during Kosovo war, 222;
    as China's adversary, 83; Deng Xiaoping
    and normalization of diplomatic relation-
    ship with, 155; and doctrine of massive
    retaliation, 74, 79, 237; as nuclear power,
    108, 245–46; as threat, 69, 92–93, 107–10,
    127–31, 202–3, 276; trade wars and, 276;
    Vietnam invasion and, 127–28
uranium, 248–50

Vietnam, 67, 116, 155; China's 1979 invasion
    of, 163–65; escalation of US involvement
    in, 115, 127–32; Mao on US engagement
    in, 128; poor performance of PLA during
    invasion of 1979, 163–65; as strategic
    lesson, 121; US engagement in, 108, 110

Walden, Andrew, 116, 118
Waltz, Kenneth, 14–15, 22, 23
Wang Binzhang, 256
Wang Dezhao, 248
Wang Dongxing, 153, 155, 156n
Wang Hongguang, 232
Warsaw Pact, 98
Wayaobu meeting, 50, 59, 61–62
Wei Ming, 248
"Winning informatized local wars." *See* 2014
    strategic guideline
"Winning local wars under high-technology
    conditions." *See* 1993 strategic guideline
World War II: strategic lessons from, 78–79,
    84, 98, 131–32
Wu De, 153, 155, 156n
Wu Lengxi, 255
Wu Xiuquan, 156

Xiang Shouzhi, 260
Xiao Ke, 100
Xi Jinping, 36, 233–34, 241, 245, 273,
    275–77
Xu Caihou, 277
Xue Litai, 237
Xu Huizi, 200

Xu Qinxian, 194
Xu Shiyou, 132, 134
Xu Xiangqian, 102, 115, 147–48, 150, 153,
    160, 277

Yang Baibing, 194, 197, 198–99, 200
Yang Chengzong, 248
Yang Dezhi, 150, 156–61, 164, 173–74, 261,
    262, 271
Yang Shangkun, 179–80, 193–94, 197–98,
    262, 264
Yang Yong, 156, 158–59
Yang Zhiyuan, 220–21
Yao Qin, 255
Yao Yilin, 192
Ye Fei, 162–63
Ye Jianying, 77, 79, 88–89, 92, 109, 145, 147,
    152–53, 160, 161, 246, 261, 265
YiTa Incident, 109–10, 128
Yu Qiuli, 127
Yu Yongbo, 198

Zhang Aiping, 240, 251–54, 258–59
Zhang Guotao, 45n, 48, 58
Zhang Qihua, 245
Zhang Wannian, 170–71, 198–201, 206–8,
    211–13, 223, 271
Zhang Zhen, 73, 156, 158, 160, 170–73, 178,
    189–90, 198, 200, 205–6, 271
Zhao Erlu, 258
Zhao Ziyang, 36, 156, 192, 194
Zhenbao (Damansky) Island, 6, 27, 108, 114,
    135, 139, 141
Zhou Enlai, 54, 81, 82, 89, 145, 237; attempt
    to remove from party leadership, 80; and
    Central Special Commission, 253; death
    of, 152; and delegation of military affairs
    to Peng Dehuai, 81; and five-year plan for
    military development, 82; Hua Guofeng
    as replacement, 152; Mao and, 47, 125,
    132; and Nationalist threat, 110–11; and
    nuclear strategy, 237–39, 242, 244,
    247–56; and strategic planning, 111; and
    US as threat, 109–10, 130
Zhou Yongkang, 277
Zhu De, 43, 52, 62, 132, 248, 289n95
Zhu Kezhen, 248
Zhukov, Georgy, 98–99
Zhu Rongji, 193, 198
Zisk, Kimberly Marten, 13, 18, 27
Zunyi meeting, 49, 59, 62

CPSIA information can be obtained
at www.ICGtesting.com
Printed in the USA
JSHW021301210821
18026JS00003B/15